COMPARATIVE STATISTICS
IN THE 19TH CENTURY

PIONEERS OF DEMOGRAPHY

A series of collective reprints of the more important milestones in the development of historical demography.

THIS SERIES INCLUDES:

The earliest classics: John Graunt and Gregory King
Mortality in pre-industrial times: the contemporary verdict
Enclosure and population
The population of Ireland before the 19th century
Population and disease in early industrial England
Comparative statistics in the 19th century
Slum conditions in London and Dublin
Mortality in mid 19th century Britain
Rates of mortality
J.-B. Bertrand: *A historical relation of the plague at Marseilles in the year 1720*
T. Short: *Comparative history of the increase and decrease of mankind*
T. Short: *New observations on city, town and country bills of mortality*
W. Black: *An arithmetical and medical analysis of the diseases and mortality of the human species*
E. H. Greenhow: *Papers relating to the sanitary state of the people of England* (General Board of Health Papers)

Each volume contains a new introduction.

COMPARATIVE STATISTICS
IN THE 19TH CENTURY

F. Bisset Hawkins M.D.

ELEMENTS OF MEDICAL STATISTICS

LONDON 1829

*

M. A. Quetelet

A TREATISE ON MAN

AND THE DEVELOPMENT OF HIS FACULTIES

EDINBURGH 1842

With an introduction

by

RICHARD WALL

1973

GREGG INTERNATIONAL PUBLISHERS LIMITED

ISBN 0 576 53289 4

Printed in Germany

INTRODUCTION

The 'Elements of Medical Statistics' and 'A Treatise on Man' were written when their authors were still comparatively youthful. Francis Bisset Hawkins and Lambert Adolphe Jacques Quetelet were born in the same year (1796). Ahead of Quetelet lay forty years of active academic life, defending and elaborating the arguments of the 'Treatise', promoting, participating in and organising statistical conferences. In 1846, as President of the Statistical Committee, he supervised the taking of the 1846 Belgian Census with all its impressive detail on all such unlikely and widely differing subjects as fire insurance, language and the number of looms and other equipment used in industrial enterprises.[1] Hawkins was not an international figure like Quetelet; nevertheless he was to have a long career in public service being successively a Factory Commissioner, Inspector of Prisons, Metropolitan Commissioner in Lunacy and Commissioner for the Government of the Model Prison at Pentonville.[2] According to Munk, Hawkins was instrumental in securing the insertion of information about cause of death when civil registration was set up in 1837. Glass, however, in his account of the events leading up to this makes no mention of Hawkins although he does note the presence of Quetelet as a witness before the Select Committee of 1833, the body primarily responsible for the change to civil registration.[3] This similarity of interests is naturally reflected in their writing, each drawing on the work of the other. It is particularly appropriate therefore that two of their early works should now appear together.

It has to be admitted, however, that later comment has not always been favourable. 'Tendentious', 'uncritical' and 'descriptive' are just some of the epithets that have been applied to the work of Hawkins.[4] Neither, on examination, has Quetelet fared much better. Undoubtedly the central figure in the period which has been dubbed 'The Era of Enthusiasm' for statistical enquiries, most commentators have been prepared to recognise his influence on his contemporaries.[5] In the field of statistics as in human biology, anthropology and criminology he has been seen as a pioneer. His influence on Buckle, Francis Dalton and Florence Nightingale is equally clear.[6] Yet in the midst of all this praise many have been quick to decry his theories. He has been variously accused of attributing physiological laws to results even though all the disturbing causes have not been eliminated,[7] ignoring the particular in pursuit of the average[8] and introducing a spurious precision into projections of population growth.[9] Meanwhile other writers have been searching for his antecedents pointing out that Quetelet was not the first to assemble statistics on marriage and suicide, not the first to use the phrase 'moral statistics' nor even the first to champion the idea of predictability in the annual rate of crime,[10] a predictability that in fact counts for very little since

Quetelet makes clear that this only applied while the causes themselves were unchanged. But to concentrate on these issues is to do less than justice to what has been widely called Quetelet's 'epoch making synthesis of social concern and mathematical method'.[11] Undoubtedly far more space than we have at present would be necessary for a full assessment of the significance of Quetelet's work. All that we can hope to do here is to draw attention to those aspects which throw most light on the demographic characteristics of nineteenth-century society. It must also be kept in mind that we are judging not one man but no less than the work of a whole generation of statisticians, demographers and doctors. This is because Quetelet summarised not merely the results of his own research but also those of his leading contemporaries, thus saving their studies from the danger of oblivion in the back numbers of specialised journals.

In this he duplicated the work of Hawkins who had just this object in mind.[12] Quetelet of course went much further covering a much wider range of subjects (Hawkins for instance has very little to say about the weight and stature of the 'average' man), but more than this he reassembled this scattered data so that it formed a coherent pattern. Hawkins does not attempt this and he has very little of his own research work to produce. For him, 'facts' on their own were of value (p.v.). Yet even so the 'Medical statistics is not just an essay in bibliography for on the basis of the comparative material he had gathered, Hawkins advanced an argument which, if it could be accepted, would overturn most current hypotheses concerning the demography of early nineteenth-century Europe. Great Britain, according to Hawkins, was the most healthy country with which he was acquainted (whether he included the United States in this computation is not clear), the result of a trend that could be traced back at least as far as 1770. Nor was this improvement limited to any particular industry or class, for the man of affluence, the pauper-patient, the inmate of the jail were all enjoying a better and longer life (p. 30). In England, men, animals and vegetables all flourished because of the care bestowed on their culture (p. 233).

We will examine these claims in detail in a moment but first we must pause to consider how firm were the facts on which Hawkins based his arguments. He was not unaware of the dubious authenticity of some, or the lack of essential detail in others and the dangers involved in forming general principles from an insufficient number of observations – he makes this quite clear in his introduction – but having said this he calmly proceeds as if all possible objections have been satisfied. But this is clearly not so. For example, definitions of what constituted an illegitimate birth are not likely to have been standard throughout Europe. Neither are definitions of still-births. In Norway for instance, they included those dying up to 24 hours *after* birth.[13] When proportions of events differ between one country and another, we are therefore in some doubt as to whether this is an indication of a real difference in social *mores* or simply the result of a difference of definition. Nowhere is this more important than with the question of suicide. Pre-industrial rates were usually in the range of 4–6 per hundred thousand inhabitants.[14] Yet Hawkins gives figures for Copenhagen of 100 per hundred thousand. This one might well imagine to be an error yet for Berlin and Paris he had figures of 34 and 49 per hundred thousand respectively, dwarfing even the figure of 25.9 per hundred thousand recorded for San Francisco in 1950 which Peter Laslett singles out as being exceptionally high. It has sometimes been thought that suicide might be under-registered because of juries being too free with verdicts of lunacy,[15] but here it seems to be necessary to allow for the possibility of over-registration, perhaps through cases of drunkenness resulting in death being classified as suicide on the grounds that the person's own folly had brought his untimely end. If the figure is anywhere near genuine then it suggests that the onset of urbanisation on a scale hitherto unparalleled did bring with it the tensions and strains which sociological theory forecasts. Hawkins also discusses the sex ratio, marital status and age of the victims but Simpson has cautioned against accepting such figures blindly. To take two examples, the majority of consummated suicides are male, but more women than men fail in the attempt; similarly the number of suicides is proportionately higher for the older age groups, but it is conceivable that there is less reluctance to conceal a suicide when the person is elderly.[16]

But to return to Hawkins' main thesis. As far as England was concerned, his findings were based largely on the baptism, marriage and burial totals assembled by John Rickman, a source which today inspires little confidence. Indeed one recent authority (Krause) has gone so far as to say that, allowing for under-registration, the death rate probably rose during the period 1780–1820 despite the fact that the figures themselves suggest a fall.[17] The possibility of defective burial registration had earlier been pointed out by Quetelet in an Appendix to his work in which he disputed England's claim to markedly lower mortality levels (see page 110). However, Quetelet too had to rely at least in part on Rickman's figures and it would be equally wise to suspend judgement on his findings that in England the expectancy of life both at birth and from the age of 45 was somewhat higher than in Belgium whereas in the intervening ages the position was reversed.

If we put Rickman's data to one side then the evidence for the fall in mortality in the late eighteenth century becomes less compelling. Robertson's work on Warrington and Glasgow suggests a fall in both adult and child mortality after 1780 (cited by Hawkins pp. 139–142). In Warrington (but not Glasgow) the more marked improvement was in the level of child mortality. For the earlier period there is only Finlaison's work on the Tontines representing the mortality experience of what Hawkins termed 'the middle ranks of society' at two points in time (1695 and 1789). His figures certainly show a fall in mortality between the two dates, the most marked improvement being in the level of child mortality (see page 15). Whereas life expectancy at the age of ten increased by only 26 per cent, and by 29 per cent at the age of 50, at birth the improvement was as much as 40 per cent. The somewhat unlikely possibility that rather more prosperous and hence perhaps longer lived persons were puchasing Tontines in the latter period should of course always be borne in mind.

It might be thought that Hawkins was on somewhat firmer ground when he asserted that fewer patients were now dying in the confines of medical institutions. The hospital reports which form the major source seem clear on this point. At St. Thomas's in London the mortality of in-patients was 1 in 10 in 1698 and the same in 1741 but had fallen to 1 in 14 for the decade 1773 to 1783 and 1 in 16 during the first decade of the nineteenth century (pp. 77–8). In the London maternity hospitals the number of women dying had been as high as 1 in 42 in 1750 but had fallen to 1 in 288 for the period 1789–1798 (pp. 120–1). These figures were far and away better than the majority recorded for continental hospitals (compare pages 102–111), a verdict with which Quetelet concurred.[18] But continental institutions were notoriously unhealthy. To take an extreme example, in a bad year as many as 90 per cent of the infants abandoned by their parents and admitted to the Foundling Hospitals would die within 12 months of birth. If doubts have arisen this is principally because of a persuasive article by McKeown and Brown,[19] in which they argued that few of the additions to medical knowledge in the eighteenth century were of any help in prolonging life while the danger of infection in the closely confined wards of hospitals meant that often there was a greater chance of recovery if one remained at home. It should be noted that the authors did not in fact claim that there was no variation over time in the level of mortality in the hospitals, indeed they saw some sign of a fall but argued that this was part of a wider phenomenon affecting the chances of survival in the home as well as in institutions.[20] Another reason why one might query some of the figures is that they were subject to considerable fluctuation from one year to another. The classic example is provided by Willan who, in his study of mortality at the British Lying-In Hospital, made it an incredible 1 in 914 for the year 1799–1800 but as Marshall has pointed out, if he had taken instead the period 1799–1803 he would have found it as much as 1 in 187.5 (well above Hawkins' figure for the preceeding decade).[21] Differences in policy regarding the admission of patients are also a possibility. Hawkins was well aware of this, distinguishing the mortality of the insane and pregnant from the 'general' and noting the proportion of fatalities arising from 'surgical' as opposed to 'physical' cases (p. 76). But rather more subtle differences may have escaped him. At the Norwich and Norfolk hospital for instance, according to a recent study, the list of persons excluded from treatment included most paupers, all cases of 'infectious' and 'incurable' disease *and* all those able to pay for their treatment.[22] It is unlikely, though, that such factors could alone account for so consistent a fall in mortality and one which can be observed in hospitals on the continent, as well as in England. Hawkins' explanation of the trend is thus of considerable interest. Better medical knowledge is mentioned but not stressed – instead most emphasis is placed on growing national prosperity and greater attention given to cleanliness and ventilation in the hospitals.[23] The mortality of the provincial hospital was lower than that of its Metropolitan counterpart because of the smaller size of the town and of the hospital (p. 81), and the one figure he gives for private practice (although there is no information on the status of the patients) is lower again (p. 122). From Paris came evidence that the mortality even in hospitals was largely determined by one's position in society. Of the wandering poor as many as 1 in 4 died after admission, of servants or others employed in buildings 1 in 10, and of the Guard of Paris only 1 in 21.

Where Hawkins' argument is broad Quetelet's is particular. Take his examination of the factors which determine the ratio of the sexes at birth. There are any number of factors to choose from, climatic, racial, environmental (urban–rural) as well as the age of each parent. There was also Prévost's suggestion that the process of family formation was more likely to cease after the birth of a son than after the birth of a daughter, an exercise of moral restraint which has recently been seen to be the key factor behind the fall in fertility in early twentieth-century England.[24] Quetelet did not dismiss this idea out of hand (indeed he later argued at some length that those who married early in life did, through a fear of producing too large a family, practise family limitation so successfully that their families were no larger in size than those of the couples who married when in their early thirties), but, as far as the possible influence on the sex ratio is concerned, he gave most emphasis to the age difference between the spouses. These factors and many others have been alternatively accepted and rejected by later writers. On one thing almost all are agreed, and that is that there are important differences to explain. Indeed there is a certain plausibility about why, for instance, fewer boys should be live-born in the town than in the country, for elsewhere Quetelet makes clear that rather more males are still-born and that still-births were more frequent in town than in the country.[25] Yet it would be advisable to bear in mind a recent study which reaches the surprising conclusion that providing a sufficient number of observations are made, none of the factors so far discussed can be shown to influence the sex ratio to any marked degree.[21]

An important element in Quetelet's reasoning was that factors which determined the distribution of births, marriages and deaths could equally help explain the distribution of quite different events such as various types of crime. Occasionally this sort of argument leads him astray as when he connects the fact that rather more men than women in the towns died while still in their early twenties (possibly a statistical artifact caused by the in-migration of young adult males) with a rise in 'the passions' which had its most marked effect in the comparatively large numbers of men of the same age group who found themselves before the criminal courts. Further than this he saw the very type of crime changing with the age of the criminal. In youth when the passions were strong, seduction, particularly of the weakest, was the most likely offence; with greater maturity, the ability to reason developed sufficiently for the planning of assassinations, while finally, in old age, the criminal practised the art of deception, this taking the place of the strength lost, no doubt prematurely, as a result of his earlier dissipations (see pp. 93–4). The old criminal was, therefore, the most depraved. Not only had he a life of crime behind him, but, Quetelet held, in general development of reason and the onset of old age should lead not to more crime but to less since reason struck at the potential criminal's inclination and old-age at his ability.

Quetelet also devoted particular attention to the variation in numbers of recorded events over time periods ranging from years down to days. The seasonal pattern in the distribution of births, marriages and deaths has attracted much attention from other writers and we cannot dwell on it here except to note that for births as well as deaths, Quetelet found the seasonal pattern stronger in the country than in the town (pp. 20, 35). But Quetelet has also much to say on the seasonal pattern of crime, seeing crime against property as more especially a phenomenon of colder months, with crimes against the person (homicide, assault and the like) primarily as an affair of the summer, this also being the maximum period for both suicide and insanity (pp. 76–80). As for the time of day, some rather insubstantial evidence pointed to a larger proportion of deaths as well as births occurring in the six hour period after midnight (pp. 20, 37); for suicide the critical period appears to have been 6 a.m.–8 a.m. (p. 81). It seems difficult to know what to make of all this and what possible mechanism Quetelet thought was at work. It has sometimes been said that he thought in terms of the direct involvement of the physical environment[27] and Quetelet was certainly far from explicit on this point (he cites, without comment, an observation by Villermé that the greatest number of conceptions nearly coincides with the greatest number of rapes) although in his discussion of crime figures he does make clear that it is the greater prevalence of misery and want that causes the winter peak of crimes against property (p. 90).

Another novel feature of Quetelet's work was the space he devoted to a consideration of the weight and stature of the individual. Such measurements had of course been taken in the past. The earliest figures Quetelet had available came for the year 1783 (p. 65) and earlier sources were available[28] but the subject had not hitherto received such detailed treatment. Many of his findings that boys were taller than girls even at birth, that girls were *relatively* as tall at 16 as boys at 18, and that the offspring of the poor, whether they are identified by occupation of parent or by place of residence, were both shorter and lighter than their social superiors, for example undergraduates at the University of Cambridge,[29] now seem commonplace although this was clearly not so when the propositions were first formulated. Before proceeding any further it would be as well to consider the doubtful value of some of these figures. Not only did Quetelet rely on cross-sectional and not longitudinal observations (that is, the tabulations of successive age groups relate to different persons and not to the same persons as they became older), but he was forced to derive his Belgian data from a variety of sources. For example, 'young persons' were measured and weighed in the schools and medical hospital, and adults (except for the very old who consisted entirely of patients in one of the other hospitals in Brussels) were drawn from the population at large with the exception that the number of people from the lower orders was particularly deficient. Since the respective average height and weight of these groups might always have been different, any growth curve constructed on the basis of these figures would be doubly unreliable. Nor does this exhaust the list of difficulties for many measurements were made regardless of shoes and clothes, and Quetelet's corrections may not always have been sufficiently accurate.[30] It is too tempting, however, given the nature of the subject with all that it implies, for the rate of growth at a time when the standard of living and in particular nutritional levels were far lower than today, to put his figures altogether to one side. If for example we look at the children of the poorest inhabitants identified by Rowntree in his classic study of York in the opening year of the twentieth century, these turn out to be considerably heavier and taller than the Lancashire children of the 1830s.[31] An additional sign of privation, particularly when young, was the prolongation of the period of growth until a person was well into his twenties. Maximum height was thus not only lower, but achieved later. It would be interesting to speculate on the significance of this for a period when many of the persons in this age group would still be unmarried and subservient, if not to their parents (who given the higher mortality might well be dead) then at least to the more senior members of the community whether master, employer or merely neighbour, although whether such small differences in height had any effect on the chance of marriage at an early age is another matter.

One more feature of this section of Quetelet's study deserves comment and that is the tabulation of the distribution of weight at birth, one of the most critical factors even today influencing the chances of the infant's survival. Unfortunately Quetelet attempts no longitudinal study – we know that 2 out of the 119 infants born at the Foundling Hospital weighed less than 2 kg (4.40 lbs) and that a further 10 weighed less than 2.5 kg (5.5 lbs) but we do not know their fate. This evidence, if it exists, would be well worth a thorough investigation. In passing, it is worth noting that the average weight at birth of 3.20 kg (7.04 lbs) for boys and 2.91 kgs (6.40 lbs) for girls does not differ so markedly from that of the present day western world.[32]

In retrospect Quetelet's achievement was not that he pioneered new statistical techniques. He relied heavily, as Helen Walker pointed out some years ago, on normal distribution.[33] This can be seen most clearly in his introduction (p. x) where he argues that even if the 'best' cases are excluded i.e. those which seem to give the most reasonable result, and a sufficient number of observations are taken, then the mean will not be affected. To resolve a multi-causal situation he proposed distinguishing all the probable causes and assigning an appropriate weight to each but the technique of correlation lay in the future and it cannot be said that he succeeded in determining whether it was race, climate, or the economic environment which exerted the predominant influence on the pace of man's journey from birth to the tomb. Quetelet was certainly a champion of the use of numbers – he has a statistician's contempt for all kinds of literary evidence (see his remarks on Shakespeare on p. 22) – but his real achievement was what might best be termed his commonsense approach to every discussion in which he took part. Take, for example, his criticism (p. 18) of Sadler who had asserted that when marriages rose, births fell and that when deaths were high so too were marriages, the population thus maintaining itself in a state of equilibrium. Quetelet questions both the figures and the interpretation arguing, with reference to the latter, that since in a period of heavy mortality the number of people having to remarry must rise there will be a consequent fall in the number of births per marriage although overall fertility may remain unchanged or even be higher. We may feel, however, that at times Quetelet enunciated theories when the basic data were untested and almost certainly unreliable, a fault of which he was very much aware (p. 103). This was only to be expected in an age when experiment was the order of the day, when each fresh enquiry seemed to open a whole new area of study. Some were even studying the behaviour of animals and relating this to humans. Hawkins quotes with approval in connection with the high level of urban mortality experiments by Jenner and Baron which show that the loss of open range and natural nourishment has a strong tendency to first disorganise and then destroy animals. Hawkins also mentions (p. 136) experiments on a human population by Professor Boër, carried out with the express encouragement of Emperor Joseph II, that were decidedly less successful: the majority of the twenty infants in the Foundling Hospital at Vienna who were being given a variety of diets to establish which would be the most beneficial unfortunately dying before any conclusions could be drawn. Although, by the early nineteenth century, certain passages to the tomb (the phrase is Quetelet's) had been closed, many were still wide open.

RICHARD WALL
Cambridge Group for the
History of Population,
April 1973

Notes

[1] Details from H. Westergaard, *Contributions to the History of Statistics* (1932), pp. 139, 145

[2] Biographical details and a synopsis of his Reports on the condition of the manufacturing districts and on the prisons are to be found in William Munk, *A Roll of the Royal College of Physicians*, III (1878), pp. 303–4. He died in 1894. M. Greenwood, *Medical Statistics from Graunt to Farr* (1948), p. 68

[3] D. Glass 'Some Aspects of the Development of Demography'. *Journal of the Royal Society of Arts* (1955–56), p. 860

[4] The first two by Greenwood (1948), p. 69, the latter by E. Grebenik in P. M. Hauser and O. D. Duncan, *The Study of Population* (1959), p. 191

[5] Although even here there have been reservations, both Lorrimer and Shrylock holding the Quetelet's vision of quantitative social physics commanded little acceptance. See F. Lorrimer 'The Development of Demography' in Hauser and Duncan (1959), p. 159; R. H. Shrylock, *The Development of Modern Medicine* (1936), p. 142

[6] H. Walker, *Studies in the History of Statistical Method* (1929), pp. 41–3

[7] Westergaard (1932), p. 165

[8] This is a very common charge and can be found for instance in E. Durkheim, *Suicide, A Study in Sociology*, ed. Simpson G. (1968), pp. 302–304, and H. Mannheim *Comparative Criminology* (1965), p. 97.

[9] D. Eversley, *Social Theories of Fertility in the Malthusian Debate* (1959), pp. 195–6

[10] These remarks are based on S. Diamond's introduction to an earlier reprint of Quetelet's treatise (1969), pp. IX–X. Diamond stresses to the extent which Quetelet's theories reflect Saint–Simonist influences.

[11] Diamond (1969), p. VII

[12] Hawkins, *Elements of Medical Statistics* (1828) p. V

[13] M. Drake, *Population and Society in Norway* 1735–1865 (1969), p. 14

[14] S. E. Sprott, *The English Debate on Suicide* (1961) p. 161; P. Laslett, *The World we have lost* (1971) p. 146

[15] ibid.

[16] See Simpson's introduction to Durkheim on suicide (1968).

[17] J. Krause, 'English population movements 1700–1850' in M. Drake, ed., *Population and Industrialisation* (1969), p. 124

[18] L. A. J. Quetelet, *A Treatise on Man* (1842), p. 46

[19] T. McKeown and R. G. Brown 'Medical evidence related to English population changes in the 18th century', reprinted in M. Drake (1969)

[20] McKeown and Brown (1969) p. 46

[21] T. H. Marshall, 'The Population Problem during the Industrial Revolution' reprinted in D. Glass and D. Eversley eds., *Population and History* (1965), p. 258

[22] S. Cherry, 'The role of the provincial hospital. The Norfolk and Norwich Hospital, 1771–1880', *Population Studies* pp. 26, 2 (1972), 295

[23] See pp. 77–8, 230. Quetelet took a broadly similar view, see pp. 43, 57 of his *Treatise*.

[24] H. J. Habakkuk, *Population Growth and Economic Development Since 1750* (1971), pp. 62–5

[25] See pp. 24, 29, although in fact the Table on p. 30 for urban and rural areas of Belgium suggests otherwise.

[26] See M. S. Teitelbaum, 'Factors associated with the sex ratio in human populations' in G. A. Harrison and A. J. Boyce, *The Structure of Human Populations* (1972). This reference I owe to M. Louis Duchesne.

[27] e.g. Mannheim (1965), pp. 14, 203

[28] See the Appendix by the translator, p. 119. The number of observations on which the figures were based was not given. This is only one of several notes which the translator, Dr. John Knox, who was a lecturer in Anatomy at the University of Edinburgh, added when he either wished to supplement or to disagree with what Quetelet had said.

[29] Note slight correction to the latter figures in the Appendix pp. 113–4.

[30] See in particular the objection by the translator on p. 60 that Lancashire children may have worn clogs rather than shoes.

[31] Compare the figures on pp. 60, 65, 119, with those in B. Seebohm, Rowntree, *Poverty, A study of Town Life*, Nelson's Edition (1913) pp. 250–2. The secular trend is in fact well documented: see in particular J. M. Tanner, *Growth at Adolescence* (1962), pp. 143–52 and bibliography,

[32] According to Tanner citing T. McKeown and R. G. Record, weight and height at birth is not dependent on the genotype of the child but reflects the maternal uterine environment although this itself is influenced by genetic as well as environmental factors. Tanner (1962), pp. 89, 119–120

[33] Walker (1929), p. 42

ELEMENTS

OF

MEDICAL STATISTICS;

CONTAINING THE SUBSTANCE OF

The Gulstonian Lectures

DELIVERED AT

THE ROYAL COLLEGE OF PHYSICIANS:

WITH NUMEROUS ADDITIONS,

ILLUSTRATIVE OF

THE COMPARATIVE SALUBRITY, LONGEVITY, MORTALITY,
AND PREVALENCE OF DISEASES
IN THE PRINCIPAL COUNTRIES AND CITIES OF THE
CIVILIZED WORLD.

———

BY F. BISSET HAWKINS, M.D.

OF EXETER COLLEGE, OXFORD;

FELLOW OF THE ROYAL COLLEGE OF PHYSICIANS;

AND PHYSICIAN TO THE WESTMINSTER GENERAL DISPENSARY.

———

LONDON:

PRINTED FOR

LONGMAN, REES, ORME, BROWN, AND GREEN,
PATERNOSTER-ROW.

1829.

Republished in 1973 by Gregg International Publishers Limited
Westmead, Farnborough, Hants, England

PREFACE.

MUCH has been done towards an illustration of the Medical Statistics of various Countries, Cities, Towns, and Hospitals, and excellent essays have been made on some separate branches. A great variety of important single facts has been gradually exhibited, by writers engaged on their own particular topics, by medical and other journals. Many of these, from their fugitive form, or insulated situation, have been neglected or forgotten; and *Reports*, which had been matured with severe labour and disinterested patience, have sometimes appeared valueless, because unaccompanied with the materials of comparison. We naturally turn away from the mere register of occurrences which does not seem to tend to establish a principle, or to contain the elements of generalisation.

But a favourable moment is, perhaps, at length arrived for arranging these scattered fragments into the rudiments of a system, and for comparing together, in close apposition, the documents afforded by different countries and institutions, which at present lie far asunder. No one can be more deeply aware than myself of the difficulties, and even dangers, of the subject; of the dubious authenticity, and frequent fluctuation of the necessary details; and of the precarious nature of any general principles attempted to be framed out of facts, which have, for the most part, endured the test of only a few years, and which have only recently become the object of enquiry or scrutiny. But an extensive assemblage and classification of such facts possess an historical and local value, whatsoever may be the fate of the reasonings deduced from them.

Independently of the light which this study throws upon Medical Science, it affords the most valuable illustrations of the history, manners, and customs of mankind, and a just criterion of the progressive or retrograde movements of society. Political philosophy can make few steps without an occasional recourse to its aid, and none at all without a reference to its stores, on explaining the principles which regulate the population of states. Malthus, who may be in some degree considered as the father of that subject, from the maturity to which he has reared it, remarks, that " we may promise ourselves a clearer insight into the internal structure of human society from those enquiries. But the science may be said yet to be in its infancy, and many of the objects, on which it would be desirable to have information, have been either omitted, or not stated with sufficient accuracy." * Some of these deficiencies have been partly supplied since the time when they were pointed out by this distinguished writer, and others are at present occupying the attention of medical practitioners and political philosophers in various parts of the world. I should be amply rewarded if the present humble essay should form a temporary repository of the most important of their labours; if it should become one of the early milestones on a road which is comparatively new, rugged as yet and uninviting to the distant traveller, but which gradually discloses the most interesting prospects, and will at length, if I do not deceive myself by premature anticipation, largely recompense the patient adventurer.

I am not aware of the existence of any work in the literature of Europe which treats the subject in all its parts, or which takes so extensive a range as the present; a circumstance which will doubtless form the best apology for any inaccuracies or omissions, inseparable from a first attempt to sketch the outlines of a system. In 1792 *Finke* † published at Leipsic a system

---

* Essay on the Principle of Population. 6th ed. i. 19.

† Versuch einer Allgemeinen Medicinisch-praktischen Geographie. 3 vols. 8vo.

of Medical Geography, elaborated with minute industry from the scanty materials afforded by that period, but divided under the heads of different countries and cities, not aiming at classification, comparison, nor general views, and inapplicable to the present time.　Professor *Berard* * of Montpelier has lately published a valuable lecture delivered at the opening of his Course of Hygiene, in which many of the most important facts of Medical Statistics are enumerated and generalised : it has repeatedly enriched the following pages.　Tommasini †, the eminent professor of Bologna, is, I believe, the only author who has written a particular essay on the necessity of applying Statistics to illustrate the practice of medicine.

It would have been easy to have trebled the size of this volume, but to many it will already appear too long, and the actual demand for this sort of knowledge would scarcely warrant a greater trial of patience : if a favourable reception should afford me an opportunity of extending it, I shall seek to supply some omissions which are at present unavoidable, and others which a first experiment rendered prudent.

---

* Discours sur les Améliorations Progressives de la Santé Publique par l'Influence de la Civilisation.　Paris, 1826.

† Della Necessita di sottopere ad una Statistica i fatti piu importanti della Medicina Pratica.　Bologna, 1821.

I have endeavoured to avoid fatiguing the reader, and overloading the page with constant references ; but every remarkable fact is traced to its source, and a sufficient number of authorities are cited throughout to form even a *Bibliography* of the subject.

As this essay does not aspire to the character of original composition, but is merely a *collection*, I beg to make one general acknowledgment of the numerous instances in which entire sentences have been copied from various writers. The gratification of the reader would have been often diminished by any alterations of expression, and the attempt would only have violated the genuineness of a relation, or have diluted the strength of an argument.

Golden Square,
March, 1829.

TABLE OF CONTENTS.

ELEMENTS

OF

MEDICAL STATISTICS.

CHAPTER I.

UTILITY AND HISTORY OF THE SUBJECT —COMPARISON
BETWEEN THE VALUE OF LIFE IN ANCIENT AND
MODERN TIMES.

THE word *Statistics* appears to have been first
used about the middle of the last century by
Achenwal, a professor at Göttingen, to express
a summary view of the physical, moral, and
political condition of states. Many important
facts, which belong to the domain of statistics,
had been published long before this appellation
had been applied to them.

But some of the details thus collected for
general purposes, were found to throw light upon
health and disease; and, on the other hand,
it was often necessary to have recourse to
medical authorities, in order to elucidate various

B

points of the general picture. A combination of these scattered features forms *Medical Statistics,* an elementary specimen of which it is the object of the following pages to present. We may perhaps define it, in a few words, to be the application of numbers to illustrate the natural history of man in health and disease.

The *probability* of life, and the *mean* life, are two expressions which often occur in such enquiries. By the *probable* life is understood the age to which one-half of all who are born in a particular country or city attain. The *mean* life implies the result of adding together the number of years attained by a given number of persons, and of dividing the sum total among each of them in an equal proportion.

Statistics has become the key to several sciences, opening in a manner the most convincing, simple, and summary, their gradual progress, their actual condition, their relations to each other, the success which they have attained, or the deficiencies which remain to be supplied. Its application to the objects of government has created political economy ; and there is reason to believe, that a careful cultivation of it, in reference to the natural history of man in health and disease, would materially assist the completion of a philosophy of medicine, by pointing out to the physicians of every part of the world the comparative merits of various modes of practice, the history of disease in different ages and countries, the increase and decrease of particular maladies, the tendency of certain situations, professions, and modes of life to protect or to expose ; and by indicating, as the basis of prognosis, those extended tabular views of the duration and termination of diseases, which are furnished, at successive periods, by hospitals and civic registers.

Medical statistics affords the most convincing proofs of the efficacy of medicine : it is one of the easiest arguments that can be employed to refute the vulgar notion (and one sometimes carelessly countenanced by medical men), that nature is alone sufficient for the cure of disease, and that art as frequently impedes as it accelerates her course. The powers of self-restoration are in no diseases more conspicuous than in fever. But if we form a statistical comparison of fever treated by art, with the results of fever consigned to the care of nature, we shall derive an indisputable conclusion in favour of our profession. * Hippocrates has left a frank and explicit statement of the history and fate of forty-two cases of acute disease, in which it does not seem that any therapeutical plan was adopted, if we except glysters and suppositories in a few, and blood-letting in one. Amongst these were

* Blane, Select Dissertations.

thirty-seven cases of continued fever, without local affection. Of the thirty-seven, twenty-one died, above half of the whole. But if we examine the returns of the Fever Hospital of London, we find (in 1825) that the total mortality was less than one in seven; and half of these deaths occurred within seventy-two hours of the admission of the patients, — a circumstance which indicates that several entered at a period of disease when the hope of recovery was extinct. In the Dublin Fever Hospital we find a still lower mortality: the average from 1804 to 1812 was one in twelve: and in the clinical wards at Edinburgh, in 1818, the mortality of fever was also about one in twelve. Of five cases of local inflammations, which Hippocrates records, four were fatal; of all his forty-two patients, in short, twenty-five were lost: a termination which throws no shade over his skill, but only brings to light his love of truth. The mortality belonged to the age, and not to the physician; and we may reasonably infer, that under other practitioners of his time and country, it was even more severe. It is curious to observe, that of the five cases of local inflammation, the only one which survived was the solitary instance in which bleeding was employed, — a pleurisy. We perceive, that one out of two acute cases may recover by the almost unassisted efforts of nature, but that under the medical protection of our own age and country, six out of seven, or even eleven out of twelve, are likely to survive, according to the period of the disease at which they are placed under treatment.

Medical statistics alone enables us to form an estimate of the influence of various mechanical improvements on the air of certain districts. The town of Portsmouth, for instance, is built upon a low portion of the marshy island of Portsea : it was formerly very subject to inter-mittent fever; but since it was paved and drained in 1769, this disorder has no longer prevailed ; while Hilsea, and other parts of the island of Portsea, retained the aguish disposition until1793, when a drainage was made, which subdued its force. *   The population of Portsmouth has pro-gressively increased, and yet its salubrity has maintained an equal pace.   The mortality in 1800, was one in twenty-eight ; in the next census of 1811, it had declined to one in thirty-eight ; at the same time that the mortality of Plymouth amounted to one in twenty-eight.

No documents remain to inform us of the rate of mortality, or of longevity, amongst the Greeks.   A few facts on these points have de-scended respecting the Romans.   In a small tract of country, in the reign of Vespasian, fifty-four persons were enumerated who had at-

---

* Blane, Select Diss.

tained their 100th year, forty who were between 100 and 140, and two individuals who had lived above a century and a half : a calculation which is highly favourable, but which only relates to a particular rural district. If we were inclined to attach any weight to Lucian on this subject, his testimony might be produced : in his Καταπλους, he informs us, that, out of 1000 persons who died, 398 were above sixty years of age ; but this was probably a vague assertion, hazarded in the humour of the moment, since it is totally opposed to the statements of Domitius Ulpianus. This earliest authority on the subject of longevity was a lawyer in the reign of Alexander Severus, of whom he became the secretary and principal minister. From the want of hospitals among the Romans, from the humble condition of their medical attendants, from their gross sensuality, inactive habits, abuse of the bath, and manner of dress, as well as from the unhealthy state of their situation (which even then appears to have been a source of alarm), we might have anticipated that longevity would not be common; and the authority of Ulpian corroborates the opinion. According to him, registers of population, puberty, age, sex, disease, and death, were kept with exactness by the censors, from the time of Servius Tullius to Justinian, and comprehend a period of ten consecutive centuries. But, unfortunately, these registers embrace the citizens of Rome alone, and not that large part of the population composed of slaves. The inferences to be drawn from them relate accordingly to select, or *picked* lives, and not to the mass of society. From observations formed on 1000 years, the expectation, or mean term of Roman life, has been fixed at thirty years. To make a just comparison of the value of life in Rome and in England, we must select subjects in England similarly circumstanced, of a condition relatively easy : and the result discloses an extension of life remarkably in our favour. Mr. Finlayson has ascertained, from very extensive observation, on the decrement of life prevailing among the nominees of the *tontines*, and other life-annuities granted by authority of Parliament, during the last forty years, that the expectation of life is above fifty years for persons thus situated, which affords our easy classes a superiority of twenty years above the Roman citizen. The expectation of life for the whole mass of Britain is at least one in forty-five, which affords to all our classes a superiority of fifteen years above even the easy classes of the Romans.

The mean term of life among the easy classes of Paris is at present forty-two, which gives them an advantage of twelve years above the Romans.

It appears that the probability of life to the *whole* population of Florence, is the same in the

present century as that of the easy classes of
Rome in the third century.

The following appear to have been the
probabilities of life among the Roman citizens
in the third century of the Christian æra. *

From Birth to 20 years of age, 30 years.

20	to 25	28
25	to 30	25
30	to 35	22
35	to 40	20
40	to 45	18
45	to 50	13
50	to 55	9
55	to 60	7
60	to 65	5

It is interesting to compare with these results
the conclusions of Finlayson indicated above. At
twenty years of age, Finlayson affords a probability of forty years. At forty he allows
twenty-nine, and at fifty so many as twenty-two.
At sixty, Finlayson admits fifteen. And as the
documents of Ulpian appear to afford no sufficient
data beyond the age of sixty-five, we may infer
that the number of Romans who passed that
period was not very numerous; whereas the
proportion of such in our own country is large;
and, indeed, throughout Europe at present, since

---

* Berard, Discours sur les Améliorations, &c. p. 69.

Blumenbach asserts, that, after an accurate examination of many bills of mortality, he has ascertained a remarkable fact, that a considerable proportion of Europeans attain their eighty-fourth year, while, on the other hand, few exceed it. *

In more modern times, the observances of the Christian religion appear, alone, to have revived the registry of births and burials. After the foundation of churches and monasteries, lists were composed of those who were baptized and who died in the Christian faith; and such appears to have been the later origin of statistical tables, relating to the physical and moral history of man. The ravages of the *plague* seem to have impressed on the ministers of Henry the Eighth the necessity of accurate registers of the burials in every parish.

At Geneva, good mortuary tables have been preserved since 1560, and the results are in the highest degree curious and satisfactory. It appears that, at the time of the Reformation, half the children born did not reach six years of age; in the seventeenth century, the probability of life was about eleven and a half years; in the eighteenth century, it increased to above twenty-seven years. We arrive at the remarkable conclusion, that, in the space of about three

---

* Institutiones Physiologicæ.

hundred years, the probability of life to a citizen of Geneva at his birth, has become five times greater. The *mean life* was thus, in one century, eighteen years; in the next, it grew to twenty-three; in the middle of the next, it rose to thirty-two; and, finally, during the present century, from 1815 to 1826, it amounts to thirty-six years.

The first of the *continued* weekly bills of mortality extant at the Parish Clerks' Hall in London, begins in 1603, the first year of the reign of James the First; since which period, an uninterrupted account has been maintained; and as they appear to have been originally undertaken during the pressure of the *plague*, so, after some discontinuance, they were permanently renewed under another severe visitation of the same evil. These bills now contain ninety-seven parishes within the walls, seventeen without the walls, twenty-nine out-parishes in Middlesex and Surrey, and ten parishes in the city and liberties of Westminster; but the great extension of London since 1660 renders them imperfect: the parishes of St. Marylebone, and of St. Pancras, are not included. Another deficiency is the absence of any account of the births and deaths among the dissenters from the established church. These points might be easily remedied; but a more difficult task, in the present state of our medical police, would be to improve the actual manner of ascertaining the mode of death of every individual. The *sworn searchers,* whose office is to *visit* and to *view* every corpse, are persons of no medical knowledge ; they are dismissed with a gratuity, and are satisfied with the first answer given to them by the relatives of the deceased. Nevertheless, these registers afford some approximation to the truth. Compared with each other through a long series of years, they throw considerable light on the fluctuations of disease, on the influence of weather, and on the retrograde or progressive state of the public health. Under an improved arrangement, they might prove in a high degree auxiliary to the medical sciences, to the police of health, and to political philosophy.

Captain John Graunt, of London, has the honour of being the first writer who ever directed the attention of the world to the comparative births and deaths of different cities, years, seasons, sexes ; to the comparative mortality of disease ; to the proportion of births to deaths ; and to the relation of the *town* to the *country* in these respects. In his work, entitled " *Natural and Political Observations upon Bills of Mortality,*" which was first published in 1661, he displays a singular genius for observation, in a field where no footstep can be traced before his own. He was really the creator of the new science of *Statistics.*

The most industrious labourer who followed him in the same mine, was Süssmilch, whose celebrated and often-quoted work belongs to the department of Natural Theology, but abounds in all the official and other tables which that period afforded. *

The gradual accumulation of registers in the principal states of Europe, had furnished a large stock of materials, but the fruit was not as yet sufficiently ripe to afford a valuable harvest. His object seems to have been rather to draw certain general conclusions, which apply to the whole civilised globe taken in mass, than to estimate the comparative degree in which various countries and cities enjoy, or are deficient in, health and longevity. He adopts the idea of Montesquieu, and many early writers, that Europe requires laws to favour the propagation of the species, and that it is one of the principal duties of governments to attend to the number of marriages.

Süssmilch estimates the nearest average of the mortality of all countries, taking towns and villages together, as one in thirty-six. Büsching, a celebrated geographer, makes it, about the same period, from one in thirty-two to one in

---

* Göttliche Ordnung in d. Veründd. d. Menschl. Geschl. a. d. Geb., d. Tod. u. der Fortpflanz dess. erwiesen. Berlin, 1742.

thirty-seven. About eighty years have now elapsed since then; and a surprising improvement in the physical condition of man has progressively developed itself. In almost every civilised country of Europe, we find every succeeding ten years produce a smaller annual proportion of deaths ; and in Britain the value of life is nearly doubled, if we compare Büsching's rate of one in thirty-two, with the actual rate afforded in 1821, of about one in sixty.

Dr. Odier of Geneva, in the fourth volume of the *Bibliothèque Britannique ;* and Dr. Heberden, junior, in his valuable " *Observations on the Increase and Decrease of different Diseases,*" published in 1801, appear to be the first writers who had the merit of disclosing this improvement in life in their respective countries. Sir Gilbert Blane, Mr. Rickman, and Mr. Finlayson, in England, Dr. Villermé in France, and Dr. Casper in Germany, have subsequently laboured with zeal in the same path of enquiry ; and have obtained results the most interesting to human nature, because uniformly agreeing in its tendency to improvement. Their statements rest on demonstrated conclusions, and not on the conjectures and questionable inferences with which the ordinary reasonings on the natural history of man abound. Great obligations are also due to the *Edinburgh Medical Journal,* and to the Geo-

graphical Section of the *Bulletin Universel,* for
the various information and reasonings which
they have afforded in every branch of medical
statistics.

CHAP. II.

PROGRESSIVE CHANGES AND PRESENT STATE OF MOR-
TALITY IN GREAT BRITAIN. — ILLUSTRATIVE TABLES.

THE earliest account of mortality in England
relates to the plague, which spread from the
north-western parts of Asia over all Europe, and
reached England in 1349. In some parts of the
kingdom, two-thirds or more of the inhabitants
were carried off; but, on the average, one-half
was computed to have perished.

We have no data for the mortality of Britain
during the following centuries; but, in 1695, a
tontine was created by Parliament, called the
Million Act; and Mr. Finlayson has deduced,
from observations on the mortality which took
place among the nominees, that the mean duration of life at birth was about thirty-seven years,
reckoning from 1695; but above fifty-two years,
reckoning from 1789. At ten years of age it
was thirty-eight from the first period, but forty-
eight from the second. At fifty years of age it
was seventeen from the first, but twenty-two
from the second. The persons upon whom the
calculation is made are select lives, taken from

the middle ranks of society; but, as they are similar cases, the comparison must be admitted to be fair. But a corresponding change in the health and duration of life of the total mass of society has equally occurred : this is easily deducible from a comparison of the census taken every ten years. In 1780, the annual mortality of England and Wales was 1 in 40. In 1790, it diminished to 1 in 45. In 1801, it continued to diminish, but not at the same rate ; it became 1 in 47. The moderate improvement of this census is the effect of the scarcity by which England was afflicted in 1795 and 1800. In 1811, the reduction in deaths proceeds: the annual amount is 1 in 50, or 1 in 52; and finally, in 1821, the yearly mortality sinks to 1 in 60, or 1 in 58 (which last proportion Mr. Rickman considers to be nearest to the truth); so that, on the whole, it has decreased from 1 in 40, to 1 in 58, nearly one-third in forty years. The mortality of the several counties in England alone ranges between 1 in 47 and 1 in 72; Middlesex and Sussex being the two extremes. In Wales, Pembrokeshire, and Anglesey, have only one death yearly in eighty-three individuals, which is the lowest genuine rate of mortality that has been published in any part of Europe. But even in Middlesex, where the rate is higher than in any other county, let us remark the change which has supervened in only 10 years: in 1811, it was 1 in 36; in 1821, eleven more lives are added, to make 1 in 47. The mortality of every county is mainly influenced by the proportion of large towns which it includes; thus, the mortality of Hampshire, which has several such, is 1 in 58; but in Sussex, where they are less numerous, it is only 1 in 72; and in Cornwall, for a similar reason, only 1 in 71. Kent, Surrey, Lancashire, Warwickshire, and Cheshire are the counties where, next to Middlesex, the deaths are most numerous. Kent is subject to ague; more than half the population of Surrey live within the walls of the metropolis; Lancashire and Warwickshire are counties which enjoy advantages from nature, but these are counterbalanced by their large manufacturing towns.

In Lincolnshire, the amount is only 1 in 62, although it is particularly the seat of ague; but this moderate share of mortality is probably due to the large proportion of dry and elevated districts to the fenny; if not to the circumstance which Dr. Wells has remarked, that phthisis pulmonalis is but little observed in places infested with the exhalations which produce intermittent fever.*

----

* Blane, Select Dissertations.

But the decline in the mortality is even more remarkable in our cities than in the rural districts. While the metropolis has extended itself in all directions, and multiplied its inhabitants to an enormous amount; or, in other words, while the seeming sources of its unhealthiness have been largely augmented, it has actually become more friendly to health. Not only its comparative mortality is greatly diminished within the last half century, but its absolute mortality in respect to preceding centuries.* In the year 1697, for example, the total deaths were about 21,000; whereas, a hundred years after, in 1797, the amount was only 17,000; and when we consider the great increase of the inhabitants of the out-parishes at the latter period, the change in the health of London will be seen in a powerful light. But it is singular that this healthy condition seems to have been particularly produced within the last 50 or 60 years; during the very period in which it has most rapidly enlarged its limits and its population. In the middle of last century, the annual mortality was about 1 in 20; it is now (or by the census of 1821) about 1 in 40. So that, in the space of 70 years, the chances of existence are exactly doubled in London; which is a progress and final result without a parallel in the history of

---

* Bateman, Reports on the Diseases of London.   1819.

any other age or country. The annual mortality
in the year 1700 was about 1 in 25. It seems
to have increased from that time to 1720; to
have attained its highest point from 1720 to
1750; and from that period to the present to
have maintained a constant and gradual decline.
Its increase about the middle of the last century
has been attributed to the great abuse of spirituous liquors, which was at length checked by
the imposition of high duties. In 1801, the decrease was to 1 in 35; or, if the returns are
corrected according to Dr. Price's estimate of
omissions, 1 in 30. In 1811, we find 1 in 38;
and there is every reason to imagine that in the
next census, which will be taken three years
hence, the annual number of deaths in London
will not exceed 1 in 42. One city alone, in
Europe or in England, approaches to London in
the value of life proportionately to its size; it is
the second in England in number of inhabitants,
the seat of manufactures — Manchester. The
mortality of Manchester was, about the middle
of last century, 1 in 25; in 1770, 1 in 28. Forty
years after, in 1811, the annual deaths are diminished almost beyond belief, to 1 in 74; but
the improvement does not stop even there, for,
in 1821, they appear to become still fewer,
although the population has been quadrupled
during the 60 years through which the deaths
have so diminished. It is due to the memory of

Dr. Percival and Dr. Ferriar, that we ascribe a large share of this improvement of health to certain regulations of police, particularly with respect to ventilation, recommended and introduced by them into Manchester.* Liverpool and Birmingham have made a considerable progress since 1811, but they fall infinitely short of Manchester. In 1811, the annual deaths of Liverpool were 1 in 30 ; in 1820, they were 1 in 40. The average of Birmingham, in 1811, was 1 in 34 ; in 1821, it was 1 in 43.

In discussing the mortality of manufacturing towns or districts, it is just to remark that the small proportion is not always *real ;* because a constant influx of *adults* is likely to render the number of deaths less considerable than that which would occur in a stationary population composed of all ages.

The following Table of the Baptisms, Burials, and Marriages in England, during twenty years, has been formed by Mr. Rickman : —

---

* Blane.

NUMBER OF BAPTISMS, BURIALS, AND MARRIAGES.

YEAR.	BAPTISMS.			BURIALS.			MARRIAGES.
	Males.	Females.	Total.	Males.	Females.	Total.	
1801	120,521	116,508	237,029	101,352	103,082	204,434	67,228
1802	139,889	133,948	273,837	99,504	100,385	199,889	90,396
1803	150,220	143,888	294,108	102,459	101,269	203,728	94,379
1804	150,583	144,009	294,592	91,538	89,639	181,177	85,738
1805	149,333	142,868	292,201	91,086	90,154	181,240	79,586
1806	147,376	144,553	291,929	92,289	91,163	183,452	80,754
1807	153,787	146,507	300,294	97,996	97,855	195,851	83,923
1808	151,565	144,509	296,074	102,614	98,149	200,763	82,248
1809	152,812	147,177	299,989	97,894	93,577	191,471	83,369
1810	152,591	146,262	298,853	104,907	103,277	208,184	84,470
1811	155,671	149,186	304,857	94,971	93,572	188,543	86,389
1812	153,949	148,005	301,954	95,957	94,445	190,402	82,066
1813	160,685	153,747	314,432	93,726	92,751	186,477	83,860
1814	163,282	155,524	318,806	103,525	102,878	206,403	92,804
1815	176,233	168,698	344,931	99,442	97,966	197,408	99,944
1816	168,801	161,398	330,199	103,954	102,005	205,959	91,946
1817	169,337	162,246	331,583	101,040	98,229	199,269	88,234
1818	169,181	162,203	331,384	107,724	105,900	213,624	92,779
1819	171,107	162,154	333,261	106,749	106,815	213,564	95,571
1820	176,311	167,349	343,660	104,329	104,020	208,349	96,833

On account of the acknowledged omissions in the registers of deaths in most of the parishes of Scotland, few just inferences can be drawn from them. In the parish of Crossmichael, in Kirkcudbright, the mortality at the close of the last century was published as only 1 in 98 ; a proportion which would imply the most unheard-of healthiness ; but there can be little doubt that it was principally occasioned by defects in the registry of interments. From the returns of 99 parishes, which alone were given in the Population Abstracts of 1801, it appears that the average mortality was 1 in 56 ; and if the details were just,

Scotland might at that period boast of the least considerable number of deaths ascertained to exist in any country. We have seen that in 20 years subsequent, England has attained to a still more favourable proportion; and I have not been able to ascertain how far Scotland has kept pace with her. The expectation of an infant's life in Scotland was, in the middle of last century, 31 years at birth, when calculated for the whole country; but in some parishes it was 40 and 46.

In the peculiar circumstances of Ireland, it would be very interesting to know the average mortality. But, unfortunately, no correct parochial registers have been kept; and the information, however much to be desired, is unattainable.

The following Table of the Annual Baptisms, Burials, and Marriages of the several Counties of England, has been formed by Mr. Rickman, on an average of the ten years from 1811 to 1821: —

ANNUAL PROPORTIONS.			COUNTIES
One Baptism to	One Burial to	One Marriage to	OF
36	62	131	BEDFORD.
34	58	145	BERKS.
35	56	144	BUCKINGHAM.
32	58	126	CAMBRIDGE.
36	55	136	CHESTER.
34	71	151	CORNWALL.
34	58	154	CUMBERLAND.
35	63	153	DERBY.
32	61	127	DEVON.
36	66	154	DORSET.
34	55	143	DURHAM.
35	59	150	ESSEX.
37	64	119	GLOUCESTER.
38	63	170	HEREFORD.
34	58	179	HERTFORD.
35	63	132	HUNTINGDON.
31	50	130	KENT.
32	55	126	LANCASTER.
36	59	133	LEICESTER.
32	62	138	LINCOLN.
38	47	106	MIDDLESEX.
47	70	154	MONMOUTH.
33	61	136	NORFOLK.
36	58	134	NORTHAMPTON.
38	58	145	NORTHUMBERLAND.
33	58	133	NOTTINGHAM.
35	61	153	OXFORD.
36	62	148	RUTLAND.
35	58	155	SALOP (Shropshire).
37	63	149	SOMERSET.
32	58	117	SOUTHAMPTON (Hampshire)
32	56	128	STAFFORD.
35	67	139	SUFFOLK.
40	52	148	SURREY.

| ANNUAL PROPORTIONS. | | | COUNTIES |
One Baptism to	One Burial to	One Marriage to	OF
33	72	151	SUSSEX.
37	52	123	WARWICK.
35	58	155	WESTMORLAND.
37	66	145	WILTS.
34	56	143	WORCESTER.
33	57	127	YORK, EAST RIDING.
36	63	151	Do. NORTH RIDING.
35.	61	131	Do. WEST RIDING.
35	57	133	ENGLAND.
41	69	156	WALES.
35	58	134	

To explain the rate of increase of the population of England, the female sex is chosen, as it affords a more accurate standard, from the circumstance of being less exposed to the influence of immigration and emigration.

FEMALES.

1801.	Increase p. Cent.	1811.	Increase p. Cent.	1821.
5,492,354	14 or 14.02	6,262,716	15$\frac{4}{5}$ or 15.82	7,253,728

The following Tables of the Number of Individuals living at various Ages are formed by Mr. Rickman from the census of 1821, and relate to a supposed given proportion of 10,000 males, and 10,000 females : —

MALES.

	Under 5 Years.	5 to 10	10 to 15	15 to 20	20 to 30	30 to 40	40 to 50	50 to 60	60 to 70	70 to 80	80 to 90	90 to 100	100 and upwards.
ENGLAND (collectively)	1538	1343	1169	988	1470	1155	941.0	665.6	447.6	221.9	56.25	4.15	.12

FEMALES.

	Under 5 Years.	5 to 10	10 to 15	15 to 20	20 to 30	30 to 40	40 to 50	50 to 60	60 to 70	70 to 80	80 to 90	90 to 100	100 and upwards.
ENGLAND (collectively)	1444	1268	1056	995	1684	1210	932.6	653.3	458.0	228.2	64.85	5.75	.22

MALES.

	Under 5 Years.	5 to 10	10 to 15	15 to 20	20 to 30	30 to 40	40 to 50	50 to 60	60 to 70	70 to 80	80 to 90	90 to 100	100 and upwards.
WALES (collectively)	1514	1407	1210	1009	1433	1109	871.4	646.3	474.8	243.6	74.09	7.54	.09

FEMALES.

	Under 5 Years.	5 to 10	10 to 15	15 to 20	20 to 30	30 to 40	40 to 50	50 to 60	60 to 70	70 to 80	80 to 90	90 to 100	100 and upwards.
WALES (collectively)	1382	1281	1093	1003	1560	1163	911.6	672.6	535.5	281.4	104.76	10.95	.50

MALES.

	Under 5 Years.	5 to 10	10 to 15	15 to 20	20 to 30	30 to 40	40 to 50	50 to 60	60 to 70	70 to 80	80 to 90	90 to 100	100 and upwards.
SCOTLAND (collectively)	1494	1357	1247	1032	1490	1095	895.4	649	458.1	216.3	58.22	6.71	.43

FEMALES.

	Under 5 Years.	5 to 10	10 to 15	15 to 20	20 to 30	30 to 40	40 to 50	50 to 60	60 to 70	70 to 80	80 to 90	90 to 100	100 and upwards.
SCOTLAND (collectively)	1294	1177	1057	1048	1769	1204	937.9	711.6	502.2	225.5	65.18	7.42	.60

Ages of the Inhabitants of *London* arranged
under the same divisions. *Fractions are omitted
below* 90.

	Under 5 Years.	5 to 10	10 to 15	15 to 20	20 to 30	30 to 40	40 to 50	50 to 60	60 to 70	70 to 80	80 to 90	90 to 100	100 and upwards.
Males	1397	1095	936	865	1718	1548	1203	730	353	128	22	1.69	.21
Females	1216	995	834	959	2062	1567	1092	690	388	156	34	3.93	.32

CHAP. III.

THE SUPERIOR SALUBRITY OF GREAT BRITAIN PROVED
BY A GENERAL COMPARISON WITH OTHER COUNTRIES.

On the continent of Europe, we find that changes in the duration of life have been experienced, similar in nature, and following the same laws, as those of our own country, but very inferior in degree. In France, for instance, the annual deaths in 1781 were 1 in 29 for the whole population; in 1802, they were 1 in 30; in 1823, they were 1 in 40. In Paris, about the middle of last century, the mortality was 1 in 25. At present it is about 1 in 32. As far back as the 14th century, M. Villermé has calculated from some manuscript documents that it was 1 in 16 or 17; and if the authority is good, this last is a most interesting fact, as it is almost the only statistical fragment which remains to characterise that early age. In Sweden, we find that from 1755 to 1775 the annual deaths were 1 in 35; from 1775 to 1795, they were 1 in 37; and, finally, in 1823, they had diminished to 1 in 48. And thus the annual mortality of Berlin

was 1 in 28 from 1747 to 1755 ; but less than
1 in 34 from 1816 to 1822.

Since the late peace, the principal governments of Europe have paid much attention to
statistics, and we possess very instructive returns
from nearly all the countries, cities, and hospitals on the Continent. A comparison of these
results enables us to submit a very interesting
conclusion, and one which we are not aware to
have been as yet generally received, namely,
that the mortality of Great Britain, its cities, and
its hospitals, is greatly inferior to that of any
other country in Europe ; and that it is incon-
testable that Great Britain is at present the most
healthy country with which we are acquainted ;
and that it has been gradually tending to that
point for the last 50 years. In the comparisons
which we shall have occasion to make, in order
to support this assertion, we shall carefully abstain from reproducing the tables of remote
periods, which have been often previously discussed, and shall be confined to the most recent
and genuine details. It is remarkable, that this
superior value of life in Great Britain is not
confined to any particular districts, or classes of
individuals.   To whatever point we turn our
view, the advantage is still the same : the man
of affluence, the pauper-patient of the hospital,
the sailor and the soldier on active service, the
prisoner of war, the inmate of a gaol, all enjoy a

better tenure of existence from this country than from any other of which we have been able to consult the records. It has been long the fashion, both abroad and at home, to exhaust every variety of reproach on the climate of our country, and particularly on the atmosphere of London; and yet we shall find that the most favoured spots in Europe, the places which have long been selected as the resort of invalids, and the fountains of health, are far more fatal to life than even this great metropolis.

If we compare the total mass of Britain with the entire population of any other nation of Europe, the superiority is equally marked. The annual deaths on the average throughout England and Wales are nearly 1 in 60. The country which approaches most nearly to us is the Pays de Vaud, where the mortality is 1 in 49. Sweden and Holland have at present the same standard, namely, 1 in 48. The next on the list is France, where one inhabitant dies annually in 40, a proportion precisely similar to that of London. The kingdoms of Prussia and Naples follow after; they range between 33 and 35; the kingdom of Wirtemberg is also at 33.

The annual proportion of deaths at Montpelier was greater 30 years ago, and is greater at present, than in London; and although the mortality of great cities is usually much larger than that of provinces or counties, yet the mortality

of London is exactly the same at present as that
of the department of the Herault, the southern
and fertile, and long supposed most salubrious
district of France, of which Montpelier is the
capital.   Finke, a German writer who wrote on
medical geography in 1792, speaks with surprise
and reprobation of the custom which then prevailed in England of sending invalids to the
south of France; and declares that the cutting
winds of those quarters annually destroyed many
of those wanderers in quest of a milder sky.

The annual mortality of Nice, though a small
town, and enjoying a factitious reputation of salubrity, is 1 in 31; of Naples, is 1 in 28. Leghorn
is more fortunate, and sinks to 1 in 35.   We instance those places as being the frequent resort
of invalids; but how astonishing is the superiority of England, when we compare with these
even our great manufacturing towns, such as
Manchester, 1 in 74; such as even Birmingham,
1 in 43; or even this overgrown metropolis,
where the deaths are only 1 in 40.   But if we
take indiscriminately the other great cities of
Europe, their inferiority in respect to the value
of life is equally pointed; in Paris, for instance,
the annual deaths are about 1 in 32, in Lyons
and Strasburg the same, in Barcelona the same:
Berlin approaches a little nearer to London, it
reckons 1 in 34.   Madrid loses 1 in 29. Rome,
Amsterdam, and Vienna, are last in the scale of

life; in Rome the deaths are annually 1 i 2 ’ at Amsterdam they are so numerous as 1 in 24, and at Vienna 1 in 22½ : we perceive that the inhabitant of London has almost a twofold advantage in this respect.

CHAP. IV.

MEDICAL STATISTICS OF COUNTRIES.

Iᴛ is generally calculated that the 20th part of every population is labouring under illness, and that the 100th part has some severe disease. If this were a fact certain, and applicable to every country, we should possess an easy standard for comparing the number of cures; but every season, every successive year, and even the influence of political events, are continually producing a fluctuation in the amount of sickness and of recovery.

FRANCE.

A great variety has always existed in the physical constitution of the natives of the different provinces of France, accordingly as they approach the Flemish, Gascon, Norman, or Breton race. The operation of the conscription has brought to light a great diversity in their height, their capability of supporting the fatigues of war, and in the number and nature of the diseases which were produced as pleas of exemption from service i   the respective districts.

The state of the population in France, formed on an average of the 6 years from 1817 to 1823, presents the following results (*Revue Encyclopédique*, 1825–6) : —

			Among 1000 of whom occur
Mean population	-	30,319,444	
—— annual marriages	-	218,917	7·23
———— births	-	957,876	31·59
———————— male	-	494,227	16·30
———————— female	-	463,649	15·29
Legitimate births	-	892,677	29·44
Illegitimate births	-	65,199	2·15
Total deaths	-	764,848	25·23
———— male	-	386,453	12·75
———— female	-	378,395	12·48
Increase of the population	-	85,255	6·36

This calculation may be considered doubly correct, because it is verified, and some errors of the press corrected in the Bulletin Universel.

About half the children born live to twenty years, and about a third to 45 years.

The lowest annual mortality is at the age of 10 ; it is then only 1 in 130. At the age of 40 it is 1 in 53.

The probability of life to a man of 40 is 23 years.

The number of men of the age of 20 to 21 is about 260,000.

M. Villermé has ascertained that the mortality increases amongst the poor, and diminishes to the affluent. In the wealthy departments of France, life is, on the average, protracted twelve

years and a half beyond its course in those
which are poor.

The least mortality occurs in France in the
districts where ease and happiness are most common; as in the departments of the *Calvados,*
of *l'Orne,* and *de la Sarthe.* In these one individual dies annually in 50; but how painful a
contrast is presented by the twelfth municipal
arrondissement of Paris, where the annual deaths
are about 1 in 24.

But without taking the metropolis into comparison, let us contrast a prosperous rural district with a poor one, as the two departments of
the *Calvados* and *l'Orne,* with the less fortunate
ones of *l'Indre* and *le Cher.*

In the two rich depart-ments scarcely one fourth of a given number of individuals die before 5 years of age. One half die at 45, three fourths are dead at 70.

In the two poor depart-ments one fourth die before completing the first year. One half between 15 and 20, three fourths at 50 in one department, and before 55 in the other. *

Such is the influence of condition, or the
absence of fatigue and privation on the frame,
that during the eight years from 1816 to 1823
the mean height of young men fit for military
service has been found to be in *Paris* 5 feet,

---

* At least such was the case in 1821, according to
Villermé.

2 inches, and 1½ lines, but only 5 feet, 1 inch, and 9½ lines for the suburbs of Sceaux and St. Denis. The same fact has been ascertained in the department of the Rhone, where a similar disproportion exists between the inhabitans of Lyons and of its suburb Villefranche, from 1806 to 1810.

PRUSSIA.

The following is the mean return of the seven years from 1816 to 1822. The average of each year presents,

Inhabitants	-	-	11,017,022
Marriages	-	-	110,238
Total births	-	-	478,069
Illegitimate births	-	-	33,925
Deaths	-	-	30,542

One birth amongst thirteen was illegitimate, but in the proportion of 1 in 12 in towns, and 1 in 16 in the country.

Since 1822, a new census has been taken for 1825, which affords the following results : —

Inhabitants	-	12,255,867
Of whom were	-	4,487,009 below 14 years of age.
————	-	7,010,240 from 14 to 60 ———
————	-	758,618 above 60 ———

The females were less numerous than the males in the first period, but more numerous in the second and third.

D 3

At the end of 1824 the entire population was
estimated to exceed rather than to fall short of
twelve millions. The average *yearly* increase,
during the nine years, from 1816 to 1824, was
more than 172,100, making a total of 1,549,109
in that period. This increase is owing to the
greater number of-births, to the diminished mortality, and to the settlement of strangers. The
immigration compared with the *emigration* affords a yearly excess of 38,000 individuals, on
an average of seven years. According to the
present annual increase, Dupin considers that
the population would double itself in twenty-six
years.

The mortality of Prussia is about 1 in 35.
In 1817, 1 male died in 33, and 1 female in
36 ; and of the legitimate children, 2 in 10 died
during the first year, of the *illegitimate*, 3 in 10.
Mr. Kunth ascribes the present improved condition of mortality to the cheapness of provisions since 1819, in addition to the improvements in medical and moral institutions. On
the contrary, during two years of high prices,
1816 and 1817, the mortality increased and the
births diminished.

The number of marriages in 1817 was ascertained to be greater than occurs in other
countries, 1 in 94. This circumstance is probably founded on the great facility of obtaining
a *divorce,* which in that year allowed 1 pair in 37

to change their partners. The proportion of divorces has, however, slightly decreased from that year to 1823, when it was lower by about one tenth.

The births were, in 1817, 1 in 23⅓ of the whole population. The number of illegitimate births, as well as of divorces, seems to experience a small progressive diminution of late years; in 1816, 1 subject in 312 was illegitimate; in 1819, 1 in 349; in 1821, it was 1 in 323.

A great increase in the number of *Jewish* inhabitants has been recently observed. They amounted in 1817 to above 127,000; in 1824 they had increased to nearly 150,000, an augmentation of above 21,000 in 7 years. During the five years from 1820 to 1824, it is pleasing to find, that more than 500 Jews have become converts to Christianity. A Berlin newspaper endeavours to explain their rapid growth by a greater fecundity, and an inferior mortality of their race; it adds a cause more susceptible of proof in an increasing proportion of their illegitimate births.

The total number of physicians, surgeons, and others employed in the practice of medicine, including those engaged in pharmacy, was 15,987, for the whole of Prussia, in 1824. *

* Uber die Med. Statist. Verhältnisse der Med. Personen zu der Bevölk. im Preuss. St. bey Casper. Berlin, 1826.

BAVARIA.

In the kingdom of *Bavaria* Rudhart states the mortality of the *Circle* of the *Iser* at 1 in 29, and that of the *Circle* of the *Upper Mayn* at 1 in 38. One seventh of the whole population inhabits the cities of the first and second order; the other six sevenths inhabit the country and the small towns. The population appears to be least considerable wherever the seignorial properties are the most numerous; one circle only out of the seven affords an exception.*

KINGDOM OF HANOVER.

During the year 1823, 52,807 children were born. The number of still-born infants in that year was 2021. Amongst the 52,807 children 4063 were illegitimate. The deaths were 32,220, the marriages were 12,317. The population is rapidly increasing under an excellent government.

AUSTRIA.

Professor Kudler, who has particularly devoted himself to the statistics of the southern part †, observes, that according to the present

---

* Uber den Zustand des Königreichs Baiern. Stutg. 1825.
† Steyermärk. Zeitschrift. 1821.

progress of the population in *Hungary*, it would
require 150 years to double itself, in the Lower
Austria 176 years, in Bohemia 230 years, in
Gallicia 248 years, and in Moravia (comprehending the Austrian Silesia) it would require so
much as 296 years in which to double itself.
Styria, from the great variations in its population,
does not admit of a similar computation. These
are remarkable facts, and throw much comparative light on the slow progress of some parts of
Austria towards prosperity. In some provinces
of Austria the anomaly is presented of a greater
number of female births than of male. This is
not the case, however, in the Lombardo-Vene-
tian provinces. The average number of individuals to each family in Styria is 5. The number
of marriages in Styria has latterly suffered a
slight diminution from temporary want. In
1803 there were 100 marriages amongst 586
inhabitants, in 1820 there were 100 to 608 inhabitants. The mean duration of a marriage is
in Styria from 22 to 23 years. The average of
births in 1819 and 1820 is in the proportion of
1 to 25 inhabitants. About a sixth part of all
the births is illegitimate. A remarkable diminution of mortality is perceptible in Styria, as in
most other countries.

> In 1812 the deaths were 29,206.
> In 1817 —— —— 28,008.
> In 1819 —— —— 21,162.
> In 1820 —— —— 19,451.

In general, the male deaths exceed the female in Styria, as elsewhere. The proportion is usually 50 male to 49 female deaths. The mortality of Styria (taken solely amongst those who are registered for the *Conscription*) is 1 death annually in 38 inhabitants. The average number of inhabitants to a house is about four.

We have dwelt longer on this province from the circumstance of its remoteness, simple habits of life, and general freedom from foreign intermixture.

KINGDOM OF THE NETHERLANDS.

The change in the duration of life, which has taken place in the kingdom of the Netherlands, has rendered the old tables of the probabilities of life formed by Kerseboam insufficient for actual use. Mr. Quetelet has recently constructed a new scale for the Netherlands with great care, and his enquiries have brought to light some curious facts.

Mr. Quetelet has found, universally in the kingdom, that the mortality is the greatest in those parts which are the most populous, the nearest to the sea, where the ground is most low and marshy. The value of life in Holland seems to have increased since the middle of last century, when Süssmilch makes the annual deaths of 39 villages of Holland about 1 in 23 ; and at present we find the mean average for the whole kingdom 1 in 48. The births are 1 to 27.

ICELAND.

From the report transmitted by the Bishop of Iceland to the Danish government it appears that the births in that island amounted in 1819 to 1326; there were also 33 still-births. Among the 1326 births, 564 were male, and 576 female : 186 were illegitimate. The deaths in the same yea* amounted to 1264, 622 of the male sex, and 642 of females : 42 of the deaths were occasioned by accidents, of which 31 were persons drowned. The population is about 48,000.

Among the 1264 deaths not one individual had exceeded 100 years of age. Of the 17 deaths between the age of 90 and 100, 11 were women, and 6 men. The same advantage on the side of the females subsisted between the age of 70 and 90. 152 deaths were from the age of 60 to 70.

SWEDEN.

The population in 1823 amounted to 2,687,457. The births in 1823 were 98,259, of which 7210 were illegitimate. That list does not include 2539 still-born. Among 99,322 women in labour 1422 had twins, and 27 had triplets. Among the deaths in 1823, only 5 persons died above 100 years of age, of whom one was a man, and *four* women. The marriages were 23,993, amongst which ten men married for the fourth

time, one for the fifth, and one for the sixth time.
The number of women who had borne children
from the age of 45 to 50 was 1462, and beyond
the age of 50 were 53.   The total number of
physicians and surgeons in Sweden was lately
only 391, and in Norway 118.

Amongst the deaths enumerated for the whole
kingdom in 1823 are 428 children accidentally
smothered by mothers and nurses.   Persons
drowned 1060.   Persons frozen 43.   Deaths
from intoxication 43.   Deaths by accidents that
cannot be described 576 ; exclusively of numerous deaths from suffocation by charcoal fires.

DENMARK.

In the year 1822 there was 1 illegitimate
birth to every 12 births for the whole kingdom,
but in 1823 so many as 1 to every 11.*

In respect to the number of deaf and dumb
in Denmark, we find 64 in the institution of
Copenhagen in 1824, of whom 40 were boys,
and 24 girls.   There were also in Zealand 109, in
Laaland and Falster 17, in Funen 58, and in
Guttand about 90.   In Sleswick, also, an institution exists which admits 75.

The proportion of still-births was in 1826
1610 to 38,316 other births.

---

* Messager Français du Nord, Oct. 1825.

FINLAND.

The births in the grand duchy of *Finland* were in 1823 49,168, of which 747 were twins, 18 triplets, 3023 illegitimate, and 1192 still-born. The deaths in the same year were 29,578 ; so many as 15,251 were below the age of 10 years, 2231 were between the age of 10 and 25, 4265 between 25 and 50, and 9821 were above the age of 50.*

RUSSIA.

The returns formerly afforded by Russia presented such extraordinary results, that it was impossible to receive them without considerable suspicion. It seems to be generally believed, that in the statistical accounts which have been occasionally sent forth a certain degree of colouring was admitted ; a few objects protruded, and others thrown into shade ; as when in the progress of the Empress Catherine through her provinces artificial villages were created in the distance to amuse with an image of prosperity. About the year 1768 the total mortality of the empire was estimated by Hermann at about 1 in 60. It would be tedious to enumerate the causes which confused or falsified the lists at that period. After 1796 they were better kept. The real

* St. Petersburg. Zeitschrift. 1825.

sum of annual deaths appears at present to be 1 in 41, according to an authentic report published by the synod of the Greek church, which includes the most numerous part of the population.

The tables of *longevity* repeatedly published in Russia are regarded with distrust* ; as it appears to have been only in 1764 that Catherine II. enjoined a certain form of registering baptisms and burials. Edicts had been previously issued, but had not been obeyed ; and even at this moment it is asserted that very few of the provincial priests are capable of making the necessary entries.†

CANTON DE VAUD.

In the *Canton de Vaud* in 1825 the births were 4974 (23 more than in 1824), the deaths were 3310 (46 more than in 1824), and the marriages were 1248 (108 less than in 1824). About one seventh of all the births were stillborn. The deaths at the age of 70, and above, were 46 men and 53 women ; at the age of 80, and above, 60 men and 43 women ; at the age of 90, and above, 8 men and 18 women.

---

* Bulletin Universel, section Géographique, t. i. p. 448. 1824.

† During the four years, from 1823 to 1826, 50,980 persons died suddenly throughout the Russian empire.

VENETIAN PROVINCES.

An official statement has lately been published, under the sanction of the Austrian government, of the statistics of the provinces called Venetian, including Venice, Vicenza, Padua, Treviso, Polesina, Bellona, Verona, and Friuli.*

As the climate of Italy is often a subject of discussion, we shall extract from this memoir the

Greatest heat of these provinces 28°(Reaumur).
Mean — — — 10°. ——

Greatest cold is 9° in some of the mountainous districts ; 15° and even 18°.

The heat and cold are always higher at Venice than at Padua.

The following is the state of weather observed at Padua during three years. The proportion of days was

	Serene.	Rain and Snow.	Cloudy and variable.	Quantity of Rain.	
In 1821	154	68	143	24	9·7
1822	186	55	124	17	4·8
1823	141	74	131	24	3·8

The number of inhabitants is 274 to the square mile (of 60 to a degree).

The average proportion of annual births is about 1 in 22 ;

---

* Quadri. Prospetto Statistico delle Provincie Venete. Ven. 1326–7.

Marriages, 1 in 107 ;

Deaths,   1 in 28.

In 1815, 1816, 1817, a scarcity prevailed, and, accordingly, the births and marriages diminished, and the deaths increased. In 1817 the mortality amounted even to nearly 1 in 14. The proportion of the poor are estimated at 1 in 26 ; but the term is not to be applied in the same general sense as in England. The number of children exposed is as 1 in 321 of the whole population. The population in 1766 was 361,491 families ; in 1827 it had increased to 397,098 families : a trifling augmentation, which marks the adverse fortunes of Italy.

KINGDOM OF THE TWO SICILIES.

Quattromani states in his *Itinerario delle due Sicilie* *, that, for the whole of that kingdom,

The mean temperature is 11° 18' (Reaumur);

The greatest heat is   -   31° ;

The greatest cold (on the mountain Ariano) is 8° below zero.

The following is a comparative view of the mortality, births, and marriages of the kingdom of the Two Sicilies during three recent years : †—

---

* Napoli. 1827.

† Annali Universali di Statistica. 1826.

	Deaths.	Births.	Marriages.
In 1822	1 in 35	1 in 24	1 in 111
1823	1 in 33	1 in 24	1 in 110
1824	1 in 27	1 in 23	1 in 127

AMERICA.

Perhaps it may be not uninteresting to compare the conditions of life in the United States with those of the southern parts of America. Here, as in the north of Europe, with respect to the south, we find a considerable superiority. Mr. Bristed states the average annual deaths throughout the United States at 1 in 40 (which is precisely the rate observed in France). In the healthiest districts of the United States it is 1 in 56; and in the most unhealthy 1 in 35.

The annual proportion of births in the United States has been estimated at 1 to 20 individuals. The proportion of males to females is 26 to 25.

With respect to the physical statistics of a *tropical climate* Humboldt has furnished some curious particulars : they are the only important ones which have been published. The vices of the mother-government had been introduced into *New Spain*, and particularly a very unequal distribution of landed property : these, and the circumstance of a very large part of the population being Indians in a distressed state, and inferior in industry and energy, had long retarded

E

the progress of its population.   During the last
half of the eighteenth century the excess of
births above deaths had become very great.
Humboldt found the mean proportion of about
100 burials to 170 baptisms.   But the proportion of deaths was very remarkable; and these
numerous births and burials show in a striking
point of view the early marriages and early
deaths of a tropical climate, and the more rapid
passing away of each generation.*   In one district the annual mortality was 1 in 26, in another
it was 1 in 29; but the average for the whole
kingdom of New Spain was 1 in 30 annually;
which is a greater proportion of deaths than now
occurs in any country of Europe with whose
details we are acquainted.

AFRICA.

   The following table of the births and deaths
at the Cape of Good Hope is interesting as it
relates to Africa, and as displaying the proportion of each, during a series of years, among the
white and black population.   It was printed in
1826 by order of the House of Commons.   The
total population amounted to 81,964 in the year
1812, and to 105,336 in the year 1820.

---

* Malthus.

| IN THE YEARS | CHRISTIANS. | | | | SLAVES. | | | | TOTAL OF | |
| | BIRTHS. | | DEATHS. | | BIRTHS. | | DEATHS. | | | |
	Male	Female	Male	Female	Male	Female	Male	Female	BIRTHS.	DEATHS.
1812	523	528	226	229	78	66	149	72	1425	811
1813	686	706	292	177	188	234	141	91	2156	888
1814	802	825	242	238	230	183	189	93	2363	960
1815	888	894	287	193	221	193	185	123	2540	974
1816	805	892	305	207	325	294	210	112	2723	1090
1817	918	927	520	227	487	467	264	143	3195	1206
1818	814	832	340	247	516	482	270	152	3058	1277
1819	810	815	340	224	506	509	255	118	3001	1251
1820	881	898	375	264	463	464	248	130	3124	1406

ISLE OF BOURBON.

The *Isle of Bourbon* presents some curious facts respecting the different rate of births and deaths which prevails among the French colonists of that island, the free blacks, and the slaves. Mr. Thomas, who has passed eight years there, and who has occupied an official situation, has lately obtained a prize from the Academy of Sciences at Paris for his statistical researches on this island, which occupy three folio volumes. The French colonists (or whites) increase very rapidly; not by the arrival of new-comers (of whom the annual average is only a fiftieth), but by the great excess of births over deaths, which is in the proportion of about 9 to 5. The births are to the whole population in the proportion of 1 to about $24\frac{1}{2}$, and the annual deaths are 1 in $44\frac{8}{10}$; a mortality inferior to that of the kingdom of France. One birth is illegitimate among $7\frac{2}{5}$.

E 2

The marriages are 1 to 100 individuals, and the average of births to each marriage is $3\frac{6}{10}$. It has been supposed, that in warm countries more girls are born than boys; but the Isle of Bourbon affords a contrary result, since, during the six years from 1818 to 1823, a sixtieth part more has been born of boys than of girls.

The progress of the *slave* population is very opposite, and marks well the intimate connection subsisting between social position and physical developement. From 1818 to 1824 it has diminished by one sixth, and is decreasing more and more rapidly, so that the proprietors are anticipating, at a short distance of time, the necessity of cultivating less ground, and of abandoning the productions which require particular labour. So great is the mortality, and so few the births, that, according to Thomas, " il s'en faudrait de 423 individus par année moyenne, que le nombre des naissances pût reparer les pertes occasionées par la mort dans cette classe d'hommes." The black population lose, at this rate, about three per cent. annually, while the whites are annually gaining about $1\frac{2}{3}$ per cent. It must be observed, however, on one hand, that the females of the white population nearly equal the males, while among the blacks the males exceed the females in the proportion of 28 to 17; but to counterbalance this advantage, the climate must be more congenial to the African temperament than to the European.

Among 5069 of the free blacks, or intermediate class, the average deaths of four recent years were only 82; the average births were 213. The greater part of these births were illegitimate: the annual average of marriages was less than 23. These free blacks hold a condition in society nearly similar to that of the whites; and their superior longevity and reproduction must be ascribed to the favourable influence of liberty. Their mortality is much less than that of the French colonists, because, with advantages of comparative prosperity, they combine the occupation of a native soil.*

---

* Rapport sur le Prix de Statistique decerné par l'Acad. R. des Sciences, pour l'Année 1827. Paris.

CHAP. V.

MEDICAL STATISTICS OF CITIES.

It is well known, that in any given country
the deaths of a city are more numerous than
those of the rural districts. This difference
is principally felt in the first five years of life,
when many more die in London than in the
country. From 5 years of age to 20 the
deaths in London are fewer. Between 20 and
50 many more die in London, on account of
the large annual influx from the country. In
all cities a large portion of disease and death is
to be assigned to the constant importation from
the country of individuals who have attained to
maturity; but having been previously habituated
to frequent exercise in a pure atmosphere, and
to a simple regular diet, are gradually sacrificed
to confined air, sedentary habits, or a capricious
and over-stimulating food. These causes are
not equally fatal to those who have passed their
early years within the walls of a city; and after
the age of 50 the proportion of deaths in
London is smaller than in the country. Jenner,
and very recently Dr. Baron, have made some

curious experiments on animals, which indicate that a loss of their open range and natural nourishment has with them, also, a tendency to disorganise and to destroy. Dr. Baron placed a family of young rabbits in a confined situation, and fed them with coarse green food, such as cabbage and grass. They were perfectly healthy when put up : in about a month one of them died : the primary stop of disorganisation was evinced in a number of transparent vesicles studded over the external surface of its liver.

In another, which died nine days after, the disease had advanced to the formation of tubercles on the liver. The liver of a third, which died four days later still, had nearly lost its true structure, so universally was it pervaded with tubercles. Two days subsequently a fourth died: a considerable number of hydatids were attached to the lower surface of the liver. At this time Dr. Baron removed three young rabbits from the place where their companions had died to another situation, dry and clean, and to their proper and accustomed food. The lives of these remaining three were obviously saved by this change. He obtained similar results from experiments of the same nature performed on other animals.

GLASGOW.

Mr. Cleland has published very valuable "*Statistical Tables relative to Glasgow**," from which we shall select a few particulars. During the seven years from 1816 to 1822 the average annual mortality was 1 in 46·78. During the 26 years from 1801 to 1826, the average annual deaths have been 1 to 44·41 persons.

Among the 26,109 registered burials for the six years ending with 1826, 1831 were of still-born children.

Glasgow has suffered much from typhus fever and epidemic dysentery, evils which have, probably, owed their origin or their extension to the distresses incidental to a large manufacturing population. Vaccination has reduced the general mortality, principally that which occurred under five years of age.

The details afforded in Mr. Cleland's work are more accurate, probably, than any others relating to our population, from the zeal which the authorities of Glasgow displayed in collecting them.

The average number of individuals to a family is $4\frac{681}{1000}$.

The number of children below 12 years is to the rest of the population *one fourth* $\frac{56}{1000}$.

---

* Third edit. 8vo. Glasgow, 1823.

The number of persons on the average inhabiting each room is $2\frac{1}{2}$.

The number of married men compared to the other males is 21,473 to 47,521. Of married women compared to other females is 21,473 to 56,730.

PARIS.

Villermé estimates the actual mortality of Paris at 1 in $32\frac{6}{10}$. In the 17th century it was 1 in 25 or 26.

Büsching mentions in his *Geography* that about the middle of the 18th century 1 man in 25 was reckoned to die annually at Paris. In the 14th century, from facts furnished by a manuscript of that age, the mortality is calculated by Villermé as 1 in 16 or 17.

Formerly, the number of deaths considerably exceeded the births; at present, the number of births exceeds the deaths.

There are more boys born dead than girls and yet, during the first three months after birth, the deaths of boys are far more numerous than of girls.

The conceptions are most numerous, but the births least abundant, in June. March and April furnish the most numerous births; and next stand January and February.

The poor and the rich occupy the two ex-

tremities of the scale of mortality. Compare, for
instance, the twelfth municipal arrondissement,
where there are the most poor, with the first,
where the rich are in the highest proportion.
The following is a table of their deaths and population : —

Arrondissement.	Inhabitants.	Deaths in private Dwellings in				
		1817	1818	1819	1820	1821
1st.	45,854	778	787	904	863	985
12th.	66,893	1492	1679	1611	1633	1865

But this disproportion is still further increased
by the greater number of inhabitants of the poor
arrondissement who die in the hospitals and
hospices; and altogether Villermé concludes that
where there are 50 deaths in the rich arrondissement there are 100 in the poor one.

There is 1 annual birth to above 32 inhabitants of the rich arrondissement, and about 1
to 26 of the poor arrondissement, and notwithstanding, there are not in proportion more
children from 0 to 5 years of age in the latter
than in the former, because, although the poor
produce more children than the rich they do
not nourish them so well.

Of 9806 illegitimate children born in Paris in
1823 the enormous proportion of 7585 were
abandoned by their parents. Of 100 infants
thus abandoned it is found that at least six
twelfths perish in the first year of their existence. In 1818, 120 died out of 133.

In 1822 and 1823, 1768 children died of the small-pox. The number of gratuitous vaccinations was 4445.

The number of violent deaths in 1823 was 690, of which 390 were cases of suicide.

Reviewing, on one side, the great political, moral, and physical events which have occurred at *Paris* during a succession of years, and on the other the progress of its population, Villermé has ascertained, that whenever the people have suffered from *any* cause, the deaths have correspondingly increased, the births have decreased, and the mean duration of life has been shortened. In periods of prosperity he has found results directly opposite to these. The mean duration of life in Paris is 32 years and some months.

It was formerly estimated, that one third of the inhabitants of Paris died in the hospitals ; but Dupin has lately calculated that half the deaths in Paris take place in the hospitals and other asylums of charity. Not a fourth part of the inhabitants are buried at private cost.

GENEVA.

If we turn to Switzerland, we find the average mortality of the city of Geneva, during the four years ending in 1823, about 1 in 43; which it may be curious to compare with some of our large manufacturing cities, such as Manchester, where the deaths were in 1811 only 1 in 74 ; or Glasgow, where in the 10 years from 1811 to 1820, they were 1 in 45. The deaths at Birmingham seem of the same amount as those of Geneva at the same period, although its population is four times more numerous.

ST. PETERSBURGH.

The latest returns from St. Petersburgh which yield the average of deaths, from 1813 to 1822, afford the same rate which was stated 40 years ago, namely 1 in 37 annually. It is probable that the last account is more correct than the former. The births during the ten years from 1813 to 1822 were greatly inferior to the burials, a result contrary to what usually happens under circumstances of improvement. The proportion of births was 100 to 134 burials. The Russians explain this, by the presence of a large number of persons from the provinces, who fix their abode in St. Petersburgh and die there. But this occurs also in every other great metropolis, although Petersburgh and Stockholm are, we believe, the only ones which at present exhibit this preponderance of death over production.

The mortality of St. Petersburgh appears to have been formerly too favourably estimated.

Mr. Krafft makes it, from 1781 to 1785, about 1 in 37. But there is reason to think, that in forming this calculation the deaths in the hospitals, prisons, and foundling-house, had been either entirely omitted or incorrectly delivered.

The number of deaths from *accidents* at Petersburgh was 412 in the year 1824.

BERLIN.

From 1747 to 1755, the annual mortality of Berlin was 1 in 28. Between 1796 and 1799 it improved to 1 in $29\frac{1}{11}$. Here the beneficial change was retarded by the ravages, the losses, the disappointments of war, and from 1802 to 1806 it had retrograded to 1 in 27 ; but from 1816 to 1822, a period of exultation and tranquillity to the Prussians, the value of life took a remarkable leap, and the annual deaths fell to less than 1 in 34. *

Extreme longevity does not appear to be common at Berlin. † During the 10 years from 1812 to 1821 only one individual died between 103 and 104 years old. Eight died during the same period between the age of 100 and 103 :

---

* I. L. Casper. De Vi Variolæ Vaccinæ in Mortalitatem, &c. Ber. 1824.

† I. E. Marsch. Operis de rationibus Prodromus quibus mors Berolini est censenda, Diss. I. Medico-Statistica. Berol, 1828.

24 from 95 to 100, and 116 from 90 to 95. And this was amongst a population of 190,000 (exclusive of the military). A few examples of very great age are not, however, to be considered as arguments of superior salubrity in any place, nor is the absence of such instances a proof of insalubrity : that alone is to be considered as a test of health, when a large mass of the population attain to the natural period of life.

VIENNA.

The annual mortality of Vienna was estimated in the middle of the last century at about 1 in 20. It has not improved in the same degree with several other European cities. Wertheim brought it to 1 in 24, in his *Medical Topography* of 1810. But Dr. Stelzig of Prague has very recently examined the subject, and fixes it at 1 in $22\frac{1}{2}$. On an average of 10 recent years, one marriage takes place annually among 124 inhabitants, and three births occur to each marriage. The stillborn are in the proportion of 1 among 25 births. On an average of 20 recent years, 338 infants die out of 1000 at the end of the first year. Among 10,530 deaths, scarcely 38 persons are found who have attained the age of 90 ; and an individual of 105 to 115 is hardly seen once in a lustrum.

The excessive spirit of regulation, the dread

of novelty, the restrictions imposed on the medical profession, and political causes which need not to be enumerated, appear to have retarded the natural progress of this city. The overweening *paternity* of the government interferes with the trivial concerns of the citizens, in the same manner in which an arbitrary and untaught father sometimes restrains the useful impulses of his children, while he permits an easy vent to their baser propensities.

PRAGUE.

Prague, the capital of Bohemia, contains a population about one third of that of Vienna, and is more healthy, as might be supposed. Dr. Stelzig has made some curious comparisons between the two cities. The mortality of Prague is 1 in $24\frac{1}{2}$. The superior longevity of the *Jews* is strongly marked in this city: on separating the Jewish from the Christian deaths, only one death is found to occur annually among 26 Jews, but 1 among $22\frac{1}{2}$ Christians. On an average of 20 years, 423 infants die out of 1000 at the end of the first year. Up to the 30th year the mortality is rather larger here than at Vienna and other capitals of Germany; but from 30 to 70 years of age the mortality is here much less. Not a year passes (according to the tables produced by Stelzig) in which among 4000 deaths we may not find at least 50 individuals of 90 years of age, 14 of 95, 9 of 100, and nearly 5 who reckon from 105 to 115 years. In this longevity the women enjoy a superiority of $\frac{2}{3}$ over the men. The greater part of the instances of the *highest* age is here composed of individuals earning a laborious subsistence, and of married ones. According to an average of several years no nobleman, no wealthy person, no bachelor, and no unmarried woman have *passed* the age of 95. This is an interesting fact, but it is an *extreme* and an insulated one, and does not militate against the general *conservative* tendency of prosperity which a variety of evidence seems to establish. The chances of exceeding the age of 90 are $\frac{2}{3}$ greater at Prague than at Vienna.

On an average of 10 years, one marriage occurs annually at Prague amongst 138 individuals, and there are above four births to a marriage for the entire population. But a singularity again occurs with respect to the *Jewish* portion : the average of births to a Jewish marriage is here above $4\frac{1}{2}$, while that of a Christian marriage is only $3\frac{1}{2}$. The proportion of male births to female is 21 to 20, but the greater mortality of the former nearly equalises the sexes.*

* Monatschrift der Gesellschaft des Vaterländisch. Museum in Böhmen. Januar. 1827.

PALERMO.

At *Palermo,* in 1823, the mortality was 1 in 31 ; the male deaths were most numerous up to the age of 55, but after that period the female deaths were most numerous. The deaths in private dwellings were 3964, in the hospitals 1067. January, October, and November were the most fatal months; and April, May, and June the most healthy. The proportion of births to the whole population was 1 to 25. January, March, and October had the greatest number of births; June, July, and August had the fewest. The marriages were 978 in a population of 164,793. The proportion of illegitimate births is 1 to 10 legitimate ones.

LEGHORN.

Doctors Gordini and Orsini have published some interesting researches into the medical statistics of Leghorn.* Their enquiries relate to the seven years from 1818 to 1825. The average number of annual births is 1 to 25 or 26 of the entire population. The total number of children abandoned by their parents during these seven years was 1281; and the deaths among these

---

* Ricerche di Statistica Medica della Citta di Livorno. 4°. Liv. 1826.

F

which occurred at Leghorn were only 102 ; but
this very small proportion is only apparent, as,
at the end of two òr three days, the infants are
transported to Pisa.   The average annual mortality of the entire population (taken on the seven
years) is about 1 in 35.

A curious difference appears with respect to
the non-Catholic part of the population, which
is composed of Protestants and Jews.   Among
these the annual births are only 1 in 38 or 39,
and the annual deaths only 1 in 48 or 49.   The
less degree of mortality is explained by the
greater *affluence* of this part of the population ;
and the less proportion of births, perhaps, depends on a principle which is not yet established,
but which rests on some facts ; namely, that the
proportion of births diminishes in a community
as it advances in civilisation and prosperity.

ROME.

In the recently-discovered fragment of Cicero
(de Republicâ) an intimation is conveyed that
the neighbourhood of Rome has been always
unwholesome.   Speaking of the choice of situation made by Romulus, he observes, "Locum
" delegit in regione pestilenti salubrem."

The population appears to have been gradually
decreasing until the late peace, which has gently
revived it.   In 1800 there were above 150,000

inhabitants, in 1810 only 123,000. Within a few years it has gained an accession of about 10,000.

On an average of the ten years from 1816 to 1825, the annual mortality is 1 in 24·76. The number of births is in the proportion of 1 in 30·23. The annual marriages are about 1 in 106. The mean number of children to a marriage is 3·30. The greatest number of poor in the hospitals is 3044 in the year 1818, and the lowest number is 1290 in the year 1824.

There can be little doubt that the force of the aguish disposition of Rome might be considerably weakened by steady and well-directed efforts supported by a proportionate capital; but it is to be feared that such a combination of circumstances will not readily meet at Rome. In 1816, 17 out of the 22 French students were attacked with intermittent fevers. The Villa Medici, in which they reside, was formerly healthy; but water brought at a great expense to embellish the garden had been suffered to stagnate there.

NAPLES.

The annual mortality of Naples has been lately estimated at 1 in 28¼. The births are annually to the inhabitants as 1 in 23¾. The population consisted, on the 1st of January, 1828, of 167,175 males, and 187,028 females. Of 14,989 births

in 1826, 1875 new-born children were abandoned by their parents; and of this number
1362 belonged to the city, and 513 were sent in
from the provinces. The sudden deaths were
330. The *suicides* were only 13, a remarkably
small proportion for a population of above 350,000.
Eleven persons died in 1826 aged above 100;
and fifty-three aged from 90 to 100. (Giornale
di Napoli, 1827.)

BRUSSELS.

It appears that at Brussels the month of May
is the most favourable for conception; and that
the most unfavourable period of the year is the
close of October.

Of 1000 infants of both sexes, born on the
same day at Brussels, about half die before
reaching the age of 26 years. The mortality of
Brussels is at present large : the battle of Water-
loo has left a remarkable influence, and during
several subsequent years has changed the ordinary average : it appears to be about 1 in 25 or
26. The greatest number of deaths occurs in
January, the lowest number in July. The lowest
number of births and deaths happen precisely at
the same time, in July ; and the greatest number
of births and deaths happen also at the same
time, nearly, in February and January.

AMSTERDAM.

The population of Amsterdam has decreased in consequence of declining commerce and political changes ; and it is curious to find that its mortality increases with the progress of decay. January is the most fatal month, and November next ; June is the least fatal. In 1815, when the condition of Amsterdam became more tranquil, we perceive a sudden increase of births. In 1814, a year of turbulence, they were only 6128; in 1815 they rose to 7050.

In 1777 the annual deaths were 1 in 27 ; a very small proportion for that period, when Amsterdam was one of the most healthy cities of Europe in this light, as it was also one of the most flourishing. The deaths have now increased to 1 in 24 ; and it seems to be one of the least healthy as it is also one of the least prosperous—a condition which we trust will not be permanent under its improved government.

The late terrible visitations of Groningen and other parts of North Holland have led to many enquiries respecting the public health, and to plans for its improvement. Among others is a decree, that after the 1st of January, 1829, no burials shall be permitted to take place in towns or churches.

STOCKHOLM.

The population amounted, at the end of 1823, to 73,210, which is less by 2356 than it contained in 1820. In 1824 the births were 2697, and the deaths 2944. The marriages were 689. Drunkenness appears here, as at Berlin, to produce a large share of the mortality. In a recent year this city exhibited a singular instance of an excess of 1439 more deaths than births; a symptom which it is painful to observe in a brave and industrious people. This disproportion existed particularly amongst the garrison, and is ascribed to immoderate use of brandy. Our authority affirms that this vice destroys the happiness and prosperity of Sweden more effectually than any war has ever accomplished.*

COPENHAGEN.

The number of births was, in 1822, 3764; of which 786 were illegitimate, or about 1 to every 5 births. †

UNITED STATES.

Doctors Niles, junior, and Rush ‡, have supplied some very interesting details on the mor-

---

* Baron Von Fahnenberg in a letter to the Literary Gazette, Jan. 1829.

† Messag. Franc. du Nord, Oct. 1825.

‡ Medical Statistics ; or, Comparative View of the Morality in New York, &c. New York, 1827.

tality of the United States, and particularly on the different degrees of mortality between the *white* and *black* inhabitants, a subject to which allusions will be found in other parts of this work.

NEW YORK.

The annual mortality of the *whites* at New York, on an average of the seven years from 1820 to 1826 is 1 in 40. The deaths of the *entire* population were in 1826 1 in 35.

The annual mortality among the *blacks alone* is, on the same average, so great as 1 in 19.

PHILADELPHIA.

Here the annual deaths among the whites are 1 in 34, but among the blacks still 1 in 19. Of the *entire population in* 1826 1 in 31. In Philadelphia during 20 years have died 7 from 110 to 120 years of age, 59 between 100 and 110, 327 from 90 to 100.

BALTIMORE.

Here the state of the black population improves. The annual mortality of the whites is 1 in 39, and of the blacks 1 in 33. In this city the *slaves* appear to enjoy a longer existence than the *free blacks,* which is probably owing to the intemperance and improvidence of the latter when left to their own control.

BOSTON.

The deaths among the entire population fluctuate between 1 in 32, as in 1821 ; and 1 in 49, as in 1826.

NEW YORK.

We shall enter a little more fully into the statistics of New York. The average temperature throughout the year is 55° of Fahrenheit. In winter the thermometer rarely sinks lower than 10° or 20° below the freezing point, and in a few hours the cold always moderates. The vicinity of the Atlantic and of the gulf-stream conduces to soften the rigour of winter. The snow seldom continues longer than two or three weeks, in January or February, and early in March the winter closes. The highest temperature in summer is seldom more than 80° or 90°, and is never of long continuance. Sudden changes of temperature frequently occur in summer and winter — one of the causes, probably, of the early decay of female beauty.

Accurate printed records of the deaths in this city were first printed in 1815. The returns are now made weekly to the city inspector, and published in the papers, and at the end of every year a minute annual report is given. From the report for 1827 we shall make a few selections : —

Total deaths	-	5181
Men	- -	1536
Women	- -	991
Boys	- -	1457
Girls	- -	1197

The above list marks the superior longevity of the female sex more strongly than any of which we are in possession.

The greatest number of deaths occurred in July, August, September, and October, the least number in May and June.

The number of deaths at one year and under was - - - - 1336

between 1 and 2 years	-	546
between 2 and 5 years	-	389
between 5 and 10 years	-	185
between 10 and 20 years	-	192
between 20 and 30 years	-	682
between 30 and 40 years	-	657
between 40 and 50 years	-	501
between 50 and 60 years	-	285
between 60 and 70 years	-	221
between 70 and 80 years	-	124
between 80 and 90 years	-	50
between 90 and 100 years	-	12
above 100 years	- -	1

The still-born were 291. The sudden deaths are marked 9. The unknown causes of death are marked 153. The number of persons drowned was 68. Deaths by accidents 42. The burned or scalded 29. The deaths from drinking cold water are 21. No official record of births is preserved.

CHAP. VI.

MEDICAL STATISTICS OF GENERAL HOSPITALS.

THE principal end of hospitals is the relief of the sick poor; but another benefit may be derived from them, an abstract of their multiplied experience, without which, their utility, as a source of information to our profession, is greatly abridged. Such reports not only tend to improve the economical arrangement of hospitals, but also collect and accumulate a store of evidence on the history of disease, which can scarcely be acquired in the most extensive private practice.

Mr. Milne, one of the most eminent writers of the present day on the probabilities of life, remarks, that in reading the writings of the physicians who have treated these subjects it is impossible not to regret that they have been so little attended to by the profession in general, and that bills of mortality have not been more generally kept in such a way as to throw the light, which they alone can do, on the causes of the increase and decrease of different diseases, and of the great differences that are found between the degrees of mortality in different situations, and among different classes of the people.

Some persons appear to have hastily concluded, that the mortality of an hospital affords little information as to the economy or practice prevailing in it, and have even ventured on the paradox of supposing, that the deaths will become more numerous as the discipline is improved, and as the skill of the officers increases ; because, under such circumstances, the most severe cases alone will be selected, and will be speedily discharged to make way for new ones. This argument appears to be founded chiefly on a solitary fact, originally produced by Joseph Frank *, namely, that at the Hôtel Dieu, in the 9th year of the French Republic, the mortality was 1 in 7, and in the next year rose to 1 in 6, although the interior economy was much ameliorated, and in the following year was so high as 1 in 4. But the real solution of this change appears to have been due to the exclusion, at that time, from the Hôtel Dieu of all pregnant and insane cases, such as had been previously received there in abundance, but whose mortality is much

---

* Reise nach Paris, London, u. e. grossen theil d. übr. Englands u. Schottlands, in beziehung auf Spitäler, &c. Wien. 1804—1806.

less than that of the common objects of a
general hospital, and whose presence accordingly
tended to diminish the annual amount. In
respect to hospitals destined for particular complaints, as syphilitic or cutaneous, or in regard
to lying-in or military hospitals, it would be
unjust to form comparisons, except with others
of a similar kind; but the general hospitals of
the principal cities of Europe may be fairly
approximated, with an occasional allowance for
the larger number of accidents which occur in
great commercial cities. The mortality at St.
George's Hospital is greater than that at the
Edinburgh Infirmary, on this account, perhaps,
because in one year (1825) we find that of 1025
in-patients admitted 664 were cases of accidents,
or about two thirds of the whole number. On
the whole, we shall generally find, that in every
city the mortality of the hospitals has gradually
declined in proportion to the increase of prosperity and to the diffusion of knowledge; and
wherever it maintains a high standard, there the
lower orders will correspond in their condition
of want and debasement, and the medical profession will be seen to occupy but a low place in
public estimation.

Next to the influence of *national* causes, the
mortality of hospitals is most affected by position
and internal economy. These circumstances
appear more powerful than even the various

merits of *practice ;* and, happily for mankind, they are advantages of a definite nature, easily comprehended, and, of late years, generally demanded. The case was formerly very different, when a singular prejudice or indifference existed in respect to ventilation. At the Leeds Hospital no case of compound fracture, nor of trepan, survived.* At the Hôtel Dieu of Paris compound fractures were also almost always fatal, and few survived amputation.† The system which will bear improper air with impunity during health becomes keenly susceptible of its mischief when diseased, and a change of air will often restore where the strictest diet has failed.

Something must also be allowed for the habit of selection or rejection which prevails at particular hospitals, or under particular officers.

Mortality is *seldom* to be assigned to the influence of bad practice, which, probably, does not often *destroy* life. An accomplished friend made particular notes on the comparative mortality under three physicians in the same hospital ; one was *expectant,* one *tonic,* the other *eclectic.* The mortality was the same, but the length of the disorder, the character of the convalescence, and the chances of relapse were very different.

The earliest statement which we possess of

---

* Howard.   † Zimmerman.

the mortality of our hospitals is in Sir William
Petty's work on Political Arithmetic, from which
it appears, that in the year 1685 the proportion
of the deaths to the cures in St. Bartholomew's
and St. Thomas's Hospitals was about 1 to 7.
The annual printed report of St. Thomas's Hospital for 1689 is still preserved: the mortality
was then about 1 in 10.   In 1741, the report
of St. Thomas's Hospital gives about 1 in 10.
During the ten years from 1773 to 1783 the
mortality at St. Thomas's became still smaller,
it was 1 in 14.   About the year 1783, some
improvements were made with respect to cleanliness and ventilation, and during the ten subsequent years the annual deaths were accordingly still fewer than before, less than 1 in 15.
During the ten years intervening between 1803
and 1813 the improvement continued, and the
proportion fell to only 1 in 16.   The average
during the 50 years from 1764 to 1813 was remarkably small, only 1 in 15.   The average
deaths of the physician's cases during ten years
were 1 in 9.*

The following are the annual Reports of
St. Thomas's and St. Bartholomew's Hospitals
for 1827 : —

---

* Blane, in Medico-Chirurgical Transactions, and Select
Dissertations.

ST. THOMAS'S HOSPITAL.

There have been cured and discharged from St.
Thomas's Hospital in Southwark, the last year, of
wounded, maimed, sick, and diseased persons,
3151 in-patients, and 9343 out-patients, including
casualties, many of whom have been relieved with
money and necessaries at their departure, to accommodate and support them in their journies to
their several habitations   -   -   -   12,494
Buried   -   -   -   -   -   259
Remaining under cure,   { In-patients   -   438
                        { Out-patients   -   441

ST. BARTHOLOMEW'S HOSPITAL.

Patients admitted, cured, and discharged, during the
last year, 4916 in-patients, 4318 out-patients, and
3173 casualty patients, many of whom have been
supplied with money, clothes, and other necessaries, to enable them to return to their several
habitations   -   -   -   -   12,407
Buried   -   -   -   -   350
                   { In-patients   476
Remaining under cure, { Out-patients   -   320
                   { Casualty patients   -   164

The first annual report of St. George's Hospital is for the year 1734, when patients were
first received. It yields a proportion of about
1 death in 8 in-patients. The two reports of
1825 and 1827 afford about 1 in 9. But there
is no doubt that when the new building is
opened the estimate will be still more favourable. The printed report of 1828 observes : —

" It is well known that the closeness of the wards in the old building has long been a subject of the deepest regret to the physicians and surgeons who have observed its effect in preventing or retarding the cure of their patients; and this evil must, in some degree, be increased by the new building partially obstructing the ventilation of the old. It is hoped, therefore, that the noble spirit which has shown itself in the commencement of this undertaking will not leave its work incomplete, nor relax its exertions till it has attained that inestimable blessing for the suffering poor, an airy, well-arranged hospital, of a size commensurate with the wants, and worthy of the opulence and charity, of the western part of the metropolis." We may remark, that a large part of the in-patients usually admitted are cases of *accidents,* a circumstance which marks the eminent utility of this institution, and explains, perhaps, a principal source of the mortality.

In the provincial hospitals of the kingdom the mortality will be generally found lower than in the metropolitan, which will also be seen to occur in France and in Germany. This circumstance is owing to the smaller population of the town, and to the usually smaller size of the hospital. In Dublin and Edinburgh the mortality of the public institutions appears to be less than in London. If we take the hos-

G

pital at Bath we find a similar result : the
mortality is there inferior to what occurs in
Dublin or Edinburgh. At the *Bath United
Hospital*, during 1827, 280 in-patients were
received under the physician's care, and 14
only died, or 1 in 20. During the same year
271 in-patients were received under the surgeon's
care, and 16 died, or about 1 in 17.

It appears clear, that the congregation of a
large mass of persons has a greater or less
tendency (according to circumstances) to promote the formation of disease, and to propagate
and exasperate it when once produced. On this
account a large town is usually less favourable
to health than a small one, and a large hospital
than a small one, and it would be probably
found, on observation, that a large *ward* in any
hospital is less healthy than a small one. These
tendencies may be occasionally retarded by
particular exertions to counteract them, but the
principle will remain unimpaired. Perhaps it
might be useful to preserve these facts in view
in the construction of new hospitals : a city
would be better served by several small hospitals than by a few large ones, without alluding to the greater convenience of transport,
visits, and study.

Dublin appears to have suffered more con-
tinuously from epidemic fever than any other
great city of Europe which has not sustained

the pressure of war. The causes of this calamitous state are attributed by the resident
physicians to want of employment, poverty, and
sometimes to famine among the lower classes;
and (if we continue to use the strong language
of one of the eye-witnesses) to circumstances
" unhappily deeply laid in the frame of society,
and arising from manners and habits generated
by ages of civil and moral degradation, which
has checked the natural progress of civilisation,
— exhibiting a population increasing, but not
improving." We may reasonably trust that
this gloomy picture will soon cease to own an
original in our own empire.

The mortality of the *Fever Hospital* has gradually and steadily diminished of late years : —

From 1804 to 1812 it was 1 in 12 ;
From 1812 to 1814 it was 1 in 15 ;
And in 1815 it was only 1 in 20 :

and we may add, that whatever may be, or
may have been, the condition of the humbler
inhabitants, the mortality of its hospitals and
asylums, taken all together, is greatly inferior to
that of all the *similar* institutions of Paris taken
together. At Paris the rate of these was in
1822 about 1 in 8, but at Dublin, as appears
from the following table, about 1 in 13, in a late
year

Return of the Admissions, Discharges, and Deaths, in the Hospitals of Dublin, from the 1st of August, 1826, to the 1st of August, 1827.

	ADMITTED.			DISCHARGED.			DIED.		
	Males.	Females.	Total.	Males.	Females.	Total.	Males.	Females.	Total.
House and Asylum -	22	287	513	140	187	327	66	97	163
Lunatics - -	38	34	72	6	9	15	35	34	69
Hardwicke Fever Hospital	1508	1407	2915	1408	1337	2745	102	81	183
Wellesley Fever ditto	869	1362	2231	753	1228	1981	62	92	154
Whitworth Chronic ditto	514	625	1139	400	532	932	113	112	225
Richmond Surgical ditto	733	347	1080	673	320	993	55	20	75
Mendicant Cells -	570	2961	3531	570	2981	3551	2		2
Total	4458	7023	11481	3950	6594	10544	435	436	871

An excellent Report (the thirty-third) has lately been published by the medical and surgical officers of the Glasgow Royal Infirmary of the cases and operations which occurred in it during 1827. It contains above 200 patients. In the medical department the number of females slightly exceeded. The average mortality of the male patients was 1 in $8\frac{2}{3}$; of the female only 1 in $10\frac{1}{4}$. The mortality has been greatly swelled by the prevalence of two formidable epidemics, typhus fever and dysentery. The typhus patients alone constitute fully one half of the whole, amounting to 1078. This fever was peculiarly fatal; the deaths of males being about 1 in 7, and of females somewhat above 1 in 10. The dysentery was also uncommonly severe; the deaths of males were above 1 in 8, of females 1 in 10. The decided bias of nearly the whole of the diseases of this year was towards *asthenia;* a tendency which was to be anticipated from the privations of the lower classes, arising from suspended commerce and languishing manufactures.

The number of surgical cases was 795 : here there is a large excess of male cases, 511, and only 284 females. The average rate of death among the former was 1 in $14\frac{1}{6}$; and among the latter 1 in $14\frac{1}{3}$. The operations amounted to 80, of which one half may be reckoned capital or important. Lithotomy was performed only five times.

G 3

In the whole year only 42 cases of phthisis pulmonalis were received, and 2 of phthisis laryngea. Scrofula and sibbens each afford 6 instances. Of scirrhus and cancer there are 30 cases. Of diseased liver there are 15. Hysteria presents 15 : syphilis 69.*

The mortality of the Edinburgh Royal Infirmary, on an average of the 10 years previous to 1818, was 1 in 16 of all admitted, — a rate similar to that recorded of St. Thomas's Hospital by Blane. My friend Dr. Moncrieff of Edinburgh has favoured me with a minute report of the practice at the *New Town Dispensary* during more than three years. I shall first lay this valuable and laborious document before the reader, and shall then subjoin the results of the Royal Infirmary obtained during the 10 years above alluded to.

---

* Glasgow Medical Journal, Number I. Glasgow, 1828.

QUARTERLY REPORTS OF THE EDINBURGH NEW TOWN DISPENSARY.

Quarter ending December 1. 1821. — Total Number of Patients, 1171.

Diseases.	Number of Cases.	Number of Deaths.	Males.	Ages of Males.	Females.	Ages of Females.
Febris continua	34	1	1	12	2	3. 5. m.
Hydrocephalus	7	4	2	2½. 4	1	13
Phrenitis	3	1				
Paralysis	5	1	1	40		
Convulsio	3	1	1	8 months		
Pneumonia	26	3	1	36	2	46. 66
Peripneumonia	2	2			2	64. 75
Carditis	2	2	1	21	1	40
Hæmop. and phthisis	29	6	2	60. 40.	4	14. 45. 60
Hydrothorax	3	1			1	40
Pertussis	21	6	2	7 m. 10	4	16 m. 14 days. 2. 2½. 3
Hepatitis, ac. and chron.	10	1			1	46
Hematemesis	3	1	1	65	1	55
Enteritis	5	2	1	40	1	40
Peritonitis	4	1				
Hydrops	17	4	1	52	3	21. 63. 63.
Morbus coxarius	2	1	1	6		
Variola	6	1	1	18 months		
Gangraena cruris	1	1			1	74
Ulcus	31	1			1	18 months
Ustio	17	1			1	2
Total		42	16		26	

Quarter ending March 1. 1822. — Total Number of Patients, 1487.

Diseases.	Number of Cases.	Number of Deaths.	Males.	Ages of Males.	Females.	Ages of Females.
Febris continua	25	2	1	49	1	41
Feb. inf. remitt.	44	1	1	3		
Phrenitis	1	1	1	42		
Hydrocephalus	7	4	1	14 months	3	10 m. 2½. 6
Convulsio	3	2	1	22 months	2	5 months
Catarrhus	179	3	1	60	2	5 wks. 60
Pneumonia	62	5	4	6 m. 18 m. 18 m. 40	1	76
Bronchitis	7	1	1	22 months		
Carditis	1	1	1	50		
Haemop. and phthisis	37	9	6	11. 19. 37. 47. 48. 60	3	30. 45. 59
Hydrothorax	7	2	2	14. 53		
Pertussis	46	6	4	14 wks. 13 m. 2. 3	2	2½. 2½. twins
Hepatitis, ac. and chron.	12	2			2	40. 65
Enteritis	3	1			1	40
Diarrhœa	50-	1			1	60
Tabes mesenterica	9	4			4	7 m. 17 m. 3. 6
Hydrops	10	4			4	20. 60. 60. 63
Erysipelas	20	2	1	45	1	3
Variola	4	2			2	5 m. 13
Ulcus	44	2	1	6 months	1	15 months
Total	55	26			29	

Quarter ending June 1. 1822. — Total Number of Patients, 1322.

Diseases.	Number of Cases.	Number of Deaths.	Males.	Ages of Males.	Females.	Ages of Females.
Febris continua	34	1	1	60		
Feb. dentitionis	10	1	1	20 months		
Hydrocephalus	8	8	4	16 m. 8. 9. 9.	4	13 m. 1. 7. 7
Convulsio	2	2	2	7 m. 14 m.		
Cynanche trachealis	2	2	1	5	1	3
Pneumonia	30	2			2	31. 48
Pericarditis	1	2	1	60		
Haemop. and phthisis	28	6	4	34. 58. 60. 70	2	2. 50
Hydrothorax	5	1			1	56
Angina pectoris	3	1	1	40		
Pertussis	13	2			2	8 m. 5
Hepatitis ac. and chron.	10	1	1	44		
Scirrhus pylori	2	2			2	50. 62
Enteritis	6	2	1	40	1	32
Peritonitis	1	1			1	65.
Diarrhœa	46	1			1	60
Cholera	1	1			1	60
Hydrops	19	1			1	45
Hydrops ovarii	1	1			1	45
Rheumatismus ac.and chr.	59	1			1	35 gangræna reg. sacræ
Syphilis	20	1	1	19		
Erysipelas	18	1	1	21		
Ustio	11	2	1	8	1	2
Total		42	20		22	

Quarter ending September 1. 1822. — *Total Number of Patients, 1407.*

Diseases.	Number of Cases.	Number of Deaths.	Males.	Ages of Males.	Females.	Ages of Females.
Febris continua	40	2	1	40	1	2
Feb. dentitionis	13	2	1	8 months	1	6 months
Hydrocephalus	5	2	1	4	1	3
Catarrhus	86	1	1	62		
Pneumonia	21	2			2	26. 55
Carditis	1	1	1	36		
Hæmop. and phthisis	37	9	3	22. 28. 60	6	20 m. 7. 25. 31. 54. 60
Hydrothorax	2	1	1	51		
Pertussis	14	2	1	18 months	1	13 months
Hepatitis ac. and chron.	12	1	1	60		
Icterus	4	1			1	26
Intus-susceptio	1	1			1	9 months
Peritonitis	5	1			1	56
Diarrhœa	64	2	1	9 months	1	25
Cholera	8	1			1	35
Hydrops	11	1	1	60		
Scrofula	24	1	1	9 months		
Syphilis	31	1			1	40
Variola	15	2	1	4	1	14 months
Phlegmon	29	1			1	4
Total		35	15		20	

Quarter ending December 1. 1822. — Total Number of Patients, 1439.

Diseases.	Number of Cases.	Number of Deaths.	Males.	Ages of Males.	Females.	Ages of Females.
Febris continua	43	1	1	24		
Feb. inf. remitt.	14	1	1	3		
Hydrocephalus	3	1			1	16 months
Apoplexia	2	2	1	35	1	60
Catarrhus	143	1			1	78
Pneumonia	25	4	2	24. 40	2	3. 60
Hæmop. and phthisis	29	4	1	19	3	22. 35. 50
Pertussis	12	2	2	9 m. 15 m.		
Hepatitis ac. and chron.	7	1			1	50
Peritonitis	2	1	1	52		
Cystitis, ulcus vesicæ	1	1	1	58		
Tabes mesenterica	6	1	1	21 months		
Hydrops	16	2	1	79	1	12
Scarlatina and sequelæ	4	2			2	3. 4
Variola	17	6	1	1	5	8 m. 1. 2. 3. 4
Total		30	13		17	

Quarter ending March 1. 1823. — Total Number of Patients, 1708.

Diseases.	Number of Cases.	Number of Deaths.	Males.	Ages of Males.	Females.	Ages of Females.
Febris continua	36	2	1	45	1	48
Feb. inf. remitt.	39	1	-	-	1	16 months
Hydrocephalus	9	9	4	4m. 10m. 4. 5	5	18 m. 3. 4. 4. 6
Delirium tremens	1	2	1	40	-	-
Apoplexia	2	2	1	76	1	18
Paralysis	6	1	1	59	-	-
Convulsio	3	1	1	2 weeks	-	-
Catarrhus	328	2	1	7 weeks	1	5 months
Pneumonia	26	1	-	-	1	60
Bronchitis	2	1	-	-	1	9 months
Hæmop. and phthisis	36	6	2	21. 40	4	3. 18. 27. 57
Asthma	21	3	1	67	2	45. 65
Hydrothorax	10	9	5	40. 56. 60.` 65. 68	4	34. 38. 40. 55
Pertussis	5	1	-	16 months	-	-
Hepatitis ac. and chron.	12	3	2	26. 40	1	36
Ulcus ventriculi	1	1	-	-	1	49
Enteritis	5	1	1	50	-	-
Strictura duodeni	1	1	-	-	1	55
Peritonitis	5	1	-	-	1	11
Tabes mesenterica	3	2	1	8	1	15 months
Hydrops	14	3	1	17 m.	2	5. 60
Scarlatina and sequelæ	17	1	1	8	-	-
Variola	39	12	4	1 m. 14 m. 2. 4	8	4 m. 9 m. 9 m. 9 m. 11 m. 3. 3. 5.
Ulcus	32	1	-	-	1	50
Total		66	29		37	

Quarter ending June 1. 1823. — Total Number of Patients, 1838.

Diseases.	Number of Cases.	Number of Deaths.	Males.	Ages of Males.	Females.	Ages of Females.
Feb. inf. remitt.	31	1			1	2
Hydrocephalus	10	5	2	2. 8	3	5. 12
Convulsio	1	1	1	9 months		
Cynanche tonsillaris	36	1			1	7 months
Catarrhus	334	2	2	61. 76		
Pneumonia	32	7	3	9 m. 2¼. 38	4	11 m. 14 m. 50. 80
Pleuritis	26	2			2	4. 80
Bronchitis	3	2	2	35. 60		
Haemop. and phthisis	34	9	7	30. 40. 40. 40. 60. 63. 72	2	4. 50
Asthma	15	1	1	60		
Hydrothorax	6	1			1	67
Angina pectoris	3	1	1	74		
Aneurisma aortæ	2	1	1	42		
Pertussis	4	1	1	5		
Hepatitis ac. and chron.	7	2	2	47. 65		
Enteritis	5	1	1	71		
Peritonitis	3	1			1	45
Diarrhœa	69	2	2	13 m. 14		
Dysenteria	8	1	1	63		
Tabes mesenterica	4	1	1	17 months		
Hydrops	8	2	1	28	1	51
Rachitis	2	1	1	8 months		
Rubeola and sequelæ	62	2	1	7	1	6
Erysipelas	17	2	1	65 husband	1	60 wife
Variola	14	6	4	18 m. 20 m. 3. 4	2	2. 2
Gangræna ani, &c.	1	1			1	2½
Total		57	36		21	

Quarter ending September 1. 1823. — Total Number of Patients, 1999.

Diseases.	Number of Cases.	Number of Deaths.	Males.	Ages of Males.	Females.	Ages of Females.
Febris continua	34	2	2	5. 23	5	9 weeks. 20 m. 2. 2½. 3
Hydrocephalus	8	7	2	3. 9	1	69
Apoplexia	1	1	-	-		
Paralysis	8	1	1	70		
Convulsio	5	2	1	7 months	1	9
Pneumonia	20	2	2	8 m. 17 m.		
Hæmop. and phthisis	50	8	2	21 m. 17	6	14. 22. 28. 30. 32. 35
Angina pectoris	3	2	1	40	1	14
Hepatitis ac. and chron.	7	1	-	-	1	50
Ulcus ventriculi	1	1	1	48		
Hæmatemesis	4	1	-	-	1	24
Enteritis	9	1	-	-	1	15
Intus-susceptia	1	1	1	5 weeks		
Peritonitis	6	1	1	4		
Diarrhœa	56	2	-	-	2	8 m. 9 m.
Tabes mesenteric	7	2	-	-	2	2. 8
Rubeola and sequelæ	338	20	9	6 m. 15 m. 18 m. 1½. 1½. 2. 2. 3. 4	11	4 m. 8 m. 9 m. 15 m. 16 m. 21 m. 1. 1. 2. 2½. 4
Erysipelas	21	1	1	20		
Variola	14	2	1	15 m.	1	10 m.
Total		58	25		33	

Quarter ending December 1. 1823. — Total Number of Patients, 1794.

Diseases.	Number of Cases.	Number of Deaths.	Males.	Ages of Males.	Females.	Ages of Females.
Hydrocephalus	6	6	3	11 m. 3. 4	3	18 m. 2½. 18
Delirium tremens	1	1	1	55		
Apoplexia	2	1	1	66		
Convulsio	2	2	2	1 m. 2 m.		
Cynanche maligna	2	2	1	27	1	6 m.
Cynanche laryngea	7	1	1	39	1	9 m.
Catarrhus	177	1				
Pneumonia	16	2	2	9 m. 50	7	1. 21. 25. 38. 45. 45. 45
Hæmop. and phthisis	42	11	4	10. 27. 38. 50		
Asthma	16	1	1	48	1	69
Hydrothorax	5	1				
Angina pectoris	1	1	1	60	1	48
Hepatitis ac. and chron.	14	1			1	2½
Enteritis	6	2	1	31	2	34. 42
Peritonitis	6	2			1	15 m.
Diarrhœa	82	2	1	2	1	2½
Tabes mesenterica	8	1			1	56
Hydrops	20	2	1	3	2	6 m. 1
Rubeola and sequelæ	35	6	4	9 m. 1. 1½. 2	2	6 m. 1
Scarlatina and sequelæ	38	4	3	2. 4. 8	3	3
Variola	19	3			3	11 m. 11 m. 16 m.
Fracturæ	4	1			1 costarum.	70
Total		54	27		27	

Quarter ending March 1. 1824. — Total Number of Patients, 1429.

Diseases.	Number of Cases.	Number of Deaths.	Males.	Ages of Males.	Females.	Ages of Females.
Febris continua	22	1	-	-	1	18
Paralysis	9	1	1	73	1	45
Mania	1	1	-	-	1	8 m.
Cynanche maligna	1	1	-	-	1	-
Cynanche trachealis	8	5	3	1. 23 m. 3	2	19 m. 4
Catarrhus	197	3	1	63	2	22 m. 80
Pneumonia	16	2	1	4 m.	1	-
Pleuritis	22	2	1	80	1	70
Hæmop. and phthisis	28	12	5	7 m. 18. 19. 28.65.	7	10. 23. 26. 28. 30. 40. 51
Hydrothorax	5	3	2	41.78.	1	4
Angina pectoris	1	1	1	46		
Pertussis	3	1	1	10 m.		
Schirrus pancreatis	1	1			1	47
Hæmatemesis	2	1			1	24
Enteritis	4	1			1	42
Diarrhœa	56	3	1	35	2	7 wks. 50
Tabes mesenterica	3	1	1	22 m.		
Hydrops	8	1			1	50
Morbus spinalis	3	1	1	22		
Syphilis	20	1			1	4 m. erup. syphilit.
Rubeola and sequelæ	1	1			1	4
Scarlatina and seq.	26	3	1	12	2	15 m. 9
Erysipelas	17	2	2	19. 50		
Variola	2	1			1	6
Tumores	15	1	1	42 tumor colli		
Vulnus	11	1			1	45 vulnus genu
Total		52	23		29	

Quarter ending June 1. 1824. — *Total Number of Patients, 1879.*

Diseases.	Number of Cases.	Number of Deaths.	Males.	Ages of Male.	Females.	Ages of Females.
Febris continua	40	1		-	1	21½
Hydrocephalus	7	7	6	11m.16m. 16m. 20m. 2.12	1	17
Apoplexia	2	2	1	55	1	60
Paralysis	1	1		-	1	60
Convulsio	3	1		-	1	20 weeks
Cynanche laryngea	1	1	1	57		
Cynanche trachealis	5	1	1	2		
Catarrhus	228	2	1	9 months	1	15 weeks
Pneumonia	32	4	2	18 m. 63	2	4 m. 8 m.
Carditis	1	1		-	1	10
Haemop. and phthisis	48	6	4	40. 43. 48. 50	2	30. 53
Asthma	17	1	1	35		
Hydrothorax	4	2	1	60	1	63
Angina pectoris	6	1	1	13		
Aneurisma aortæ	1	1	1	37		
Pertussis	1	1	1	9 months		
Enteritis	2	1		-	1	16
Peritonitis	3	2	2	10. 52		
Tabes mesenterica	4	1		-	1	19 months
Suppuratio renis	1	1	1	45		
Hydrops	22	3	2	44. 70	1	68
Scarlatina and sequelæ	61	2	2	14 m. 4		
Variola	14	1	1	15 months		
Gangræna	1	1	1	78		
Total		45	30		15	

H

Quarter ending September 1. 1824. — Total Number of Patients, 1486.

Diseases.	Number of Cases.	Number of Deaths.	Males.	Ages of Males.	Females.	Ages of Females.
Febris continua	15	1	1	2		
Hydrocephalus	4	4	2	11 m. 5	2	9 m. 14
Paralysis	8	2	2	56. 70		
Mania	2	1	1	41		
Convulsio	3	1	1	2		
Cynanche maligna	1	1	1	7 months		
Cynanche trachealis	2	2	1	2	1	7 months
Pneumonia	27	1			1	6 months
Bronchitis	3	2	2	2½. 3	4	19. 25. 30. 45
Hæmop. and phthisis	31	7	3	2. 35. 48	1	61
Asthma	6	1			1	39
Hydrothorax	3	1	1	40		
Hepatitis ac. and chr.	8	1			1	23
Hæmatemesis	5	1			1	18 months
Diarrhœa	92	3	2	10 months	1	20 months
Tabes mesenterica	5	2	1	7 months	1	70
Enteritis	2	1				
Retentio urinæ	1	1	1	75		
Rheumatismus ac. and chr.	72	1			1	59
Morbus spinalis	2	1			1	20
Scarlatina and sequelæ	17	1	1	10		
Variola	21	9	6	6 m. 18 m. 18 m. 2. 3. 4	3	9 m. 18 m. 3
Total		45	26		19	

Quarter ending December 1. 1824.— Total Number of Patients, 1377.

Diseases.	Number of Cases.	Number of Deaths.	Males.	Ages of Males.	Females.	Ages of Females.
Febris continua -	23	3	2	11. 17	1	12
Feb. inf. remittens -	23	1	1	7	1	5
Hydrocephalus -	4	4	3	10 m. 15 m. 10		
Paralysis -	3	3	3	36. 70. 80		
Cynanche trachealis -	4	3	1	5	2	11 m. 3
Catarrhus -	165	1	1	78		
Pneumonia -	29	3	2	16 m. 2½	1	13 m.
Pleuritis -	14	2	2	3. 35		
Bronchitis -	3	2	1	5	1	2
Hæmop. and phthisis -	21	5	2	38. 44	3	30. 32. 40
Asthma -	4	1	1	56		
Hydrothorax -	6	2	1	60	1	38
Pneumothorax -	1	1	1	18		
Pertussis -	43	7	2	6 m. 11 m.	5	7 m. 7 m. 2. 2. 4
Scirrhus pylori -	2	1	1	55		
Gastritis -	2	1				
Enteritis -	6	1	1	7 months	1	48
Diarrhœa -	66	2	1	35	1	3
Cholera -	7	1			1	14 days
Tabes mesenterica -	2	1	1	16 months		
Cancer recti -	1	1				
Hydrops -	13	3			1	35
Scrofula -	10	1	1	8	3	23. 70. 76
Syphilis -	20	1				
Rubeola and sequelæ	5	1		:	1	45
Scarlatina and seq. -	14	1			1	9 months
Variola -	24	8	2	3. 5	6	6 m. 2. 2. 2. 2½. 3
Total -		61	30		31	

H 2

Abstract of the Quarterly Reports.

	Number of Cases.	Number of Deaths.		
		Males.	Females.	Total.
Quarter ending December 1. 1821.	1171	16	26	42
———————— March 1. 1822. -	1487	26	29	55
———————— June 1. 1822. -	1322	20	22	42
———————— September 1. 1822.	1407	15	20	35
——————— December 1. 1822.	1439	13	17	30
———————— March 1. 1823. -	1708	29	36	66
———————— June 1. 1823. -	1838	36	21	57
———————— September 1. 1823.	1999	25	33	58
——————— December 1. 1823.	1794	27	27	54
——————— March 1. 1824. -	1429	23	29	52
———————— June 1. 1824. -	1879	30	15	45
——————— September 1. 1824.	1486	26	19	45
——————— December 1. 1824.	1377	30	31	61

List of Patients admitted into the Royal Infirmary of Edinburgh for Ten Years previous to the 1st of January, 1818. (Extracted from the printed Report of the Committee of Contributors to that Institution, appointed to enquire into the State of the Hospital, by the General Court of Contributors, held on the 5th of January, 1818.)

Years of Admission.	Total admitted, exclusive of those remaining in the Hospital annually.	Cured.	Relieved.	Dismissed with Advice.	Dismissed as improper.	Dismissed as irregular.	Dismissed by their own Desire.	Died.
1808	1787	1279	144	77	65	17	91	121
1809	1646	1184	138	36	75	22	105	109
1810	1854	1375	143	59	55	29	68	108
1811	2146	1712	131	58	52	26	55	121
1812	2018	1572	148	33	57	22	66	88
1813	1774	1352	174	28	84	9	86	96
1814	1884	1280	198	26	73	23	118	108
1815	1628	1065	168	46	82	37	135	111
1816	1798	1189	183	49	79	34	127	123
1817	2250	1506	234	4	51	135	110	142
Total from 1808 to 1817, both inclusive	18785	13514	1661	416	673	354	961	1127
Average for the above period	$1878\frac{5}{10}$	$1351\frac{4}{10}$	$166\frac{1}{10}$	$41\frac{6}{10}$	$67\frac{3}{10}$	$35\frac{4}{10}$	$96\frac{1}{10}$	$112\frac{7}{10}$

H 3

PARIS.

The hospitals of Paris received and treated during the year 1822, 47,393 individuals.

The *hospices* afforded refuge to 13,216.

The *administration* supported 19,557 deserted children.

The average period of residence in the hospitals was about 35 days.

The mortality in the hospitals (classing all together) was 1 in 8·42.

The mortality in the *hospices* was 1 in 6·71.

The *daily* expense of each patient in the hospitals was 1 franc, 76 centimes, and 72 dixièmes (about eighteen-pence English).

The daily expense of each inmate of the *hospices* was 84 centimes, and 58 dixièmes (about eight-pence English).

The number of individuals maintained in the hospitals and *hospices* has greatly increased since 1786, when Tenon published his *Report*. In 1822 the number of sick treated in the hospitals exceeded, by 2074, that of 1786 ; the number of the aged of both sexes received in the *hospices* exceeded, by 1828, that of 1786 ; the number of deserted children supported by the administration exceeded, by 2873, that of 1786; a circumstance not arising from a real increase in the proportion of illegitimate births, but from a diminution of the mortality, which previously devoured these unfortunate beings. Vaccination, greater attention to their comforts, and a better choice of nurses, have combined to reduce the mortality of the children supported in the country to about the half of its former amount.

During the years 1817, 1818, 1819, 1820, and 1821, the annual average of deaths in private dwellings was 13,320, and in hospitals and *hospices* 8595 ; so that the proportion of deaths in such establishments, to deaths *at home*, is at Paris in the relation of 64 to 100.*

Some facts adduced by Villermé † tend to prove that the mortality of the various patients in the hospitals of Paris is considerably influenced by the goodness or meanness of their condition, by the quantity of their wages, and the nature of their work. The mortality of the lowest class, composed chiefly of persons working or wandering in the streets, is about 1 in 4. Of the class of servants and artisans who are employed more in the interior of dwellings, the mortality is about 1 in 10. The mortality of the soldiers of the *Guard of Paris* is only 1 in 21 in their hospital.

If we examine the progress of several years at the *Hôtel Dieu*, a slow but gradual improvement will appear. Between the years 1770 and

* Villermé.
† Mém. de l'Acad. R. de Médecine, t. i. Paris, 1828.

1780 the mortality was about 1 in 4 of all admitted; at this period it would be difficult to
imagine, as some have done, that high mortality
is a proof of well-regulated hospitals, since *Hunc-
zowski* declares that he often saw on the same
bed a dead body lying by the side of two dying
patients and of one convalescent.

The mortality of the Hôtel Dieu, in the year
1822, was 1 in $6\frac{82}{100}$ on the *whole* number admitted, namely, about 1 in $6\frac{3}{4}$ of the physicians'
cases, and 1 in 12 for the surgeons'. We observe
that the mortality of the two sexes differs; that
of the females is greater than of the men, being
1 in 5 of the first, and only 1 in 7 of the last.
The duration of each patient's stay was about
the same for both sexes, namely, about 25 days;
and the length of stay about the same for both
medical and surgical cases. The ages which
afforded the most disease were from 15 to 40
for the men, and from 15 to 32 for the women.
The surgical cases are here the least fatal, being
chiefly composed of slight injuries; while the
medical cases abound in acute disorders, moribund and aged objects, previously exhausted
by want, or by improper treatment.

In the *Charité*, another general hospital, the
mortality is 1 in $5\frac{53}{100}$ in the same year. At the
hospital St. Louis, on the other hand, which is
not a general hospital, out chiefly confined to
cutaneous and scrofulous complaints, rheumatism, and ulcers, the annual mortality is

greatly inferior, being only 1 in about 14, while the duration of the cases is much longer, being 60 days.

PROVINCIAL HOSPITALS OF FRANCE.

In the provincial hospitals of France the mortality is much less than in those of the capital: at Lyons the mortality of the Hôtel Dieu is about 1 in 11; at Montpelier the average of all the medical institutions is about 1 in 10. We have previously remarked, that as the mortality of great cities is usually superior to that of towns, so the annual deaths of metropolitan hospitals will usually exceed the proportion of provincial ones; and, generally, that in any large hospital the proportion of deaths will exceed that of a small one.

BERLIN.

The mortality of the great general hospital, the *Charité*, on an average of 20 years, from 1796 to 1817, was about 1 in 6; and this fact forms a remarkable contrast with *St. Thomas*'s Hospital in London, at the same period, where the deaths were only 1 in 16. And yet in addition to the usual cases of a general hospital, the Charité was receiving all this time an abundant supply of lying-in women, and of the insane, whose presence would tend to lower the total sum of death. The medical cases were to the surgical in the proportion of about 6 to 1 of all admitted. It can contain 1000 patients; and many are received who pay a small sum for separate rooms and superior accommodation ; a plan which is also encouraged at the great hospital of Vienna, and appears to deserve imitation in our own cities, particularly where the funds of an hospital are not of a permanent nature.

The most fatal disease experienced by the inhabitants during the present century has been the epidemic typhus, which destroyed 1575 individuals in the year 1813, and 1323 in the year 1814. This scourge was introduced by the return of the French army from Russia ; but among all the calamities which Buonaparte poured upon Prussia, it has been perhaps the most easily repaired.

In the *garrison* hospitals of Prussia were received, during the year 1822, 96,895 patients : 3811 of these remained from the preceding year. The number of those discharged cured, during the year, was 91,413 ; the lost or missing 25 ; discharged incurable 452 ; died 1123 ; remained at end of the year above 3800. The mortality was thus about 1 in 85. Amongst the deaths, 33 were drowned by accident, and 48 were suicides. Amongst all these patients only one death from small-pox occurred, and seven from scarlet fever. There was only one death of a maniac, and only one from disease of the heart. The deaths from consumption of the lungs were 270. Deaths from apoplexy 85, of whom about a fourth did not apply for assistance. Deaths from strangulated hernia 2, and from universal syphilis 2.

VIENNA.

The great hospital of Vienna includes a variety of establishments, but the annual mortality of the whole is about 1 in 6. The mortality of the sick wards is about 1 in 7. The total number of beds is about 2000, contained in 111 rooms.

About a ninth part of the whole population of Vienna were contained in its hospitals and asylums during 1824, which is a much smaller proportion than exists at Paris.

PESTH.

At Pesth, the present capital of Hungary, the annual deaths at the civil hospital were, in 1826, 1 in 6; the same proportion that exists at the metropolis of Austria, on whose government it depends, and under whose mistaken policy it equally languishes.

From the 1st of November, 1825, to the last day of June, 1826, were received

With internal disorders - 718, of whom 151 died.
With external disorders - 373, of whom 20 died.
Pregnant women - 39
New-born infants - 39, of whom 1 died. *

* A. Jankovich. Mem. Clin. in Nosocomio Civ. Pesthiensi. 1826.

DRESDEN.

At Dresden the annual mortality of the city hospital was, in 1816, 1 in 7 ; and this amount must be chiefly imputed to the crowded and badly ventilated state of the hospital ; for the prosperous and enlightened character of the place would otherwise yield, probably, a better result.

MUNICH.

The hospital at Munich is one of the most modern and of the best regulated. The report óf 1819 affords only 1 death in 9, of above 3500 patients admitted, — the lowest mortality of any hospital of the same dimensions in Germany, but the city of Munich is also one of the most happily circumstanced. The deaths of both sexes were exactly equal, and the greatest number took place in March and April. The following is a table of the diseases treated in this year : —

Cholera	2	Gangræna	16	Scirrhus ventriculi	5
Erysipelas	160	Angina	27	Scabies	393
Febris biliosa	51	Arthritis	86	Hæmoptoe	17
—— catarrhalis	77	Enteritis	7	Phthisis	101
—— ephemera	7	Hemiplegia and Paralysis }	26	Hydrops	84
—— exanthematica	35			Peripneumonia and Pleuritis }	76
—— humoralis	59	Rachitis	1		
—— inflammatoria	15	Syphilis	147	Rheumatismus	163
—— intermittens	47	Struma	3	Apoplexy	12
—— nervosa	112	Vitium cordis	7	Amaurosis	1
—— pituitosa	10	Scirrhus pylori	1		

The mortality of the hospitals of the small towns of Germany appears to be often half, or even one third of that of the great cities; but I shall not enter into details respecting them, because I have no sufficient data from our own provincial hospitals of the same size with which a comparison might be formed. I may mention that this is particularly the case at Bonn, at Göttingen, and at Heidelberg : at the last town, which is thriving, placed in a most fertile situation, and of comparatively simple habits, the deaths at the hospital were, in 1825, only 1 in 21 ; but it must be observed that only 285 were admitted in the whole year. The average stay of each patient was about thirty-two days, which is seven more than the average stay at the Hôtel Dieu of Paris. The mortality of the out-patients was about half of the rate of the in-patients.

RUSSIA.

With respect to the general hospitals in Russia, it was found * in 1811 that the average mortality of those which contained above 30 patients was 1 in 9, but of those which contained less than 30, only 1 in 10. In 1812, a period of

---

* C. T. Herrmann. Mém. de l'Acad. des Sciences de Petersbourg, tom. ix. Petersb. 1824.

war, 7000 more patients were admitted than in
the preceding year. The annual average of
deaths at the Imperial Hospital for the sick
poor at Petersburgh has been for fourteen
years ending in 1817 so high as 1 in 4½, the
greatest proportion of any general hospital of
the same extent, and at the same period. The
sick are most numerous in April and May, and
in September and October.

In the year 1816, the in-patients amounted at
the above hospital to 2043, of whom 1378 were
cured, and 461 died. The out-patients were
26,968, of whom 4072 died. The operations for
the *stone* do not appear to have been so frequent
as might have been expected in a country where
that disease is very common. Thirty-two operations occurred from 1803 to 1817 : nineteen
patients recovered, twelve died, and one remained under treatment at the time of the
report.*

In the *poor-houses*, or *asylums*, of Russia, there
were 5044 admissions in the year 1811, and 519
deaths. They are 45 in number, and hold 1169
individuals. In 17 *orphan-houses* (which are not
to be confounded with the *foundling hospitals*)
1472 were received in 1811, and 977 in 1812.
The average mortality was 1 in 3⅓ during the
first year, and 1 in ⁄₇ during the second year.

---

* Mém. sur l'Etat actuel de l'Hôpital Imperial. Petersb.
1817.

PAYS DE VAUD.

The Cantonal Hospital of the *Pays de Vaud* received, in 1825, 344 patients : of whom 193 were cured, 40 were relieved, 15 were incurable, 16 died, and 50 remained. (*Feuille du Canton de Vaud.* 1826.)

GENEVA.

The mortality of the hospital at Geneva, during the year 1823, was about 1 in 11. The deaths of the sexes were exactly equal ; and the mean age of the patients who died was nearly the same for both sexes, being fifty-three years for the men, and fifty-six for the women. The average stay of each patient was 26 days, being nearly the same as at the Hôtel Dieu of Paris. The average stay of the patients who died was 22 days. About a third of all the patients were soldiers, whose presence contributed (as appears invariably to be the case) to dilute or lower the amount of fatal cases.

BRUSSELS.

The mortality of the hospital of St. Pierre at Brussels was in the year 1823 1 in 9 for the adult patients : exactly the same proportion prevailed for the two sexes, although a large part of the female ones were cases of labour : the deaths among the children, many of whom were foundlings, were 1 in 6.

AMSTERDAM.

The average mortality of the chief hospital, St. Pieter's Gasthuis, during the twenty years from 1798 to 1817, was about 1 in 8. The mortality of the male patients was about 1 in 7, of the females 1 in 9. The average loss of all the foundlings received in the noble establishment appropriated to them has been, during the twenty years from 1800 to 1819, about 1 in $8\frac{1}{4}$; a very low proportion when compared with many other similar institutions, but owing to the excellent arrangement and care observed throughout.*

In the chief hospital, during the year 1823, only two operations for the *stone* occurred, and six for *cataract*.

PIEDMONT.

The proportion of deaths to recoveries at the general hospital of Genoa was, in 1821, in 6. The proportion of the hospital St. Giovanni at Turin was, in the same year, 1 to 7. The medical practitioners in the kingdom of Sardinia

---

* Nieuwenhuijs. Geneeskundige Plaatsbeschrijving. Amst. 1816—1820.

are chiefly divided between the doctrines of
Brown and Broussais : the new contra-stimulant
theory has few partisans.

MILAN.

At Milan the mortality of the Great Hospital
was, during the three disastrous years ending in
1814, about 1 in 6. In 1823 it had improved
to 1 in 7. The number treated during 1823
was 13,278, of whom the males formed 8582, and
the females only 4696. The deaths were 1901,
of which 1073 were male cases, and 828 female.
The proportion, according to age, was *

From the age of 1 to 10 — 77
——————— 51 to 60 — 370 the highest proportion.
——————— 81 to 91 — 21 the lowest.
——————— 41 to 51 — 350

The mortality of the *clinic* during 1812, 1813,
and 1814, was 1 in 8, at which period *Rasori*
was the professor. The patients treated were
4852, and the deaths were 558. Rasori himself
communicated this statement to me.

Melchiorre Gioja, in his *Filosofia della Statistica* †, one of the most elaborate productions of
the present century, has given some curious tables
explanatory of the intimate connection and re-

* *From the document preserved in the office of the hospital.*
† 2 tom. 4to. Milano. 1826. Tom. ii. pp. 359—416.

I

action subsisting between the price of wheat, the quantity of disease, the number of children abandoned by their parents, and the mortality not only in hospitals but in private dwellings. We may premise that the price of wheat was very high in the years 1815, 1816, and 1817.

TABLE I.

The number of children exposed at the *Luogo Pio* of *St. Catherine* at Milan, and the number of sick in the Great Hospital of that city, in years of want, and at other periods.

Years.	Exposed.	Mean Number of exposed.	Number of Sick.	Mean Number of Sick.	Price of the Moggio of Wheat.	Mean Price of the Moggio of Wheat.
1815	2280	from 1818 to 1825 inclusively (1750)	17,974	from 1818 to 1825 inclusively (14,010)	59 lire	from 1818 to 1825 inclusively (25 lire)
1816	2625		20,993		75	
1817	3082		23,350		63	

TABLE II.

The mortality in the private dwellings and hospitals of Milan in years of scarcity, compared with the average mortality of other years.

Years.	Deaths in Private Dwellings.	Mean Number of Deaths in Private Dwellings.	Deaths in Hospitals.	Mean Deaths in Hospitals.	Total Mortality.	Mean Total Mortality.
1815	3824	from 1818 to 1825 (3305)	2680	from 1818 to 1825 (2028)	6504	from 1818 to 1825 (5333)
1816	3966		3085		7051	
1817	3806		4620		8426	

PAVIA.

At Pavia the most minute records are preserved of all which passes in the medical institutions. The tables which register their
transactions abound in the most interesting details, and we gladly render justice on this
point to the *Austrian* government, which, beyond all others, exacts from its medical officers the
most comprehensive and instructive reports.
We must refer for a specimen of this minuteness
to the Clinical Annals, lately published by Professor Hildenbrand. The total mortality of the
hospital of *San Matteo della Pietà*, in 1823, was
$10\frac{3644}{5247}$ per cent. It receives lying-in women as
well as general cases. The mortality of the
medical clinic was $6\frac{248}{2447}$ per cent. ; of the surgical clinic, $6\frac{17}{23}$ per cent. ; and of the obstetric
clinic, $6\frac{4}{51}$ per cent. The total number treated in
the year was 3201 men and 2086 women. 42
patients were brought in moribund. The surgical operations were 120. The mortality of
the foundlings *in* their hospital was about 12
per cent., but of those *put out* to nurse about
8 per cent. An accurate register is preserved
of the *veterinary* clinic : the mortality is about
6 per cent.

PADUA.

The cases of the medical clinic, at which Brera is professor, were in the scholastic season of 1820–21 149. The deaths were 10. Of the male cases 62 were acute, 21 were chronic, and 6 of the whole were incurable. Of the female cases 47 were acute, 19 were chronic, and of the whole 8 were incurable. The average duration of every disease was about 25 days, including the convalescence. The duration of the male and female cases was nearly the same. We perceive that the mortality was about the same as at the medical clinic of Pavia, about six per cent. The average cost of medicines for each patient was about four shillings, and the average cost of the food of each patient was about the same sum.

BOLOGNA.

Professor Tommasini has published the following report of the diseases and mortality in the clinical wards under his care, during the three scholastic seasons, 1816–17, 1817–18, and 1818–19. This detail is the more interesting, because he is one of the most zealous and enlightened partisans of the contra-stimulant doctrine, and is surpassed by no one in earnest attention to the patients committed to his care.

	Entered.	Died.	Mortality per cent.
Acute inflammations, including 15 rheumatisms and 8 *exanthems* - -	209	21	$10\frac{1}{21}$
Chronic phlogoses, including 13 dropsies, which depended on a *lento-phlogistic* condition - -	38	5	$13\frac{1}{6}$
Synocha and catarrhal fever -	35	0	0
Synochus, nervous fever, or typhus -	57	4	$7\frac{1}{57}$
Affections from a deficiency of stimulus	4	0	0
Simple intermittent fever, and complicated with physconia - -	45	0	0
Hæmorrhages - - -	17	1	$5\frac{15}{17}$
Convulsions - - -	18	1	$5\frac{5}{9}$
Asthmatic affections - -	4	0	0
Torpors, hemiplegia, and apoplexy -	10	1	10
Irritative affections - -	10	0	0
Hydrophobia - - -	2	2	100
Pellagra - - - -	1	0	0
Scrofulous disorders - -	3	0	0
Total - -	453	35	$7\frac{3}{4}$

LEGHORN.

During the seven years from 1818 to 1825 the average annual mortality of the male patients at the hospitals of Leghorn has been 1 in $7\frac{1}{6}$, and of the female patients 1 in $7\frac{1}{2}$.* On the other hand, as has been observed in other places, the deaths among the sick soldiery were only 110 to 7878 patients.

---

* Gordini ed Orsini. Ricerche, &c. Liv. 1826.

PALERMO.

The number of sick received at the Great Hospital of Palermo in 1823 amounted to 4221. The deaths were 515 ; a proportion of 12 per cent.

SPAIN.

The materials for comparison which this country has supplied are very scanty.

The two principal hospitals at *Madrid* are the *General Hospital* for men alone, and the *Hospital of the Passion* for women. According to a French traveller * 11,959 men and 3271 women were treated in these two hospitals in the year 1814, of whom 722 of the former, and 465 of the latter, died. In 1818, of 10,807 male patients, 9150 were cured, and 860 died ; and of 3693 women, 2956 were cured, and 423 died. But the report which we quote does not express that these were all in-patients, and affords little information, from its want of minuteness.

In the hospital of *Valencia* in 1786 were received 4800 civil patients, of whom 639 died ; and 890 soldiers, of whom only 27 died.

The general hospital of *Santa Cruz*, at *Bar-*

---

* D'Hautefort, Coup-d'œil sur Lisbonne et Madrid. Paris, 1820.

celona, receives the sick, the insane, and foundlings. The following is a report of its pro-
ceedings, furnished by the *Europeo,* an intelligent periodical journal of Barcelona, which has
now ceased to exist : —

GENERAL DISEASES.

Years.	Existing.	Entries.	Cured.	Died.	Remaining.
1820	469	3800	3366	5	495
1821	495	3866	3664	754	243
1822	243				388
1823	388	3456	3231	539	304

Compared with the returns of some great hospitals, this is considerably in favour of Barcelona.
The following is the report of the *insane* at the
same hospital : —

Years.	Existing.	Entries.	Cured.	Died.	Remaining.
1820	142	131	74	39	160
1821	160	113	76	34	142
1822	142				
1823		73	54	43	

The blank spaces exist in the original.

CHAP. VII.

STATISTICS OF LYING-IN HOSPITALS, AND OF THE
STILL-BORN.

The most prominent fact afforded by medical
statistics, next to the diminished mortality of
infancy, is the peculiar change which has supervened within the last 100 years in the fate of
lying-in women. In 1750, at the British Lying-
in Hospital of London, 1 woman died out of
42 ; in 1780, only 1 died in 60 ; and, finally,
the improvement became so great, that only 1
case was fatal out of 288, in the 10 years between 1789 and 1798. The proportion of still-
born children was at that time about 1 to 25 ;
and of women having twins was about 1 to 84.
The deaths of the children during all this period
preserved a constant proportion to the fate of
the mothers. In 1750, one child died out of 15 ;
in 1780, 1 in 44 ; and in the last decade, from
1789 to 1798, only 1 in 77.

Let us compare with this statement the situation of the lying-in women, about the same time,
in France. Tenon, a distinguished French
writer on hospitals, assures us, that the mortality
of the lying-in women at the Hôtel Dieu of

Paris (where they were then admitted) was about 1 in 15, while that of the British hospital was only 1 in 60 ; and the still-born were 1 in 13 at the former, while 1 in 25 at the latter. But it is pleasing to observe that this state of things no longer exists at Paris : the mortality of the Lying-in Hospital there was in 1822 1 in 30 ; which is at least the double of what at present occurs in our lying-in institutions. At the City of London Lying-in Hospital, in 1826, the deaths were 1 to 70 ; but, compared with the average of the Dublin Lying-in Hospital during 70 years, the present deaths at the Paris hospital are about treble in amount. The average stay of each female admitted into the Paris hospital was about 22 days.

The loss at the Dublin hospital was only 12 women among 2675 delivered, in the year 1822. The following is the official report of the results observed there during nearly 70 years, from its origin in 1757 to 1825 : —

Proportion of males and females born, about 12 males to 11 females.
————————— children dying in the hospital, about 1 to 19.
————————— children still born, about 1 to 17.
————————— women having twins (and more), about 1 to 60.
————————— women dying in child-bed, about 1 to 89.
————————— women having three and four children, about 1 to 4000.

The deaths at the Lying-in Hospital at Stockholm were, in 1822, about the same as at Paris, being 1 in 29. In 472 deliveries were 11 cases of twins, 1 triplet, and the still-born were 36. Of the 21 deaths of mothers 16 were from puerperal fever; and 12 of the new-born infants had ophthalmia purulenta, which is a very common affection, also, of the foundlings at Paris. A beneficial change has occurred at Berlin, corresponding to what has been seen at London and Paris. From 1796 to 1806 one lying-in woman died out of 32 received into the Charité Hospital at Berlin; but in the ensuing 10 years, from 1807 to 1817, only 1 fatal case occurred amongst 45. The average fate of pregnancy throughout the whole kingdom of Prussia in the year 1817 has been published under the sanction of that government : it is the only document of so comprehensive a nature, and embracing all ranks of society, which has yet been published. According to it 1 mother dies in that country out of 112 ; and as it relates to the rich equally as to the poor, and to rural districts as well as to cities, it places in a strong light the very low mortality of the Dublin Hospital, which in 1814 lost only 1 in 100 of women, always poor, and often miserable.

The following report of the obstetric practice in a healthy provincial town (*Lewes*) has been published by Mr. Mantell :* —

---

* London Medical Gazette, vol. ii. p. 782. 1828.

During the last 15 years occurred 2410 cases.

Arm presentations four, or 1 in 600.

Cases in which turning was necessary eight, or 1 in 300.

Cases of embryotomy, three : in one the fœtus dead ; in two, destroyed : 1 in 800.

Puerperal convulsions six : three delivered by natural efforts ; one, the child turned ; one by forceps ; one convulsions *after* delivery : 1 in 400.

Fatal cases only two : one uterine hæmorrhage, fifth month after pregnancy, occasioned by too early exertion, died 48 hours after delivery ; and one fatal syncope, without any apparent cause, died twelve hours after delivery : 1 in 1200.

This document forms a remarkable contrast with the registers of the lying-in hospitals of great cities. It proceeds from a gentleman whose name is familiar to the friends of science.

The mortality at the Edinburgh Lying-in Hospital is about 1 in 100. The following table shows also the number of still-born, and other particulars, obtained at that institution, during a period of nearly three years : —

EDINBURGH GENERAL LYING-IN HOSPITAL.

WOMEN.				CHILDREN.				
Year.	Number of Patients.	Died.	Disease.	Male.	Female.	Died.	Still-born.	Abortion.
1826	196	1	Peritonitis.	97	104	4	12	2
1827	218	2	Phthisis.	116	103	3	11	
1828	149	1	Exhaustion.					
to 29th		1	Peritonitis.	76	74	5	8	3
Sept.								

STATISTICS OF THE STILL-BORN.

It appears that 1 infant out of 32 is still-born in Prussia. The proportion of the still-born is also in Hanover about 1 in 30.

The varieties in the number of the still-born at different places are very difficult of explanation, or baffle it entirely. At Edinburgh, in the middle of last century, the proportion is said to have been 1 in 25, at the very time when at Strasburg it was 1 in 8. At Strasburg the number is now lessened, but continues larger than elsewhere. On an average of 20 years it has beeen 1 in 11 there, at present it is one in 12½ of all births. In Sweden and in Finland, on the contrary, it is only 1 in 40. Generally speaking, the still-born are more frequent in towns than in the country, and more common amongst the poorer classes than the affluent. At Stuttgard it has been remarked, that the number of the still-born augments nearly in the same proportion as that of the illegitimate births, and it may be added that of the legitimate children in Prussia, only 2 out of 10 die in the first year, but of the illegitimate ones, 3 in 11.

The proportion of the still-born has continued nearly the same for the last 50 years at Berlin : it is at present 1 in 19½. According to Caspar, the rate in some other cities is,

London and Vienna, 1 in 24 ;
Paris and Dresden, 1 in 19 ;
Hamburg, 1 in 15.

It is scarcely necessary to prove that abortions and still-births are far more frequent amongst the unmarried than among married women. If we observe what happens among the most unfortunate of the former, as in the Hospital *des Vénériens* at Paris, the excessive proportion of two children out of seven are born dead ; and in a similar establishment at Hamburg the proportion is 1 in 3. If we take a whole town, as Göttingen, only 3 per cent. of the children born in marriage are still-born, but so many as 15 per cent. of those born out of wedlock. *

---

* Casper. Beiträge, &c.

CHAP. VIII.

STATISTICS OF FOUNDLING HOSPITALS, AND OF THE
DISEASES OF CHILDREN. — REMARKABLE DIMINUTION
WHICH HAS GRADUALLY OCCURRED IN THE MOR-
TALITY OF INFANCY.

BENEATH the thin layer of brilliant colours
which some writers delight in spreading over the
ancient nations, we perceive lurking a deep and
dark corruption, which is not least visible in
their base contempt of infant life, and astonishing
indifference towards their own offspring. No
where are the superior virtue and judgment of
modern times more strongly disclosed than by a
comparison on this point of duty. Every succeeding century, and every advance on the road
of Christianity, are marked by increased attention
to the physical treatment of children, and by a
diminution in their mortality.

Aristotle was of opinion, that where the *exposure* of children was not allowed the number
of those actually produced ought to be limited.
If the children exceed the number prescribed by
the law, he recommends to induce miscarriage
before the fœtus is formed.* But (so short-

---

* Aristot. Περι Πολιτειας, vii. 16.

sighted is every vicious counsel) this unnatural permission would have had an effect directly opposite to the intention, and would have rather increased than diminished the population of a country ; marriage would be prematurely encouraged by the prospect of easy means of relief, and parental tenderness would frequently interpose to rescue the offspring.*

Among the ancient Persians it was a common custom to bury children alive. In most of the Grecian states infanticide was not merely permitted, but actually enforced by law. Of all the nations of antiquity the Romans were most unrelenting in their treatment of infants. The law of the Twelve Tables sanctioned this barbarous practice, and such was the custom of Rome from her first origin to the time of Constantine. Christianity first opposed a barrier to the crime. The Phœnicians and Carthaginians were no strangers to it. At a later period traces are visible in the history of the Vesigoths. The Chinese are notorious for cruelty in the exposure and murder of their children. This habit was among the Hindoos until lately still more prevalent. The number of infants murdered in the provinces of Cutch and Guzerat alone amounted, according to the lowest computation, to 3000

---

* Malthus on Population.

annually.* Within a few years, through the benevolent exertions of England, infanticide has
been completely abolished in many provinces of
India. †

Mr. Duncan, the Marquis Wellesley, and Co-
lonel Walker, have been mainly instrumental in
accomplishing this reform; and this event, in conjunction with the recent resolution of the East
India Company to oppose by forcible measures
the immolation of widows, would leave the most
noble monument of the British sway in the East,
even if it had achieved there no other trophies of
enlightened benevolence.

If any one be desirous of tracing the worldly
or civil influence of Christianity, he may meet
with abundant satisfaction in considering the
sudden growth of asylums for the *sick* and the
destitute, which accompanied its progress, and
which may be sought in vain in the history of
antiquity. The boasted and over-rated triumphs
of Greece and Rome record no provision for the
friendless : to pamper the vices and to flatter
the ambition of a few selfish and proud individuals, who carelessly frowned from a barren
eminence on the servile and detesting crowd

---

* Buchanan, Researches in Asia.

† Beck, Elements of Medical Jurisprudence. Philadelphia.
See also Foderé, Essai Historique et Moral sur la Pauvreté
des Nations, la Population, la Mendicité, les Hôpitaux, et
les Enfans Trouvés. 8vo. Paris. 1825.

below, was the principal object of their buildings and of their institutions.

Foundling hospitals gradually flowed from the admirable spirit of charity thus introduced ; and whatever we may think of their *policy*, the feeling which created them can only excite respect. We cannot help agreeing, however, with Malthus, Beck, and others, that their utility, under any system of *indiscriminate* admission, is highly questionable. It will presently be seen that they have done very little towards the *preservation of infant life ;* and it is certain that the facilities which they afford corrupt the maternal instinct, and offer a premium to seduction. Altogether we have reason to congratulate ourselves that England contains so few, and that the only one in Great Britain (of whose existence we are aware) subsists under limits which counteract abuse.

The Foundling Hospital of London deserves priority of mention, not merely on account of its excellent economy and the good health of its inmates, but from its standing alone in the principle of rejecting *secret* or *indiscriminate* entries. It acted originally on the same system as other foundling hospitals, but has happily changed it to introduce examination of the mother's previous character, and a special application on her part. So far is this difficulty from encouraging *infanticide*, that the crime is rare in London; and

K

far from being unfavourable to the preservation of infants, in scarcely any situation is their death so probable as in the hospitals where they are admitted clandestinely.

The number of children at present residing in the Foundling Hospital of London is 310, and 130 more are in the country. They are received at any age under twelve months, and are immediately sent to wet-nurses in the neighbouring counties. Every child has a separate nurse. She receives 3s. 6d. a week, and a small allowance more is made for clothing, and for the attendance of an apothecary on the spot. The nurses receive additional premiums on rearing the child to a certain age. The children remain five years in the country; on their return are instructed, and supported in the hospital until the age of 14 or 15, when they are placed in service or apprenticed. Their appearance is singularly neat, fresh, orderly, and cheerful. During the 20 years, ending in December, 1827, the mortality from the period of admission to 14 years of age has been only 25 per cent. *

The mortality which at a former period prevailed in the Foundling Hospital of Dublin resulted from neglect and injudicious management: it was so formidable as to become the subject of parliamentary enquiry; when it appeared that of 10,272 sick children sent to the *Infirmary* at-

---

* Mr. Lievesley, the Secretary, favoured me with this fact.

tached to the hospital, during the 21 years ending in 1796, 45 only were recovered ; a statement which, at this moment, seems incredible. Of the above number, no less than 10,201 were stated to be affected with syphilitic symptoms; but so great has been the change of late years in this respect, that scarcely one child in 30 is now contaminated with them.   Under the new system a happy change has taken place : various improvements have combined to diminish the mortality ; among others, the use of house wet-nurses, instead of spoon-feeding, has been very beneficial ; and the number of lives preserved has been so considerable, that the wages paid to country nurses have annually increased since 1803, when about 8000*l.* were paid to them, up to 1811, when the sum amounted to about 16,000*l.* From June, 1805, to June, 1806, 2168 infants were taken into the house, and only 486 died there, — a very small proportion for that period.

From 1800 to 1811, 11,111 infants were brought in by distressed parents, and 14,974 were abandoned. But it must be remembered, to the credit of Dublin, that its Foundling Hospital is not at all confined to the city, but receives inmates equally from every part of Ireland, and even several from England ; since this is the only hospital in the United Kingdom which receives any infant left at the door with-

out enquiry. The exertions made to instruct
the children, as they advance, in useful arts, and
the general attention paid to their education,
appear to distinguish this establishment very
honourably.

In Edinburgh an attempt has been occasionally made to form a Foundling Hospital,
but has failed from the opinion of its injury to
morality.

The number of children abandoned by their
parents at *Paris* in 1827 amounted to 8084.*

In every hospital where foundlings are indiscriminately received the mortality appears to be
beyond the control of all attention or skill. In
Paris, at present, of 1000 foundlings admitted,
251 are ascertained to die during the first few
days, and 235 more on their road to the country
nurses, or before the end of the first year; so
that at that period only half remain alive. It
seems that the frail tenure by which an infant
holds its life will not allow of a remitted attention, even for a few hours; and that the deser-
tion of a child by its mother, at the very time
when of all others it stands most in need of her
care, is in the event nearly equivalent to its
destruction. †

A great difference exists between the mortality of the children reared in the populous

---

* Annuaire pour l'An 1829.   Paris.
† Malthus.

quarters of Paris, where the streets are narrow and the inhabitants poor, and of those who are bred in the provinces. In Normandy it has been stated that only one child dies out of eight during the first year ; while in the worst parts of Paris, about 9 out of 10 have been said to die during the same period, an assertion which, however, appears exaggerated. The best authorities concur in allowing that the mortality of infants has diminshed there within the last fifty years, and the administration of the hospitals declares, in 1823, that the number of infants maintained at the Foundling Hospital is greater at present from this very cause, since the abandonments are really less numerous than formerly. *

The streets at Paris *du Roule* and of the *Faubourg St. Honoré* are known to be inhabited by persons in easy circumstances; and the street *Mouffetard* is remarkable, on the contrary, for the misery and privations of its inhabitants. During the first 10 years of life, the proportion of deaths has been nearly twice as large in the Mouffetard as in the former streets. And out of a given number of deaths at home, the infants of the Mouffetard up to the age of one year have contributed as many as all the children up to the age of 10 years in the two other streets. †

---

* Resumé des Comptes Moraux. 1823.

† Mém. de l'Acad. Roy. de Médecine, tome i. Paris, 1828.

We must remark, with pleasure, that however large may be the actual mortality of the found- lings of Paris, it falls greatly short of former periods. From the year 1771 to 1777, of 31,951 who entered the hospital, 21,985 died in the first month; 3491 in the remainder of the first year; and at the end of 1777 only 4711 were alive: but, on the contrary, from the year 1789 to 1813, 109,650 were received, and only 39,330 died.*

Dr. Casper of Berlin published in 1824 an interesting collection of statistical facts, illustra- tive of the influence of vaccination on longevity, and diseases in that city. In the 10 years from 1782 to 1791, 4453 deaths occurred from small- pox. About 1800, vaccination was introduced at Berlin, and in the 10 years from 1802 to 1811 only 2955 died of small-pox; and, finally, in the 11 years from 1812 to 1822, only 555, about an eighth of the deaths which had occurred 30 years before. In 1789, one death out of every nine deaths in Berlin was occasioned by small-pox: the same proportion existed from 1801 to 1803; but from 1820 to 1822 only one death in 1635 was the result of small-pox.

In 1789, of every four children who died, one was a victim of the small-pox; but in 1820 to 1822, only one in 785. In the former year one

---

* Foderé.

child of every eight born was sacrificed to it, but in the latter only 1 in 2066. An epidemic small-pox was formerly observed to occur at Berlin at the lapse of every three years: in 1803, its recurrence was first checked by the progress of vaccination. In the subsequent years this epidemic disposition has entirely disappeared under its influence. Casper combats, by certain documents, the notion that the other diseases of infancy have become more fatal since the introduction of vaccination: so far is this from being the case at Berlin, that if we compare the two periods, 1786 to 1789, and 1819 to 1822, we shall find that in the years prior to vaccination 39 children died out of 100 by the *other* diseases incident to their age ; whereas, in the years protected by vaccination, only 34 out of 100 died by those *other* diseases.

At the Foundling Hospital of Vienna died annually above one half of all received, according to the average published in 1810. Since that time the fatality amongst this class has been much lessened by sending them to be nursed in the country ; and when placed there, it has been found to fluctuate according to the plenty or scarcity of the current season. Before the introduction of vaccination, the destiny of childhood was still more precarious. From 1783 to 1793 considerably more than half of all the deaths occurred before the fifth year of age.

Every effort to rear the foundlings within the
walls of the hospital formerly proved vain. In
the most favourable years only 30 children out
of 100 lived to 12 months of age ; in the average
years 20 out of 100 attained 12 months, but in
bad years not even 10. The Emperor Joseph II.
was anxious to improve their condition, and even
desired Professor Boër to make a series of experiments with all kinds of food, that it might
be ascertained if *diet* had any influence on the
mortality. Twenty children were accordingly
chosen as the subjects of experiment, and fed
with various articles ; but no conclusions were
obtained as to their comparative merits, since
the greater part of the subjects died within a few
months. But in 1813, the government wisely
determined that the Foundling Hospital should
serve merely as a depôt for the children, until
they could be transferred to the care of nurses
in the country. The medical faculty made a
report, in which they ascribed the mortality not
to deficiency of nourishment, nor of cleanliness,
nor of attention, but to the confinement of so
many children together in a small space, to the
vitiated atmosphere, to the noise, and to contagion, particularly with respect to diarrhœa. In
1822, under the new system of nursing in the
country, the deaths had diminished from 1 in 2
(as in 1810) to 1 in 4½.

At the Foundling Hospital of *Stockholm* 525
children were received in 1822, and 101 died,

or 19⅓ per cent. ; 15 died in the first month, 6 in the second, 19 in the third, 15 in the fourth, 10 in the fifth, 3 in the seventh, when a marked diminution in the deaths commences.

From careful enquiries which *Malthus* made of the attendants at the Foundling Hospital at Petersburgh, in 1787, he understood that 100 deaths per month, and 10 admissions per day, was the common average.

The foundling hospitals both at Petersburgh and at Moscow have been always most carefully and liberally conducted, and yet at the latter city, during the 20 years subsequent to 1786, when the hospital was first instituted, of 37,000 children received, 35,000 at least are computed to have died. In 1811, the foundlings admitted into the hospitals appropriated to them were 2517, and the deaths were 1038. In 1812, 2699 were admitted, and the deaths were 1348.*

This evil has latterly increased in Russia : the admissions have increased, and the deaths have been augmented in proportion. In the province of Archangel, were, in 1812, 417 foundlings, and 377 of them were swept away in the same year.

At Barcelona, in 1821, the fifth part of all the children born was abandoned to the Foundling Hospital : 437 were admitted during the year, and 463 died. The number of

---

* C.T. Herrmann. Mém. de l'Acad. des Sciences de Petersbourg, t. ix. Petersb. 1824.

children remaining at the end of the former
year is not stated, so that the exact proportion of deaths to admissions does not appear.
During the year 1823, which was that in which
the *counter-revolution* was effected, the deaths
greatly exceed the births, contrary to what had
previously happened; and so few were even the
illegitimate births, that only 229 foundlings were
admitted to the hospital during the very time that
339 died in it. This fact remarkably indicates
the influence of political events in suspending
the usual operation of habit and passion. We
have no information respecting the foundling
hospitals of Portugal, but the proportion of illegitimate births at Lisbon is rated so high as
1 in 3, and at Oporto, one half of all births.

The French established a foundling hospital at
Geneva during their occupation, but it exists no
longer. In the *Pays de Vaud* the proportion of
illegitimate children was about 1 in 100 births,
before the arrival of the French, an event which
is considered by the Swiss to have left a permanent taint on their morality. The proportion
has since diminished: it is now about 1 in 20.

The Foundling Hospital at Florence is well
managed, and the mortality is not great, only
1 in 10, on account of the speedy removal of
the infants into the country. A considerable
number of the children were formerly the victims
of what was supposed to be a syphilitic taint.

After a few weeks, or even days, they became
pale and thin, were often covered with pustules
and small ulcers *circa genitalia* and neighbouring parts, grew cachectic, and finally died
in a state of marasmus. The use of mercury
in this disorder was unavailing. Dr. Breschet
of Paris has observed a similar complaint in
the Foundling Hospital there, and believes that
it has no connection with syphilis. His observations render it probable that it arises from an
insidious inflammation of the abdominal viscera;
and his view is confirmed by the diminution of
the mortality since a treatment founded upon it
has been adopted.

The mortality of the Foundling Hospital at
Naples is 1 in 5 annually.

During the year 1823, 597 foundlings were
received at the hospital at Palermo, and 429
died, or 72 per cent.*

Various writers have discussed the singular
improvement which the progress of medical
knowledge, in combination with the growth of
general prosperity, has accomplished during the
present century in the mortality of children.
Sir Gilbert Blane and Dr. Casper must be named
among the most powerful advocates of this
interesting fact; but Mr. Roberton, one of the
surgeons of the Manchester Lying-in Hospital,

* Bulletino Universale di Scienze, &c. No. 52. 1825.

has recently published the most complete work which at present exists on the subject.[*] To this book, and to the very excellent illustrations of it contained in the Edinburgh Medical and Surgical Journal [†], all who wish to possess the facts which determine the question in this country must direct their attention.

Mr. Roberton furnishes us with a number of local tables from different parts of the kingdom, and the result indicates that the mortality of children is much larger in cities than in small towns, and more considerable in small towns than in the country. The causes are very apparent, particularly the bad air of crowded rooms, the poverty produced by more frequent and sudden vicissitudes of employment, the greater number of illegitimate births, to which must be added a less obvious but very destructive influence in the practice which prevails among the lower classes in towns of giving *unmixed spirits* to infants. Mr. Roberton declares that at Manchester the child is initiated by sucking a finger dipped into the poison. There is reason to believe, however, that this practice is not unknown to nurses among the higher classes of

---

[*] Observations on the Mortality and Physical Management of Children. London. 1827.

[†] See the masterly review in the number for April, 1828, page 373.

this and other countries. The late Professor Gregory used to relate such instances in his lectures; and a celebrated diagnostic trait is recorded at Berlin of the late eminent physician *Heim*, who being suddenly summoned to attend an infant of the court in much apparent danger, roused the anger of the anxious circle by declaring that the child was only *drunk*, and subsequently verified his assertion at the expense of the nurse.

Several facts are scattered through this work illustrative of the diminution of infantile mortality in several parts of Europe. We shall here only add a few examples drawn from our own country. In *Warrington*, a manufacturing town, whose population is about 13,000, the average annual mortality of the nine years subsequent to 1772 was 1 in 26·48, and of these deaths 55·12 per cent. were of children *under ten years* of age. But the annual average of all deaths during the eight years after 1817 was 1 in 37·4, and of these the proportion *under ten years* diminishes to 44·65 per cent. An improvement nearly similar has occurred at Glasgow, on comparing the six years subsequent to 1782 with the six years previous to 1812. And here we remark with pleasure the correction of an important error which Dr. Watt had committed, and which requires the more notice, since it has been frequently repeated both at home and abroad as an argument against the efficacy of vaccination.

Mr. Roberton has the merit of having detected this important mistake. His view is confirmed by the ingenious writer in the Edinburgh Medical Journal, and we cannot explain it better than by using the words of the latter. Doctor Watt inferred from an examination of the Glasgow tables that the mortality of children had *not* improved between the two periods mentioned above; and that as a manifest diminution had taken place through the abatement of small-pox, the improvement must have been compensated by a corresponding increase of deaths from other infantile diseases, and especially from measles. Dr. Casper pointed out the error of this opinion in its application to Berlin. Mr. Roberton has still more strongly contradicted the conclusions of Watt by neutralising his own data. The statement of Watt was founded on the fact, that for six years subsequent to 1782 the deaths *under ten* were 53·48 per cent. of the total deaths, whereas in the six years previous to 1812 they formed 55·43 per cent. But unfortunatly for the accuracy of his inference, Watt did not take into account the great improvement which has arisen during the interval in the *total* mortality, and omitted to make the requisite correction, namely, by referring the infantile deaths to the population, instead of the general mortality. The result of this alteration will be easily perceived. In the

early period the average annual mortality was
1 in 26·7, and of the deaths 53·48 per cent. were
under ten ; that is, among every 1000 of the
population there died annually 37·45, *of whom*
20·03 *were under ten.* In the latter period the
annual mortality was 1 in 40·8, and of the deaths
55·43 per cent. were *under ten ;* that is, in every
1000 inhabitants 24·51 died annually, of *whom*
13·58 *were under ten.* So that in reality the
deaths among children in a given number of inhabitants had decreased to two thirds of what
they were in the former period.

It would exhaust the patience of the reader to
enter with minuteness into the influence of vaccination in diminishing the deaths from small-
pox in different countries. That blessing has
been checked in our own country by the caprice
of the lower classes; but we shall state its effects
in a country where the measure is enforced by
the government. The following is an official
return of the deaths in *Sweden* : —

In the year 1779 the small-pox destroyed 15,000 persons.

1784	-	-	-	-	12,000
1800	-	-	-	-	12,800
1801	-	-	-	-	6,000
1822	-	-		-	11
1823	-	-	-	-	37

As it is well ascertained that *illegitimate*
children die in a much larger proportion than

those who are born in marriage, we should be glad to compare the rate of such births in England with the average of other countries. We are, however, only able to produce a single instance. Mr. Roberton states that the proportion at Manchester was about 300, on an average of the three years, 1824, 1825, and 1826, or about 1 in 12 of all the births. This affords an estimate highly favourable in comparison with the cities of the Continent, and especially if we consider its large population of adults.

To illustrate the mortality arising from various diseases at different periods of childhood, Mr. Roberton has published a valuable table taken from the register at the *Rusholme Road Cemetery* in Manchester. He informs us that it is kept with unusual care ; and he has selected a period of four years subsequent to April, 1821, and including 2056 deaths under the age of 10. Of these, 994 (chiefly within the first year of life) arise from what are called in popular language convulsions, infantile decline, water in the brain, tooth fever and teething, worm fever, and bowel complaints.

Table of the Diseases which cause Death at various periods of Infancy.

Diseases.	Under 1 Month.	Between 1 and 2.	2 and 3.	3 and 6.	6 and 9.	9 and 12.	1 and 2 Years.	2 and 3.	3 and 5.	5 and 10.	Total.
Measles	—	1	1	5	8	25	117	72	50	20	299
Scarlet fever	—	—	—	—	1	—	—	1	4	2	8
Small-pox	—	1	2	5	25	17	49	30	44	14	187
Quinsey	—	—	—	—	—	—	—	—	—	1	1
Erysipelas	—	—	—	1	—	—	—	—	—	—	1
Swine-pox	—	—	—	—	—	—	—	—	1	—	1
Chin-cough	—	2	3	17	17	16	48	24	17	6	150
Croup	—	—	—	3	2	3	9	10	12	2	41
Inflammation of the lungs	—	1	3	14	36	17	42	12	21	9	155
Do. of the bowels	4	2	—	4	8	3	7	6	1	3	38
Do. of the brain	—	—	—	1	—	1	—	—	—	1	3
Inflammatory fever	—	—	—	—	—	—	1	—	—	2	3
Inflammation of the liver	—	—	—	—	—	—	2	—	—	—	2
Do. of the kidneys	—	—	—	—	—	—	1	—	—	—	1
Ulcerated throat	—	—	—	—	—	—	—	—	—	1	1
Mortification	—	—	—	—	—	—	—	—	—	1	1
Water in the brain	1	—	1	14	16	8	39	18	10	18	125
Convulsions	121	85	42	49	14	9	9	1	1	1	332
Fits	—	2	—	4	2	1	1	4	4	—	18
Asthma	—	—	—	—	—	—	—	1	1	—	2
Water in the chest	—	—	1	—	—	—	—	—	1	—	2
Disorder of the nerves	—	—	—	—	1	—	—	—	—	—	1
Dropsy	—	—	—	—	—	—	—	—	—	3	3
Brain fever	—	—	—	—	—	—	1	1	—	5	7
Continued do.	1	—	—	—	1	1	2	3	1	—	9
Typhus do.	—	—	—	—	—	—	1	1	—	6	8
Worm do.	—	—	—	—	—	—	2	7	1	1	11
Tooth do. and teething	—	—	—	12	34	47	78	9	1	—	181
Remittent do.	—	—	—	—	—	—	—	1	—	—	1
Rheumatic do.	—	—	—	—	—	—	—	—	—	1	1
Putrid do.	—	—	—	—	—	—	1	1	—	—	2
Cholera Morbus	1	1	2	6	1	4	4	1	—	1	21
Bowel complaints	5	11	7	17	15	12	10	4	2	2	85
Black thrush	—	—	—	2	—	1	1	—	—	—	4
Bilious complaints	—	—	—	1	1	—	—	—	—	—	2
Jaundice	—	—	1	—	—	—	—	—	—	—	1
Violent vomiting	—	—	—	—	—	—	1	—	—	—	1
Stoppage in the bowels	1	—	—	1	—	1	—	—	1	—	4
Infantile decline	7	10	9	39	34	22	66	—	20	23	260
Consumption	—	—	—	—	—	—	—	—	6	12	18
Decline after measles	—	—	—	—	—	—	3	1	1	—	5
Stricture of the bowels	—	—	—	2	—	—	1	—	1	—	4
Defect in the internal organisation	—	—	—	—	—	—	—	1	—	—	1
Inflammation of the head	—	—	2	—	—	—	—	1	—	1	4
Tumour on the hip	—	—	—	—	1	—	—	—	—	—	1
Inflammation in the groin	—	—	—	1	—	—	—	—	—	—	1
Inflammation in the neck	—	—	—	1	—	—	—	—	—	—	1
White swelling	—	—	—	—	1	—	—	—	—	—	1
Accidents	1	—	—	1	—	1	4	6	7	13	33
Unknown and lingering complaints	4	—	—	1	—	4	1	1	2	1	14
	146	116	74	201	218	193	501	246	210	151	2056

Mr. Robertson infers from this table the great importance of devoting an increased attention to the physical management of children. Upon this chiefly depends the healthy condition of their digestive organs; and we perceive, from the above table, that a large portion of their mortality originates in disorders of the first passages.

CHAP. IX.

STATISTICS OF ASYLUMS FOR THE INSANE.

A VERY general opinion exists of the increase of maniacal disorders, and it is probably correct; but it can be founded on general arguments alone, because it is only within a comparatively recent date that public asylums for the insane have become common throughout Europe, and they are at present very unequally distributed over its surface. The growth of such institutions is obviously due to the increased benevolence of modern times, and is not to be ascribed *so much* to the present particular pressure of the evil, as to the disposition, which is happily diffusing itself over Christian countries, to relieve every description of suffering.

Esquirol will not admit that insanity is specially increasing, but affirms that this notion arises only from the greater attention at present bestowed by the public on it, (an attention which is partly owing to the excellent essays which have appeared on the subject,) and from the improved economy of lunatic asylums, which attracts a larger share of inmates. (*Mém. Acad, R. de Méd.* t. 1.)

It is very difficult, perhaps impossible, in the
present state of our information, to compare the
prevalence of mania in different countries, because the documents furnished by each relate
chiefly to the patients confined in public asylums,
and rarely include the numerous portion remaining at home, or in the houses of private
superintendants. Even the returns of hospitals
afford little light on this point, because the proportion of such establishments to the wants of
the population varies much in the respective
districts.

The clergymen of all the parishes in Scotland
(except fifty) made a return in 1818, which
reckons,

In public asylums	-	441 } 600 }	in all 4833.
In private asylums	-	159 }	
With their friends	-	1356 }	
And at large	-	2877 }	

Of 4647 of the above, the large proportion of
3495 is stated to be fatuous and idiotic. The
proportion of idiots in Switzerland is also very
great ; and we may remark that, in both countries, scrofula is very prevalent. *

A return made from Scotland to parliament,
in 1826, states the number to be about 600 in
public asylums and licensed houses : an estimate

* Morison, Outlines of Lectures on Mental Diseases.
Lond. 1826. p. 73.

which, compared with the former more detailed account, proves the insufficiency of such documents to explain the relative prevalence of this disease in different countries.

The most complete report of the causes of insanity is derived from the *Bicêtre* and *Salpêtrière.* During the five years from 1815 to 1820 4404 cases have been received in these asylums ; of whom 1763 were men, and 2641 women. The following are the principal causes enumerated for both sexes : * —

	Men	Women.
Consequence of other diseases -	236	—
Consequence of pregnancy -	—	189
Consequence of the critical age, and of deranged menstruation -	—	693
From onanism and debauchery -	52	101
From hysteria - -	—	116
From ambition - - -	134	—
From religion - -	54	30
From love - - -	76	18
From misfortune - -	122	87
From chagrin - - -	115	107
From political events - -	78	—
From fright - - -	—	44

Esquirol has prepared a table explaining the *professions* of 164 persons thus afflicted. They occur in the following precedence : — Mer-

* Recherches Statistiques sur la Ville de Paris, &c. d'après les Ordres de M. le Comte de Chabrol, t. iii. 4to., Paris, 1826.

chants 50, soldiers 33, students 25, agents 21, advocates and notaries 11, artists 8, medical men 4, chemists 4, labourers 3, sailors 3, engineers 2.

In almost every country, except France, the number of male lunatics seems to exceed the females ; and this exception may be easily understood to arise from the prominent and active part which the French woman usually plays in society, and even in retail trade. Of 2507 insane cases admitted into the public hospitals at Paris, 1095 were men, and 1412 women ; but at Esquirol's private asylum, from 1802 to 1814, the men were 191, and the women 144. At Charenton, also, the male cases preponderated, from 1815 to 1823. The proportion at Lyons was 60 men, and 150 women.

In England : — of 7904 lunatics confined in private houses, from 1812 to 1824, the men were so many as 4461, and the women only 3443. Dr. Burrows remarks that, among the better classes confined in such houses in London and its environs, the proportion of men to women is nearly the same. He quotes from Esquirol a just compliment to Englishwomen, who, according to that author, are less subject to insanity than their French sisters, from their more solid education, their more domestic life, and the less active share which they take in the business of society. Casper, a German physician, writes in a similar

strain : he describes the female inmates of the
French lunatic hospitals as coquettish and forward to an extreme point, and the toilette of
those at the Salpêtrière as ridiculous ; and con-
trasts the decent deportment and dress of the
women who are found in the English asylums.
At Bethlehem only one female addressed him,
and the object of her enquiry was connected
with the name of the German poet Gessner.

In Scotland and Ireland the proportion of
the sexes affected with this complaint is nearly
equal. At Zurich, in 1823, the sexes were
nearly equal. In the hospitals of Berlin and
Vienna the men have a large majority. With
respect to Italy : in the asylum at Turin, the
men in one year were 180, and the women 97 ;
at the *Incurabili* of Genoa the men were 55
and the women 60 ; at the Senavra of Milan
the number of women considerably exceeded,
from 1802 to 1826, when 2799 men and 3207
women were received. In Pennsylvania, in
1812, the cases were two males to one female.
Dr. Burrows, from whom these proportions are
copied, believes that among the pauper lunatics
of London a majority of females would be found.
He adds, very justly, that *drunkenness* renders
this disease more generally prevalent among men
than among women. * At the Salpêtrière of Paris,

---

* Burrows' Commentaries on Insanity. 1828.

L 4

a 20th part of the female lunatics are reckoned
to have become insane through prostitution. *
At Amsterdam the females maintain a constant
superiority in number, but in several of the
smaller towns of Holland the men exceed.

It appears from calculations made by Esquirol
and Georget that the mortality of the male
sex, in this disease, is most considerable from
the age of 30 to 40, and of the female sex from
40 to 60.

Horn has calculated that the most frequent
age for the invasion of mania is 30 to 35 for
men, and from 25 to 30 and from 45 to 50
for women.

Mania seems to be rare in Spain, as is also
suicide ; in Copenhagen, on the contrary, whose
inhabitants are of a northern temperament, and
far more advanced in knowledge, both evils are
very common.

In the whole state of New York, in 1825,
819 persons were reported as lunatics. We may
add, that the deaf and dumb were 645 in the
same year.

Mania is stated to be very unfrequent in South
America, and among the Indian tribes ; and to
be very prevalent in China. †

---

* Burrows' Commentaries on Insanity.   1828.
† Morison, Outlines, &c.

This appears really to be one of the few important disorders which increase with the progress of civilisation and refinement. It is, perhaps, on this account, more common in our own than in other countries ; but it is almost a solitary mourner in the train of prosperity, and is lost in the crowd of blessings which attend the extension of education and of affluence.

It must be remarked, that any public calamity has a tendency to increase the victims of this malady. The price of bread rose high in France in 1816; the lower classes suffered greatly; and in 1817, the Salpêtrière received a *double* complement of entries. In 1815, a similar scarcity prevailed in Ireland, and the number of insane at the Cork asylum is said to have suddenly risen from 74 to 210. In 1816 and 1817, a scarcity of grain was experienced in the Netherlands, and the lunatic asylums of Ghent, Louvain, Antwerp, Bruges, and Gheel acquired a remarkable accession of inmates.

With respect to the cures and mortality of such establishments, abundant materials exist, from which we shall select only a few.

In the kingdom of the Netherlands, of 4000 patients received in the public asylums of late years, 1577 were cured or discharged, and 1254 died. According to Nieuwenhuijs, 1248 entered the establishment near *Amsterdam* from 1797 to

1817, and 604 died. (*Guislain, Traité sur l'Aliénation Mentale. Amst.* 1826.)

At the Charité of Berlin, 413 insane were admitted from 1805 to 1815, and 117 died. The proportion of cures to admissions was 1 to 2 in 1816. (*Horn.*)

Müller informs us that 528 were admitted into the Asylum at Würtzburg from 1802 to 1823. Of these, 62 went away with some amendment, 17 left while under treatment, 292 were perfectly restored, and 78 died. (*Die Irrenanst. zu Würtzburg.*)

The Senavra Hospital at Milan presents the following results during the 25 years from 1802 to 1826. Most of the patients are of the poorest class, chiefly inhabitants of the low and swampy grounds in the neighbourhood of Milan, who have become the victims of *pellagra*, a disease which appears often to induce mental derangement. *

Proportion of males to females	87 to 100
Proportion of males to females cured	57 to 59
Proportion of males to females dying	40 to 45
Proportion of cures to admissions is	58 to 100
Proportion of deaths to admissions is	42 to 100

Dr. Burrows, junior, observed striking malformation of the cranium among many of the

---

* Burrows' Commentaries, 523.

patients; several of them had the goitrous throat. The diet is good : extreme neatness and good order reign throughout.

At the Wakefield asylum, since it was opened in 1819, the proportion of deaths to admissions in males has been 28 in 100; in females $19\frac{1}{2}$ in 100; in both sexes taken together 24 in 100.

At the Lancaster asylum, from 1817 to 1825, the proportion of deaths to admissions in males has been 25 in 100; in females 23 in 100; in both sexes together $24\frac{1}{2}$ in 100.

The deaths in the York Retreat, from 1796 to 1819, have been about 20 in 100.

At the Bicêtre and Salpêtrière, during 1822, 1823, and 1824, the proportion of deaths to admissions in males was 25 in 100; in females 19 in 100; in both sexes together 22 in 100.*

Puerperal insanity constitutes one-twelfth of all the insane women admitted into the Salpêtrière, and sometimes a tenth. Among the upper ranks in Paris it appears still more frequent; Esquirol found the proportion in his private practice to be one in seven. Of 92 cases of puerperal insanity received during four years at the Salpêtrière, 6 died, or 1 in 15. It appears to be more frequent from delivery than from suckling, and more than half recover unless the predisposition be very strong.

---

* Burrows' Commentaries, 556.

Esquirol divides insanity into two species, simple and complicated, and each species into four varieties. The proportion of poor women so affected at the Salpêtrière, and of those in his *private* establishment, who are persons in good circumstances, he has thus arranged.*

Simple Species.	In Salpêt.	In private Est.
1. Acute demency	10	11
2. Chronic demency	43	32
3. Senile demency	35	2
4. Intermittent demency	7	2
Complicated Species.		
1. Melancholic demency	34	20
2. Maniacal demency	21	8
3. Convulsive demency	4	6
4. Epileptic demency	30	
	out of 289 Epileptics.	

Disorders of the uterine system constitute one fourth of the number, the progress of age more than a fifth, and mania and melancholia conjointly a seventh.

The most frequent *fatal* cases in the Glasgow asylum, of late years, are from apoplexy, palsy, atrophy, exhaustion, and pulmonary and dropsical affections.

In the Lancaster county asylum, atrophy, hydrothorax, and bowel complaints chiefly occur.†

* Burrows' Commentaries.   † Ibid.

We subjoin a classification of the affections of which the patients of the Paris lunatic hospitals have died, during the years 1822, 1823, and 1824.*

Organic diseases of the brain and its membranes -	418
Diseases of the thoracic organs - -	198
Inflammations of the abdominal organs - -	306
Cutaneous inflammations - - -	3
Cachexies - - - - -	110
Surgical diseases - - -	47
Diseases undetermined - - -	9
	1091

* Compte Rendu, &c.

CHAP. X.

MORTALITY OF PRISONS.

With respect to the mortality of *prisons*, we have some very curious details from France, but very few of other countries. The highest mortality any where known amongst adults is at the Depôt of Mendicity of St. Denis, at Paris. Here the annual deaths are nearly 1 in 3 of every prisoner admitted. But the inmates are usually vagrants picked up in the streets of the capital, without asylum or resource, the victims of calamity, disease, or debauchery. Many are afterwards placed in other depôts, and when there appear to improve in bodily health under the power of habit, so that their mortality is ultimately reduced to 1 in 6, although their treatment is not bettered. At the generality of the prisons of Paris, as the Force, St. Pelagie, Conciergerie, &c., the ordinary rate of death is about 1 in 23 annually. Dr. Villermé deduces from this rate a conclusion, that residence in a prison abridges life of 20 years; and he applies the remark equally to prisoners for debt. On the other hand, in a solitary instance, a remarkable exception presents itself: the galley-slaves of

France are better fed and clothed than the other prisoners; they work in the open air, and are usually callous to the impressions of memory or of hope; the mortality of these beings is so low as 1 in 49, while that of the whole French nation is 1 in 40. But this small proportion of deaths is partly due to the absence of children from their list, as well as of men beyond 70, at which last age they are released.

These results are obtained by Dr. Villermé from the years 1815—1818.* The official newspaper, *Le Moniteur*, has endeavoured to disprove his statements, and to diminish the mortality; but it has drawn its calculations only from the first eleven months of 1824, and it allows that in 1818 the mortality of the Depôt of St. Denis was 1 in 7. Dr. Villermé has replied at length to its objections.

The annual mortality of the principal prisons in the Netherlands has been lately published by *Quetelet* as 1 in 27.†

The prisons of London present a record very different from the above, and in the whole range of medical statistics it would be difficult to find a more striking contrast. I am fortunately enabled to adduce the testimony of my

---

* Des Prisons telles qu'elles sont, et telles qu'elles devraient être. 1820.

† Mém. Acad. R. de Bruxelles, t. vi. Brux. 1827.

eminent friend Mr. Samuel Cooper, the author of the valuable *Dictionary of Surgery*, who, in his capacity of surgeon to the *King's Bench* and *Fleet* prisons, has furnished me with the following document.

Of 300 prisoners received in the Fleet prison during the year ending the 9th of March, 1828, only four died, which is a mortality *of* 1 *in* 75. The diseases of which they died were, one of *fever*, aged 40; one of pleurisy, aged 45; and two of consumption, aged 28 and 70. Mr. Cooper finds that the average mortality of the *King's Bench* and *Fleet* prisons ranges between 1 in 50 and 1 in 55.

So great was the care taken of prisoners of war in this country, that in the year 1813, the mortality amongst them was only 1 in 55, not one half of what occurs to the whole population of Rome, although these persons were labouring under most of the privations which embitter or enfeeble existence.

CHAP. XI.

COMPARATIVE PREVALENCE OF SUICIDE IN DIFFERENT PERIODS AND COUNTRIES.

SUICIDE is so frequent a topic of allusion in medical writings, and so often depends on the deranged state of body or mind, that it seems to merit a place in medical statistics. We have here a very pleasing conclusion to draw in respect to England, as, in spite of ancient prejudices entertained against our supposed propensity, it really appears that the English are less disposed to suicide than any other people who have attained a similar grade of civilisation.

Dr. Burrows has the merit of having first vindicated our country from the conjectural report of a peculiar proneness to suicide, which, like some other current accusations of England, had been so often repeated abroad and at home, that it was at length established into an axiom. The happy superiority which England enjoys in many respects ensures a prompt circulation to any charge which can be produced against a point supposed to be vulnerable. The proofs which Dr. Burrows published have been by

M

some foreigners rejected as unsatisfactory, on account of the acknowledged imperfections of the bills of mortality, in which the suicides of London are recorded. But even if those returns had been multiplied by four, five, or six, certainly a liberal allowance for deficiences, the proportion, in relation to our population, would have been inferior to the returns of some of the cities of the Continent. Fortunately, however, a document has been more recently published, which enables me to satisfy all who have no secret wish to retain an unfounded prejudice. It is well known that a coroner and jury are summoned to investigate every suicide which occurs in Westminster. Mr. Higgs, the coroner of the city of Westminster, made, in 1825, a report of the suicides committed in Westminster during the 13 years previous. In order to furnish easy means of comparison, we must premise that the population of Westminster, according to the census of 1821, was 182,444. We may add, for the use of strangers, that it is the centre of dissipation for the whole empire. During the 13 years from 1812 to 1824, the *total* number of suicides was only 290, a number which, *if trebled*, would be inferior in proportion to the returns made by the great cities of France and Germany.

The number of males in this table is 207, of females only 83, which is a proportion of

5 to 2. The *Novembers* of these 13 years produce only 22, while the rate of the *Junes* is 34.
In the years 1812, 1815, 1820, and 1824, November did not afford one suicide. The least prolific
months were May and September, next August
and October, and then November. During the
latter eight years, a reduction occurred on the
average of nearly six per annum. The annual
average is a little more than 22 during the whole
term. From motives of humanity, the juries
gave a verdict of *insanity* in all but five instances.
In 1825, a year marked by commercial distresses, the total number was 24 : of these, two
women had been seduced and abandoned, and
one man cut his throat through jealousy, eight
poisoned themselves, and eight were found
hanging.

The annual number returned by the bills of
mortality for London usually ranges between
30 and 50. After making every allowance, we
may estimate the number of suicides annually
accomplished in London and Westminster at
about 100. In England and France a majority
of the victims appear to be *unmarried.* In
France, the proportion of married men to single
amongst suicides has been rated as only 2 to 3.*

Other countries certainly present a darker

---

* Dict. Sciences Medic. art. Celibat.

picture. We are not surprized at finding the
number of 1300 recorded for Versailles in 1793,
a year of political storm, and of dreadful anticipation to its inhabitants. In 1806, Falret
asserts that the suicides of Rouen amounted to
60 during the months of June and July alone.
Professor Grohmann notes a remarkable increase
at Hamburg : — in 1816 the number was only 2,
in 1820 it rose to 10, and 1822 produced so
many as 59. In the small district of Frank-
fort-on-the-Main the number in 1823 was 100.

In 1806 there were 300 at Copenhagen : — of
late years the annual average has been 100 in
100,000 inhabitants. In Berlin, according to
Casper, the proportion is 34 annually in every
100,000 inhabitants, and in Paris 49. The increase in Prussia, and particularly in Berlin,
is extraordinary. In the 17 years following
1758, the proportion at Berlin was 1 suicide
in 1800 deaths. But in the 10 years following
1787 the proportion is seen to double itself, becoming 1 in 900 deaths. In the 10 years following 1798, it is trebled; and in the 10 years
ending in 1822 it arose to the formidable height
of 1 in every 100 deaths. These numbers, large
as is their amount, do not include many who are
found drowned in the river, and whose fate is
dubious. In 1817, the proportion for the whole
Prussian nation was 1 in every 400 deaths. We
must remark on the comparative frequency of

this crime amongst *boys* in France and Germany. We should not venture to state the curious fact of the existence of a *suicide club* in Prussia, except on the authority of Dr. Casper, an eminent statistical writer resident in Berlin, a city where every work is submitted to the *censure*. This club consisted of six persons, who avowed openly their intention of destroying themselves, and endeavoured to gain proselytes. Their absurdity excited more laughter than belief, but three instances occurred of conformity to principle, and at length all the six evinced their sincerity: the last shot himself in 1817.

In Berlin it seems to be more frequent among weavers and soldiers than in other classes of society, and, on the whole, is principally seen among the lower classes. It is more common among the females of Paris than among those of Berlin, in a twofold average; which might be anticipated from the more retired and unambitious path of the German woman. During six recent years, 18 cases happened at Berlin of individuals under the age of puberty, and 11 of men above 70. So far more numerous are the *civic* cases than the *rural* ones in Prussia, that while the proportion in its towns is 14 in every 100,000 inhabitants, the country exhibits only four in the same number.

Dr. Casper, the enlightened writer who has collected many of the above facts, and who has ingeniously commented upon them, attributes a large share of the increase in Berlin to *drunkenness*. From 1812 to 1821, a fourth of all the number arose from this evil ; and it is probable that many assigned to other causes were really indebted to this. The increase of liquor shops at Berlin will illustrate this, as in 1822 one house in every four was appropriated to this trade ; an arrangement which allots 130 of the total population to the maintenance of each house ; but after the deductions of the diseased and the young, a very inferior proportion.

The crime appears to find very few victims in *Spain :* in the whole of that country only 16 instances are officially reported to have occurred during the year 1826. In all *Sweden*, in 1823, there were only 151 suicides. Only 13 suicides occurred in the city of Naples during the year 1826 : the same number happened in 1823, and only seven in 1824.

During the four years from 1823 to 1826 only 4087 suicides occurred throughout the empire of Russia.

Imitation, — a principle which, it is to be feared, is but too frequently the cause of other offences, — seems occasionally to produce suicide. At a meeting of the French Academy of Medicine, *Costel* lately mentioned, that a soldier at the Hôtel of Invalids hung himself on a post, and was shortly afterwards *imitated* by *twelve* other invalids; but that the disposition ceased on the removal of the fatal post. Dr. Burrows relates some similar instances. In a regiment at Malta suicides became alarmingly common. The commander, having vainly tried other means, resolved to deny Christian burial to the next suicide. Another instance occurred. The regiment was drawn out, the corpse was stripped naked, placed on a hurdle, and thrown into the fosse with every mark of indignity. The spirit of imitation immediately ceased. Primrose relates that the women of Lyons were seized with a propensity to commit suicide by throwing themselves into the *wells* of that city. In 1813, in the little village of St. Pierre Monjau, in the Valais, one woman hung herself: many others followed her example; and had it not been for the interposition of the civil authorities, the contagion might have spread.

At the meeting of the French Academy, alluded to above, Esquirol related six cases occurring of persons being seized with the propensity to destroy their children since the trial of Madame *Cornie* for that crime.*

There is reason to believe that suicide, as well as other evils, has a tendency to propagate itself in this country by the long and laboured details

---

* Burrows, Commentaries on Insanity, p. 438.

which are so often circulated in our news-
papers. The attention once drawn to a particular
subject, gradually attaches itself fondly to the
topic, in unoccupied or ill-governed minds.
And, as if not satiated with the vices arising on
our own soil, our journals are perpetually ran-
sacking foreign countries to produce varnished
tales of misery and crime, or to excite a sardonic
laugh over the ruins of human nature.

At New York the number of suicides has
varied annually from 13 to 29, between the years
1816 and 1826. At Philadelphia the number
has fluctuated between 2 and 13 annually, from
1820 to 1826. At Baltimore between 2 and 7
from 1819 to 1826.

The most remarkable body of information
which has yet appeared on the statistics of suicide is due to the industry of Dr. *Falret* of
Paris. M. de Montyon, a wealthy and zealous
philanthropist, bequeathed at his death various
legacies devoted to the benefit of mankind; and
among them, a prize for the best statistical essay.
Dr. Falret contributed one on the present subject, which, although it did not obtain the preference, has been deservedly rewarded by the
Minister of the Interior with a second medal.
Some of his tables relate to the suicides registered by the police of Paris from the year 1794
to the year 1825 inclusive, and others to the
sudden deaths which have also been recorded

by the police, during the 30 years ending in 1823.

The entire number of suicides entered by the police at Paris during the 30 years from 1794 to 1823 was 6782. Of these 4720 were accomplished. Two thirds were of the male sex. The average number for each of the 10 years commencing from 1794 was only 107, but for each of the 10 years ending in 1823 the average was so great as 334.

Not quite a third of the whole number were *married :* of this married third 960 were men, and 735 were women.

As to the *age* of the suicides, we are surprized by finding that 181 were below the age of 15, and that 497 were between 15 and 20. The period of life which affords the largest list is between 35 and 45. Drowning was the mode of death most frequently chosen; the second mode is by fire-arms; and next follow in succession, *precipitation*, strangling, cutting or pointed intruments, the vapour of charcoal, and, lastly, poison. It must be admitted, that a considerable number of those enrolled as suicides fall rather within the philosophical than the popular acceptation of that term; since many owed their end to drunkenness, and other physical causes.

The *moral* causes entered on the police-registers are instructive, in the light which they

throw upon national character.   Amongst them
are enumerated of

Unfortunate love	-	254	instances,	
			of which 157 were female.	
Jealousy and envy	-	92	- -	53
Wounded self-love	-	53	- -	equal in both sexes.
Dishonour and calumny		125	- -	97 male.
Remorse	-	49	- -	37
Disappointed ambition		122	- -	110
Reverse of fortune		322	- -	283
Gaming	- -	155	- -	141
Other misconduct		287	- -	208
Domestic chagrin	-	728	- -	524
Misery	- -	905	- -	511
Fanaticism	-	16	- -	1
Misanthropy	-	3	- -	3

The results of these tables are favourable to
the character of the female sex; and not least
in the circumstance, that, of 1758 instances,
where causes are not assigned by the police
(from ignorance or from a prudent silence),
1381 belong to males.

September was the month most prolific of
suicide; March and October approach most
nearly to it: January, February, December,
and November fall greatly below them in number.   The five months of spring and summer,
between March and September, are, on the
whole, the most productive season of the year. *

---

* Rapport sur le Prix de Statistique decerné par l'Acad.
Roy. des Sciences, pour l'Année 1827.

The number of persons taken out of the river amounted in 1820 to 260. From enquiries made in that year the inference was drawn, that 64 per cent. of the drowned have destroyed themselves. About an eighth part of the whole number were restored to life.

A *suicide club* is *said* to have existed lately at Paris, but the members were not likely to become numerous: they were 12, and the leading regulation directed, that one member should be annually selected to put an end to himself.

Among Roman Catholics the disposition to suicide appears far less prevalent than in Protestant communities. * It would be easy to dilate on the sources of this disproportion. Blumerbach made the observation in respect to Switzerland, and Casper has established it relatively to Germany. It is very rare among the *Jews* of Germany, partly from the dread of ridicule which disinclines them towards taverns, and partly from the beneficence of the wealthy members towards the indigent of their own race.

Climate, then, cannot be considered as a cause, and no one will hereafter ascribe it to changes of weather.

---

* Casper, Beiträge, zur Medicinischen Statistik und Staatsarzneikunde, 85. Berlin. 1825.

Although the average of most countries affords a large majority of male suicides, yet, in particular districts, the proportion varies. My friend, Dr. Macmichael, informs me, that the Middlesex Hospital (which is situated in a parish overstocked with the victims of prostitution) received during 16 recent months 20 cases of *attempted* suicide by poison, of which no less than 16 were females.

We may conclude, that it is more frequent in the lower ranks than in the middle ones : in nearly 152,000 persons insured at the *Equitable Office* only 15 cases occurred during 20 years.

CHAP. XII.

COMPARATIVE PREVALENCE, INCREASE, AND DECREASE
OF DISEASES IN DIFFERENT COUNTRIES AND CITIES.

THE progress of refinement is commonly de-
nounced as a fountain of new maladies, continually branching out into fresh streams of evil,
and gradually destroying the roots of the supposed natural health of man. But the history
of medicine is far from favouring this idea ; and
if a few diseases not previously described have
sprung into modern notoriety, a catalogue of
ancient ones more numerous and more formidable
is become nearly extinct. We shall first offer a
few tables of the diseases which at present prevail in some of the most remarkable parts of the
globe, and shall afterwards throw a restrospective
glance on those which were the bane of former
ages.

PRUSSIA.

The government of Prussia deserves the highest praise for the encouragement which it affords
to statistical enquiries. The following table presents a summary of the causes of death in that

country during the year 1817, and was published under the sanction of the director of the
Statistical Office of Prussia. It explains the proportion among 10,000 males, 10,000 females, and
10,000 of both sexes combined.

	Males.	Females.	Sexes combined.
Of old age - - -	950	1080	1013
Chronic diseases - -	4205	4291	4241
Acute diseases - -	2241	2573	2008
Sudden death - -	770	676	0725
External diseases - -	244	199	0222
Unknown diseases - -	710	693	0702
By disease in general -	8170	8022	8098
Infants still-born - -	507	409	0460
Women in child-birth -		273	0132
Small-pox - - -	95	98	0096
Hydrophobia - - -	7	8	0007
Accidents and violence -	233	100	0169
Suicide - - - -	39	10	0025
	880	898	0889
General Total -	10,000	10,000	10,000

According to the computation of the late Dr.
Friedlander, the following are the general inferences from the above table. In time of peace,
the 10th part of the population of Prussia arrive
at the natural term of life. Accidents (including
the small pox) produce about an 11th part of
the deaths. Four fifths die of disease. Amongst

10,000 births, 310 are still-born, or a 32d part;
and 89 mothers perish, or 1 in 112. A ninth
part of the deaths of children is owing to neglect
of vaccination.*

FRANCE.

According to the report of the Council of
Health for 1823, pulmonary phthisis destroys
about a fifth part of the inhabitants of *Paris*, and
pulmonary catarrh a 12th part. Apoplexy and
intestinal catarrh are next on the list of fatality,
and are followed by *gastritis*, scirrhous and can-
cerous affections : convulsions, the small-pox,
and croup, are the most destructive diseases of
infants.

Dr. Falret has found, on examination of the
registers of *sudden deaths* preserved by the
police of *Paris* during the 30 years from
1794 to 1823, that *apoplexy* has been more
frequent, by one third, during the 10 years following 1804 than during the 10 which preceded it. Amongst 2297 cases recorded for
30 years, 1670 were male and only 627 female. He has ascertained that the greater number occurred between the age of 55 and 65,
and next between 45 and 55. The period of

---

* Dict. des Sciences Medicales, art. Statistique.

life between 35 and 45, and that between 65 and 75, afford an equal proportion. As to the influence of *seasons*, the spring, and particularly the winter, produced the most considerable number; the summer was least fatal, and the autumn forms nearly the mean.*

We subjoin the principal causes of death to all the inhabitants of Paris during the year 1818, distinguishing the sexes. The nomenclature is unfortunately obscured by the vagueness of the modern French nosology.

	Men.	Women.
Fevers, putrid or adynamic -	400	443
——— malignant or ataxic -	391	424
——— undetermined - -	171	319
Phlegmasiæ, cutaneous - -	746	649
————— of mucous membranes -	1237	1453
————— serous membranes -	202	281
————— cellular texture, and pa- ⎱ ronchymatous organs ⎰	1454	1858
Comatose affections - -	496	503
Spasmodic affections - -	787	732
Local nervous affections - -	501	512
General organic lesions - -	1895	2063
Particular organic lesions - -	802	900
Gangrenous inflammations -	80	101
Died in child-bed - -		75

RUSSIA.

According to *Krafft*, pleurisies destroy one fourth of the whole population of *Petersburg*,

---

* Rapport sur le Prix de Statistique decerné par l'Acad. Roy. des Sciences, pour l'Année 1827.

fevers one third, and consumptions one sixth. These three forms of disease constitute five sevenths of all the deaths. From his observations it would appear that the half of all who are born there attain to the age of 25, a proportion which should indicate a degree of health in *early* life very uncommon in large cities, but *after twenty* a mortality much greater than occurs in any other town in Europe, and which is justly attributed to the immoderate use of brandy.*

ICELAND.

The most common disorders in Iceland are phthisis, and complaints of the thorax : the males are most subject to those from their exposure and early toils. Besides the ordinary ailments of infancy, the *trismus nuscentium*, or locked-jaw of infancy, is considered as a scourge of the island. It often becomes epidemic, and cuts off the infants of a whole district. The sea, the cold, and the snow destroy a large proportion of the inhabitants, according to the journal cited below, and yet the proportion of deaths is not so large as in some of the southern parts of Europe : it appears not to exceed 1 in 38 or 39 annually. Nervous and catarrhal fevers frequently occur

* Malthus and Tooke

N

epidemically, and prove very fatal. The itch is the most common disorder in the island, through the uncleanly habits of the people.*

SWEDEN.

From *Nicander*'s table of the deaths from disease in Sweden and Finland during the 21 years ending in 1795, 134 persons died annually of pulmonary consumption throughout the entire kingdom among every 100,000, but in the *city* of Stockholm five times that proportion were its annual victims, and in Carlscrona (a less populous town) about twice the former proportion. In 1823, 309 individuals, throughout Sweden, died of measles, 5 of hydrophobia, and 152 of venereal diseases.

UNITED STATES.

At New York, phthisis appears to engross a fifth, and sometimes only a sixth of all the deaths. At Philadelphia, a seventh, and sometimes only an eighth.

The following table shows the deaths which have occurred in every month at New York, from the diseases under-mentioned, during the 11 years from 1816 to 1826. †

---

* Notiz. ans d. Geb. der Natur und Heilkunde. Aug. 1824.

† Medical Statistics; or, a Comparative View of the Mor-

Diseases.	Jan.	Feb.	Mar.	April.	May.	June.	July.	Aug.	Sept.	Oct.	Nov.	Dec.	Total.
Phthisis -	660	659	644	664	616	510	591	663	579	585	645	650	7466
Acute diseases of the lungs	220	292	254	230	210	114	117	105	92	141	152	172	2069
Fevers - -	178	137	158	186	211	245	262	374	497	441	305	211	3205
Dropsies -	244	257	241	245	259	242	272	308	269	259	210	245	3044
Dysentery -	22	14	29	7	16	28	233	489	378	203	79	36	1544
Cholera infantum (10 years)	2	2	2	1	5	32	246	527	288	108	14	18	1245
Croup - -	137	106	122	106	91	66	69	6	84	140	139	122	1239
Marasmus -	68	66	85	95	79	69	80	12	139	135	89	84	1115
Gastro-enteritis	48	54	56	60	60	76	121	9	94	69	67	59	861
Hooping-cough	53	66	42	33	37	31	73	10	105	71	56	49	721
Apoplexy -	49	59	56	47	57	45	109	57	45	59	55	57	697
Measles -	48	42	46	45	32	44	65	7	45	39	24	45	552
Intemperance	49	32	33	31	49	47	46	43	44	47	63	47	531
Diseases of liver	48	46	34	35	34	39	57	44	36	64	41	50	528
Palsy - -	42	42	44	31	28	28	31	38	25	41	34	44	428

This table not only indicates the diseases which are most fatal at New York, but also explains the influence of the seasons on each complaint. We perceive that phthisis, dropsies, disorders of the liver, and palsies, which are chronic affections, are not more or less fatal in particular months. On the contrary, the effect of season is very marked on all the acute disorders. To understand better the inferences, we should state that the population of New York was, in 1816, above 110,000, and that it has gradually increased to 176,000 in 1826. Of 718 blacks who died in 1827, about 100 were victims of phthisis.

tality of New York, Philadelphia, Baltimore, and Boston. By N. Niles, jun. M. D. and J. D. Rush, M. D. 8vo. New York, 1827.

N 2

The deaths from small-pox were 149 in the year 1827, which is an excess of 91 above the year 1826.

WEST INDIES.

Dr. Alison, in his very instructive essay on the Pathology of Scrofulous Diseases *, has inserted a communication from Dr. Ferguson on the deaths and chief diseases occurring in the army, in the Windward and Leeward Islands, in the West Indies, from March 1816 till March 1817, distinguishing the deaths among the white and the black troops. The average strength of the army, during the year, was 7337 whites, and 5772 blacks; and of these there died, —

	Whites.	Proportion to the whole.	Blacks.	Proportion to the whole.
Of fever - -	477	1 in 15·3	38	1 in 151·8
Of dysentery - -	342	1 in 21·4	98	1 in 58·9
Of pulmonic complaints	82	1 in 89·1	128	1 in 45
	901		264	

We perceive that fever caused ten times as great a mortality among the white troops as among the blacks, and dysentery nearly three times as great; but that pulmonary complaints caused

* Transactions of the Medico-Chirurgical Society of Edinburgh, vol. i.

twice as great a mortality among the blacks as among the whites. The blacks were thus attacked chiefly in the elevated situations in the interior of the islands, where the heat is least oppressive.

IRELAND.

The following table * exhibits the diseases which prevail among the poor of Dublin, and the comparative number afflicted with each, as they appear on an average of several years, from the reports of the different Dispensary Institutions : —

Apoplexy	-	-	21	Dropsy, anasarca	-	337
Amaurosis	-	-	18	———— ascites	-	240
Amenorrhœa and chlorosis	-	-	285	———— of the chest	-	84
				———— of the ovarium		9
Asthenia	-	-	75	Erysipelas	-	-	105
After-pains	-	-	24	Ear-ache	-	-	36
Catarrh	-	-	123	Epilepsy	-	-	12
Cholera	-	-	354	Fever not contagious	-	105
Colic	-	-	216	—— intermittent	-	102
—— of Poitou	-	15	Hæmorrhage from the lungs	-	-	156
Cough and dyspnœa	-	3765	———— from the nose	-	-	30
Consumption	-	-	387				
Dysentery	-	-	345	———— from the stomach	-	-	15
Deafness	-	-	66				
Diarrhœa	-	-	381				

* History of Dublin, by Warburton, Whitelow, and Walsh, vol. ii. p. 1343. Lond. 1818.

Hæmorrhage from the uterus, and abortion		93
Heart-burn	-	36
Head-ache and vertigo		306
Hemicrania	-	18
Herpetic eruptions	-	153
Hooping-cough	-	15
Hysteria	-	48
Hydrophobia	-	3
Hypochondriasis	-	15
Inflammation of the eye		507
—————— ear		6
—————— intestines		21
————— kidneys		3
—————— lungs		243
—————— liver		90
—————— mamma		15
—————— peritonæum		42
————— parotid gland		21
—————— tonsils		642
—————— trachæa		3
Indigestion	-	792
Idrosis	-	12
Insanity	-	30
Itch	-	93
Jaundice	-	39
Leucorrhœa	-	162
Lumbago and sciatica	-	297
Measles	-	108
Menorrhagia	-	165
Nettle-rash	-	24
Opacity of the cornea	-	36
Peripnenmonia notha	-	162
Pleuritic stitches	-	1020
Pains of the stomach and bowels	-	75
Paralytic affections	-	90
Palpitations	-	135
Piles	-	69
Petechiæ et purpura hæmorrhagica	-	12
Prurigo	-	30
Psoropthalmia	-	45
Porrigo capilis et barbæ	-	66
Pulmonary consumption		399
Rheumatism, acute	-	533
—————— chronic	-	549
Retroversio uteri	-	3
Rickets	-	6
Scarlatina	-	1024
Small-pox	-	114
St. Vitus's dance	-	3
Scrofula	-	42
Spasms	-	15
Typhus	-	807
Tabes mesenterica	-	15
Tape-worm	-	12
Tenesmus	-	135
Tooth-ache	-	57
Trismus dolorificus	-	6
Venereal complaints	-	78
Vomiting	-	147
Worms	-	216
Wry-neck	-	18
Water on the brain	-	42

ENGLAND.

In respect to the increase and decrease of diseases in England, an important table has been lately published by Mr. Morgan, the Actuary of the *Equitable Insurance Office.* It gives a complete statement of the supposed causes of the deaths which occurred among the persons whose lives were insured in that office from 1800 to 1821. The number of individuals insured during that time is stated by Mr. Morgan to have been nearly 152,000. They were composed chiefly of the middle or easy classes, and of every age from ten years upwards. Mr. Morgan, who was formerly a member of the medical profession, considers this table as a fair estimate of the diseases of this country, — but, we must add, more especially of its middle classes. The certificates of the diseases were principally signed by medical men. We perceive that the total deaths were 1930. The greatest number of deaths under any one head is 262 for *natural decay and old age.* This is a remarkable feature, because it indicates that about a seventh part of the deaths were not apparently owing to disease. Apoplexy is next the most fatal agent ; consumption follows far behind. General fever then presents itself. The principal diseases follow in this order,—Dropsy, palsy ;—hydrothorax makes one 19th of the whole, and its chief victims were between 50 and 60 years of age ; — then diseases of the liver, inflammation of the bowels, and of the lungs. The cases of calculous disorder

N 4

were 8.   There is not a single death from small-pox, measles, nor scarlet fever.

Angina pectoris presents a large proportion of 44.   Gout affords 26 deaths.

The deaths from *accidents* were 19.

The deaths from consumption are scarcely 1 in 12, which is very different from the usual proportion in the general population, and indicates, in this particular, as in so many others, the conservative power of affluence.

But the fatality of consumption has begun to diminish also in regard to the general population of London.   At the close of last century the deaths from this disease had gradually increased from about 15 per cent. to 26 per cent. of the total mortality.   From 1799 to 1808 they still increased, being then above 27 per cent.   From 1808 to 1818 they however declined to 23 per cent., and from 1818 to 1825 they have become still less numerous, being at length only 22 per cent., nearly the same proportion as at Paris : at Vienna it is about 17 per cent.

DISEASES.	AGES.								
	10 to 20.	20 to 30.	30 to 40.	40 to 50.	50 to 60.	60 to 70.	70 to 80.	80, &c.	Total.
Angina pectoris - -	—	—	5	11	12	9	4	3	44
Apoplexy - -	1	3	19	38	69	69	38	5	242
Asthma - - -	—	—	—	2	19	19	11	2	53
Atrophy - -	—	—	3	4	6	11	1	—	25
Cancer - -	—	—	1	4	10	8	1	1	25
Childbirth - -	—	—	2	2	—	—	—	—	4
Consumption - -	2	9	34	31	44	28	5	—	153
Convulsion fits -	—	—	3	4	1	3	—	—	11
Decay (natural) and old age - }	—	—	—	—	5	72	127	58	262
Diabetes -	—	—	—	2	2	—	1	1	6
Dropsy - -	1	—	7	28	38	41	20	2	137
—— in the chest -	—	1	3	18	34	28	16	—	100
Dysentery - -	—	—	1	1	2	4	4	—	12
Disease of the stomach and digestive organs }	—	—	5	4	8	8	1	—	26
Disease of the liver -	—	2	5	24	23	21	4	—	79
—— bladder and urinary passages }	—	—	2	4	15	23	15	—	59
Epilepsy - -	—	—	2	3	2	1	2	—	10
Erysipelas - -	—	1	3	2	3	2	2	—	10
Fever, general - -	—	6	18	33	33	39	15	2	146
—— bilious - -	—	1	4	8	9	4	1	1	28
—— nervous - -	—	3	3	13	6	8	3	—	36
—— inflammatory -	—	—	—	4	6	3	2	—	15
—— putrid - -	—	2	7	4	6	7	—	—	26
Gout - -	—	—	1	4	4	11	6	—	26
Inflammation of the bowels	1	2	11	13	15	25	9	1	77
—————— lungs -	—	—	9	4	24	22	12	2	73
—————— brain -	—	3	7	5	5	3	—	—	23
—————— chest & peripneumony - }	1	1	1	1	6	7	4	1	22
Palsy - -	—	1	3	8	26	42	34	2	116
Quincy - -	—	—	—	1	1	1	—	—	3
Rupture of a vessel -	—	—	7	14	13	12	3	—	49
Slain in war - -	1	1	1	1	—	—	—	—	4
Stone - -	—	—	—	—	1	2	4	1	8
Suicide - -	—	1	2	3	7	2	—	—	15
Water in the brain -	—	—	—	1	3	1	—	—	5
	7	37	166	299	458	536	345	82	1930

One of the most interesting and important
contributions which could be made to medical

literature would be a detailed history of the *origin, progress,* and *revolutions* of diseases in different times and countries, comprehending an ample estimate of the influence which political and moral events have exercised on their fluctuations, and indicating the measures of police and of domestic economy, which analogy may suggest to restrain or to divert their future current. This remarkable section of the philosophy of medicine remains as yet unwritten, if we except the excellent essays which Heberden and Blane alone have supplied towards its illustration. The facts and reflections which these authors have communicated in a concise form are of the greatest value, and will probably be more highly appreciated in a distant century than at the present moment. This chapter would be incomplete without a brief statement of the results which they have presented, and we are not acquainted with any other sources of collective information on the subject. It must be premised that they relate chiefly to what has occurred in our own country.

I. Some diseases have arisen, and have since disappeared. Of this description are the *leprosy* and the *sweating sickness.* The leprosy appears to have committed the most extensive ravages, and to have had hospitals erected solely for its relief. It became general throughout Europe in the twelfth century, and is supposed to have been imported by the Crusades. It has not been known in Europe since the beginning of the sixteenth century. The sweating sickness is supposed to have been introduced into England by the army which invaded it under Henry VII. It prevailed from 1485 till 1551, and in some years during one month in autumn with a fatality nearly approaching to the plague.

II. The diseases which have arisen but have not disappeared are the small-pox, the measles, perhaps all the other specific contagions, and syphilis. Though the exact period of the origin of each cannot be ascertained, we have reason to believe that there has been a time when no one of these was known.

III. The diseases which have prevailed with various degrees of frequency and fatality at different periods are the plague, the dysentery, intermittent fever, typhus fever, the small-pox, syphilis, the scurvy, and the rickets. The first occurrence of the *plague* in English annals is in the year 430. The last year in which it was epidemic here was 1665, and the last year in which we find it mentioned in the bills of mortality is 1679. In another part of this work allusion is made to the causes of its discontinuance. Not only the bills of mortality but professional and other writings afford the most incontrovertible evidence of the great and rapid decline of dysentery and intermittent fevers. A considerable mortality is assigned to the *scurvy* in the London *Bills* of the seventeenth century : the scanty supply of fresh vegetable food for man, and of winter fodder for cattle (which made it necessary to slaughter and salt them for winter use), and the uncleanness and dampness of the streets and houses, explain its prevalence at that time, and its extinction at the present. Even at sea, it is now nearly as uncommon as at land, in consequence of the improved diet, cleanliness, and general supply of lemon-juice. There is no doubt of the great decrease of *rickets*, in common with the other complaints of children. It was first described by Glisson, and is first enumerated in the bills of mortality for the year 1634.

IV. Some diseases are more prevalent in modern times than formerly ; such as the scarlet fever, consumption, gout, dropsy, palsy, apoplexy, mania, and generally all those diseases of which the brain and nerves are the seat. The increase of opulence, which enables a larger proportion of society to exist without the necessity of bodily labour, the diffusion of intellectual pursuits, the increasing number of sedentary occupations, and the multiplication of political interests, have all conspired to bring the latter class of diseases into more conspicuous action ; and they will probably be developed in every country in the proportion in which these conditions arise or proceed.

The diseases which chiefly occur in *savage* nations appear to be fevers, fluxes, and rheumatisms. One cause of exemption from many diseases, is, probably, the loss in infancy of all those children who are weak and sickly, but who are preserved in civilised society by skill and nursing, until they become in more advanced years the victims of other diseases.

If we agree with Blane in referring the remote causes of all predominent disorders to three general heads, namely, the vitiated exhalations and secretions of the human body, the noxious exhalations of the earth, and depraved habits of life, it will be easily perceived that the greater number of diseases are by their nature very much subject to human control. And the triumph which has been already obtained over several maladies by the progress of knowledge, and of affluence, affords great encouragement to our endeavours to conquer others. Without alluding to the diminution of small-pox by vaccination, the counteraction of typhus by means of cleanliness and ventilation, and of agues by draining marshes, by construction of sewers, and by cleansing the streets, are proofs of the empire of human art over disease. It would not be difficult to multiply instances, but it will occur to every one,

that the introduction of *linen* and soap, the
greater facility of procuring fuel, the more ample supply of water, the widening of streets, and
the increasing abundance and choice of provisions, have contributed in various degrees to
banish some diseases, and to mitigate others.*
Altogether it appears that the two extremities of
social life, its infancy and its maturity, are the
most exempt from the visitations of disease, and
that the intervening period of transition from
barbarism to high civilisation has been the
scene on which disease has been most active
and most prominent, and on which it has exhibited its most ghastly forms.

---

* Blane, in Med. Chir. Trans. vol. iv. and in Select Dissertations, and Heberden on Increase and Decrease of
different Diseases, 4to. 1801.

CHAP. XIII.

STATISTICS OF CLIMATE IN RELATION TO HEALTH AND DISEASE.

CLIMATOLOGY would fill an entire volume with highly interesting statistical facts, but we can here only select from its domain a few of the details most nearly allied to medicine.

Hippocrates first indicated the path to be pursued in examining the *air, waters,* and *places,* and has bequeathed an excellent description and generalisation of those subjects as he found them in his own country, and in the neighbouring ones. Unfortunately the rules which he lays down have been misapplied to explain the circumstances of other regions, and here they have been necessarily found erroneous. The failure is not to be imputed to that original observer, but to those who have inconsiderately wandered from the scene of his remarks. If we select his characteristics of a northern climate, and apply them to the Asturias, a province of Spain seated in the latitude of Northern Greece, we are disappointed on perceiving that the reigning diseases are a species of *lepra,* dysenteries, scrofulous tumours, and other affections of the nature which Hippocrates attributes to a southern exposure.*

The *exposure* and the *winds* form the basis of the climates of Hippocrates. We may enumerate the following causes of a climate; namely, the action of the sun on the atmosphere; the interior temperature of the globe; the elevation above the level of the sea; the general inclination of the surface, and its local exposures; the positions of its mountains in relation to the cardinal points; the neighbourhood of great seas, and their relative situation; the geological nature of the soil; the degree of cultivation and of population at which a country has arrived; and the reigning winds. †

Malte-Brun has developed an idea of *Kant*, in founding a classification of climates on the principal combinations of qualities which characterise them. An examination of the *four climates* of *Hippocrates* convinced him of the impossibility of founding a classification on their causes, because all these causes vary with geographical circumstances. Heat and cold may be accompanied with moisture and with dryness; we have hence four principal climates.

I. The *warm* and *dry* climate exists in an ex-

---

* Thierry, Obs. Médicales sur l'Espagne, and Malte-Brun, Geog. Universelle, t. ii.

† Malte-Brun, Geog. Univ. t.ii. p. 401.

treme degree in the deserts of Sahara and
of Arabia : water is here invaluable ; men and
animals are few in number ; the olive tint and
bilious temperament predominate among the
fierce inhabitants.

II. The *warm* and *moist* climate is that of
Bengal, of Mesopotamia, of the coasts of Zan-
guebar, of Senegambia, of Guiana, of Panama :
an eternal verdure embellishes it, and it is the
birthplace of the giants of the vegetable kingdom : the reptiles are enormous ; the human
race is robust, and its generations rapid, but its
character approaches the brute; the skin is
black, and the temperament phlegmatic.

III. The *cold* and *dry* climate nourishes a
vigorous but not luxuriant vegetation : the waters
are generally pure, but hard ; the animals and
the men enjoy strength and health ; there is an
equilibrium between the moral and physical
qualities. Generation is slow but regular: the
sanguine temperament and the white skin predominate in this climate, which includes the
largest portion of Europe and of Asia.

IV. The *cold* and *moist* climate, in its extreme degree, such as is experienced in Siberia
and in the north of Canada, envelopes the atmosphere with unwholesome mists, and reduces
vegetation to a few stinted shrubs, and to creeping
mosses : the animals are clothed in a thick fur,
under which they pass half the year torpidly :

o

man is large, but feeble and heavy, and is only occupied in defending his physical existence against the severity of nature : the copper-red skin and the melancholic temperament seem to spring from this constitution of climate.*

The temperate *zone* is the most favourable to health, but as its extremities approach the frigid and the torrid zones, they partake of the dispositions peculiar to these; and in proportion as they border more nearly on either, are more subject to the morbific influence arising from vicissitudes of seasons and of weather. Between the 40th and 60th degree the succession of the four seasons is the most regular and the most sensible, without, however, exposing the health of man. It is between these latitudes that the most civilised and prosperous nations are found : the natural term of life is here more generally attained; diseases are less virulent, less rapid in their progress, less unsightly, less fatal.

In forming a *medical* estimate of climate within the temperate zone, we do not balance heat or cold in the scale of latitude so much as we examine *localities*. The neighbourhood of the *sea*, for instance, produces a variety of modifications. In high latitudes, the coasts and the islands are less cold than the interior of con-

---

* Geographie Universelle, t. ii. p. 422.

tinents. In warm climates, the maritime parts
are cooler than the middle of plains. The port
of Bergen, in Norway, is not so often frozen as
the Seine. The months of winter are much less
cold at Plymouth than at Paris. although the
mean heat of the year is rather less at the former
place than at the latter.* *Mountains* also affect
a climate in various ways. The Alps are considered to have an essential part in maintaining
the mildness of Italy ; and on the contrary, the
the central and southern parts of Russia suffer
cold disproportioned to their latitude and exposure, partly through the want of a chain of
northern mountains, which might weaken the
force of the winds coming from the White Sea
and the Oural mountains. † But the protection
which mountains afford against winds sometimes
operates unfavourably : an insupportable heat
occurs in some vallies : in those which are deep
and narrow, and which receive the dry winds
only very obliquely, the air stagnates, there is a
perpetual fog, the water loses its purity, and a
race of beings vegetates scarcely sensible to impressions, rachitic, scrofulous, and cachectic in a
degree which is never witnessed in more fortunate situations. Plains of a moderate height
are usually healthy : the lower plains, which are

---

* Malte-Brun.   † Ibid.

contiguous to mountains, lakes, or marshes, remarkably depress our principal organs.

We are compelled to attach a much lower importance to the influence of *climate*, both in health and disease, than was formerly assumed. In Europe, at least, the maladies of the individual appear to depend much more upon his habits and condition, and occasional local peculiarities, than upon the varieties of climate. One of the most important prerogatives of man is his inherent power of accommodating himself to every climate; but this power is modified by the degree of prudence which governs him; and a large proportion of European deaths in tropical climates is owing to the neglect of a suitable diet, and to insufficient self-restraint. Isert (in his voyage to Guinea) attributes the mortality of the Europeans, in that region, to their licentious mode of living, which is totally misplaced in that climate. Niebuhr, also, who saw all the companions of his travels perish around him, remarks, in his account of Arabia, that their diseases arose from their European mode of life, such as eating too much animal food, and exposing themselves to the cold evening air.*

West imagines that females suffer less from

* Rudolphi, Grundriss der Physiologie, i.

changes of climate than men; but the cause of this is probably due to their more regular, provident, and temperate habits, and to their comparative exemption from exposure to inclemency of weather, or excessive labour.

The stronger and more rapid are the changes of climate the more striking is its influence. Thus we have found it most conducive to the health of our troops not to transport them immediately from England to the West Indies, but to send them, in the first instance, to Gibraltar, in order to accustom them, gradually, to a hot climate. The stranger, indeed, does not usually suffer so much on his first arrival, because his strength is then unenfeebled ; but after a time his frame becomes more susceptible through the previous respite. The inhabitant of warmer climates, when transplanted to the North, suffers chiefly from scrofula, in all its degrees. John Hunter used to observe, in his lectures, that nearly all the monkies which are brought into this country ultimately perish through scrofulous affections.

It appears certain that a greater degree of health and longevity is enjoyed in the northern than in the southern countries of Europe and of America; but the superiority of the former in civilisation, prudence, and good government, probably outweighs the variety of latitude. Two of the most formidable diseases with which we

are acquainted originate in a debasement of
condition and feeling, the plica polonica, and
the pellagra. The plica polonica (says Dr.
Kerckhoff) is commonly to be met with among
the poor alone, who wallow in filth and misery,
and particularly among the Jews, who are pro-
verbially negligent of their persons; he consequently contends, that it is no more endemic
to Poland than to any other country. The
pellagra is found chiefly in the wretched hovels
of the Milanese and Venetian peasantry. It is
observed to spread in proportion to the poverty
of the times, and seems to spring from a confined air, disregard of cleanliness, and bad food.
Mere locality seems alone to produce some
complaints; and Dr. Foderé principally ascribes
the frequency of goître in the Passes of the
Valais to the stagnation of air which occurs in
confined and narrow situations. A similar cause
is also assigned at Salzburg, where goître is
prevalent. In 1806, the proportion of persons
afflicted with goître in the department of Mont
Blanc, was 1 in 33 or 34 of the whole population. It is found also in South America, at the
foot of the Andes, and it is curious to remark
that the remedy there empirically employed is a
marine fucus.

According to Foderé, the same valley only
produces cretinism and goître in its narrow
part: as we approach towards the summit of

its side, the inhabitants become free from those diseases.

Dry and elevated countries are most subject to acute disorders; and chronic ones, on the contrary, are more frequent in low and damp situations. Even in the same city this principle is sometimes illustrated; for in the higher part of it few diseases present themselves, and those of an acute kind, while in the lower quarters they are frequent, and more chronic.

The inhabitants of cities are most subject to nervous affections, scrofula, rachitis, and pulmonary phthisis; while a residence in the country disposes more generally to inflammatory complaints. A long-continued stay in hospitals, prisons, ships, and barracks, predisposes to dysentery, to scurvy, and to dropsy. *

It is only in tropical regions that climate appears to tyrannise over our frame, and to defy the efforts of skill or prudence. Yet even in the epidemic cholera of India, we perceive that the mortality of the European troops is greatly inferior to that of the natives : — 767 soldiers were attacked, and 211 of them died; while of the natives, 4065 were attacked, and 1544 died, which yields a fatality of $27\frac{1}{2}$ in 100 of the troops, but so overwhelming a proportion as 38

* Chomel, Pathologie Générale.

in 100 of the natives. According to the report of the diseases of the *northern* division of the army of the Presidency of *Madras*, for a period of six years, from 1815 to 1820, the proportion of sickness among the European troops was 93 per cent. and amongst the native troops 66 per cent. The proportion of deaths per cent. among the Europeans was 6 ; among the natives 3. These proportions vary considerably in the different divisions of the army. *

In the tropical fever of Jamaica in 1808 there were 200 deaths in 494 cases.

From the Report of the Commissioners of Inquiry into the State of the Colony of *Sierra Leone*, ordered by the House of Commons to be printed, in May, 1827, it appears, that from the original settlement in 1787 to 1826 the total number of settlers arrived in that colony (including all classes) was 21,944, and of all these only 13,020 remained. It is painful to witness these destructive fruits of a plan originally dictated by the benevolent desire of civilising the native Africans. The fine island of *Fernando Po* affords a better prospect. According to a recent letter of Captain Owen, not a single death had occurred there during nearly four months, in a colony of 650 persons. †

---

* Annesley, Sketches of Diseases of India, 8vo. 1825.
† Quarterly Review, No. 77. p. 181.

The influence of climate on the diseases of Europe is very conspicuous in one particular point, the great variety in the fatality of different months and seasons to different cities. The observation of Celsus on this head was doubtless formerly applicable to Rome, but it is totally contrary to the actual state of London, where the autumn now appears the most healthy, and next follow the summer, the winter, and least healthy of all is spring.* At Montpelier, on the contrary, March appears one of the most healthy, and August one of the least healthy months. Petersburgh appears to correspond pretty nearly with London. At Paris, also, the greatest mortality occurs in April, and the lowest in July. At Berlin, also, March is the most fatal month, and November the least so. Padua and Milan, on the contrary, coincide more nearly with Montpelier, and with the axiom of Celsus. But this distribution of the seasons in London appears to have only existed within the last 100 years. Graunt observed, at the close of the 17th century, that in London " the unhealthful season was the autumn." It was in that season that the plague, remittent fever, and small-pox, were always most prevalent and fatal. The important improvements which subsequently were effected in the domestic economy of London gradually

* Bateman.

reversed this ancient order : they did not transfer disease from one season to another, but removed the evils of the unhealthy periods, without the addition of any new source of mischief to the others. We can hardly find a happier illustration of the practical benefits of progressive knowledge in promoting the general interests of mankind, nor a better example of the mutual dependence of all arts, sciences, and professions, on each other. Villermé believes that in healthy districts winter and spring are most fatal, and that winter is more fatal in the north than in the south. In marshy countries he finds July, August, September, and October the most fatal months, and that the evaporation of the marshes is most fatal from 1 to 6 years of age.

When we speak of a healthy climate, it is gratifying to reflect that in most instances it is man himself who has in a great measure created these climates of health. Twenty centuries ago, England, France, and Germany, resembled Canada, and Chinese Tartary, countries situated like Europe, at a mean distance between the equator and the pole. Macchiavelli, in his early age, seems to have anticipated this truth : he remarks, in his quaint language, " Unhealthy countries become wholesome by the multitude of men who inhabit them ; who at the same time are occupied in cultivating the earth, and who make the earth sane : the fires which they kindle purify the air : these advantages nature herself does not produce."

It is only by constant efforts of industry that the salubrity of any spot is maintained : when these are relaxed, or when prosperity and civilisation decline, the seeds of disease are immediately deposited in the earth. The aguish disposition has been observed to increase at Rome in the same proportion that its population has diminished. On the other hand, it is well known that the climate of the United States has been remarkably improved by draining, cutting down trees, and the operations of agriculture ; and that spots which were impracticable, or fatal to the early settlers, at present afford a comfortable residence. The improvement that is continually taking place in the climate of America proves that the power of man extends to features of nature, which from the magnitude and variety of their causes seemed entirely beyond his control. At Guiana, in South America, within five degrees of the line, the inhabitants, living amidst immense forests, were a century ago obliged to alleviate the severity of the cold by evening fires. But by clearing the surface of the country even the duration of the rainy season has been shortened, and the warmth is so increased that a fire would now be deemed an annoyance. It thunders continually in the woods, but rarely in the cultivated parts.*

It appears certain that the climate of Europe has undergone a great change. If we compare its actual state with the accounts of ancient writers, a remarkable discrepancy is observed, which can only be explained by the influence of industry on the improvement of the soil; and there is reason to believe that America will partake of the same happy amelioration when an equal length of gradual toil has been bestowed upon her. We are told by Cæsar, that the vine could not be cultivated in Gaul on account of its winter-cold. The rein-deer, now found only in the zone of Lapland, was then an inhabitant of the Pyrenees. The Tiber was frequently frozen over, and the ground about Rome covered with snow for several weeks together, which almost never happens in our times. †

Even on nations exposed to the same scorching sun the influence of *diet* seems to be more powerful in forming the constitution and the character than mere climate, as is evinced in the wide diversity existing between the Hindoo and the Malay. The *nature of the soil* is the earliest element which operates in creating a national character; but religion and government produce

* Ure's Dictionary of Chemistry, 3d edit. p. 329.
† Ibid.

a second, a more essential, a moral climate, which ultimately determines not merely the health of citizens, but the existence of a state.*

---

* See, on the diseases of various climates, *Geographische Nosologie, von F. Schnurrer*, M. D. 8vo.   Stuttgart, 1813. and the large work of Finke, cited in the preface ; also Annesley on the Diseases of India, 2 vols. 4to.

CHAP. XIV.

INFLUENCE OF VARIOUS CONDITIONS, PROFESSIONS, AND
MODES OF LIFE ON LONGEVITY. — AVERAGE QUAN-
TITY OF DISEASE ATTENDANT ON PARTICULAR PUR-
SUITS.

THE comparative mortality and longevity of
the various classes of society seem to have
been formerly balanced by conjecture alone;
and it appears to have been even a prevalent
opinion, that poverty was favourable to long life;
that it exempted from numerous diseases which
follow in the train of luxury and wealth, and that
the affluent individual, if desirous of attaining to
old age, would find it his interest to imitate the
habits or diet of the peasant. The contrary has
been brought to light during the present century
by a rich variety of facts; and the present conclusion is, that, in general terms, poverty, cold,
and moisture (which two latter circumstances
are generally included in the first), are the greatest enemies to the enjoyment of health and long
life, and that competence, or an easy condition,
is the strongest safeguard of the body. Of an
equal number of infants taken among the poor
and the easy classes, it will be found, at least in

France (where the argument has been the most agitated), that the proportion of deaths among the former is double ; and that wherever is the greatest portion of misery, there will also attend the largest share of mortality. In epidemic visitations, the mortality begins and ends with the poorer classes, and on these are their principal ravages exhausted. It seems to be partly on this account, that women (at least in England) die in a less frequent proportion, and are longer lived on the average than men, because they are usually more secluded from the conflict of life, are less exposed to vicissitudes of weather, and to severe labour. In France, on the contrary, where the women, in every rank, take a more active part in worldly affairs, and where, among the lower orders, they perform a large part of the manual and out-of-door employments, their mortality (on a late average formed during the six years from 1817 to 1823) appears to be nearly the same as that of the men. Buffon had previously observed, that in most rural districts the mortality of females was somewhat higher than of males, on account of toils unsuited to their frame, which they were there compelled to undergo, and which, it may be added, usually imprint on the female peasant of continental Europe the stamp of old age before she has attained the age of 40.

Mr. Finlaison affirms, that the mortality of

the female sex, at every period of life, is less
than that of the male at a corresponding age,
excepting under ten years of age, when no
difference appears between the two; and also
in extreme old age, as when beyond 85, when
he likewise perceives no distinction. Dr. Price
and other writers have considered that the two
periods of life most fatal to women were from
45 to 52, and from 20 to 35. But all Mr. Finlaison's observations lead him to a conclusion
directly opposite, namely, that the mortality of
females is less between 30 and 35 than at 20;
and that there is no foundation for the belief that
it is greater from 45 to 52.

In the Paris tables of mortality for the year
1818, it appears that the mortality of women is
not greater at the *critical* period of life than at
any other, and that it increases at an advanced
age.

The conservative tendency of an easy condition is strongly marked by the very inferior
degree of mortality and of disease which occurs
among persons insured at the various life-offices.
The Equitable Office had always employed the
corrected Northampton tables of the probabilities of life. But Mr. Morgan, the actuary,
found in 1810 that the actual deaths which had
occurred among 83,000 persons insured during
30 years was in the proportion of only 2 to 3 of
what had been anticipated by the tables. And

among these *selected* lives the mortality of the
women is still less than that of the men; because in the middle classes they enjoy a remarkable exemption from fatigue and difficulty. To
illustrate the low rate of mortality among such
picked lives, or among persons in the enjoyment
of competence, it may be mentioned, that the
annual average of deaths amongst the persons
insured at the Equitable from 1800 to 1820 was
only about 1 in 81$\frac{1}{2}$. Of 1000 members of the
University Club, only 35 died in 3 years, which
is a still lower rate, about 1 in 90 annually. Of
10,000 pupils who passed in different years
through Pestalozzi's institution in Switzerland,
it is even asserted that not one died during his
residence there. These were youths chiefly,
but of all countries, constitutions, and ages;
generally, it is to be observed, of easy circumstances. Pestalozzi, also, paid particular attention to their bodily exercises.

On the other hand, let us observe how great
is the mortality of man in his lowest state of
want and degradation. It was formerly computed that a 5th or 6th part of the negro slaves
died annually. The free Africans who serve in
our troops have been said to lose annually only
3 men out of 100, while the slaves were losing
17 in 100. At present, however, their mortality
decreases in proportion to the superior care taken

P

of them : of about 20,000 slaves landed at Rio
Janeiro in 1823, only 1400 had died on the
voyage ; which would still form an enormous
proportion for Europeans, but is a happy contrast to the former returns of a slave-ship.

In *schools* the annual number of deaths is
very small, as might be anticipated from the
age at which they are generally frequented.
A considerable difference would probably be
found between the mortality of *civic* and of *rural*
schools.

The annual average of deaths at Christ's Hospital, in London, during the 40 years ending in
1799, was 1 in 150. The mortality of Heriot's
Hospital, at Edinburgh, (which is composed of
children from the age of seven to fourteen) has
been only 1 in 235, on an average of the last
17 years. The annual deaths at the Edinburgh
High School and *Academy* are only 1 in 833 :
the pupils are the children chiefly of the middle
and higher classes, and many live in the houses
of their parents ; circumstances which have a
more powerful influence than is generally estimated on health and longevity, and which are
strongly illustrated by the above fact.

During the terrible progress of epidemic fever
in Ireland, in the years 1817, 1818, and 1819,
it was generally remarked throughout the
country that fever did not spread through

families in comfortable circumstances; and, indeed, it might be asserted, that the danger of such extension diminished accordingly as the persons visited by sickness were more elevated in society. While fever raged in almost every part of Ireland, it is curious to remark that the *army* suffered comparatively little from it, because the private soldier is better fed, lodged, and clothed than the peasant of Ireland. The prevalence was nearly twice greater among the inhabitants than among the army. *

Duvillard has ascertained in France that the mortality of the married is less than that of the single; and a similar result appears to have been observed elswhere.

Cultivation of the sciences appears particularly favourable to longevity, in spite of various assertions formerly made to the contrary: it almost seems that the man who labours chiefly with his mind has a fairer prospect of life than the one whose body alone is occupied. Franchini† has enumerated 104 Italian mathematicians of different epochs: he has ascertained the ages at which 70 of these died, and among the 70 are 18 who had attained the age of 80, and

---

* Barker and Cheyne, Account of the Fever lately epidemical in Ireland. 2 vols. 8vo. London, 1821.

† Saggio della Storia delle Matematiche. Lucca, 1821.

2 of 90 ; and this, too, in a southern climate, which is not generally very favourable to old age. In France 152 men of science and letters have been taken at random : half the number appear to have cultivated science, and about half to have been devoted to general literature : on adding together the age at which each had died, it was found that the average result would be above 69 years for each of the 152 individuals.*

On the mortality of particular trades very few materials exist, although many remarks are to be found on the diseases to which they are subject.†

A statement has been lately published of the deaths which occurred among a society of fifty *plumbers.* During seven years 14 members have died, all under 36 years of age, and through diseases induced by their business.

Dr. Alison believes that there is hardly an instance of a *mason* regularly employed in hewing stones at Edinburgh living free from phthisical symptoms to the age of 50.

It does not require much reflection to perceive that *want*, or privation, not merely shortens the

---

* Berard, Discours, &c.

† Ramazzini, De Morbis Artificum.   Also the French translation, with notes, by Patissier.   Also Gosse, in the Quarterly Journal of Foreign Medicine and Surgery, vol. ii.

natural term of life, but that it has a tendency to produce several diseases, some of which, when once formed, gradually communicate themselves to those who are placed in more fortunate circumstances. The greater part of epidemic diseases in Europe originate in an impoverished state of the lower orders, by whatever cause induced. A season of scarcity, the march of armies, war, or the absence of accustomed employment, all conspire to generate among the poor a disease which often reaches to the rich; and if other arguments could not supply attention to the necessitous part of society, expedience, and consideration of self, must always render it abundantly politic on the part of the opulent to anticipate and remedy the effects of such casualties. Maclean declares that scarcity is the most powerful auxiliary cause of the *plague*. Even in 1758, when a scarcity existed in England, which was considered not real, but artificial, Sir R. Manningham, a physician of London, thought it necessary to call the attention of the public to the danger of an impending pestilence. He observes, that " the plague of pestilence may be much easier produced in this country by an artificial famine than by any infection of the plague itself from foreign parts." We must conclude with Dr. Heberden, *junior*, that the presence of infectious matter is not alone sufficient to make the plague epidemical, but that some concurrent state of the air, and of the human body, is likewise necessary ; and that our long exemption from this evil is not so much to be attributed to any accidental absence of its exciting causes, as to our own change of manners, our love of cleanliness and of ventilation, which have produced amongst us, if not an incapability, at least a great unaptness, any longer to receive it.

The superior health enjoyed by the British *army* and *navy*, when at a distance from their own home, has often been a subject of surprise and exultation. We will go back above half a century, and quote the sentiments of an eminent foreigner on this subject. Alluding to the events of the Seven Years' War, *Müller* remarks that "the resources of military talents were never more successfully applied by any modern people than by the Britons during that contest : so much care was taken to provide for all the wants of the soldiery, that the ordinary mortality *among the wounded*, was not more than 1 in 20 ; and out of 14,000 men who were employed in the year 1760 in cruizing in the Bay of Biscay, scarcely 20 were attacked by disease."

If we follow the steps of the late war, we shall find one remarkable anecdote which requires no comment. During the ten months from the siege of Burgos to the battle of Vittoria inclusive, the total sick and wounded which passed through the hospitals was above 95,000. But through the exertions of the medical officers, the army took the field preparatory to the battle with a sick list under 5000. But this was not all; during twenty successive days it marched towards the enemy, and in less than one month after it had defeated them, it mustered, *within 30 men*, as strong as before the action, and this, too, without any reinforcement from home.* No general, most assuredly, either of modern or ancient times, has ever been so deeply indebted to his medical companions as the commander of our Peninsular troops. Even in the Portuguese hospitals, they accomplished the most important improvements; and the hospital occupied by our royal artillery at Lisbon (a place the most hostile to cleanliness) is characterised by Dr. Carter as a model of neatness and good order. †

Even on the barren rock of Gibraltar our garrison has been trained to the enjoyment of a more secure existence than that which is enjoyed by some cities on the Continent. It appears from a recent report, that its mortality was only 1 in 48 (exclusive of the years in which epidemic fever prevailed).

---

* Edinb. Med. Journal. January, 1820.
† Short Account of Hospitals. Lond. 1819.

It may be not uninteresting to compare with these facts the fate of the disabled soldier in remoter times. Xenophon, Cæsar, and Polybius, who are very copious on the details of war, make no mention of hospitals of any kind ; and one of the commentators on Vegetius intimates that each Roman legion (containing three thousand or four thousand men) had *one* medical officer alone attached to it.*

To mark the improvement of health in our navy, we may compare the fate of Commodore Anson's crew with a ship placed in similar circumstances 50 years after. Anson was 143 days at sea without touching at any place of refreshment. On his arrival at Juan Fernandez, half of his companions alone survived ; and of the remaining 200, only eight were capable of duty. But in 1794, the Suffolk, a 74 gun-ship, passed 162 days also without any communication with land, and arrived in India without the loss of even one man, and with no case of scurvy, or of any other dangerous disease, at the time of disembarkation. The success which attended the efforts of Cooke, and subsequently of Captain Parry, in checking the inroads of disease upon their crews, is universally known. So great a change has thus been wrought in the

---

* Blane, Select Dissertations.

effective strength of our sailors, that two ships
of war are computed to be now capable of more
service than three of the same rate under the
former system. The total mortality of the whole
British navy, in all parts of the world, including
those who were lying in hospitals, was, in 1813,
only 1 in 42. *

On the other hand, we must assign a portion
of the good health enjoyed by our army and
navy to the influence of *moral* causes, such as
national spirit, and general success. The operation of moral causes on the health of soldiers
was strongly evinced in the French army during
its disastrous campaigns of 1813 and 1814: the
number of its diseases preserved a terrible proportion to its losses, and augmented with every
failure. †

With respect to the average quantity of sickness prevailing in our *army*, it appears from the
official returns at the Adjutant-General's office,
that, in 24 monthly musters of 313,695 men,
all under 50 years of age, there were 14,049
disqualified for military duty by indisposition ;
from which it results that each man, on an
average, suffered $2\frac{33}{100}$ weeks' sickness in the
year. Supposing that, after the age of 50, the
sickness in the army should follow the course of

---

* Blane, Select Dissertations.
† Chomel, Pathologie Genéralé.

mortality indicated by the Carlisle tables (which apply to a population in mass), the result would be, from 50 to 60, above four weeks' illness, and from 60 to 70, above eight weeks' illness, during the year.

If this rate be compared to that which seems to occur among the members of *friendly socie-ties* (chiefly composed of artisans and agricultural labourers), the advantage is much in favour of the latter. The Highland Society reports the average of sickness under the age of 50 to be only ·76 decimal parts of a week; between 50 and 60 to be $1\frac{88}{100}$ weeks, and between 60 and 70 to be $5\frac{63}{100}$ weeks, in every year.

Messrs. Finlaison and Davies, after much consideration, are of opinion, that this report of the Highland Society falls short of the proportion of sickness which would be experienced in the practice of friendly societies in *England*, in the same degree that the sickness of the army is excessive. They are, therefore, satisfied, that a mean between the two would be a very near approximation to the sickness that in reality occurs. Such a mean exhibits $1\frac{33}{100}$ weeks under the age of 50; $2\frac{97}{100}$ weeks from 50 to 60, and $7\frac{23}{100}$ weeks from 60 to 70, in every year. *

---

* Report made by Messrs. Finlaison and Davies, in answer to the reference made to them by the Committee on Friendly Societies. Printed by order of the House of Commons, 1827.

The number on the sick list of every army appears much larger than the proportion which occurs in other classes of life ; but, on the other hand, the *deaths* of a military hospital are uniformly far less numerous than those of a civil one. This may partly depend on the reluctance of the labouring classes to enter a hospital, except in extreme cases ; and on the natural promptitude which disposes the private soldier to escape duty, and to improve his fare, by becoming the inmate of a residence more comfortable than his usual one. The examination of the bodily condition of the soldier, before his admission, and the composition of an army, which excludes both extreme youth and advanced age, as well as the regularity of exercise and of hours, concur to produce a very simple catalogue of diseases, and a disposition to recovery, such as is seldom, if ever, witnessed in general hospitals.

Soldiers appear to enjoy a better prospect of longevity than sailors, and this is probably owing to their inferior exposure to severe labour, inclemencies of weather, and privations in the article of food. The mortality of Greenwich Hospital, on an average of 10 years, is about 240 annually in 3000 men. At the Hospital of Chelsea the mortality is less considerable, but the amount is not in my possession. At Chelsea, however, the number of invalids is small in comparison, and we are always to bear in mind the tendency of large accumulations of individuals to detract somewhat from the chances of health and of life.

CHAP. XV.

STATISTICS OF THE SEXES.—COMPARATIVE FRUITFULNESS
OF MARRIAGE IN VARIOUS COUNTRIES.

HUFELAND asserts, from extensive examination, that the relative numbers of the sexes are in all parts of the world the same, namely, 21 males to 20 females.   But a greater number of still-births generally occurs among males, and there is also a greater mortality of males in infancy; so that at the age of 14 or 15 the sexes are nearly equal.

According to Casper, the proportion of females to males, among the still-born at Berlin, is so remarkably small, that in every 48 still-births 28 are males, and only 20 of the other sex, but this minority is not universal.   In the kingdom of Hanover the proportion has been nearly equal, or exactly adapted to the relative numbers of the sexes.

The proportion of males to females born at the Dublin Lying-in Hospital, during 70 years, has been about 12 to 11.

Some travellers have imagined, that in warm climates a greater number of females is born than of males; an idea, probably, originally excited by the number of women who are secluded in the mansions of the richer inhabitants of the East. On reports of this nature, Montesquieu concluded that polygamy is excusable in certain regions. But we are not aware of a single statistical fact which has been brought to support the theory; while, on the other hand, from the registers of baptisms preserved by the Danish missionaries of Tranquebar, from the lists formed by the Dutch at Amboyna and at Batavia, and from the information procured at Bagdad and at Bombay by Niebuhr, we have every reason to believe that the proportion of the sexes is the same in the East as in Europe.

Some curious facts have been communicated to the French Academy of Sciences by M. Giron de Buzareingues, relative to the inequalities which occur in different departments of France, in the proportion of male and female births. Of course they are not cited here as establishing a general principle : their value must be determined by a series of observations in other places.

M. Giron has made several experiments on sheep, horses, and birds, which indicate, that when the male is too young, and the female in full vigour, the proportion of female births exceeds that of male, and *vice versâ*. He affirms that, by attention to this circumstance, we may at will produce an excess of males, or of females, in our flocks, studs, and poultry-yards.

Pursuing these enquiries with regard to the

human species, he divides individuals into different classes : the first is composed of persons whose employments tend to develope their bodily powers ; the second, of those whose business tends to enervate ; the third, of those whose occupations are of a mixed description. He found that in the first class the number of male births exceeded the average proportion of male to female births throughout France ; that in the second class the number of female births exceeded the average proportion of female to male births throughout France ; and that in the third class the proportion of male to female births was nearly the same as the average proportion throughout France.

He arrives at the conclusion, that the pursuits of agriculture tend to the increase of the male population, and that the habits of commerce, and of manufactures, favour an augmentation of the female population.

The variety in the proportion of births to a marriage in various countries is a subject of discussion which it is far more easy to lay before the reader in detail than to explain. M. Benoiston de Chateauneuf has lately read before the Academy of Sciences at Paris a most elaborate memoir on this topic. We shall avail ourselves of many of the facts which he has stated, without repeating his conclusions, which do not always correspond with the examples :

he believes, for instance, that the fecundity of marriage is less in those countries which are deficient in agriculture, industry, or liberty, whereas we shall perceive a contrary tendency in most of the following examples.

In England, from 1800 to 1810, the proportion of births to marriages, as corrected by Malthus, was 4 to 1, and from 1810 to 1821 about 4·22 to 1.

In France the proportion of births to a marriage is 4·21.

In Holland, 4·20.

In Scotland, 4·2. (M. Chateauneuf finds this to have been the general average for the ten years ending in 1793, from comparing the tables contained in 17 out of the 21 volumes published by Sinclair on the Statistics of Scotland.)

In Prussia, according to Hoffmann, $3\frac{1}{8}$.

In Wirtemberg, according to Memminger, $4\frac{13}{20}$.

In Sweden, 3·62.

In Russia, 5·25.

In Portugal, 5·14.

In the province of Bergamo, 5·24.

In the government of Venice, 5·45.

In Savoy, 5·65.

In the canton of Friburg, 5·35.

In Bohemia, 5·27.

The proportion of the southern provinces of France is 4·34, but of some of the northern only

4·00. This was also observed to be the case fifty years ago. M. Chateauneuf inclines to the opinion, that fecundity is greater in the south than in the north.

At St. Domingo, in 1788, three marriages only afforded an average of two births among the blacks, while the average of births to the whites was three to each union.

Within the limits of every country numerous varieties exist. At Paris the average is scarcely 2.44, while in some villages of Scotland it is so high as 7.

Some of these estimates, however, are differently given by other writers ; and altogether it is a subject on which it would be at present premature to generalise.

Mr. Sadler proposes to demonstrate, that the fecundity of human beings is, *cæteris paribus*, in the inverse ratio of the condensation of their numbers, and that the variation in that fecundity is effectuated not by the misery but by the happiness and prosperity of the species. He promises in a future work to produce the details on which this view is founded.* Muret †, so long ago as 1766, appears to have entertained a somewhat similar opinion. He was astonished at finding that the proportion of births in the

---

Ireland, its Evils, and their Remedies. 8vo. Lond. 1828.
† Mém. Soc. Economique de Berne.

Pays de Vaud was much less than in other
countries, although the duration of life was
greater ; and came to the conclusion, that healthy
countries, having less fecundity, will not over-
people themselves ; and that the unhealthy
countries, by their extraordinary fecundity, will
be able to sustain their population. We shall
pursue this subject in the ensuing chapter.

CHAP. XVI.

APPLICATION OF MEDICAL STATISTICS TO ILLUSTRATE
THE PRINCIPLE OF POPULATION. — CONCLUSION. —
GENERAL PRINCIPLES.

WHEREVER registers of births, deaths, and marriages have been kept for a long period, it has
been uniformly found that improvement in the
public health, and the absence of epidemics,
have been attended by a diminished proportion
of marriages and of births. In the degree in
which a nation advances in prosperity and civilisation, premature and imprudent marriages become less frequent, and the number of births is
accordingly lessened. Thus in England the
annual proportion of marriages has diminished
since the early part of the last century, when it
was estimated at 1 amongst 115 individuals. The
census of 1801 lowered the proportion to 1 in
123, that of 1811 to 1 in 126, and, finally, in
1821 we find only 1 in 131. Accordingly the
proportion of births was in 1801 as 1 in 34·8 of
the population, in 1811 it was 1 in 35·3, and
in 1821 only 1 in 36·58. Malthus remarks,
that " marriages, births, and deaths diminish
generally in proportion to the increasing healthi-

ness of a country ;" and we have had repeated
occasion to remark the connection and re-action
which subsist between the prosperity and the
health of a country or city.

Süssmilch has given many instances of this
gradual diminution of marriages, which evince
the dependence of the marriages on the deaths
in all old countries.* These views are so calculated to dispel the apprehensions which a superficial observer might entertain of the future over-
growth of population, while viewing the gradual
improvement in the tenure of life, that I shall
wander a little from my road to produce the
consolatory reflections of *Say*, one of the leading
authorities in Political Economy, and assuredly
no juvenile enthusiast. " Independently of
those causes which, in different states, destroy
the proportion between the number of births
and that of the population, there is another cause
which, in a particular country, totally changes
this proportion, — it is the mean duration of life.
In fact, as the number of men cannot exceed
their means of subsistence, *if men live longer, a
less number is born*, and the human race is maintained at its complement with fewer births and
with fewer deaths, a contingency much more favourable to its happiness. That the duration of
the mean life has become prolonged among the

Malthus, Suppl. Encyclopæd. Brit. art. Population.

chief part of the civilised nations of the globe, is
a fact which can no longer be doubted. Since
we have used linen next to the skin instead of
wool * ; since we have inhabited more airy
dwellings ; since we have paid more attention
to cleanliness, and bestowed more enlightened
cares on infancy ; since we have learned to
remedy evils formerly incurable, and to prevent
the invasion of certain diseases like the small-
pox, — the life of man is sensibly lengthened.
This is not the reason which makes the population more numerous (for such an effect never
takes place permanently, except by means of
an augmentation of production) ; but it is the
reason that causes a certain number of people to
renew themselves less frequently. There are
very great advantages in this new form of our
peopling ; but it is not my present object
to explain them ; I have remarked on them
elsewhere. † Several positive and curious facts
confirm this observation. We know, for instance,
that the population of Paris has considerably increased since the middle of the eighteenth century. It did not then amount to 600,000 souls;

* La Reine Isabeau de Bavière, femme de Charles VI., fut
la première personne en France qui porta des chemises de
toile. Auparavant, on avait des chemises de serge, et les
maladies de la peau etaient bien plus fréquentes et plus
difficiles à guérir. (*Say.*)

† Traité d'Economie Politique. 3d ed. ii. 391.

it now exceeds 800,000. Nevertheless, the number of births is scarcely increased! *Lalande* finds that the mean number of annual births from 1745 to 1756 was 23,391; and the mean annual number of births in the years 1817—1821, was only 24,214; that is to say, only 823 births more than at the former period. The population has increased one third, and the number of births one twenty-eighth part. One child was formerly born amongst $25\frac{65}{100}$ inhabitants; and at present there is only one child born amongst more than 33 inhabitants. We may make a similar observation on the movement of the population of London."*

The researches of Mr. F. Villot† tend to mark the later period at which marriages are contracted in an advanced state of society, and the less considerable number of births which is likely to result. On examining the marriage-registers of Paris kept during the eighteenth century, he finds, that the average age of the man at the moment of marriage was about 29 years, and that of the woman about 24 years. The average age of the father on the birth of *a son* was about 33 years, and of a mother about 28 years.

---

* Revue Encyclopedique. Sept. 1827.

† Memoir read at the Acad. of Sciences, in July, 1828, by F. Villot, Archivist, and Director of the Statistical Office of Paris.

After enumerating so many varieties in the distribution of mortality, it remains to consider shortly the causes which diminish it, and which, in our own country, have rendered that diminution so conspicuous.

The *particular* causes have been generally admitted for some years : such as improvements in ventilation and in the general economy of hospitals; the common adoption of a more rational treatment of disease, and particularly of the antiphlogistic plan, which, under various names, has acquired an almost universal currency. The particular causes chiefly affect disease already formed, and promote a favourable termination.

The *general* causes act on the entire mass of a nation, and operate in the prevention of disease. Some of these have already been the subject of remark.

Among the general causes, the increase of commercial and agricultural industry has multiplied the comforts of the lower classes, and has enabled them to procure a more spacious dwelling, more frequent changes of clothing, and more abundant and more wholesome food ; insomuch, that the average mortality and health of every nation are mainly determined by the degree in which its government has encouraged these pursuits, or has checked their free course. So intimate a connection subsists between po-

litical changes and the public health, that where-
èver feudal distinctions have been abolished,
wherever the artisan or the peasant have been
released from arbitrary enactments, there also
the life of the lower classes has acquired a new
vigour ; and it is certain, that even bodily
strength and the power of enduring hardships
are divided among the nations of the earth in
a proportion relative to their prosperity and
civilisation. *

We may easily conceive the different constitution of body and of mind which is likely to grow
upon the unemployed inhabitant of a decayed
city, who gloomily wanders without an object
through silent streets whose pavement is choked
with grass ; and upon the active citizen who
feels himself a constituent member of a flourishing community, and who is attracted on all sides
by invitations to the exercise of his faculties.

It is indisputable, that the average proportion
of deaths in England and her cities is less than
that of any other country of Europe.   And it

---

* The experiments which Péron made with Regnier's
dynamometer illustrate this assertion.   The details are
seen in his *Voyage aux Terres Australes.* He found that
the natives of New Holland are stronger in the hands and
loins than those of Van Dieman's Land, the natives of the
Isle of Timor than those of New Holland ; but the French
were stronger than all these, and the English were stronger
than the French.

may be added, that the powers of body and of mind are preserved to a late period in higher perfection here than in other countries: nowhere are the advances of age so slowly perceived, and nowhere so little manifested on the exterior. An analogous condition of health and vigour may be also observed in our animals and in our vegetation; and if it should be replied, that this excellence is owing to the care bestowed on their culture, the answer applies equally to the human being, on whom more attention is here bestowed, and who is really an object of greater value here than elsewhere.

If political and moral circumstances actually possess so preponderant an influence on the production of disease, and on the guidance of its fatality, it seems to be incumbent on our profession to study their progress, and to profit by their results. A peculiar set of diseases appears to belong to every age, and it may be almost affirmed, that there is also a mode of treatment adapted to every age. But the science of medicine, purified from obsolete mysteries, no longer idly promises to extend existence beyond the term originally assigned to it, and only endeavours to conduct the feeble and the unfortunate in safety to the natural boundaries of their present being. And altogether we must conclude, that the causes which shorten life are generally those which render it miserable ; and that wherever a people enjoys a higher degree of prosperity, of rational freedom, and of moral dignity, there also will a greater number of individuals reap the full harvest of their years.

THE END.

A TREATISE ON MAN

AND THE DEVELOPMENT OF HIS FACULTIES.

By M. A. QUETELET,

PERPETUAL SECRETARY OF THE ROYAL ACADEMY OF BRUSSELS, CORRESPONDING
MEMBER OF THE INSTITUTE OF FRANCE, ETC.

NOW FIRST TRANSLATED INTO ENGLISH.

EDINBURGH:

PUBLISHED BY WILLIAM AND ROBERT CHAMBERS.

1842.

Republished in 1973 by Gregg International Publishers Limited
Westmead, Farnborough, Hants, England

PUBLISHERS' NOTICE.

THE present work was first printed and issued in Paris in 1835, with the title, " Sur L'Homme, et le Développement de ses Facultés, par M. A. Quetelet, Secrétaire Perpetuel de l'Académie Royale de Bruxelles," &c. &c. (2 volumes 8vo.) Previous to its appearance, the author had attained a high reputation among men of science, being distinguished peculiarly by the cautious, accurate, and comprehensive character of all.his researches, and by his skill and acumen in applying the important science of numbers to every subject which he investigated. The treatise " Sur L'Homme" brought him a large accession of well-merited fame. It was the first attempt made to apply the art of calculation to the social movements of the human being, and to examine by it his moral anatomy, with the view of detecting the real sources and amount of the evils under which he labours, and, ulteriorly, of remedying them when known. Of the nature of the remarkable truths developed by M. Quetelet, it would not be proper here to speak; nor is it necessary, as the work itself will sufficiently indicate and explain them. Suffice it to state, that the impression made by the treatise over the whole of continental Europe, through criticisms, republications, and translations, has been very great. Fully convinced of its value, Messrs Chambers gladly embraced a proposal which was made to them to publish an English translation, and to present it in such a form and at such a price as might be most calculated to promote its diffusion throughout all sections of the community.

On learning that a British edition was in progress, M. Quetelet came forward in the most handsome manner, and proffered a new preface, which accordingly is presented here in a translated form. In this composition, the object of the author has been, at once to defend his treatise from objections brought against it subsequently to the issue of the original Parisian edition, and also to point out in what manner he intended, in his projected continuations of the work, to follow up and elucidate the principles already laid down by him. It will probably be admitted by the majority of readers, that he has most ably defended his views and estimate of the physical, moral, and intellectual qualities of man, with their results upon his position in society. He has refuted the objections brought against his mode of reasoning ; and has cleared himself of the charge of being either a materialist or a fatalist. He shows, also, that he is no theorist or system-maker, but simply wishes to arrive at truth by the only legitimate way, namely, the examination of *facts* —the incontrovertible facts furnished by statistical data. Lastly, he conveys the important information, that the experience of every additional year, since the first publication of his treatise, proves, in the most remarkable manner, the accuracy both of his statistical tables and the inferences founded upon them. His section on crime, in particular, however startling it may have appeared to the world, has been shown, by fresh statistical information, to merit credit in every particular. On these accounts, the publishers are confident that the prefatory matter with which they have been favoured by the distinguished Belgian philosopher, will be felt by the public greatly to enhance the value of the present edition.

It seems only necessary to add, that the present translation has been effected under the able superintendence of Dr R. KNOX, F.R.S.E., Corresponding Member of the French Academy of Medicine, and Lecturer on Anatomy in Edinburgh ; and that the work, in its passage through the press, has been indebted to the editorial care of Mr THOMAS SMIBERT, who has also translated the manuscript preface of M. Quetelet. Considering its native value, and these acquired advantages, the publishers present it with the confident hope that it will form a valuable addition to the philosophical literature of their country.

EDINBURGH, *November* 5, 1841.

CONTENTS.

PREFACE OF M. QUETELET,

DRAWN UP EXPRESSLY FOR THE PEOPLE'S EDITION OF HIS WORK ON MAN.

THE plan which has been pursued by me in the composition of this work, is a vast and comprehensive one. It was therefore natural, that, before drawing up a sequel to it, I should endeavour to learn the opinions of competent persons respecting the character of my researches, and the mode of execution which had been adopted in my treatise.* But in presenting, as it were, only the vestibule of the edifice, I might justly entertain fears lest sufficient light had not been cast on the matter, and lest I should not have been able to make it clear how all the portions of the vast whole were to arrive at agreement and consistency among themselves. In this state of things, it struck me that I could not do better than show, by particular examples, in what manner it is expedient in general to proceed in this line of inquiry, and in what light I viewed the analysis of man, under the triple relations of his physical, moral, and intellectual qualities.

The development of the three examples which I have chosen, will themselves give birth to as many works, the materials of which I am collecting with all the activity and speed that other engagements incidental to my position will permit. Whilst waiting till I can terminate these labours, I have deemed it right to give here an indication of them, and this will afford me, at the same time, an opportunity of clearing up some points in my published treatise, which may have been imperfectly understood.

As regards the *physique* of man, subjects of research are not wanting; but, besides that many of these subjects—as, for example, that of population—have frequently been discussed, and by men of great ability, they do not appear to me to be all equally suited to the end which I propose to attain; some are even complicated by their intimate dependence on moral phenomena, and these I wish to steer clear of as far as possible. The interest excited by the first researches into the growth of the human being, and the happy applications made of them in England, determined my choice of a subject, leading me to direct attention to the proportions of the human frame at different ages, and the causes which modify them. The subject appertains at once to science and the fine arts; and my relations in society permitted me to count upon the assistance of men of enlightenment, who promised to co-operate with me in my inquiries.

The study of the proportions of the human frame was carried very far by the Grecian artists, but they have left us no other monuments of their knowledge than those admirable works of sculpture, which the moderns regard to this day as models, and to which they resort for their finest inspirations. The principal artists of the era of the revival of letters, such as Leon Baptista Alberti, Michael Angelo, Leonardo da Vinci, Albert Durer, with many others who comprehended what art ought to borrow from science, felt the neces-

* The work upon Man was published at Paris in 1835. In the year following, a copy of it was printed at Brussels; and, in 1838, Dr Riecke gave a German translation of the work, enriched with notes. The Brussels copy was published without my participation, and indeed against my will; such was not the case with the German version, concerning which I had communications with Dr Riecke.

sity of resorting to observation, in order to rebuild in some sort the ruined monument of ancient artistical skill. They studied nature in a philosophical manner; sought to strike out the limits within which they ought to confine themselves in order to be truthlike, without taking away from each age, and one may say from any passion, its individual character; and from those profound studies which kept them ever before the face of nature, they deduced original views and new models, destined to distinguish for ever that celebrated age. The proportions of the human body did not alone attract their attention: anatomy, perspective, and chemistry, formed parts of their studies; nothing was neglected; and some of these great artists even gained for themselves a first place among the geometers of their day. Their successors have not devoted themselves to such serious studies, and hence it so frequently happens that they are reduced to content themselves, either with copying from those who went before them, or with working after individual models, whose proportions they modify according to mere caprice, without having any just or proper ideas of the beautiful.

It would be an error, doubtless, to suppose that science *makes* the artist; yet it lends to him the most powerful assistance. In general, it is difficult to keep it within due limits; and I shall even freely admit, that Albert Durer, in his work upon the proportions of the human frame, has imparted to it a certain scientific dryness, which lessens its utility. One finds there more of the geometer than the artist, and the geometer, moreover, such as he was at a time when it had not yet been discovered how much the rules of style enhance the value of scientific works, and, above all, of those which appertain at the same time to the domain of the fine arts.

After the example of Leon Baptista Alberti, whom he followed closely in the order of time, Albert Durer commences by stating the divisions of the body, in parts or proportions of the total height taken by him as *unity*. Changing afterwards his measure of proportions, he takes as unity the size of the head, and assigns successively the proportions of several individuals, giving them seven, eight, nine, and even ten heads of height [or, in other words, a body corresponding to the measurement of so many heads]. The scale thus formed by him has been received into all studios; and, without reverting *very* often to the measurements which their predecessors had taken from nature or from the works of the Greeks, artists have, for the most part, bound themselves down to follow a blind routine. Noble exceptions, however, have presented themselves. Nicholas Poussin, one of the most profound thinkers whom the arts have produced, took care to correct and regulate by the *antique* the proportions which Leon Baptista Alberti and Albert Durer had given from the living model. At a later period, also, some labours have been undertaken on this subject; and I may mention, in particular, those of the sculptor, Shadow of Berlin.

My aim has been, not only to go once more through the task of Albert Durer, but to execute it also on an extended scale. The German artist had his art exclusively in view, and confined himself to the observation and exhibition of man when fully developed, and at an age when he presents himself under the most advantageous forms. In order to keep faithfully by the plan which I had chalked out, I have viewed the individual from the hour of his birth; I have sought to determine, for that epoch, the different relations of bulk, subsisting between the various parts of his frame; and to ascertain how far these relations become modified during his development, what they are in the flower of his age, and in what position they remain up to the instant of decay. It is only by long and laborious study, and by the comparison of a vast number of individuals, that it will be possible to succeed in establishing correct average proportions for each age, and in settling the limits betwixt which they can be made to vary, without ceasing to be accurate and faithful to nature—our first and great guide in this difficult study.

If the inquiry into the average bodily proportions be of high importance, in order to attain to the type of beauty in the arts, not less great is the interest attached to the subject of the limits within which variations of them must be kept, in order not to shock the taste, and in order to retain the means of giving character to individual forms, of shadowing forth strength, grace, and dignity of figure, and of preserving to art that variety which constitutes its principal charm. Although *artistical* limits will always be less extended than the *natural* limits, yet it is to be observed that, by the term natural limits, I understand those within which the human proportions may vary, not only without constituting deformities and monstrous aberrations from nature, but also without wounding the eye by a want of harmony.

In order that the taste may be satisfied, it is necessary to present to it a whole of which it can seize readily all the parts, and mark their relations of bulk. But what are the natural limits spoken of? They are doubtless difficult to establish; nevertheless, every one has an idea of them, more or less exact, which he carries with him in his decisions. It is to determine these in a more precise manner that our endeavours ought to be directed. " This statue is beautiful," people will say ; but they will agree in finding that the arms are too long. Without such a defect, it would have possessed more grace. The defect, at the same time, does not constitute a monstrosity, not even an anomaly ; it may be conceived to exist in nature, and even without displeasing the taste ; but it wounds the eye in a work of art, open to more severe rules of judgment.

In order to discover to what extent tastes and forms might vary in different countries, I have endeavoured to compare the proportions of the models, which, in the opinion of the artists of Paris, Rome, Belgium, and other places, united the most perfect graces of form ; and I have been surprised to find how little variety of opinion exists, in different places, regarding what they concurred in terming the beautiful. Changes of bodily proportions characterise nations to a much smaller degree than differences in physiognomical expression, in delicacy and suppleness of members, and in ease, greater or lesser, of gait—all of them qualities modified singularly by education, climate, and habitudes.

Nor am I to confine myself, in my extended inquiry, to the comparison of actual models, estimated as types of the beautiful ; I propose also to unite my results to those which artists left to us at the revival of the arts, and, above all, to what we can gather of the knowledge of the ancients on this point, from a study of their works. These comparisons, I conceive, will present hints interesting to history and art ; they will prove of not less importance to the natural history of man. Analogous labours, undertaken in different quarters of the globe, would enable us to appreciate all that distinguishes race from race, and to discover the relative points of bulk most liable to variation ; they would also furnish for the future valuable elements of comparison, not yet possessed by science.

All the sciences tend necessarily to the acquirement of greater precision in their appreciations. The study of diseases, and of the deformities to which they give place, has shown the benefit derivable from corporeal measurements, effected under enlightened views; but in order to recognise whatever is an anomaly, it is essentially necessary to have established the type constituting the normal or healthy condition. In order to be of use to science, I have deemed it necessary to direct my researches in a particular manner to the dimensions of the chest, which seem most frequently to merit consideration in the state of illness; and the same region is the one where the greatest malformations are most often to be observed.

The relative proportions of the human head merit equally our serious attention, serving, as they do at this day, for a basis, so to speak, of a new science. One of the individuals whose writings have spread the greatest interest respecting the study of phrenology, Mr George Combe, addressed to me, on the subject of the work on Man, the following words, which I shall beg leave to transcribe here, on account of the ingenious hints which they convey on the subject under consideration :—" Allow me to observe, that I desire much to see the physiology of the brain made the basis of such investigations, because I am convinced that the size, quantity, and proportions of the brain in individuals, have an influence over the development of their faculties, which is fundamental—that is to say, the brain determines the strength and the bent of the natural dispositions, and also the kind and degree of the intellectual capacity ; and all external influences merely direct these to certain objects in preference to others, excite them to action, or impede their manifestations, but without changing the primitive character. Criminals, for instance, have the animal organs largely developed, and those of the moral and intellectual faculties, or at least the moral, deficient ; and the causes of the regularity in the number of crimes will be found in the causes which produce a given number of defective brains annually ; and crimes must be diminished by lessening the production of imperfect brains, or by treating those who have them as moral patients, and preventing them from abusing their propensities. Your researches are exceedingly interesting and useful, and all that I mean to say is, that this element is wanting to render them complete."

Nothing, doubtless, could be more interesting, above all in studying the moral development of man, than to be able to follow simultaneously the development of the organs which seem most directly connected with our actions, and to estimate to what extent the instrument is in concord with the effects produced by it. But for that purpose, it would be necessary that the science should be farther advanced than it really is ; and that we should know the modifications which the head and brain of man undergo, from birth to the period of complete development, as well as the epochs at which the divers organs, regarded as the seats of such and such passions and propensities, manifest themselves, and what are their degrees of increase, actual and proportionate. This science, it seems to me, leaves as yet much to desire, and for the mere reason that it is yet in its infancy. I conceive that, in its actual condition, time would be more profitably expended in separating two kinds of studies which, in their results, might respectively control each other, than in seeking to amalgamate them, by which might be incurred the risk of falling into theoretic ideas, and quitting the path to truth. I shall explain myself by an example. Observation shows, that, in our state of society, it is about the age of twenty-five when the propensity to crime is at the maximum, especially as far as murder is concerned ; this is a fact fully established, and of which new evidence is given every year by the statistical records of France. Now, supposing that phrenology had made sufficient inquiries into the development of the organs, it might be possible to determine whether or not the age of twenty-five is really that at which the destructive organs have reached their greatest development, and if they sustain a progressive diminution afterwards, or are repressed by other and more powerful organs.

In considering matters under this point of view, it would be necessary first to study the progressive and proportionate growth of the brain and its several parts, and the development also of our moral and intellectual qualities. Comparisons might then be established to determine if the development of the faculties, and of the cerebral organs regarded as specially connected with them, takes place in a simultaneous manner. But to explain the actions by the organs, to render the one subordinate to the exercise of the other, would be to ramble widely from the course I have followed; for I am less desirous to explain phenomena than to establish their existence.

I have always comprehended with difficulty, moreover, how persons, pre-occupied doubtless by other ideas, have seen any tendency to materialism in the exposition of a series of facts deduced from statistical documents. In giving to my work the title of Social Physics, I have had no other aim than to collect, in a uniform order, the phenomena affecting man, nearly as physical science brings together the phenomena appertaining to the material world. If certain deplorable facts present themselves with an alarming regularity, to whom is blame to be ascribed? Ought charges of materialism to be brought against him who points out that regularity? What I have read and heard on the subject of my work, proves to me that I have not carried conviction to every mind, and that I have frequently been judged with prejudice. Judgments upon books are formed with even more haste and levity than judgments upon men. Writings are talked of without being known; and people take up an opinion for or against, in consequence of decisions of which it would cost them some trouble to determine the source. These are evils which must be borne with patience, and the more so because they are common. "There are few works on political economy," said Malthus to me, "which have been more spoken of and less read than mine." All the absurdities which have been spoken and written respecting the illustrious English author, are well known. Certainly, by an appeal against such decisions, he would have all to gain, and nothing to lose, before a less prejudiced tribunal.

One of the facts which appears to have excited the greatest alarm, out of all pointed to in my work, is naturally that relating to the constancy with which crime is committed. From the examination of numbers, I believed myself justified in inferring, as a natural consequence, that, in given circumstances, and under the influence of the same causes, we may reckon upon witnessing the repetition of the same effects, the reproduction of the same crimes, and the same convictions. What has resulted from this exposition? Timorous persons have raised the cry of fatalism. If, however, some one said, " Man is born free; nothing can force his free-will; he underlies the influence of no external causes; cease to assimilate him to a machine, or to pretend to modify his actions. Therefore, ye legislators, repeal your laws; overturn your prisons; break your chains in pieces; your convictions and penalties are of no avail; they are so many acts of barbarous revenge. Ye philosophers and priests, speak no more of ameliorations, social or religious; you are materialists, because you assume to mould society like a piece of gross clay; you are fatalists, because you believe yourselves predestined to influence man in the exercise of his free-will, and to direct the course of his actions." If, I say, any one held such language to us, we should be disgusted with its excessive folly. And wherefore? Because we are thoroughly convinced that laws, education, and reli-

gion, exercise a salutary influence on society, and that moral causes have their certain effects. Am I a fatalist, then, when I declare that you have greater reason for so thinking than you had imagined? That is the real state of the question; we differ only about degrees. Which of us is in error? To determine this, it is necessary to examine our motives for conviction. Mine, like yours, rest first of all on observation. We both call in experience to the support of our opinions; but, in your case, the experience is based on vague uncertainties, whilst I, more circumspect, strive never to lose sight of those scientific principles which ought to guide the observer in all his investigations. My aim is not to defend systems, or bolster up theories; I confine myself to the citation of facts, such as society presents to our view. If these facts be legitimately established, it follows that we must accept of and accommodate our reason to them.

Now, what do these facts teach us? I repeat, that in a given state of society, resting under the influence of certain causes, regular effects are produced, which oscillate, as it were, around a fixed mean point, without undergoing any sensible alterations. Observe, that I have said *under the influence of the same causes;* if the causes were changed, the effects also would necessarily be modified. As laws and the principles of religion and morality are influencing causes, I have then not only the hope, but, what you have not, the positive conviction, that society may be ameliorated and reformed. Expect not, however, that efforts for the moral regeneration of man can be immediately crowned with success; operations upon masses are ever slow in progress, and their effects necessarily distant.

But, it may be again asked, what becomes of human free-will and agency? In the face of facts, I have not to occupy myself with that question, so often debated. I cannot altogether pass it by, nevertheless, in silence, because it seems to me to involve one of the most admirable laws of conservation in nature—a law which presents a new proof of the wisdom of the Creator, and of which you have not caught even a glimpse in your narrow views of the moral organisation of man. It is necessary, then, to admit that free-will exercises itself within indefinite limits, if one wishes not to incur the reproach of denying it altogether. But, with all the follies which have passed through the head of man, with all the perverse inclinations which have desolated society, what would have become of our race during so many past ages? All these scourges have passed by, and neither man nor his faculties have undergone sensible alterations, as far at least as our observations can determine. This is because the same finger which has fixed limits to the sea, has set similar bounds to the passions of men—because the same voice has said to both, " Hitherto shalt thou come, and no farther!"

What! when it is necessary to take the most simple resolve, we are under the domination of our habitudes, our wants, our social relations, and a host of causes which, all of them, draw us about in a hundred different ways. These influences are so powerful, that we have no difficulty in telling, even when referring to persons whom we are scarcely acquainted with, or even know not at all, what is the resolution to which they will lead such parties. Whence, then, this certainty of foresight, exemplified by you daily, if you were not convinced, at the outset, that it is extremely probable the empire of causes will carry it over free-will. In considering the moral world *a priori,* you give to this free-will the most entire latitude; and when you come to practice, when you speak of what passes around you, you constantly fall into contradiction with yourselves. You foretell the conduct of individuals, in whose case oscillations may take place within limits so large, that it would be contrary to all the principles of the theory of probabilities to take them for the types of calculations, or to found upon them the most petty inferences. Be more consistent with yourselves.

Could you possibly be afraid of applying the calculation of chances to moral phenomena, and of the afflicting consequences which may be inferred from that inquiry, when it is extended to crimes and to quarters the most disgraceful to society? "I should guard myself," said a scientific friend, whose philanthropic views I otherwise respect—"I should guard myself, had I arrived at the afflicting results of which you speak, against grieving others with the relation of them. Draw a veil over the hideous spectacle; and if you believe that you possess the truth, imitate with respect to it the sage circumspection of Fontenelle." But is the anatomy of man not a more painful science still?—that science which leads us to dip our hands into the blood of our fellow-beings, to pry with impassible curiosity into parts and organs which once palpitated with life? And yet who dreams at this day of raising his voice against the study? Who does not applaud, on the contrary, the numerous advantages which it has conferred on humanity? The time is come for studying the moral anatomy of man also, and for uncovering its most afflicting aspects, with the view of providing remedies.

This study is a difficult one. Speculative philosophy has long been occupied with it; but there are questions not to be resolved by such means; speculation has its limits, as observation also has. Every propensity and every passion, develops itself in a manner more or less rapid, attains a degree of maximum intensity, and declines in general by shades not yet fully recognised. It is with the intellectual as with the moral faculties of man; they both have their laws of development. With regard to some of them, these laws march in a parallel relation; others are interwoven in their growth, or stand in manifest opposition. Now, these are the laws which it is necessary to ascertain and comprehend, not in a vague manner, but with such precision as to enable us to establish numerically the degree of intensity for each age. There lay, if I do not deceive myself, the novel feature of my labours; thence sprung, at least, the chief meed of praise, and the criticisms which I have received; and it is this principle which I must strive to justify by my ulterior labours, because I was compelled to limit myself, in a first essay, to simple indications.

The analysis of the moral man through his actions, and of the intellectual man through his productions, seems to me calculated to form one of the most interesting parts of the sciences of observation, applied to anthropology. It may be seen, in my work, that the course which I have adopted is that followed by the natural philosopher, in order to grasp the laws that regulate the material world. By the seizure of facts, I seek to rise to an appreciation of the causes whence they spring.* As I could only indicate this course summarily, and the difficulties embarrassing it, I have been desirous to show, by two examples, selected and

treated in a searching manner, how the course in question should be followed. The one has for its object the examination of works of literature, philosophy, science, the fine arts, &c., and of the ages at which they have been produced, with the results to be deduced from the whole. The other example concerns the development of the propensity to crime, upon a scale more extended than I had yet had an opportunity of forming. After these last new researches, I conceive I may now confidently say, that the *tables of criminality* for different ages, given in my published treatise, merit at least as much faith as the tables of mortality, and verify themselves within perhaps even narrower limits; so that crime pursues its path with even more constancy than death. Twelve years have elapsed since the data furnished by the tribunals of justice in France were collected with great care and exactitude, and since the ages of criminals were first marked; and, in each succeeding year, they have reckoned from about 7000 to 8000 individuals accused before the courts of assize; and it is still betwixt the ages of twenty-one and twenty-five, that, all things being equal, the greatest number of persons are to be found in that position. I have taken, for the same years, and for the city of Paris, the mortality of a period of ten years, and have found, that, though my observations included a much larger number of persons, and these pertaining to a much more homogeneous population, the mortality of the capital proceeded with less regularity than the crimes of the kingdom, and that each age paid a more uniform and constant tribute to the jail than to the tomb.

An objection has been made to my views, which appears somewhat valid at a first glance. It has been forcibly reproduced by a writer of merit, who, while treating my work with liberality, has drawn together all the gravest objections brought forward against it. I shall take leave to cite his words. "We now reach the most delicate portion of M. Quetelet's work—the development of the intellectual and moral qualities, the social system. Here the field is not the same; we have no longer to do with phenomena vital and regular, or with those laws to which man is subjected along with the brutes, and which operate continually without his intervention, or constitute instincts in him too powerful to be resisted. We have to consider things which he is at liberty to do or not to do—acts which he may consummate or not consummate at choice. We enter into the domain of the human will—free, bold, and independent. Can science follow man in this new route? Will it be able to appreciate, in a manner at once comprehensive and exact, the results of the physiological and moral constitution of the mind and soul which distinguish him from other animals? Contented to follow, up to this point, the material phenomena revealed by evident facts, can science sound the heart of man, dive into the mysteries of spiritual being, and tear away for the human race the veil which the moralist can with

* This appreciation is in general very difficult, and has given rise to grave errors. One of the chief causes of these errors seems to me to spring from the *incomplete enumerations*, made when it is sought to give an account of the causes which have led to any result. Thus, it is recognised that in some locality crimes are very numerous, and an attempt is made to explain that unfavourable state of things. How do most writers and even statisticians proceed in such a case? In place of passing in review all the causes which can lead to crime, of weighing their influences, and of inquiring into those, above all, which have acted with the greatest energy, they only attend, in the prejudiced state of their minds, to one alone, often the least influential of all, to which they ascribe the effects produced by the whole. They have been led in this manner to conclude that popular instruction produces crime, because, in such and such a kingdom, the provinces where it chiefly abounds send the greatest number of children to schools; as if the degree of instruction, and the kind of instruction, and other elements, did not all enter equally into the question. The true talent of the observer, it seems to me, whatever be the phenomena of which he

seeks to estimate the causes, consists in a complete enumeration of these, and in distinguishing between such as are entitled to weight, and such as may be overlooked without inconvenience. It is this fine insight, this delicate tact, principal attributes of superior intelligences, which constitute the great observer, the true philosopher. To wander from this course is to step into error, and to become entangled in those interminable disputes which afflict the sciences, and, above all, those whose phenomena are most complex. The medical sciences offer sad examples of this evil. Maladies are in general the result of an infinity of causes; and wherefore attribute them, then, to one of these more than to another? It may be conceived that two physicians, in citing each a different cause as the origin of one disease, may be both in the right, since each may have found the cause stated by him to have predominated in the case under his notice; the only err in neglecting the other influential causes which the have not had the chance of observing, because the number of their observations was too limited. This is the history of man of the theories and systems, alternately adopted and rejected in medicine.

difficulty raise in order to judge one individual? Risks she not being stranded in the conflict with these supreme mysteries of intelligence? Upon what constant facts, upon what fundamental points, can she lean for support? The facts of birth, growth, and decay, are the same for all men; but what are held by one people to be intelligence, genius, morality, and crime, will these not be deemed by another people error, poverty of intellect, immorality, and lawful actions? Finally, will not the free-will and agency of man disconcert all calculations? Or, at least, will not the errors in such calculations be too considerable in number and extent to leave them any real value?"*

I have already spoken of free-will, and have shown how little it influences the number of crimes, and the ages of criminals; I shall not return, therefore, to that subject. The next most serious objection which seems to present itself here is, that the facts upon which one is compelled to rest have not the same identical value, as in the case of birth, death, and marriage, when the population is treated of; but that these facts may vary through many different shades, and may even be qualified amongst different nations, in consequence of what is crime with one being viewed as something lawful with another.

We must here understand ourselves fully. I can admit that a certain act, which is punished before the French tribunals, may not be so in other places, or have been so in other times. This is, then, an error of denomination which should be corrected, and which would but prove at most that virtues and crimes, estimated in relation to different times, have a contingent value merely, not an absolute one. The essential point here is, that the fact, qualified in one manner or another, should be the same. But it will be said, that it is not identically the same, and that even where the laws take care to specify and define different crimes, those which are ranged under the same head may still vary within pretty extensive limits. This is equivalent to saying, that the observations have not all the precision necessary, and that the estimate cannot be perfect. Now, this is a fact which I myself readily admit and regret; for, if the observations were precise, I should march on, in the new path which I have sought to open up, with as much assurance as in other quarters of the vast field of the sciences of observation. In every instance, it is not my method that is defective; proper observations alone fail me. But will it be ever impossible to have them perfectly precise? I believe that even at present we have them sufficiently so to enter, at least, on the great problem under consideration. Name them as you will, the actions which society stamps as crimes, and of which it punishes the authors, are reproduced every year, in almost exactly the same numbers; examined more closely, they are found to divide themselves into almost exactly the same categories; and, if their number were sufficiently large, we might carry farther our distinctions and subdivisions, and should always find there the same regularity. It will then remain correct to say, that a given species of actions is more common at one given age than at any other given age.

Is it really true, moreover, that the designation of crime may be so very arbitrary, and that that which has been set down as poisoning or assassination, for example, may testify to no evil inclination? Although we are here in a new field, where facts cannot be estimated mechanically, as in the physical sciences, the difference, nevertheless, is not to be held so great as it may appear at first sight. Even the physical sciences sometimes rest on facts which are not identically the same, as deaths and births should be; and which may lead to appreciations and conclusions more or less great. With the use even of an instrument, when one wishes to discover a temperature, a magnetic declination, or the force and direction of a

wind, does one really find the quantities which are sought? When one measures an individual, is the real height positively discovered? Errors, greater or lesser, may be committed; and observation alone can recognise the limits within which they range. Has the consideration of the average life of man been rejected, because that average rests upon numbers which vary, without doubt, within limits as extended as can be conceived?

But, to reply by the same argument brought against myself, if, in place of reckoning diseases, one wished to specify their nature, and to indicate, as statisticians do, the number of voluntary, violent, and accidental deaths, as well as those produced by natural maladies, without entering at all into the classifications which might be formed of these, would not one lie open to the same objections? Must we refrain from making up a list of suicides, because death may there have been caused by unknown hands, or by accidents of which no one is cognisant, or by some natural means which have operated instantaneously, and left no visible traces behind? And how often does it happen that the author of a suicide only lends his hands involuntarily to a crime of which another has guiltily reduced him to become the victim? One would require to renounce entirely the sciences of observation, if every such difficulty in the way were to be admitted as a let and barrier; and these are only more apparent in my researches, because we are less familiarised with their character.

The same writer whom I have cited, combats me on another point. I have attempted to give an example of the analysis of the development of the passions, which tends to show that their maximum energy is reached about the age of twenty-five years. "So that," said I, "if there existed an art which, in its exercise, developed itself in a ratio with the passions, and without requiring preliminary studies, its maximum of development would occur about the age of twenty-five."* "To this reasoning let us oppose an example," says the Genevese philosopher. "If there has been a writer who has shone brilliantly, and deeply impressed the public, by reason, not of his works and learning, but of the impulses of the passions, certainly Jean Jacques Rousseau is that man. Now, it was not before the age of forty, fifteen years later than the period signalised as the maximum one of his passions, that Rousseau commenced to write." What would be the reply of the author now quoted, whose writings on population are justly esteemed, if I were to say to him in my turn, that the death of J. J. Rousseau did not take place till after the age of 65 years; that is to say, a long period after the epoch signalised by the law of mortality calculated for Geneva, and after he had long passed the average life of man. Must we then conclude that the tables of mortality for Geneva should be rejected? What does one individual example prove in such matters?

I would remark, besides, that the words cited from my work, when viewed isolately, are far from expressing the idea which I wished to attach to them. The works of genius upon which our judgments bear are in general complex; for there is no work, constructed by genius, which does not suppose the exercise of various of its faculties. A skilful analysis could alone make out the part of each of them; I would suggest for this purpose the idea of a work which should have for its object the analytic examination of the development of our intellectual faculties for each age. Now, I have aimed to present, in the work here reproduced, only an essay, only a particular example, of such an analysis, "which tends to show that the maximum of energy of the passions occurs about the age of twenty-five." The minimum is not then determined; and even when it shall be, by a sufficient number of observations, one will no more be able to apply it to any given individual in particular, than

* Bibliothèque Universelle de Genève, July 1835, p. 313. Article of M. E. Mallet.

* "On Man," vol. ii. page 119. Brussels edition.

one could make use of a table of mortality to determine the period of his decease. It should be well understood that social physics never can pretend to discover laws which will verify themselves in every particular, in the case of isolated individuals. The science will have rendered a service sufficiently vast, in giving more precise views upon a host of points, of which vague glimpses only were before possessed. Thus, men speak generally of the age of the passions; they admit, then, that there is an epoch of the life at which the passions act with greater energy? How know they this? Doubtless, by the observation of man. Well, it is observation which the science of social physics will employ, but observation conducted in a more certain manner, after scientific principles, and not resting on fugitive glances of which one can preserve no durable traces.

I trust I may be permitted to notice here another objection which has been made, on the subject of the value which I believed it proper to attribute to average qualities. "You believe, then," it has been said to me, "that the type of health would be a mean betwixt all the constitutions existing—all the states of health? But then you must grant at least that your type would be more perfect if the average were struck upon those alone who were in health." This argument may appear at first sight an embarrassing one; but, when examined more closely, it may easily be shown to rest upon no solid foundations. I believe I might even say, retorting in some measure the argument, that, if the average were taken upon all men, the healthy excepted, it would remain still the same. This only would result, that, in order to obtain that average with an equal degree of precision, it would be necessary to draw it from an infinitely greater number of individuals. We may consider maladies like deviations from the normal state, be it more or be it less; and it is betwixt these contrary conditions that the state of health would be found.

We aim at a target—an end—marked by a point. The arrows go to right and left, high or low, according to the address of the shooters. In the mean time, after a considerable number of trials, the butt, which has not yet been touched, perhaps, a single time, becomes so well pointed out by the marks around it, that they would aid at once in rediscovering it, if it should chance to be lost sight of. Nay, more than this; even aims the most unfortunate may be made to conduce to this end; commencing with those marks which are farthest away, if they be sufficiently numerous, one may learn from them the real position of the point they surround.

This figurative reasoning is applicable, it may easily be conceived, to all inquiries into the physical sciences, and even the moral also, where the point in view is to arrive at means or averages. As stated in the considerations presented at the close of my work, every quality, taken within suitable limits, is essentially good; it is only in its extreme deviations from the mean that it becomes bad. The study of these deviations or anomalies may serve to aid in the determination of the normal state, if it cannot be established in a direct manner. This presumes, it is true, that human nature, in its aberrations, has not a tendency to deviate from the mean in one sense in preference to another, as those who aim at a mark might have a tendency to shoot always too high or too low. Now, nothing proves the existence of any such tendency.

It may be imagined, after the preceding remarks, how much importance I attach to the consideration of *limits*, which seem to me of two kinds, *ordinary* or natural, and *extraordinary* or beyond the natural. The first limits comprise within them the qualities which deviate more or less from the mean, without attracting attention by excess on one side or the other. When the deviations become greater, they constitute the extraordinary class, having itself its limits, on the outer verge of which are things preternatural, or monstrosities. Thus, the men who fall, in respect of height, outside of the ordinary limits, are giants or dwarfs; and if the excess or the deficiency of height surpasses the extraordinary limits, they may be regarded as monstrosities. From the view of the human constitution, also, we may find the state of health and of sickness, and also a condition to be called extraordinary or preternatural. We must conceive the same distinctions in the moral world.

Narrow as may be the natural limits, they are yet too extended, as I have pointed out, when we wish to approach the beautiful in the arts. Artistical limits do not tolerate certain proportions, which nevertheless constitute neither physical defects nor infirmities.

The consideration of limits, upon which I insist, has convinced me more and more of the important part which they play in the social order. One of the most interesting observations which I have had occasion to make, is, that they narrow themselves through the influence of civilisation, which affords, in my eyes, the most convincing proof of human perfectibility. On the one side we approach more closely to what is good and beautiful; on the other, vice and suffering are shut up within narrower limits; and we have to dread less the monstrosities, physical and moral, which have the power to throw perturbation into the social framework. The distinctions which I had already established with care in my work, ought to have proved, methinks, to some less prejudiced judges, how far I am from a blind fatalism, which would regard man as unfit to exercise free-will, or meliorate the future condition of his race.

ON MAN.

INTRODUCTORY.

MAN is born, grows up, and dies, according to certain laws which have never been properly investigated, either as a whole or in the mode of their mutual reactions. Hitherto, the science of Man has been limited to researches, more or less complete, respecting some of its laws, to results deduced from single or insulated observations, and to theories often based on mere glimpses; and these constitute pretty nearly all the materials it possesses. It must be admitted, however, that for nearly two centuries various distinguished men have studiously inquired into the rate of reproduction and mortality of mankind; the differences which age, sex, profession, climate, and seasons, produce in regard of births and deaths, have been assiduously studied. But they have neglected to put forward, with sufficient prominence, the study of his physical development (*bodily growth*), and they have neglected to mark by numbers how individual man increases with respect to weight and height—how, in short, his forces are developed, the sensibility of his organs, and his other physical faculties. They have not determined the age at which his faculties reach their maximum or highest energy, nor the time when they commence to decline. Neither have they determined the relative value of his faculties at different epochs or periods of his life, nor the mode according to which they mutually influence each other, nor the modifying causes. In like manner, the progressive development of moral and intellectual man has scarcely occupied their attention; nor have they noted how the faculties of his mind are at every age influenced by those of the body, nor how his faculties mutually react.

It will be evident that I do not speak here of the speculative sciences, which, for a long time, have unravelled with great acuteness the greater part of the questions within their scope, and which they could attempt directly, avoiding, however, all numerical appreciation of the facts. The void resulting from this neglect must be filled up by the sciences of observation; for, either from a distrust in their own strength, or a repugnance in supposing it possible to reduce to fixed laws what seemed to flow from the most capricious of causes, it has hitherto been deemed expedient by learned men to abandon the line of inquiry employed in the investigation of the other laws of nature, so soon as the moral phenomena of mankind became the object of research. It must also be admitted, in explanation, that observations having for their object the *Science of Man*, present difficulties exceedingly great, and, to merit confidence, must be collected upon a scale far too extended to be attempted by an individual philosopher. Thus, we need not be at all surprised if facts respecting the increase of human weight and height from birth, be not readily found—if even the development of man's bodily strength be not exactly known; and it ought to excite no surprise, if, on these interesting points, the results be confined to mere sketches.

The study of the development of the intellectual qualities present, perhaps, still greater difficulties; but the result will show that these difficulties are more apparent than real.

With respect to the physical or animal forces, it is readily enough admitted that their development depends on the action of nature, and is thus regulated by laws which in certain cases admit of being determined by numbers; but it is asserted, that in respect of the moral or intellectual faculties, over which our volition exercises an influence, it would seem to approach an absurdity, to inquire into laws influenced by a cause at once so capricious and so anomalous as the human will. Hence it has happened that, in the study of man, a difficulty, seemingly insurmountable, was encountered at the very first step; but this difficulty is connected principally with the solution of a question which we shall now examine.

Are Human Actions regulated by Fixed Laws?

Experience alone can with certainty solve a problem which no *à priori* reasoning could determine. It is of primary importance to keep out of view man as he exists in an insulated, separate, or in an individual state, and to regard him only as a fraction of the species. In thus setting aside his individual nature, we get quit of all which is accidental, and the individual peculiarities, which exercise scarcely any influence over the mass, become effaced of their own accord, allowing the observer to seize the general results.

Thus, to explain our meaning by an example—we may instance the case of a person examining too nearly a small portion of a very large circle, and who, consequently, would see in this detached portion merely a certain quantity of physical points, grouped in a more or less irregular manner, and so, indeed, as to seem as if they had been arranged by chance, notwithstanding the care with which the original figure may have been traced. But, placing himself at a greater distance, the eye embraces of necessity a greater number of points, and already a degree of regularity is observable over a certain extent of the segment of the circle; and, by removing still farther from the object, the observer loses sight of the individual points, no longer observes any accidental or odd arrangements amongst them, but discovers at once the law presiding over their general arrangements, and the precise nature of the circle so traced. But let us suppose, as might happen, that the different points of the arch, instead of being material points, were small animated beings, free to act according to their will, in a very circumscribed sphere, yet these spontaneous motions would not be perceived by the eye placed at a suitable distance.

It is in this way that we propose studying the laws which relate to the human species; for, by examining them too closely, it becomes impossible to apprehend them correctly, and the observer sees only individual peculiarities, which are infinite. Even in those cases where the individuals exactly resemble each other, it might still happen that, by examining them separately, some of the most singular laws to which they are subject, under certain influences, might escape for ever the notice of the observer. To him, for example, who had examined the laws of light merely in a single drop of water, the brilliant phenomenon of the rainbow would be totally unintelligible—it might even happen that the idea of the possible existence of such an appearance would never have occurred to him unless accidentally placed in favourable circumstances to observe it.

What idea should we have of the mortality of mankind by observing only individuals? Instead of the admirable laws to which it is subject, our knowledge would be limited to a series of incoherent facts, leading to a total misapprehension of the laws of nature.

The remarks we make respecting human mortality, may be equally extended to man's physical and moral faculties. To attain a knowledge of the general laws regulating these latter (moral) faculties, a sufficient number of observations must be collected, in order to bring out what is constant, and to set aside what is purely accidental. If, in order to facilitate this study, all human actions could be registered, it might be supposed that their numbers would vary from year to year as widely as human caprice. But this is not what we in reality observe, at least for that class of actions of which we have succeeded in obtaining a registry. I shall quote but a single example; but it merits the attention of all philosophic minds. In every thing which relates to crimes, the same numbers are reproduced so constantly, that it becomes impossible to misapprehend it — even in respect to those crimes which seem perfectly beyond human foresight, such as murders committed in general at the close of quarrels, arising without a motive, and under other circumstances to all appearance the most fortuitous or accidental: nevertheless, experience proves that murders are committed annually, not only pretty nearly to the same extent, but even that the instruments employed are in the same proportions. Now, if this occurs in the case of crimes whose origin seems to be purely accidental, what shall we say of those admitted to be the result of reflection?*

This remarkable constancy with which the same crimes appear annually in the same order, drawing down on their perpetrators the same punishments, is a singular fact, which we owe to the statistics of the tribunals. In various writings, I have done my utmost to put this evidence clearly before the public :† I have never failed annually to re-

* The following is the result of the reports of criminal justice in France, &c. :—

	1826.	1827.	1828.	1829.	1830.	1831.
Murders in general, -	241	234	227	231	205	266
Gun and pistol, - -	56	64	60	61	57	88
Sabre, sword, stiletto, poniard, dagger, &c.,	15	7	8	7	12	30
Knife, - - - - -	39	40	34	46	44	34
Cudgels, cane, &c., -	23	28	31	24	12	21
Stones, - - - - -	20	20	21	21	11	9
Cutting, stabbing, and bruising instruments,	35	40	42	45	46	49
Strangulations, - - -	2	5	2	2	2	4
By precipitating and drowning, - - - -	6	16	6	1	4	3
Kicks and blows with the fist, - - - -	28	12	21	23	17	26
Fire, - - - - - -	..	1	..	1	..	..
Unknown, - - - -	17	1	2	..	2	2

† See page 43 of the *Recherches Statistique*, &c., 1809; page 178 of the fifth volume of the *Corresp. Mathematique;* page 214 of the same collection, in the observations on the constancy observed in the number of crimes committed ; page 80 of the *Recherches sur le Penchant au Crime,* &c. [Inquiries into the Propensity to Crime, &c.] After having repeated positively the same statement so many times, I read the following words I confess with surprise, in 1838, in an Essay on the Moral Statistics of France (*Statistique Morale de la France*), the author of which honours me with his correspondence, and is acquainted with my writings :—

peat, that there is a *budget* which we pay with frightful regularity—it is that of prisons, dungeons, and scaffolds. Now, it is this budget which, above all, we ought to endeavour to reduce ; and every year, the numbers have confirmed my previous statements to such a degree, that I might have said, perhaps with more precision, " there is a tribute which man pays with more regularity than that which he owes to nature, or to the treasure of the state, namely, that which he pays to crime." Sad condition of humanity! We might even preuict annually how many individuals will stain their hands with the blood of their fellow-men, how many will be forgers, how many will deal in poison, pretty nearly in the same way as we may foretell the annual births and deaths.

Society includes within itself the germs of all the crimes committed, and at the same time the necessary facilities for their development. It is the social state, in some measure, which prepares these crimes, and the criminal is merely the instrument to execute them. Every social state supposes, then, a certain number and a certain order of crimes, these being merely the necessary consequences of its organisation. This observation, so discouraging at first sight, becomes, on the contrary, consolatory, when examined more nearly, by showing the possibility of ameliorating the human race, by modifying their institutions, their habits, the amount of their information, and, generally, all which influences their mode of existence. In fact, this observation is merely the extension of a law already well known to all who have studied the physical condition of society in a philosophic manner: it is, that so long as the same *causes* exist, we must expect a repetition of the same *effects.* What has induced some to believe that moral phenomena did not obey this law, has been the too great influence ascribed at all times to man himself over his actions : it is a remarkable fact in the history of science, that the more extended human knowledge has become, the more limited human power, in that respect, has constantly appeared. This globe, of which man imagines himself the haughty possessor, becomes, in the eyes of the astronomer, merely a grain of dust floating in the immensity of space: an earthquake, a tempest, an inundation, may destroy in an instant an entire people, or ruin the labours of twenty ages. On the other hand, when man appears most influenced by his own actions, we see paid an annual tribute to nature of births and deaths, as regular as may be. In the regular reproduction of crime, we see again reproduced another proof of the narrow field in which he exercises his individual activity. But if each step in the career of science thus gradually diminishes his importance, his pride has a compensation in the greater idea of his intellectual power, by which he has been enabled to perceive those laws which seem to be, by their nature, placed for ever beyond his grasp.

It would appear, then, that moral phenomena, when observed on a great scale, are found to resemble physical phenomena ; and we thus arrive, in inquiries of this kind, at the fundamental principle, that *the greater the number of individuals observed, the more do individual peculiarities, whether physical or moral, become effaced, and leave in a prominent point of view the general facts, by virtue of which society exists and is preserved.* It belongs only to a few men, gifted with superior genius, to alter sensibly the social state ; and

" Each year reproduces the same number of crimes, in the same order, in the same regions. Each class of crimes has its peculiar and invariable distribution, according to the sex, age, season ; all are accompanied, in equal proportions, with accessory facts, unimportant in appearance, and, but for their return, inexplicable. It becomes necessary to give examples of this fixity in this constancy in the reproduction of facts *hitherto considered as inexplicable* (insaisissables dans leur ensemble), *and as being subject to no law.*" I shall make only *one* observation, which is, that I never considered the number of crimes invariable. I believe, on the contrary, in the perfectibility of the human species.

even this alteration, or action, requires a considerable time to transmit fully its effects. If the power which man possesses of modifying his actions, was communicated immediately to the social system, every kind of prevision or prejudgment would become impossible, and we should expect in vain to find in the past lessons for the future.* But it is not so: when active causes have once established themselves, they display an evident action, even for a long time after efforts have been made to oppose and destroy them; and too much care, therefore, cannot be bestowed in pointing them out, and in suggesting the most efficacious means to modify them in a useful manner. This reaction of man upon himself, is one of his noblest attributes; it offers, indeed, the finest field for the display of his activity. As a member of the social body, he is subjected every instant to the necessity of these causes, and pays them a regular tribute; but as a man, employing all the energy of his intellectual faculties, he in some measure masters these causes, and modifies their effects, thus constantly endeavouring to improve his condition.

How the Laws relative to Man ought to be Studied and Interpreted.

We have just seen that man is placed under the influence of regular and periodic causes, affecting not merely his physical qualities, but likewise his actions; and that these lead to effects equally regular and periodic. Now, these causes, and their mode of action, or the laws to which they give rise, may be determined by a close inquiry; but, as has been already said, in order to succeed, we must study the masses, with the view of separating from our observations all that is fortuitous or individual. Every thing being equal, the calculation of probabilities shows, that in the direct ratio to the number of individuals observed, we approach the nearer to the truth.

By the manner, then, in which these laws have been determined, they present no longer any thing individual; and, consequently, can be applied to individuals only within certain limits. Every application which one might attempt to make to a man in particular, must be essentially false, in the same way as if we were to pretend to determine the precise period of a person's death by looking into the tables of mortality.

Such tables, in respect to particular cases, can give only approximations; and the doctrine of probabilities shows here also that the results deduced from them, and the results observed, agree always the better the greater the number of the individuals to whom they refer. Thus, although the tables of mortality teach us no direct application to an individual, yet they offer very certain results when applied to a great number of persons; and upon these general results, assurance societies calculate their annual profits. We endeavour here to be well understood respecting the nature and value of the laws we propose inquiring into. It is the social body which forms the object of our researches, and not the peculiarities distinguishing the individuals composing it. This study interests, in an especial manner, the philosopher and the legislator: the literary man and the artist, on the contrary, will endeavour to understand, in preference, those peculiarities which we endeavour to separate from our results, and which constitute, as it were, the physiognomical and pictorial aspect of society.

Moreover, the laws which relate to the social body are not essentially invariable; they change with the nature of the causes producing them. The progress of civilisation, for example, has changed the laws respecting mortality, and must have exercised an influence over the physical and moral condition of man. Tables constructed to show the intensity of the disposition

* [The supposed civilisation of Russia by Peter the Great, and of Prussia by Frederick II., form no real exceptions to the statements of M. Quetelet.]

to crime at different ages, although for several years they may have offered pretty nearly the same results, may yet become gradually modified: it is to effect this modification that the friends of humanity ought to turn their attention. The study of the social body, which we have in view, has for its object to leave this important subject no longer to a kind of empiricism, but to offer the means of recognising directly the causes which influence society, and to measure even that influence itself.

These causes, once known, present no sudden changes, but are modified gradually. Future events may be foreseen by a knowledge of the past, or conjectures may even comprise a period of several years, without fear of experience producing results unconfined by the limits previously assigned them. Now, these limits are proportionally widened as our conjectures embrace a wider series of years.

Of the Causes which Influence Man.

The laws presiding over the development of man, and modifying his actions, are in general the result of his organisation, of his education or knowledge, means or wealth, institutions, local influences, and an endless variety of other causes, always very difficult to discover, and some of which may probably never be made out.

Of all these influencing causes, some are purely physical, others inherent in our nature. Man, in fact, possesses in himself a moral force securing to him the empire over all living beings on this globe; but their destination forms a mysterious problem, whose solution will probably escape us for ever. By means of these moral forces, man is distinguished from other animals. By means of them, also, he possesses the power of modifying, at least in appearance, the laws of nature affecting him, and perhaps by causing a progressive movement, tends to approach a happier physical condition.*

The forces which characterise man, are living forces in their nature; but do they act in a constant manner, and has man, at all epochs, possessed the same quantity—in a word, does there exist any thing analogous to the active or living forces in nature? What, moreover, is their destination? Can they influence the progress of the system, or compromise its existence? or, perhaps, like the internal forces of a system, may they not modify in something its progress, or the conditions of its stability? Analogy leads us to believe, that in the social state we may expect to find in general all the principles of conservation observed in the natural phenomena.

Plants and animals appear to obey, like the planets, the eternal laws of nature, and were it not for the intervention of man, these laws could be verified just as easily in the one case as in the other; but man exercises, both on himself and on all around, *a disturbing action*, the intensity of which takes a development in proportion to his intellect, and the effects of which are such, that society does not resemble itself at any two different epochs.

It would be important to determine, in all the laws affecting the human species, what belongs to nature and what belongs to the disturbing force of man; it appears at least certain, that the effects of this force are slow, and might almost be called *secular perturbations*. However this may be, if they really were

* Buffon explains very well the power possessed by man in modifying nature's works:—" All these modern and recent examples prove, that man has but recently known the extent of his power, and that even yet he does not know it sufficiently; it depends entirely on the exercise of his intellect: thus, the more he observes, the more he will cultivate nature, and the more extensive will be his means to subject nature's works to himself. And what might he not effect upon himself—I mean on his own species—if the will were always governed by the judgment? Who could predict limits to the moral and physical perfectibility of human nature?" &c.—*Epoques de la Nature*.

developed with much rapidity, we could not, with the few elements we possess in respect to the past, draw important conclusions in regard to the future.

We must then do as astronomers have done in the theory of arbitrary constants—and as the early statisticians did in calculating the laws of human mortality —make an abstraction at first of the effects of the disturbing force, and return to it afterwards when a long series of documents permits us to do so.

Thus, to bring out my meaning, in calculating the different tables of mortality, the medium duration of human life has been shown to vary for different countries, and even for different provinces, though these may be quite contiguous. But these differences might depend as much on the nature of the climate as on man himself; and hence the necessity of determining what belonged to the one, what to the other. For this purpose, one might select an assemblage of circumstances proving that the forces of nature remain the same; and if the results obtained at different epochs were also identical, then follows the natural conclusión that the disturbing force of man amounted to nothing. Now, this attempt has been made, and at Geneva, for example, it has been found that the average duration of life, or the medium life, has successively become longer. Now, we are at least entitled to conclude from this the existence of the disturbing force of man, and to form the first idea of the energy of its effects on this point of the globe, so long as it is not proved that causes foreign to man may have altered the fertility of the soil, the state of the atmosphere, temperature, or given rise to some other alteration in the climate. But hitherto we know only the result of different forces, which it would be impossible to estimate individually, and of which we cannot even furnish a complete list. Thus we are disposed to believe that the forces which have prolonged at Geneva the duration of the average life of man, have arisen from the circumstances of his having improved his habitations, rendering them more healthy and more commodious; of his having ameliorated his pecuniary circumstances, his food, and institutions; of his having been able to withdraw himself from the influence of certain diseases, &c.; and it might even have happened that the disturbing force of man may have altered for the better the nature of the climate, by drainage, clearing the forests, or by other changes.

Of the Object of this Work.

The purpose of this work is to study in their effects the causes, whether natural or disturbing, which influence human development; to endeavour to measure the influence of these causes, and the mode according to which they mutually modify each other.

It is not at all my intention to propose a Theory of Man, but merely to ascertain by proof the facts and the phenomena which affect him, and to endeavour, by observation, to discover the laws forming the connecting links of these phenomena. The *social* man, whom I here consider, resembles the centre of gravity in bodies: he is the centre around which oscillate the social elements—in fact, so to speak, he is a fictitious being, for whom every thing proceeds conformably to the medium results obtained for society in general. It is this being whom we must consider in establishing the basis of social physics, throwing out of view peculiar or anomalous cases, and disregarding any inquiry tending to show that such or such an individual may attain a greater or less development in one of his faculties.

Let us suppose, for example, that we endeavoured to discover the disturbing influence of man in modifying his physical strength. By means of the *dynamometer* (measurer of strength), we may first estimate the strength of the hands, or of the loins, in a great number of persons of different ages, from infancy to extreme old age, and the results obtained in this way for a country will give two scales of forces deserving of our confidence in the direct proportion of the number of observations made, and in the care with which they have been made. By comparing at a later period these scales, obtained by the same means and under the same influences, but at different periods of time, we shall discover whether the disturbing action or influence of man has diminished or augmented the quantity of this strength. Now, it is this variation which the whole system undergoes, that it is important to point out in social physics. We may even in this way determine changes happening in the different classes of society, but without descending to individuals. A man, in consequence of gigantic height, or by herculean strength, may attract the attention of the naturalist or the physiologist; but in social physics his importance would disappear before that of another individual, who, after having ascertained experimentally the means of developing advantageously the height and strength, may succeed in putting them in practice, thus producing results either affecting the whole system or one of its parts. After having considered man at different epochs, and as belonging to different nations—after having successively ascertained the several elements of his physical and moral condition, and pointed out, at the same time, the variations in the quantity of materials which he produces and which he consumes, in the increase or decrease of his wealth, and the changes occurring in his position with respect to other nations—we must next determine the laws to which man has been subject in the different races, from their origin; that is to say, we must follow the progress of the centres of gravity in each part of the system, just as we determined the laws relating to man in each nation, by the entire mass of the observations made upon the individuals composing that nation. Under this point of view, nations would be, in respect to the social system, what individuals are in respect to nations; each would have their laws of increase and decrease, and have a share, more or less important, in the perturbations of the system. Now, it is only from the whole of the laws which relate to different races, that we can afterwards decide on what belongs, whether to the equilibrium or to the movement of the system; for we do not know at present which of these two states actually exists. What we see daily proves to us sufficiently the effects of internal actions and forces reacting on each other; but the centre of gravity of the system, if we may so say, and the direction of the movement, are unknown; it may even happen, that whilst the motion of all the parts of the system is progressive or retrograde, the centre may remain unvaryingly in equilibrio.

Perhaps we may be asked, how it can be possible to determine absolutely the value of the disturbing power of man—that is to say, the differences, more or less great, which the social system produces, from that state or condition in which he would be placed if left to the forces of nature alone? Such a problem, if it could be solved, would unquestionably be interesting, but scarcely useful, since such a condition does not exist in nature, seeing that man has at all times been in possession of an intellectual force, and has never been reduced to live merely as animals do. It is of more consequence, indeed, to determine if the effects of his disturbing power vary in a manner more or less advantageous.

From what we have said, the object of scientific research, then, should be to inquire—

1. What are the laws of human reproduction, growth, and physical force—growth of his intellectual powers, and of his disposition, more or less great, to good or evil; the laws regulating the development of his passions and tastes; the mode of succession of the materials he produces or consumes; the laws of human mortality, &c.

2. What influence has nature over man; what is the measure of its influence, and of its disturbing

ON MAN.

ON MAN.

forces; what have been their effects for such and such a period; and what the social elements chiefly affected by them.

3. Finally, can human forces compromise the stability of the social system? I am not sure if these questions may ever be answered; but to me it seems that their solution would form some of the noblest and most interesting results of human research. Convinced of this truth, I have already made some efforts to reply to the first series of these questions; and still more, to make my ideas understood, and to point out the route which ought to be followed, I have endeavoured also to demonstrate how to detect the influencing causes, and to determine the degree of their respective actions. Whatever idea may be formed of these researches, I trust it will still be admitted, that in respect to the development of the human faculties, a great number of observations and results have been accumulated which science did not previously possess.

I wish it also to be understood, that I consider this work as but a sketch of a vast plan, to be completed only by infinite care and immense researches. I have room, therefore, for hope that the leading idea, as to the composition of the work, may be alone criticised; and that, in respect to the filling up of the details, necessarily very incomplete in some parts, from want of materials, a lenient criticism may also be vouchsafed. I have thought it my duty, however, in the suitable place, to point out these deficiencies.

On the Importance or Dignity of the Inquiries Relative to Man.

The nature of the researches in this work, and the view which I have taken of the social system, have in them a something positive, which at first sight may startle some minds. Some may be disposed to see in it a tendency to materialism; others, misunderstanding my ideas, may view them as an attempt to exaggerate the field of the exact sciences, and to place the geometrician upon ground which does not belong to him; they may reproach me for engaging in absurd speculations, and with inquiring into measures where things do not admit of being measured.

In respect to the charge of materialism, it has been reproduced so often and so regularly on every occasion when science attempted to make a new step, and when the spirit of philosophy, breaking through its ancient barriers, attempted a new road, that it seems almost superfluous at the present day to reply to it, the more especially that the fanatical spirit is no longer backed with chains and tortures. It can scarcely now be esteemed an insult to the Divinity, that man exercises the noblest of his faculties by directing his meditations towards the sublimest laws of the universe, by endeavouring to explain the admirable economy and the infinite wisdom which presided at its formation. Who would venture to accuse of dryness those philosophic minds, which have substituted for the narrow and paltry world, as known to the ancients, the knowledge of our magnificent solar system, and have so vastly removed the limits of our starry heaven, that genius can no longer guess its extent but with religious awe? Certainly, the knowledge of the wonderful laws which regulate the system of the world, gives us a much nobler idea of the power of the Divinity, than that of the world which sublime superstition wished to impose upon us. If the animal pride of man be lowered, on observing how small the spot is which he occupies upon the grain of dust of which he at one time made his universe, how much, on the other hand, ought his intelligence to be pleased at the extent of its power, shown in investigating so deeply the secrets of the heavens!

Having thus observed the progress made by astronomical science in regard to worlds, why should not we endeavour to follow the same course in respect to man? Would it not be an absurdity to suppose, that, whilst all is regulated by such admirable laws, man's existence alone should be capricious, and possessed of no conservative principle? We need not hesitate in asserting, that such a supposition, and not the researches we propose making, would be injustice to the Creative Power.

In respect to the second objection, I shall endeavour to answer it when estimating the moral and intellectual faculties of man.

BOOK FIRST.

DEVELOPMENT OF THE PHYSICAL QUALITIES OF MAN.

1. The Determination of the Average Man in General.

WE have said that, in the course of our researches, the first step to be made would be to determine the average man, amongst different nations, both physical and moral. Perhaps the possibility of such an appreciation of physical qualities, which admit of direct measurement, will be granted us: but what is the course to be pursued in regard of the moral qualities? How can we ever maintain, without absurdity, that the courage of one man is to that of another as five is to six, for example, almost as we should speak of their stature? Should we not laugh at the pretension of a geometrician, who seriously maintained that he had calculated that the genius of Homer is to that of Virgil as three to two? Certainly, such pretensions would be absurd and ridiculous. It is proper, then, first of all, to agree upon the meaning of words, and to examine if that which we aim at is possible, not in the actual state of science, but in such a state as science will some day arrive at. We cannot, indeed, demand from those who employ themselves with social physics, more than we should have done from those who foresaw the possibility of forming an astronomical theory, at a period when defective astronomical observations and false theories, or their total absence, with insufficient means of calculation, only existed. It was especially necessary to be certain of the means of performing such a task; it was afterwards necessary to collect precise observations with zeal and perseverance, to create and render perfect the methods for using them, and thus to prepare all the necessary elements of the edifice to be erected. Now, this is the course which I think it proper to pursue in forming a system of social physics. I hold that we should examine if it is possible to obtain the means of performing the desired task, and, firstly, if it is possible to determine the average man.

This determination will be the subject of the three first books of this work. We shall, first of all, consider man in a physical relation; then we shall consider him with respect to his moral and intellectual qualities.

2. Of the Determination of the Physical Qualities of the Average Man.

Amongst the elements pertaining to man, some are susceptible of a *direct* appreciation, and the numbers which represent them are true mathematical quantities: such are, in general, the physical qualities. Thus the weight and stature of a man may be measured directly, and we may afterwards compare them with the weight and stature of another man. In comparing the different men of a nation in this manner, we arrive at average values, which are the weight and stature proper to be assigned to the average man of this nation: as a sequel to such an inquiry, we might then say that the Englishman is of greater height and larger size than the Frenchman or Italian. This mode of proceeding is analogous to that pursued in physics,* in determining the temperature of different countries, and comparing them with each other: thus, we say justly, that at Paris, the mean temperature of the summer is 18 degrees cent., although the thermometer has almost always been either higher or lower than this point. We conceive, moreover, that the ratio which exists between the weight or stature of the average man peculiar to one of the three mentioned countries, may vary in course of time.

In certain cases, we employ *non-material* measures, as when we attempt to appreciate the average duration of life for any particular nation, or to estimate at what age the average man of that nation ceases to exist. Life is measured by duration, and this measurement admits of quite as much precision as we employ in physics.

Lastly, we may employ *conventional* measurements, as when we estimate the riches, productions, and consumption of one country, and compare them with those of another. All these calculations have already been made by economists, with greater or less accuracy; therefore they cannot appear strange to us.

There are elements pertaining to man, which cannot be measured directly, and which are only appreciable *by their effects:* of this number is the strength of man. We are of opinion that it is not absurd to say that such a man is twice as strong as another when pressing with his hands, if this pressure, applied against an obstacle, produces effects which are as two to one. Only, it then becomes necessary to admit that causes are proportionate to effects; and it is necessary to take great care, in estimating the effects, to place the individuals in similar circumstances. Thus, for example, we might make serious errors in employing the dynamometer of Régnier indiscriminately for all persons, because the size of the hands, or the height of the stature, may have some influence, so that one handles the instrument with a greater or less degree of facility.

It results from what has preceded, that, in the determination of the average man, considered with respect to physical qualities, the greatest difficulty consists in collecting exact observations in sufficient number to arrive at results which deserve some degree of confidence.

In the first book, we shall examine all which relates to the life of man, his reproduction, and mortality; in the second, we shall be occupied with the development of his stature, weight, strength, and his physical qualities in general.

CHAPTER I.

OF BIRTHS IN GENERAL, AND OF FECUNDITY.

1. Of Births.

THE act of birth is connected with conception, in the same manner as the effect is connected with the cause which produces it: to the first we attach the idea of necessity, and to the second that of free will.† As in other subjects, we generally lose sight of causes which have acted long anterior to the effects we observe; our attention is not attracted to the regularity with which births are produced—we are accustomed to regard them as natural phenomena, with which the will of man is but feebly concerned. If we observe the influence of seasons, places, years of abundance or scarcity, &c., it is rather as acting on our physical than on our moral qualities—it is as modifying the facility and not the volition which we have in reproduction.

Moreover, we have a very natural dislike to consider our will as influenced by physical causes.

Whatever be the nature of the causes which produce births in greater or less number, with more or less regularity, the thing most important to be known is the result which follows; we shall afterwards be able to inquire what nature performs, and what belongs to the disturbing action of man. In order to facilitate this inquiry, we shall first examine successively how births are produced, taking into consideration the times, places, sexes, seasons, hours of the day, and other causes which are external to the man; and thereby we shall be more able to compare the influence of these causes with those which man exercises, in virtue of his mode of existence and of his political and religious institutions.

2. Of Fecundity.

Taken in an absolute sense, the annual number of births of a country has only an indifferent degree of importance, but it acquires a very great value when we compare it with the other elements of population of this country. We may first employ it to measure the *fecundity*, by comparing it with the actual number of the population or with the annual number of marriages. In the first case, we obtain a measure of the *fecundity of the population*, and in the second case of that of the *fecundity of marriages*. Statisticians avail themselves of both these measures or data, which nevertheless require to be used with great care.

When we compare two countries with respect to the fecundity of marriages, we must be very cautious only to compare the number of *legitimate* births with the number of marriages. We conceive, indeed, that in a country where all the births were indiscriminately reported, with the number of registered marriages, the fecundity would appear too great, and the error would be more considerable, according as there were more illegitimate births and fewer marriages regularly confirmed. The opposite error would take place in a country where more importance was given to establishing the annual number of marriages than that of births. In general, it is necessary to distrust the number expressing the fecundity of the marriages of a country, when the civil records are carelessly kept, or when the registrations are not made uniformly. I think England may be especially pointed out as presenting numbers which have often led those inquirers into error who have availed themselves of them.*

Malthus observes, that the ratio of births to marriages, taken as a measure of fecundity, supposes a stationary population: if the population were increasing, for example, its increase would be more rapid, and the real fecundity of marriages would the more exceed the proportion of births to marriages.† This able economist points out several other circumstances which it is proper to consider in estimating fecundity, such as marriages for the second or third time, late marriages sanctioned by local customs, and frequent emigrations or immigrations.‡

As it respects political economy, the number which expresses the fecundity of a population is perhaps more important than that which expresses the fecundity of marriages. Indeed, the economist is generally more concerned with the increase which the population receives than with the manner in which this increase takes place. The fecundity of marriages might be exactly the same in two different countries, without the population being the same. In countries, for example, where prudent foresight renders marriages less numerous, there will be fewer births; on

---

* [The term physics, as here used, is synonymous with the terms natural or experimental philosophy, as used in this country.]

† We generally consider the duration of pregnancy to be nine months. I do not know whether researches have been made to ascertain if any causes exist influencing this duration, and if their influence has been calculated.

* Malthus—Essai sur le Principe de Population, tome ii. p. 212. Geneva Edition: 1830.

† The words of Mr Malthus are (3d ed., vol. ii. p. 6)—" The more rapid is the increase of population, the more will the real prolificness of marriages exceed the proportion of births to marriages in the registers."

‡ Ibid., tome ii. p. 219. English Edition, book ii. ch. 9.

the contrary, in countries whose inhabitants are improvident and careless, and in new countries, where the immigrations are numerous and where the settlements are formed by persons generally at a reproductive age, we find a great fecundity in the population. These are important distinctions to be made, to avoid all kinds of error, either in making estimates or in the approximating of numbers.

Another very common error in statistical works proceeds from an erroneous estimate of the population: scarcely sufficient attention has been hitherto paid to this subject. When census are not accurately made, we generally obtain too small a number as the amount of the population, and the fecundity, calculated from it, must appear too great. This is an error which I point out here, because I have committed it myself in my first essays on statistics and in speaking of the fecundity of the ancient kingdom of the Netherlands: it resulted from this circumstance that certain provinces were found in a very unfavourable state compared with others; but a deeper examination has shown me what caused my mistakes, and has led me to solicit the government, with active entreaty, for a census, henceforth become necessary; which was effectually accomplished in 1829.

There is one particular case in which the ratio between the fecundity of one country and that of another remains exactly the same, whether we estimate it according to the population or according to the annual number of marriages; this is when the populations of the countries which we compare are homogeneous or composed of the same elements—when, on both sides, we annually count the same number of marriages to the same number of inhabitants.*

I thought I ought to present the preceding observations on the calculation of fecundity, before examining all which relates to births. We shall now proceed more safely in endeavouring successively to appreciate the influence which *natural* and *disturbing* causes exercise over births.

~~~~~~~~

CHAPTER II.

OF THE INFLUENCE OF NATURAL CAUSES ON THE NUMBER
OF BIRTHS.

1. Influence of the Sexes.

THERE is a very remarkable fact, which has been long ago observed, although we do not yet know the true causes of it. It is this—that more boys are born annually than girls. Now, since the proportion of male to female births does not differ much from unity, or is almost the same for the different countries for which it has been calculated, it has been necessary to have recourse to numerous observations to determine it with more precision. After more than fourteen and a half millions of observations made in

* Some calculations which I shall advance will make this easily understood. Let f be the fecundity of a country, n the annual number of births, m that of marriages, c the remainder of the population, and f', n', m', and c', respectively, the same numbers for another country; we shall have for the fecundity of marriages the proportion

$$f : f' :: \frac{n}{m} : \frac{n'}{m'}.$$

Now, if the populations be homogeneous, as in the case which we are supposing, we shall also have

$$\frac{m}{c+m} = \frac{m'}{c'+m'}.$$

Now, if we multiply both terms of the latter ratio of the proportion by this equality, we shall have

$$f : f' :: \frac{n}{c+m} : \frac{n'}{c'+m'};$$

—a result agreeable to what is advanced in the text, since the terms of the latter ratio represent the fecundity of the population.

B

France, from 1817 to 1831, the value of this ratio has been as 106·38 to 100; and its average value has varied but little, taking one year with another.*

To know whether climate influences the ratio in question, thirty of the most southern departments of France have been considered separately. The births in these departments, from 1817 to 1831, have been 2,119,162 males, and 1,990,720 females; the ratio of the first number to the second is as 105·95 to 100—nearly the same as for the whole of France. This result would lead us to conclude, that the superior number of male to female births does not depend, in any sensible degree, on climate.[†]

However, in order to ascertain more decidedly the influence exercised by climate, it will be proper to extend our researches beyond the limits of France. Taking our data from the principal European states, we find the following results, according to M. Bickes, who has collected more than seventy millions of observations : [‡]—

STATES AND PROVINCES.	Males to 100 Females.
Russia, - - - - - -	108·91
The province of Milan, - - -	107·61
Mecklenburg, - - - -	107·07
France, - - - - -	106·55
Belgium and Holland, - - -	106·44
Brandenburg and Pomerania, -	106·27
Kingdom of the Two Sicilies, -	106·13
Austrian Monarchy, - - -	106·10
Silesia and Saxony, - - -	106·05
Prussian States (*en masse*), -	105·94
Westphalia and Grand Dutchy of the Rhine, -	105·96
Kingdom of Wurtemburg, -	105·69
Eastern Prussia and Dutchy of Posen,- -	105·66
Kingdom of Bohemia, - -	105·33
Great Britain, - - - -	104·75
Sweden, - - - - -	104·62
Average for Europe, -	106.

Some travellers have thought that hot climates are more favourable to female births; but numbers have not confirmed this opinion, at least from what we have just seen in Europe. However, more observations than we possess are necessary, and especially observations collected near the equator, before we can affirm that the influence of climates is absolutely insensible. The following are the observations made at the Cape of Good Hope, on the white population § residing there, and also on the slave population : ||—

Years.	Free Births.		Slave Births.	
	Males.	Females.	Males.	Females.
1813, - -	686	706	188	234
1814, -	802	825	230	183
1815, - -	833	804	221	193
1816, - -	805	892	325	294
1817, - -	918	927	467	467
1818, -	814	832	516	482
1819, -	810	815	505	509
1820, - -	881	893	463	464
Total,	6604	6780	2936	2826

Thus, among the free births, the females numerically exceed those of the males; and this result is reproduced every year.[¶]

* Annuaire du Bureau des Longitudes, 1834. † Ibid.
‡ Memorial Encycl. Mai 1832.
§ Journal Asiatique, Juillet 1826; and Sadler, tome ii. p. 371.
|| Elements of Medical Statistics, by Hawkins, p. 51.
¶ [It appears to the translator, that the predominance of female over male births, amongst the white race of the Cape of Good Hope, is not so much owing to climate as to the peculiarity of race: the free white population of the Cape are, as near as may be, purely Saxon, descended from the old Dutch families, who originally settled there about two hundred and seventy years ago. They have preserved the purity of their blood with great care,

It appears that residence in town or country is not without its influence on the ratio of births of the two sexes, as we may judge from the Belgic documents:—

Years.	Births in the Towns.			Births in the Country.		
	Boys.	Girls.	Ratio.	Boys.	Girls.	Ratio.
1815 to 1824,	164,376	154,110	106·66	472,221	441,502	106·96
1825 to 1829,	87,516	83,122	105·29	256,751	241,989	106·10

The number of boys, compared with that of girls, has then been smaller in town than in the country: it is to be observed, that both ratios have sensibly diminished during the latter period.

This influence of town residence, tending to diminish the proportional number of births, is also observed in other countries. This is seen in the following table, in which M. Bickes has found another kind of influence, namely, legitimacy of birth:*—

STATES AND PROVINCES.	Boys to 100 Girls.	
	Legitimate.	Illegitimate.
France, - - -	106·69	104·78
Austrian monarchy, - - -	106·15	104·32
Prussian monarchy, -	106·17	102·89
Sweden, - - -	104·73	103·12
Wurtemburg, - - -	105·97	103·54
Bohemia, - - -	105·65	100·44
Province of Milan, -	107·79	102·30
Eastern Prussia and Posen, -	105·81	103·60
Brandenburg and Pomerania, -	106·65	102·42
Silesia and Saxony, - -	106·30	103·27
Westphalia and the Dutchy of the Lower Rhine, - -	106·07	101·55

CITIES.		
Paris, - - -	103·82	103·42
Amsterdam, - - -	105·00	108·83
Leghorn, - - -	104·68	93·21
Frankfort-on-the-Maine, -	102·83	107·84
Leipsic, - - -	106·16	105·94

Thus all the documents relative to states agree in giving a larger proportional number of boys for legitimate than for illegitimate births. This difference is much less conspicuous for towns. M. Bickes has extended his researches concerning legitimate births to a great number of cities; and the average of the ratios, which I have calculated, gives 104·74, a value which is very sensibly inferior to that which all the European states give.

M. Poisson, some years ago, made researches into this singular circumstance, that the ratio of male to female births, for natural children, differs sensibly from the general ratio of France taken altogether; and he has obtained, from the documents of 1817 to 1826 inclusively, 21-20ths instead of 16-15ths. M. Mathieu also had arrived at a similar result.†

With the view of throwing more light on this interesting subject, Mr Babbage has also carefully collected the numbers of several different countries, and presented them, with all the desirable details, in a letter, which is inserted in Brewster's Journal of Sciences, new series, No. I. I have extracted the principal results.

intermingling as little as possible with the dark races, whether Caffre or Hottentot. Generally speaking, they hold the mulatto in great dislike and contempt ; so that, amongst the pure Dutch of the Cape, a mulatto, however slightly tinged, has hitherto had little chance of acquiring a proper status in society. With respect to M. Quetelet's table of births, it seems probable that an excess of boys over girls is a law chiefly with the Celtic and Sarmatian races, and that in respect to the pure Saxon race, there exists either an opposite law, namely, the excess of females over males, or, perhaps, as near as may be, an equality ; but the translator inclines to the opinion that the excess will be in the females with respect to the Saxon race.]

* Zeitung fur das Gesammte Medicinal wesen. Also, An. de Hygiène, Oct. 1832.

† Annuaire et le tome ix. des Mémoires de l'Academie des Sciences, p. 239.

	Legitimate Births.		Number of Births observed.	Illegitimate Births.		Number of Births observed.
	Female.	Male.		Female.	Male.	
France,	10,000	10,657	9,656,135	10,000	10,484	673,047
Naples,	10,000	10,452	1,059,055	10,000	10,367	51,309
Prussia,	10,000	10,609	3,672,251	10,000	10,278	212,804
Westphalia,	10,000	10,471	151,169	10,000	10,039	19,950
Montpellier,	10,000	10,707	25,064	10,000	10,081	2,735
Averages,	10,000	10,575		10,000	10,250	

In quoting these numbers, M. Prévost observes, that, independently of the physiological cause which gives a greater facility to male births, there exists an accessory cause in legitimate births especially, which still further increases this facility, and which he attributes to a sort of preference generally given to children of the male sex. "Is not the end of this preference," says he, "to prevent, after male births, the increase of the family, and consequently to increase the proportional ratio of the latter? Parents have one son : if different causes impede the increase of their family, they will perhaps be less uneasy at this privation, when their first wish is accomplished, than they would have been if they had not had male children. Would not this diminution of births, after one or two sons, tend to increase the ratio of male births?"* Without denying the influence which this moral restraint may exercise in certain cases, I think it altogether insufficient to explain the results which I shall soon advance.

M. Giron de Buzareignes has also communicated to the Parisian Academy of Sciences some researches made in France, on the births of children of both sexes.† He divides society into three classes : the first is composed of persons whose occupations tend to develop the physical qualities ; the second, of persons whose occupations tend to weaken these powers ; and, lastly, the third, of persons whose occupations are of a mixed kind. According to this observer, the proportional number of male births in the first class will be greater than that which France furnishes in general ; in the second class, it will be the contrary ; and in the third, both numbers will be equal. Thus, agricultural occupations are favourable to the development of male births, whilst commerce and manufactures produce an opposite effect. This observation agrees very well with the results which have been previously pointed out for town and country, but it does not sustain an equal examination when applied to the different states of Europe.

M. Bickes, who is much inclined to question the opinion advanced by M. Giron de Buzareignes, has presented a new explanation of the causes which occasion the ratio of the sexes to vary. According to him, "It is in the blood (the constitution, the race) of people or nations, who differ more or less from each other in this respect, that the powers or causes reside, whatever they may be, which determine the production of many boys. Political and civil institutions, customs, habitual occupations, mode of life, wealth, indigence, &c.—all these things have no influence on the respective ratio according to which the two sexes come into the world." We should have much difficulty to explain by this means how, in the same people, the ratio of births of the two sexes presents such sensible differences in town and country. As to the effect of legitimacy on the preponderance of female births, M. Bickes thinks that the first cause of it cannot be demonstrated.‡ We shall soon find other obstacles to his hypothesis. Professor Hofacker has made some researches in Germany, on the influence of the age of parents on male and female births, whence it results, that in general, when the mother is older than the father, fewer boys than girls are

* Bibliothèque Universelle de Genève. Oct. 1829, p. 140, et seq.
† Bulletin de M. Férassac, tome xii. p. 3.
‡ Annales de Hygiène, Oct. 1832, p. 459.

born; the same is the case when the parents are of equal ages; but the more the father's age exceeds that of the mother, so is the ratio of boys greater.

The different results of M. Hofacker are brought together in the following table:—

Ages of the Man and Woman.	Boys to 100 Girls.
The man being younger than the woman,	90·6
,, ,, as old as the woman,	90·0
,, ,, older from 3 to 6 years,	103·4
,, ,, ,, from 6 to 9 years,	124·7
,, ,, ,, from 9 to 18 years,	143·7
,, ,, ,, by 18 years and upwards,	200·0
The man from 24 to 36—the woman from 16 to 26 years,	116·6
,, ,, ,, ,, ,, 36 to 46 ,,	95·4
,, ,, 36 to 48 years, ,, young,	176·9
,, ,, ,, ,, middle-aged,	114·3
,, ,, ,, ,, older,	109·2
,, ,, 48 to 60 years, ,, middle-aged,	190·0
,, ,, ,, ,, older,	164·3

If these results were deduced from sufficiently numerous observations, and so accurate as to deserve entire confidence, and if they were verified in other countries, they would present a very powerful argument in favour of the hypothesis, that the births of one or the other sex can be made to predominate at will. We must regret that there are still so few proper documents to elucidate this delicate question; the only ones which I have succeeded in procuring are found in the work of Mr Sadler on the "Law of Population." I shall first present a table extracted from the registers of the peers of England, and let it be observed that it only includes first marriages:—

Difference of Ages: the Husband being—	Number of Marriages.	Births.		Ratio of Births.		Children by each Marriage.
		Male.	Female.	Male.	Female.	
Younger,	54	122	141	865	100	4·87
As old,	18	54	57	948	100	6·17
Older from 1 to 6 years,	126	366	353	1037	100	5·71
6 to 11,	107	327	258	1267	100	5·47
11 to 16,	43	143	97	1474	100	5·58
16 and upwards,	33	93	57	1632	100	4·55
Total,	381	1105	963			

These results agree perfectly with those of M. Hofacker. I have calculated in the latter column the fecundity of the marriages, which has likewise a value depending on the respective ages of the espoused.

In examining the influence of the age of the parents on births, Mr Sadler has been led to the following conclusions:—The ratio in which the sexes are born is regulated by the difference of age of the parents, in such a manner that the sex of the father or the mother will preponderate beyond the average of the total number of births, according to the party which has the excess of age. On the other hand, the sex which is in excess will have a mortality depending on the period which separates the age of the parents, so that the sexes will be balanced in numbers, towards the ordinary period of marriage.

It is thus that Mr Sadler explains how the proportional number of male births is not so great in the manufacturing towns of England as in the country, where men marry later, and present a greater difference of age to the women whom they espouse.* He also extends his explanation to the difference which is observed between legitimate and illegitimate births.

Mr Sadler, moreover, finds, that in considering the age of the father or the mother separately, we do not

* It is a fact which appears well established by several statisticians, and by Mr Milne in particular (Traité des Annuités, vol ii. p. 493), that precocious marriages generally produce a greater number of daughters.

observe any difference of facility in producing infants of one sex rather than of another. This facility, according to him, only depends on the relative ages of the parents: this he deduces from the following numbers, extracted from registers of marriages:—

Age of the Couples at the time of Marriage.*	Number of Marriages.	Births.		Ratio of Births.		Fecundity.
		Male.	Female.	Male.	Female.	
Under 21,	54	143	124	1153	1000	4·94
21 to 26,	307	668	712	938	1000	4·50
26 to 31,	284	696	609	1143	1000	4·59
31 to 36,	137	298	263	1133	1000	4·10
36 to 41,	90	149	151	987	1000	3·33
41 to 46,	58	93	83	1120	1000	3·04
46 to 51,	51	79	83	952	1000	3·17
51 to 61,	30	27	17	1588	1000	1·47
61 and upwards,	16	5	8	625	1000	0·81
Total,	1027	2158	2050	1052	1000	4·10

Ages of the Wives of the Couples.	Number of Marriages.	Births.		Ratio of Births.		Fecundity.
		Male.	Female.	Male.	Female.	
Under 16,	13	37	33	1121	1000	5·38
16 to 21,	177	502	387	1299	1000	5·02
21 to 26,	191	512	485	1055	1000	5·22
26 to 31,	60	115	92	1250	1000	3·43
31 to 36,	21	40	36	1110	1000	3·62
36 and upwards,	9	13	13	1000	1000	2·89
Total,	471	1219	1046	1165	1000	4·81

Since these numbers are generally small, it would perhaps have been better had they been arranged under fewer heads. It appears to me that we might reduce them to the three following: under 26 years, from 26 to 36 years, and upwards of 36 years. We then obtain respectively 970, 1140, 1032 male births for 1000 female ones, when taking the couples; and 1161, 1211, 1000, when taking the wives. We see that the period between 26 and 36 years gives a few more male births.

Lastly, in extending his researches to widows and widowers, Mr Sadler further finds, from the registers of English couples, that the widowers tend to produce more female children.

Age of the Widowers or Widows at the time of Marriage.	Number of 2d & 3d Wedlocks.	Births.		Ratio of the Births.		Children by Marriage.
		Male.	Female.	Male.	Female.	
22 to 27,	5	21	33	91·3	100	8·80
27 to 32,	18	33	39	84·6	100	4·00
32 to 37,	24	51	66	77·3	100	4·87
37 to 42,	17	29	32	90·6	100	3·58
42 to 47,	16	30	38	79·0	100	4·25
47 to 52,	15	30	43	69·9	100	4·87
52 and upwards,	12	10	15	66·7	100	2·08
Total,	107	204	256	79·7	100	4·30

The ratio is so marked, that we find it almost corresponds to the different ages.

It results from the examination of the probable causes which may produce the inequality between the births of male and female children which has just been pointed out, that the most influential, if we may trust to the few documents which science at present possesses, is evidently that which the difference of age of the parents produces: we might even think that the other causes which have been pointed out, are in some manner the effects of it. Indeed, it ge-

* All the numbers of this and the following table have been taken from fruitful first marriages.

nerally happens throughout Europe, that men, when they marry, are five or six years older than women, so that the preponderance of male births will be almost the same, as is established by the researches of Hofacker and Sadler, who give, as the ratio of births of both sexes, the number 103·5 nearly, when the father is from 1 to 6 years older than the mother. Now, we think that this ratio will be larger or smaller, according as the difference of age of the parents is greater or less in the different nations, in town or country, among the persons whose connexions are legitimate or illegitimate; and, lastly, according to all the circumstances which may cause the ages to vary at which production takes place; so that the age of the parents will be the principal regulator which determines the magnitude of the ratio between the births of the two sexes. Hence we see how important it is to direct our researches to the age at which marriage takes place, especially since the greater or less mortality of children depends on these ages.*

2. Influence of Age on the Fecundity of Marriages.

We have just seen that the relative age of the parties exercises a sensible influence on the ratio of male births: it is natural to suppose, that it will have still more influence with regard to the number of births, or the fecundity. I am not acquainted with much on this subject besides the researches of Mr Sadler, which were undertaken with the design of showing that the age of parents, considered apart, has no influence on the ratio of male to female births. I have introduced them above, taking care to calculate the number expressing the fecundity in the last column. However, since the numbers of Mr Sadler are generally small, I have thought proper to receive fewer divisions of ages, which will give a greater probability to my particular results: we may sum up all these results in the following table:—

According to the Registers of English Couples.	Number of Children procreated by one Individual; being at the time of Marriage—		
	Under 26 years.	Between 26 and 36.	More than 36 years.
Husbands, - -	5·11	4·43	2·84
Wives, - -	5·13	3·49	2·80
Widowers & Widows.	8·80 †	4·50	3·66

We see that the fecundity of marriages, all things being equal, diminishes in proportion to the increas-

* [Assuming as a fact, an assertion which has been often made, that thoughtless and premature marriages, that is, when both sexes are very young, take place to a much greater extent in Ireland than in most other countries, records of such marriages would go far to solve the difficult question proposed above by M. Quetelet: such records, if they exist, might be compared with those of Holland, where it is presumed that a moral condition of the people exists, which is the antithesis to the Irish character. A comparison of these records with each other would go far to solve the question. Should it be found that the male sex still predominates in births in Ireland, it would then be clear that the theory of age proposed by M. Buzareignes, and supported by M. Quetelet, would be at fault, whilst that of Bickes, or the theory of race, which is the view supported by the translator, would be the true one.

It is quite possible, however, that both causes may have their influence; but a glance at the table, page 12, proves indisputably, as far as such records go, that, commencing in Eastern Europe with the Sclavonic race, amongst whom we find the disproportion of boys to girls greatest, and passing through the mixed Sclavonic and Saxon races of Prussia, and through the Celtic nations of France and the north of Italy, to Westphalia, Great Britain, and Sweden, where the Saxon race exists in its greatest purity, we find the disproportion between boys and girls constantly decreasing, and are entitled, therefore, to conclude, that whatever other causes may be in operation, blood or race comes in for at least a considerable share in the effects.]

† This number being founded on five marriages only, which produced 44 children, cannot be entitled to much confidence.

ing age of the parties. To observe the influence of age itself on the fecundity of individuals, it would be necessary to compute the probability of life in marrying; for it is very evident that he who has yet twice as long to live as another person, may hope, all things being equal, to procreate more children. It is very true, on the other hand, that those who marry young have some fear lest they should have too numerous a family; which is not the case when persons marry at a more advanced age. In supposing, as a kind of limit, that, all things being equal, the fecundity depends on the probability of life, it would be necessary for each age to divide each of the ratios previously found by the corresponding number which expresses the length of the probable life. Now, in admitting approximatively 36, 32, and 21 years, as the probability of life of the individuals of the first class; afterwards, for the women, 40, 34, and 23 years; and, lastly, for the widows, 38, 33, and 22 years, we shall have, as the relative values of fecundity—

According to the Registers of English Couples.	Number of Children procreated by one Individual; being at the time of Marriage—		
	Under 26 years.	Between 26 and 36.	More than 36 years.
Husbands, - -	0·142	0·138	0·135
Wives, - -	0·128	0·103	0·125
Widowers & Widows,	0·131	0·136	0·166

These numbers, which only express the relative fecundity, serve, moreover, to show that the greatest aptitude for reproduction is evidently, among the individuals whom we are considering, before the age of 26 years; moreover, we see that it is not sensibly diminished in men until the 36th year. The data for females are too few to be relied on, since they only include nine women more than 36 years of age.

When we consider the respective ages of the husbands, we find, still availing ourselves of the numbers furnished by Mr Sadler, and which we have quoted above, that the fecundity of marriages reaches its greatest value when the ages of the married persons are the same, or when the man is from 1 to 6 years older than the woman: it does not sensibly diminish, if the difference of age does not exceed 16 years; but when it is greater, or when the man is younger than the woman, the fecundity seems to be at its *minimum*. These are results which it is in some measure easy to foresee. Moreover, I only proposed to point out these researches, without pretending to go deeply into them, since adequate data are still wanting.

Mr Sadler, in another part of his work, has ascertained the number of children produced by the wives of those couples in England whose ages at the time of marriage he has been able to determine: putting down all the marriages this time, whether they were fruitful or not, or were born during the first or second time of wedlock; and these are his results:—

Age at the time of Marriage.	Number of Marriages.	Number of Children.	Mortality of Children before the Marriageable Age.	Births by Marriage.	Deaths for one Birth.
12 to 15,	32	141	40	4·40	0·283
16 to 19,	172	797	166	4·63	0·208
20 to 23,	198	1033	195	5·21	0·188
24 to 27,	86	467	180	5·43	0·171

We see here that, from 12 to 27 years, the fecundity of women continues to increase. At first view, this result appears contrary to those which have been previously obtained; but it is proper to observe, that he is considering marriages in general, and not, as we have previously supposed, fruitful marriages in particular. We have seen that, on this latter hypothesis, the fecundity of women does not perceptibly vary under the age of 26 years. We can then only attribute the difference to this, that many women, married late in life, continue barren. Moreover, it results from the calculations of Mr Sadler, that the children procreated by too premature marriages are more subject to mortality than others. It is, besides, very odd, that the statistician, who has calculated the preceding tables with a definite object, has not extended their application beyond the age of 27 years. It is also much to be desired that he had ascertained the ratio of fruitful to barren women, for the different ages at which marriages have taken place.

Not to choose the individuals whom he examines from a privileged class, Mr Sadler has also given a table from 2860 cases of child-birth, attended by Dr Granville in several of the principal benevolent establishments in London : we shall quote it here.

Age at the time of Marriage.	Number of Marriages.	Children at the full period.	Children living at the time of Birth.	Dead Children.	Deaths for one Birth.	Average No. of Births during one year of Marriage.	Children by Marriage.
13 to 16,	74	376	209	167	0·44	0·46	5·08
17 to 20,	354	1307	751	556	0·43	0·50	3.70
21 to 24,	283	823	474	349	0·42	0·52	2·91
25 to 28,	110	287	170	117	0·41	0·55	2·61
29 to 32,*	38	67	46	31	0·31	0·59	2·03

This table deserves to be carefully examined. We first observe that the mortality of children is somewhat less, in proportion as the marriages are less precocious ; afterwards, the numbers of the seventh column, which Mr Sadler gives as having been calculated by Mr Finlayson from accounts taken of the ages of the delivered women, whom he does not know or of whom he takes no account, would tend to show that fecundity is greater as the woman is younger, and on this side of the term of 32 years. Nevertheless, from the last column, which I have added, and which I have made from the numbers of the table, it is easy to see that, if the annual fecundity be less, the *fruitful women* who have married early, all things being equal, have produced more children ; which brings us back to the observation already made on the wives of peers. It is singular that Mr Sadler should not have examined the fecundity in both these cases : it seems to me, that he would have found less solid arguments in favour of the law of population which he endeavours to establish.

We certainly see, from the numbers of Mr Finlayson, that there is a somewhat greater annual fecundity for women married late ; but it does not compensate for the excess of absolute fecundity of those who have married early. Generally, when a man marries a woman very young, he endeavours to take care of her, and her family may become numerous without his object being to make it so : on the contrary, if he marry a person grown up, he no longer thinks care so necessary ; and, on the other hand, if he wishes to have a family, the time becomes more precious to him, as the age of his wife is advanced.†

It seems to me that the following consequences naturally follow from what has been said :—

1. Too premature marriages bring on sterility, and produce children who have less likelihood of living.

2. A marriage, if it be not barren, produces the same number of births, at whatever period it takes place, provided that the man's age does not exceed 33, or that of the woman 26 years. After these ages, the number of children produced diminishes.

3. From the preceding result, and from a consideration of the probability of life, we may infer that it

* It is evident that there are errors in this line, which we thought necessary to copy exactly.

† The table of Mr Finlayson, which is more extended than that of Mr Sadler, gives 0·78 as the annual fecundity of a woman from 33 to 36 years of age, and 1·12 for one from 37 to 39 years of age.

is before the age of 33 years of the man, and 26 of the woman, that we observe the greatest fecundity.

4. If we may reckon the respective ages of married persons, we find that, all things being equal, the marriages most productive are those in which the man is at least as old as the woman, or older, yet not much exceeding her time of life.

After these observations, it becomes interesting to examine if man, in our climate, conforms to the laws which nature appears to have attached to fecundity, and if he reproduces at the most appropriate period of life. To establish this period, it would be necessary to know the age of parents at the time of the birth of their children. From the want of these documents, we may recur to the ages at which marriages take place, and admit, with sufficient probability, as an average term, that the birth of the first-born takes place within the first year which follows marriage.

In this hypothesis, it will be necessary to recur to tables of population ; and some calculations, founded on the probability of life, will assist us in determining the marriage ages. The following table will explain the course which we have followed. The second and the fourth columns, from the Belgic population table, inform us of the number of men and women who are married, and who are of the age stated in the first column ; moreover, also, whether they are yet married, or in the state of widowhood. The third and fifth columns point out what becomes of the same individuals in the period which follows, taking their mortality into account. The calculations have not been extended beyond 56 years, since the results after that period could only be very doubtful.

Age.	Married Men or Widowers.		Married Women or Widows.	
	Number of the Tables.	Number when Reduced.	Number of the Tables.	Number when Reduced.
From 14 to 16, -	0	0	4	4
.. 16 to 20, -	96	91	403	987
.. 20 to 25, -	3,278	3,029	5,981	5,594
.. 25 to 30, -	14,025	13,175	16,256	15,204
.. 30 to 35, -	20,879	19,628	21,928	20,552
.. 35 to 40, -	19,374	18,140	22,660	21,143
.. 40 to 45, -	18,951	17,512	22,188	20,566
.. 45 to 50, -	18,350	16,583	19,950	18,312
.. 50 to 53, -	11,708	10,864	12,453	11,697
.. 53 to 56, -	9,925	9,087	10,130	9,432

Now, to arrive at the number of marriages which have taken place between 20 and 25 years among the men, it will be sufficient to take from the number of married individuals of this age the number of those who were so before arriving at the age of 20 years : it will be necessary, moreover, to take into consideration the mortality of the latter ; so that from 3278 we take away 91: the remainder, 3187, gives the number of marriages which have been made. In the same manner, the number of marriages which have been made between 25 and 30 years, will be calculated by taking 3029 from 14,025. We proceed in the same manner with the succeeding numbers ; for the two classes which exceed fifty years, we must remember that they only include three years. To avoid any confusion in the calculation, we have, in the following results, employed the numbers of an average year of each period.

Age.	Marriages which have taken place.	
	Men.	Women.
From 14 to 16 years,	0	2
.. 16 to 20 ..	24	80
.. 20 to 25 ..	637	1118
.. 25 to 30 ..	2199	2132
.. 30 to 35 ..	1541	1345
.. 35 to 40 ..	51	422
.. 40 to 45 ..	162	209
.. 45 to 50 ..	169	123
.. 50 to 53 ..	586	489
.. 53 to 56 ..	313	522

Some negative quantities are presented among these numbers, which may arise from a greater mortality than that which we have supposed; or from this circumstance, that at certain times there are *lacunæ*, or voids, in the population; or still more from the declarations of married persons having been made falsely, to conceal their age, or from other motives. We observe, indeed, that of the four negative numbers, three of them fall near the period of 50 years, which is overrated. Several persons, to give a round number, as is observed in other population-tables, will probably have declared themselves to be 50 years old, when they had not attained that term by some months, or even when they had already passed it by some years. As to the negative number between 35 and 40 years for the men, it corresponds to the direful period of the French wars, in which the Belgians took part: the men of this age entered on their 19th year some time between 1808 and 1813.

Considering what has just been said, we see that men in Belgium do not marry before 16, and probably not before 18 years of age: some women have married between 14 and 16 years of age. *The greatest number of marriages, both of men and women, take place between their 26th and 30th years:* women, however, reach the adult period earlier than men; the *maximum* would seem to fall about the 29th year for men, and after the 27th for women.

The number of marriages diminishes very sensibly after the 35th year; and it may be considered as almost nothing, for females at least, after the 40th year. Indeed, the total, between 40 and 56 years, is only 53. The number 53 is only relative to the numbers of the table, and not to what really takes place. Of the men, there is a certain number who marry at even more advanced ages: thus, the preceding table gives 162 from 40 to 45 years, 169 from 45 to 50, and 273 from 50 to 53 years.

From this research, it would result that a man's first child would be born to him when he was about 30 years of age, and the woman being about the age of 28: this would give the duration of a generation in Belgium; it is also the average duration of life nearly. We shall especially insist on this coincidence.

It is also very remarkable, that marriages only become frequent when men have passed the stormy period of the passions, and of the greatest tendency to crime, which happens about the 24th year: this is also the time when the development of the physical qualities has terminated, and the intellectual ones attain a greater energy.

According to M. Friedlander, to whom we are indebted for the article *Mortalité* in the *Dictionnaire des Sciences Medicales*, it would be about the 30th year that the greatest number of accouchements take place in Sweden and Finland. The following are the results which he has presented, from sixteen years' observation, made prior to 1795 :—

Age of the Women Delivered.	Average Number of Women alive.	Annual Number of Births.	Number of Women to 10 Births.	Ratio of Women to 1000 Births.
15 to 20 years,	134,548	3,298	408	33·
20 to 25 ··	129,748	16,507	78	165·
25 to 30 ··	121,707	26,329	46	263·
30 to 35 ··	111,373	25,618	43	256·
35 to 40 ··	97,543	18,093	54	181·
40 to 45 ··	90,852	8,518	106	85·
45 to 50 ··	78,897	1,694	465	17·
Upwards of 50 years,	69,268	39	17,760	0·4
				1000·4

It is to be desired that such observations as these, which may be obtained with sufficient accuracy from the registers of the civil state, were more numerous; and that all which relates to the age of the parents,

and to the period of the conception or birth of their children, might be stated more carefully for the future.

3. Influence of Places.

One of the first subjects of investigation presented to the mind, when studying the circumstances connected with births, is the determination of the influence of climate on fecundity. Unfortunately, the data which we possess on this important subject are so incomplete, and modified by so many accessory causes, that it is almost impossible to separate them from matter foreign to the question, and lay hold of results deserving of confidence. Opinions, also, vary much on this subject; and we are still ignorant whether, all things being equal, the north or the south is most favourable to fecundity.

If it be the fecundity of the population which we compare, we find, even in neighbouring countries, the most striking discordances; because, errors of numbers being taken away, the accessory causes are almost always more active than the influence of climate. To give an example of this, I shall quote the ratio of the births to the population of different countries, from the medical statistics of Mr Hawkins.*

STATES AND COLONIES.		Number of Inhabitants to one Birth.
Iceland, 1819, -	- - - -	37·0
England, -	- - - - -	35·0
Cape of Good Hope, 1820,	- - -	33·7
France, -	- - - - -	31·6
Sweden,	- - - - -	27·0
Isle of Bourbon, -	- - -	24·5
The Two Sicilies,	- - - -	24·0
Prussia, -	- - - -	23·3
Venice, -	- - - -	22·0
United States,	- - - -	20·0

It would be impossible to find any agreement between these numbers and the degrees of latitude to which they refer, which might indicate the influence of climate. Even without going beyond France, we find very great discordances for some selected departments. Thus, the ratio for that kingdom is one birth to 32 inhabitants; whilst the ratio for the departments of Orne and Finisterre has been one to 44·83, and 25·97 respectively, for the five years 1826–30. On the other hand, taking the most southern departments of France indiscriminately, we do not find any sensible difference from those of the north. There is a province in America, called Guanaxuato, which in 1825 had one birth to 16·08 inhabitants:† this ratio, and that of the department of Orne, may almost be considered as forming the limit of the known ratios of different countries.

Since the examination of the influence of climate on the fecundity of the population is rendered perplexing by the existence of powerful influences of other kinds, we ought first to endeavour to ascertain the latter, in order to be able to judge what would be the fecundity of the *same* population, placed in two different climates. Moreover, the difficulty of obtaining an exact enumeration of the population, adds to the singular complexity of this research.

By taking the fecundity of marriages into account in considering the hypothesis of a homogeneous population, and only making use of the ascertained number of marriages and legitimate births, we may hope to arrive at more conclusive results on the influence of climate. M. Benoiston de Châteauneuf considered this interesting question in a notice " On the Intensity of the Fecundity of Europe at the Commencement of

* Elements of Medical Statistics, by E. Bisset Hawkins. London : 1829.

† Bibliothèque Universelle, 1833. On the Proportional Mortality of Norman Populations, by Sir F. D'Ivernois.

the Nineteenth Century."* We shall take this philosopher as our guide in our remarks on the fecundity of marriages.

"If we divide Europe into two climates only—one of which, commencing at Portugal and terminating at the Low Countries, will thus extend from the 40th to the 50th degree of north latitude, and represent the southern division; whilst the other, going from Brussels to Stockholm, or from the 50th to the 67th degree, will represent the northern division—we shall find that, in the former, 100 marriages give 457 births; and in the latter, the same number of unions only produces 430.

The difference becomes still greater, if we merely compare the two extreme temperatures with each other. In Portugal, 5·10 children are born to each marriage; in Sweden, 3·62 only.

Finally, without going out of France, we may find new proofs of this observation. 'The fecundity,' says Moheau, 'increases from the north to the south of France. There, the average number of births by marriage is annually 5·03, and in the provinces of the north it is only 4·64.'

What was true in our case, fifty years ago, is also true now. The average of births, taken for five years (1821–25), is 4·34 by marriage in our provinces in the south (Dauphiny, Languedoc, Provence), and in Flanders and Picardy it is only 4·00.†

These facts suffice to show that we ought not to accuse those writers of inaccuracy who first affirmed that fecundity was greater in warm than in cold climates: they were in the right.

But if we extend these researches—and if, in extending them to many countries, we generalise still more —then the differences of climate, temperature, and position disappear, their influence ceases to be manifested, and nature obeys other laws."

According to M. Benoiston, there are born, each year, by marriage—

STATES AND PROVINCES.	Children to one Marriage.
In Portugal,	5·14
·· the province of Bergamasco (Italy),	5·24
·· the government of Venice,	5·45
·· Savoy,	5·65
·· Roussillon (Eastern Pyrenees),	5·17
·· a part of Dauphiny,	5·39
·· ·· Lyonnais,	5·68
·· ·· Anjou,	5·09
·· ·· Poitou,	5·46
·· ·· Brittany,	5·52
·· ·· Franche-Comté,	5·01
·· ·· Alsace,	5·03
·· the canton of Fribourg,	5·35
·· a part of Scotland,	5·13
·· Bohemia,	5·27
·· Muscovy,	5·25
·· Eastern and Western Flanders,	5·27

"These different countries present a very great fecundity, and we may observe that eight of them are mountainous (Brittany, Franche-Comté, Roussillon, Comté de Nice, Savoy, Fribourg, Bohemia, Bergamasco): we also see that these are in general fertile countries, where the produce of the ground is adequate to the necessities of the people.

It appears that in maritime countries the births are also more numerous than in inland states; and the same is successively the case for wine, pasturage, corn, and forest countries."

The following table for Belgium presents some interesting details :—

* Annales des Sciences Naturelles, Dec. 1836.

† M. Benoiston de Châteauneuf informs us that he has deducted a certain number for natural children, but he does not say whether the same has been done for the rest of Europe.

Provinces.	Population in 1830.	Births: 1825-29.	Marriages : 1825-29.	Inhabitants To one Birth.	To one Mar.	Children to 100 Marriages.
Antwerp,	354,974	11,018	2,392	32	149	4·48*
Brabant,	556,146	18,893	4,035	29	137	4·68
Flanders, East	733,938	24,148	4,246	30	173	5·19
·· West,	601,678	20,315	4,145	30	169	4·90
Liege,	369,937	11,837	2,382	31	155	4·72
Hainau,	604,957	20,016	4,323	30	140	4·51
Limbourg,	337,703	10,589	2,422	32	139	4·37
Namur,	212,725	11,018	1,378	32	154	4·57
Luxembourg,†	292,151	10,477	2,278	28	128	4·67
Kingdom,	4,064,209	135,140	28,076	30	144	4·72

We see at first that the fecundity, estimated either in the ratio of the population or of the marriages, presents little difference, which is an evidence that the population is so far homogeneous; and we shall truly find this to be the case a little farther on. Luxembourg and Brabant, which have produced the greatest number of births in proportion to the population, are also the two provinces which, all things being equal, present the greatest number of marriages. The Flemings have fewer marriages, but the marriages are more fruitful there than in the rest of the kingdom, which explains why the ratio of births is exactly equal to that of the whole of Belgium. Moreover, it becomes difficult, from the small extent of this country, to recognise the effects of some of the influential causes which have been pointed out above, and especially difference of climate.

It is here necessary to make an essential remark, which is, that generally, in estimating the fecundity of marriages in Belgium, the total number of births has been compared with the total number of marriages, without making any deduction for illegitimate children; and I myself confess that, owing to the want of documents, I have not made this deduction in my works. I have reason to think, from some partial data, that the proportion of illegitimate to legitimate births would differ very little from that of France, where 100 marriages produce 408 births, taking them indiscriminately, and of these only 379 are legitimate births, that is to say, 29 less. In supposing, then, that legitimate and illegitimate children are in the same ratio to each other in Belgium as in France, the figure expressing the fecundity of marriages would not be more than about 4·4, which still gives it a very high value compared with other countries.

The distinction of first, second, and third times of wedlock, becomes equally important to enable us to work out the share of each of the influential causes with precision. In countries, indeed, where successive marriages are easily accomplished, the figure expressing the fecundity of marriages should be very small, for the fecundity of woman is not without limits; and the ratio of births to marriages should necessarily change, if the marriages become more numerous, while the number of births yet remains the same.

Among the causes influencing the number which expresses the fecundity, we ought to rank the circumstance of a town or country residence. During the decennial period of 1803 to 1813, the only one for which we may form calculations in Belgium, we find that 100 marriages have produced 484 births in the town, and 450 in the country;‡ but we might still reasonably object, that, legitimate not having been

* The fecundity of marriages has been calculated for the years between 1803 and 1829: the numbers of this province are not very accurate, since the population is not exactly known.

† The population of Luxembourg is that of 1825: the average of the marriages for this province and for Limbourg has only been taken for three instead of five years; the same also for the kingdom.

‡ Recherches sur la Reproduction et la Mortalité.

distinguished from illegitimate births, this difference can only be deceptive.

If we seek to establish the ratio of the energy of fecundation to the population, we generally find, taking only the figure of the fecundity of the great cities of Europe, that it has a superior value to that of the adjacent country districts. We may see, in the *Bulletin des Sciences Géographiques* for April 1831, a table of the changes of the population of the principal cities of Europe, which, if the elements of it are exact, gives one birth for 22·4 inhabitants, as the average of 78 cities there noted. The cities which present the extremes of the series are—Utrecht, 19·0; Liverpool, 18·0; Oporto, 19·6; London, 40·8; St Petersburg, 46·7.[*]

When we make the distinction between city and country for Belgium, we also find that the number of births, compared to the population, is greater in the cities: it has been 1 to 29·1 between the years 1825 and 1829. In the country, its value has been 1 to 30·4: and hence it would really appear, that there is a more active cause of fecundity in cities than in the country.

M. Villermé, in his work on Monthly Births,[†] has shown that unhealthy periods, principally those of epidemics produced by marsh miasmata, are unfavourable to fecundity. This philosopher has found a direct proof of it in the number of conceptions, which diminishes at those periods of the year when marshy emanations are most intense.

Mr Sadler, in his work on the Law of Population, has examined the relation which exists between the number of marriages, of births, and of deaths: in extending his comparisons to the numbers of different countries, and especially to those of England, France, and the old kingdom of the Low Countries, he has generally found, that *places which annually produce the greatest number of marriages are those where the fecundity of marriages is the smallest*, being, as it were, a sort of compensation which prevents the population of a country making too rapid an advance. The same author finds, *that the countries where marriages are very numerous, are also those which have a greater mortality*. We may form some idea of his results from the following table, which is a summary of the values obtained for France :—

Table showing that the Preventive Obstacle diminishes the Fecundity of Marriages, and that the Fecundity is regulated by the amount of Mortality.

Proportion of Marriages.	Number of Departments.	Legitimate Births to one Marriage.	Inhabitants to one Death.
1 to 110 to 120 Inhabitants,	4	3·79	35·4
·· 120 to 130 ··	15	3·79	39·2
·· 130 to 140 ··	23	4·17	39·0
·· 140 to 150 ··	18	4·36	40·6
·· 150 to 160 ··	10	4·43	40·3
·· 160 to 170 ··	9	4·48	42·7
·· 170 and more,	6	4·84	46·4

These facts, established by Mr Sadler, are verified by the numbers which the different parts of England furnish. Mr Sadler has also availed himself of the documents which I had given for the ancient kingdom of the Low Countries, and found a new confirmation of his results. I shall also present this table, which is instructive on many points.

In comparing countries with each other, after having compared the parts of which they are composed, and in making use of the data which would seem to deserve most confidence, we find :—

* The smallness of this ratio for St Petersburg, is owing to the peculiar state of the population, which contains a much greater number of men than of women.

† Annales de Hygiène, Janvier 1831.

Kingdoms.	Inhabitants			Fecundity.
	For one Marriage.	For one Birth.	For one Death.	
Prussia,*	102·	23·1	36·2	4·23
England,†	128·	34·0	49·0	3·77
France,‡	131·4	32·2	39·7	3·79
Belgium,§	144·	30·0	43·0	4·72

These results do not so well agree with the principles which Mr Sadler has deduced from his particular observations.

Provinces.	Inhabitants for one Marriage.	Births for one Marriage.	Average.	Inhabitants for one Death.	Average.
Limbourg,	90·3	3·09		4·75	
One marriage for less than 100 inhabitants,		3·09	3·09	4·75	4·75
Holland, Northern,	104·4	4·50		34·5	
·· Southern,	113·3	4·74		35·5	
Zealand,	113·7	5·49		31·4	
Utrecht,	118·2	4·86		36·3	
One marriage for 100 to 120 inhabitants,		19·59	4·89	137·2	34·3
Overyssel,	121·9	4·60		48·5	
Friesland,	128·7	5·75		46·1	
Drent,	130·3	4·89		55·0	
Guelderland,	131·1	4·75		53·7	
Hainau,	136·5	4·98		51·1	
Flanders, Western,	137·7	5·01		40·7	
One marriage for 120 to 140 inhabitants,		29·78	4·96	290·1	48·3
Brabant, Southern,	142·2	5·45		38·2	
Antwerp,	142·9	4·65		48·8	
Groningen,	149·3	5·17		49·3	
Luxembourg,	149·9	5·37		53·8	
Brabant, Northern,	150·0	5·14		51·4	
Liege,	154·1	5·33		46·2	
One marriage for 140 to 160 inhabitants,		31·11	5·18	287·7	47·9
Flanders, Eastern,	165·3	5·82		44·8	
One marriage for 160 or more inhabitants,		5·82	5·82	44·8	44·8

After considering all the documents produced by Mr Sadler in support of his observation, it seems to me that we might truly admit as very probable, that a great mortality induces many marriages, and that marriages are less productive in proportion as they are more numerous. But I think that the author is too eager to draw arguments from them against the anti-populationist, whom he strives to defeat when attempting to make particular theories prevail. It seems to me that the facts which he cites, in order to acquire all the importance which he is desirous of giving them, should be supported by another statistical document, namely, the number of marriages of the first, second, and third wedlocks. It is said that deaths make way for marriages; this is what the researches of Mr Sadler prove: it is also said that mortality increases fecundity; and Mr Sadler opposes the results at which he has arrived to this assertion. It is here, I think, that the error

* Babbage in Brewster's Journal of Sciences, No. I., new series.
† Rickman—Preface to the Abstract of the Population, 1821.
‡ Annuaire du Bureau des Longitudes de Paris.
§ Annuaire de l'Observatoire de Bruxelles.

will be found. Firstly, it is necessary not to confound the fecundity of the marriages with the fecundity of the population : then, on the other hand, in a country where the mortality would be very great, especially among adult persons, the marriages of second and third wedlocks would be more numerous, and each marriage would thus produce, during its continuance, a fewer number of children; although, in point of fact, the fecundity of the population were very great. For example, in the provinces of France which have the least mortality, and, as Mr Sadler observes, the fewest marriages, we find the greatest number of children to each marriage. This latter observation appears to me to be a necessary consequence of the former : a woman, who has five children by one marriage, might, the mortality being greater, have these five children by two successive marriages, or even by a greater number. It would be very natural, then, that the fecundity of marriages should appear to have diminished. It is even evident, according to the mode of reasoning I have just employed, that it would be necessary to admit that, *all things being equal, in a country where mortality becomes greater, marriages should become more numerous, and the fecundity of marriages, on the contrary, decrease.* This result, which I deduce from purely rational considerations, is found to be supported by the facts brought forward by Mr Sadler; but it does not follow that the absolute fecundity of this country should decrease, or that the country should have a smaller annual number of births. I think the contrary, and believe that I can prove it a little farther on.

What so often renders statistical results difficult of interpretation is, that facts are assumed as simple which in their nature are complex. Thus, it appears to me impossible to determine any thing concerning the fecundity of the women of a country merely from the ratio of marriages to legitimate births: we necessarily ought to consider the mortality of the country we are examining, and take the marriages of second or third wedlocks into account. I regret that M. Benoiston de Châteauneuf, in his interesting work on the Fecundity of Europe, has not paid attention to this element: I think he might have overcome several difficulties which his subject presented to him, (which was extremely complex), and have explained some apparent anomalies.

It will also be necessary henceforth, in all researches on fecundity, to consider the age of marriage in the different localities. For example, it is evident, if persons do not marry at the same age in the country as in cities, that, all things being equal, we ought to expect to find different numbers for the fecundity of marriages. The same will be the case when we compare certain northern states, where marriage takes place very late, with southern countries, where it occurs very early. I repeat again, that the more we study the phenomena of population, the more complexity we find in them; but, at the same time, we have the hope of succeeding, by an analysis conducted with sagacity, and by using good materials, in ascertaining the causes on which they depend, and in estimating the degree of influence of each of these causes.

4. Influence of Years.

We possess different documents, which inform us of the fecundity of marriages of the same country at different periods, and which thus allow us to judge whether, all things being equal, this fecundity has undergone variations independent of the annual changes resulting from a more or less prosperous state of things, such as those which would arise from changes in the nature of the climate, or from the progressive advancement of civilisation. In making use of the Prussian documents furnished by Süssmilch, and retaining the periods of this philosopher, we find at first :

Periods.	Average Number			Baptisms. to one Marriage.
	of Marriages.	of Baptisms.	of Deaths.	
1693 to 1697, -	5,747	19,715	14,962	3·43
1698 to 1702, -	9,070	24,112	14,474	3·97
1703 to 1708, -	6,042	26,886	16,430	4·42
1709 to 1711, -	5,835	18,833	85,955	3·23
1712 to 1716, -	4,965	21,603	11,948	4·35
1717 to 1721, -	4,324	21,396	12,039	4·95
1722 to 1726, -	4,719	21,452	12,063	4·55
1727 to 1731, -	4,808	20,559	12,825	4·28
1732 to 1735, -	5,424	22,692	15,475	4·18
1736 to 1737, -	5,522	20,394	25,425	3·69
1738 to 1742, -	5,582	22,069	15,255	3·96
1743 to 1746, -	5,469	25,275	15,117	4·62
1747 to 1751, -	6,423	28,235	17,272	4·40
1752 to 1756, -	5,599	28,392	19,154	5·07
1816 to 1823, -	109,237	480,632	307,113	5·40 *
1827, -	106,270	524,062	368,578	4·93 †

The numbers belonging to the commencement of this century are births in general, whilst those of Süssmilch only include baptisms ; which may cause a difference, the amount of which I do not know how to obtain. In order to arrive at the accidental causes, I have taken periods somewhat more extended than the preceding.

From 1693 to 1708, -	-	3·94 baptisms to one marriage.
·· 1709 to 1721, -	-	4·18 ··
·· 1722 to 1735, -	-	4·36 ··
·· 1736 to 1746, -	-	4·09 ··
·· 1747 to 1756, -	-	4·73 ··
·· 1816 to 1823, -	-	4·40 births to one marriage.
·· 1827, -	-	4·93 ··

Average, - 4·37

For England, we find, according to Messrs Rickman and Sadler, vol. ii. p. 478—

1760,	-	3·66 baptisms to one marriage.
1770,	-	3·61 ··
1780,	-	3·56 ··
1785,	-	3·66 ··
1790,	-	3·59 ··
1795,	-	3·53 ··
1800,	-	3·40 ··
1805,	-	3·50 ··
1810,	-	3·60 ··

Average, 3·57

Mr Sadler gives, for the fecundity of the years 1680 to 1730, the numbers 4·65 and 4·25, which would seem to prove that the fecundity has diminished; but it might also happen that this apparent increase depended on the manner in which the numbers have been collected.[‡]

Sweden gives the following results :[§]—

From 1749 to 1758,	-	4·20 births to one marriage.
·· 1759 to 1764, -		4·05 ··
·· 1821 to 1826,	-	4·03 ··

Average, - 4·09

And I have found for the ancient kingdom of the Low Countries—

From 1803 to 1812,	-	4·69 births to one marriage.
·· 1815 to 1824, -		4·74 ··
·· 1825 to 1830,	-	4·831 ··

Average, - 4·72

It would result from the examples which have been presented, that the fecundity of marriages does not sensibly vary in the same country and in the course of a century, when we include periods of time suffi-

* Babbage, in Brewster's Journal of Sciences, No. I., new series.
† Bulletin des Sciences, Janvier 1830.
‡ We might also attribute it to greater prudence and circumspection. It has also been observed, that the proportional number of marriages, for the last half century, has progressively diminished in England.— (SAY — *Cours d'Economie Politique*, p. 7, ch. 2.
§ Sadler, vol. ii. pp. 258, 262.

ciently great to remove the accidental causes attending years of greater or less prosperity.

It is remarkable that epidemics, periods of great scarcity, and all severe scourges, do not merely exercise a sensible influence on the number of deaths, but also on the amount of marriages and births. It does not certainly follow that, because provisions are rather dearer one year, that there should necessarily be fewer births and marriages, because the influence of this increase of price may be masked by some other cause; but when the dearness of provisions is very decided, and when there is truly a scarcity, we have the greatest likelihood of finding it manifested in the books of marriages and births. This is what we shall easily find on inspecting the following table for the kingdom of the Netherlands:—

Years.	Births.		Deaths.		Marriages.	Price of Wheat.	Half a Hectolitre of Rye.
	Town.	Country.	Town.	Country.			
						florins.	florins.
1815, -	59,737	135,625	49,007	88,592	48,854	4·90	3·50
1816, -	58,095	138,507	47,327	88,796	40,801	9·56	7·17
1817, -	55,207	122,348	55,240	97,368	33,881	6·79	4·28
1818, -	55,665	128,041	49,169	91,247	39,218	5·18	3·82
1819, -	61,788	143,504	49,738	98,659	42,401	3·72	2·52
1820, -	61,263	133,685	50,681	94,496	43,258	3·74	2·08
1821, -	65,356	145,003	49,706	88,414	44,796	3·71	1·87
1822, -	67,794	151,747	52,078	95,475	46,949	3·30	2·46
1823, -	65,318	148,299	48,815	91,877	45,424	2·95	1·96
1824, -	67,030	151,636	47,662	87,253	44,665	2·48	1·51
1825, -	68,078	153,813	50,689	95,449	47,097	3·12	2·08
1826, -	67,919	153,970	58,749	110,155	48,054	4·02	2·96
Total,	753,250	1,706,178	608,861	1,127,781	525,398		
Aver.,	62,770	142,182	50,739	93,981	43,783	4·48	3·03

The year 1817 presents a much greater number of deaths, for the cities and country, than the preceding years, whilst the births and marriages, on the contrary, have been much fewer: this year was really a year of scarcity, as was also the preceding one. We may observe that, during the period from 1709 to 1711, the same effect took place in Prussia, according to the numbers of Süssmilch, which have been quoted above, but from another cause—the pestilence which ravaged that country in 1710. The increase of mortality, also, has been accompanied by a falling off in the number of baptisms, and that of marriages has likewise fallen, but more particularly in the succeeding years, which has undoubtedly been owing to the vacuity which was formed in the class of adult persons. A singular mistake in figures, led one of the first economists of this century to conclude that the births were multiplied, as if to make up for the void left by the pestilence: indeed, after such scourges, it is not unusual to see the population regain its relation to the means of subsistence by an increase of births. In general, privations are not only mortal to the human species, but even arrest its development: their influence is not always felt immediately—we often perceive that a long time after the cause has ceased to operate. In 1826, the price of bread rose again in Belgium, and we also see that the mortality became greater, and the number of marriages and births which the preceding year presented, underwent a sensible diminution.* However, these latter elements, especially the figure of births, are, from their nature, less subject to variation than the number of deaths.

On the contrary, in the years 1821 and 1824, the price of grain was at the lowest, and these are the years which, with respect to the increase of the population, have presented the least degree of mortality; they are also followed by years which present more marriages and births. The changes in the price of bread have also as marked an influence in the country as in town: it is perhaps less observable in the births.

* We have for the following years:—

Years.	Births in Town.	Births in Country.	Marriages.
1827, - -	64,100	143,288	45,632
1828, - -	68,674	153,166	47,400

5. Influence of Seasons.

The seasons have a marked influence on all the relations of man; they operate on his physical as well as his moral nature. Thus, the vehemence of his passions, and the intensity of his inclination to crime, are modified according to temperature and climate; and the same also holds in respect to his reproductive faculty and mortality. Physiologists have already observed the influence of the seasons on the births and deaths of mankind; but their results, in general, do not agree much with each other, because they are modified by the locality, the period, and the habits of the people to whom they applied. In 1824, I published some particular researches on this interesting subject, in the Nouveaux Mémoires de l'Académie de Bruxelles.* The result of these researches was, that the number of births and deaths increases and decreases alternately; and that these numbers reach their maximum towards the month of January for deaths, and towards the month of February for births; and their minimum about six months after, in July.† These conclusions were afterwards confirmed by the principal cities of the Low Countries; and the general results of the kingdom were found to agree with the numbers first obtained for Brussels. These researches became the subject of several interesting letters from M. Villermé,‡ who, in the Annales de Hygiène, has since treated the same subject to its fullest extent, and has shown that the periods of maximum and minimum approach or recede according to the climate and habits of the people.

We shall commence by stating the number of births in the cities and country of the ancient kingdom of the Low Countries, during the twelve years from 1815 to 1826 inclusive. For the better understanding of these numbers, we have taken into account the unequal length of the months, and have taken quantities corresponding to months of 31 days: we have also assumed as unity, in the two last columns, the average of the total number of births, both for town and country.

Months—1815 to 1826.	Births.		Births.	
	Town.	Country.	Town.	Country.
January, - - -	68,255	159,787	1·067	1·102
February, - - -	71,820	170,699	1·122	1·177
March, - - -	69,267	164,851	1·083	1·137
April, - - -	66,225	147,118	1·035	1·014
May, - - -	62,102	134,446	0·971	0·927
June, - - -	58,730	125,026	0·918	0·862
July, - - -	57,151	121,512	0·893	0·838
August, - - -	59,620	131,657	0·932	0·908
September, - - -	62,731	144,389	0·980	0·995
October, - - -	62,500	146,362	0·977	1·009
November, - - -	64,273	146,285	1·005	1·009
December, - - -	65,120	148,186	1·018	1·022

Let us first observe, that the influence of the seasons is much more apparent in the country than in town; which appears natural, since, in the latter case, there are fewer means of maintaining an equality of temperature. The maximum of births in February supposes the maximum of conceptions to happen in the month of May, when the vital powers regain all their activity, after the rigours of winter.

* Sur les Lois des Naissances et de la Mortalité à Bruxelles, tome iii. p. 501. See also the Correspondance Mathematique et Physique, tomes i. and ii.

† The thirty-fourth volume of the Mémoires de l'Académie Royale de Turin, published in 1830, contains two letters of Professor Vanswinden on the same subject, which inform us that this philosopher had already arrived at the same result as early as 1798. It is to be regretted that we were not sooner acquainted with these, as also with the researches of M. Balbo, Sur l'Influence des Saisons. It would appear from these researches that deaths have not so regular a course as with us.

‡ See the letters addressed to me by M. Villermé in the Correspondance Mathematique et Physique, tome ii., and in the Recherches sur la Population, les Naissances, &c., dans le Royaume des Pays Bas, p. 15.

Should we not be correct in concluding, from the preceding results, that climates most favourable to fecundity are those which enjoy a mild temperature, and that excess of cold or heat should prove unfavourable to human procreation. This induction is in accordance with the results which have been made known above, on the influence of climates.

Now, if we wish to estimate the different causes which may modify the influence of seasons, we cannot follow a better guide than M. Villermé; and, not to modify the conclusions which he has deduced from his laborious researches concerning climates, we shall copy them verbatim, referring for them to the work of this savant, *De la Distribution par Mois des Conceptions et des Naissances de l'Homme.* (*Ann. de Hygiène.*)

" The direct or indirect influence of the annual revolution of the earth around the sun, of the great changes of temperature which this revolution causes, and of certain meteorological conditions, on conception, and consequently on the births of the human race, appears, then, very evident. But this induction, well founded as it may be, can only be really proved when, at the other side of the equatorial line, where the seasons succeed each other in the same order as on this side, but at contrary times, we see the periodic return of similar results occurring at similar seasons.

Well, in the republic of Buenos Ayres, the only country of the southern hemisphere of which I have been able to procure monthly results of births, the latter are so distributed that the greatest monthly numbers occur in July, August, and September, that is to say, in winter; and the fewest numbers in January and May, or in summer. The alternation of maximum and minimum follows that of the seasons precisely.

The influence of the different positions of the sun with respect to the earth, on the monthly distribution of conceptions, and consequently of births, is therefore very certain.

There is another consequence: the maximum and minimum periods of conception approach each other in hot countries, and recede from each other in cold ones, especially the period of minimum.

Finally, it results from all the facts which have been cited, that in our state of civilisation we are, at least in some measure, subjected to the different periodic influences of the kind we are considering, which are manifested by plants and animals."

6. Influence of the Hours of the Day.

Curiosity led me to investigate, if there existed any relation between the different hours of the day and the moments of births:* I have been assisted in this department by the data which M. Guiétte, then connected with the Lying-in Hospital, Brussels, communicated to me; these data are the result of eleven years' observations, from 1811 to 1822. I have since communicated them to M. Villermé, who has found them perfectly analogous to the results obtained at the Lying-in Hospital of Paris, but which are still unpublished, so far as I know.

With these observations, which, up to the present time, are very few, I present the indications of still-born children, at periods of six hours, according to the numbers observed by M. Guiétte in 1827–28.

Hours.	Births: 1811-1822.	Still-born: 1811-1822.	Births: 1827-1828.
After midnight, -	798	53	145
Before mid-day, -	614	51	119
After mid-day, -	574	59	119
Before midnight, -	694	55	148
Total, - -	2680	218	531

* Correspondance Mathématique et Physique, 1827, tome iii. p. 42; and Recherches sur la Population, p. 21.

We see, from these data, that births are more numerous during the night than in the day-time: the ratio for the years between 1811 and 1822 is 1492 to 1188, or 1·26 to 1; and for the two years of the observations of M. Guiétte, 293 to 238, or 1·23 to 1: therefore, about five children are born during the night to every four born during the day.

These observations have given rise to similar ones: Dr Buek of Hamburg, treating the same subject, has arrived at the following results:* the numbers are reduced to 1000 :—

Births.	Winter.	Spring.	Summer.	Autumn.	Average.
After midnight,	325	320	291	312	312
Before mid-day,	270	252	256	216	249
After mid-day,	190	136	189	225	183
Before midnight,	215	292	264	247	256

These numbers give the ratio of night to day, as 1·31 to 1. It would appear from these particular data, that births are generally most numerous towards the hours of midnight and mid-day.

As to still-born children, the hourly difference is not appreciable, from the small number of observations which have been collected.

~~~~~~~~~

CHAPTER III.

OF THE INFLUENCE OF DISTURBING CAUSES ON THE NUMBER OF BIRTHS.

1. Influence of Professions, Food, &c.

IF it be true that every thing which has a direct influence on the physical constitution of man, either weakening or strengthening it, has also an influence on his reproductive tendency, and causes the number and kind of births, and also the times at which they take place, to vary, we cannot doubt the influence of professions, trades, and modes of life, minor causes necessarily included in the preceding general ones.

It is to be regretted, however, that we have no particular researches on this interesting point. M. Benoiston, in his *Mémoire sur l'Intensité de la Fécondité en Europe,* has felt the importance of it, and has laboured to verify one particular fact, which seems to require further examination. We generally think that the fecundity of marriage is low among fishermen, and ascribe it to the phosphorus contained in the fish on which they live. But deeper researches have shown, that the alleged fact is at least doubtful; for it is found that the maritime departments of France, inhabited by fishermen, have almost exactly the same fecundity as the rest of the kingdom.

M. Villermé, in his work *Sur les Naissances par Mois,* has endeavoured to ascertain if the usual severe labour of the country diminishes fecundity, or changes the periods of conception; but he has not been able to obtain any conclusive results.

It appears that the influence of professions is generally masked by other modifying causes, which act so powerfully that, considering the statistical elements which we possess, we cannot appreciate the influence of professions in a satisfactory manner. All that we can decide, from researches which have hitherto been made, is, that it is weak, and especially depends on the quantity and nature of the food, and the development of the physical powers. " There is no principle of political economy on which authors are more fully agreed," M. Benoiston† says, " than that the population of a state is always in proportion to the amount of its produce. It is by virtue of this law, which has

* Nachricht von dem Gesundheits—Zutande der Stadt Hamburg, von N. H. Julius. Hamburg: 1829.
† Sur l'Influence de la Fécondité en Europe.

few exceptions, that we do not see a great number of births among a poor and oppressed people, who have neither agriculture, industry, nor liberty. So far is such from being the case, that slave populations decline instead of increase. It is an acknowledged fact, that in St Domingo, in 1788, three marriages among the blacks only produced two children, whilst each marriage of the white people produced three." *

I do not know whether it is an unfounded prejudice, that in Protestant states, clergymen have generally a larger family than the other professions—at least, this opinion was generally believed in the ancient kingdom of the Low Countries. But the fact may be explained, not only from the nature of the profession, but also because the income of clergymen often increases with the number of their children.

2. The Influence of Morality.

When speaking of legitimate and illegitimate births, we showed that a state of concubinage tends to produce fewer male children: the same would be the effect of all habits which enervate the powers—they also diminish the number of conceptions. It also seems to be well established, that prostitutes either produce fewer children or are barren. The too early approximation of the sexes induces similar effects, and produces children which have a less probability of life.

Habits of order and foresight ought also to exercise a considerable influence on the number of marriages, and consequently of births. The man whose condition is unsettled, if he allow himself to be governed by reason, dreads to divide with a family the vicissitudes of fortune to which he is exposed; many economists have also maintained, and with reason, that the most efficacious mode of preventing an excess of population in a country, is to diffuse knowledge and sentiments of order and foresight. It is evident that the people of a country would not seek so much to contract alliances and load the future with trouble, if each individual found a difficulty in providing for his own subsistence. The great fecundity of Ireland has been cited as an example of the influence which depression and improvidence may exercise over productiveness.† When man no longer reasons, when he is demoralised by misery, and just lives from day to day, the cares of a family no more affect him then than the care of his own existence; and, impelled by momentary gratification, he begets children, careless of the future, and, if we may use the expression, resigns to that Providence who has supported him, all the care of the progeny to which he has given existence.

Foresight may also render marriages less fruitful, because a man is less eager in reproduction if he fears that his family, becoming too numerous, may one day feel the finger of distress, or be under the necessity of undergoing privations and renouncing a certain degree of ease to which they have been accustomed. I do not doubt but that particular researches, undertaken with the design of elucidating this interesting point, will some day confirm these conjectures: they would be of the greatest utility in pointing out the course to be pursued in the instruction which it is proper to give to the people.

One of the most striking examples of the effects of the indolence, poverty, and demoralisation of a people, is given by the province of Guanaxato in Mexico, where 100 births take place annually for every 1608 inhabitants, and 100 deaths for every 1970. " Some traveller," says M. D'Ivernois, " who has observed the sad concurrence of excessive mortality, fecundity, and poverty, in Mexico, attributes it to the banana, which almost ensures them an adequate quantity of

food : others charge the raging heat of the climate, which begets an insurmountable aversion to labour, and leaves the inhabitants of this indolent region in a manner insensible to every other desire but that which impels the sexes towards each other. Hence the myriads of children, the greater part of whom do not live to be weaned, or only appear on the registers to give place immediately to others ; and the surviving ones commence the inert and brief existence of their predecessors, like them the victims of the indolence, apathy, and perpetual misery to which they are habituated, without experiencing the necessity of extricating themselves, any more than their parents had done. To form an idea of what takes place in this republic, we must read the report of a Swiss who visited it in 1830. Nothing can equal the amount of physical, moral, and political evil, with which he has supplied his hideous account. Although he neglected to ascertain the number of births, he has guessed it, since he calls Mexico a *barbarous China.*"

The criminal documents of France inform us of an equally curious circumstance, namely, that the period of the maximum of conceptions nearly coincides with that of the greatest number of rapes. M. Villermé rationally remarks, that this coincidence may lead us to think that those who are guilty, are sometimes obliged in an irresistible manner, not having the free command of the will. This conjecture acquires the greatest degree of probability from the researches which I shall explain further on, when considering the tendency to crime : we shall there see how worthy this subject is of the attention of philosophers and legislators.

The production of illegitimate children deserves an attentive consideration for many reasons : in a political view, especially, it ought to become the subject of the most serious researches, since its tendency is to diffuse through society a continually increasing number of individuals deprived of the means of existence, and who become a burden to the state. On the other hand, these individuals, generally possessing a feeble organisation,* as we shall soon see, rarely arrive at maturity ; so that they do not even afford the hope of compensating some day for the sacrifices which have been made for them. According to Mr Babbage (Letter to the Right Hon. T. P. Courtenay), we reckon—

	For 1000 Legitimate Children—	For 1 Illegitimate Child—
In France, - -	69·7 illegitimate.	14·3 legitimate.
Kingdom of Naples, -	48·4 ..	20·6 ..
Prussia, - - -	76·4 ..	13·1 ..
Westphalia, - -	88·1 ..	11·4 ..
Cities of Westphalia,	217·4 ..	4·6 ..
Montpellier, - -	91·6 ..	10·9 ..

We see that, in the cities of Westphalia, the number of illegitimate children is exceedingly great. About fifty years ago, at Stockholm, Gottingen, and Leipsic, one-sixth of the births were illegitimate ; one-fourth at Cassel ; and one-seventh at Jena.† From Berlin, we obtain the following results :—

From 1783 to 1793,	26,572 births, of whom 2,834 illegitimate, or 9 to 1
.. 1794 to 1798, 30,165	.. 3,006 .. 9 to 1
.. 1799 to 1803, 31,638	.. 3,800 .. 8 to 1
.. 1804 to 1808, 30,459	.. 4,941 .. 6 to 1
.. 1819 to 1822, 26,971	.. 4,319 .. 6 to 1
.. 1783 to 1822, 145,705	.. 18,890 .. 7 to 1

The number of illegitimate births has therefore been increasing. The following are the numbers for Paris, for the last few years, according to the *Annuaires du Bureau des Longitudes* :—

---

* Traité du Commerce des Colonies, p. 218.
† See an article by M. D'Ivernois, inserted by the *Bibliothèque Universelle de Genève*, Mars 1830.

* [It is curious to observe how precisely opposite to the truth, as established by statistics, the generally received opinions of mankind have been on most points.—See Shakspeare's Historical Plays—*King Lear* and *King John*.]
† Casper, Beitrage, &c.

Years.	Births.		Legitimate Births to 1 Illegitimate.
	Legitimate.	Illegitimate.	
1823, - -	27,070	9,806	2·76
1824, - -	28,812	10,221	2·82
1825, - ,,	29,253	10,039	2·91
1826, -	29,970	10,502	2·85
1827, -	29,806	10,392	2·86
1828, -	29,601	10,475	2·81
1829, - -	28,721	9,953	2·88
1830, -	28,587	10,007	2·85
1831,* - -	29,530	10,378	2·83
1832,* -	26,283	9,237	2·84
Average, -	287,633	101,010	2·84

Thus, for 28 births there have been almost exactly 10 illegitimate children: I think this ratio is the most unfavourable of any which has hitherto been made known.†

* In these numbers, 1099 and 1065 children, acknowledged and legitimatised subsequent to birth, are not included.

† [The views of M. Quetelet on this subject do not appear to embrace all the causes of illegitimacy. It may happen that in countries where the means of subsistence are of difficult attainment, parties, from prudential considerations, will not enter the married state. This is visibly the case in Scotland, where the illegitimate births are very numerous, but, from the want of national registers, cannot be stated. The ratio of illegitimates, we have reason to believe, is much greater in Scotland than in Ireland, where matrimony is entered upon with little regard for the future. Thus, extreme prudence may be said to lead to immorality. The possibility of effecting retrospective marriage (that is, dating it from before the birth of the illegitimate children), is another frequent cause of illegitimacy in Scotland; and it may be added, that the demand for wet-nurses by the higher class of mothers for their infants, forms another prevailing cause of illegitimacy, at least in large towns.

For the purpose of throwing light on this important subject in social statistics, we beg to subjoin the following passages from the Sixth Annual Report of the Poor-Law Commissioners of England, for 1840 : they occur in the report handed in from Sir Edmund Head on the Law of Bastardy:—" Mr Laing, in his recent Tour in Sweden, gives most instructive evidence as to the number and causes of illegitimate births in that country. It appears that the proportion of illegitimate to legitimate births in all Sweden, from 1820 to 1830, is as 1 in 14·6, and in Stockholm as high as 1 to 2 3. Mr Laing goes on to remark—' There are two minor causes, both, however, showing a degraded moral feeling, which were stated to me as contributing much to this lax state of female morals. One is, that no woman in the middle or higher ranks, or who can afford to do otherwise, ever nurses her own child. A girl who has got a child is not therefore in a worse, but in a better situation, as she is pretty sure of getting a place for two years, which is the ordinary time of nursing. The illegitimacy of the child is in this community rather a recommendation of the mother, as the family is not troubled with the father or friends. As to the girl's own child, there is a foundling hospital, the second minor cause; in that it can be reared at a trifling expense, during the time the mother is out nursing. The unchaste are, therefore, in point of fact, better off than the chaste of the female sex in this town.'—Laing's Sweden, pp. 115, 117. It is well known that the results of the unrestricted reception of bastard children into the foundling hospitals in Belgium made it necessary for the government to take steps, in 1834, for discouraging the operation of, if not for repealing, the law under which it took place. I do not know what the present state of this question in that country is.—(See Senior, Foreign Poor-Laws, p. 137.) The legislation of the French Republic, by the laws of 27th Frimaire year 5, and 30th Ventôse year 5, explained by an edict of 19th January 1811, was most favourable to the mothers of bastards, and relieved them from all care of their own offspring. M. de Beaumont says— ' On sait qu'une loi de la révolution récompensait les filles mères d'enfants naturels.'—(L'Irlande, ii. 122, note 2.)

Under the influence of these laws, which only carried out the principle involved in our former practice, the illegitimate children increased from 1·47th (which they were, on an average of seven years, in 1780) to 1·14th, in 1825. (See Senior, Foreign Poor-Laws, p. 120 ; M'Culloch, notes to Adam Smith, p. 162, n.)—Malthus (vol. i. p. 375) reckoned the illegitimate births in France, at the time he was writing, as 1-11th of the whole.

Since writing the above, I have received the Annuaire du Bureau des Longitudes, for 1840, which gives the most recent information on French statistics.

3. The Influence of Political and Religious Institutions.

Nothing appears more adapted to multiply the population of a state, without inducing injury, than multiplying the products of agriculture and industry, and, at the same time, ensuring a prudent degree of liberty, which may be a guarantee for the public confidence. The absence of liberal institutions, which excite the activity of man, and at the same time increase his energy and comfort, must produce the effects which are observed in the East, where population languishes and decreases. On the contrary, in the United States, population increases with a rapidity which has no parallel in Europe. M. Villermé* observes, that at the period of the French revolution, " when the tithes, duties on wine, salt, feudal tenures, &c., and corporations and wardenships, had just been abolished (that is to say, when petty workmen and cultivators, in a word, the persons of no property, by far the most numerous class in the nation, found themselves all at once in a state of unaccustomed ease and competency, which they celebrated through the greatest part of the territory by feasts, and rejoicings, and more abundant food), the number of births increased, to diminish gradually afterwards."

Years of war and peace have likewise a marked influence on the population : we shall only quote one example at present. From the date of the wars of the empire, it was insinuated that the French population, far from being reduced, only made greater increases. M. D'Ivernois, who has succeeded in procuring the number of births and deaths for this period, has endeavoured to verify this assertion, so often repeated : he has, moreover, established two remarkable facts.† " Whoever investigates births, learns that,

It appears that in 1838 the number of births in Paris was

29,743 { 20,454 legitimate.
        { 9,289 illegitimate.

The illegitimate were therefore 31·2 per cent., or, to the legitimate, as 1 to 2·2 - a proportion larger than that existing at Stockholm.

In the whole of France, in 1837,

The total number of births was 943,349 { 873,520 legitimate.
                                        { 69,829 illegitimate.

That is, 7·4 per cent., or as 1 to 12·5.

The ' mouvement moyen' of the population, calculated on the twenty-one years from 1817 to 1837, gives, as the annual number of births,

968,752 { 899,451 legitimate.
        { 69,301 illegitimate.

That is, the illegitimate to the legitimate as 1 to 12·979.

It thus appears that the proportion of illegitimate births is greater in France than in Sweden, the former being as 1 to 12·979, and the latter as 1 in 14·6, according to Mr Laing (p. 115), while the morality of France would seem to have deteriorated since the calculation of Peuchet. I fear that there are rural districts in this country in which the proportion of illegitimate to legitimate births is far more unfavourable than that existing in the French empire. The population of the county of Radnor, in 1831, was 24,661. According to Mr Rickman, the number of baptisms registered in 1830 was

                         649
                         26 add for unentered births and baptisms.
                         —
                         675 total.

The number of illegitimate children born in 1830 is stated, on the same authority, to be 100 ; that is to say, 1 in 6·75, or more than twice as many in proportion as in France. This will not seem incredible, when we find from the table published in the appendix to the Second Annual Report of the Poor-Law Commissioners, that the average annual number of bastards chargeable to the parishes of the county of Radnor, in 1835 and 1836, was 417, or 1·59th of the whole population of the county, according to the census of 1831 ; and it is not to be wondered at that there are at present fifteen women with bastard children inmates of the workhouse of the Knighton Union, of which the population is only 8719 —census 1831."]—Note by the Publishers.

* Sur la Distribution par Mois, &c.
† Bibliothèque Universelle de Genève.

since the return of peace, the inhabitants of Normandy have been attempting to repair as soon as possible the breaches caused by the war. We are likewise informed, that, as soon as the breaches were filled up, the births have so exactly regained what may be considered as their former ratio of increase, that in 1830, the last year of which the returns are known, the births do not exceed the deaths by 5000, which, in a population of 2,645,798 inhabitants, is the slowest rate of increase we know of. The slight variations of the Norman registers for the third of a century, and their stationary condition during the year 1819, authorise us in regarding this movement of the population as the law which had for a long time regulated, and probably will long continue to regulate, the renewal of generations. The second fact, relative to deaths, informs us also, that far from being diminished, they have undergone a slight increase during the peace. But not to exaggerate the latter, we should always remember that, during the time of Napoleon, the soldiers who died abroad, or in the hospitals at home, were never put on the state registers; whilst, from the period of the restoration, the bureau of the civil state has inserted all military deaths, except, perhaps, those who have perished in the short expeditions to Spain and Algiers."

Political and religious prejudices appear to have been at all times favourable to the multiplication of the species; and great productiveness was considered as an unequivocal proof of celestial benediction and a prosperous state, without considering whether the births were in proportion to the means of subsistence.* It is astonishing that learned economists have fallen into the same notion. Have they not, in many instances, confounded the effect with the cause? However this may be, when a nation, after having been in a languishing state, regains its prosperity, we generally see an increase of fruitfulness; but we should err if we were to conclude that this increased fertility, which is only an effect of the better condition of the people, is, on the contrary, the source of it.

We cannot doubt that the overthrow of powerful religious bodies in several countries, the suppression of a great number of festivals formerly held sacred by the church, such as a less rigorous observance of Lent, and other similar causes, may not in our time have modified the degree of fecundity. From the researches of M. Villermé, it appears that in almost all Catholic countries, Lent, observed as it now is, and especially as it used to be, seems evidently to diminish the number of conceptions, at least during its continuance.

We have already seen that the time of marriage influences both the number and kind of births which the marriage produces. M. Villermé has endeavoured to ascertain if the number of marriages which are contracted during the different months of the year, has a direct ratio to the number of conceptions, and he has come to the following conclusions:—1st, that this ratio is scarcely perceptible; 2d, that, nevertheless, marriages appear to be more fruitful during the early months than afterwards; and, 3d, that it is not proved, probable as it may seem, that a woman is more likely to become pregnant within the first week or two of her marriage, if she marry in April, May, June, or July, than if she wedded at any other time of the year.

CHAPTER IV.

OF STILL-BORN CHILDREN.

In concluding what we have to say concerning births, and before examining the subject of deaths, I thought

* When a seventh son was born, it was customary for the prince to hold it at the baptismal font. This practice has not become obsolete in Belgium, and we might quote several examples in which the magistrate or one of his officers has been the representative of the monarch in such cases.

it necessary to say something on still-births, whose equivocal existence seems to belong as much to the annals of life as of death.

To take a general idea of the subject at first, it will be proper to state the ratio of still to live births, in the different countries of Europe, according to the calculations of the principal statisticians.*

PLACES.			Births to 1 Still-Birth.	Authors.
Strasburg,	-	-	11	Friedlander.
Hamburg,	-	-	15	Casper.
Dresden,	-	-	17	Rambach.
Paris,	-	-	19	Baumann.
Berlin,	-	-	20	Casper.
Vienna,	-	-	24	..
London,	-	-	27	Black.
Brunswick,	-	-	33	Rambach.
Stockholm,	-	-	36	Wargentin.

The average of this table would give about 1 still-birth to 22 living ones: this ratio differs slightly from that of Berlin, which has continued almost the same for the last sixty years. The following are the values which have been obtained, taking periods of several years:—

PERIODS.						Births to 1 Still-Birth.
From 1758 to 1763,	-	-	-	-	-	23·5
.. 1764 to 1769,	-	-	-	-	-	20·2
.. 1770 to 1774,	-	-	-	-	-	17·7
.. 1785 to 1792,	-	-	-	-	-	18·6
.. 1793 to 1800,	-	-	-	-	-	20·0
.. 1801 to 1808,	-	-	-	-	-	18·6
.. 1812 to 1821,	-	-	-	-	-	19·7
Average,						19·8

Few statistical documents are more liable to be faulty than those which belong to still-births; however, when the same ratio is so nearly maintained throughout, and within periods so close to each other, and when the data have been collected under different administrations, we have strong reason to believe that it is not far from the truth.

Casper thinks that the number of still-births, compared with live-births, is greater in town than in country; but he does not quote any results in proof of this assertion, which, however, is quite justified by the numbers which I have found for Western Flanders (Recherches sur la Reproduction et la Mortalité). The following are the values obtained for the years from 1827 to 1830 inclusive:—

	Average Number of		Ratio.
	Live-Births.	Still-Births.	
Town, - - - -	5,424	266	20·4
Country, - - - -	14,637	383	38·2

The ratio of still-births to live-births in town, is almost exactly the same as at Berlin; but it differs very much from that of the country, indeed it is almost double. It is natural, then, to inquire, whence arises the great danger which in town threatens the life of the child before it is born? May we not attribute it, in some measure, to the use of corsets and the habit of tight-lacing?

What is still more remarkable is, that the mortality is greater among boys than girls: thus, of 2597 still-births which have been counted for Western Flanders, 1517 were male and 1080 female children, which gives a ratio of 14 to 10 nearly. This difference is considerable, and since it is nearly the same for the tables of each particular year, we must ascribe it to a special cause. At Berlin, from 1785 to 1794, the computation is 1518 still-births of the male and 1210 of the female sex: also, from 1819 to 1822, 771 boys

* Dr Casper, in his Memoir on the Mortality of Children at Berlin, has presented some interesting researches on still-births, of the principal results of which I have availed myself.—Uber die Sterblickheit der Kinder in Berlin—Bietrage zur Medicinischen Statistick, &c. 8vo. Berlin: 1825.

and 533 girls came into the world without life. M. Casper says the ratio appears to be 28 to 20; it is, then, exactly the same as for Western Flanders. This new identity of results is very remarkable; and it will be interesting to investigate the causes of a circumstance which is so unfavourable to the male sex. If we were desirous of guessing at this point, we might say, with those who suppose that a male conception requires a certain excess of energy in the woman, that this excess of energy was absent or wanting during the growth of the fœtus, and that energy failing, the child would suffer more from it, if a boy, than a girl. Hence the disproportion of dead births between the two sexes; hence, also, the greater mortality of boys immediately after birth, and during the period of suckling, at which time they are still in some measure connected with the mother. It is also evident that women in town, who are more delicate than those in the country, will be more liable to bring forth still children, and especially when they are pregnant of boys.

We possess statistical documents of still-births for the city of Amsterdam,* which it will be interesting to compare with the preceding. The following are the original numbers furnished for the years from 1821 to 1832:—

Number of Still-Births and of Births for Amsterdam.

Years.	Still-Births.			Births.		
	Boys.	Girls.	Total.	Boys.	Girls.	Total.
1821, -	288	246	534	3,742	3,600	7,342
1822, -	280	222	502	3,887	3,713	7,600
1823, -	268	198	466	3,734	3,448	7,182
1824, -	266	216	482	4,011	3,849	7,860
1825, -	207	128	335	3,802	3,550	7,352
1826, -	231	173	404	3,803	3,635	7,438
1827, -	..	..	..	3,524	3,366	6,890
1828, -	..	..	..	3,679	3,529	7,208
1829, -	..	..	..	3,785	3,618	7,403
1830, -	241	169	410	3,727	3,579	7,306
1831, -	208	168	376	3,843	3,499	7,342
1832, -	210	151	361	3,351	3,101	6,452
Average,	244	186	430	3,741	3,541	7,282

We therefore calculate 1 still-birth for 16·9 births, which is a very unfavourable proportion from what we have seen above. The number of still-births of the male sex likewise here exceeds that of still-births of the other sex; and this would appear to be a general law, since none of the papers which have been quoted are contrary to it, and in all cases the difference is very considerable, and nearly about the same. Here the average numbers are in the ratio of 244 to 186, or 13 to 10 nearly.

The *Annuaires du Bureau des Longitudes* give the following data for Paris:—

Years.	Still-Births.			Births.		
	Boys.	Girls.	Total.	Boys.	Girls.	Total.
1823, -	847	662	1,509	13,752	13,318	27,070
1824, -	810	677	1,487	14,647	14,165	28,812
1825, -	846	675	1,521	14,989	14,264	29,253
1826, -	810	737	1,547	15,187	14,783	29,970
1827, -	904	727	1,631	15,074	14,732	29,806
1828, -	883	743	1,626	15,117	14,484	29,601
1829, -	925	788	1,713	14,760	13,961	28,721
1830, -	943	784	1,727	14,488	14,099	28,587
1831, -	954	755	1,709	15,116	14,414	29,530†
1832, -	994	726	1,720	13,494	12,789	26,283
Average,	8,916	7,274	16,190	146,624	141,009	287,639

* Jaarboekje par Lobatto. See also a memoir by M. Engeltrum, a prize-essay at Utrecht, and printed in 1830. The author counts, for the hospital at Amsterdam, from 1821 to 1826—
Births—Legitimate, 488   Dead births, 28   Ratio, 17 to 1
.. Illegitimate, 1770   151   .. 12 to 1
† In these numbers, 1099 and 1065 children, who were acknowledged and legitimatised after birth, are not included.

From this table, we calculate the still-births to births, in Paris, as 1 to 17·7—almost the same as for Amsterdam and Berlin. This ratio does not seem to differ much from that of large towns, which may be generally considered as 1 to 18. We see here, also, that the dead births of the male are more numerous than those of the female sex: the ratio is 12·2 to 10.

The official tables for the Prussian monarchy in 1827, and for Denmark in 1828, furnish the following results:*—

	Births.	Still-Births.	Ratio.
Prussian Monarchy, -	490,660	16,726	29 to 1
Denmark—{Boys, -	19,954	882	23 to 1
{Girls, -	18,840	690	27 to 1

These numbers, also, are similar to those which have been already given.

If we regard the influence of the seasons on still-births, the following are the data of Berlin, and for Western Flanders, during the five years from 1827 to 1831 inclusive:—

Months.	Still-Births at Berlin.	Still Births in Flanders.		
		Town.	Country.	Total.
January, -	117	140	225	365
February, -	123	141	197	338
March, -	120	115	205	310
April, -	112	100	160	260
May, -	110	102	162	264
June, -	98	104	162	266
July, -	92	117	153	270
August, -	108	108	136	244
September, -	89	108	139	247
October, -	104	110	152	262
November, -	124	90	143	233
December, -	121	106	179	285
	1,305	1,341	2,013	3,354

These data tend to show that the number of still-births is greater during winter, and at the end of winter, than in summer.

M. Casper has examined some particular circumstances which may influence the number of still-births, such as illegitimate conceptions, venereal diseases, the abuse of strong drinks, &c. Thus, at Gottingen, in 100 births, there are 3 dead births of legitimate children, and 15 of illegitimate children. At Berlin, the dead births in 100 illegitimate births have been, for half the last century, three times as numerous as the dead births among 100 legitimate children : and this state of things has not improved ; for, during the four years from 1819 to 1822, it is computed there were—

	Living Children.	Dead Children.	Ratio.
Legitimate births, -	22,643	937	25
Illegitimate births, -	4,002	317	12 †

Indeed, a woman generally takes less care to preserve the child which she carries in her bosom, when it is illegitimate. Moreover, it is necessary to add, that those children, who are almost always the fruit of misconduct, presuppose less vigour and soundness in the parents. M. Duges says, that at the Venereal Hospital in Paris, he has found two premature births to six or seven accouchements.‡ At Hamburg, during the year 1820, in one house which contained scarcely any but public women affected with the venereal disease, of 18 illegitimate births, 6 were dead births ; and in another house in the same city, likewise partly occupied by public women, the still-births were 11 out of 93.

These different examples prove too well the great influence which the condition of mothers exercises over the children of which they are pregnant, and

* Bulletin de M. Ferussac, Janv. and Mai 1830.
† The official tables of the whole Prussian monarchy for 1827 gave (*Bulletin de M. Ferussac,* Janv. 1830, p. 118) 490,660 births, of which 16,726 were still-births, a ratio of 29 to 1.
‡ Recherches sur les Maladies des Nouveaux Nés. Paris : 1824.

convince us of the utility of researches into still-births, and the causes which may multiply the number of them.

While considering the mortality of new born children, it is proper also to examine the fate of the mothers. According to Willan, the mortality in the great Lying-in Hospital of London, into which about 5000 women were annually admitted, was—

	Of the Mothers.	Of the Children.
From 1749 to 1758,	1 in 42	1 in 15
,, 1759 to 1768,	1 in 50	1 in 20
,, 1769 to 1778,	1 in 55	1 in 42
,, 1779 to 1788,	1 in 60	1 in 44
,, 1789 to 1798,	1 in 288	1 in 77 *

Mr Hawkins observed the mortality in the London Hospital in 1826, to be 1 in 70. According to the same statistician, in the Lying-in Hospital of Dublin, from the time of its foundation in 1757 to 1825—

The loss of children has been,	1 in 19
,, still-births,	1 in 17
,, mothers,	1 in 89

At the same hospital, also, twin cases have occurred in the proportion of 1 to 60 accouchements ; and three or more children in the proportion of 1 to 4000.

According to Tenon, at the end of the last century the mortality at the Hotel-Dieu of Paris, was 1 woman in 15, and 1 still-born child to 13 births ; but in 1822, the mortality at La Maternité was not more than 1 woman in 30. At the same time, in the Maternité of Stockholm, the proportion was almost the same as at Paris, or 1 woman in 29.

At the Lying-in Hospital of Edinburgh, during the years 1826, 27, and 28, the loss was only 1 woman in 100.

According to Casper,[†] the mortality of confined women at Berlin, has been—

From 1758 to 1763,	1 in 95
,, 1764 to 1774,	1 in 82
,, 1785 to 1794,	1 in 141
,, 1819 to 1822,	1 in 152

Here, again, we see how much the mortality depends on the care taken of the woman and child at the time of confinement. The greatest mortality which has been noticed, was that of the Hotel-Dieu of Paris at the end of the last century : it was 1 woman in 15 for the mothers, whilst in London it was reduced to 1 in 238, or nineteen times less.

~~~~~~~~~~~

CHAPTER V.

ON THE INFLUENCE OF NATURAL CAUSES ON MORTALITY.

1. Influence of Locality.

WE possess, in general, fewer documents respecting births than respecting deaths ; for this reason, perhaps, that man takes less interest in what regards his entry into life than his exit from it. The laws regulating births he views more as an object of curiosity, whilst it is of the highest moment for him to know all his chances of life and death. Nevertheless, in inquiring into the mortality, it behoves us to proceed with the greatest caution, and not to hold, as many authors have done, all numerical statements to be of the same importance.

The mortality is generally estimated by the ratio of deaths to the population. Now, if it be in general difficult to ascertain, by the registers of a country, the precise number of deaths, it is still more difficult to determine exactly the total numbers of the population. A census is a very delicate operation, which can be executed only from time to time. and will be found productive of very different results, according

* From Elements of Medical Statistics, by Mr Hawkins.
† Beitrage, p. 180.

to the care bestowed in its execution. In places, for example, where there may exist an interest for concealment of numbers, we should naturally expect to find a low estimate of the people, and in consequence too high an estimate of the mortality ; hence the necessity for extreme caution in comparing one country with another, or the same country with itself at different periods.

The influence which climate exercises over the mortality of the human species, deserves to be first considered. But climatology, taking the word in its most extended sense, is a science still too little advanced to engage our attention here :* we absolutely want data, and particularly comparative data, with respect to countries out of Europe, and even some European countries themselves, where political sciences have not been sufficiently cultivated. It becomes thus impossible to appreciate at all correctly the effects of temperature, and its relations to moisture and dryness, the direction of the winds, of running streams, &c. We ought, therefore, in our first view, to leave out these latter circumstances, and busy ourselves only with the most general results.

If we, in the first place, consider only Europe, and if we divide this part of the globe into three principal regions, with a view of setting aside as far as possible accidental causes, we may arrive at means to solve the problem which now occupies us. It would be better, also, to adopt the results of late years, thus giving a more extended comparison.

Countries.	Periods.	1 Death in	Authorities.
North of Europe.			
Sweden & Norway,	1820	41·1	Marshall.
Denmark,	1819	45·0	Moreau de Jonnes.[†]
Russia,	about 1829	27·0	Sir F. D'Ivernois.[‡]
England,	1821 to 1831	51·0	Potter & Rickman.
Central Europe.			
Prussia,	1816 to 1823	36·2	Babbage.
Poland,	1829	44·0	Moreau de Jonnes.
Germany,	1825 to 1828	45·0	..
Belgium,	1825 to 1829	43·1	An. de l'Ob. de Brux.
France,	1817 to 1831	39·7	An. du B. de Long.
Holland,	1815 to 1825	38·0	{ Rech. Statistique { sur les Pays Bas.
Austrian Empire,	1828	40·0	Moreau de Jonnes.
Switzerland,	1827 to 1828	40·0	..
South of Europe.			
Portugal,	1815 to 1819	40·0	..
Spain,	1801 to 1826	40·0	..
Italy,	1822 to 1826	30·0	..
Greece,	1828	30·0	..
Turkey in Europe,	1828	–30·0	..
Naples and Sicily,	1822 to 1824	32·0	Bisset Hawkins.

As several of the authors just quoted have merely given ratios, without the numbers from which these were deduced, I have been forced to take the averages from the ratios themselves, and not from the numbers, which would have been more exact. Upon the whole, we shall probably approach the truth in stating the mortality in Europe to be as follows :—

In the North of Europe,	1 Death for 41·1 Inhabitants.
Central Europe,	,, 40·3 ,,
Southern Europe,	,, 33·7 ,,

Whatever distrust the numbers relating to mortality may excite in us, I believe it may be admitted, that upon the whole the mortality is greater in the

* See the Researches of Sir J. Clarke in England on the Influence of Climate on Chronic Diseases—(Annales d'Hygiène, Avril 1830.) See also La Philosophie de la Statistique, par Melchoir Gioja, 2 vols. 4to, 1826.

‡ The numbers of M. Moreau de Jonnes are taken from a notice on the Mortality of the Different Countries of Europe : it is to be regretted that the author has not stated the sources of his information.

‡ Bibliothèque Universelle, Oct. 1833, p. 154.

south of Europe than in the north or centre, without anticipating the cause of this difference, and whether it depends on the political institutions or on the nature of the climate itself. It is England which turns the balance in favour of the north of Europe; and were it left out, the centre of Europe would present the least mortality. If we now quit the limits of Europe to consider those localities nearer the equinoctial line, and more exposed to extreme temperature, we have, according to M. Moreau de Jonnes[*]—

Under the Latitude	Places.		
6° 10′	Batavia,	1 Death for 26 Inhabitants.	
10° 10′	Trinidad,	..	27 ..
13° 54′	St Lucia,	..	27 ..
14° 44′	Martinique,	..	28 ..
15° 59′	Guadaloupe,	..	27 ..
18° 36′	Bombay,	..	20 ..
23° 11′	Havannah,	..	33 ..

This last table seems to prove that the mortality increases as we approach the equinoctial line. Still, these numbers must be received with distrust, because amongst the places referred to there are several cities, and the mortality in cities, as we shall shortly see, is generally greater than in the country. We must also regret that we have so few data in respect to places still nearer the equinoctial line. According to M. Thomas, the mortality of whites in the island of Bourbon is only 1 in 44·8; and from documents published in England in 1826, by order of the House of Commons, the mortality at the Cape of Good Hope is still less.[†]

Amongst the local causes which influence mortality, I have mentioned that of a town or country residence; this influence is sufficiently well marked. In Belgium, for example, the following have been the results of late years:—

	Population.	Average Number of Deaths.	1 Death to
Cities,	998,118	27,026	36·9 Inhabitants.
Country,	3,066,091	65,265	46·9 ..

We see that the ratios of mortality are almost as 4 to 3. This difference will be particularly apparent, if we examine the mortality of the principal cities of Europe.

* In Iceland, from 1825 to 1831, it has been computed that there is 1 death for 30·0 inhabitants, which would tend to show that excess of cold is as injurious to man as excess of heat.—*Bibliothèque Universelle*, Oct. 1833, p. 177.

† Elements of Medical Statistics, p. 51.

[The reader will be pleased to observe, that the question of the influence of climate on mortality is a more intricate one than perhaps our distinguished author was fully aware of. Firstly, it involves the simple question as to the influence of climate over the mortality of any particular race of men, who have been known to inhabit that country from time immemorial, or at least beyond the usual historic periods; secondly, it involves the question of the influence of climate over the mortality of another race foreign to the country, or who have migrated to it within historic periods. The numbers, for example, in the above table, placed opposite Batavia, have nothing whatever to do with the effects of climate over the native Javanese, but express merely the fearful mortality which sweeps off the Saxon foreigners migrating to a climate which nature never intended they should inhabit. On the other hand, the climate at the Cape of Good Hope, the healthiest perhaps in the world, seems equally favourable to all the three races inhabiting the colony and its frontier, namely, the aboriginal Hottentot and the invading Caffre and Saxon. We shall afterwards endeavour to show, that by putting the above table in comparison with the preceding one, a great and important element of statistics has been left out, and Quetelet has given us the statistics of Java and Bombay, as if the native inhabitants had ceased to exist; whereas it is manifest that the effects of climate over the migratory part of the human race, the Celt and Saxon, should be stated apart, and not mingled up with, or rather substituted for, the natural statistics of countries which probably can never retain possession of, whatever be the extent of their emigrations.]

C

Cities.	Inhabitants to 1 Death, according to		Inhabitants to 1 Birth, according to	
	Czoerning.	B. Hawkins.	Czoerning.	B. Hawkins.
North of Europe.				
London, - -	51·9	40·0	40·8	29·5 *
Glasgow, -		46·8		27·7
St Petersburg,	34·9	37·0	46·7	
Moscow, -	33·0		28·5	
Copenhagen, -	30·3		30·0	
Stockholm, -	24·3	24·9	27·0	24·8
Central Europe.				
Lyons, - -	32·3	32·0	27·5	
Amsterdam, -	31·0	24·0	26·0	
Paris, - -	30·6	32·5	27·0	
Bordeaux, -	29·0		24·0	
Hamburg, -	30·0		25·5	
Dresden, - -	27·7		23·0	
Brussels, -	25·5	26·0	21·0	
Berlin, - -	25·0	34·0	21·0	
Prague, - -	24·5	24·4	23·3	
Vienna, - -	22·5	22·5	20·0	
Southern Europe.				
Madrid, - -	36·0	35·0	26·0	
Leghorn, -	35·0	31·0	25·5	
Palermo, -	33·0		24·0	
Lisbon, -	31·1	28·2	28·3	52·5
Naples, -	29·0	52·0	24·0	25·0
Barcelona, -	27·0	24·8	27·0	
Rome, •	24·1		31·0	23·6
Venice, -	19·4		26·5	
Bergamo, -	18·0		20·0	30·2

Comparing this table with the preceding one, it is easy to observe that the mortality of cities is generally much greater than that of those countries to which they belong. I think this fact established, notwithstanding the inaccuracies inherent in such calculations.

We venture to conclude, then, with a high degree of probability, that in the actual state of things the mortality is less in temperate climates than in the north or south, and that it is greater in cities than in the country.[†]

If we consider each country in particular, we shall afterwards find, according to the localities, very great differences. Thus in France, in the department of the Orme, there is 1 death for 52·4, and in that of Finisterre, there is 1 for 30·4 inhabitants—a remarkable difference for places so near each other. In the former kingdom of the Low Countries, and during the period from 1815 to 1834, in the province of Zealand, there was 1 death for 28·5 inhabitants, and in the province of Namur, 1 for 51·8 inhabitants. We must here remark, that a great mortality keeps pace with the great fecundity. In the localities just quoted, for example, there were—

Countries.	Inhabitants		
	for one Birth.	for one Marriage.	for one Death.
Department of Orme, -	44·8	147·5	52·4
... Finisterre,	26·0	113·9	30·4
Province of Namur, -	30·1	141·0	51·8
... Zealand, -	21·9	113·2	28·5

* Topographisch-Historich Beschreibung von Reichenberg. See *Bulletin des Sciences Geographiques*, Avril 1833.

† M. Villermé informs me that he has arrived at the same conclusion, in an unpublished work, *On the Laws of Population, or the Relation of Medicine to Political Economy*.

[There is an inherent inexactness in these calculations which it is extremely difficult to get rid of. Norway, for example, and Sweden, and even the northern parts of Russia in Europe, are each of them inhabited by two races of men, of whom it is impossible to say, from a want of historic evidence, which formed the primitive race. The Fins, inhabiting the north of Sweden and Norway, and even of Russia, and perhaps also the Laplanders, are perfectly distinct races from their Scandinavian and Sarmatian masters, and of course their statistics ought to be considered apart.]

Thus Zealand and the department of Finisterre had more marriages, births, and deaths, than the department of Orme and the province of Namur. I declare that I have often been tempted to attribute these discrepancies to a faulty census of the population; but more attentive researches have induced me to believe that this state of things is dependent on local causes. In the province of Zealand, for example, continually buried in a humid atmosphere, there prevail fevers and other diseases causing this excess in the mortality; and this, reacting on the amount of subsistence, naturally increases the marriages and births.

What we have observed in these provinces may also be noticed in other countries, where we equally observe a great mortality and a great fecundity. Of this truth, England and the republic of Guanaxuato offer striking examples:—

States.	Inhabitants		
	to one Marriage.	to one Birth.	to one Death.
England, - - - -	134·00	35·00	58·00
Guanaxuato,* -	69·76	16·08	19·70

These are, so to speak, the two extreme limits in the scale of population, and, we may also add, in the scale of civilisation.

It may be said, that a country proceeds onwards to a more prosperous condition, when fewer citizens are produced, and when those existing are better preserved. The increase then is entirely to its advantage; for, if the fecundity be less, the useful men are more numerous, and generations are not renewed with such rapidity, to the great detriment of the nation.

Man, during his early years, lives at the expense of society; he contracts a debt which ought one day to be paid; and if he dies before having been enabled to do so, his existence has rather been a loss, or cost, to his fellow-citizens than an advantage. Is it desired to know what he costs? Let us take the lowest price: from birth to the age of twelve or sixteen, the expenses attending the support of a child in the hospitals of this kingdom (the Low Countries) amounted to about 1110 francs, say 1000 only, and this rate is certainly not too high, even for France.† Every person, then, who escapes from infancy has contracted a kind of debt, of which the minimum is 1000 francs, which society pays for the support of a child abandoned to its charity. Now, there are born in France annually more than 960,000 children, of whom 9–20ths are cut off previous to their having become of the smallest utility to the state; these 432,000 unfortunate persons may be viewed as so many friendless strangers, who, without fortune and without industry, have come to take part in the consumption of the general produce, and have then withdrawn themselves, leaving only, as traces of their existence, sorrowful adieus and eternal regrets. The expense they have caused, without reckoning the time devoted to them, amounts to the enormous sum of 432,000,000 of francs. And if we consider, on the other hand, the griefs caused by their departure, griefs which no human sacrifices can compensate, it is easy to see how worthy this subject is of the attention of the statesman and of the true philosopher. We cannot too often repeat, that the prosperity of states consists less in the multiplication than in the conservation of the individuals composing it.

The assertion that a great mortality unhappily coexists with a great fecundity, seems opposed to the

* According to M. D'Ivernois (Bibliothèque Universelle de Genève, 1833.)

† [In this country, the cost of bringing up a child to the age of twelve, on the lowest calculation, could scarcely be considered as lower than £144. We of course mean that he shall be brought up with due regard to his future health and strength.]

observations of Mr Sadler; but, as I have already remarked, the fecundity of marriages must not be confounded with the fecundity of the population; I have even shown, that, all things being equal, a great mortality is rather productive of a less fecundity of marriages, because second and third marriages are more multiplied, and the duration of marriages becomes then less.

To examine the question which now occupies us, the absolute number of births and of deaths must be compared with that of the population.

The following table contains some results in respect to the different countries already quoted:—

States.	Inhabitants			
	For one Death.		For one Birth.	
England, - - -	51·0	51·0	35·0	35·0
Sweden, - - -	47·0	45·0	27·0	28·5
Belgium, - - -	43·1		30·0	
France, - - -	39·7		31·6	
Holland, - - -	38·0	36·5	27·0	26·5
Prussia, - - -	36·2		23·3	
Sicily and Naples, -	32·0		24·0	
Guanaxuato, - -	19·7	19·7	16·1	16·1

I regret that the actual state of statistics does not allow me to present the observations of a greater number of countries. Still I think that these data prove an intimate ratio to exist between the mortality and the fecundity. And this ratio exists also between the different provinces of the same country.

In classing the cities according to their mortality, we find, according to the medium value of the numbers given above, leaving out St Petersburg, in respect to which there is evidently some error:—

Cities.	Inhabitants to one Death.		Inhabitants to one Birth.	
London, - - -	46·0	46·4	40·8	35·2
Glasgow, - - -	46·8		29·5	
Madrid, - - -	36·0		26·0	
Leghorn, - - -	35·0		25·5	
Moscow, - - -	33·0		28·5	
Lyons, - - -	32·2		27·5	
Palermo, - - -	32·0	32·3	24·5	27·0
Paris, - - -	31·4		27·0	
Lisbon, - - -	31·1		28·3	
Copenhagen, - -	30·3		30·0	
Hamburg, - - -	30·0		25·5	
Barcelona, - - -	29·5		27·0	
Berlin, - - -	29·0		21·0	
Bordeaux, - - -	29·0		24·0	
Naples, - - -	28·6		23·8	
Dresden, - - -	27·7		23·0	
Amsterdam, - -	27·5	26·6	26·0	24·2
Brussels, - - -	25·8		21·0	
Stockholm, - - -	24·6		27·0	
Prague, - - -	24·5		23·3	
Rome, - - -	24·4		30·6	
Vienna, - - -	22·5		20·0	
Venice, - - -	19·4	18·7	26·5	23·2
Bergamo, - - -	18·0		20·0	

The numbers thus cited tend, then, to show, that there exists a direct relation between the intensity of the mortality and that of the fecundity, or, in other terms, that the number of births is regulated by the number of deaths. This confirms fully the ideas of the economists who admit that the population tends always to a certain level, regulated by the quantity of the products. And in those localities where there exist particular causes of a greater mortality, it must happen that the generations are shorter, and succeed each other more rapidly.

We may remark, moreover, that in the countries we have just compared, the number of deaths is less than that of births; and this happens also in respect to the cities, with the exception of Stockholm, Rome, Venice, and Bergamo. It may, moreover, be observed, that these numbers have a greater tendency to become equal in proportion to the direct extent of

ON MAN. 29

the mortality, with the exception of England and its cities; we have, in fact, for the

LOCALITIES.	Ratio of Births to Deaths.
England,	1·46
Sweden and Belgium,	1·58
France, Holland, Prussia, Naples and Sicily,	1·37
The republic of Guanaxuato,	1·23
Cities having more than 40 inhabitants to 1 death,	1·15
,, 30 to 40	1·20
,, 20 to 30	1·10
,, less than 20	0·81

In studying the influence of localities on a less extensive scale, and in comparing the different parts of the same province, we frequently arrive at very dissimilar results: thus, as the country is level or mountainous, intersected with forests or marshes, the numbers which the mortality may offer will be found to differ very sensibly. M. Bossi, in the *Statistique du Départment de l'Ain*, gives a striking example: with a view to study the influences of localities, he divided the department into four portions, and from documents collected during the years 1812, 1813, and 1814, he obtained the following results:—

	Inhabitants to one Death annually.	Inhabitants to one Marriage annually.	Inhabitants to one Birth annually.
In mountain parishes,	38·3	179	34·8
On the sea-side,	26·6	145	28·8
In corn districts,	24·6	135	27·5
In stagnant and marshy districts,	20·8	107	26·1

These remarkable results offer a new confirmation of the direct ratio which exists generally between deaths, marriages, and births. It may be seen, also, how the neighbourhood of marshes and stagnant waters may become fatal. M. Villermé cites a remarkable example of the influence of marshes. "At Vareggio," observes M. Villermé,[*] "in the principality of Lucca, the inhabitants, few in number, barbarous, and miserable, were annually, from time immemorial, attacked about the same period with agues; but in 1741, floodgates were constructed, which permitted the escape into the sea of the waters from the marshes, preventing at the same time the ingress of the ocean to these marshes, both from tides and storms. This contrivance, which permanently suppressed the marsh, also expelled the fevers. In brief, the canton of Vareggio is at the present day one of the healthiest, most industrious, and richest on the coast of Tuscany; and a part of those families whose boorish ancestors sunk under the epidemics of the *arria cativa*, without knowledge to protect themselves, enjoy a health, a vigour, a longevity, and a moral character, unknown to their ancestors."

Similar epidemics prevail at fixed epochs on the borders of the Escaut, producing what are there called the fevers of the polders: these fevers follow great heat, and cause Zealand to approach the condition of Vareggio, and of the marshy countries quoted by M. Bossi.

M. Villermé pointed out to me a new example of the increase of mortality caused by the influence of marshes. In the Isle of Ely, from 1813 to 1830 inclusive, in 10,000 deaths, from birth to the most advanced age, there were 4732 before the age of 10, whilst in all the other agricultural districts of England together there were but 3505 deaths. In the Isle of Ely, also, there were 3712 deaths from 10 to 40 years in 10,000 deaths, which took place from 10 years to extreme old age; and only 3142 in the other agricultural districts which were not marshy.[†]

* Des Epidémics (An. d'Hygiène, Janv. 1833, p. 9.)
† See the letter of M. Villermé inserted in the *Bulletin de l'Academie de Bruxelles*, No. 23, for June 1834.

We owe, also, to M. Villermé a very curious memoir on the mortality of Paris and other large cities,[*] showing that wealth, independent circumstances, and misery, constitute, in the actual state of things, in respect to the inhabitants of the different quarters of Paris, the principal causes to which must be attributed the striking differences observed in the rate of mortality. The distance or proximity of the Seine, the nature of the soil, its depression to the east or west, the elevated grounds shutting in Paris to the north or south, the peculiar exposure of certain quarters, the different kinds of water made use of—are all circumstances modifying in some measure the general climate of the city; yet they do not seem to produce sensible differences in respect to the mortality. To make this more apparent, I have collected in a single table the principal results arrived at by M. Villermé: the numbers refer to the periods from 1822 to 1826.

Arrondissement.†	Inhabitants to one Death in Private Dwellings.	Surface occupied by the Buildings.	Surface occupied by one Individual in the Houses.	Localities not Taxed.‡	Average Value of one Locality.	Taxed Localities.	
						Personal Contribution.	By a patent of more than 30 francs.
			metres.		francs.		
2	71	0·75	26	0·11	605	0·40	0·47
3	67	0·55	15	0·07	426	0·38	0·44
1	66	0·57	65	0·11	498	0·49	0·35
5	64	0·46	19	0·22	226	0·28	0·36
4	62	0·59	7	0·15	328	0·23	0·49
11	61	0·55	22	0·19	258	0·30	0·32
7	59	0·82	11	0·22	217	0·29	0·35
6	58	0·62	13	0·21	242	0·20	0·45
9	50	0·60	16	0·31	172	0·26	0·30
10	49	0·53	46	0·23	285	0·46	0·24
8	46	0·46	47	0·32	173	0·25	0·31
12	44	0·64	37	0·38	148	0·19	0·29

2. Influence of Sexes.

The influence of the sexes is extremely evident in every thing which pertains to death; it has already been shown to be so before the birth of the child. During the four years from 1827 to 1830, there have been in Western Flanders 2597 still-born children, 1517 of which were males and 1080 females, which gives a ratio of about 3 to 2. This difference is considerable, and as we find it appear annually, it must have a special cause.

Again, this mortality affects male children not only before their birth, but pretty nearly during the ten or twelve months which follow that event; that is to say, pretty nearly during the period of lactation, as may be seen from the following documents respecting Western Flanders:—

* An. d'Hygiène, July 1830.

† The 2d arrondissement comprises the following quarters:— Chaussée d'Antin, Palais-Royal, Feydeau, and Faubourg Montmartre; the 3d, Montmartre, Faubourg Poissonnière, St Eustache, and Mail; the 1st, Roule, Champs-Elysées, Place-Vendôme, and Tuileries; the 4th, St Honoré, Louvre, Marchés, and Banque; the 5th, Faubourg St Denis, Porte St Martin, Bonne-Nouvelle, and Mont-Orgueil; the 11th, Luxembourg, Ecole de Medicine, Sorbonne, and Palais-de-Justice; the 7th, St Avoie, Mont-de-Piété, Marché St Jean, and Arcis; the 6th, Porte St Denis, St Martin-des-Champs, Lombard, and Temple; the 9th, Ile St Louis, Hotel-de-Ville, Cité, and Arsenal; the 10th, Monnaie, St Thomas d'Aquin, Invalides, and Faubourg St Germain; the 8th, St Antoine, Quinze-Vingts, Marais, and Popincourt; the 12th, Jardin du Roi, St Marcel, St Jaques, and L'Observatoire.

‡ All the localities of each quarter have been reduced to 100, so as to show how many of that number there are who pay no tax, how many are taxed by personal contribution, and how many by patent. The untaxed localities represent the poor.

Ages.	Cities.		Ratio.	Country.		Ratio.
	Boys.	Girls.		Boys.	Girls.	
0 to 1 month,	3,717	2,786	1·33	8,180	5,769	1·42
1 to 2 ..	900	662	1·36	2,012	1,609	1·25
2 to 3 ..	607	500	1·21	1,480	1,161	1·27
3 to 4 ..	532	382	1·39	1,192	984	1·22
4 to 5 ..	403	322	1·25	968	774	1·25
5 to 6 ..	346	329	1·05	831	707	1·18
6 to 8 ..	569	508	1·12	1,331	1,117	1·20
8 to 12 .·.	1,148	1,030	1·11	2,505	2,453	1·02
1 to 2 years,	2,563	2,409	1·06	4,994	4,920	1·02
2 to 3 ..	1,383	1,337	1·03	2,927	2,879	1·02
3 to 4 ..	908	908	1·00	1,606	1,748	0·92
4 to 5 ..	556	583	1·96	1,200	1,184	0·99

It appears, then, beyond doubt, *that there is a particular cause of mortality which attacks male-children, by preference, before and immediately after their birth.* The effects are such, that the ratio of deaths before birth is as 3 to 2; during the two first months after birth the ratio is 4 to 3; during the third, fourth, and fifth months, 5 to 4; and after the eighth or the tenth month, a difference scarcely exists.

The inequality in the number of deaths for children of both sexes, towards the period of birth, is a remarkable fact in the natural history of man, and merits the attention of physiologists. It cannot be attributed to the excess of male births over female births, seeing that the ratio of these last numbers is scarcely from 20 to 19; this ratio could, at the most, explain the difference of mortality in ages beyond the first year.

The influence of sex shows itself at different ages in a manner more or less curious: an idea may be formed of this by an inspection of the following table, constructed from numbers collected in the different provinces of Belgium :—

Age.	Male Deaths to one Female Death.	
	City.	Country.
Still-born, - - - -	1·33	1·70
From 0 to 1 month, - -	1·33	1·37
.. 1 to 2 .. - -	1·37	1·20
.. 2 to 3 .. - - -	1·22	1·21
.. 3 to 6 .. - -	1·24	1·16
.. 6 to 12 .. - -	1·06	1·03
.. 1 to 2 years, - -	1·06	0·97
.. 2 to 5 .. - -	1·00	0·94
.. 5 to 14 .. - -	0·90	0·93
.. 14 to 18 ..·· - - -	0·82	0·75
.. 18 to 21 .. - -	0·98	0·92
.. 21 to 26 .. - -	1·24	1·11
.. 26 to 30 .. - -	1·00	0·86
.. 30 to 40 .. - - -	0·88	0·63
.. 40 to 50 .. - -	1·02	0·83
.. 50 to 60 .. - - -	1·07	1·18
.. 60 to 70 .. - -	0·96	1·05
.. 70 to 80 .. - - -	0·77	1·00
.. 80 to 100 .. - -	0·68	0·92

This table gives the ratio between the deaths of the two sexes for each year, without regard to population. The numbers for the country may, moreover, be considered as representing faithfully the amount of the relative mortality, because at each age the individuals of both sexes are nearly equal in number, which is not the case in cities, at least with respect to aged men. The ratio of cities in respect to the population is in general very great for those of advanced years; there exist, nevertheless, the same alternations of increase and of decrease as in the ratio calculated for the country.

Thus, about the period of birth, there die more males than females; about the age of two years, the mortality of both sexes becomes pretty nearly equal; that of women thereafter increases, and becomes sensibly greater between the ages of 14 and 18 years, that is to say, after puberty; between 21 and 26, the most active epoch of the passions, the mortality of the male exceeds that of the female; from 26 to 30, epoch of marriage, the mortality is once more equalised, but becomes sensibly greater for women during the whole period of fecundity: when that period ceases, the mortality diminishes, and this condition or ratio continues until the final period of existence for both.

The great mortality of the female peasantry (*femmes de la campagne*) during the period of child-bearing, may be owing to the laborious duties of their station, which they are thus called on to perform at a period requiring the greatest care.[*] These laborious agricultural employments are, on the contrary, from their regularity, very far from being equally prejudicial to man. The male inhabitants of towns suffer much at this period of life from irregular conduct, and the facilities offered for following the dictates of passion.

3. Influence of Age.

Of all the causes which modify the mortality of man, none exercises a greater influence than age. This influence is universally acknowledged, and its appreciation is one of the first objects to which the doctrine of the calculation of probabilities was directed. The first table of mortality appears to be dated in 1693; it was composed by the astronomer Halley, who constructed it from documents of the city of Breslaw. Similar tables have been constructed since that time for the principal European countries; yet there are few in which the distinction of the sexes has been observed. Even France does not possess a general mortality table keeping in view this distinction; and all the assurance societies continue to base their calculations on the hypothesis that the mortality is the same for both sexes. Nevertheless, the English have observed the necessity for modifying their rates of insurance; and Mr Finlayson, secretary for the national debt, has perfectly shown that the greater mortality of men ought to be kept in view.

The tables which I give here for Belgium, keep in view not only the distinction of the sexes, but notice, for the first time, the differences caused by a town or country residence. I have taken care, also, to indicate the mortality during the early months following birth. The data employed in the construction of these tables have been collected with care for a period of three years, from the registries of the civil state in Belgium. To enable the reader to compare these results, I have taken the same basis, and calculated the mortality, assuming 10,000 births for each of the sexes in town and country. A fifth table shows the mortality of the kingdom, without regard to the differences just alluded to.

Age.	Table of Mortality of Belgium.				General Table: Town and Country; Men and Women.
	Town.		Country.		
	Men.	Women.	Men.	Women.	
Birth,	10,000	10,000	10,000	10,000	100,000
1 month,	8840	9129	8826	9209	90,396
2 ..	8550	8916	8664	8988	87,936
3 ..	8361	8760	8470	8829	86,175
4 ..	8195	8641	8314	8694	84,720
5 ..	8069	8540	8187	8587	83,571
6 ..	7961	8437	8078	8490	82,526
1 year,	7426	7932	7575	8001	77,528
18 months,	6954	7500	7173	7603	73,367
2 years,	6626	7179	6920	7326	70,536
3 ..	6194	6761	6537	6931	66,531
4 ..	5911	6477	6326	6691	64,102
5 ..	5738	6295	6169	6528	62,448
6 ..	5621	6176	6038	6395	61,166
7 ..	5547	6095	5939	6299	60,249
8 ..	5481	6026	5962	6215	59,487
9 ..	5424	5966	5792	6147	58,829
10 ..	5384	5916	5734	6082	58,258
11 ..	5352	5873	5683	6018	57,749
12 ..	5323	5833	5634	5960	57,289
13 ..	5298	5807	5589	5908	56,871
14 ..	5271	5771	5546	5862	56,467
15 ..	5241	5732	5502	5796	56,028

[*] [The reader will be pleased to observe that M. Quetelet alludes here to the whole period of child bearing in the female peasantry, as contrasted with the habits of towns; on the other hand, it is a fact generally admitted, although we know not the precise data on which the opinion is founded, that the individual accouchements are not only safer but much easier in the country than in towns.]

Age.	Town.		Country.		General Table: Town and Country; Men and Women.
	Men.	Women.	Men.	Women.	
16 years,	5209	5689	5456	5725	55,570
17 ..	5171	5645	5408	5668	55,087
18 ..	5131	5690	5357	5608	54,575
19 ..	5087	5551	5302	5546	54,030
20 ..	5038	5500	5242	5484	53,450
21 ..	4978	5445	5178	5421	52,810
22 ..	4908	5387	5109	5356	52,172
23 ..	4827	5326	5036	5289	51,465
24 ..	4740	5264	4958	5222	50,732
25 ..	4662	5201	4881	5153	49,995
26 ..	4590	5138	4805	5085	49,298
27 ..	4523	5074	4734	5016	48,602
28 ..	4459	5010	4673	4948	47,965
29 ..	4397	4946	4620	4880	47,350
30 ..	4335	4881	4572	4812	46,758
31 ..	4275	4816	4525	4744	46,170
32 ..	4214	4751	4478	4677	45,584
33 ..	4154	4686	4431	4609	44,996
34 ..	4094	4622	4384	4542	44,409
35 ..	4034	4558	4337	4474	43,823
36 ..	3976	4490	4296	4401	43,236
37 ..	3918	4418	4255	4329	42,650
38 ..	3860	4347	4215	4257	42,064
39 ..	3802	4277	4174	4185	41,476
40 ..	3744	4208	4134	4112	40,889
41 ..	3678	4148	4090	4041	40,300
42 ..	3611	4088	4044	3971	39,697
43 ..	3544	4027	3995	3901	39,106
44 ..	3477	3967	3943	3831	38,504
45 ..	3411	3907	3887	3761	37,900
46 ..	3352	3846	3827	3701	37,295
47 ..	3293	3783	3767	3640	36,690
48 ..	3233	3720	3707	3579	36,084
49 ..	3174	3656	3647	3519	35,477
50 ..	3115	3592	3588	3458	34,789
51 ..	3040	3520	3512	3392	34,153
52 ..	2962	3448	3435	3323	33,418
53 ..	2881	3375	3358	3256	32,676
54 ..	2810	3300	3276	3187	31,930
55 ..	2739	3225	3194	3118	31,179
56 ..	2667	3150	3111	3049	30,424
57 ..	2583	3090	3026	2982	29,656
58 ..	2499	3010	2939	2912	28,975
59 ..	2415	2939	2851	2840	28,081
60 ..	2329	2862	2767	2762	27,242
61 ..	2239	2779	2677	2677	26,356
62 ..	2146	2689	2587	2586	25,423
63 ..	2051	2595	2495	2495	24,465
64 ..	1956	2498	2387	2405	23,478
65 ..	1859	2397	2277	2310	22,462
66 ..	1754	2292	2163	2200	21,362
67 ..	1649	2187	2049	2006	20,263
68 ..	1556	2085	1942	1983	19,219
69 ..	1466	1983	1835	1875	18,175
70 ..	1372	1864	1713	1758	17,017
71 ..	1279	1741	1587	1642	15,060
72 ..	1184	1627	1474	1530	14,749
73 ..	1087	1514	1358	1420	13,638
74 ..	989	1389	1236	1300	12,461
75 ..	891	1261	1114	1182	11,273
76 ..	806	1134	996	1061	10,120
77 ..	721	1011	882	940	9014
78 ..	631	900	770	832	7910
79 ..	541	789	664	723	6853
80 ..	463	682	566	619	5867
81 ..	394	585	482	535	5031
82 ..	332	495	414	460	4299
83 ..	273	411	353	390	3627
84 ..	225	346	294	323	3016
85 ..	184	289	239	262	2464
86 ..	150	239	191	211	1989
87 ..	120	192	152	168	1585
88 ..	93	150	117	132	1233
89 ..	69	116	88	97	924
90 ..	49	86	67	71	682
91 ..	37	65	48	54	510
92 ..	28	47	33	40	367
93 ..	18	33	27	32	282
94 ..	11	24	20	24	207
95 ..	9	18	14	18	153
96 ..	5	12	10	12	105
97 ..	4	8	7	7	67
98 ..	2	4	4	4	39
99 ..	1	2	2	2	20
100 ..		1	1	1	10
101 ..					5
102 ..					2
103 ..					1
104 ..					0

Table of Mortality of Belgium—(*Continued*.)

An inspection of this table shows that the probable value or duration of life after birth is in general about 25 years, that is to say, that at the age of 25, the number of children born at the same time is reduced to one-half. Keeping in view the distinction of the sexes, we find that the probable life of girls (*filles*, unmarried females) is longer than that of boys (unmarried males); in fact, it is 27 years in the country, and more than 28 in cities, whilst for unmarried males it is less than 24 years in the country, and less than 21 in cities.

Towards the age of five years, the chances of prolonged life are the greatest, whatever be the sex or place of abode; at this epoch, the probable duration of life of women in city, and men in the country, is 50 years, and of 48 years for women in the country, and men in the city.

This age of five years, when the more urgent dangers of infancy have ceased, is very remarkable in the natural history of man: in proportion as we recede from it, the probable duration of life becomes shorter and shorter; thus, at the age of 40, it is only 27 years for the inhabitants of the country, and for women inhabiting towns, and of 25 years only for men inhabiting towns; for those who have reached 60 years, the probable duration of life is from 12 to 13 years; and with the octogenarian it is reduced to four years.

In general, the mortality is greater for man inhabiting towns, owing, without doubt, to the irregularities and excesses to which he is exposed.

The value, then, of the average life in Belgium is 32·15 years; for men inhabiting cities, 29·24, and for the male agricultural population, 31·97; for women inhabiting cities, 33·28, and 32·95 in the country. According to Mr Rickman's last work, the average life in England would be 33 years, 32 for the men and 34 for the women.[*] In France, it is estimated at 32·2, calculated from the numbers of births.[†] Finally, these calculations presume the population to be stationary, and we shall afterwards have occasion to see that they lead to serious errors.

I shall next make a more attentive examination of the different critical periods of man and woman, as well as of the degrees of duration of life (*viability, existibility*) at different ages.

What first occupies our attention, is the great mortality of children after birth: to have an accurate idea of this, it is sufficient to consider that, in town as well as country, four times as many children die within the first month after birth as in the second; and almost as many as during the second and third years, although the mortality then is very great. Indeed, the table of mortality shows, that one-tenth die within the first month after birth. This number is equal to the aggregate number of deaths of the survivors between 7 and 24 years of age, or between 24 and 40 years; or, still further, it is equal to the number of survivors who reach the age of 76 years. MM. Milne Edwards and Villermé have made some interesting researches on the mortality of new-born children; Toaldo, in Italy, attributes it chiefly to the custom of taking the infants to church immediately after birth, where they often endure the severest cold, and are exposed naked to the waters of baptism.

The mortality is so great, especially for male children, that, from the first year after birth, the number is already reduced one-fourth. The loss of boys in towns is such, that at the fifth year, out of 10,000, there are only 5738 remaining.

The age of five years is very remarkable, because the mortality, which until that time is very great, is suddenly reduced, and becomes extremely small until the age of puberty. At the age of five years, the probability of life attains its maximum, that is to say, man may reckon upon a longer existence.

The epoch which precedes puberty, and which

[*] Preface to The Abstract, &c., p. 46.
[†] Annuaire du Bureau des Longitudes for 1834, p. 102.

commences at 13 in town and 14 in the country, is equally deserving of attention: it also presents a maximum of a peculiar kind—it might be called the maximum of *viability*; it is the period when man can most depend upon his actual existence, and when he can wager with most probability that he will not die the moment after.

After the age of puberty, the mortality becomes greater, especially among women: this increase is even perceptible among women in the country.

Towards the age of 24, there is a peculiar circumstance connected with men; namely, a maximum which is not observed in the curve of the mortality of women. (See the table of curves at the end of the volume). The period of this maximum coincides with that when man shows the greatest inclination to crime;* it is the stormy age of passion, which occupies a most conspicuous place in the moral life of man. The mortality afterwards diminishes insensibly, and reaches for men in town and country a new minimum about the age of 30.

The reason why these periods of maximum and minimum are not observed in the curve of female mortality, proceeds undoubtedly from the circumstance, that the effect which the development of the passions in woman might have over the deaths is combined with the effect resulting from the dangers of childbearing; for, after the age of 24 years, the deaths of women continue to increase, and, taken from 28 to 45 years, exceed the number of deaths of men. The difference is very apparent between 30 and 40 years.†

From 60 to 65 years, also a remarkable period, viability loses much of its energy, that is to say, the probability of life becomes very small.

Lastly, the length of one century appears to be the limit of man's existence. Very few exceed this bound. On the 1st of January 1831, of sixteen centenarians found in Belgium, fourteen of them lived in the three provinces of Hainault, Namur, and Luxembourg. Limbourg and Eastern Flanders had each one, and none were found in the provinces of Brabant, Anvers, Western Flanders, and Liege. The three oldest individuals were 104, 110, and 111 years—they belonged to the province of Luxembourg; the others did not exceed 102 years.

Of the sixteen centenarians, nine belonged to the male sex; none of them had been soldiers: it is remarkable that all these persons had been, or still were married, and generally were living in very ordinary circumstances. It is generally thought that the greater number of centenarians are males, although the average life of females is longer.

A German physiologist, M. Burdach, has published some very singular approximative comparisons of human mortality and the periods of human life.‡ This philosopher divides life into 10 periods of 400 weeks each; and thus makes an age of the first dentition, of adolescence, of youth, &c.; in the first period is found a secondary one of 40 weeks, the age of lactation.

To complete the documents relative to mortality at different ages, it would be necessary to consider the dangers to which man is exposed every moment. Indeed, when we say that the infant at birth has a probable life of 25 years, we know nothing of the dangers to which he may be exposed during this period. It is for the purpose of considering these dangers that I have constructed the following table, which points out the actual degree of mortality of

---

* *Recherches sur le Penchant au Crime aux differens Ages.* See also the third book of this work.

† It has long been thought that the time of cessation of the monthly period was more fatal to women than the other periods of life. M. Benoiston de Châteauneuf has shown that this opinion is groundless, in a *Memoire sur la Mortalité des Femmes de l'Age de 40 à 50 Ans.* Paris: 1822.

‡ *Die Zeitrechnung des Menschlichen-lebens* Licpsie: 1829.

---

each age, that is to say, the probability of dying within a very limited period. This table is calculated from the one on mortality: the inverse ratio of each number, placed opposite, may be considered as the relative degree of the duration of the life of man at different ages, or the relative probability of living:—

Age.	Degrees. of Mortality.	Degrees. of Viability.	Age.	Degrees. of Mortality.	Degrees. of Viability.
1 month,	960	1	23	12	85
2 ··	273	4	24	12	82
3 ··	200	5	25	12	83
4 ··	168	6	30	11	95
5 ··	135	7	35	11	90
6 ··	127	8	40	12	83
1 year,	115	9	45	13	77
2 ··	77	13	50	15	67
3 ··	60	17	55	20	50
4 ··	27	37	60	27	37
5 ··	21	48	65	39	26
6 ··	15	67	70	57	18
7 ··	12	83	75	187	11
8 ··	10	100	80	29	8
10 ··	8	131	85	174	6
14 ··	6	161	90	250	4
15 ··	7	155	95	283	3
20 ··	10	100	100	4217	2

I have endeavoured to render these numbers sensible to the eye by the construction of a curve *a b c d e*. (See Plate 2, placed at the end of the volume). The greater or less divergence from the axis A B, indicates the greater or less degree of viability. Thus we see that, about the age of 14, viability is greatest: it afterwards presents an anomaly between the 15th and 30th years. This curve has been constructed for men and women indiscriminately: the dotted line serves for females. Its form is more regular than that of males alone: it descends in a continuous manner from the point *m*, which corresponds to the 13th year, to the point *n*, corresponding to the 50th, where it is confounded with the other curve. We see that viability after puberty diminishes more rapidly in females than males; it is also less during the time of childbearing, from the 27th to the 45th year, but greatest at the age of the passions, about the 24th year. The curve of viability has a striking similarity to that of the propensity to crime, and a still greater similarity to that showing the development of the physical powers.

The age of shortest viability would be then immediately after birth, and the age of longest viability immediately before puberty: the viability of the child after the first month of life is greater than that of the man near 100 years old.

Towards the 75th year, it is scarcely greater than for the infant about the sixth month after birth.

We shall add to what has already been said, the law of the duration of diseases, expressed in weeks and fractions of a week, as M. Villermé has given it in the *Annales d'Hygiène* for January 1830, according to the documents of the philanthropic Highland Society of Scotland.

Age.	Weeks of sickness for one Person.	Age.	Weeks of sickness for one Person.
21st year,	0·575	55th year,	1·821
25th ··	0·585	57th ··	2·018
30th ··	0·621	60th ··	2·246
35th ··	0·675	63d ··	3·100
40th ··	0·758	65th ··	4·400
45th ··	0·962	67th ··	6·000
50th ··	1·361	70th ··	10·701

The committee of the Scotch Society which has collected these data, thinks that below the age of 20 the average annual duration of diseases ought to be estimated at three days, or nearly; and above 70 years, also, for the working class, about 4 months, or 16½ weeks. These researches coincide very well with the measures of viability given above.

M. Villermé has also been investigating the law of mortality of each age during epidemics,[*] and he has been led to conclude that it *seems* to agree with the general law of mortality according to age, that is to say, that those who, all things being equal, have the least probability of life, are those who fall most readily, when attacked by epidemics :[†] thus, one epidemic attacks more particularly children, another old persons. Well, of an equal number of diseases at each age, the mortality of children is greater the younger they are, and when old persons are attacked, the older they are.

This observation is confirmed by the researches of Duvillard on death caused by the small-pox ; by those which have been collected after the sweating miliary fever, which was epidemic in 1821 in the department of Oise ; and by several others quoted by M. Villermé.

"According to the unanimous accounts from different parts of Germany," says this philosopher, "accounts which fully confirm the official report on the ravages of cholera-morbus in the city of Paris and department of the Seine, the children under four or five years, and the old persons of advanced age, attacked by this malady, almost always die, whilst young people less frequently fall under it.

Indeed, some researches which I have made on the influence of marshes, show that the same circumstance attends the fevers or epidemic maladies resulting from them (marshes) ; for of an equal number of sick persons, more young children died than of all the others, and after these the old persons.

The influenza, or catarrhal fever, which prevailed through a great part of France during the spring and summer of 1831, and which especially attacked adults and old persons, at least in Paris, has principally been fatal to the latter when very old.

All these facts concerning diseases so different, render it extremely probable that the mortality occasioned by epidemics commonly follows, as has been already stated, for the sick persons who are attacked by them, the general law of the mortality according to age.

Hence the inference, that epidemics which attack the two extremes of life, are, every thing considered, the most fatal and deadly."

4. Influence of Years.

It has been observed that the annual number of deaths may, in certain circumstances, be considerably modified by scarcity, wars, and other scourges.

The influence of famine had been confirmed long ago ; nevertheless, an English statistician, Mr Sadler, recently thought he perceived in the relative numbers of England almost the opposite of what his predecessors found. Similar discordances between the results of observers have often been quoted by superficial persons to establish the small importance of statistical inquiries, instead of seeking for the true cause of them.

Now, to explain the difficulty which here presents itself, it is necessary to observe, in the first place, that mortality does not increase just at the moment when bread becomes dearer—the excess of mortality is only induced by the diseases and privations which poor people are obliged to endure at periods of distress ; so that, during the greater part of the time, the influence of the scourge on the registers of mortality only becomes visible several months, and sometimes a year, after its commencement. The consequences, moreover, do not stop suddenly : the price of bread may

have resumed its ordinary course, or even become lower, and yet the excess of deaths may be still very sensible.

We should be wrong in admitting, also, that the smallest fluctuations in the prices of bread ought proportionally to show themselves in the number of deaths : in the midst of so many causes modifying mortality, a single one, in order to leave manifest traces, must be strongly marked. We must not, then, ascribe, as Mr Sadler has done, the same importance to every year from the time that the price of grain had somewhat exceeded the average—we must keep to those years in which there was a positive scarcity ; and, above all, we must not suppose the mortality to proceed equally with the price of provisions. An examination of the tables showing the movement of the population in Belgium from 1815 to 1826 inclusive, will point this out. We may there observe, that the price of wheat and rye reached their maximum in 1816 ; but the effects of the scarcity over the deaths and births became apparent only the year following. Were we to follow Mr Sadler's plan, the calamitous year of 1816 would be arranged among the happy ones, since, comparatively to the other years, there were fewer deaths. To proceed as Mr Sadler has done, we ought to compare the deaths of the four years from 1815 to 1818, during which the prices of grain exceeded the average, with those of the four following years, and we have as a medium of each period—

	Average of Deaths—	
	In Town.	In Country.
Years of famine, - - -	50,186	91,501
.. plenty, - - -	51,015	95,222

Observe how this conclusive table would lead to results entirely opposed to those we have obtained.

We cannot be too much on our guard against conclusions drawn from statistical documents, and especially against the methods of reasoning which may be employed. The greatest sagacity is necessary to distinguish the degree of importance to be attached to each influencing element ; and we have frequent proofs that even clever men have been led into absurdities by ascribing to certain causes influences produced by other causes which they had neglected to take into consideration.

The fatal influence of the years 1816 and 1817 shows itself not only in the general results of deaths for all Belgium, but also, as has been remarked,[*] in the particular results in the foundling hospitals, and in houses of refuge. This may be judged of by the following numbers :—

Years.	Foundling Hospitals.		Mendicity Houses : Inhabitants to one Death.
	Population.	Deaths.	
1815, - - -	10,739	1,597	8·25
1816, - - -	11,176	1,455	10·15
1817, - - -	11,829	1,793	5·49
1818, - - -	12,813	1,290	6·79
1819, - - -	13,248	1,346	9·29

We ought to attribute this greater mortality to the individuals admitted into the hospitals and mendicity houses having been already sufferers from the famine, and not to the privations which they had to undergo in these establishments. The number of admissions of foundlings, which, one year with another, never exceeded 3000, reached to 3945 in 1817 : it is this which has rendered the mortality greater, because the in-

---

[*] An. d'Hygiène, Janv. 1833, p. 31.

[†] [Typhus fever, which occasionally spreads epidemically, seems to form an exception to this law.]

[*] Page 35 of Recherches sur la Population, les Naissances, &c., dans le Royaume des Pays Bas. See also, on the Mortality of 1817, the Statistique Nationale of M. Ed. Smits.

fants exposed at this critical time had within them the germs of death already.*

Another observation which may be made on the preceding numbers, is the dreadful mortality of mendicity houses, which was about 4 or 5 times as great as in the least healthy provinces of Belgium: we may say the same for the houses for foundlings. This confirms the very judicious remarks which have been made by MM. Villermé and Benoiston de Châteauneuf, in the *Annales d'Hygiène*, on the unequal mortality of the rich and poor. The deaths in the prisons of Belgium were incomparably less numerous than in the houses of mendicity. At Vilvorde, in 1824, 1825, and 1826, there was 1 to 28 inhabitants; at Saint-Bernard, 1 to 22 in the year 1826; and at Ghent, about the same period, 1 to 44 only: this ratio is somewhat less than that for the whole kingdom. We ought to make a distinction between the prisons and houses of mendicity, because the individuals who enter these latter establishments rarely make a stay of 7 or 8 months, and generally arrive there, as has been already stated, with a constitution undermined by privation and disease; on the contrary, those who enter prison after having undergone sentence, are generally in a less unfavourable state of health, and the average duration of their confinement is not less than 5 years.†

In investigating the influence of years of peace or war, it seems to me that in general the same degree of confusion has been made. A country in time of war suffers, indeed, because its male population falls, on the one hand, either in engagements, or in consequence of fatigue and privation; and, on the other hand, the chances of reproduction become fewer; the country, moreover, suffers, because its industry and activity are impeded, or because importations of all kinds, especially of grain, are diminished: but a nation might be engaged in war without any of these causes undergoing a very sensible alteration. It would be then deceptive to look for the effects of it in the tables of mortality. It is in this manner that Mr Sadler* also denies the influence of years of war, when making use of English data; and without inquiring whether the means of subsistence, the imports, and the exports, had undergone any change, or whether the nation had been deprived of a part of the male population more than at another time. I think that we might more accurately appreciate this influence in such a country as Holland or Belgium, several provinces of which have a great maritime trade, and the ports of which have long been closed. Thus I shall collect the numbers given during the two decennial periods which have preceded and followed 1814: the one includes the years from 1804 to 1813 inclusive, and we shall take it as a period of war; the other extends from 1815 to 1824, and forms a time of peace:†—

Provinces.	Deaths.		Births.		Marriages.	
	1st Period.	2d Period.	1st Period.	2d Period.	1st Period.	2d Period.
Brabant, Northern, - -	75,771	69,507	89,488	100,963	21,210	20,330
. . Southern, -	118,356	119,109	145,256	169,181	30,862	36,423
Limbourg, - - -	75,679	70,549	91,397	101,781	20,453	22,960
Gueldres, - - -	53,764	59,818	67,308	90,862	15,627	19,337
Liege, - - - -	74,683	82,698	102,949	113,623	22,671	24,387
Flanders, East, - -	169,966	162,834	207,334	218,839	42,549	43,120
. . West, - -	144,726	141,310	179,099	191,139	37,663	37,882
Hainault, - - -	110,344	118,289	158,762	183,198	37,093	39,591
Holland, Northern, -	143,108	121,725	122,275	145,744	33,533	34,789
. . Southern, -	136,457	123,850	135,703	165,741	32,498	34,942
Zealand, - - - -	46,237	42,436	45,805	55,331	10,731	10,645
Namur, - - -	30,519	34,134	48,557	58,690	11,406	12,592
Antwerp, - - -	87,126	70,623	96,058	101,471	21,579	23,075
Utrecht, - - -	31,150	29,928	36,065	41,033	8,674	8,982
Friesland, - - -	45,337	38,219	49,354	65,565	14,186	15,327
Overyssel, - - -	31,483	37,479	43,114	51,951	9,960	11,629
Groningen, - - -	37,026	30,539	41,592	51,673	11,940	11,492
Drenthe, - - -	9,418	9,859	13,254	16,723	3,691	3,954
Luxembourg, - - -	66,406	58,695	91,809	92,242	20,412	18,740
Total, - -	1,487,606	1,421,600	1,765,179	2,015,646	406,743	430,247

* Gioja, in his *Filosofia della Statistica*, has taken the same years, 1815, 1816, and 1817, as examples of the influence of famine on mortality. The following are the results at which he has arrived; they do not require any comment:—

Number of Children exposed at the *Luogo pio* de Sainte-Catherine, at Milan, and of the sick persons in the large hospital of that city.

Years.	Children Exposed.	Annual Average Number.	Sick Persons.	Annual Average Number.	Price of one muid of Wheat.	Annual Average Price.
1815,	2280	1750	17,974	14,010	59 liv.	25 liv.
1816,	2625	(from 1818	20,993	(from 1818	75 ..	(from 1818
1817,	3082	to 1825).	23,350	to 1825).	63 ..	to 1825).

Mortality in the private houses and hospitals of Milan.

Years.	In Private Houses.	Annual Average Number.	Deaths in the Hospitals.	Annual Average Number.	Total of the Deaths.	Annual Average Number.
1815,	3324	3305	2680	2028	6504	5333
1816,	3996	(from 1818	3085	(from 1818	7051	(from 1818
1817,	3806	to 1825).	4620	to 1825).	8426	to 1825).

† Annales d'Hygiène.

This table shows us at first that in all the provinces, without exception, the number of births has been greater during the decennial period of peace than during that of war; the number of deaths, on the contrary, has been smaller, except in some provinces in the interior, such as Gueldres, Overyssel, Drenthe, Brabant (Southern), Hainault, Liege, and Namur; yet the difference in several of them may be owing to the increase of population, and it must be observed that these provinces are chiefly agricultural, and that Hainault, Namur, and Liege, were actively engaged in the clearing of lands and toil of arms. The number of marriages has varied very little during the two periods.

The provinces which have very sensibly suffered by mortality were those especially which are maritime, and whose ports were closed for a considerable time. Thus the two Hollands and Zealand had more deaths than births. This state of things ceased at the peace. It seems to me that the results contained in this table

* [Mr Sadler seems to have been anxious to maintain the accuracy of the old saw, " few die of want, thousands of surfeit." Like most ancient adages, the truth will be found by as near as may be reversing it.]

† See, on the influence of the wars of the French Empire, the observations of M. F. D'Ivernois, the results of which have been given at page 23.

are as conclusive as can be desired, and show to what extent wars influence mortality, by impeding the activity of the people and injuring their industry.

We may here find an apparent contradiction to what has been stated elsewhere. I have observed that the deaths generally, in becoming more numerous, likewise increase the number of marriages and births; but the obstacle to the multiplication of marriages was that very state of war, the influence of which I have just been showing—a state which removed the major part of the young men from society. Nevertheless, we observe that the number of marriages has been almost the same during the two periods; and I find a new confirmation of my conjectures. The great mortality ought to have shortened the duration of marriages, and brought on more marriages of second and third unions, which have, by that cause, been less fruitful, and produced fewer births. I particularly insist on this fact, which appears to me very remarkable, namely, that the fecundity of marriages has been incomparably less during the first period.

Remarks somewhat similar should be made for the influence of years of famine. Here the contradiction appears greater. A great number of deaths has frequently been accompanied by fewer marriages; this was owing to the want which momentarily induced the death exciting a fear to undertake new establishments, so that persons did not pass rapidly from the state of widowhood. What has been observed concerning the deaths, which, by multiplying, multiply the marriages and births, ought only then to be generally understood for those countries which are not under the influence of accidental causes, such as wars, epidemics, famines, &c.

5. Influence of Seasons.*

The number of deaths, like that of births, undergoes very sensible variations according to the different months of the year. Numerous researches have already been presented on this subject, and it has been acknowledged that, in our climate, the rigours of winter are in general mortal to the human species.[†] The following table, prepared from the documents of Belgium, and according to the same principles as that which has been given for births, will present a first example of the influence of seasons on mortality:—

Months: 1815 to 1826.	Deaths.		Ratio.	
	Town.	Country.	Town.	Country.
January, -	59,892	116,129	1·158	1·212
February, -	56,267	114,758	1·088	1·198
March, -	54,277	114,244	1·050	1·192
April, -	51,818	107,264	1·002	1·120
May, -	48,911	93,714	0·946	0·978
June, -	46,607	84,464	0·901	0·882
July, -	45,212	77,555	0·874	0·809
August, -	47,032	78,302	0·910	0·822
September,	50,191	85,131	0·971	0·888
October, -	51,649	89,514	0·999	0·934
November, -	52,908	89,585	1·024	0·935
December, -	55,631	93,705	1·076	1·030
Average, -	51,700	95,822	1·000	1·000

* The greater part of what follows has been extracted from a memoir *Sur l'Influence des Saisons et des Ages sur la Mortalité*, which I presented to the Royal Academy of Sciences of the Institute in 1833. I had already published some observations on this subject in the first volumes of my *Correspondance Mathematique et Physique*.

† [Another old saw, and as like the preceding as possible in its almost inconceivable want of any foundation in truth, was, that "an open winter, or a green Christmas, make a fat churchyard:" like the former saw supported by Mr Sadler, it may readily be shown that a precisely reverse statement will approach the truth as near as possible: this had been long suspected by Dr Heberden. In the climate and locality of Edinburgh, for example, the first setting-in of frost is annually accompanied by a great increase of mortality; it also aggravates both the number of cases of typhus fever and the deaths therefrom, occasionally to an alarming extent.]

Let us here again remark that the influence of the seasons is more evident in the country than in town, where there is a greater combination of means to withstand the inequality of temperatures.

The terms of maximum and minimum do not take place at the same time in all climates; in some, they even appear to have been shifted by civilisation, which has caused local causes of epidemics to disappear. These epidemics were especially caused by high temperatures in marshy places or the interior of cities. M. Villermé has pointed out a very striking example for the city of Paris (*An. d'Hygiène*), in the following table of the months, arranged in the order of the decreasing number of deaths of an average day:—

13 Years at the end of the 17th Century.	20 Years up to 1722, including the 13th of the preceding Column.	20 Years from 1723 to 1742.	20 Years from 1743 to 1762.	20 Years from 1763 to 1782.	The 10 Years which terminated in 1817— (1814 is taken away.)	The 10 Years from 1817 to 1826.
Sept.	Feb.	April.	April.	April.	April.	April.
Dec.	Sept.	March.	March.	March.	March.	March.
Jan.	April.	May.	Feb.	Feb.	Feb.	May.
Nov.	Jan.	Feb.	May.	Jan.	Jan.	Jan.
March.	March.	Jan.	Jan.	May.	May.	Feb.
May.	May.	Dec.	June.	Dec.	Dec.	June.
Aug.	Oct.	June.	Dec.	June.	June.	Sept.
Feb.	Nov.	Sept.	Nov.	Nov.	Sept.	Dec.
Oct.	Dec.	Aug.	Oct.	Oct.	Nov.	Aug.
April.	Aug.	Oct.	Sept.	Sept.	Oct.	Oct.
June.	June.	Nov.	July.	July.	Aug.	Nov.
July.	July.	July.	Aug.	Aug.	July.	July.

This table is founded on two millions of deaths: it results from this (says M. Villermé), that from the progressive diminution of the epidemics which so often desolated Paris formerly, at the end of summer, the annual period of the maximum of mortality in this city has been shifted. During the years of the 17th century of which we have accounts, this maximum took place in autumn, but now it is in spring. Formerly the minimum was observed at the beginning of summer, but in the present age it is a little later. This proof of the ameliorations which have been made in Paris, since the end of the reign of Louis XIV. (continues M. Villermé), either in the healthy state of the city itself, or in the lot and condition of the inhabitants, is decisive; for we may affirm that the changes which we have just confirmed, belong, not to an increase of mortality during the season which at present gives the maximum, but to a diminution during the season which formerly contained the greatest number of deaths.

M. Villermé makes the observation, that the epidemics which result from famine always exercise their ravages at annual periods, when food is most scarce, difficult to obtain, or the diseases which induce painful conditions of life, for a great number of men, are more numerous or much more aggravated; and they cease after harvest, which brings back abundance. For example, in the ancient kingdom of Holland and the Netherlands, at the end of the bad harvest of 1816, the excess of deaths became very sensible during the following year, and particularly during the months which preceded the new harvest.

With respect to epidemics, independent of famine, they seem to be generally combined with summer or hot weather, and the first months of autumn, at least in our climate. This seems to be especially the case from the researches of M. Friedlander for London, Dantzic, Malta, Lavalette, and Aleppo.*

According to Wargentin, the maximum of mortality for Stockholm would take place in the month of August; and according to M. Mourgue, it is the same for Montpellier. The displacement of the maximum in these cities may be owing to local causes. It ap-

* Des Epidemics, &c., An. d'Hygiène, p. 27.

pears, at least in most European countries, that the maximum of deaths generally takes place at the end of winter, and the minimum about the middle of summer.

But this observation was so complex that we sought to analyse the particular facts which it sums up. It was interesting to see if the rigours of winter were equally fatal at all ages, and if the maxima and minima of deaths invariably took place in the same months, at different periods of life, or whether they varied according to these periods.

I have examined this thorny question with care, notwithstanding the long and irksome calculations which I was obliged to undertake. To perfect my researches as much as possible, I have taken into account town or country residence, and the distinction of sexes, so that the tables which I have formed are at the same time tables of mortality for the different months, for men and women, for town and country.* I do not think that this subject has ever been considered in a sufficiently comprehensive manner; there were, however, some special works, particularly on the mortality of new-born children. MM. Villermé and Milne Edwards had observed that the mortality of new-born children increases during the heat of summer, and still more during the cold of winter;† but their numbers, belonging to the three months which follow birth, do not establish distinctions for each particular month, nor for the more advanced months.

According to the researches made in Belgium, the maximum of deaths in summer was not sensible during the first month after birth: but, setting out from this period, it takes place in August, and is most conspicuous towards the middle of the first year; the two minima, which were confounded during the first month, afterwards diverge more and more until the fifth and sixth months, and are placed the one in April the other in November: they afterwards approximate again, to be again confounded, after the first year, and to form a single minimum in September. This singular result is found again when we consider the tables for the mortality of the sexes separately; it is found again, in making the distinction of town and country; but the maximum of summer is manifest in town from the first month after birth.

When we consider the number of deaths which take place soon after birth, it becomes necessary to take into account the excess of births which takes place after the winter: now, in taking an account of this excess, we find that it does not sensibly influence the results previously announced. It is always correct, then, to say, that the greatest mortality, in the first year which succeeds birth, is observed during winter, that it diminishes in spring, increases a little during the heat of summer, and afterwards undergoes a new diminution on the near approach of winter; so that a mild temperature is most fitly adapted to tender infancy, while excess of heat and excess of cold are prejudicial to it, either because these excesses directly influence an organisation which is still very delicate, or because they act through the intermedium of the mother who supports it.

After the first year, the mortality of children is entirely altered; we only observe one maximum and one minimum; the maximum appears after winter, and the minimum in summer. From the age of eight to twelve, these terms are slightly altered, and advance in the order of the months, until near the epoch of puberty, in such a manner that the maximum of deaths is observed in May and the minimum in October. Near puberty, the maximum recedes until the 25th year, and is invariably placed in the month of February, until the most remote age. As to the minimum, it does not again leave the month of October, but it establishes a second in the month of July, which remains there till the end of the mortal career; so that between these two minima, placed three months distant from each other, we observe a secondary maximum, scarcely apparent indeed, during the month of September.

Thus, when man and woman have attained their physical development (about the age of 25 years), they are like children during the first year, most subject to mortality after the heat of summer and the rigours of winter.

The table which follows will assist the reader to understand these results, and their numerical appreciation. It is well to be aware, that in the calculations I have taken account of the unequal lengths of the months. On the other hand, that we may perceive at one glance the law of mortality with respect to seasons and ages, I have constructed a series of lines, which, by their greater or less divergence from the horizontal line, indicate the greater or less divergence from the average mortality. (See the figured table, plate 1).

Table Showing the Influence of Seasons and Age on Mortality.

Ages.	Jan.	Feb.	March.	April.	May.	June.	July.	Aug.	Sept.	Oct.	Nov.	Dec.
From 0 to 1 month,	1·39	1·28	1·21	1·02	0·93	0·82	0·78	0·79	0·86	0·91	0·93	1·07
„ 1 to 3 „	1·39	1·18	1·15	0·95	0·89	0·83	0·83	0·94	0·83	0·92	0·97	1·13
„ 3 to 6 „	1·24	1·06	1·02	0·90	0·95	0·95	0·99	1·06	0·99	0·94	0·86	1·02
„ 6 to 12 „	1·28	1·21	1·27	1·18	1·06	0·84	0·76	0·87	0·81	0·82	0·86	1·03
„ 12 to 18 „	1·10	1·11	1·24	1·30	1·25	1·03	0·88	0·81	0·74	0·77	0·78	0·98
„ 18 to 24 „	1·23	1·18	1·21	1·18	1·03	0·84	0·80	0·76	0·75	0·81	1·01	1·18
„ 2 to 3 years,	1·22	1·13	1·30	1·27	1·12	0·94	0·82	0·73	0·76	0·78	0·91	1·01
„ 3 to 5 „	1·23	1·16	1·26	1·29	1·13	0·94	0·78	0·74	0·73	0·79	0·89	1·05
„ 5 to 8 „	1·20	1·17	1·32	1·24	1·20	0·96	0·78	0·74	0·76	0·75	0·85	1·02
„ 8 to 12 „	1·08	1·06	1·27	1·34	1·21	0·99	0·48	0·82	0·81	0·76	0·80	0·96
„ 12 to 16 „	0·95	0·95	1·14	1·14	1·19	1·04	0·97	0·95	0·96	0·81	0·86	1·04
„ 16 to 20 „	0·93	0·94	1·07	1·18	1·15	1·03	1·00	0·99	0·89	0·87	0·95	1·01
„ 20 to 25 „	0·97	1·00	1·09	1·02	1·09	0·96	0·90	0·92	0·96	0·95	1·03	1·11
„ 25 to 30 „	1·05	1·04	1·11	1·06	1·02	1·02	0·91	0·96	0·95	0·93	0·97	0·97
„ 30 to 40 „	1·11	1·13	1·11	1·04	0·99	0·92	0·85	0·94	0·99	0·95	0·94	1·03
„ 40 to 50 „	1·17	1·15	1·13	1·05	0·99	0·86	0·86	0·94	0·93	0·87	0·95	1·11
„ 50 to 65 „	1·30	1·22	1·11	1·02	0·93	0·85	0·77	0·85	0·89	0·90	1·00	1·15
„ 65 to 75 „	1·43	1·32	1·18	0·99	0·91	0·77	0·71	0·80	0·88	0·86	0·98	1·17
„ 75 to 90 „	1·47	1·39	1·16	1·01	0·87	0·77	0·67	0·75	0·84	0·84	1·00	1·21
„ 90 & upwards,	1·53	1·43	1·25	0·96	0·84	0·75	0·64	0·66	0·76	0·74	1·03	1·29
Average, - -	1·26	1·20	1·17	1·08	1·00	0·88	0·80	0·84	0·86	0·86	0·94	1·09

* These researches are founded on the official documents intrusted to me by the *Bureau de Statistique* established by the minister of the interior. They comprise about 400,000 of different ages, and apply to all Belgium for the years 1827 to 1831. However, the occupation of Maestricht and Luxembourg, has left some vacancies in the tables prepared for the eastern part of the kingdom. † An. d'Hygiène, 1829.

We may see, from the preceding table, that at no period of life is the influence of the seasons on mortality more perceptible than in old age; and at no age less than between 20 and 25, when the physical man, fully developed, enjoys the plenitude of his power.

The absolute maxima and minima are very evident between 1 and 12 years, and after the age of 50, since they afford numbers which, especially in the latter period, are as 1 to 2 and 2½. It is not so with the secondary maxima of summer: the numbers which they present differ so little from those of the minima between which they fall, that we may,,for some periods, attribute the difference to the almost inevitable errors in this species of observations, if they did not manifest themselves in the same manner for several successive years, and even in the partial tables, making a distinction of sexes.

Now, if we establish this latter distinction, we shall find that, for the different epochs of life taken separately, the numbers minima and maxima, both absolute and secondary, fall almost exactly on the same months, and that their ratios have almost the same values; but it is not so with the absolute number of deaths for each sex. Thus, as we have already seen, during the first year after birth, more boys die than girls, and the ratio of deaths for the two sexes is almost the same for each month. Besides, we may judge better by comparing the deaths which have taken place at the same epochs and in the same localities. I am contented to compare the principal ages with each other, and I have assumed as unity the number of male deaths.

Months.	1st Month.	1 to 2 Years.	12 to 16 Years.	16 to 20 Years.	20 to 25 Years.	40 to 50 Years.	90 and upwards.
January,	0·75	0·95	1·32	1·04	0·83	1·21	1·18
February,	0·70	0·91	1·42	1·08	0·83	1·22	1·30
March, -	0·79	0·90	1·11	1·17	0·78	1·18	1·50
April, -	0·73	0·94	1·23	1·18	0·80	1·21	1·44
May, -	0·75	0·96	1·45	0·97	0·80	1·30	1·40
June, -	0·67	0·97	1·28	1·16	0·73	1·18	1·20
July, -	0·70	1·00	1·32	1·08	0·78	1·17	1·42
August,	0·79	0·92	1·20	0·98	0·77	1·08	1·08
September,	0·79	0·98	1·31	1·01	0·73	1·06	1·47
October,	0·67	0·99	1·22	1·01	0·68	1·11	1·50
November,	0·76	1·05	1·20	0·99	0·64	1·11	1·68
December,	0·76	1·05	1·20	0·96	0·64	1·18	1·48

In making the distinction of town and country, I have not found any essential difference in the results concerning the influence of seasons on mortality. I was also equally occupied in investigating the influence which the seasons might have on the number of still-born infants; but the results which I have obtained have already been quoted at page 25.

Since my first researches on the relations which exist at different ages, between the seasons and the mortality, a similar work, by M. Lombard of Geneva,* has appeared. I have had the satisfaction to see that the conclusions of this philosopher almost exactly coincide with my own; although they only include 17,623 deaths, it is easy to perceive that they establish nearly the same facts as those observed in Belgium. Some displacements of the maxima may proceed from the combined influence of different causes, which must naturally vary with the localities. Thus the tables of Geneva give for the first month after birth results conformable to those of Belgium, and we do not perceive any secondary maximum in summer, except for infants between one month and two years old — though this secondary maximum is evidently later than in Belgium, and appears in the months of September and October. It is to be regretted that the numbers for Geneva do not make the distinction of children of early age, since their mortality differs so much, according to my observations. M. Lombard does not admit that this secondary maximum of deaths, which he finds in September and October, for children of one or two years old, may be caused by the continuance of heat, to which cause MM. Villermé and Edwards attribute it: he thinks that it might be attri-

* De l'Influence des Saisons sur la Mortalité à differens Ages.

buted "to the difference of temperature between day and night, which is never greater than at this time of the year." This difference, according to him, principally affects the digestive tube, an organ which, in the child, is very liable to contract serious disease. The secondary maximum of September, for the most advanced years, which I also find in his numbers, still remains to be explained; moreover, the two causes assumed are both probable.

6. Influence of the Hours or Time of Day.

The different parts of the day (day and night) seem to exercise an influence over the number of deaths similar to that by the same cause over births; but to arrive at satisfactory conclusions respecting this point, more numerous observations are required. The only data I have been able to obtain are drawn from the records of the Hospital Saint-Pierre at Brussels for a period of 30 years :*—

Hours.	Deaths.
After midnight, 12 to 6 o'clock, - - -	1397
Before mid-day, 6 to 12 noon, - - - - -	1321
After mid-day, 12 to 6 P. M., - - - - -	1458
Before midnight, 6 to 12, - - - - -	1074
	5250

The difference of day and night is not so well marked for the births; and, contrary to what we observed in regard to the births, most deaths take place in the day time. The two first parts of the day present nearly the same number of deaths, the difference affecting chiefly the 6 hours following mid-day and the 6 hours preceding midnight.

The inquiries of Dr Buek of Hamburg do not agree so well with ours on this point as they did in regard to the births. The following table contains the results, as he has given them, the seasons having been taken into consideration, and their sum reduced to 1000.

Deaths.†	Winter.	Spring.	Summer.	Autumn.	Medium or Average.
After midnight,	315	321	292	281	306
Before noon, -	243	260	236	220	242
After noon, - -	194	211	220	227	211
Before midnight,	248	207	252	272	241

These numbers agree with the preceding only in this respect, that the number for the first part of the day exceeds that for the second. The ratio in respect to Hamburg is 548 to 452, and for Brussels 2718 to 2532; and this is also what we observe with respect to births. But I repeat, in order to entitle them to confidence, these researches ought to be very considerably extended.

CHAPTER VI.

ON THE INFLUENCE OF DISTURBING CAUSES ON THE NUMBER OF DEATHS.

1. Influence of Professions, Degree of Affluence, &c.

IT is scarcely possible, in the actual state of science, to determine precisely the different chances of mortality to which man is exposed in different social conditions: the elements which we have been able to collect, to determine this point, are at present too scanty; however, they enable us to prove that the influence of professions, for instance, may cause a considerable variation in the degree of mortality. It is the same with the affluence and mode of subsistence of a people. To obtain conclusive ideas on these important points, I am going to bring forward the principal results which have been arrived at.

Statisticians at the present day appear to acknow-

* For the details, see Correspondance Mathematique, 1827, vol. iii. page 42, and the Recherches sur la Reproduction, &c.

† [Although the word Naissance is found here in the original work, it is quite evident that the author means Deces, or Deaths.]

ledge that the chances of mortality are much more numerous in manufacturing than in agricultural countries, and in the interior of cities than in the middle of the country. We have already had several proofs in what has gone before, and we can produce some fresh ones—I do not say for town and country, for we have seen that the difference of mortality is too apparent to require us to return to it again—but for manufacturing provinces.

If we first look at England, we shall there find very evident differences between the manufacturing and agricultural provinces. The following are some results which have been communicated to me by M. Villermé, who has deduced them from the new documents published in England by Mr Rickman, for the years 1813 to 1830 inclusive :—

Localities.	Of 10,000 Deaths which have taken place	
	From Birth to the most advanced Age, before the Age of 10 Years had been completed, there were—	From the Age of 10 Years to the greatest degree of longevity, from the 10th to the 40th, there were—
In the whole of the agricultural districts, - - -	3,505	3,142
In the whole of the districts partly agricultural and partly manufacturing, - -	3,828	3,319
In the whole of the manufacturing districts, - -	4,355	3,727

We here see very evidently that all the advantages are on the side of the agricultural districts.

In the Netherlands, the most agricultural province is Gueldres: the mortality there is only 1 in 53·7 individuals, whilst in the commercial provinces of Holland it is 1 in 35.

In Belgium, the provinces generally displaying the fewest deaths are those of Luxembourg, Namur, and Hainault; these are also essentially agricultural provinces, although the two latter have some manufacturing towns.

France presents similar results, but which will appear less conclusive, because the departments most exposed to mortality are certainly the manufacturing departments in general; but since these are also those which include the greatest cities in the kingdom, we cannot exactly discern whether it is really the professions of the inhabitants or their dense crowding which causes the excess of mortality.

It would appear evident that the most favourable state for man is a regular life, which produces a sufficiency for his wants, and which is not agitated by the passions or irregularities of town life. In the agricultural state, man generally attains a state of comparative affluence: he does not undergo, as in the manufacturing districts, the alternate changes of superfluity and want—he is less acquainted with these two extremes which subject him to privations or drive him to excesses.

Misery, with the privations which it brings in its train, is one of the most powerful causes of mortality. Several statisticians have endeavoured to demonstrate this observation; and again, very recently, M. Benoiston de Châteauneuf has given a new confirmation of it in a paper entitled "On the Duration of Life in the Rich and in the Poor."* The author, to whom we are indebted for a valuable collection of researches on the mortality of man in his different social conditions, has made, on the one hand, an abstract of the deaths of 1600 persons of the highest rank, among which are 157 sovereigns or princes; on the other hand, he has taken from the civil registers of the state the deaths of 2000 persons in the 12th arrondissement of Paris,

* See the *Moniteur* for May 11, 1829.

which contains a population of workmen of all kinds, ragmen, sweepers, delvers, day-labourers, &c., a class subjected to pain, anxiety, and hard labour, who live in want, and die in hospitals. These researches, which bring together the extremes of wealth and poverty, have given the following results :—

Age.	Mortality		
	of the Common rank.*	of the Rich.	of the Poor.
25 to 30 years,	1·41	0·00	2·22
30 to 35 „	1·56	0·85	1·43
35 to 40 „	1·71	1·20	1·85
40 to 45 „	1·91	0·85	1·87
45 to 50 „	2·21	1·59	2·39
50 to 55 „	2·68	1·81	2·58
55 to 60 „	3·39	1·68	4·60
60 to 65 „	4·41	3·06	5·76
65 to 70 „	5·85	4·31	9·25
70 to 75 „	7·80	6·80	14·14
75 to 80 „	10·32	8·09	14·59
80 to 85 „	13·15	11·58	..
85 to 90 „	13·55	16·29	..
90 to 95 „	14·05	..	..

The registers of insurance societies likewise tend to point out the greater mortality of the poor. The Equitable Society had always employed the tables of mortality of Northampton; but the secretary, Mr Morgan, showed, in 1810, that the deaths of 83,000 insured persons, which had taken place in the space of 30 years, were in the ratio of 2 to 3 compared with those given in the tables. Among these *select* persons, the mortality of females is still lower than that of males, because, in the middle class, women are more exempt from anxiety and fatigue, as well as the fatal effects of passion and irregularities of conduct. In general, among the persons insured by the Equitable Society, the average death annually was only 1 in 81·5 from the year 1800 to 1820.†

On the other hand, to take an extreme limit also, if we consider man in the state of greatest misery and deepest degradation, it is calculated that one negro slave dies annually out of 5 or 6, whilst the free Africans who served in the English troops only lost 1 man in 33·3.‡

It is likewise proper that we should duly understand the word *riches*, when speaking of population : a great abundance of goods is often only a ready means of gratifying the passions and giving way to excesses of every kind. The most favourable state of a people is that in which they have the means of providing for every real want, without exceeding the bounds of temperance, and without creating artificial wants. It is to be observed, as M. de Tracey very judiciously remarks, that the people are almost always richer in nations called *poor* than in those called *rich*. Thus, there is no nation possessed of more wealth than England, yet a great part of the population subsist on public money.§ The rich province of Flanders certainly contains more poor than Luxembourg, where great fortunes are rare; but here the population live in a state of general affluence, and find the means of procuring moderate incomes, and which never vary from day to day, as in the manufacturing districts. The same may be said of Switzerland, and agricultural countries generally.

According to Mr Hawkins, the mortality of the whole marine of England, in the different parts of the world, without excepting the population in hospitals, was in 1813 1 in 42. The same author thinks that

* According to the table of M. Duvillard.

† M. D'Ivernois has quoted several striking examples of longevity among insured and select persons in the affluent classes of Geneva.—(*Bib. Universelle*).

‡ Elements of Medical Statistics, p. 208, *et seq.*

§ [M. Quetelet here refers to the exorbitant sums levied in England in the form of poor-rates, and which amounted to £4,123,604 in the year 1838. No alteration of consequence has since taken place in the annual expenditure on this score.]

the troops on land have a still smaller mortality than the seamen.

M. Benoiston de Châteauneuf has also been occupied with investigations on the mortality of the French army compared with that of the rest of the population, and he has been led to several curious results, which I shall endeavour to state succinctly.*

M. de Châteauneuf here likewise finds that the privileged class is that which is the best fed, and undergoes the least fatigue: thus, according to the documents of France, the mortality of the soldier was a little greater than that of the mass of the people; the guard has fewer deaths than the army; and the sub-officer dies more rarely than the soldier, both in the guard and army.

If we investigate the influence of seasons on the mortality of soldiers, the following are the results which we obtain for the deaths of the infantry from 1820 to 1826:—

Seasons.	Months.	Deaths.
Winter.	January, February, March,	4·168
Spring.	April, May, June,	4·182
Summer.	July, August, September,	4·463
Autumn.	October, November, December,	4·279
		17·092

The maximum of deaths falls in summer. But without taking notice of the astronomic calculation which fixes the period of the seasons, if we determine the seasons by their influence on the atmosphere alone, after the manner of several German and Italian physicians, we have a new division as follows:—

Seasons.	Months.	Deaths.
Winter.	December, January, February,	3·996
Spring.	March, April, May,	4·357
Summer.	June, July, August,	4·143
Autumn.	September, October, November,	4·596
		17·092

The maximum of deaths is no longer in summer, but takes place in autumn. Thus, in whatever way we divide the year, whether into half-years, quarters, or seasons, the intensity of mortality reaches its minimum in winter. Taking the numbers of each month, we find two minima and two maxima: these results differ less from those of civil life than M. de Châteauneuf thinks, who, moreover, when he composed his memoir, was not acquainted with the influence of seasons on different ages. We may form an opinion of it by bringing together the numbers of France, and those which I have found for Belgium.

Months.	Deaths in France from 1820 to 1826.	Deaths in Belgium	
		From 16 to 20 Years.	From 20 to 25 Years.
January,	1·402	0·93	0·97
February,	1·334	0·94	1·00
March,	1·432	1·07	1·09
April,	1·475	1·18	1·02
May,	1·450	1·15	1·09
June,	1·257	1·03	0·96
July,	1·279	1·00	0·90
August,	1·607	0·99	0·92
September,	1·577	0·89	0·96
October,	1·638	0·87	0·95
November,	1·381	0·95	1·03
December,	1·260	1·01	1·11
Total,	17·092	12·00	12·00

We see, however, that after the great heats of summer, the soldier is exposed to a degree of mortality which is not observed in civil life.

If we consider the different regions of France, we shall find that the inhabitants of the provinces in the

* Essai sur la Mortalité de l'Infanterie Française (An. d'Hygiène, tome x. 2d part.) See also a memoir by M. le Comte Morozo, Sur la Mortalité des Troupes Piémontaises, in the Memoires de l'Academie de Turin.

north are more capable of bearing the fatigues of service than those of the south; but none appear less fitted for service than those of the centre.

M. de Châteauneuf has also endeavoured to investigate what causes the increase of mortality of the soldier, and he has examined the influence of several causes, such as duels, venereal diseases, suicides, nostalgia, phthisis, &c. This able statistician had already examined in another work the influence of certain professions on the development of pulmonary phthisis,* and he had arrived at several interesting conclusions. M. Lombard of Geneva has since been occupied with the same subject of research,† and has collected a great number of facts, of the principal results of which we ought not to be ignorant.

After having discussed the data afforded him by five different lists, formed for Paris, Hamburg, Vienna, and Geneva, M. Lombard has put them together, and divided the professions into three classes, according as they are favourable, indifferent, or unfavourable to the development of phthisis, or, in other terms, according as they have a greater, equal, or smaller number, than the general average.

The following is the general list:—

I.—PROFESSIONS PLACED ABOVE THE AVERAGE.

A.—Among Men.

1. *In all the lists.*—Sculptors, printers, hatters, polishers, gendarmes, brushmakers, soldiers, jewellers, tailors, millers, mattress-makers, lacemen or embroiderers, lemonade-makers, domestics, and hairdressers.

2. *In the majority of the lists.*—Copy-writers, cooks, turners, joiners, barbers, shoemakers, and coopers.

3. *In one list only.*—Ironmongers, vinedressers,‡ commissioners, old-clothesmen, tinmen, *porteurs de lessive*, paviers, paviers, engravers, mechanics, calico-printers, doorkeepers, showmen, springmakers, enamellers, design-painters, street-sweepers, pastry-cooks, showmakers, instructors, carters, brokers, sundial-makers, showpillar-makers, upholsterers, Protestant ministers,§ iron-merchants, lime-makers, basket-makers, shepherds, teachers of arithmetic, police-officers, servants in place, feather-sellers, crystal-cutters, gauze-weavers, sportsmen, and ribbon-makers.

B.—Among Women.

1. *In all the lists.*— Seamstresses, shoemakers, glovers, and embroiderers.

2. *In the majority of the lists.*—Polishers.

3. *In one list only.*—Makers of watch-needles, clockmakers, milliners, teachers, laundresses, old-clotheswomen, toilet and mercer-women, hatters, bookbinders, knitters, jewel-makers or dealers, feather-makers or dealers, florists, brushmakers, and racemakers.

II.—PROFESSIONS WITHIN THE LISTS, SOMETIMES ABOVE THE AVERAGE, SOMETIMES BELOW IT.

A.—Among Men.

Students, plasterers, stone-cutters, saddlers, delvers, clockmakers, waggoners, cellarmen, ‖ goldsmiths, stocking-makers, charcoal-makers, gilders, musicians, sawyers, and glaziers.¶

* An. d'Hygiène, tome vi. partie 1, July 1831.
† Idem, tome xi. partie 1, Jan. 1834.
‡ This result is founded solely on six deaths, and requires confirmation.—*Note by M. Lombard.*
§ The number of consumptive persons is increased by the deaths of several English ecclesiastics, who arrived out of health at Geneva.—*M. Lombard.*
‖ The first eight may be considered as belonging to the first class, that is to say, to those among whom the number of phthisical persons is above the average; in fact, they are so placed in the Geneva list, which may be considered more exact than the other.—*M. Lombard.*
¶ The remark made in the preceding note will apply to the last seven professions, which, in the Geneva list, are placed below the average.—*M. Lombard.*

B.—Among Women.

Housekeepers, day-labourers, spinners, weavers, gauzemakers, gilders, stocking-menders, and mantua-makers.

III.—PROFESSIONS BELOW THE AVERAGE.

A.—Among Men.

1. *In all the lists.*—Coachmen, quarrymen, carpenters, tavern-keepers, butchers, porters at the market and message-boys, porters, tanners, bleachers, bargemen, confectioners, slaters, foundry-men, and orderlies.

2. *In the majority of the lists.*—Bakers, smiths, farriers, locksmiths, masons, and weavers.

3. *In one list only.*—Surgeons, braziers, cutlers, different merchants, woodcutters, advocates, sedan-carriers, chamois-leather-dressers, agriculturists, men of letters, negotiators, grocers, persons employed under government, bookbinders, governors of colleges, commissioners, loaders, clogmakers, merchant-drapers, druggists, annuitants, veteran officers, grooms, messengers, bankers, magistrates, dyers, physicians, coal-measurers, notaries, carvers, lawyers, money-changers, breeches-makers, candle-makers, tobacco-merchants, librarians, harness-makers, blanket-weavers, furbishers, plumbers, wood-merchants, professors, chocolate-makers, funeral assistants, landlords, cheesemongers, skin-dealers, furriers, chimney-sweepers, agents, architects, gunsmiths, packers, pinmakers, assizers of wood, vermicelli-makers, teachers of foreign languages, needle-makers, spinners, cotton-weavers, marble-cutters, starch-manufacturers, ragmen, water-carriers, toymen, stuff-manufacturers, shop-boys, miners, merchant-mercers, and combmakers.

B.—Among Women.

1. *In all the lists.*—Carders of mattresses, sicknurses, retailers, bleachers, gardeners.

2. *In the majority of the lists.*—Women employed in doing tailor-work.

3. *In one list only.*—Fringe-makers, embroiderers, winders, gauzemakers, ragwomen, cotton-spinners, watch-chainmakers, calico-printers, cooks, domestics, annuitants, washerwomen, merchant-grocers, counterpane-makers, butchers, midwives, bakers, female porters, and leech-appliers.

Next, passing to the causes which may influence the frequency of phthisis in the different professions, M. Lombard arrives at the following conclusions:—

1. The circumstances which multiply phthisis, are misery, sedentary life and absence of muscular exercise, shocks sustained in workshops, a curved posture, the impure air of shops, the inhalation of certain mineral or vegetable vapours, and, lastly, air loaded with thick or impalpable dust, or light, elastic, filamentous bodies.

2. The circumstances which exercise a preservative influence, are riches, active life, and fresh air, regular exercise of all parts of the body, inhalation of watery vapour,* or animal and vegetable emanations.

If we want to ascertain the degree of influence of each of these causes, in the production of phthisis, among the workmen who are found exposed to them, it may be considered as being as follows:—

Average number of phthisical persons, 114 in 1000.

I.—Noxious Influences.

1. Mineral and vegetable emanations,	0·176
2. Dust of different kinds,	0·145
3. Sedentary life,	0·140
4. Life passed in workshops,	0·138
5. Dry hot air,	0·127
6. Bent posture,	0·122
7. Movement of the arm, striking the chest,	0·116

* [The theory evidently alluded to in the text, that the inhabitants of marshy countries were less liable to pulmonary phthisis than others, was supported for a while by a few medical men, but afterwards entirely abandoned.]

II.—Preservative Influences.

1. Active life, muscular exercise,	0·089
2. Exercise of the voice,	0·075
3. Life passed in the open air,	0·073
4. Animal emanations,	0·060
5. Watery vapours,	0·053

There are, then, many other researches which have for their object the determination of the influence of professions on mortality:* it would be difficult to present a summary here, since the facts at present collected are very few; however, I cannot pass over in total silence the researches of Casper of Berlin, who, by his labours in medical statistics, has taken a distinguished rank in science.† Casper finds that the profession of medicine is perhaps more exposed to mortality than any other, contrary to the prejudices so generally received; and he has observed that theologians occupy the other extreme in the scale of mortality. Undoubtedly, we must here include under the name of theologians, the clergymen and not the learned men who descend into theological studies; which may make a great difference, for the activity of mind, carried to a certain degree, may become as prejudicial, as a regular and quiet life is advantageous, to the preservation of man. The following table, presented by Casper, points this out clearly:—

Of 100 theologians, there have attained the age of 70

and upwards,	42
Agriculturists and foresters,	40
Superintendants,	35
Commercial and industrious men,	35
Military men,	32
Subalterns,	32
Advocates,	29
Artists,	28
Teachers, professors,	27
Physicians,	24

It would seem to follow from this table, that mental labour is more injurious to man than bodily, but that the most injurious state is that where fatigue of body is joined to that of the mind. A sedentary life, which is not exposed to any kind of excess, appears, on the contrary, to be most favourable. The summary which follows will suffice to point out the extremes.

Of 1000 deaths, there were as follows:—

Age.	Physicians.	Theologians.	Ratio.
From 23 to 32 years,	82	43	1·91
·· 33 to 42 ··	149	58	2·57
·· 43 to 52 ··	160	64	2·50
·· 53 to 62 ··	210	180	1·17
·· 63 to 72 ··	228	328	0·70
·· 73 to 82 ··	141	257	0·55
·· 83 to 92 ··	30	70	0·43
	1000	1000	

I do not know whether we have any precise researches on the influence which study in general has on the constitution of children and young persons. This subject deserves a serious examination at the present day, especially since many parents, by improper attention, and sometimes from motives of self-love or very censurable cupidity, bring up their children as we should grow plants in a hot-house, to enjoy their flowers and fruits the sooner. Numerous examples have shown how short these fruits endure, and how subject those are who produce them to premature decay: we have seen few of these prodigies preserve their reputation beyond the period of infancy, or withstand the excessive efforts of an organisation too feeble for the labours imposed upon it. We shall also have occasion to examine, when speaking of mental alienation, to what extent excessive studies, especially in the exact sciences, may predispose to this dreadful malady, or even entirely ruin the most happy organisation.

* See especially, in the *Annales d'Hygiène*, different memoirs by MM. Parent Duchatelet, D'Arcet, Leuret, Marc, Villermé, Benoiston de Châteauneuf, &c.
† Gazette Medicale Hebdomadaire de Berlin, 3d January 1834; and An. d'Hygiène, April 1834.

There are diseases, of more or less danger, inherent in the habits of individuals, and the quality of the food and drink which they use. Of this number appears to be stone in the bladder, which especially afflicts certain localities. I am under obligations to M. Civiale, for different data on this cruel scourge, which is now combated with so much success; and I thought that those respecting age were not without interest in a work the object of which is the study of the development of man. Although the observations are at present scanty, it appears certain that the disposition to this disease is the greatest in childhood: we may judge from the following table:—

Ages.	Patients affected with Stone.			
	Lunéville.	Bristol.	Norwich and Norfolk.	Leeds.
From 0 to 10 years,	943	46	255	83
„ 10 to 20 „	377	65	99	21
„ 20 to 30 „	106	41	47	21
„ 30 to 40 „	38	34	46	12
„ 40 to 50 „	23	37	41	28
„ 50 to 60 „	18	28	92	21
„ 60 to 70 „	16	18	63	9
„ 70 & upwards,	5	2	6	2
Total, - -	1526	371	649	197

It is about the age of five years especially, that the number of calculous patients appears to be the greatest. Indeed, at Lunéville, the following numbers have been observed from year to year, commencing at infancy and reaching to the 10th year:—0, 17, 79, 131, 145, 143, 116, 119, 84, and 75.

It would appear that after puberty age had no great influence on the predisposition to this disease, especially taking into account the number of individuals of each age which a population contains.

The difference of the sexes has a marked influence: it is generally supposed that about 21 men are affected with the disease to one woman; this would be inferred from the following table:—

Places.	Stone Cases.		
	Men.	Women.	Men to 1 Woman.
Lunéville, - - -	1463	63	23
Bristol, - - -	348	7	49
Paris, - - -	423	16	26
Ulm, - - -	123	4	31
Leeds, - - -	188	9	21
Norwich and Norfolk, -	618	31	20
Lombardy, -	758	36	41
Diction. de Medicine, -	312	44	7
Practice of M. Civiale, -	419	10	42
Total, - - -	4652	220	21·14

Women, like men, have a greater disposition to stone in infancy than at a more advanced age; as to the danger of death from it, we may calculate on about 1 death to 5·3 cases nearly, in different countries, when lithotomy is had recourse to. The danger of operation is least during infancy.

2. Influence of Morals.

Up to the present time, we possess few researches on the influence which morals may have on the number of deaths in a nation, excepting in the case of violent deaths. This is a vast field open to the investigations of statisticians, who might arrive at results no less interesting for the preservation of society than for moral and political philosophy.

We have already seen, from the preceding researches, what advantage an industrious and prudent people has, with respect to mortality, over a depraved and indolent one. In establishing a parallel between England and the unfortunate republic of Guanaxuato, I have shown that, proportion still being kept in view, the deaths were almost three times as numerous in the latter as in the former country. We have likewise seen that the mortality was much less in the higher classes of society than in the lower; and this state of things is not merely owing to abundance on the one hand and privations, on the other, but also to rational and temperate habits, more regulated passions, and less rapid transitions in their mode of living.

The violence of the passions seems to have considerable influence in shortening the duration of human life. Thus, when the physical man is fully developed, about the age of twenty, it would be supposed that he ought to resist all the destructive tendencies of his nature; but the contrary is the case. This excess of mortality, which is not observed in females, continues in man until very near the age of thirty, a period at which the fire of the passions is somewhat deadened. We shall be better enabled to understand this critical period in the life of the male, when we have examined the development of his moral nature.

It is particularly in epidemics that we are enabled to recognise the influence of morals on the number of deaths. We have been enabled to judge, especially during the ravages of cholera in Europe, how much intemperance has been fatal to those who gave themselves up to it. Opinions have been greatly at variance on the nature and curative means of this scourge, but all agree in establishing the fact which I have stated.*

From numerous observations, it appears that the fear of a disease may singularly predispose to an attack of it: the moral influences here exercise a remarkable action over the physical, and one which deserves the greatest attention from philosophers. This interesting subject has already been made the object of many researches; but it has scarcely been examined by that rigorous method of analysis which has for some time been applied to science. Persons have been seen to fall down dead, through the violent excitement of a passion; others have been seen, labouring under a presentiment of death, really to die, when their excited imagination had made them dread death. It would be extremely interesting to determine what are the passions most dangerous to excite inordinately, and at what point fear may cause death. These researches would induce essential modifications in our habits and institutions. Thus, the custom of attending with religious forms on the patient whose condition is hopeless, may cause death in many cases; and we cannot but applaud the precautions taken in certain countries, of discharging these forms from the commencement of the disease, when it only presents symptoms of slight danger. Religious ceremonies then appear less like the signal of a passage to another state of existence.

I shall also class among the disturbing causes which increase mortality, man's tendency to self-destruction, or to destroy his species, although he shares it in common with animals, who are obedient only to the laws of nature. But here the tendency is manifested under entirely different forms; thus, destruction of man by man is a crime or a virtue, according to the manner in which it takes place: and it would be very difficult to assign the limits of two such opposite conditions, especially if we regard the difference of times and places. An historical account of the displacement of this limit in different nations, would of itself be a work of the highest interest, and would show us under what phases humanity has been fated to appear.

* [The translator's experience in respect to cholera has a tendency to modify M. Quetelet's opinion. So far as he observed, the temperate and the intemperate fell equally under this terrible scourge; in fact, its origin, progress, and disappearance, are quite a mystery. It can scarcely now be said that a single well-established fact respecting this disease was made out by the medical profession in Europe.]

An examination of such questions as these, however, will more naturally find a place when I consider the development of the moral qualities of man, and have to speak of duelling and homicide. This will also be the place to treat of the destruction of man by his fellow-man, when on a larger scale, and in modes consecrated by our manners and institutions; for our ideas of war belong also to moral statistics.

I have just shown, by different examples, how much mortality is influenced by morals: another no less striking example of this influence is that which still-births afford, when we have made the distinction between legitimate and illegitimate ones. The fatal heritage of vice does not affect the child before its birth only, it pursues it still, for a long time after it has escaped this first danger, and misery often aggravates the evil. Thus, it follows from the researches of Baumann and Süssmilch, that the mortality presents the following ratio, all things being equal :—

Still-births,	1 legitimate,	2·0 illegitimate.
1st month after birth,	1	2·4 ..
2d and 3d month,	1 ..	2·0 ~
4th, 5th, and 6th month,	1 ..	1·7 ..
Remainder of the year,	1 ;.	1·5 ..
2d year,	1 ..	1·4 ..
3d and 4th year,	1 ..	1·3 ..

The difference continues very evident until the seventh year; so that, according to Baumann, only one-tenth of illegitimate children will arrive at maturity. This result just explains what is observed in the republic of Guanaxuato, " where nothing can equal the mass of physical, moral, and political pollution." *

Casper gives a table of the mortality of children at Berlin,† from which it appears that of 28,705 children who died before the age of 15 years, during the decennial period from 1813 to 1822, there were 5598 illegitimate, which gave annually 2311 deaths of illegitimate, and 160 of legitimate children, before the age of 15. But according to this savant, about the same period, 5663 legitimate children were born, and 1080 illegitimate ones. The ratio of deaths, therefore, was 1 to 2·5 for the first, and 1 to 1·9 for the second.

What especially tends to increase the mortality of illegitimate children is, that the greater number of them are abandoned to public charity. The absence of the cares of a mother, at a time when they are most needed, and the other privations of every kind, which are the necessary consequences of such an abandonment, sufficiently explain the great mortality which generally exists in foundling hospitals.

To understand this mortality, M. Benoiston de Châteauneuf, in his *Considerations sur les Enfans Trouvés,*‡ thus estimates the mortality of infancy in Europe during the century which has just elapsed :—

	Minimum.	Maximum.
From 0 to 1 year,	19 in the hundred.	45½ in the hundred.
.. 0 to 3 years,	26½ ..	50 ..
.. 0 to 4 ..	30 ..	53 ..
.. 0 to 10 ..	35 ..	55 6-7ths ..

According to this savant, the mortality of foundlings in several cities of Europe was, from birth to the end of the first year—

At Petersburg, in 1788,	- - -	40 per cent.
.. Florence, ditto,	- - - -	40 ..
.. Barcelona, in 1790,	- - - -	60 ..
.. Paris, in 1789,	- - - -	80 ..
.. Dublin, in 1791,	- - - -	91 ..

" From birth to four years old, at Rome, Madrid, Dublin, and Paris, we find 50, 62, 76, and 98 in the hundred.§

* Sir F. D'Ivernois, *Sur la Mortalité Proportionnelle.*
† Beitrage, p. 173.
‡ Paris, 1824, 1 vol. 8vo.
§ M. de Gérando, in his excellent work *Le Visiteur du Pauvre,* makes the mortality 1 in 7 of the children which the civil hos-

Lastly, at the end of 20 years, of 19,420 children received into the house at Dublin, only 2000 remained alive, and 7000 at Moscow out of 37,600. What an awful destruction! War and epidemics are less terrible to the human race. And let no one suppose that modern times have produced more happy results, or that this dismal catalogue, which we might still extend, at the present day presents fewer numbers. According to the authentic accounts which we have before us, at Madrid, in 1817, there died, either in hospital or country, 67 children out of 100 ; at Vienna, in 1811, 92 ; at Brussels, from 1812 to 1817, 79. At this period, the hospital, which was small, unhealthy, and badly ventilated, was removed to another quarter of the city, and from that time there has been a considerable decrease of the average number of deaths, which is not more than 56 in the 100." *

What has preceded, sufficiently shows what influence well-directed conduct may exercise over the life and death of foundlings. This is not the place to examine how far these institutions should be approved of, where unfortunates are collected together ; but it may be interesting to know how much the number of foundlings and deserted children has increased since these institutions arose. At Paris, for example, the ratio of their number to that of births, in one century, makes the following progress :—

Years.	Ratio in 100.	Years.	Ratio in 100.
From 1710 to 1720,	- - - 9·73	From 1770 to 1780,	- - 33·66
.. 1720 to 1730,	- - - 11·37	.. 1780 to 1790,	- - 28·70
.. 1730 to 1740,	- - - 14·48	.. 1790 to 1800,	- - 17·69
.. 1740 to 1750,	- - - 18·21	.. 1800 to 1810,	- - 20·95
.. 1750 to 1760,	- - - 23·71	.. 1810 to 1820,	- - 22·88
.. 1760 to 1770,	- - 30·75		

We see that the proportion rises rapidly during the latter years of the reign of Louis XV.; it diminishes more than two-thirds under the Convention ; it increases again under the imperial government ; and has been stationary since the revolution.

M. de Châteauneuf, from whom I borrow the greater number of the preceding data, gives the following ratios for some of the principal cities of Europe :—

		Foundlings.
Lisbon, from 1815 to 1819,		26·26 in 100 births.
Madrid, ...		25·58 ..
Rome, .. 1801 to 1807,		27·90 ..
Paris, .. 1815 to 1821,	- -	20·91 ..
Brussels, .. 1816 to 1821,		14·68 ..
Vienna, .. 1815 to 1821,	- -	23·43 ..
Petersburg, 1820,		45·00 ..
Moscow,	- - -	27·94 ..
County of Nice,	- -	6·06 ..
Savoy,	- - -	5·83 ..

Thus, in the greater number of the cities quoted previously, nearly one-fourth of the children are exposed. This state of things is very apt to give rise to reflections on the misery and immorality of great cities. Paris annually produces about 21 foundlings to 100 births, whilst the rest of France only produces 3·52. It is true that this disproportion would be much less, if throughout France there were the same facility as at Paris of sending children to the hospitals ; and it is also just to remark, that many children are sent to Paris, who do not belong to the city. In Belgium the following values have been obtained, according to the results of the ten years preceding 1833 :†—

pitals in Paris send out to be supported (p. 205) ; but we must observe, that these children vary from 1 day to 12 years of age : and in this the numbers agree with those of M. Benoiston, at p. 76 of his *Considerations,* &c.

* I have found, from the average results of the eight years from 1815 to 1822, that the mortality of the hospital at Brussels was 66·38 in the 100 : at this period, it had a greater mortality than any of the nineteen hospitals in the kingdom ; the average mortality has been 45·07 in 100.—See *Recherches sur les Naissances, &c.*
† See Correspondance Mathematique et Physique, tome viii. livraison 2, p. 135.

Provinces.	Births: Annual Average.	Foundlings and Deserted.	Foundlings to 100 Births.
Antwerp,	11,018	2156·5	19·6
Brabant,	18,893	2307·4	12·2
Flanders, West	20,315	480·5	2·3
.. East,	24,148	693·8	2·9
Hainault,	20,016	1830·2	9·1
Liege,	11,837	212·2	1·9
Namur,	6,399	844·9	13·2
The kingdom,*	112,626	8525·5	7·6

It is very difficult to explain the differences which are presented by the several provinces of such a country as Belgium, unless as regards the facility which mothers find, in certain localities, of exposing their children. On this subject, we ought to read the observations of M. Gouroff, one of the persons who has paid most attention to all that concerns foundlings.† "The city of London, the population of which is 1,250,000, in the space of five years from 1819 to 1823, has only had 151 children exposed; and the number of illegitimate children received into eighty-four workhouses, during the same period, only reaches to 4668 ; and, moreover, about one-fifth of these children are supported at the expense of the father. What a striking contrast is Paris, which, having only two-thirds the population of London, has had, within the same years, 25,327 children, all maintained at the expense of the state!

Do we still ask for a more certain proof of the influence which foundling hospitals have in multiplying the abandonments of infants? Mayence had no establishment of this kind ; and from 1799 to 1811, there were 30 children exposed. Napoleon ordered a 'tour' to be established in this city. It was opened on the 7th November 1811, and existed until the month of March 1815, when the Grand-Duke of Hesse-Darmstadt caused it to be suppressed. During these three years and four months, the house received 516 foundlings. When it was once suppressed, as the habit of exposing the children had not taken root in the people, all things returned to their former order : in the course of the nine following years, only seven children were exposed."

When proposing the reform of foundling hospitals, M. de Gouroff does not desire it to be done precipitately. "On the contrary, it requires reflection, time, and patience, to prepare and gradually execute the measures which ought to precede it, and to avoid the error committed in some of the cities of Belgium, which, in 1823, that they might not be burdened with the expense of the children left out of doors, suppressed the 'tours.' Immediately the lives of several new-born infants were sacrificed, and public opinion obliged the government to order their re-establishment."

The principal conclusions of the work of M. de Gouroff are :—

1. That in Catholic countries, or rather in those where asylums have been opened to all children indiscriminately who are abandoned at the time of birth, these little unfortunates are much more common, much more numerous, than elsewhere.

2. That in these asylums there is a frightful mortality, and quite beyond the proportion of the greatest mortality which cuts off other children, even in the most indigent classes.

3. That infanticide is scarcely prevented by foundling hospitals ; or rather, that, in order to prevent a few infanticides, whether direct or indirect, through the effect of unrelieved exposure, these houses do themselves destroy an incomparably greater number of children.‡

* Except the provinces of Liege and Luxembourg.
† Essai sur l'Histoire des Enfans Trouvés. 8vo. Paris : 1829.
‡ [Perhaps the question is not very fairly stated by M. de Gouroff. Infanticide, when direct, is a horrible crime, in fact, mur-

3. Influence of Knowledge and of Political and Religious Institutions.

Civilisation, which sweetens the existence of man, has also prolonged it : the progress of knowledge has contributed to the health of the individual houses and interior of cities, and has gradually caused marshy lands and the other sources of the epidemics which habitually harassed our ancestors, to disappear. Knowledge, by multiplying the commercial relations of nations, has also rendered famines less frequent and formidable ; the chances of which, on the one hand, have been diminished by bettering the culture of the earth, and varying the means of subsistence : medical science and public hygiène have likewise found out valuable means for resisting mortality ; whilst the development of industry, and the securities which society received from more liberal institutions, have contributed to diffuse affluence and the most active means of preservation.

At the present day, it appears clearly established, that in countries where civilisation makes the greatest progress, we may also observe the greatest diminution of mortality. However, we must not exaggerate these advantages, as has been done in respect to some countries : the greater accuracy statistical documents acquire, the more numerous appear the prejudices which have been entertained on this subject. England is placed in an advantageous position, which has always fixed the attention of savants when studying the theory of population ; but it is perhaps to this kingdom that my remark is most applicable. If we examine what has been the mortality from the commencement of the eighteenth century, we shall find, according to two of her most eminent statisticians :*—

Years.	Inhabitants to one Death.
1700,	43
1750,	42
1776 to 1800 inclusive,	48
1806 to 1810 ,,	49
1816 to 1820 ,,	55
1826 to 1830 ,,	51

According to these numbers, there would be a very sensible decrease of mortality ; but we know that very numerous omissions have taken place in the figures of mortality. Mr Rickman himself thinks that, in consequence of these omissions, we ought to reckon 1 death in 49 inhabitants, instead of 1 in 51, for the five last years ; whilst, according to Mr Hawkins, the mortality for 1822 would have been 1 in 60.† On the other hand, the census may likewise have been faulty. Moreover, it might be objected, that these inaccuracies, if they could be corrected, would probably only place in a clearer light a still greater difference of mortality, since the figure of mortality is generally smaller in proportion as there is more negligence in collecting it. That would suppose always that the census of the population is correct.

The changes which have taken place in great towns should especially receive our attention. For example, in 1697, the total number of deaths in London rose to 21,000 ; however, a century after, in 1797, the number was only 17,000, notwithstanding the increase of the population.‡ These advantages have been

der ; but the exposure of a child is a misdemeanour ; so that foundling hospitals were established in Catholic countries without doubt with a view to prevent crime, and it is astonishing and almost incredible that they have not succeeded in effecting even this : in other respects, they themselves are an evil of the first magnitude.]
* Mr Marshall gives 5,475,000 and 6,467,000 as the population of England and Wales in 1700 and 1750 ; and the deaths 132,728 and 154,686. The other ratios are drawn from the last work of Mr Rickman.
† Elements of Medical Statistics, by F. Bisset Hawkins.
‡ Ibid., p. 13.

obtained especially between 50 to 60 years ago, since which time the city has increased with great rapidity in extent and population. In the middle of the last century, the annual mortality was still 1 in 20; at present, it is only 1 in 40, according to the census of 1821; so that it has exactly diminished one-half. It is then correct to say, that the mortality, towards the end of the last century, had undergone an increase, which may be attributed to the excessive abuse of spirituous liquors which then prevailed.

The towns of Manchester, Liverpool, and Birmingham, have presented almost the same decrease of mortality as London. It is very difficult to believe that some error may not have crept into such estimates.

France, like England, has experienced a diminution of mortality, if we may refer to ancient documents.* According to M. Villermé, it was computed in 1781, that 1 death took place to 29 inhabitants; in 1802, 1 in 30; and now, 1 in 40.†

In Sweden, from 1755 to 1775, 1 death took place to 35 inhabitants; in 1775 to 1795, 1 to 37; and in 1823, 1 to 48.

Likewise, at Berlin, from 1747 to 1755, the annual mortality was 1 to 28; and from 1816 to 1822, the ratio was less than 1 to 34.

M. Moreau de Jonnes, in a notice on the mortality of Europe, has presented the following table, which likewise tends to prove the influence of civilisation on the number of deaths, in periods of which the intervals have been marked by social ameliorations.‡

Countries.	Years.	One Death to	Years.	One Death to
Sweden, - -	1754 to 1768	31·0	1821 to 1825	45·0
Denmark, -	1751 to 1754	32·0	1819	45·0
Germany, - -	1788	32·0	1825	45·0
Prussia, -	1717	30·0	1821 to.1824	39·0
Wurtemburg, -	1749 to 1754	31·0	1825	45·0
Austria, -	1822	40·0	1825 to 1830	43·0
Holland, -	1800	26·0	1824	40.0
England, -	1690	33·0	1821	58·0
Great Britain, -	1785 to 1789	43·0	1800 to 1804	47·0
France, -	1776	25·5	1825 to 1827	39·5
Canton de Vaud,	1756 to 1766	35·0	1824	47·0
Lombardy, -	1767 to 1774	27·5	1827 to 1828	31·0
States of the Church,	1767	21·5	1829	28·0
Scotland, - -	1801	44·0	1821	50·0

I repeat, that I am far from giving my belief to the prosperous state which these figures seem to point out. However, we cannot but be inclined to admit that deaths have diminished with the development of civilisation and affluence. Some countries have afterwards lost their population, or at least it has remained stationary, when those advantages were lost which they previously enjoyed. Thus, the opulent city of Amsterdam, which, by its activity, has for some time been unrivalled in Europe, is affected by the diminution of its commerce. In 1727, the mortality there was 1 to 27, and it still preserved the same value, according to the average results of the 12 years which preceded 1832. The deaths really rose to the number of 7336; and on the 1st of January 1830, of 202,175 persons, 90,292 were males, and

* Mr Finlayson has succeeded in obtaining the registers of tontine-holders, both in France under Louis XIV. and in England under William III., and he is convinced that the life of the French tontine-holder at that time was longer than the English one.—See on the question the observations of M. D'Ivernois, Bibliothèque Universelle, Oct. 1833, p. 146.

† It is well to premise, that the mortality calculated for the beginning of the present century is extremely uncertain.—See the judicious remarks of Sir F. D'Ivernois in the Bibliothèque Universelle de Genève, 1833.

‡ It is to be regretted that the author has not pointed out the sources of his information: his results would have had much more value. Several numbers of this table must certainly appear very doubtful.

111,883 females. The following table will show the number of deaths, year by year:*—

Deaths in the City of Amsterdam.†

Years.	Deaths.			Births. Total.
	Male.	Female.	Total.	
1821, - -	3,618	3,507	7,125	7,342
1822, - -	4,041	3,957	7,998	7,600
1823, - -	3,279	3,355	6,634	7,182
1824, - -	3,082	2,994	6,076	7,860
1825, - -	3,184	3,118	6,302	7,352
1826,‡ -	4,351	4,457	8,808	7,438
1827, - -	4,133	4,107	8,240	6,890
1828, - -	3,562	3,516	7,078	7,208
1829, - -	4,056	3,942	7,998	7,403
1830, - -	3,387	3,427	6,814	7,306
1831, - -	3,479	3,659	7,138	7,342
1832,§ - -	4,057	3,765	7,822	6,452
Average,	3.686	3,650	7,336	7,282

In comparing the births with the deaths which have taken place during the years pointed out in the table above, we see that they have been in average value numerically inferior to the number of deaths; in fact, there have been annually 7282 births, and 7336 deaths. It is true that Amsterdam has been troubled by several scourges; nevertheless, it constantly appears that its population is not on the increase, which is an almost infallible index of the loss of prosperity, when the average life does not attain a high value.

If we consider the ages on which the mortality falls, we shall have a new proof of the influence which our institutions and habits have in modifying it. In speaking of still-births, we have shown how much their number may be increased in the interior of cities, and especially in the midst of excesses of every kind, which give rise to demoralisation; we have, moreover, seen that the children who are born under these unfortunate circumstances, have fewer chances of living, especially if the parents are in misery. Different dangers gather round their early years, and wait upon the whole course of their career: thus, without speaking of those to which, by our nature, we are exposed, some belong to our manners, others to our religious institutions, and lastly, others to our political institutions. As to those which belong to our manners, I have already attempted to point them out; I have also shown the influence which certain religious institutions may have—baptism, for example—on tender infancy; the Lent and fasts on our reproductive powers, and probably on our vitality; and religious ceremonies and the preparatives for death on the minds of the sick. Moreover, we may join to these active causes, which modify the amount of population, the state of celibacy which is imposed on a class of persons, whose number, during the sway of Catholicism, was much greater than it is in our own day.

Amongst political institutions, the levying of soldiers, and wars, are likewise, notwithstanding all that has been said on the point, ever recurring causes of mortality, and causes so much the more afflicting, because they fall on the healthiest and most valuable part of the population—on the man who has just attained his full physical development, and is prepared to repay to society the debt which the infinite cares of

* Jaarbockje, by Lobatto, different years.

† The five years from 1816 to 1820 have given—

1816,	- - - - -	6,233	6,615
1817,	- - - - -	8,416 (a)	7,040
1818,	- - - - -	6,300	6,888
1819,	- - - - -	6,557	7,154
1820,	- - - - -	7,066	6,850
Average,	- - - -	6,914	6,909

(a) This was a year of scarcity.

‡ Period of the epidemic of Groningen.
§ Year of the cholera.

his infancy have contracted. In some countries even, by too extensive an enlistment into the army of men before they had time to become fully developed, they are exposed to new chances of death; or, by the fatigues of war, the vigour of the new generation is prematurely undermined.

Governments dispose, in some sort, of the lives of the men whom they have constantly under their influence, from the moment of birth to the day of their death. I shall not here speak of the kind of governments: we know too well that those which are favourable to despotism arrest the development of the species; and, on the other hand, how much a prudent degree of liberty, by seconding every individual industry and exertion, gives to man the means of providing for his preservation. I shall not speak of the immense distance which exists between the degree of mortality of the slave and his master, notwithstanding all the excesses to which the latter class give themselves up;* but I cannot omit taking a rapid view of the mortality in institutions created by man for the protection of society, and giving a glance at the influences of vaccination, hospitals, asylums, prisons, &c. My design is not so much to treat this subject deeply, as to show to what extent the numbers may vary, according to the locality.

In most civilised countries, there are enactments on vaccination, of greater or less severity, which are enforced with proportionate rigour. According to Casper, and several other savants who have written on the ravages caused by small-pox, it would appear that formerly generations were decimated by this scourge, that is to say, one-tenth of the human race died from it. Duvillard† has found—1st, that in the natural state, of 100 individuals of 30 years of age, scarcely four individuals have escaped an attack of small-pox; 2d, that two-thirds of all infants are attacked by it sooner or later; 3d, that small-pox, in the early years after birth, destroys, on the greatest average, one out of every three who are affected with it; 4th, and one dies out of every seven or eight affected, at whatever age it may be. Such was the state of things before the discovery of vaccination; it has since been much ameliorated. However, in 1817, 745 persons died in Paris of small-pox; in 1818, 993; and in 1822, the number was as many as 1084. Also, at St Petersburg, in 1821, 408 deaths took place from it; and at Vienna, 238 in 1822; whilst in London, during that year, there were 712. Prussia has been much better dealt with than other countries; during the two years 1820 and 1821, taken together, only 1 in 7204 persons died from it, whilst France lost 1 in 4218 the last two years. The following are the data of Berlin, for almost half a century:—

From 1782 to 1791 inclusive,	- -	4,453 deaths.
.. 1792 to 1801	- - -	4,990 ..
.. 1802 to 1811	- - -	2,955 ..
.. 1812 to 1822	- - -	555 ..

The number of deaths for the last period, which is extremely small in comparison with the preceding years, would be still less if the deaths for 1814 and 1815 were subtracted, during which time vaccination was neglected. Indeed, these two years had 411 deaths from it, so that during the remaining there was only 114. Moreover, we should fall into a serious error, as M. Villermé* has said, if we counted as gain to the population all those individuals who had been vaccinated, and not carried off by the small-pox. " An epidemic, or any other malady against which we endeavour to secure ourselves," says M. Villermé, " indeed suppresses one cause of death, but from that circumstance the probability of dying from other diseases becomes greater. In other words, by closing one of the gates of death, we open the others wider, so that more persons pass through these latter, which is not saying that mortality should be equally rapid. Consequently, vaccination, and every preservative against epidemic disease, or any disease whatever, does not increase the population of old Europe directly; but, what is still better, it alleviates the lot of those whom it snatches from the chances of small-pox, it diminishes the number of the blind, it preserves the native beauty of the person, and increases the average duration of life."

We may, then, regard the valuable discovery of Jenner as a real conquest of knowledge. We especially recognise the progress of civilisation, in all that which was hideous and miserable being removed from society: perhaps a feebly enlightened philanthropy has been too zealous, and in seeking to avoid certain evils, given rise to others. Nothing can more excite our compassion, than the feeble infant which a mother in her distress abandons to public charity; notwithstanding, an excess of pity may become an encouragement to vice, and a real burden always increasing on society.†

It appears that it is this dread which has prevented the formation of a foundling hospital in Edinburgh.‡ Moreover, it has been shown how dreadful the mortality is in the greater number of these establishments, notwithstanding all the efforts of art, which has combated them with some success. Mr Hawkins, in his Elements of Medical Statistics,§ says that the mortality in the foundling hospital in Dublin was so great, that it became the object of parliamentary inquiry: of 10,272 sick children sent to the infirmary attached to the hospital, during 21 years ending in 1796, only

---

* Des Epidemics, Jan. 1833.

† [No one now disputes that the poor ought to be the objects of national and legislative care; but great differences exist as to the amount of provision which ought to be made for them. One party contend, that not only the infirm and aged poor, but the able-bodied also, when out of work, are entitled to an ample support. Another, in which Dr Chalmers takes the lead, would only extend a limited public provision, in very necessitous cases, and that only after aid from relations and neighbours of the parties had been found to fail. The principle of the modern English poor-law appears a fair medium between the two extremes: it affords out-of-door relief to the infirm, the aged, and the helplessly young, and to the able-bodied in necessity holds out accommodation in work-houses, where the provision is a little inferior to that usually enjoyed by the independent labourer, so that it may act as a test of real necessity, and not be an attraction to sloth. It has long been a favourite doctrine with the second of the extreme parties, that provision of every kind vitiates a population, by taking away motives for self-dependence; but it has been shown more satisfactorily, on the other hand, that when a population is allowed to sink below a certain point of comfort, it tends to become excessive, in consequence of the recklessness which attends a state of great misery. Unquestionably, the interest, as well as humanity, of every civilised nation, is concerned in making provisions to prevent any portion of the population sinking into very abject circumstances.—Publishers' Note.]

‡ In Edinburgh, an attempt has occasionally been made to form a foundling hospital, but has failed, from the opinion of its injury to morality.—Hawkins, Elements of Med. Stat., p. 132.

§ Page 130.

---

* The mortality of Europeans at Batavia appears to be as great as that of the slave population; but it would seem that the chances of mortality are increased for the adult man who is transported to a climate very different to that in which he was developed. This is confirmed by the following table, which M. Moreau de Jonnes, unfortunately without mentioning his sources:—

Batavia, 1805,	- -	Europeans,	1 death to	11·0 persons.
"	"	Slaves,	"	13·0 "
"	"	Chinese,	"	29·6 "
"	"	Javanese,	"	40·0 "
Bombay, 1815,	- -	Europeans,	"	18·5 "
"	"	Mussulmans,	"	17·5 "
"	"	Parsees,	"	24·0 "
Guadaloupe, 1811 to 1824,	Whites,	"	23·5 "
"	"	Free Blacks,	"	35·0 "
Martinico, 1815,	-	Whites,	"	24·0 "
"	"	Free Blacks,	"	33·0 "
Grenada,	- -	Slaves,	"	22·0 "
St Lucia,	- -	Slaves,	"	20·0 "

† Analyse et Tableaux de l'Influence de la Petite-Vérole.

45 were preserved!—10,201 of these unfortunate children were affected with syphilitic symptoms, whilst of late there has only been 1 in 30. We have also shown how much art and good management have diminished the mortality of lying-in institutions. My object in speaking of these establishments was not, of course, to present a complete table; but to show how political institutions and philanthropic establishments may cause the degree of mortality to vary, whatever other causes of variation there may be. It is with the same object that I think I ought to take a view of the mortality of hospitals in different countries. This difficult subject may give rise to serious errors, because all hospitals do not receive patients affected with disease of equal severity or advancement. It is requisite, therefore, to use much reserve, and especially only to compare those hospitals with each other which admit the same kind of patients. In this I shall follow Mr F. B. Hawkins as my guide, and borrow the numbers which he gives in his Elements.

In 1685, in the Hospitals of St Bartholomew and
St Thomas, the Mortality was   - - 1 in 7
~ 1689—St Thomas, - - - - - - 1 in 10
~ 1741   ~   - - - - - - - 1 in 10
From 1773 to 1783, - - - - - 1 in 14
~ 1783 to 1793, - - - - - - 1 in 15
~ 1803 to 1813, - - - - - - 1 in 16

According to the first report of St George s Hospital, for 1734, the mortality was 1 in 8; from 1825 to 1827, it was 1 in 9.
The mortality in the Royal Infirmary of Edinburgh, for the decennial period which terminated 1818, was 1 in 16, or the same as St Thomas's.*
M. Casper, in his researches on the state of the poor in Paris,† has presented a table, including the proportion of deaths and duration of stay in the hospitals and asylums of Paris. Since these data deserve confidence, from the sources from which they have been drawn, and from the care which the author has taken to test them, I have thought proper to extract the following numbers:—

Hospitals of Paris—1822.	Mortality.	Average duration of Stay.
Hotel-Dieu, - - - -	1 in 6·8	25·2 days.
Pitié, - - - - -	~ 8·2	28·0 ~
Charité, - - - -	~ 5·5	30·6 ~
St Antoine, - - - -	~ 6·7	31·6 ~
Necker, - - - - -	~ 5·6	33·6 ~
Cochin, - - - - -	~ 8.3	25·8 ~
Beaujon, - - - -	~ 6·2	30·8 ~
St Louis, - - - -	~ 14·4	60·3 ~
Veneriens, - - - -	~ 33·2	66·4 ~
Enfans Malades, - - -	~ 4·4	51·3 ~
Maison d'Accouchemens, - -	~ 28·0	21·1 ~
Foundling Hospital—indoor patients,	~ 4·3	12·2 ~
~ ~ outdoor patients,	~ 6·2	
Maison Royale de Santé, - -	~ 5·8	24·7 ~
Maison de Santé (Veneriens), -	~ 113·0	41·0 ~

Asylums of Paris—1822.

Salpétrière, - - - -	~ 8·4	
Institute de St Perine, - -	~ 9·1	302·0 ~
Bicêtre, - - - -	~ 7·6	
Incurables—men, - - -	~ 6·7	
~ women, - - -	~ 11·1	64·0 ~
Hospice des Ménages, - -	~ 11·8	31·5 ~
~ des Orphelins, - -	~ 75·3	
~ de la Rochefoucauld, -	~ 8·4	

It appears that the mortality of hospitals, in the remainder of France, is not so great as at Paris. Thus,

* [The mortality of the Royal Infirmary of Edinburgh has since that period, namely in 1838-39, risen to 1 in 6, chiefly, as is supposed, from the frightful mortality caused by typhus fever.]
† Beiträge—Das Armen-und Armen Kranken-wezen in Paris.

at the Hotel-Dieu of Lyons, it is only 1 in 11; at Montpellier 1 in 10, for the average of all the hospitals. The following is a summary of the mortality in the principal hospitals of Europe,* which may be compared with the preceding data:—

	Mortality.
Berlin—La Charité, from 1796 to 1817, -	1 in 6 nearly.
Vienna—Large Hospital, - - -	.. 6 ..
Pesth in Hungary—Civil Hospital, 1826, -	.. 6 ..
Dresden—City Hospital, 1816,	- .. 7 ..
Munich—New Hospital, 1819, - -	.. 9 ..
Petersburg—Imperial Hospital, 1817,†	- .. 4·5
Geneva—Hospital, 1823, - - -	.. 11 ..
Brussels—St Peter's, 1823, - -	.. 9 ..
Amsterdam—St Peter's, 1798 to 1817,	- .. 8 ..
Turin and Genoa, 1821, - - -	.. 7 ..
Milan—Large Hospital, 1812 to 1814,	.. 6 ..
Pavia—San-Matheo della Pieta, 1823,‡	- .. 10·7
Bologna—Clinic of Tommasini, 1816 to 1819,	.. 7·7
Leghorn, 1818 to 1825,	- - .. 7·3
Palermo—Large Hospital, 1823, -	- .. 8·2

It would appear, from these documents, that the mortality in the principal hospitals on the continent is generally greater than in those of England. We may be astonished, moreover, in comparing the principal states of Europe, that we do not find great differences, especially when we consider the influence which the local position and resources may have, without speaking of the different plans of medical treatment which may be pursued. Mr Hawkins has made a very curious remark on the latter subject. "We rarely ought to attribute mortality to bad treatment, which probably seldom destroys the patient. A friend took particular notes on the comparative mortality under three physicians, in one hospital. The practice of the one was eclectic, the second expectant, and the third tonic. The mortality was the same, but the duration of indisposition, the character of the convalescence, and the chances of relapse, were very different." §

This is not the place to speak of hospitals for mental infirmity, on the mortality of which we still have little accurate information. I shall have occasion to speak of them when considering the development of the moral and intellectual faculties, and the diseases to which they are subject. Neither shall I stay to consider the mortality of mendicity houses, these establishments being very few in Europe, and based on plans so different as not to admit of comparison. But I ought not to omit mentioning the great mortality observed in those of the old kingdom of the Low Countries. In the seven depôts which were formed at different places in the kingdom, and between the years 1811 and 1822, there annually died of the average population 1 in 8·9; that is to say, as many as in hospitals, whilst the mortality of the whole kingdom was 1 in 43·8. "The mortality in the mendicity houses is indeed more dreadful, since the population of these establishments does not include persons of tender years. We must not forget that a great number of old and infirm persons of both sexes occupy these abodes, and that the state of extreme emaciation in which they are found in general, when they arrive, brings with it the developed seed of a speedy dissolution, and should undoubtedly be classed with the causes to which we must attribute this fatal result. This latter circumstance was made especially remarkable in the disastrous year 1816. A multitude

* Elements of Med. Stat.
† With respect to the hospitals of Russia in 1811, the mortality in establishments containing more than 30 patients was 1 in 9, and 1 in 10 in those which had fewer than 30 patients.
‡ Women are received there during labour.
§ [In fevers of all descriptions, and epidemics, as the plague, cholera, &c., there seems much reason to fear that medical attendance is generally of little avail. On this subject, the translator will be found to treat in the appendix.]

of unfortunate persons then only entered these houses to die in a few days after their arrival, and the greater number of the remainder expired, in the following years, from weakness. On the other hand, it is not impossible that the sudden transition from the most dreadful privation to a diet which comparatively may appear superabundant, here exercised a more deplorable influence than with a little more precaution it could have done. A third observation, which ought not to be passed over in silence, is, that in order to find the laws of mortality in an establishment whose population is moveable, it is not sufficient to compare the number of deaths with the daily entries, but it is also necessary to attend to the number of individuals to whom this number of entries have a reference. The greater this latter number, especially in asylums of human misery and infirmity, the more chances are there for the mortality to appear great."[*]

The mortality which has just been pointed out is no doubt very considerable; but I do not think that it has ever fallen in any of the mendicity houses of Belgium lower than it was towards the commencement of this century in the mendicity houses of France. Indeed, according to M. Villermé,[†] the mortality at Laon, during a period of thirteen years ending in 1826, was 1 person in 4·32; at Nancy in 1789, 1 in 5, and in 1801 it was 1 in 3·22; at Auch, during a period of five years, at least 1 in 3; at Metz 1 in 8·13 in 1789, and 1 in 2·22 in 1801. This dreadful mortality cannot be compared to any thing except what took place, also about the commencement of the century, in one of the principal prisons of Belgium: it is scarcely credible that, in the prison of Vilvorde, there died

In 1802, 1 prisoner in 1·27 of the average population.

.. 1803,	..	1·67	..	..
.. 1804,	..	1·91	..	..
.. 1805,	..	7·77	..	..
.. 1806,	..	20·31	..	..
.. 1807,	..	30·36	..	..

In 1801, the evil had not begun to exist; it was in 1802 when it attained its greatest intensity. In 1805, M. Chaban, prefect of the ancient department of Dyle, and M. Rouppe, inspector-general of the prison, began some improvements, which could not be completed until 1807.[‡] M. Villermé, who has also taken care to register this remarkable mortality, in his work on the Mortality of Prisons, adds the following reflections:— "After these last facts, what need be said to show the power of the government? I do not think that imprisonment should always be barbarously severe, but I think the bad discipline almost always renders it so. Those who are intrusted with the care of prisoners, having never made researches of the present kind, what they have said of them has often appeared as clamorous sympathy merely. But when we take the numbers of the men, and determine the annual proportion of their deaths, every thing is reduced to a simple calculation, the elements of which may be verified. If it be correct, all the evil or all the good which the figure expresses is real."

To understand to what extent the evil reached in the prison of Vilvorde, and how defective the discipline of it was, it is sufficient to quote the mortality since this period. At the same time, I shall give the mortality of two other large prisons in Belgium.[§]

[*] These judicious observations are extracted from the notes with which M. le Baron Reverberg has enriched my *Recherches sur les Populations, les Naissances, &c.*

[†] Mortalité dans les Prisons, *An. d'Hygiène*, tome i. p. 9.

[‡] Tableau Statistique de la Maison de Détention de Vilvorde, par M. Rouppe.

[§] Rapport sur l'Etat Actuel des Prisons en Belgique, &c., par Ed. Ducpétiaux.

Years.	Deaths on the Average Population.		
	At Vilvorde House of Confinement.	St Bernard House of Correction.	Ghent House of Confinement.
1825, - -	29·00	18·71	31·60
1826, - -	29·00	22·08	45·90
1827, - -	29·62	17·81	77·53
1828, - -	48·14	17·99	51·35
1829, - -	29·74	15·06	101·67
1830, - -	36·66	11·93	101·08
1831, - -	39,78	30·51	57·90

We may now be enabled to judge if the mortality of men left to themselves, and giving themselves up to the greatest excesses, may not be aggravated rather than otherwise, by a negligent and unenlightened administration : men during the most dreadful pestilences, and soldiers during the most destructive wars, have not been exposed to such a mortality as the prisoners of Vilvorde, during the early years of the present century.

The evil was far from being so great during the same period in the prison-house of Ghent; indeed, there was only 1 death to 20·4 prisoners in 1801 ; in 1789 there was only 1 death to 25·8 prisoners. According to M. Villermé, the annual mortality in the prisons of the department of the Seine has ·been, during the years 1815, 1816, 1817, and 1818, as follows :—

At la Grande Force,	-	-	1 in 40·88 prisoners.
.. the Madelonnettes,	-	-	.. 38·03 ..
.. the Conciergerie,	-	-	.. 32·06 ..
.. la Petite Force,	-	-	.. 26·63 ..
.. Sainte-Pélagie,	-	-	.. 24·48 ..
.. the Bicêtre,	-	-	.. 18·75 ..
.. the Sainte-Lazare,	-	-	.. 17·92 ..
.. the Mendicity House at St Denis,	-	.. 3·97 ..

We see that in the department of· the Seine the mortality of the depôt of mendicity is also much greater than that of the prisons, and appears frequently to result from the injured constitutions of the poor, and their privations and miseries before entering prison [the depôts?], and from the impossibility they found of procuring the necessaries of life.[*]

The prisons in the departments of France are generally far from presenting as favourable results as those of the department of the Seine; indeed, the mortality in the central houses (*maisons centrales*) and of those of justice and correction, were—

At Montpellier, 1822,	-	-	1 in 9·33 prisoners.
.. Riom, 1821 to 1827,	-	-	.. 9·87 ..
.. Baulieu near Caen, 1814 to 1825,	-	.. 11·59 ..
.. Melun, 1817 to 1825,	-	-	.. 14·81 ..
.. Gaillon, 1817 to 1825,	-	-	.. 11·36 ..
.. Metz, 1801,	-	-	.. 18·43 ..
.. Toulouse, 1822 to 1824,	-	-	.. 35·07 † ..
.. Lyons, 1820 to 1826,	-	-	.. 43·00 ‡ ..
.. Saint-Flour, 1813 to 1826,	-	-	.. 47·00 ..
.. Rouen, 1815 to 1826—Maison de Justice,	-	.. 51·18 § ..
.. .. 1820 to 1825—Bicêtre,	-	.. 59·07 ‖ ..

It is calculated that, for the average period of confinement in 1827, there was 1 death to 22 sentenced, in the central houses of imprisonment of France ; and the average ratio was 1 in 16 for the men, and 1 in 26 for the women. M. Villermé, from whom I bor-

[*] Mortalité dans les Prisons, p. 5.

[†] In 1814, a year of misery, with a crowded prison, 1 prisoner died out of 7·95.

[‡] One in 19, from 1800 to 1805 inclusive ; 1 in 31, from 1806 to 1812 ; 1 in 34, from 1813 to 1819.

[§] The infirmaries have been better organised, and the nursing better conducted. The mortality in 1812, 1813 and 1814, was 1 in 4·06 !

[‖] The mortality was 1 in 8·46 from 1811 to 1814 ; 1 in 20·70 from 1816 to 1820 ; after this period, those condemned to one year of confinement and more were withdrawn.

row the preceding data, estimates the mortality of the galley-slaves' prison as follows :—

At Rochefort, from 1816 to 1828,	1 in 11·51
.. Toulon, ...	.. 20·55
.. Brest, ...	.. 27·06
.. L'Orient, ...	.. 39·17

We have often taken the prisons of Switzerland and the United States as patterns; it may be interesting, therefore, to know the mortality there.*

Penitentiary of Berne, ...	1 in 25·00
Lausanne, from 1808 to 1825, old method,	.. 21·49
.. .. from 1826 to 1829, new method,	.. 12·25
.. .. from 1830 to 1831,	.. 36·00
.. Geneva, 1826 to 1831,	.. 49·00
Prison of Philadelphia (Pennsylvania),	.. 16·66
.. of Newgate (New York),	.. 18·80
Penitentiary of Sing-sing (New York), 12 years,	.. 36·58
.. Wethersfield (Connecticut),	.. 44·40
.. Baltimore (Maryland),	.. 48·57
.. Auburn (New York),	.. 55·95
.. Charlestown (Massachusetts),	.. 58·40

It is to be regretted that census of the mortality of prisons in England is wanting; it only appears that it is very small. This subject is perhaps more entitled to the attention of statisticians than any other, for there are few which present values so liable to change, and consequently the discipline should be more enlightened. Indeed, we have seen that, according to the negligence or zeal of the governors of prisons, the mortality of the establishment need not exceed what it is in ordinary society, or may become more dreadful than the most destructive scourges. The loss of liberty, and the humiliation connected with the condemned state, are punishments so great, that we need not aggravate them by a mortality unequalled by all the other scourges to which the species is exposed. The mortality of prisons has diminished in almost all establishments without exception; it is a fresh benefit resulting from the diffusion of knowledge, and I dare say from the care with which statisticians have brought forward results on which we did not possess any precise data, and which consequently produced less impression, because we readily deceived ourselves as to the nature of the evil.† I cannot better conclude this chapter than by quoting the principal conclusions to which M. Villermé has been led—one of the men who has thrown most light on this important subject :‡—

1st, The mortality of prisoners is generally much greater than that of free people.

2d, It is in the direct ratio of the bad management of prisons, the state of misery and nakedness of those detained therein, and the privations and sufferings which they passed through before imprisonment.

3d, If the management or discipline is almost powerless in correcting these latter causes, it may always, by care and understanding, prevent or very much extenuate the former.

4th, If, taking away the difference owing to locality and good or bad treatment, we arrange the prisoners in the order of their mortality, they stand as follows :—

Accused.
Condemned.
Detained in mendicity houses.

* Rapport sur l'Etat Actuel des Prisons en Belgique.
† Mortalité des Prisons, &c.
‡ One of the most remarkable works which has been written on the amelioration of prisons, and the moral reformation of the inmates, is that of Dr Julius of Berlin—*Vorle-sungen über die Gefängniss Kunde*, 8vo. Berlin, 1828. This work has been translated into French. The author, who has investigated the state of prisons with the most remarkable zeal, has been called to Berlin by the Prussian government, to give public lectures on the objects of his researches. He has published a collection called *Jahrbücher der Straf-und Besserungs-Anstalten, Erziehungshäuser, &c.*, more especially containing information on crimes and prisons. See also the works of Mr Lucas.

5th, To appreciate the effects of the salubrity or insalubrity, of the good or bad management of each prison, and the different chances of life of each class of prisoners, the best means will be to determine the annual proportion of deaths, not by comparing the latter to the total number of the inmates, but to their average annual population.

6th, Ignorance of the lot of prisoners, of their wants, especially of the wants and the fate of the poorest of them, is the first cause to which may be attributed the excessive mortality shown by the numbers we have quoted.

CHAPTER VII.

RELATIONS OF POPULATION TO SOCIAL PROSPERITY.

1. Of Population and its Increase.

UNTIL now I have been considering the principal facts which relate to the birth, life, reproduction, and mortality of man, but without examining his condition in the social mass. This research, however, is the philosophical end towards which all our efforts should lead: we cannot dissemble as to the great difficulties which it at present presents, notwithstanding it has exercised the sagacity of several writers of the highest merit; and it is with the greatest deference that I present some new observations, which I think capable of receiving useful application.

Populations arise imperceptibly; it is only when they have reached a certain degree of development that we begin to think of their existence. This increase is more or less rapid, and it proceeds either from an excess of births over deaths, or from immigrations, or both. In general, it is a mark of wellbeing, and of the means of existence being superior to the wants of the actual population. If we approach or exceed this limit, the state of increase soon stops, or a contrary condition may take place. It is then interesting to examine how different countries are populated, what are the means of subsistence and the rate of increase of the people, and to assign the limit which they may reach without danger. After that, the consideration is, to know the composition of the population, and if the constituent elements are advantageously distributed, and contribute, in a more or less efficient manner, to the well-being of the whole. But it would be proper first to take the questions of highest moment, and to establish, in a summary and clear manner, the ideas on population promulgated by the most distinguished economists.

It appears incontestible, that population would increase in a geometrical ratio, if no obstacle were presented to its development.

The means of subsistence are not developed so rapidly; and, according to Malthus, in the most favourable circumstances for industry, they can never increase quicker than in an arithmetical ratio.*

* *Essay on the Principle of Population*, vol. i. p. 15. (Translation of MM. Prévost, Geneva, 1830). This law of the increase of subsistence may appear doubtful, and the ideas of economists are very different on this subject. Mr Senior thinks that there is a tendency in the means of subsistence to increase faster than the population.—See *Two Lectures on Population*, p. 49. On this subject we may also consult the correspondence between this gentleman and Mr Malthus. Mr M'Culloch, in the notes on Dr Smith's *Wealth of Nations*, vol. iv. p. 133, thinks, on the contrary, that the progression established by Mr Malthus is too high for the countries where the best lands are already under cultivation. Since these things cannot be decided until all parts of the globe are under culture, it would be difficult to establish any thing experimentally, of a positive nature, on this head; for if a population consume all the products of the land which they inhabit, they may still, by the exchange of other produce, supply themselves with what before was wanted, and in this case they will receive new accessions: thus the multiplication of machinery, by seconding human labour in England, has allowed the means of subsistence to undergo an increase since the com-

The obstacle to population, then, is the want of food, proceeding from the difference of ratio which these two quantities follow in their respective increases. When a population, in its development, has arrived at the level of its means of subsistence, it ought to stop at this limit, from human foresight; or if it have the misfortune to overleap this limit, it must be forcibly brought back by an excess of mortality.

The obstacles to population, therefore, may be arranged under two heads—the one acts by preventing the growth of population, and the other by destroying it in proportion as it is formed. The sum of the first forms what may be called the *privative obstacle*, that of the second the *destructive obstacle*.*

Mr Malthus has analysed, with great sagacity, the principal obstacles to its increase which population has met with; he has determined, with no less credit, the limit which it cannot pass without being exposed to the greatest danger. However, it may be necessary to remark, notwithstanding the researches of the English philosopher, and of the economists who have followed in his track, that the *modus operandi* of the obstacles has not been clearly made out. The law has not been established by virtue of which they operate: in a word, they have not afforded the means of carrying the theory of population into the domain of mathematical science, to which it seems particularly to belong.† Hence it results, that the discussion of this delicate point has not been completed at the present day, and the dangers attending society have perhaps been exaggerated, from not finding sufficient security in the action of the obstacles against an evil, the dreadful rapidity of which followed a geometrical progression.

To endeavour to fill up so important a *lacuna*, I have made numerous researches, the details of which it will be superfluous here to present; and an attentive examination of the state of the question has proved to me, that the theory of population may be reduced to the two following principles, which I consider will hereafter serve as fundamental principles in the analysis of the development of population, and of the causes which influence it.

Population tends to increase in a geometrical ratio.

The resistance, or sum of the obstacles to its development, is, all things being equal, as the square of the rapidity with which it tends to increase.

The obstacles to rapidity of increase of a population, really operate, then, like the resistance which the media oppose to the passage of bodies through them. This extension of one of the laws of physics, which is most happily confirmed when we apply it to the documents which society supplies, presents a new example of the analogies which are found in many cases between the laws regulating material phenomena and those which apply to man. So that, of the two principles which I take as the basis of the mathematical theory of population, the one is generally admitted by all economists, and scarcely appears contestible, and the other has been verified in all the applications where we had to

mencement of the present century, which appears to me to be greater than an arithmetical ratio. We cannot but continue to look upon the products of industry as equal to the products of agriculture, until the exchange of money for food becomes impossible by too great a development of the population on the surface of the globe.

* Malthus—*Essay*, &c. p. 20, tome i. In the view which I have adopted, the destructive obstacle acts generally by natural powers, and the privative obstacle by the disturbing powers of man.

† May I be allowed to recall the ideas on this point which I expressed in 1827, at the opening of a public course on the history of the sciences?—" It is to be observed," I said, " that the more progress the physical sciences have made, accordingly have they tended to enter within the bounds of mathematical science, which is a sort of centre to which they converge. We might even judge of the degree of perfection to which a science is capable of being carried, by the greater or less facility with which it admits of calculation."

consider the movements and the obstacles in a continuous manner.

However, notwithstanding the prejudices we might have in favour of them, it would undoubtedly be necessary to reject them, if, by submitting them to analysis, they could not support this proof to the extremest detail.

I thought, therefore, that I ought to examine, first of all, the consequences which the theory involved, and I have had the satisfaction to find them entirely conformable to the results of experience. Thus, when population can develop itself freely and without impediment, it increases in a geometrical ratio; if it be developed in the midst of obstacles of every kind, which tend to arrest it, and which operate in an uniform manner, that is to say, if the *social state does not change*, the population does not increase in an indefinite manner, but tends more and more to become stationary. Hence it results, that population finds, in its very tendency to increase, those causes which ought to prevent the fatal catastrophes which might be feared from too great fullness, if I may so express myself, brought on in a sudden manner, and before which all human prudence would fail. The experience of our old Europe proves very fully, that population arrives at its state of equilibrium, increases, or recedes, by generally following one law of continuity. The bound which it cannot pass is variable, and depends on the quantity of food: population can never be developed so rapidly as to strike suddenly against this bound; the obstacles which previously arise, having the same tendency, are too numerous to render a violent shock possible. Nature does not raise a smaller tribute of deaths; but since we pay this tribute in detail, it is less sensible to us than if we required suddenly to discharge it.

It is thus that the greater part of our population has progressively arrived at the level of the means of subsistence, by continually preserving a tendency to develop, and consequently to reproduce an excess of mortality, nearly in the same manner as the cloud suspended in the air has a continual tendency to descend and diffuse the fullness which it holds. In the midst of the causes innumerable which may disturb this state of equilibrium, population advances or recedes almost in the same manner as we see the cloud ascend or descend according to the temperature, direction of the winds, and a crowd of other atmospherical circumstances, which, however, does not prevent its always reaching a certain average height, depending on its constitution and the obstacle which the resistance of the air opposes to its descent.

When the social system undergoes any changes, the obstacles always preserve the same mode of action; but their intensity may vary in an infinite manner, so that the development of population may be infinitely modified likewise. If we possessed exact census for different periods, the analysis would show the intensity of the causes which have been able to accelerate or oppose the development of population, and the circumstances which have given origin to them. Supposing, for example, that a population which increases continually in an arithmetical progression, the constant difference of which is also known, we might determine, by means of the two laws announced above, what energy the obstacles have successively opposed to the development of the population; in other terms, the law according to which these obstacles have been enabled to manifest themselves. It will suffice to know the law according to which a population is developed, to deduce, at least approximatively, the law according to which the obstacles have developed themselves, and *vice versa*. But such problems as these belong exclusively to analysis; I can only point them out here, reserving a return to them in a special work.

I have said that, when the state of equilibrium has been once attained, population would become stationary, or at least would oscillate around a fixed state, in consequence of corresponding variations produced by climate and amount of food; but since it is essential to the nature of man to endeavour to increase the quantity of his produce by a greater degree of manual and intellectual labour, population may be enabled to find the means of development; in such a manner that, if all the physical circumstances were the same in the different countries of Europe, there could not be a better measure of produce and industry than the density of the population found there. The specific population is indeed the result of all the influential elements of a country, and should be found carried to a limit which is in relation to all the facilities which a country could present for its development during the preceding periods.

In adopting the measure of productive power, in a first approximation, it may be interesting to know the specific population of each country, that is to say, the number of inhabitants on a square league of ground: for this purpose I shall adopt the numbers given by M. Balbi in the *Precis de la Geographie Universelle de Malte-Brun*, liv. 16. I thought it necessary to omit the small states having fewer than one million of souls.

	Inhabitants to a Square League (of 25 to the Degree.)
Low Countries,	1829
Lombardo-Venetian kingdom,	1711
Wurtemburg,	1502
England (properly so called),	1457
Kingdom of Saxony,	1252
States of Sardinia,	1122
France,	1062
States of the Church,	1043
Bavaria,	968
Prussian monarchy,	792
Switzerland,	783
Hungary,	750
Kingdom of Naples and Sicily,	747
Spain,	641
Denmark,	616
Portugal,	446
Turkey,	324
Russia,	161
Sweden and Norway,	82

The Low Countries, Lombardy, Wurtemburg, and England, are, then, the countries which really support the densest populations in Europe, and consequently those which, all things being equal, should produce the most for their suitable support. Portugal, Turkey, Russia, Sweden, and Denmark, on the contrary, have populations of less density. Now, since the people of these countries have been increasing for many centuries back, with all the facilities which their locality and institutions allowed, it is to be presumed that if they are not the same in the different countries of Europe, there have been some obstacles to their propagation, either in the lands not being equally fertile, or because it has been more difficult to develop the trade and industry of man, or because there was not a secure basis for social institutions, or, lastly, owing to moral causes, and the other motives, the influence of which on the number of births and deaths I have examined.

There is also an important distinction to be established, and which, because it has not been observed, has often thrown strange confusion into all questions on population; namely, that it is necessary to know not only of how many individuals a people is composed, but also in what manner each individual obtains the means necessary for his own existence. There is an infinity of shades among the people: some have a more cultivated mind, more industry, and more wants; one individual alone consumes by himself what otherwise might support three persons, or even more; but these three men would live miserably, and propagate as a people as miserable as themselves. It would then be inaccurate to say that, because the last nation has a population three times as dense as the first, that it produced three times as much. In order that the figures of the preceding table may be compared with

each other, it is necessary to multiply them individually by a constant coefficient, being what is necessary for one individual of each nation to supply his wants. We should also be wrong in judging that, because one nation had a stationary population, it made no progress. The state of industry and knowledge may ameliorate the condition of the population very much, without any traces of it being discernible (namely, the amelioration). This increase of wellbeing, all things being equal, is measured by the quantity of things which one individual consumes, and in an equitable division of the matter which is consumed. This constant coefficient is destined to play an important part in the theory of population. It is this which defines the limit towards which population tends in its successive growth, almost in the same manner as the point at which a body remains *in equilibrio* in any medium, is regulated by its density. In general, when a population is stationary, according as the consumption of the inhabitant increases or diminishes, in such proportion may the people be said to be made richer or poorer.

Because a population is increasing, we must not conclude any longer that its prosperity increases. It is necessary, first, to consider the constant coefficient, which is the measure of the degree of comfort of the individual, just as, on the other hand, the specific population is the measure of the degree of affluence or comfort of any country. When we wish to establish comparisons between the people, it is of the greatest importance to consult the quality, if I may so express myself, as well as the quantity.

In general, statisticians continue to employ the annual increase of the population, to calculate in what time it would double itself, although experience almost constantly falsifies the results of their calculations. This inquiry, which leads us into the hypothesis that there is no obstacle to the development of a people, can scarcely be directly applied to old Europe, any more than we should expect to see the results of experience accord with those of the theory of the fall of bodies through a vacuum. These calculations, for the most part, are only suited to satisfy curiosity, since they belong to an hypothesis which cannot be realised, or at least is available only within very narrow limits.

If a country, by virtue of its increasing civilisation, takes a new impulse, and from the increase of its produce carries onwards the boundary which limits the extent of its population, it would be in the most favourable circumstances, by a geometrical progression, that it would first tend to reach that boundary; but this rapidity of increase would soon abate, from the effect of obstacles, and would soon be extinguished. The same applies to a decreasing population; but the motion takes place in the opposite direction. Analysis supplies us with some formula, which very accurately express these different states.

Countries most happily divided, scarcely present a population increasing in a geometrical ratio. England, however, is a striking example, which ought to occupy the highest degree of attention. After having been stationary, or even retrograde, at the commencement of the last century, its population then began to increase progressively, undergoing various oscillations until the middle of the century, when, receiving a second impulse, it began to take an arithmetical ratio. A fresh and more energetic impulse was given to it at the commencement of the present century, and it has not since ceased to increase in a geometrical ratio; so that it has passed through states contrary to those of a population which tends to its limit, and where the obstacles go on increasing. Here the obstacles have been diminishing in consequence of the immense progress of industry, and the introduction of such an incredible quantity of machinery, the products of which represent a population which England is far from possessing.

Years.	Population.*	Decennial Increase.	Annual Increase per cent.	Period required for the Population to double itself.
1700, -	5,134,516	— 68,179	—0·13	— 500 years.
1710, -	5,066,337	+279,014	+υ.з4	+ 129 ..
1720, -	5,345,351	342,642	0·62	112 ..
1730, -	5,687,993	141,712	0·25	278 ..
1740, -	5,829,705	209,979	0·35	197 ..
1750, -	6,039,684	440,046	0·70	100 ..
1760, -	6,479,730	747,856	1·09	63 ..
1770, -	7,227,586	587,241	0·78	89 ..
1780, -	7,814,827	725,911	0·89	77 ..
1790, -	8,540,738	646,438	0·73	96 ..
1800, -	9,187,176	1,220,380	1·25	56 ..
1810, -	10,407,556	1,550,005	1·39	49 ..
1820, -	11,957,565	1,883,186	1·46	43 ..
1830, -	13,840,751	..	..	.. ..

The same ratio of increase does not take place twice successively during the period included in this table, except for late years, when a geometrical progression is very marked, the value of which is 1·38. From 1760 to 1800, the progression was arithmetical, and the constant difference had an annual value of 67686·1. Availing myself of these numbers, I have calculated the successive values of the population, placing by the side of my results the observed values.

Periods.	Population.		
	Observed.	Calculated.	Difference.
1760, - -	6,479,730	6,479,730	0
1770, - -	7,227,586	7,156,591	— 70,995
1780, - -	7,814,827	7,833,453	+ 18,636
1790, - -	8,540,738	8,510,314	— 30,424
1800, - -	9,187,176	9,187,176	0
1810, - -	10,407,556	10,531,900	+ 124,344
1820, - -	11,957,565	12,073,400	+ 115,835
1830, - -	13,840,751	13,840,751	0

These differences between the calculated and observed results do not exceed the limits of the fluctuations which attend the results of different years ; the greatest difference of one period of ten years does not amount to 125,000 inhabitants ; this inequality does not amount to 1-80th of the population.*

We are about to find a second very instructive example, and a much less complicated one, in what takes place in the United States of America, a new country which rose to liberty by one effort, proud of the industry of its inhabitants and the fertility of its soil. Population immediately developed itself there with a rapidity most astonishing, and unknown altogether in this old Europe ; immigration also added still further to the excess of births over deaths. But this rapid increase was soon met by obstacles which multiplied, and the rapidity of increase, great as it was, became uniform. It is an arithmetical and not a geometrical progression which is observed. Such are the facts presented by the population of the United States, which has been so often quoted as an example, and which has not been attended to with sufficient scrutiny. I quote the printed numbers of Professor Rau.† They are, moreover, conformable to those which have been given by other statisticians.

Years.	Inhabitants.	Annual Increase.
1780, - - -	2,051,000	6·2 in 100
1790, - - -	3,929,326	3·0 ..
1800, - - -	5,306,035	3·1 ..
1810, - - -	7,239,703	2·87 ..
1820, - -	9,654,415	1·9 ..
1825, - - -	10,438,000	1·9 ..

* The value of the population is given according to the numbers of Mr Rickman, *Preface to the Abstract, &c.*, 1831, p. 45. Mr Rickman, at page 24, gives as the annual increase for the periods 1801, 1811, 1821, 1831, the values 1·41, 1·57, and 1·54 ; the difference of my results may be occasioned by the method of calculation employed. I thought proper to compare the annual increase, not to the population of the first year of each period, but to that of an average year of this period.

† *Bulletin de M. Ferussac*, Fév. 1831. See also the numbers given by M. Warden in the *Bulletins de la Société Philomathique*, 1832.

I shall first observe, that the population has made almost regular increases from year to year, so that its successive values form an increasing arithmetical progression, of which the difference between one year and another may be considered as of the value of 190,822.* Proceeding with this hypothesis, we shall have—

Years.	Inhabitants.	Annual Increase.
1780, - - -	2,051,000	6·3 in 100
1790, - -	3,959,220	3·7 ..
1800, - -	5,867,440	2·8 ..
1810, - -	7,775,660	2·2 ..
1820, - -	9,683,890	1·9 ..
1825, - -	10,637,990	.. ..

Thus, although in fact population has received considerable increases, things are still in the same state as in 1780 ; there is as much room and food for new comers, because, nearly every year, about 190,822 individuals come to occupy the wastes which remain to be inhabited. These increases are less sensible when we calculate them, as is generally done, by comparing them to the population. The population is, indeed, less prolific, because the care taken to fill the places which remain vacant, is divided amongst a greater number of persons.†

In the greater number of the countries of Europe, population is increasing, and it is according to the value of the annual increase that statisticians have established their calculations to determine the period at which each of the populations would be found to have doubled. I here quote the results obtained by two gentlemen whose names are esteemed in science.

Countries.	According to Professor Rau.		According to M. Ch. Dupin.	
	Annual Increase.	Period required in which to Double.	Increase.	Period required in which to Double.
Ireland,	2.45	28 6 years.		
Hungary, -	2·4	20·2 ..		
Spain, -	1·66	41·9 ..		
England, -	1·65	42·3 ..	1·67	42·0 years.
Prussia, -	..	..	2.70	26·0 ..
Prussia on the Rhine,	1·33	52·33 ..	..	..
Austria, -	1·3	53·6 ..	1·01	69·0 ..
Bavaria, -	1·08	64·6 ..	..	..
Low Countries,	0·94	74·8 ..	1·24	56·5 ..
Kingdom of Naples,	0·83	83·5 ..	1·11	63·0 ..
France, -	0·63	110·3 ..	0·65	105·0 ..
Sweden, - -	0·58	118·0 ..	..	..
Kingdom of Lombardy,	0·45	152 8 ..	..	..
Russia, -	..	..	1·05	66·0 ..

* Representing this difference by d, and P standing for the population in 1780, and x for the number of years which have elapsed, we have for the population of this xth year $Px = P + dx$: it is according to this formula that the numbers of the following table have been calculated. It also follows that the increase a relative to the population, had, as a general value, or for a period of n years after the xth,

$$a = \frac{2 d}{Px + Px + n}$$

It is according to this formula that the successive increases of the population have been calculated. If by means of lines we represented the degree of increase of the population in proportion to the years, we should have on one hand a straight line, and on the other an hyperbola. The asymptote marks the limit towards which the increases tend.

† The theory would, moreover, prove, that at first the population has been smaller than the table indicates, for at the end of the last century it should have been more numerous. I hear, indeed, from M. Warden, that the United States, from political motives, and in order to acquire more importance, have, during the time of war, exaggerated the amount of the population, especially in the interior of the country, where strangers can exercise less inquisitive control.

If the doubling of the population were indeed to take place according to this table, we should certainly have to fear a dreadful catastrophe, owing to the means of subsistence not being able to follow so rapid a development; but we have already seen that it is only in very rare cases that a continued and rapid increase can take place. If such catastrophes could happen, we should already have seen them long ago in Europe. No doubt, the mortality may be accidentally increased by famines, pestilence, and other plagues; but these evils, the influence of which civilisation tends to diminish, may take place in countries which have not yet reached their bound.

The calculation of the annual increase of the population is not the only source of deception in estimating the doubling of populations. The subject is still open to great errors in other respects. It will almost always be impossible to agree upon these matters, unless we quote the years and the numbers according to which the increases take place. Many authors only estimate the increase of population from one or two years of observation, and are thus exposed to the greatest errors. This is mixing the influences which we wish to determine, with those resulting from an infinity of causes, which may often cause the former to be entirely misunderstood. It appears to me, that, in order to pronounce with any degree of certainty on the state of a country, we must at least employ the results of ten years' observation; that is to say, of periods during which institutions have remained the same, and no remarkable events have taken place. Thus we might hope to find out the influence of accidental causes, and only retain what results from the nature of the country, its institutions, and the industry of the people. It is especially necessary to avoid taking any numbers of critical years, and those years immediately succeeding them. At the present day, Europe is enjoying a respite after long and bloody wars—after more or less stagnation of commerce; and, under the influence of more liberal institutions, it is easy to understand that produce should become more abundant, and population increase; but does this give any reason to suppose that the increase shall continue the same? It appears to me, that this would be a great error, and I do not fear to appeal the point to experience.

It is very remarkable that a population is more numerous, if it have been constantly stationary during a certain number of years, than if, during the same period, it has been alternately increasing and decreasing, when the ratio of the increase itself has been equal to the ratio of the decrease, the effect of one year not compensating that of another. This seems, at the first view, to be a paradox; we may nevertheless be assured of its truth. If we seek to find what becomes of a given number of individuals after $m + n$ years (m indicating the years during which the population has been stationary, and n those during which it has received an increase or decrease of a determinate quantity), we find that the number of survivors continues the same, in whatever manner the years $m + n$ have succeeded each other. Thus, whether a population increases regularly during ten years, and then is stationary for twenty more—whether these two periods succeed each other in an inverse order, or are intermixed—a given number of individuals who shall be born, will present the same number of survivors when the thirty years have passed over.[*]

2. Of Tables of Population.

Populations present very great differences, according to the manner in which the individuals who compose them are grouped, either by families or houses; however, when considering only one country, these differences are less apparent. In the country of Belgium, for example, we have about five individuals to one family, and this number is a little smaller in town. We also calculate, almost exactly, in each province and in the country, 106 families to 100 houses, whilst we find 125 to 174 in towns.

We observe, also, that in the country of Belgium the individuals of both sexes are nearly balanced. It is not so in towns; the number of men is every where smaller than that of women. This difference may be owing to the greater mortality of men, as well as to the more frequent employment of female domestic servants. In the country, on the contrary, male servants are most sought after for cultivating lands.

If we divide the population of the two sexes into three classes, namely, unmarried, married, and widowers, we shall have, still preserving the distinction of town and country—

In Town.	In 1000 Men.			In 1000 Women.		
	Unmarried.	Married.	Widowers.	Unmarried.	Married.	Widows.
Flanders, East,	652	311	37	643	281	76
" West,	646	317	37	638	278	84
Brabant, -	629	332	39	625	284	91
Hainault, -	642	316	42	604	307	89
Liege, -	635	323	42	624	293	83
Anvers, -	655	312	33	646	276	78
Namur, -	663	297	40	622	291	87
In the Country.						
Flanders, East,	687	276	36	661	272	67
" West,	671	293	36	645	288	67
Brabant, -	652	313	35	623	311	66
Hainault, -	647	317	36	611	318	71
Liege, -	646	312	42	618	305	77
Anvers, -	672	289	39	639	289	72
Namur, -	634	331	35	596	332	72

Whence we see that,

1. In general, two-thirds of the population are unmarried; the other third is composed of married persons or widowed.

2. Taking 1000 individuals of each sex, the unmarried males are rather more numerous than the unmarried females: it is the same with the married men.

3. The unmarried are still more numerous in country than in town; so that we find the greatest number of unmarried persons out of 1000 in the country, who are also males.

4. The number of widows is almost double the number of widowers.

This latter result, which is very remarkable, becomes more striking when we compare the number of widowers with that of widows.

Provinces.	Widowers to 100 Widows.	
	City.	Rural Districts.
Flanders, East, - -	44	53
" West, - -	39	53
Anvers, - - -	38	55
Brabant, - - -	37	53
Hainault, - - -	46	50
Namur, - - -	45	47
Liege, - - -	46	52

Thus the number of widowers, compared with the number of widows, is incontrovertibly more numerous in town than in country, and especially in the provinces of Brabant, Anvers, and Western Flanders.

This circumstance may be owing to men marrying later in town than in country. Indeed, we shall observe that the three provinces which have just been pointed out, are those which, all things being equal,

---

[*] Recherches Statistique sur le Royaume des Pays-Bas, p. 61, et seq.

have the greatest part of their population shut up in the cities. Men have also more facility of passing from the state of widowhood than women.

The distribution of the population according to age, has long occupied the attention of statisticians more than any other element. Tables of population are of two kinds—the one kind are obtained directly by a census, the other are deduced from tables of mortality. When we may rely on the accuracy of the census, the former are always preferable to the latter, and more faithfully represent the actual state of the population.

The table which I here present is the result of a great census made in Belgium about the end of, 1829 ; it has been calculated from original documents, and I think I can guarantee its accuracy. In the *Recherches sur la Reproduction et la Mortalité*, all the documents belonging to it may be seen.

TABLE OF THE POPULATION FOR BELGIUM.

1,000,000 Persons are taken as a basis, and classed according to the indications of the Table.

Age.	Men.				Age.	Women.			
	Unmarried.	Married.	Widowers.	Total.		Unmarried.	Married.	Widows.	Total.
0 years,	317,202	146,164	17,949	481,315	0 years,	335,930	146,053	36,702	518,685
1 „	303,058	146,164	17,949	467,171	1 „	322,212	146,053	36,702	504,967
2 „	288,997	146,164	17,949	453,110	2 „	308,595	146,053	36,702	491,350
3 „	276,369	146,164	17,949	440,482	3 „	296,379	146,053	36,702	479,134
4 „	263,815	146,164	17,949	427,928	4 „	284,204	146,053	36,702	466,959
5 „	251,389	146,164	17,949	415,502	5 „	272,087	146,053	36,702	454,842
6 „	239,166	146,164	17,949	403,279	6 „	260,449	146,053	36,702	443,204
8 „	216,910	146,164	17,949	381,023	8 „	238,863	146,053	36,702	421,618
10 „	195,861	146,164	17,949	359,974	10 „	218,646	146,053	36,702	401,401
12 „	176,439	146,164	17,949	340,552	12 „	199,828	146,053	36,702	382,583
14 „	158,023	146,164	17,949	322,136	14 „	181,683	146,053	36,702	364,438
16 „	137,837	146,164	17,949	301,950	16 „	162,364	146,049	36,702	345,115
20 „	104,088	146,072	17,945	268,105	20 „	128,083	145,654	36,694	310,431
25 „	66,240	142,847	17,892	226,979	25 „	89,884	139,767	36,600	266,251
30 „	39,818	129,077	17,637	186,532	30 „	63,823	123,892	26,219	223,934
35 „	25,465	108,696	17,139	151,300	35 „	47,243	102,762	35,421	185,426
40 „	18,187	89,973	16,488	124,648	40 „	36,216	81,499	34,024	151,739
45 „	13,736	71,939	15,571	101,246	45 „	28,249	61,419	31,916	121,584
50 „	10,311	54,700	14,460	79,471	50 „	21,857	44,218	29,167	95,242
53 „	8,404	44,050	13,402	65,856	53 „	18,089	34,223	26,709	79,021
58 „	6,962	35,231	12,296	54,489	56 „	15,095	26,417	24,385	65,897
59 „	5,694	27,787	11,164	44,645	59 „	12,535	20,090	21,719	54,344
62 „	4,430	20,764	9,693	34,887	62 „	9,948	14,672	18,608	43,228
65 „	3,434	15,120	8,242	26,796	65 „	7,749	10,301	15,683	33,783
67 „	2,817	11,599	7,112	21,528	67 „	6,049	7,685	13,416	27,150
69 „	2,317	9,020	6,113	17,450	69 „	4,940	5,732	11,387	22,059
71 „	1,772	6,540	5,100	13,412	71 „	3,773	4,054	9,175	17,002
73 „	1,391	4,976	4,286	10,653	73 „	2,994	2,963	7,571	13,528
75 „	1,027	3,575	3,389	7,991	75 „	2,254	2,030	5,930	10,214
77 „	710	2,369	2,538	5,618	77 „	1,589	1,300	4,369	7,258
79 „	482	1,517	1,845	3,844	79 „	1,065	814	3,102	5,001
81 „	305	831	1,191	2,327	81 „	680	451	1,968	3,099
83 „	198	516	804	1,518	83 „	454	259	1,350	2,063
85 „	123	302	510	935	85 „	276	144	864	1,284
87 „	76	161	300	537	87 „	154	78	502	734
89 „	39	80	172	291	89 „	88	41	299	428
90 „	26	48	123	197	90 „	60	27	216	303
91 „	17	32	79	128	91 „	39	17	143	199
92 „	14	26	57	97	92 „	29	14	109	152
93 „	11	19	41	71	93 „	18	13	76	107
94 „	7	15	31	53	94 „	12	10	54	76
95 „	5	11	22	38	95 „	10	6	38	54
96 „	4	8	16	28	96 „	6	5	24	35
97 „	1	5	10	16	97 „	3	3	18	24
98 „	1	4	6	11	98 „	2	2	10	14
99 „	0	1	5	6	99 „	1	1	5	7
100 „ and upwards,	0	0	3	3	100 „ and upwards,	1	1	2	4

Without staying, for the present, to bring forward some results which may be deduced from this table, I shall examine how far two tables of population, obtained by a census and from the list of mortality, can agree with each other.[*]

When a population is stationary, that is to say, when we have annually as many deaths as births, the tables of mortality are considered as the true tables of population. Thus, according to the general table given above, of 100,000 births, we found 77,528 children of one year, 70,536 of two years, 66,531 of three

years, and so on ; and the sum of all these individuals formed the whole population, which, according to the same table, had raised itself to 3,264,073 souls. If we then successively cut off from this sum the number of births, the number of individuals of one year old, of two years, &c., the remainder will express the number of survivors at these different ages. In this manner, we should form a table of population ; but to render it comparable to that which has been obtained directly by the census, we should also require to take 100,000 as the basis, instead of 3,264,073, and reduce all the other numbers to a proportion with it. The following table has been obtained in this indirect manner from the table of mortality, supposing the population stationary. It is found to correspond with the table of population obtained by the census, and such as has been given above, but without preserving the distinction of places and sex. We may judge of the errors which these tables present.

* We may consult some writings on census, recently published, with advantage—*Census of the Population*, by Mr Babbage, *Edin. Rev.* No. xcvii. *Letter to his Grace the Duke of Hamilton and Brandon Respecting the Parochial Registers of Scotland*, by Mr J. Cleland : Glasgow, 1834, 8vo. Notes by M. le Baron de Keverberg, being the Appendix to the *Recherches sur la Population, les Naissances, les Décès, &c., en Belgique.*

Table of the Population of Belgium.

Age.	Deduced from the Table of Mortality.	Obtained Directly by the Census.	Age.	Deduced from the Table of Mortality	Obtained Directly by the Census.
Birth,	100,000	100,000	67 years,	6,404	4,868
1 year,	96,937	97,214	69 ..	5,194	3,951
2 years,	94,562	94,446	71 ..	4,116	3,041
3 ..	92,401	91,962	73 ..	3,179	2,418
4 ..	90,361	89,489	75 ..	2,379	1,820
5 ..	88,400	87,034	77 ..	1,724	1,268
6 ..	86,487	84,648	79 ..	1,205	884
8 ..	82,768	80,274	81 ..	316	543
10 ..	79,143	76,138	83 ..	530	358
12 ..	75,500	72,314	85 ..	327	222
14 ..	72,094	68,657	87 ..	190	127
16 ..	68,648	64,707	89 ..	104	72
20 ..	61,932	57,854	90 ..	76	50
25 ..	53,952	49,323	91 ..	55	33
30 ..	46,506	41,047	92 ..	39	25
35 ..	39,524	33,673	93 ..	27	18
40 ..	32,992	27,639	94 ..	19	13
45 ..	26,908	22,283	95 ..	12	9
50 ..	21,289	17,471	96 ..	8	6
53 ..	18,154	14,488	97 ..	4	4
56 ..	15,220	12,039	98 ..	2	2
59 ..	12,495	9,899	99 ..	1	1
62 ..	9,993	7,811	100 & upwards,	1	1
65 ..	7,746	6,058			

The table of population deduced from the table of mortality gives results which are generally greater than those of the table obtained directly by the census. Thus, it indicates that in a population of 100,000 souls, there were 53,952 individuals who were more than 25 years old, and the other table gives only 49,323 individuals having more than this age. How does this difference arise, and how may it be explained?

According to several distinguished authors who have written on this subject, it would be sufficient (as we said above, if the population were *stationary*, that is, the number of births annually being constantly nearly equal to that of deaths)* to calculate the table of population from that of mortality. We shall here remark, that it would undoubtedly suffice, in the greater number of cases, where the population is stationary; but this single condition is not enough: it is also necessary that the same number of deaths correspond annually also, in order that the proportion of the survivors may remain nearly the same at the different periods of life, and that the numbers entered on the tables of mortality for each year may be reproduced almost identically. To perceive the necessity of this condition, let us suppose that we form a table of mortality for a triennial period, during which the population shall have been stationary; and let us suppose, moreover, from some cause, that the mortality during this period affected individuals of fifty years in preference, and, as a compensation, sparing those newly born, that afterwards all may be re-established in the usual order. It would happen, that the population table which we deduce from this table of mortality, will not truly represent the actual state of things: it will indicate too great a population for the fiftieth year, and too small a one for the children.

We may begin to see that a population may be stationary, without our being able to deduce from its bills of mortality, calculated for certain number of years, a table of the population. We see, on the contrary, that this calculation may be made without inconvenience, in the case where the population was not stationary. Indeed, let us suppose a stationary population, and also admit that the tables of mortality may annually present numbers identically the same; it is evident that, by multiplying each of these numbers by a constant ratio, greater or less than unity, that these multiplications will have no other effect than to make an increase or decrease, in the same

* Lacroix — Traité Elémentaire du Calcul des Probabilités, p. 210: 1833.

ratio, of all the numbers of the table of mortality, and consequently those of the table of population.*

In this manner, the bases merely of the tables will have varied: now, the base which we employ is quite arbitrary; we have adopted 100,000, so that we might have numbers which we could compare with each other, and with those of other tables. Thus, all has been done as if we had multiplied by a constant ratio each one of the numbers which are placed in the tables, whilst really the population was increasing or decreasing.

After what has been said, we see *that the necessary conditions to enable us from a table of mortality to deduce a table of population, are, that the deaths at each age preserve annually the same proportion to each other, whether the population be stationary, increasing, or decreasing.*

Applying the preceding to the tables of population given above, we conceive that the differences which they present do not simply arise from the circumstance that in Belgium the population is in a state of increase, but because the mortality has not each year struck the same ages in the same proportions; and no doubt also owing to the years having not been equally fruitful. It is necessary to observe, on the other hand, that, under the French government, certain parts of the population were decimated by wars, and consequently must present vacuities.

3. Can Data on Population Furnish any Marks of the Prosperity of a People?

In seeking to measure the prosperity of a people, the movements of the population have often been made use of. The possibility of arriving at satisfactory results, by following such a course, would undoubtedly deserve to be deeply examined. It is a question of great interest; but I confess the data alone of the population do not appear to me to be sufficient to resolve the question. Local influences, climate, customs, institutions, &c., are elements which we can scarcely neglect, when comparing one people with another : perhaps there would be less danger when comparing a people with itself at different periods, during which these elements have not undergone any sensible variation.†

* Some lines of calculation will better enable us to comprehend this mode of reasoning. Let us designate by the letters

$$a^1, a^2, a^3, a^4, a^5, \&c.,$$

the deaths observed from 0 to 1 year, from 1 to 2 years, from 2 to 3 years, &c. Moreover, let us designate by A, A^1, A^2, &c., the numbers written in the table of mortality opposite 0 year, 1 year, 2 years, 3 years, &c., so that

$$A = a + a^1 + a^2 + a^3 + a^4 + \&c.$$
$$A^1 = \qquad a^1 + a^2 + a^3 + a^4 + \&c.$$
$$A^2 = \qquad\qquad a^2 + a^3 + a^4 + \&c.$$
$$A^3 = \qquad\qquad\qquad a^3 + a^4 + \&c.$$
$$\&c.$$

We shall have, for the corresponding ages of the table of population—

$$\Sigma A = A + A^1 + A^2 + A^3 + A^4 + \&c.$$
$$\Sigma A^1 = \qquad A^1 + A^2 + A^3 + A^4 + \&c.$$
$$\Sigma A^2 = \qquad\qquad A^2 + A^3 + A^4 + \&c.$$
$$\Sigma A^3 = \qquad\qquad\qquad A^3 + A^4 + \&c.$$
$$\&c.$$

If we now multiply by n each of the numbers of the deaths, we shall have, for the numbers of the tables of mortality—

$$nA, nA^1, nA^2, nA^3, nA^4, \&c.;$$

and for the numbers of the table of population—

$$n\Sigma A, n\Sigma A^1, n\Sigma A^2, n\Sigma A^3, \&c.$$

But in certain cases we may have $n > 1$, = 1, < 1, with an increasing population, stationary or decreasing ; in both these cases, the table of population and the table of mortality will continue to present the same numbers for the same ages, if we take the same base as the starting-point.

† I shall here bring forward, in a great measure, an article which I inserted in the *Revue Encyclopédique* for August 1830.

The Academy of Moral and Political Sciences, during the Session June 7, 1834, put the following question to the meeting :—*To determine in what the misery of different countries consists, and by what signs it is manifested ; to examine the causes which produce it.*

We might be exposed to serious errors in not taking notice of the number of marriages and births of a nation; for if it be true that disheartening circumstances sometimes add evil to evil, as in Ireland, and since moral degradation is a great stimulus to precocious marriage,* it may still happen that mortality only makes greater ravages; and one of the most fatal scourges of a people is to see its generations renewed with a degree of rapidity which does not allow it to preserve useful men. Now, it generally happens that the births are regulated by the number of deaths; that is to say, the countries which produce the greatest number of children, are precisely those in which the mortality is the greatest. When reproduction is greater than the limits of prudence, it appears that the weakest part of the population is the first to feel the consequences the excess of the population passing rapidly from the cradle to the tomb. If, therefore, the number of births could be useful to show the degree of prosperity of a people, it would be more particularly in considering it in relation to the mortality. But, as I have said, the mere number of births appears to me absolutely insufficient.

I should have more distinct confidence in the number of deaths, if it only established a measure by which we might be assured of a population having attained or exceeded the limits which it could not cross without condemning itself to pauperism. M. D'Ivernois has very clearly shown† the utility of it on this head; and the publication of the work which he announces under the following title is much to be desired — *On the Average Mortality Considered as a Measure of the Comfort and Civilisation of a Nation.* This universal measure, says the author, I flatter myself I have found in the *mortuary number* of the people, by which I understand that which indicates whether the proportion of deaths annually, compared with the total number of living persons, increases or diminishes. Perhaps we may be wrong in precalculating the results; but if we observe that this measure does not change when the total amount of those alive remains the same, as well as that of deaths, we may have some fear of its precision. A population may remain numerically the same from different causes, and present a greater or less number of useful men, without our being able to say, for that reason merely, that its comfort also remains the same. If so, we should estimate a child as equal to a useful man.

To take one example only. If, from any cause whatever, the mortality in a flourishing country were to attack useful men more particularly, and spare the children, the number of deaths and that of births remaining otherwise the same, it would infallibly happen, after some years, that this population would be deteriorated, and would have lost many of the elements of prosperity; and yet the loss which it had experienced would not in any manner be detected by the measure employed. The mortuary figure would remain the same; and a considerable number of useful and productive men would be replaced by unproductive children.

Certainly we cannot deny that very strict relations exist between the happiness of a country and the movements of its population; the thing is, to ascertain how to express them. It seems to me that on this head we ought to make an important distinction. We may consider the question in two points of view. We may propose, when considering a people, to examine which are the disastrous years—those during which it has suffered more or less; or, on the other hand, we may examine, in an absolute manner, what is the number of useful men at disposal—in a word, what is its strength, which is also one of the principal

* See an article by M. D'Ivernois inserted in the *Bibliothèque Universelle de Genève,* March 1830.
† Bibliothèque Universelle, 1831.

elements of its prosperity. In the first case, the number of deaths would almost always be employed with considerable success; for a disastrous year is generally accompanied and followed by numerous privations, even amongst the most highly favoured people, and privations are mortal to the human species. Thus, if we only knew that 1817 was a year of famine for Belgium and a great number of countries, we should attain our end without trouble, because the number of deaths was greater than for the years which preceded or followed. This increased mortality was also felt in the mendicity houses, in which it was almost double what it had been heretofore, as also in the hospitals and asylums for foundlings.

As to the second manner of considering the question, I have endeavoured to show why the number of deaths merely appeared to me insufficient. It is important, indeed, to know not only how many deaths take place in the population, but also at what age these deaths occur. Some writers have employed, in such estimates, the duration of the average life, others the duration of the probable life; and they have sought to establish their valuation according to the changes which the one or the other of these values undergoes. But here we meet with an obstacle nearly similar to the one I have before pointed out; namely, that the duration of the probable life, as also that of the average life, may have a value of different kinds. This inconvenience is especially felt, when we employ the number which expresses the probable life, since, in fact, we only consider the period at which a certain number of individuals of the same age are reduced to one-half; and we do not express whether those who died first were able to make themselves useful during a longer or a shorter time, neither does it establish any thing with respect to those who survive.

Taking the figure which expresses the average duration of life, or the average of the ages to which a certain number of individuals have attained, whom we suppose to have been born at the same time, we also give the same value to one year of the life of an infant as to that of a man whose labours have been profitable to society.

There is one difficulty to which the preceding questions are liable, and which deserves particular attention, because very important and interesting considerations are connected with its solution—considerations of high moment to statistics and political economy. M. D'Ivernois, whose labours have been so beneficial to these sciences, has kindly called my attention to this difficulty, and asked my advice on this delicate point: he was desirous of knowing if two nations, who, as regarded the ratios of births and deaths, might stand at precisely the same numbers, might not have two averages of life, by virtue of the eventual difference in the order of mortality for the age of their dead.*

For the sake of simplicity, let us suppose a people who have each year the same number of births and deaths, and let us examine if the average duration of life may not vary from year to year; this question returns, in fact, to the same point as that which was proposed above. If we formed a table of mortality after the deaths of one year, and deduced the average duration of life from it, I suppose that we should find it 30 years exactly. The year following, if the mortality took place in the same manner and in the same proportion, the duration of average life would still be 30 years. But if, in the lists of deaths of this second year, we substitute an infant of one year for a man of forty, which will not affect the proportional number of births or deaths, we shall find, however, when taking account of the infant substituted for the full-

* In inserting my answer in the *Bibliothèque Universelle de Genève,* March 1831, M. D'Ivernois announces that he had come to the same conclusions as myself, and that he received similar results from M. Villermé.

grown man, that the average duration of life became rather shorter, since the sum of years which had been lived would be reduced by 39 years. We see already, that if the tables of mortality and the duration of average life were only calculated according to the observations of this year, they could not present the same identical results as for the first year. Average life would be shorter; but it is evident that society would have gained, since it preserved an useful man instead of an infant.

We conceive that, if instead of one such substitution, a greater number were made, average life, calculated according to the deaths of this year, would be found diminished in a very sensible manner; and nevertheless we should have cause to be glad at what at first appears a paradox. In fact, we should have preserved useful years to the state, in exchange for some years which are expensive to it.

But it may be objected that these 39 years are not lost to the sum of the years lived, and that the individual of 40, who has been replaced, will lengthen the average duration of life, when he dies, by the whole period which he has gained by the substitution; and, indeed, if the period of time according to which we calculate the average duration of life·is also extended, so as to comprise the death of the individual in question, it is evident that this debt of 39 years has only been deferred, and that the sum of years lived is not found affected. Thus, the average life remains the same; but it is always correct to say, that even then society has been benefited, since, for a longer or a shorter time, useful years have been substituted for expensive ones.

If, by a concurrence of circumstances which civilisation ought to produce, such substitutions are made as those we have just been considering, not for one year only but for several, and if this state of things should continue increasing, we conceive that it would become impossible, still preserving the same proportional numbers of births and deaths, to preserve the same average life: it must begin to diminish. However, how is it that such extraordinary results are not met with? It is, I think, because the substitutes are never sufficiently numerous, nor their duration long enough, to leave sensible traces amidst the other influencing elements.

However, this teaches us how necessary it is to guard against the inductions which we might draw from the average duration of life, calculated from few years of observation, and among a people in progress

or decay. By extending the preceding reasoning, we readily arrive at the following conclusions:—

1. A people may annually have figures of exactly the same value, as proportional numbers of births and deaths, without the average life continuing the same.

2. When, all things being equal, the mortality spares the perfect men and takes off the children, the duration of the average life diminishes, and vice versa: it being understood that we calculate the average life from the number of deaths.

3. The number of births, deaths, and of the average life, may preserve the same value, whilst, indeed, the population experiences great losses, or receives great benefits, which remain unobserved.

4. To estimate suitably what a population gains or loses, it is necessary, when making the division of years, to establish the average life, to take into account the *quality* of these years, and to examine whether they are *productive* or not.

When, for example, it is intended to estimate the forces which a state can command, in considering the problem in a purely physical point of view, as has been done, it appears to me that the most certain way would be, to compare the number of useful men with those who are not so. The elements of comparison, in this case, would require to be extracted from the tables of mortality, or rather from accurately constructed tables of population; and it would be necessary to inquire how many children there are, not in a condition to be useful, in a given number of individuals, and how many of the old men contribute to the benefit of society: we might divide a population into two parts, the one being less, and the other more than 15 years of age. I allow that I here suppose that a man cannot render himself more useful at 30 or 40 than at 16 or 80; but this is an inconvenience which we also find in other methods of valuation, and which, moreover, we might cause to disappear, by attributing more importance to certain years of life than to others, if extreme accuracy did not become illusory in such a case. To give us a somewhat accurate idea at first, of the manner in which the population is composed, I have here collected the most accurate data from some of the principal countries previously considered. We shall find the numbers classed separately belonging to the two categories which I have established between productive individuals and those whose maintenance may be considered as a charge to society.

Ages.	Great Britain: 1821. Marshall.	Ireland: 1821. Marshall.	England: 1821. Marshall.	England and part of Wales: 1813 to 1830. Rickman.	France: before 1789. Annuaire.	Belgium: 1829. Annuaire.	Sweden: 1820. Marshall.	United States: 1830. Marshall.
Below 5 years,	1647	1535	1472	1487	1201	1297	1307	1800
5 to 10 ··	1385	1355	1300	1307	981	1089	1010	1455
10 to 15 ··	1209	1218	1119	1114	939	946	894	1243
15 to 20 ··	1046	1219	1000	992	897	883	899	1112
20 to 30 ··	1558	1760	1583	1574	1638	1680	1711	1781
30 to 40 ··	1180	1150	1176	1181	1404	1341	1362	1091
40 to 50 ··	878	771	931	934	1161	1017	1087	688
50 to 60 ··	545	600	663	659	892	793	855	430
60 to 70 ··	348	273	460	456	577	604	586	253
70 to 80 ··	160	96	227	228	255	279	240	110
80 to 90 ··	40	23	62	63	50	66	41	31
90 to 100 ··	3·4	3	5·5	5	4·8	4·9	1	4
Above 100 ··	0·1	0·5	0·3	0·2	0·2	0·1	0	0·2
Below 15 years	4241	4108	3891	3908	3121	3332	3211	4498
Above ··	5758·5	5895·5	6105·8	6092·2	6879	6668	6782	ₒ 5500·2
Ratio,	1·36	1.43	1·57	1·56	2·20	2·00	2·11	1·22

The results of this table, although in some degree foreseen, surprised me very much. I confess I did not expect to find so great a difference between the numbers of France, Belgium, Sweden, and those of England and the United States. In the former countries, the adult population is double the other, whilst in the latter it is only one-fourth or one-third more. The United States, especially, appear to be in an extremely unfavourable condition, since they, of all countries we have been considering, present the fewest adults in the population.

The great disproportion which has been pointed out, is more especially owing to the rapid increase of population in England and the United States of late years : the greater number of the individuals proceeding from this great development of fecundity, are still little advanced in the career of life ; so that there will be a greater number of persons not adults. The prodigious increase of population which has been observed in the United States, has taken place within little more than 30 years ; we also see that the number of individuals under this age is comparatively superior to that of other countries. It is the same in England and Ireland in ascending from 20 to 30 years : Sweden, France, and Belgium, on the contrary, present populations which have slowly increased, and which may thus pretty well represent the usual proportion of adults in ordinary times.

I do not think that, up to the present time, sufficient attention has been paid to the great number of children which too rapid an increase of population throws into a country, and the smaller intrinsic value which this population momentarily receives from it, which must be a very powerful obstacle to ulterior development.

In France, Belgium, and Sweden, for example, of three inhabitants, two at least are in a state for re-production, whilst in the United States only one in two, or more accurately, six out of eleven.

In conclusion, it is production which regulates the *possible limit* of the inhabitants of a country. Civilisation narrows this limit, and tends to increase the produce which belongs to each individual, so as to increase his well-being, and secure him the means of existence. As to medicine, it is limited to close certain passages to the tomb, but only by enlarging others; for it cannot increase the list of the living, except in causing the supernumeraries to live at the expense of society. " Esculapius himself could not, by his art, confer immortality on one-half of men, except by condemning them to abstain from reproduction, unless by doubling the mortality of the other half, or by pushing production to the point of supplying the new wants which would arise." * Yet it would be also misrepresenting the immense benefits which have accrued to humanity from medicine, to deny its power in lengthening the average life of man ; but this grand conquest, due to the progress of knowledge, can only be maintained by the knowledge and foresight of men, who prevent, by celibacy, new births and new food for death.† When there takes place no sudden change, nature annually levies upon us the same tribute of deaths, from which each of us seeks as much as possible to withdraw : each is desirous to belong to the privileged class ; but the effect of this kind of fraud is not so much to diminish the amount of tribute, as to transfer it to those of our neighbours who are less favourably placed in their social position.‡

The average duration of life, could it be ascertained exactly, would furnish us with a measure of the prudence and hygienic state of a country : the consump-tion of the inhabitant would give the state of civilisation and the exigencies of climate ; and the proportional number of inhabitants, keeping in view this latter measure, would give that number which represents its production.*

BOOK SECOND.

DEVELOPMENT OF STATURE, WEIGHT, STRENGTH, &c.

APPARENTLY but little interest is attached to the determination of the stature and weight of man, or to his physical development at different ages; nor, until the present time, has any one particularly attended to this subject. Man has only been studied in his most conspicuous relations; the correlative study of his qualities, and the numerical determination of the modifications which are consequent upon age, have been neglected. This state of things leaves immense voids in science, and the result is that we generally want the necessary means for solving a great number of interesting questions, especially relating to the natural history of man. For example, we are almost totally ignorant of the ratios which may exist between the laws of development of his different faculties, and what are the elements which predominate at such or such an age : hence the critical periods of life can only be determined in a very indefinite manner.

The researches which have been made to measure the height and weight of man, especially relate either to the period of birth or to the period of complete development; but the intermediate ages have scarcely been attended to. Physiologists have connected the first of these determinations with a question in legal medicine ; they have even anticipated the period of birth, and sought to value the size and weight of the fœtus. Natural philosophers, who studied man as a mechanical agent, have rather been occupied with the determination of his weight when he has acquired complete development. La Hire has made some very remarkable researches of this kind, which prove that the subject now occupying us has a much deeper interest than that resulting from mere curiosity.

To show how little advanced is the state of the study of the progressive development of man, let us suppose that we want to establish the age of an individual, from the aggregate of his physical qualities : we may be allowed to say, that we shall not find in science any assistance for the determination of this question—we shall be reduced to mere empirical conjecture. However, legal medicine presents numerous examples where such determinations become necessary. We may ask, no doubt, if it will ever be possible to obtain them, especially for advanced ages ? This fear, well founded as it may appear, ought not, however, to lead us to reject such researches : that would not be very philosophic. If to the data furnished by the habit of observation, and the *tact* resulting therefrom, we can join physical qualities susceptible of measurement, prudence bids us not neglect them. When a physician is called to examine the body of an infant found lifeless, and when, in a legal inquiry, he, from simple inspection, establishes the presumed age of this child, it is evident that he cannot but impose his judgment on those who read the inquiry, however erroneous it may other-

---

* [" Esculape lui-même ne pourrait, par son art, donner l'immortalité à la moitié des hommes, qu'en les condamnant à ne point se reproduire, à moins de doubler la mortalité de l'autre moitié, ou de porter la production au point de fournir aux nouveaux besoins qu'il aurait fait naître."]

† By prolonging the average duration of life, the medical sciences substitute useful years for unproductive ones. The adult man has a longer career, produces more, and society has fewer infants to feed ; so that, in this point of view, medical sciences really increase production and render a new service. This remark was made to me by a friend, and I mention it here because I believe it to be true.

‡ M. Villermé has observed to me, whilst this work was in the press, that he had advanced the same idea, but under another form, in his work on epidemics.

* M. Chitti, who makes *social economy* consist in obtaining the greatest possible utility, with the least possible labour, has given the following measure of riches :—" The degree of the riches of a people, as well as those of an individual, is indicated by the ratio between the sum of the wants and the sum of the available funds which he possesses to satisfy them."—*Cours d'Economie Sociale au Musée de Bruxelles*, 3d Lecture.

wise be, since there are no elements existing for the verification of it. If, on the contrary, to the assistance of the estimate which has been made of the age, is joined the height and weight of the child, and some other physical qualities susceptible of computation; and if, moreover, there were exact tables which might enable one to ascertain, at different ages, the values of these physical qualities, and the limits within which they are found connected in individuals regularly formed, the judgment given of the age would be capable of verification—it would even become useless, if the elements of verification admitted of great accuracy. Such appreciations, then, ought not to be neglected by legal medicine, since they tend to substitute precise characters and exact data for conjectural estimates, which are always vague and often faulty.

Thus, apart from the interest which is presented by the determination of man at different ages, and in researches relating to the average man, it may present another important element, as we shall see more perfectly farther on, for the solution of the following problem of legal medicine: *To determine the age of an individual after death, from the aggregate of his physical qualities.* In this sense, weight would be one of the elements which it would be necessary to connect with the distinguishing of individuals; and this physical character naturally takes a place near that of the stature.

Researches on the height of man, and on his development, may have another useful end, that of enlightening governments on many points; as, for example, as regards the fixing of the age of recruits.

There is another element, the determination of which is equally important, and which, also, is but little known, namely, the strength. I do not flatter myself that I have filled up the voids which science presented on this subject, but I shall think myself happy if my researches may induce other persons to attempt it.

CHAPTER I.

OF THE DEVELOPMENT OF THE HEIGHT.

I do not think that, before Buffon, any inquiries had been made to determine the rate of human growth successively from birth to maturity; and even this celebrated naturalist cites only a single particular example; neither has he examined the modifying influences which age exerts on height. The only researches at all precise which science possesses, refer to the length of the child before birth, and to that of the fully developed man.*

Chaussier, who invented the *mecometre*, an instrument adapted to measure the length of children, thought that we might view as regular the increase in length of the child for six months before its birth; and he estimated this increase at two inches per month. In the *Dictionnaire des Sciences Medicales*, the length of the fœtus is estimated by the following numbers:—

	Metres.
At birth,	0·487 to 0·541
One month before birth,	0·433 to 0·487
Two months	0·379 to 0·433
Three months	0·300 to 0·379
Four months	0·216 to 0·300
Five months	0·162 to 0·216

The medium length of the child at birth would then be 0·514 metres: this estimate differs but slightly from that obtained at the Foundling Hospital in Brussels, by means, also, of Chaussier's *mecometre*. On measuring the length of fifty male and as many female

* See on this latter subject an excellent memoir of M. Villermé, inserted in the first volume of the *Annales d'Hygiène*.
† [The French metre is equal to 3 feet English and ·2808 of a decimal; or 3 feet and 2·10ths.]

children immediately at birth, the following numbers were obtained :*—

Length.		Boys.	Girls.	Total.
From 16 to 17 inches French,	-	2	4	6
.. 17 to 18	..	8	19	27
.. 18 to 19	..	28	18	46
.. 19 to 20	-	12	8	20
.. 20 to 21	..	..	1	1
		50	50	100

With regard to the mediums or averages and the limits, they have given the following values for the two sexes :—

Value.	Boys.	Girls.
Minimum,	16 inches 2 lines.†	16 inches 2 lines.
Medium,	18 .. 6 .. nearly.	18 .. 1½ .. nearly.
Maximum,	19 .. 8 ..	20 .. 6 ..

From these results it follows, that, from the period of birth, the height or length of one sex is superior to the other; being, for boys, 0·4999; for girls, 0·4896; giving thus in favour of boys a trifle less than half an inch.

By uniting these numbers to those which have been obtained in the junior schools of Brussels, the Orphan Hospital, boarding-houses, and in public life, in respect to young persons of different classes, I have been able to construct the following table, comprising the rate of growth from birth to 20 years: the height of the shoe is not included :—

Table showing the rate of Growth in the two Sexes.

Ages.	Boys.	Girls.	Difference.
	metres.	metres.	metres.
Birth, - - -	0·500	0·490	0·010
1 year, - - -	0·698	..	..
2 years, - - -	0·796	0·780	0·016
3 .. - - -	0·867	0·853	0·014
4 .. - - -	0·930	0·913	0·017
5 .. - - -	0·986	0·978	0·008
6 .. - - -	1·045	1·035	0·010
7 .. - - -	..	1·091	..
8 .. - - -	1·160	1·154	0·006
9 .. - - -	1·221	1·205	0·016
10 .. - - -	1·280	1·256	0·024
11 .. - - -	1·334	1·266	0·048
12 .. - - -	1·384	1·340	0·044
13 .. - - -	1·431	1·417	0·014
14 .. - - -	1·489	1·475	0·014
15 .. - - -	1·549	1·496	0·053
16 .. - - -	1·600	1·518	0·082
17 .. - - -	1·640	1·553	0·087
18 .. - - -	..	1·564	..
19 .. - - -	1·665	1·570	0·095
20 .. - - -	..	1·574	..
Growth terminated, -	1·684	1·579	0·105

We observe by this table that, towards the age of 16 to 17, the growth of girls is already, *relatively*, almost as much advanced as that of boys from 18 to 19.‡ Moreover, the annual growth for boys is about 56 millimetres [somewhat more than two inches] between 5 and 15 years of age; whilst for girls it is only about 52 millimetres [or rather less than two inches.] In the *Dictionnaire des Sciences Medicales*, in the article *Giants*, M. Virey attributes the lower stature of woman to the circumstance of her arriving sooner at the age of puberty, or having reached perfection, and also to her having less vital energy. We may add, that her annual growth, up to the age of puberty, is also less rapid than that of man.

* I have been greatly aided in numerous researches into the height, weight, strength, and other physical qualities of man, by Messrs Guiette and Van Esschen, Professors in the School of Medicine at Brussels, as well as by M. Plataw. Without their assistance, it would have been impossible for me to have obtained all the measurements in the various charities, hospitals, public schools, Prison of Vilvorde, &c.
† [The French line is equal to the 12th part of an inch.]
‡ [The proposition may be easier understood by stating it in this way: A girl is relatively as tall at 16 as a boy is at 18, the sex and full growth of each being taken into account.]

After having spoken of what relates to the sexes, it must be interesting t' consider the influence of a town or a country resi. ace upon human growth. Already Dr Villermé, in the second part of the *Annales d'Hygiène*, had proved, contrary to the generally received notion, that the inhabitants of towns are taller than those of the country. I have arrived at the same conclusion in respect to the inhabitants of Brabant. Extracts from the government militia registers, which I communicated at that time to Dr Villermé, were published in the fifth number of the *Annales d'Hygiène;* they gave the following numbers : —

Arrondissements.	1823.	1824.	1825.	1826.	1827.	Average.
	metres.	metres.	metres.	metres.	metres.	metres.
1. {Brussels, - - -	1·6719	1·6640	1·6631	1·6647	1·6528	1·6633
{Rural Communes, - - -	1·6325	1·6317	1·6343	1·6353	1·6296	1·6325
2. {Louvain, - - -	1·6424	1·6349	1·6399	1·6460	1·6335	1·6393
{Rural Communes, - - -	1·6296	1·6229	1·6090	1·6145	1·6127	1·6177
3. {Nivelles, - - -	1·6398	1·6446	1·6581	1·6384	1·6330	1 6428
{Rural Communes, - - -	1·6264	1·6260	1·6409	1·6431	1·6330	1·6323
Annual {Cities, - - -	1·6514	1·6478	1·6587	1·6497	1·6398	1·6485
Averages.{Rural Communes, -	1·6295	1·6269	1·6280	1,6309	1·6225	1·6275
General Average, - - - - - - -						1·6380

The averages of each year were taken from 400 individuals for Brussels, and from 150 for Louvain and Nivelles. Those of the rural parishes were deduced from 400 individuals for each district. Thus, the general average for the whole province was drawn from 3500 individuals living in towns, and from 6000 living in the country.

By these numbers, we see that the inhabitant of towns is taller than the inhabitant of the country; and in arranging the cities and rural districts according to the respective height which man attains in them *in his nineteenth year,* the order would be as follows :—Brussels, Nivelles, Louvain; and the same order for the rural districts around these towns. In spite of the differences we have thus remarked as taking place at the age of 19, it might still happen that the inhabitant of the country might attain a greater height than the inhabitant of the town previous to the completion of his full growth, in such a way that the growth of man in cities might be at first more rapid up to a certain point than in the country, and might even be nearly terminated in cities, whilst in the country the growth would be very far from having attained its complete development. And these remarks coincide pretty nearly with the deductions of Dr Villermé, in respect to the height of man in France. The doctor remarks, that "human height becomes greater, and the growth takes place more rapidly, other circumstances being equal, in proportion as the country is richer, the comfort more general, houses, clothes, and nourishment better, and labour, fatigue, and privations during infancy and youth less; or, in other words, the circumstances accompanying misery put off the period of the complete development of the body, and stint human stature."

It becomes, then, important to determine the epoch at which human growth terminates; and the government registers for Brussels, being examined with this view, gave the following results. These registers refer to a great levy made about eighteen years ago; I have divided them into three series, each comprising 300 individuals :—

19 Years.	25 Years.	30 Years.
1·6630 metre.	1·6822 metre.	1·6834 metre.
1·6695 „	1·6735 „	1·6873 „
1·6620 „	1·6692 „	1·6817 „
Medium, 1·6648 „	1·6750 „	1·6841 „

Thus we see that human growth,* as regards height, does not terminate at 19, or even invariably at 25. I

* [The translator had observed some years ago, that the male human height had evidently not attained its maximum previous to at least 30 years of age, and probably not even then. This he was led to remark by observing large numbers of students, who, leaving college at the age of 20, 21, or 22, have returned seven or eight years afterwards. Examination proved that these persons had grown very considerably, not only in breadth but also in height.]

have to regret exceedingly that the state of the government registers does not allow of my making similar researches in regard to the inhabitants of the country; we might then have known if the growth in towns terminates more rapidly than in the country, and also if man, when fully developed, is tallest in the country.

When we class the 900 individuals of whom I have spoken above, in the order of their height, we come to the following results:—

Heights.	Number of Individuals		
	of 19 Years.	of 25 Years.	of 30 Years.
From 15 to 16 decimetres,	32	17	15
.. 16 to 17, ..	173	174	163
.. 17 to 18, ..	92	103	109
.. 18 to 19, ..	3	5	12
.. 19 to 20, ..	..	1	1
	300	300	300 *

Thus, at 19, 3 individuals only were more than 18 decimetres [above 5 feet 10 inches] high; at the age of 25, there were 6; and at the age of 30 there were 13.† It seems to me that we are entitled to conclude, from the whole of these results, that human growth, in respect to height, does not terminate in Brussels even at the age of 25, which is very much opposed to the generally received opinion.

According to M. Hargenvilliers,‡ the average height of conscripts of 20 years, taken for all France, is 1·615

* [The value of the decimetre in English measures is 3 inches and ·937 decimal parts, or nearly 4 English inches.]

† In the preceding numbers were comprised the men who were rejected, or had leave to withdraw from the corps, as of under size.

‡ *Inquiries and Considerations on the Formation and Recruitment of the French Army:* 1817. M. Villermé, in his Memoir on the Height of Man in France, quotes the opinion of Tenon and also some facts, which show that, during the time of the Empire, continual wars had lowered the human stature.

[A question naturally arises here, whether the stature was actually lowered, or the young conscripts merely called on before their time of full development; but the remark of Dr Villermé suggests other considerations, well worthy the attention of statisticians—such, for example, as the effects produced in Prussia, by the maintaining of a standing army of somewhat more than 200,000 men in time of peace, it being admitted that these are the finest and best proportioned men in the kingdom. For we have first the withdrawal of the very choicest of the male population from the exercise of the arts and the cultivation of science, at precisely that period of life when they are best fitted for such pursuits; and, secondly, the effects upon the population in respect to the restraints upon marriage, and the preference given by the soldier to a debauched and irregular life. The same remarks, modified, apply to all other European nations, none of them being without standing armies of greater or less magnitude.]

E

metre [4 feet 10 inches nearly]; and of 100,000 there were as follows:—

Under 1·570 metre,	- - -	28,620
1·570 to 1·598 ··	- - -	11,580
1·598 to 1·624 ··	- - -	13,990
1·624 to 1·651 ··	- - -	14,410
1·651 to 1·678 ··	- - -	11,410
1·678 to 1·705 ··	- - -	8,780
1·705 to 1·732 ··	- - -	5,530
1·732 to 1·759 ··	- - -	3,190
Above 1·759 ··	- - -	2,490
		100,000

We might consider the inhabitants of the ancient department of Bouches-de-la-Meuse, which was partly formed of Holland, and of which the Hague was the chief place, as affording the limits of the statures observed in France from the time of the Empire. The average height of conscripts for the years 1808, 1809, and 1810, raised before the age of 20, was 1·677 metre.* On the other hand, in the ancient department of the Apennines, of which Chiavari was the chief place, the country mountainous, without industrious occupations, extremely poor, and where the men toil from a very early age and are ill fed, the average stature of the conscripts for the same three years, was 1·560 metre. " The difference of these results," says M. Villermé, " is striking. In the former place, where the stature is highest, there were but few excused or rejected even for diseases; on the contrary, in the latter place, where the stature is very low, there are many excused even for this latter cause; so that all the advantages are in favour of men of high stature."†

It is remarkable that the inequality of statures is not merely observed between the inhabitants of town and country, but is also felt in the interior of towns between individuals of different professions, and having different degrees of affluence, as M. Villermé has shown for the different arrondissements of Paris, where the stature of men seems to be, all other things being equal, in proportion to the good fortune, or at least in inverse proportion to the difficulties, toils, and privations experienced in infancy and youth.‡ Of 41 young persons between 17 and 20 years of age, measured at the Athenæum of Brussels, 13 were found between 16 and 17 decimetres, 26 between 17 and 18 decimetres, and 2 between 18 and 19 decimetres; so that the young persons between 17 and 18 were double the number of those between 16 and 17 decimetres; whilst, in the interior of the town, the number of the former is not equal to the latter, even at the age of 30 years.

The young girls measured in the Female Orphan Hospital of Brussels, and who, during their infancy, have been brought up in the country, are generally smaller than girls of the same age, in easy circumstances, who have been measured in town.

In the Prison (Maison de Détention) of Vilvorde, by forming three groups, each of 23 individuals for each sex, the average results have been—

For men.	For Women.
1·657 met.	1·572 met.
1·664 ··	1·581 ··
1·670 ··	1·585 ··
General average, - 1·664 ··	1·579 ··

* Sur la Taille, &c.

† [The translator is firmly persuaded that Dr Villermé and M. Quetelet, have failed to detect the real cause of difference of stature in those two departments: it is a question purely of race, and not of feeding or locality. The taller conscripts were Saxons, drawn from the departments of Holland and the Mouths of the Meuse; the shorter conscripts, found in the Apennines and around Chiavari, were the descendants of the ancient Celtic population of that country. The difference in stature, then, depends, in this instance, in a great measure on the difference in blood, or on the race of men: it has existed for thousands of years, and will continue so, altogether independent of locality, feeding, or government.]

‡ Annales d'Hygiène, No. 2, p. 370.

Classing them according to size, we find—

Sizes.	Men.	Women.
From 14 to 15 decimetres, - -	1	3
·· 15 to 16 ·· - - -	6	36
·· 16 to 17 ·· - -	42	27
·· 17 to 18 ·· - -	19	3
·· 18 to 19 ·· - -	1	··
	69	69

These results show that the prisoners were generally shorter than fully developed individuals measured in Brussels; their average stature being nearly equal to that of young persons of 19 years of age, and it may correspond with the average stature of the inhabitants of the province.

With the view of appreciating the modifications which painful toil in manufactories may produce on the development of children, Mr J. W. Cowell has made different observations at Manchester and Stockport; he has inserted the details in the first volume of Factory Reports, and has kindly assisted me in obtaining the results, which I have reduced to the métrical measure. The girls and boys have been measured with their shoes on; no deduction has been made for this circumstance: but, as the observations were made on the Sunday, the thickness of the soles for boys would probably be from one-half to one-third of an inch (English), and for girls from one-eighth to one-sixth of an inch. This being laid down, the following are the values obtained :*—

Average Stature of Children of the Lower Orders, at Manchester and Stockport.†

Ages.	Boys		Girls	
	Working in Factories.	not Working in Factories.	Working in Factories.	not Working in Factories.
	metres.	metres.	metres.	metres.
9 years,	1·222	1·233	1·218	1·230
10 ··	1·270	1·286	1·260	1·254
11 ··	1·302	1·296	1·299	1·323
12 ··	1·355	1·345	1·364	1·363
13 ··	1·383	1·396	1·413	1·309
14 ··	1·437	1·440	1·467	1·479
15 ··	1·515	1·474	1·486	1·502
16 ··	1·565	1·605	1·521	1·475
17 ··	1·592	1·627	1·535	1·542
18 ··	1·608	1·775	1·593	1·645

It appears, from these numbers, that the statures of male and female children do not differ much in Belgium and England: we also see that, until the age of puberty, there is no great difference in size of the children of the lower orders, whether they work in factories or not. But for the latter years of the table, there is a very sensible difference. Will it be found that the growth in factories, after puberty, is diminished, or only retarded? or, which seems more probable, does not the amelioration remarked for the lower ages proceed from the useful changes which have already been made, from the apprehension of parliamentary inquiries?‡

When, in England, we chose the terms of comparison from rather higher classes of society, we find the stature of men higher than in France or the Low

* [It has been suggested to the translator, by a gentleman well acquainted with the manufacturing districts of Yorkshire and Lancashire, that wooden clogs, and not shoes, seemed almost universally worn by the manufacturing population of these counties, more especially of Lancashire. Now, the soles and heels of these clogs are of great thickness: a question then arises with respect to Mr Cowell's measurements. If this class of the population wear clogs on Sundays, this circumstance may partially affect the value of Mr Cowell's statements.]

† The number of children measured was—factory boys, 410; others, 227: female factory children, 652; others, 201. Very few non-factory children, of the ages of 16, 17, and 18, have been measured.

‡ It has been found, by this inquiry, that in some districts the children were forced to work standing upright, with the legs fastened in tin pipes.

Countries, at least for young persons between 18 and 23 years of age. The following are the results of 80 measurements made on students of the University of Cambridge, in groups of 10 each :*—

Ten individuals,	-	58 feet 3¼ inches.
„	- - -	58 „ 6½ „
„	- - -	58 „ 9 „
„	- - -	57 „ 7½ „
„	- - -	56 „ 9½ „
„	- - -	57 „ 9¼ „
„	- - -	58 „ 3 „
„	- - -	58 „ ‥ „
Average,	- -	58
Height of one person,	-	5 feet 9 3-5th inches.

I have enumerated different causes which influence the growth of man in town, but their number increases when the researches embrace a large extent of territory; thus, the complete development stature stops more suddenly in very hot or very cold countries than in those of a moderate temperature; more suddenly in low plains than on mountainous heights, where the climate is severe. The kind of food and drink farther influence growth; and individuals have been known to grow considerably by changing their mode of life, and making use of moist food calculated to distend and increase their organisation. Some diseases, and particularly fevers, may also excite rapid and extraordinary growth. The case of a young girl is related, who, becoming unwell (*pendant ses menstrues*) by an attack of fever which she had, acquired a gigantic stature.† Lastly, it has also been remarked that lying in bed is favourable to growth, and that a man in the morning is somewhat taller than in the evening; during the day, he undergoes a degree of depression.‡

I shall now pass to a more particular examination of the law of growth of man, from birth to complete development. The numbers on which my results are based, have been collected at Brussels, and as much as possible from individuals of different classes: by the side of the observed values, I have written down the calculated ones, according to an empirical formula, which I shall explain subsequently.

* It is a custom at Cambridge to measure and weigh the young persons coming to the university, with great accuracy, at a merchant's warehouse, where a book is kept for the purpose of entering the data. It is from this book that, through the kindness of Mr Whewell, the accompanying numbers have been taken.

† See *Dictionnaire de Médicine*, article *Geant*, by Virey.

‡ [M. Quetelet has unaccountably omitted, in the above paragraph, the great cause productive of differences in stature of men and animals—to wit, difference in race or blood. The diminutive Bosjeman of Southern Africa, the athletic Caffre, reaching the full European stature, and the gigantic Boor, the descendant of the Saxon race, are as nearly alike in respect to food and climate as may be; the extraordinary differences, therefore, which these men present, are ascribable to one cause alone—a difference of blood or origin; and the historic evidence derived from ancient Rome, and from the equally authentic figures depicted in the tombs of Egyptian Thebes, prove that these differences caused by blood or race are now neither greater nor less than they were at least 4000 years ago, thus, as it were, setting at defiance all minor causes, such as food, climate, localities, &c. Whether the Hun resides in the fertile plains of Hungary, the shores of the Caspian, or the frozen regions of Scandinavia or of Lapland, the general stature of the race remains perfectly unaltered.

In respect to what M. Quetelet observes regarding the influence of rest and horizontal position on the stature, it is a fact well established that, by such a position, in bed for example, the elastic fibro-cartilages connecting the spinal bones together, seem to recover their full depth, and the stature may gain an inch or more thereby. Recruits for the army and deserters avail themselves of a knowledge of this fact, and occasionally succeed in making their identity difficult to be established.]

Table of the Growth of Man.

Ages.	Stature Observed.	Stature from Calculation.	Difference.
	metres.	metres.	metres.
Birth, - -	0·500	0·500	0·000
1 year, - - -	0·698	0·698	0·000
2 „ - - -	0·796	0·791	+ 0·005
3 „ - - -	0·867	0·864	+ 0·003
4 „ - - -	0·930	0·928	+ 0·002
5 „ - - -	0·986	0·988	— 0·002
6 „ - - -	1·045	1·047	— 0·002
7 „		1·105	
8 „ - - -	1·160	1·162	— 0·002
9 „ - - -	1·221	1·219	+ 0·002
10 „ - - -	1·280	1·275	+ 0·005
11 „ - - -	1·334	1·330	+ 0·004
12 „ - - -	1·384	1·385	— 0·001
13 „ - - -	1·431	1·439	— 0·008
14 „ - -	1·489	1·493	— 0·004
15 „ - -	1·549	1·546	+ 0·003
16 „ - - -	1·600	1·594	+ 0·006
17 „ - - -	1·640	1·634	+ 0·006
18 „		1·658	
19 „ - - -	1·665	1·669	— 0·004
25 „ - - -	1·675	1·680	— 0·005
30 „ - - -	1·684	1·684	0·000

I have endeavoured to render the preceding results *sensible* by the construction of a line, which indicates the growth at different ages, but in one-tenth of the real proportions.

Thus, supposing that the new-born infant sets out from the point *o*, and proceeds along the axis *o*A, reaching in succession the points I., II., III., IV., &c., at the age of 1, 2, 3, 4, &c., years, his head will always be at the height of the curve *o*B, at the different points 1, 2, 3, 4, &c. We see that—

1. The most rapid growth takes place immediately after birth: the child in the course of one year grows 2 decimetres [7 8-10th inches] nearly.

2. The growth of a child diminishes as its age increases, until towards the age of four or five years, the period at which it reaches the maximum of probable life. Thus, during the second year after birth, the growth is only one-half of what it was during the first; and during the third year, only about one-third.

3. Proceeding from the fourth or fifth year, the increase of stature becomes almost exactly regular until about the sixteenth year, that is to say, until the age of puberty, and the annual increase is 56 millimetres [2 2-10th inches] nearly.

4. After the age of puberty, the stature still continues to increase, but only inconsiderably: from the sixteenth to the seventeenth year, it increases 4 centimetres [1 5-10th inches]; in the two succeeding years, it only increases 2½ centimetres [or a little less than 1 inch; in exact numbers, 0·984].

5. The full growth of man does not appear to be attained at his twenty-fifth year.

In what has just been said, I have only spoken of absolute growth: if we compare the annual growth with the stature already acquired, we shall find that the child increases in size two-fifths from birth to the end of the first year; during the second year, one-seventh; during the third year, one-eleventh; during the fourth year, one-fourteenth; during the fifth year, one-fifteenth; during the sixth year, one-eighteenth, &c.; so that the relative growth is continually decreasing from the time of birth.

The curve representing the growth of females, would be a little under that of males, and would be nearly equidistant from it, until the age of eleven or twelve years, when it tends more rapidly to become parallel to the axis *o*A.

It remains for me to speak of the formula by which I have calculated the numbers shown in the table given above. Letting the co-ordinates *y* and *z* represent the stature and the age corresponding to it, we have the following equation :—

$$y + \frac{y}{1000\,(T - y)} = ax + \frac{t + x}{1 + \frac{4}{3}x};$$

t and T are two constants which indicate the stature of the child at birth, and that of the fully developed individual: their values for Brussels are 0·500 and 1·684 metre. The coefficient *a* of the first term in the second number, will be calculated according to the different localities, from the regular growth which annually takes place between the fourth and fifth, to the fifteenth or sixteenth year: for Brussels, its value has been made equal to 0·0545 metre. I think that, in giving these three constants, we may use this formula with considerable advantage for other localities.

If we make *t* = 0·49 metre, T = 1·579 metre, *a* = 0·052 metre, agreeably to the observations above quoted for calculating the law of the growth of women for Brussels, we shall have—

$$y + \frac{y}{1000\,(1\cdot579 - y)} = 0\cdot0521\;x + \frac{0\cdot49 + x}{1 + \frac{x}{2}}.$$

By using this formula, I have calculated the numbers which appear in the third column of the following table:—

Law of the Growth of Woman.

Ages.	Stature Observed.	Stature Calculated.	Difference.
	metres.	metres.	metres.
Birth,	0·490	0·490	0·000
1 year,	..	0·690	..
2 ..	0·730	0·781	— 0·001
3 ..	0·853	0·852	+ 0·001
4 ..	0·913	0·915	— 0·002
5 ..	0·978	0·974	+ 0·004
6 ..	1·035	1·031	+ 0·004
7 ..	1·091	1·086	+ 0·005
8 ..	1·154	1·141	+ 0·013
9 ..	1·205	1·195	+ 0·010
10 ..	1·256	1·248	+ 0·008
11 ..	1·286	1·299	— 0·013
12 ..	1·340	1·353	— 0·013
13 ..	1·417	1·403	+ 0·014
14 ..	1·475	1·453	+ 0·022
15 ..	1·496	1·499	— 0·003
16 ..	1·518	1·535	— 0·017
17 ..	1·553	1·555	— 0·002
18 ..	1·564	1·564	0·000
19 ..	1·570	1·569	+ 0·001
20 ..	1·574	1·572	+ 0·002
Growth terminated,	1·579	1·579	0·000

The differences between the observed numbers and the calculated ones, are greater than in the table (already given) of the growth of man. It may be owing to the circumstance, that the observations have been less numerous, and made on fewer of the different classes of society, for the one sex than for the other. What appears to give additional support to my conjecture is, the manner in which the positive and negative signs succeed each other in the differences of the observed and calculated numbers. Moreover, it is remarkable that the formula may be entirely determined, when we have been enabled to give the statures of an individual corresponding to three different ages, sufficiently distant from each other.

Although the equation of which I have availed myself in the calculations, is of the third order, it resolves itself, like those of the second, into an unknown one, when we give the successive values of the other. Considered as belonging to a curve, it points out to us that there still exists another branch than the one we are occupied with; for to each value of the abscissa *x*, there are two values of *y*.

The curve of growths *o*B has an asymptote parallel to the axes of the abscissæ, situate at a distance from this axis equal to T, which is the height of man fully developed; moreover, this curve, proceeding from the point *o*, which corresponds to birth, towards the thirteenth or fourteenth years, is sensibly confounded with an hyperbola; for in these limits, the second term of

the first order is so small as to be considered nothing, so that we shall have—

$$y = ax + \frac{t + x}{1 + \frac{x}{2}}.$$

The curve *o*B does not merely indicate the growth of man from birth to complete maturity, but also those of the other side of the axis O*o*; that is to say, for the months which precede birth, the results which it presents are conformable to those observed with regard to the fœtus. This concordance is not always manifested until towards the fifth or sixth month before birth, which is the age at which the embryo becomes a fœtus. It is, moreover, true, that before this period the child is in a state which hardly yet appears to belong to human nature. The curve singularly represents this state, if we give any significance to it; for between five and six months before birth, it suddenly passes under the axis *o*A, and the values of statures, positive as they were, become negative: the curve in the negative region is lost in infinity, approaching an asymptote which corresponds to a value of $x = -\frac{3}{4}$; or, in other words, at nine months before birth, the period of conception. Without occupying ourselves with the stature of the infant while it is still an embryo, or altogether unformed, if we confine our calculations to the growth of the fœtus about five months before birth, we shall find the following results, by the side of which are written the results of measurements given in the *Dictionnaire des Sciences Medicales*:—

Age of the Infant.	Stature Calculated.	Stature Observed.
	metres.	metres.
Birth,	0·500	From 0·487 to 0·541
1 month before birth,	0·464	” 0·433 to 0·487
2 ” ” ”	0·419	” 0·379 to 0·433
3 ” ” ”	0·361	” 0·300 to 0·379
4 ” ” ”	0·165	” 0·216 to 0·300
5 ” ” ”	0·165	” 0·162 to 0·216

The calculated values fall, for each month, between the limits of the results of the observations. Moreover, it is well to observe that these results do not carry the same degree of exactness as those obtained after birth, because of the uncertainty of the period of conception, as well as the varying duration of pregnancy. What is most important for us to observe here, in my opinion, is the law of continuity which exists for the growth of the child immediately before and after birth. Admitting the approximative calculations of M. Chaussier, it will be found that *the fœtus increases almost as much in length in one month, as a child between six and sixteen years does in one year.*

In what has preceded, I have endeavoured to point out how the development of the stature of man and woman takes place: it now remains for me to say some words on the diminution which this element undergoes by age. From a great number of observations, of which we shall make greater use when speaking of the corresponding diminution of weight, it appears that it is chiefly towards the fiftieth year that the decrease becomes most apparent, and towards the end of life it amounts to about 6 or 7 centimetres [2 3-10th inches, or 2 6-10th inches]. From the number of individuals who have been measured, those have been carefully excluded who were much round-shouldered, or who could not make themselves straight during the observation.

Ages.	Stature of Men.	Stature of Women.
40 years,	1·684 metre.	1·579 metre.
50 ..	1·674 ..	1·536 ..
60 ..	1·639 ..	1·516 ..
70 ..	1·623 ..	1·514 ..
80 ..	1·613 ..	1·506 ..
90 ..	1·613 ..	1·505 ..

It may be asked if the diminution of stature towards the end of life is not rather apparent than real, and if it be not owing to the circumstance that longevity is generally shorter for individuals of great stature. ·At least, it would be interesting to examine if the size of man has any influence on the duration of his life.

I shall endeavour, in a few words, to present such of the results of my researches as appear to me most interesting: it is almost unnecessary to observe that these results only apply to Brussels and the province of Brabant.

1. The limits of growth in the two sexes are unequal: first, because woman is born smaller than man; second, because she sooner finishes her compléte development; third, because the annual increase which she receives is smaller than that of man.

2. The stature of the inhabitant of towns, at the age of 19, is greater than that of the country person by 2 to 3 centimetres [7-10ths to 1 inch nearly].

3. It does not appear that the growth of man is entirely completed at 25 years of age.

4. Individuals who live in affluence generally exceed the average height: misery and hard labour, on the contrary, appear to be obstacles to growth.

5. The growth of the child, even from several months before birth until complete development, follows such a law of continuity, that the increase dimi nishes successively with age.

6. Between the 5th and 16th years nearly, the annual growth is pretty regular, and it is one-twelfth of the growth of the foetus during the months before birth.

7. Subsequently to the 50th year, man and woman undergo a diminution of stature which becomes more and more marked, and may amount to from 6 to 7 centimetres [2 3-10ths or 2 0-10th inches] nearly, about the age of 80 years.

~~~~~~~~~~~~~

CHAPTER II.

OF THE DEVELOPMENT OF THE WEIGHT, AND OF ITS RELATIONS TO THE DEVELOPMENT OF THE HEIGHT OF THE BODY.

1. Weight and Height at Different Ages.

RESEARCHES on the height and weight of new-born infants have been made at the Foundling Hospital of Brussels. To ascertain the weight, the ordinary balance has been used; but in the different observations, the weight of the swaddling clothes has been taken. The average values obtained for 63 male and 56 female children, are as follows :—

	Weight.	Height.
Male children,	3·20 kilogrammes.	0·496 metre.*
Female children,	2·91 ..	0·483 ..†

Thus, *from the time of birth, there is an inequality in the weight and height of children of the two sexes, and this inequality is in favour of males.* The height corresponds nearly with what I have found from other observations.

By classing the infants who furnished the preceding average values according to their total weight, we find—

Infants Weighing	Boys.	Girls.	Total.
From 1·0 to 1·5 kilog.	..	1	1
.. 1·5 to 2·0 ..	..	1	1
.. 2·0 to 2·5 ..	3	7·	10
.. 2·5 to 3·0 ..	13	14	27
.. 3·0 to 3·5 ..	28	23	51
.. 3·5 to 4·0 ..	14	7	21
.. 4·0 to 4·5 ..	5	3	8
	63	56	119

* Here those children only have been measured whose weight had been ascertained. The number of observations is greater than I could avail myself of in my former researches.

† [The kilogramme is, as nearly as possible, 2 1-5th lbs. English.]

The extremes were as follows :—

	Boys.	Girls.
Minimum,	2·34 kilog.	1·12 kilog.
Maximum,	4·50 ..	4·25 ..

Professor Richter has made researches similar to the preceding at the Foundling Hospital of Moscow ;* and, according to his observations, of 44 new-born children, the sexes of whom are not stated, the average value was 9 1-15th pounds in weight, and 18½ inches (Paris) in length. I regret that I do not know the value of the weight which he employed. The height, which is 0·501 metres, new measure, is almost precisely the same as we have found for boys. The extremes obtained by M. Richter were as follows :—

	Weight.	Height.
Minimum,	5 pounds.	15 inches.
Maximum,	11 ..	21 ..

Thus, the weight of boys varies as 1 to 2, as I have found at Brussels. The extremes of length do not differ so much, and present values which differ very little from those which we have obtained.

Moreover, the extremes, at least of weight, may differ as much as the averages. We read in the *Dictionnaire des Sciences Medicales*, article *Foetus*—" The researches made at the Foundling Hospital, on more than 20,000 infants, prove that one infant, born at the full period and well-formed, generally weighs 6¼ pounds. Only a very small number of infants have been seen at this hospital weighing 10½ pounds, or others weighing only 3 pounds, or 2 pounds and some ounces." This value of 6¼ pounds, or 3·059 kilogrammes, obtained from so great a number of observations, agrees very nearly with the value—3·055 kilogrammes—obtained for Brussels, leaving out of consideration the distinction of the sexes: the extreme values likewise present very little difference.

It is remarkable that learned men who have made observations on the weight and height of new-born infants, should have attended so little to the distinction of the sexes. Although our results are not deduced from so large a number of observations as could be desired, yet we think we may conclude, with sufficient probability, that the average values of the weight and height of children of the two sexes present a very sensible difference.

From all the researches which have been made on the relations existing between the weight and the age of the foetus, it appears that the ratios present so much uncertainty, that we can scarcely make any use of them.

It is M. Chaussier, if I am not mistaken, who has made the remark, that an infant diminishes a little in weight immediately after birth. This curious remark deserves to be carefully verified: unfortunately, I have only been able to procure seven series of observations, which do not extend beyond the seventh day after birth. The average calculations for each day present the following values :—

	Weight of the Infant.
After birth,	3·126 kilog.
On the 2d day,	3·057 ..
.. 3d ..	3·017 ..
.. 4th ..	3·035 ..
.. 5th ..	3·039 ..
.. 6th ..	3·035 ..
.. 7th ..	3·060 ..

It really appears, then, from these numbers, that *the weight of the child diminishes a little immediately after birth,* and that it does not begin to increase in a sensible manner until after the first week.

* Synops, Praxis Medico-Obstetriciæ : 1810.

Thus we see that, from birth, there is an inequality in the weight of children of the two sexes: however, we shall examine if this inequality is produced again at different ages, and examine the modifications which it undergoes. I have already stated the analogous results for height; nevertheless, I thought it would be useful to state again the new numbers which have been obtained from the individuals of both sexes, on whom observations were made to determine the weight. It was interesting to place these two elements, during their progressive development in the same individual, opposite each other.

In estimating the weight, I have generally used the balance of Sanctorius. Since this balance is not so sensible when slightly charged, and also since great care is required in placing the bodies to be weighed by it, children of tender age have been almost constantly weighed in the arms of persons whose weight had previously been taken.

The observations on children from 4 to 12 years of age, have for the most part been made in the schools of Brussels and at the Orphan Hospital. The weights of young persons have been taken more especially in the colleges and at the Medical School of Brussels. For more advanced ages, individuals of different classes have been taken, though those of the lower orders have been least numerous.

For old men, the weights have chiefly been taken in the large and magnificent hospital recently erected at Brussels. The two following tables point out the results, such as they are, for men and women.

The first column gives the ages; the second and third point out the average values of the height and weight which correspond to these different ages. The values of the height are almost the same as those previously given, except for individuals who are more than 16 or 17 years of age; which no doubt arise from individuals of the lower class having been less numerous in these than in the former observations. Indeed, I have already shown that young persons who apply themselves to study, and persons in the affluent classes generally, are taller than others. In the third column, the ratios of weight and size for different ages are calculated, their values being considered as abstract numbers. These ratios are not deduced immediately from the numbers contained in the two preceding columns, but are the average of the ratios calculated for each individual. In the last place, the four last columns point out the maximum and minimum of height and weight at each age, for individuals who are well-formed.

Table of the Size and Weight of Man at Different Ages.								Table of the Size and Weight of Woman at Different Ages.							
Ages.	Size.	Weight.	Ratio of Weight to Size.	Size Observed.		Weight Observed.		Ages.	Size.	Weight.	Ratio of Weight to Size.	Size Observed.		Weight Observed.	
				Max.	Min.	Max.	Min.					Max.	Min.	Max.	Min.
	met.	kilog.		met.	met.	kilog.	kilog.		met.	kilog.		met.	met.	kilog.	kilog.
Birth,	0·496	3·20	6·19	0·532	0·438	4·50	2·34	Birth,	0·483	2·91	6·15	0·555	0·438	4·25	1·12
1 year,	0·696	10·00	14·20	0·750	0·682	11·00	9·00	1 year,	0·690	9·30	13·50	0·704	0·660	10·5	8·3
2 ..	0·797	12·00	15·00	0·824	0·730	13·50	10·50	2 ..	0·780	11·40	14·50	0·798	0·720	12·0	8·3
3 ..	0·860	13·21	15·36	0·875	0·840	13·60	12·10	3 ..	0·850	12·45	14·70	0·895	0·795	15·8	10·5
4 ..	0·932	15·07	16·32	0·965	0·840	18·20	12·50	4 ..	0·910	14·18	15·10	0·950	0·810	15·8	11·5
5 ..	0·990	16·70	16·98	1·080	0·915	18·50	14·00	5 ..	0·974	15·50	15·70	1·085	0·876	17·5	13·3
6 ..	1·046	18·04	17·44	1·115	0·960	20·40	15·80	6 ..	1·032	16·74	16·24	1·085	0·936	20·3	13·3
7 ..	1·112	20·16	18·31	1·162	1·109	24·50	17·20	7 ..	1·096	18·45	16·85	1·177	1·050	23·4	16·0
8 ..	1·170	22·26	18·92	1·260	1·120	28·50	19·00	8 ..	1·139	19·82	17·45	1·380	1·050	23·4	16·0
9 ..	1·227	24·09	19·68	1·325	1·150	29·00	22·20	9 ..	1·200	22·44	18·65	1·380	1·110	25·7	18·3
10 ..	1·282	26·12	20·37	1·325*	1·163	32·00	22·70	10 ..	1·248	24·24	19·45	1·380	1·160	28·3	20·3
11 ..	1·327	27·85	21·58	1·405	1·215	33·80	25·00	11 ..	1·275	26·25	20·60	1·385	1·160	39·8	21·6
12 ..	1·359	31·00	22·80	1·450	1·270	36·30	25·00	12 ..	1·327	30·54	23·00	1·476	1·160	42·8	21·6
13 ..	1·403	35·32	25·30	1·490	1·300	39·50	34·60	13 ..	1·386	34·65	24·50	1·580	1·160	42·8	21·6
14 ..	1·487	40·50	27·49	1·630	1·330	45·00	37·00	14 ..	1·447	38·10	25·35	1·580	1·160	51·0	32·0
15 ..	1·559	46·41	29·88	1·658	1·380	61·50	37·00	15 ..	1·475	41·30	28·10	1·638	1·160	55·2	32·0
16 ..	1·610	53·39	33·00	1·730	1·430	61·50	40·00	16 ..	1·500	44·44	29·62	1·638	1·160	57·6	32·0
17 ..	1·670	57·40	34·25	1·790	1·467	65·50	45·00	17 ..	1·544	49·08	31·75	1·688	1·284	61·6	..
18 ..	1·700	61·26	35·67	1·790	..	67·00	45·00	18 ..	1·562	53·10	34·05	1·740	..	79·9	..
19 ..	1·706	63·32	37·00	1·800	..	70·00	48·20	20 ..	1·570	54·46	34·70	..	..	..	..
20 ..	1·711	65·00	37·99	1·838	..	72·70	..	25 ..	1·577	55·08	35·26	..	..	..	..
25 ..	1·722	68·29	39·66	1·890	..	98·50	..	30 ..	1·579	55·14	35·90	..	..	..	..
30 ..	1·722	68·90	40·02	..	..	..	..	40 ..	1·555	56·65	36·50	..	..	..	..
40 ..	1·713	68·81	40·03	..	..	..	..	50 ..	1·536	58·45	38·15	..	1·444	90·5	39·8
50 ..	1·674	67·45	40·14	..	..	..	..	60 ..	1·516	56·73	37·28	..	1·436	..	..
60 ..	1·639	65·50	40·01	..	..	..	..	70 ..	1·514	53·72	35·49	..	1·431	93·8	..
70 ..	1·623	63·03	38·83	..	..	..	49·1	80 ..	1·506	51·52	34·21	1·701	1·408	72·5	33·0
80 ..	1·613	61·22	37·96	1·820	1·467	83·00	49·7								

The numbers in the preceding tables are such as have been obtained from direct observation; but they must be subjected to two corrections—in the first place, because the persons have always been weighed in their dresses; and, secondly, because observations have not been made on all classes of society.

The first cause of error which has been pointed out, may be removed, or at least diminished to some extent. The average weight of the clothes at different ages may be determined very precisely, and then it is only necessary to subtract its value from each of the corresponding numbers of the table of weights. From different experiments, I think we may admit, as near the truth, that the average weight of the clothes at different ages is one-eighteenth of the total weight of the male body, and a twenty-fourth part of the total weight of the female. With this value, I have corrected the numbers of the preceding table, except for new-born infants, because the numbers had already undergone this correction, from direct experiment, immediately after weighing them [the infants].

The second cause of error may also be removed: indeed, we shall soon see, that of individuals of the same age, the weight may be considered as having a pretty constant relation to the size of the body. It will be sufficient, then, to know the ratios inserted in the fourth column of the preceding tables, and to have a good general table of the growths, to deduce the corresponding table of the weight. It is in making use of the *table of growths* given above, and constructed with elements collected from all classes of society, that I have calculated the following table, in which I have also made the necessary correction for clothing :—

* When a number is repeated, it is because the maximum of this year was less than that of the preceding. The inverse takes place in the column of the minima.

Table of the Development of the Height and Weight.

Ages.	Men.		Women.	
	Height.	Weight.	Height.	Weight.
	metres.	kilog.	metres.	kilog.
Birth,	0·500	3·20	0·490	2·91
1 year,	0·698	9·45	0·690	8·79
2 "	0·791	11·34	0·781	10·67
3 "	0·864	12·47	0·852	11·79
4 "	0·928	14·23	0·915	13·00
5 "	0·988	15·77	0·974	14·36
6 "	1·047	17·24	1·031	16·00
7 "	1·105	19·10	1·086	17·54
8 "	1·162	20·76	1·141	19·08
9 "	1·219	22·65	1·195	21·36
10 "	1·275	24·52	1·248	23·52
11 "	1·330	27·10	1·299	25·65
12 "	1·385	29·82	1·353	29·82
13 "	1·439	34·38	1·403	32·94
14 "	1·493	38·76	1·453	36·70
15 "	1·546	43·62	1·499	40·37
16 "	1·594	49·67	1·535	43·57
17 "	1·634	52·85	1·555	47·31
18 "	1·658	57·85	1·564	51·03
20 "	1·674	60·06	1·572	52·28
25 "	1·680	62·93	1·577	53·28
30 "	1·684	63·65	1·579	54·33
40 "	1·684	63·67	1·579	55·23
50 "	1·674	63·46	1·536	56·16
60 "	1·639	61·94	1·516	54·30
70 "	1·623	59·52	1·514	51·51
80 "	1·613	57·83	1·506	49·37
90 "	1·613	57·83	1·505	49·34

To render the preceding results more apparent, I have constructed two lines, which represent the increase of weight which men and women undergo at different ages: these lines have, for abscissæ, the ages, and for ordinates, the corresponding weights. We perceive, at the first glance, that, *at equal ages, man is generally heavier than woman; about the age of twelve years only are individuals of both sexes nearly of the same weight.* This circumstance is owing to the development of the weight being inconsiderable in both sexes, until the time of puberty, when, on the contrary, it becomes very apparent. Now, since puberty takes place sooner in woman, this acceleration causes a temporary disappearance of the inequality of weight which existed between children of both sexes, and which is, for children between one and eleven years of age, from one kilogramme to one and a half. The difference of weight of the sexes is more considerable in adult persons; it is about five kilogrammes between the sixteenth and twentieth years, and more than seven after this period.

Man reaches his maximum of weight about the age of 40, *and he begins to waste in a sensible manner about the age of* 60 : *at the age of* 80 *he has lost about six kilogrammes* [16 lbs. troy]. *His height has also diminished, and this diminution is about seven centimetres* [2 7-10ths inches].

The same observation applies to women: in old age, they generally lose from six to seven kilogrammes in weight, and seven centimetres in stature. I have taken care not to include ricketty individuals in these valuations, or badly formed persons, or even those who were round-shouldered, and unable to stand upright for many minutes.

Woman attains her maximum of weight later than man; she weighs the most about the age of 50 *years:* setting out from about the age of 19, the development of her weight is nearly stationary, until the period of procreation is passed.

The extreme limits of the weight of well-formed individuals have been 49·1 and 98·5 kilogrammes for men; and for women 39·8 and 93·8 kilogrammes.

The limits of height have been 1·467 and 1·890 metres for men; and 1·444 and 1·740 metres for women.

The average weight at 19 years, is nearly that of old persons of the two sexes.

When man and woman have attained their complete development, they weigh nearly exactly twenty times as much as at birth; whilst the height is only about three and one-fourth times what it was at the same period.

One year after birth, children of both sexes have tripled their weight; boys weigh 9·45 kilogrammes, and girls 8·79 kilogrammes, At 6 years, they have doubled this latter weight, and at 13, they have quadrupled it.

Immediately before puberty, man and woman have one-half the weight which they have after their complete development.

I am indebted to the kindness of M. Villermé for the communication of the unpublished researches of Tenon on the weight of man, which appear to have been made in 1783. They were made in a village in the environs of Paris—the village of Massy—where Tenon had his country house. These researches, which comprise observations on 60 men between 25 and 40 years of age, and as many women of the same ages, give the following results:—

	Maximum.	Minimum.	Average.
	kilog.	kilog.	kilog.
Weight of man,	83·307	51·398	62·071
" woman,	74·038	36·805	54·916

In all these observations, the weight of the clothes has been subtracted, and care has been taken not to include any female who was pregnant.

If we now compare these numbers with those I obtained at Cambridge, made on men from 18 to 23 years of age, weighed with clothes, we shall find, dividing into series of tens the 80 individuals whose weights were obtained—

	Stones.	Pounds.
1st series,	108	9
2d "	111	2¾
3d "	114	6¾
4th "	101	0¼
5th "	102	5
6th "	107	12½
7th "	103	6¼
8th "	112	2¼
Average,	107	$10\frac{27}{32}$

Which gives, for the weight of one individual, about 151 pounds, or 68·465 kilogrammes, which is nearly the weight of a man of 30 in Brabant, when weighed with his clothes on.

If, on the other hand, we compare the weight of children of the lower classes in England, we shall find the following results, which have been communicated to me by Mr J. W. Cowell, taken on 420 boys working in the factories, and 223 not working in factories; and 651 girls working in factories, and 201 not working in those places.

Average Weight of Children of the Lower Orders.

Ages.	Boys		Girls	
	Working in Factories.	not Working in Factories.	Working in Factories.	not Working in Factories.
	kilog.	kilog.	kilog.	kilog.
9 years,	23·47	24·15	23·18	22·87
10 "	25·84	27·33	24·85	24·68
11 "	28·04	26·46	27·06	27·72
12 "	29·91	30·49	29·96	29·96
13 "	32·69	34·17	33·21	32·97
14 "	34·95	35·67	37·82	37·83
15 "	40·06	39·37	39·84	42·44
16 "	44·43	50·01	43·62	41·33
17 "	47·36	53·41	45·44	46·45
18 "	48·12	57·27	48·22	55·32

These numbers were collected at Manchester and Stockport; the children were weighed in summer, and consequently were lightly clothed, and they had nothing in their pockets. We see here again, as in the height, that it is only after puberty that, at equal ages, we observe a difference in weight. The comparison of weights seems to be rather in favour of Belgic children; it is true that those of England were taken from the lower orders.

2. Relations between the Weight and Height.

If man increased equally in all his dimensions, his weight at different ages would be as the cube of his height. Now, this is not what we really observe. The increase of weight is slower, except during the first year after birth; then the proportion which we have just pointed out is pretty regularly observed. But after this period, and until near the age of puberty, the weight increases nearly as the square of the height. The development of the weight again becomes very rapid at the time of puberty, and almost stops at the twenty-fifth year. In general, we do not err much when we assume that, *during development, the squares of the weight at different ages are as the fifth powers of the height;* which naturally leads to this conclusion, in supposing the specific gravity constant, that the transverse growth of man is less than the vertical.

However, if we compare two individuals who are fully developed and well-formed with each other, to ascertain the relations existing between the weight and stature, we shall find that *the weight of developed persons, of different heights, is nearly as the square of the stature.* Whence it naturally follows, that a transverse section, giving both the breadth and thickness, is just proportioned to the height of the individual. We furthermore conclude that, proportion still being attended width predominates in individuals of small stature.

Taking twelve of the smallest individuals of both sexes, and twelve of the largest, of those who have been submitted to our observations, we have obtained the following values as the average of stature, and the ratio of weight to the stature :—

Men.	Stature.	Ratio of Weight to Stature.
The smallest, - - -	1.511 metre.	36·7 kilog.
The largest, - -	1·822 ..	41·4 ..
Women.		
The smallest, - - -	1·456 ..	35·6 ..
The largest, - - -	1·672 ..	38·0 ..

Thus, the stature of men and women, fully developed and well-formed, varied in the proportion of five to six nearly : it is almost the same with the ratios of the weight to the stature of the two sexes ; whence it naturally follows, as we have already said above, that the weight is in proportion to the square of the stature.*

Now, let us suppose that we have the individuals grouped, not according to age, but to stature, and that we have taken the average of the weight of each group, for example, and that we proceed by ten centimetres at a time : we shall have groups of children at first, then groups of children with whom some adult persons are classed, which will be the case with men commencing at 1·47 metres nearly, and women at 1·41 metres. If we afterwards reduce these numbers to a tabular form, we shall arrive at the following results, the weight of the clothes having been subtracted :—

* Calling t and T the statures, and p and P the corresponding weights of the smallest and the largest individuals, we have, in fact, almost exactly, $t : T :: 5 : 6$, by the numbers of the first column, belonging to men, and $\frac{p}{t} : \frac{P}{T} :: 5 : 6$ for those of the second; from which we find that $t : T :: \frac{p}{2} : \frac{P}{T}$, or, in other words, $t^2 : T^2 :: p : P$. It is the same with the numbers belonging to females.

Relation of Stature to Weight.

Stature.	Men.		Women.	
	Weight.	Ratio.	Weight.	Ratio.
At Birth, -	3·20	6·19	2·91	6·03
0·60 metre,	6·20	10·33	~	~
0·70 ~ -	9·30	13·27	9·06	12·94
0·80 ~ -	11·36	14·20	11·21	14·01
0·90 ~ -	13·50	15·00	13·42	14·91
1·00 ~ -	15·90	15·90	15·82	15·82
1·10 ~ -	18·50	16·82	18·30	16·64
1·20 ~ -	21·72	18·10	21·51	17·92
1·30 ~ -	26·63	20·04	26·83	20·64
1·40 ~ -	34·48	24·63	37·28	26·63
1·50 ~ -	46·29	30·86	48·00	32·00
1·60 ~ -	57·15	35·72	56·73	35·45
1·70 ~ -	63·28	37·22	65·20	38·35
1·80 ~ -	70·61	39·23	~	~
1·90 ~ -	75·56	39·77	~	~

We see that, statures being equal, woman weighs a little less than man until she attains the height of 1 metre 3 decimetres, which nearly corresponds to the period of puberty, and that she weighs a little more for higher statures. This difference, for the most part, proceeds from aged females being mingled with groups of a moderate stature sooner than males are ; and, at equal statures, as we have already stated, aged persons weigh more than young ones.

To apply the preceding to determine the age of a *non-adult* person, from a knowledge of the weight and stature only, let us suppose the height of the person to be 1·23 metre, and the weight 24 kilogrammes, he being, moreover, of the male sex. We shall immediately see, from the preceding table, that he is heavy in proportion to his stature ; the table before informs us that, by taking the height alone, he ought to be a little more than nine years of age, and considering the weight alone, he should be under ten ; so that we may pronounce, with great probability of truth, that the individual in question must be between nine and ten.

3. Weight of a Population.—Weight of the Human Skeleton.

The following table may serve to determine the weight of a population composed of men, women, and children, or of a population composed of individuals of certain limited ages : it has been formed by taking the numbers belonging to each age from a population table, and multiplying them by the weight of individuals of this age.*

Table of the Weight of a Population of 10,000 Souls.

Ages.	Men.	Women.	Total.
	kilog.	kilog.	kilog.
0 to 1 year, - -	0·894	0·803	1·697
1 to 2 ~ - -	1·462	1·324	2·786
2 to 3 ~ - -	1·504	1·372	2·876
3 to 4 ~ - -	1·676	1·485	3·161
4 to 5 ~ - -	1·964	1·658	3·522
5 to 6 ~ - -	2·017	1·765	3·782
6 to 8 ~ - -	4·251	3·786	8·037
8 to 10 ~ - -	4·768	4·318	9·086
10 to 12 ~ - -	5·263	4·827	10·090
12 to 14 ~ - -	6·332	5·977	12·309
14 to 16 ~ - -	8·805	7·801	16·606
16 to 20 ~ - -	18·902	17·700	36·602
20 to 25 ~ - -	25·292	23·308	48·600
25 to 30 ~ - -	25·603	22·770	48·373
30 to 40 ~ - -	39·396	39·548	78·944
40 to 50 ~ - -	28·720	31·470	60·190
50 to 60 ~ - -	24·122	24·634	48·756
60 to 70 ~ - -	23·620	16·458	40·118
70 to 90 ~ - -	9·620	7·808	17·428
80 and upwards, - -	2·320	1·998	4·318
Total, - - -	236·471	220·810	457·281

* The population table made use of in these calculations is one which will be found above, taken from the *Recherches sur la Mortalité et la Reproduction. Bruxelles* : 1832.

Thus, taking at once a population of 10,000 souls, without distinction of age or sex, the weight will be 457,000 kilogrammes nearly, 236,000 being that of the male portion. Thus we see that *the average weight of an individual, without reference to age or sex, is* 45·7 *kilogrammes nearly; and, considering the sexes,* 47 *kilogrammes for a man* [125 9-10ths lbs. troy], *and* 42½ *kilogrammes for a woman* [74 lbs. troy]. The whole population of Brussels, which amounts to 100,000, would weigh 4,572,810 kilogrammes; or nearly four and a half times as much as a cube of water 10 metres square: and the whole human race, computed at 737,000,000, would not weigh as much as 33 cubes of water 100 metres square: a value which at first sight appears small, since such a volume of water might be contained in a basin having a surface of less than one-third of an acre [*hectare*], and a depth of 100 metres.

To the preceding data, I shall add some measurements of the human skeleton, which have been communicated to me by MM. Van Esschen and Guiette. They will throw additional light on our present subject.

Dimensions.	Number of Skeletons.				
	No. 1.*	No. 2.†	No. 3.‡	No. 4.§	No. 5.‖
	kilog.	kilog.	kilog.	kilog.	kilog.
Weights, - - -	4·2	4·4	5·7	5·2	3·0
	met.	met.	met.	met.	met.
Statures, - -	1·685	1·640	1·667	1·755	1·500
Height of head, - -	0·138	0·134	0·136	0·135	0·135
— of spinal column,	0·590	0·560	0·563	0·550	0·470
— of pelvis, - -	0·210	0·186	0·182	0·225	0·152
Length of the upper extremities, } -	0·779	0·735	0·754	0·790	0·662
Length of the lower extremities, }	0·917	0·870	0·885	0·970	0·800

The two last skeletons, belonging to females, did not present any essential difference from the three first, which were males.

We see, from the preceding table, that the weight of a skeleton prepared some years, scarcely exceeds the weight of a child at birth.

From the foregoing, we deduce the following conclusions:—

1. From birth there is an inequality, both in weight and stature, between children of the two sexes; the average weight of a boy being 3·20 kilogrammes [8 5-10ths lbs. troy], that of a girl 2·91 kilogrammes [7 7-10ths lbs. troy]; the stature of a boy is 0·496 metres, and that of a girl 0·483 metres.

2. The weight of a child diminishes a little towards the third day after birth, and does not begin to increase sensibly until after the first week.

3. At equal ages, man is generally heavier than woman: about the age of 12 years only are the individuals of both sexes of about the same weight. Between 1 and 11 years, the difference in weight is from one kilogramme to one and a half; between 16 and 20, it is six kilogrammes nearly; and after this period eight to nine kilogrammes.

4. When man and woman have attained their full development, they weigh almost exactly twenty times as much as at birth; and their stature is about three and one-fourth times greater than it was at the same period.

* No. 1. Natural skeleton of a man of about thirty-five years of age, prepared seven years.

† No. 2. Skeleton of a man about twenty-five years of age, prepared six years.

‡ No. 3. Skeleton of a man. Age and date of the preparation unknown.

§ No. 4. Skeleton of a woman. Age and date of the preparation unknown.

‖ No. 5. Skeleton of a woman aged fifteen years, prepared one year.

5. In old age, man and woman lose about six or seven kilogrammes in weight, and seven centimetres in stature.

6. During the development of individuals of both sexes, we may consider the square of the weight, at different ages, as proportioned to the fifth power of their stature.

7. After the full development of individuals of both sexes, the weight is almost as the square of the stature.

From the two preceding relations, we infer, that increase in height is greater than the transverse increase, including breadth and thickness.

8. Man attains the maximum of his weight at about 40, and begins to waste in a sensible degree about the 60th year.

9. Woman attains the maximum of her weight about the age of 50. During the period of reproduction, namely, from the 18th to the 40th year, her weight scarcely increases in a perceptible degree.

10. The weight of individuals who have been measured, and who were fully developed and well-formed, varies within extremes which are nearly as 1 to 2; whilst the stature only varies within limits which, at the most, are as 1 to 1¼. This is inferred from the following values, furnished by observation:—

	Maximum.	Minimum.	Average.
Weight of man,	98·5 kilog.	49·1 kilog.	63·7 kilog.
— woman,	93·8 —	39·8 —	55·2 —
Stature of man,	1·890 met.	1·467 met.	1·684 met.
— woman,	1·740 —	1·408 —	1·579 —

11. At equal statures, woman weighs a little less than man before reaching the height of 1·3 metres, which almost corresponds to the period of puberty; and she weighs a little more for higher statures.

12. The average weight of an individual, without reference to age or sex, is 45·7 kilogrammes; and, taking sex into account, 47 kilogrammes for man, and 42·5 kilogrammes for woman.

~~~~~~~~~

CHAPTER III.

OF THE DEVELOPMENT OF STRENGTH OR POWER.

THE measure of strength is one of the elements which we are most anxious to ascertain with some degree of precision; not merely because this subject of investigation has occupied the attention of many observers; but since their principal object was to ascertain the useful effect of power, what they have done has a characteristic nature, which distinguishes their results from those which I propose to determine with a scientific purpose. Thus, Désaguiliers, De la Hire, Guenyveau, Coulomb, Schulze, &c., have chiefly investigated the relations which exist between the speed and the burden carried, in respect to a man employed either in carrying burdens or drawing them. I shall not enter into the details of the results which they have obtained, since they can be found in the principal treatises on practical mechanics. What is of most importance for us to know here is, I think, what relation the intensity of power which man can display (either with his hands or loins, without subjecting him to a day's labour), bears, in its development, to the age of the person: this latter question is composed of more complex elements.

To determine the different degrees of our physical power, different instruments have been proposed, the least imperfect of which is undoubtedly the dynamometer of Régnier.* However, this instrument still

* [The dynamometer cannot well be described in mere words. All that can be said of it is, that it is an instrument so contrived as to exhibit, on a dial-plate, the measure of strength resident in the arms and loins of the parties subjected to trial. M. Quetelet's observations may make this point more clear.]

leaves much to be desired ; and, fully perceiving its defects when I commenced the experiments which I am now about to state, I was far from supposing they were so great they really are. The most considerable results om its form; indeed, the dynamometer is managed with varying degrees of facility, and estimates of power, varying in accuracy, are given, according to the size of the hand and length of the fingers. This defect is especially apparent with children: it is almost necessary to employ different instruments for different ages. These inconveniences led me to think of a dynamometer, in which the two steel plates to be brought into apposition should, with a maximum of power, assume that position in the hand which was most favourable to its development: unfortunately, other labours have prevented me from prosecuting these attempts, and undertaking a new series of observations. Therefore, I must confine myself to giving the results obtained with the dynamometer of Régnier, premising that they do not present that degree of accuracy which I was anxious to give them.

I think we may even already suspect the imperfection of the dynamometer, from the discordant results obtained by different experimenters who have used it.

According to Régnier, a man from 25 to 30, is in possession of his greatest strength, and by pressing strongly with both hands, makes an effort equal to 50 kilogrammes [134 lbs. troy], and raises a weight of 13 myriagrammes [260 lbs. troy, nearly] He retains this power until nearly 50, when it begins to decrease.* The strength of woman is been considered as equal to that of a man of 15 or 16, or to two-thirds of the power of an ordinary man.

Régnier has also found that, by trying first one hand and then the other, that the right hand is generally stronger than the left; and the sum of these is commonly equal to the power of both hands acting together.

Other experiments have since been made by Peron, who has stated the results in the account of his voyage to Australasia. Ransonnet has also made dynamometric experiments in the roadstead of Havre, on 345 individuals belonging to the companies of two frigates and a brig which he commanded. Collecting the values obtained by these different observers, we have the following table:—

Persons experimented on.	Observers.	Strength.	
		Manual.	Lumbar.
		kilog.	Average.
French, from 25 to 30 years,	Régnier,	50·0	13·0
" " 25 to 45 "	Ransonnet,	46·3	14·2
" " " "	Péron,	69·2	22·1
Natives of New Holland,	"	51·8	14·8
Malays of the Island of Timor,	"	58·7	16·2

The degrees of strength of the French, according to these observations, we see differ very much: the results of Péron differing especially from those of Ransonnet and Régnier.† It would appear that Péron has made a mistake in reading the degrees of the dynamometer; at least this seems to be the case, from the correction which has subsequently been made by Freycinet and Bailly, who were of the number of persons experimented on by Péron, and who are found to have a lumbar power sensibly smaller than that placed opposite their names in the table. According

* Dictionnaire des Sciences Medicales, article Dynamometre, et Description et Usage du Dynamometre. (Journal de l'Ecole Polytechnique, Prairial, an 6.)

† M. Ransonnet has kindly favoured me with some accounts of the observations which were required of him, and made with an instrument the accuracy of which he cannot warrant, not having had an opportunity of testing it himself.

to M. Freycinet, instead of the lumbar powers stated by Péron, we must read as follows:—

15·9 myriagr. instead of 22·1, for the French.
10·1 " " 14·8, .. New Hollanders.
11·3 " " 16·2, .. Malays of Timor.

However the case may be, by considering the values of Péron as relative, it would appear that the strength of the French sailors was greater than that of savages; and this result agrees with the accounts of many voyagers.

Dynamometric experiments require the greatest precaution. I have seen the same persons obtain exceedingly different results from successive efforts. A cause of frequent error, when sufficient precaution is not taken in using the instrument of Régnier to measure the lumbar power, is, that the needle is made to move as much by pressing the instrument between the knees, as by pulling. Indeed, it is difficult to pull without bringing the knees towards each other, and thus pressing the elliptic spring in the direction of its small axis, where it yields most readily: the position in which we are placed to pull, and the height of the stature, have likewise some influence. It is also necessary to keep trying the accuracy of the instrument, especially towards the bottom of the scale, because it is generally not so sensible for small weights.

I regret that I could not increase my observations to the extent I desired; and I bring forward my results with diffidence. The number of individuals of each age experimented upon was at least 10: these persons generally belonged to the better class; and those below 25, of the young men, were generally taken in the colleges, and at the Medical School of Brussels: the young women, also, were taken from the schools and the Orphan Hospital.

It is well, in measuring the power of a person, to take the average of several successive observations, because we find the results vary slightly; and generally the first effort is more powerful than the second, the second than the third, and so on, until we arrive at a certain limit; but the difference is not very great after the first few trials.* We may find a difference of one or two degrees, or more, between the first effort and the extreme; consequently, these observations admit of great chance of error.

Observations on the Lumbar Power, estimated by means of the Dynamometer.

Ages.		Lumbar Power.		Ratio of the Strength of Men and Women.
		Men.	Women.	
		myriag.	myriag.	
6 years,	- -	2·0	..	..
7 "	- -	2·7	..	..
8 "		..	2·4	..
9 "	- - -	4·0	3·9	1·33
10 "	- - -	4·6	3·1	1·48
11 "		4·8	3·7	1·30
12 "		5·1	4·0	1·28
13 "	- -	6·9	4·4	1·57
14 "	- -	8·1	5·0	1·62
15 "	- -	8·8	5·3	1·66
16 "	- -	10·2	5·9	1·72
17 "	- -	12·6	6·4	1·97
18 "	- -	13·0	6·7	1·94
19 "	- -	13·2	6·4	2·06
20 "	- -	13·8	6·8	2·03
21 "	- -	14·6	7·2	2·05
25 "	- -	15·5	7·7	2·01
30 "		15·4	..	..
40 "	- -	12·2	..	..
50 "	- -	10·1	5·9	1·71
60 "		9·3	..	..

In this table, I have not included boys under six, and girls under eight years of age, because of the difficulty of teaching them how to handle the dyna-

* M. Edwards has told me, that after dinner he has generally observed the contrary with strong persons, the first effort being somewhat less intense than the succeeding ones.

mometer, and the errors which would have resulted therefrom. It is necessary to all the preceding values, to add the weight of the dynamometer, which is certainly a part of the resistance to overcome: this amounts to one kilogramme.

If we had extremely sensible and suitable instruments for measuring the lumbar power of children, it is evident that we could not begin to make use of them before the age of two years, since before this period the child cannot stand upright alone, nor carry an additional weight. It is to be observed that, of all the individuals figured in the table, the lumbar power is sufficient to raise a load or overcome an obstacle exceeding the weight of the individual. The load a man can carry relatively to his weight, increases with his growth until maturity, and the perfect man can raise more than double his own weight.

The lumbar power of females differs less from that of males during childhood than after complete development. During childhood, the lumbar strength of boys is about one-third more than that of girls; towards the age of puberty, one-half; and the strength of a developed man is double that of a woman.

Professions produce a very sensible difference. I have seen labouring masons and carpenters move the dynamometer 20 degrees or more. The average of several servants, between 20 and 40 years of age, has given me a value of 10 or 11 degrees.

To measure the power of the hands presents the greatest obstacles. It seems to me that it is almost impossible to rely on the accuracy of the results, unless the observations have been made with the greatest care, and by one and the same person. The first and greatest obstacle proceeds from the unequal size of the hands, and the difficulty of grasping the instrument. From all the corrections which I have made, I think I may rely on the accuracy of my own results: and, nevertheless, they differ so much from those obtained by the observers quoted, that I deliberated some time in using them, the more so since they are, like all the measures taken with Régnier's dynamometer, subject to undergo a previous correction, owing to the unequal size of the hands. To show how important this correction is, I made different trials with the dynamometers, placing my hands in different positions, and I have obtained extremely dissimilar values. We may judge better from the following:—

The dynamometer I have used is made, like all others, of a spring almost of an elliptic form: the lengths of the greater and lesser axis are 30 and 5·5 centimetres respectively; the dial and the index are so placed that the hands, when most approximated, are still 2·5 centimetres distant from each other; and pressure is made at a certain distance from the small axis, where the maximum of effect is produced. We obtain, therefore, only a part of the action which might be produced by pressing both extremities of the small axis. Moreover, it appears that the dynamometer I have used has been graduated, taking this distance into account. I was then desirous to know what would be the effect produced by increasing the distance between the hands, and I have obtained these values:—

Distance of the Hands.	Degrees of the Dynamometer.
25 mill.	80·5
35 ··	64·0
45 ··	54·5
56 ··	49·5
65 ··	44·0
75 ··	38·0
85 ··	34·6

Thus, by placing the hands so that they were each, when least distant, one centimetre from the dial, and consequently 45 millimetres from each other, I only produced an effort of 54·5 instead of 80·5—a difference of 26 degrees. Now, many persons, trying their

manual strength by the dynamometer, generally place their hands in the manner I have stated; they must then give very erroneous results. Women and children, especially, have another disadvantage in using the dynamometer, for the opening which they are obliged to allow their hands does not permit them to press with the power they are capable of. Also, I think the values I have obtained for them are generally too low.

Observations on the Power of the Hands, from Experiments with the Dynamometer.

Ages.	Power of Men			Power of Women		
	with both Hands.	with the Right Hand.	with the Left Hand.	with both Hands.	with the Right Hand.	with the Left Hand.
	kilog.	kilog.	kilog.	kilog.	kilog.	kilog.
6 years,	10·3	4·0	2·0	..	..	..
7 ··	14·0	7·0	4·0	..	..	..
8 ··	..	..	..	11·8	5·6	2·8
9 ··	20·0	8·5	5·0	15·5	4·7	4·0
10 ··	20·0	9·8	8·4	16·2	5·6	4·3
11 ··	29·2	10·7	9·2	19·5	8·2	6·7
12 ··	33·6	13·9	11·7	23·0	10·1	7·0
13 ··	39·8	16·6	15·0	26·7	11·0	8·1
14 ··	47·9	21·4	18·8	33·4	13·6	11·3
15 ··	57·1	27·8	22·6	35·6	15·0	14·1
16 ··	63·9	32·3	26·8	37·7	17·3	16·6
17 ··	71·0	36·2	31·9	40·9	20·7	18·2
18 ··	79·2	38·6	35·0	43·6	20·7	19·0
19 ··	79·4	35·4	35·0	44·9	21·6	19·7
20 ··	84·3	39·3	37·2	45·2	22·0	19·4
21 ··	86·4	43·0	38·0	47·0	23·5	20·5
25 ··	88·7	44·1	40·0	50·0	24·5	21·6
30 ··	89·0	44·7	41·3	..	..	..
40 ··	87·0	41·2	38·3	..	..	..
50 ··	74·0	36·4	33·0	47·0	23·2	20·0
60 ··	56·0	30·5	26·0	..	..	..

From this table we may infer, that the manual power of men, at different ages, is greater than that of women. The difference is generally smaller at early periods than afterwards: thus, before puberty, the ratio is 3 to 2, and it afterwards becomes 9 to 5. We also see that the hands, acting together, produce a greater effect than the sum of the effects they produce acting separately; this appears to be partly owing to the weight of the instrument, which is carried twice, and in an inconvenient manner, when the hands are used in succession. Lastly, the strongest hand is that one we use habitually, at least considering masses of people. The right hand is about one-sixth stronger than the left.

Now, if we compare the power of pressing, which I have observed, with that of MM. Régnier, Ransonnet, and Péron, we shall find the greatest differences, and which I can only attribute to the manner in which the hands were placed on the instrument, and the consequent space betwixt them. I have tried the instrument in different ways, and I think I may be certain that the indications are accurate, especially those for the average power of man. Those values which I ought to mistrust are those obtained for women and children; they appear to me to be less than they ought to be, for the reasons above stated.

According to the researches of MM. Régnier and Ransonnet, the average strength of man is not more than 46·3 or 50 kilogrammes [184 lbs. troy]; that is to say, that it does not come up to his weight; whence it follows, that a man could not lift himself by the pressure he can exercise with his hands. Now, experience evidently disproves such a result. Among the sailors experimented upon, there was probably not one who could not hold himself suspended, for some minutes at least, at the end of a cord firmly fixed at the other end. According to Péron, the manual force would be 69·2 kilogrammes: this value approaches nearer the truth. What I have found for a developed man is 89 kilogrammes [238 lbs. troy], nearly 19 kilogrammes more than the weight of a man in his dress; so that a man may hold at the end of a cord, and bear at the same time a weight as heavy; moreover, the thickness of the cord, or the form of the object which he holds, will necessarily influence the result of the experiment.[*]

We also see, from the values which I have obtained, that it is about the age of 9 or 10 years that a man begins to acquire sufficient power in his hands to hold himself suspended for a time. Woman, at any age, does not appear capable of exercising a power equivalent to her weight; yet many women, from exercise and habits of labour, at length exceed this limit. Thus we see young girls, by practising gymnastic exercises, acquire the power of raising themselves by means of cords to different heights. It would appear, then, although my values are very superior to those of the observers quoted, that they are rather below than above the truth, at least for children and women.

When the power of the hands is tried several times in succession, it happens, just as with the lumbar strength, that, all things being equal, the subsequent efforts are never so energetic as the first ones. Thus the degrees of power diminish successively, and tend to a limit. The second effort is generally weaker by 4 or 5 degrees than the first; the difference is not so great afterwards.

Trying my strength at different periods of the day, I have not observed any very great differences. The greatest effect I have been able to produce was observed on coming from a public lecture, at a time when I was slightly indisposed by an accession of fever. I was able to bring the needle of the dynamometer nearly 10 degrees beyond the point it habitually reached. In general, the strength was greater after dinner than before; it appears to vary with different times of the day, and especially with the hours of refreshment. My experiments are not so numerous as to enable me here to bring forward numerical results of sufficient accuracy; and, for the same reason, I have been obliged to defer establishing the ratios between the stature, weight, and strength of men at different ages. But it appears to me that affluence, abundance of food, and moderate exercise, favourably assist the development of the physical powers; whilst misery, want, and excess of labour, produce the contrary effect. Therefore, the man who finds himself in affluent circumstances, not merely possesses the advantages of fortune, as well as longer life and less liability to disease; he has also better opportunities for the proper development of his physical qualities.

CHAPTER IV.

INSPIRATION, PULSATION, SWIFTNESS, &c.

1. Inspiration and Pulsation.

IN individuals who are well-formed and enjoying good health, the number of inspirations and beats of the heart are generally confined within certain limits, which it may be interesting to know, as well as the average value which they have at different ages. The authors who have written on this subject generally give results which are very discordant, for early ages especially. Keplér appears to have been the first who thought of determining the number of pulsations in a given time; and we may be astonished that, in our own time, we have not more accurate results than those found in the most eminent physiological works.

The following are the numbers which different authors have given for the beats of the heart in one minute:—

Ages.	Number of Beats of the Heart, according to			
	Magendie.[*]	Rochoux.[†]	Adelon.[‡]	Dict. de Méd. vol. 21.
Birth, -	130 to 140	140	130 to 140	140
1 year, -	120 to 130	..	120	..
2 -	100 to 110	100	110	100
3 -	90 to 100	..	90	..
Puberty, -	..	..	80	80 to 90
Manhood,	..	..	70	..
Old age, -	..	..	60	..

" The number of pulsations of the fœtal heart, in a given time," says M. Paul Dubois,[§] "cannot always be easily determined; but when it can, as is usually the case, we find the number from 140 to 150 a-minute, and very frequently 144; it is very natural to think that the number of pulsations should be quick, inversely as the age of the fœtus, and yet our researches do not confirm such an opinion. Indeed, we may affirm, that, from the end of the fifth month, at which period the pulsations of the heart may be readily counted, until the end of gestation, the rhythm [measure] of the double beats has appeared exactly the same to us."

M. Billard has given results which generally do not much agree with those which have been quoted. According to this observer, of 41 children, between 1 and 10 days old, and apparently enjoying good health, he has found—

18 having fewer than 80 pulsations per minute.
2   ~   ~   80   ~   ~
1   ~   ~   89   ~   ~
4   ~   ~   100   ~   ~
10   ~   ~   110 to 129 ~   ~
1   ~   ~   130   ~   ~
2   ~   ~   145   ~   ~
2   ~   ~   150   ~   ~
1   ~   ~   180   ~   ~

Thus, in one-half of the infants, the pulse was almost the same number as of adults; and there were others, the beats of whose heart exceeded in number those of individuals of a more advanced age. These children presented no appearance of disease.

Of 36 children from 1 to 2 months old—

14 presented 80 to 85 pulsations.
1   ~   60 to 62   ~
2   ~   90   ~
2   ~   94 to 95   ~
5   ~   110 to 112   ~
2   ~   114   ~
7   ~   125 to 130   ~
3   ~   140-147 to 150 ~

Of 20 children from 2 to 3 months old—

14 presented more than 90 pulsations.
2   ~   ~   100   ~
2   ~   ~   70   ~
2   ~   ~   70 to 80 ~

It would be wrong to affirm that children uniformly present a more frequent pulse than adults.[||]

It does not appear that the number of inspirations per minute has been examined with as much care as the pulsations. Authors, in general, have not and cannot agree on this point. Haller said he made 20 inspirations per minute; Menzies says 14; Davy observed on himself 26; Thomson, also on himself, 19; Magendie, 15. But we generally say that there are 20, and that every fifth inspiration is deeper than the others.[¶]

* Physiologie. Ed. 1825.
† Dict. de Médicine, 1827.
‡ Physiologie, vol. iii. p. 417.
§ Rapport sur l'Application de l'Auscultation à la Grossesse.
|| [Notwithstanding these observations, there can be no doubt whatever that the pulsations of the heart, counted at the wrist, are uniformly much more numerous in children under six years of age than in adults.]
¶ Dictionnaire des Sciences Médicales, Art. Respiration.

I shall now present the results of experiments made at Brussels, both on inspirations and the beating of the ·heart simultaneously.

And first, according to the observations made on 18 male and as many female children, immediately after birth, the following results were obtained :—

	Pulsations.			Inspirations.		
	Aver.	Max.	Min.	Aver.	Max.	Min.
Boys, -	136	165	104	44	70	23
Girls, - -	135	165	108	44	68	27

Therefore, it appears that difference of sex does not influence these phenomena, at any ráte at birth.

The following is a classification of the preceding numbers :—

Inspirations.						Boys.	Girls.
25 to 30,	-	-	-	-	-	3	1
30 to 40,	-	-	-	-	-	3	5
40 to 50,	-	-	-	-	-	5	8
50 to 60,	-	-	-	-	-	5	3
60 to 70,	-	-	-	-	-	2	1
Pulsations.							
104 to 115,	-	-	-	-	-	2	1
116 to 125,	-	-	-	-	-	0	0
126 to 135,	-	-	-	-	-	6	7
136 to 145,	-	-	-	-	-	5	5
145 to 155,	-	-	-	-	-	0	1
155 to 165,	-	-	-	-	-	2	1

I think these results susceptible of greater accuracy. Considering the number of inspirations and pulsations in men, at different ages, I have found, per minute, for the average and extreme values, in nearly 300 individuals, as follows :—

Ages.	Pulsations.			Inspirations.		
	Aver.	Max.	Min.	Aver.	Max.	Min.
Birth,	136	165	104	44	70	23
5 years,	88	100	73	26	32	..
10 to 15,	78	98	60	..	..	..
15 to 20,	69·5	90	57	20	24	16
20 to 25,	69·7	98	61	18·7	24	14
25 to 30,	71·0	90	59	16·0	21	15
30 to 50,	70·0	112	56	18·1	23	11

It does not appear that there is a determinate ratio between the pulsations and inspirations; however, in many individuals, and I am of the number, it is as 4 to 1.

The observations made on women have been less numerous than those made on men. Moreover, it does not appear that the difference of sexes is at any period more marked than about the time of birth; perhaps there is a slight acceleration in females, at least this appears from the following numbers :—

Ages.		Pulsations.	Inspirations.
Birth,	- -	135	44
15 to 20 years,	-	78	19
20 to 25	~ -	77	17
25 to 30	~ -	72	~
30 to 50	~ -	74·5	19

The temperament, the state of the health, and a crowd of other circumstances, must cause the number of inspirations and pulsations to vary considerably in different individuals. Wakefulness and sleep have also great influence.* From a considerable number of

* [It is sufficiently singular that the chief cause modifying the number of pulsations of the heart, during the twenty-four hours, escaped the notice of M. Quetelet. He takes no account of the singular influence exercised in accelerating the pulsations by the slightest muscular exertion. The condition of sleeping or waking, to which he ascribes considerable effect, has little influence on the pulse, further than as regards a quiescent or non-quiescent state of the body. He seems also inclined to ascribe to sleep those effects which have long ago been proved to be solely attributable to another cause, viz., a diurnal revolution in the number of pulsations of the human heart.—See *Edinburgh Medical and Surgical Journal* for 1815.]

observations made carefully on a male child between 4 and 5 years cf age, I have found that, when awake, the number of pulsations was 93·4, and the number of inspirations 29·3; whilst for the same child, during sleep, I counted 77·3 pulsations, and 21·5 inspirations, on an average.* The ratio of these numbers is 1 to 1·21 for the pulsations, and 1 to 1·36 for the inspirations. Similar observations have been made on a young girl between 3 and 4 years old, and on a woman of 26 years. All these observations have presented the following average values :—

Ages.	Pulsations.			Inspirations.		
	Awake.	Asleep.	Ratio.	Awake.	Asleep.	Ratio.
Girl, 3 to 4 years,	102.3	92·0	1·11	30·2	24·8	1·22
Boy, 4 to 5 ~	93·4	77·3	1·21	29·3	21·5	1·36
Woman, 26 to 27,	77·5	67·0	1·16	27·0	20·8	1·30

It results from these observations, that sleep causes a more sensible modification of the number of inspirations than of the beats of the heart. In general, it diminishes both numbers, the first in a ratio which may be considered as 7 to 6, and the second in the ratio of 4 to 3 nearly. It is very important to consider the state of the individual in these researches, and not to make·the observations when the person is excited by walking quickly, or by passions and emotions of the mind, and still more if the person is not well in health. To observe accurately the number of inspirations is very difficult, and particularly if the individual knows that he is the object of observation. I have seen many persons unable to make such observations on themselves. We must also consider the time of the day : for instance, in the evening we are generally more excited than in the morning, and the beats of the heart, as well as the inspirations, are more rapid.† Neither is it indifferent whether we observe the person before or after a meal. Observing myself at quiet moments, but at different times of the day, I have found the average number of the beats of the heart to be 66·2, and the average number of inspirations 15·8. The first number has varied between the extremes of 74 and 56 : this latter value has been observed immediately before dinner, and the former after a public lecture, about one hour after reaching home. The number of inspirations has varied between 17 and 14·5.

MM. Leuret and Mitivié, who have recently published an interesting work on the *frequency of the pulse in the insane,‡* have sought to determine the influence of temperature and changes of the moon on this frequency; but their observations were not sufficiently numerous to deduce a numerical appreciation of so feeble an element. On the other hand, comparing young people and old persons, they have found that, contrary to the generally received opinion, the pulse of the first is slower than the second : thus they have counted in one minute,

In young persons,	- - -	65 pulsations.
~ old persons,	- - -	74 ~
~ insane women,	- - -	77 ~

The observations were made in the morning, whilst the persons were still in bed, and the pulse consequently beating slower than during the day. MM. Leuret and Mitivié have also thought that the average number of pulsations was fewer in winter than in

* [These observations of M. Quetelet are of little comparative value, from his having neglected to state the *position* of the child during the waking state, and the time of day or night.]

† [The reader is requested to suspend his judgment in respect to these observations until he has perused the documents in the appendix. Certain important elements in these observations have, as we have already said, been overlooked by M. Quetelet.]

‡ Paris, Crochard : 1832. 8vo.

summer, and that the variations do not correspond to changes of temperature.*

2. On Swiftness, and the Activity of some other Physical Qualities of Man.

There are several other physical qualities of man besides those I have just considered, which are likewise susceptible of measurement, and which have been little attended to hitherto. What is generally the best known is the swiftness and the length of the stride of man; but at present, the data for different ages are wanting, and especially when consideration is had to the weight and size of individuals.

A foot traveller can pass over six kilometres [7158 yards] an hour, and continue a long distance, which is at the rate of 100 metres [119 yards] a-minute. We calculate the length of the step at eight decimetres [31·496 inches] : thus the traveller makes 125 steps per minute, and 7500 steps in an hour. He can walk at this rate 8½ hours a-day, and continue as long as he likes, without injuring his health or strength. Then, as a fact, we suppose 51 kilometres [55,743 yards] the average distance which a traveller can walk each day, without overstretching his powers. The average weight of a man in his ordinary clothes is 70 kilogrammes [187 lbs. troy]. Thus, the pedestrian carries each day 70 kilogrammes a distance of 51 kilometres; or, which amounts to the same thing, 3570 kilogrammes the distance of one kilometre.

According to M. Ch. Dupin, from whom I borrow the preceding details,† the military step is computed to be as follows :—

	Length.	The Soldier makes per minute—
Common step,	65 cent.‡	76
Quick march,	65 „	100
Charging,		125

I regret that my own observations do not allow me to treat this subject at present in more detail, or to present a summary of the results obtained by observers who have endeavoured to ascertain the practical effect of speed combined with strength. We find, in general, that wherever the energy of man can be excited, employed as a machine, the physical qualities he can put in force have been measured with more precision. His other qualities have been less studied : thus, we know little of the average speed of man in running; we also know very little of the height and length of his leap, with the exception of the cases of those men who possessed those qualities in an extraordinary degree.

I have been endeavouring to sum up what relates to the height and extent of the leap, in some results which it may be useful to know. However, I ought to premise, that since these results for young ages have been obtained from individuals, several of whom were studying gymnastic exercises, the values may be greater than they otherwise would be. The leaps were made without taking a run, and on a plane and horizontal surface. The length was estimated by measuring the distance from the toes.

Ages.	Length of the Leap. metres.	Height of the Leap. metres.
11 years,	1·52	..
12 „	1·60	..
13 „	1·66	0·64
14 „	1·77	0·70
15 „	1·97	0·80
16 „	2·06	0·83
17 „	2·04	0·81
18 „	2·14	1·00
19 to 30,	2·18	0·93
30 to 40,	1·78	0·88

* [The observations of MM. Leuret and Mitivié have been refuted in this country—first by Dr Knox, in 1814, and afterwards by Dr Guy, in 1836.—See Anatomical and Physiological Memoirs and Medical Gazette, likewise Guy's Hospital Reports.]

† Géométrie et Méchanique des Arts et Métiers, tome iii. p. 75 : 1826.

‡ [25 5-10ths inches.]

The height of the leap was estimated by the height of an obstacle over which the person could leap, with his feet close together, and without taking any run. Estimating the length of the leap at two metres, [6 5-10ths feet] we see that it is about triple that of the ordinary or quick step of soldiers.

I ought, according to the plan I have laid down, to present a great number of other data here, which are capable of being measured, and which vary according to the ages of the persons. I ought, in some manner, to meet those views relative to man which have been put forth by Mr Babbage, with whom I have frequently had the honour to meet during my experiments. Mr Babbage, in wishing for a table of constants, had in view a measurement of every thing in the different kingdoms of nature which is capable of measurement. This gigantic plan has not deterred his countrymen, who are not accustomed to shrink from difficulties, when, by surmounting them, they can enrich science : thus, the British Association, at the meeting which took place in Cambridge in 1833, set aside a certain sum to encourage the efforts of those who seek to realise, in some measure, the ideas of Mr Babbage. I have not laboured on so grand a scale as my erudite friend ; I have only been considering man : but in another view I have rendered the problem more comprehensive, by seeking to determine the modifications which age induces on physical qualities, which cannot be considered as constant until man is fully developed, and when he has not approached the period of decay.

I recollect that Mr Babbage, in a conversation which we had together on the subject of his constants, told me that he had been investigating how many times a man could do certain things in one minute of time : for example, how many steps he could make, how many strokes of the oar the rower makes, how many blows the smith gives with his hammer, how many stitches the tailor makes, &c. ; and that he had observed that these numbers do not vary much in the different countries which he had visited. These constants partly depend on our organisation, and more especially on some of the faculties, as inspirations, pulsations, stature, &c. It would be interesting to determine the ratios which exist between the different constants, and see if they obey simple laws.

Grétry remarks somewhere in his memoirs, that the step of man is easily regulated by an air he sings, the measure being quicker or slower. Pythagoras long ago perceived a certain harmony in the number of blows struck by the forger ; this harmony was undoubtedly purely numerical, like that which he guessed at concerning the motions of worlds, and which, indeed, has been acknowledged by Kepler, who was impressed with the same ideas of harmony as the founder of the Italian school. I again repeat, that to judge of the mutual dependencies of each of our faculties, and to determine to what extent they are influenced by each other, it is necessary to have studied them successively with care, before establishing relations which require subsequent impartiality and discernment. Not until then shall we be able to know man, and the effects of all the causes by which he is influenced, whether these causes be extrinsic to him, or whether they depend merely upon his will and his organisation.

BOOK THIRD.

DEVELOPMENT OF THE MORAL AND INTELLECTUAL QUALITIES OF MAN.

1. Of the Determination of the Average Man with Regard to Moral and Intellectual Qualities.

WE have been enabled to perceive, in the two preceding books, that an appreciation of the physical qualities of the average man does not present any real difficulty, whether we can measure them directly, or whether they only become appreciable by their effects. It is not so with the moral and intellectual qualities. Indeed, I do not know that any person had thought of measuring them, before the essay I wrote on the development of the inclination to crime at different ages. At the same time, I endeavoured to mark out the course which it is proper to follow in such researches, and the real difficulties which present themselves, when we attempt to arrive at each particular result. Perhaps it will be useful to give a summary recapitulation of my ideas on the subject, before passing to the application of them.

Certain moral qualities are very analogous to physical ones; and we may value them, by admitting that they are proportioned to the effects which they produce. Thus, we cannot hesitate to say that one operative has twice or thrice the activity of another, if, all things being equal, he performs double or triple the amount of labour which the other one does. Here the effects are purely physical, and like the compression of the spring in the estimation of mechanical forces: we have only to admit the hypothesis that causes are proportioned to the effects produced by them. But in a great number of cases, this appreciation becomes impracticable. When the activity of man is exerted on immaterial labours, for example, what standard can we adopt, except the works, such as books, statues, or paintings, produced? for how can we obtain the value of the researches and thought which these works have required? The number of the works can alone give an idea of the productive power of the author, as the number of children brought into the world gives us the fecundity of a female, without taking into account the value of the work produced.

If, like the fecundity of females, the different qualities of men were manifested by deeds to which we could assign a value, we conceive that these qualities might be appreciated and compared with each other. Thus, we should not be astounded at hearing, that one man has twice the courage of another, but only one-third the genius; but, since such an appreciation has nothing definite and exact, we confine ourselves to saying that a certain individual has courage, or has not courage, or is even a coward; which in mathematical language would be expressed by saying that his courage is *positive*, *zero*, or *negative*. We say that one man has more courage than another. This opinion is formed, when, after having seen both the individuals in question in action, we think one inferior to the other, without being able to form an exact estimate of their degree of courage. Here we see how arbitrary this is, and how much such estimates are matters of debate. It might also be considered absurd in any one to attempt to express by numbers the relative courage, genius, prudence, or evil propensities of two individuals. Yet, let us examine such an impression more narrowly; let us try to find out why it is absurd; and see if the ratio for which we contend may not be laid down in some cases.

Let us suppose that two individuals are every day placed in circumstances inciting to acts of bravery, and that each one has the same readiness to seize them; moreover, let us suppose that each year we enumerate, pretty constantly, 500 acts of the one, and 300 of the other: moreover, these acts, though more or less remarkable, may be considered collectively, as having each the same value, because they are generally produced under similar circumstances. This being admitted, and considering causes as proportioned to their effects, we should have no difficulty in saying that the bravery of these two individuals is as 500 to 300, or 5 to 3. Such an appreciation would have more truth, according as the observations on which it was founded extended over a greater number of years, and varied little from one other. Here,

then, the absurdity only proceeds from the *impossibility*, in the first place, of placing two men in equally favourable circumstances to display their bravery and courage; in the second place, of enumerating each of these acts; and, lastly, of collecting a sufficient number of them, in order that the conclusion we form may be as little removed from truth as possible. Consequently, the ratio is only considered as being absurd, from the supposed *impossibility* of determining it. However, let us suppose the two individuals just spoken of are Frenchmen, and that one of them represents the generality of men between 21 and 25 years of age, and the other the generality between 35 and 40: moreover, instead of courageous acts, let us substitute thefts, of such a nature as come under the power of the criminal tribunals, and all the rest will be realised, in such a manner that we may consider it as very probable that in France the inclination to theft is almost as five to three, in men between 21 and 25, and 35 and 40. Indeed, we may admit that men between 21 and 25, who, according to the French tables of population, are as numerous as those between 35 and 40, have the same facility to commit theft as the latter; and, moreover, that the thefts coming under the judgment of the criminal tribunals, have circumstances of equal aggravation in each. If it be objected, that we can, in this consideration, only take in the thefts which come before the tribunals, I shall say that, when we calculate the mortality or fecundity of a nation, we are only acquainted with the births and deaths noted in the civil records, and that a great number may be omitted. Moreover, the probability of omissions is as great for individuals between 21 and 25, as for those between 35 and 40 years of age.

Thus we may say, first, that the individuals we compare are almost exactly in the same circumstances; second, that if we do not know the absolute number of thefts which they have committed, at least we know the probable ratio; third, that this ratio must be entitled to more confidence, since it is founded on the observations of several years, and varies within narrow limits merely. Indeed, the ratio of 5 to 3 has been calculated from the results of four years: for two years, it was exactly as 5 to 3; one time rather more, the other rather less. These differences are such, that if we measure for four days in succession, the ratio of the power of two individuals by Régnier's dynamometer, the differences between these four ratios and the general average will undoubtedly be greater than those which we have observed. Thus we may consider it as very probable, that the degrees of inclination to theft, for France in her present state, are such as we have established.

Now, let us suppose that society, in a more perfect state than its present and real one, takes the opportunity some day to register and appreciate courageous and virtuous actions, as crimes are now done, will there not be some means of measuring the relative degrees of courage or virtue at different ages? Therefore the absurdity which is now attached to an endeavour to appreciate this ratio for the average man, is more apparent than real, and is owing to the impossibility which still exists, in the actual state of society, of procuring the necessary elements of the calculation.

It appears to me that it will always be impossible to estimate the absolute degree of courage, &c., of any one particular individual: for what must be adopted as unity?—shall we be able to observe this individual long enough, and with sufficient closeness, to have a record of all his actions, whereby to estimate the value of the courageous ones; and will these actions be numerous enough to deduce any satisfactory conclusion from them? Who will guarantee that the dispositions of this individual may not be altered during the course of the observations? When we operate on a great number of individuals, these difficulties almost entirely disappear, especially if we only want to determine the ratios, and not the absolute values.

Thus 'we might estimate the tendency to certain vices or virtues, either for men at different ages or for both sexes, when we are only taking one nation into consideration: but the difficulties increase when we compare different nations, because many circumstances which in the two former cases were the same, become very dissimilar in the latter.

To make a summary of what has been said on the possibility of measuring qualities of men which are only appreciable by their effects, I think we may employ numbers in the following cases, without any imputation of absurdity:—

1. When the effects may be estimated by means of a direct measure, which gives their degree of energy, such as those produced by strength, speed, and activity, applied to material works of the same nature.*

2. When the qualities are such that the effects are almost the same, and in a ratio with the frequency of these effects, such as the fecundity of females, drunkenness, &c. If two men, placed in similar circumstances, became intoxicated regularly, the one every week, and the other twice a-week, we should say that their propensity to intoxication was as 1 to 2.

3. Lastly, we may also employ numbers, when the causes are such that it is necessary to pay as much attention to the frequency of the effects as to their energy, although the difficulties then become very great, and indeed sometimes insoluble, owing to the few data at present possessed by us. This is what we observe especially in regard to the moral and intellectual qualities, such as courage, prudence, imagination, &c. The question generally becomes simplified, when the effects really vary in energy; but these, nevertheless, under their different modifications, are in almost similar proportions. We may, then, leave energy out of the calculation, and only attend to frequency. Thus, comparing the state of man at 25 and at 45 years of age, in his tendency to commit theft, we may, without erring greatly, attend only to the frequency of the thefts at these different ages, because the different degrees of aggravation of these offences may be supposed the same in both cases. In such appreciations as these, the values we obtain have the greater likelihood of approaching the true values which are wanting, according as, all things being equal, they are more numerous—just as when we put two individuals to the proof, to form an idea of their knowledge, veracity, memory, &c., we mark the number of mistakes they make. Moreover, as I have already remarked, these modes of appreciation are almost impracticable, when two individuals are con-

* Perhaps we might reduce to the same class the effects of memory, whether considered in its readiness to apprehend or its power of retention. For example, two persons, the mind of each being equally calm, and constituted alike favourably for the experiment, will commit some pages of a book to memory, the one in two hours, the other in four hours: but the first person, after a month, will not be able to repeat the passage in question without stopping, whilst the second finds no defect of his memory until two months have elapsed. After such an experiment, the facility to apprehend (in the two individuals) is as 1 to 2, and the facility to retain in the inverse ratio: the time here serves as a measure. We should say, undoubtedly, that it is impossible to note the precise moment when we have committed the passage entirely to memory, as well as when the memory begins to be defective. But here we may act as is done in physical phenomena, which present the same inconvenience, when calculating the duration of the sensation of sight or hearing, or the loss of electricity by a moist medium, or the cooling of bodies. Memory seizes and loses in a gradual manner, and according to a certain law; but there is a ratio between the facility of seizing and retaining in different persons, independently of this law. This ratio must vary very much according to the age of persons. I think these variations may be ascertained by increasing the number of experiments, to correct what may have been defective in other observations. I do not think that the changes which age produces on sensations of sight and hearing have yet been studied: I do not speak of the other senses, the mode of operation of which is but little understood.

cerned, because the facts are not sufficiently numerous to draw any satisfactory conclusion from them; and, moreover, the individuals may alter during the course of the observations. It is not so with the average man: indeed, we can obtain a great number of observations in a short time. It would be impossible, when comparing two men, the one between 21 and 25, and the other between 35 and 40, to determine, all things being equal, their degree of proneness to theft, or any other crime, for this proneness may not have been disclosed, even in one single action, in the course of the observations; which is no longer the case when we take all men, collectively, of the same age: the number of acts or effects is then great enough to allow us, without any serious error, to neglect the different degrees of energy of these acts. Again, if we find that the number of crimes remains nearly exactly the same, from year to year, it is very probable that the result obtained will not be far from the truth.

I think all the qualities of man which are only appreciable by their effects, may be referred to the three heads I have laid down above: I also think it will be perceived that the impossibility of employing numbers at present, in such appreciations, is rather owing to the insufficiency of the data than to the inaccuracy of the methods.

If the law established for the average man is liable to some exceptions, as all the laws of nature are, yet this will be what expresses most nearly what the state of society has been; and nothing can be more important. At birth, man is possessed of the germs of all the qualities which are developed successively and in different degrees; prudence predominates in one, avarice in another, imagination in a third: we also find some tall in proportion to their age, others having a precocious imagination, and possessed of activity and vigour in old age. The single fact that we remark the existence of these differences, proves that we have some notion of a general law of development, and reason accordingly. Therefore, I am not aiming at something unheard of, but only to give more precision to these commonly vague appreciations, because they rest on incomplete or defective observations, and are almost always few in number.

After all which has been said, I think it not only not absurd, but even *possible*, to determine the average man of a nation, or of the human race; the apparent absurdity of such a research only proceeds from the want of a sufficient number of accurate observations, so that the conclusions may present the greatest possible probability of truth. In the preceding book, I have already attempted to determine the laws of the development of the physical powers of the average man: I am now going to continue my researches, and extend them to the moral and intellectual qualities.

CHAPTER I.

DEVELOPMENT OF THE INTELLECTUAL FACULTIES.

1. Development of the Intellect.

THE field we are going to traverse is immense; in the actual state of science, we must confine ourselves to simple indications, which will serve as posts to denote the first attempts made with a design of taking in and observing the whole field. It will first be necessary to determine the period at which memory, imagination, and judgment, commence, and the stages through which they successively pass in their progress to maturity; then, having established the maximum point, we may extend our inquiries to the law of their decline. I have already stated the mode in which memory is to be estimated, and I shall here endeavour to show how we ought to proceed with reason and imagination.

We can only appreciate faculties by their effects;

in other words, by the actions or works which they produce. Now, in attributing to a nation, as we should to an individual, all the works which it has produced, we may form an opinion both of the fecundity and the power of intellect of that nation, compared with others, making allowance for the influence of causes impeding their production. Afterwards, by bearing in mind the ages at which the authors have produced their works, we possess the necessary elements to follow the development of the mind, or its productive power. In such an examination, it will be necessary to separate the different kinds of works; placing together works of art or design, music, mathematics, literature, philosophy, &c., so as to perceive immediately the different shades of development of the different faculties.

This research should be repeated in passing from one nation to another, to see if the laws of development vary by locality more than by the nature of the works. It will also be necessary that these examinations be most accurate and impartial; we should not select, but take the works promiscuously, without classing them. This might be tedious and irksome; but would present curious and very unexpected results.

I shall now give an example of such an analysis of dramatic works only, and I shall take France and England as the subject of observation. To exclude all idea of system, I shall only consider those works truly deserving of mention which are given in the Repertory of Picard for France, and the British Theatre for England. I know that, in attributing as much merit to the Misanthrope as to the Sicilian, and as much to Don Sancho of Arragon as to Cinna, there can be no similarity; but here, as well as in the researches into crime, it happens that the greater number of the obstacles disappear, and the ratio of works of the first order to those of the second may be considered as being essentially the same, in the groups we have formed. Besides, when examining the degrees of merit of the different works in detail, we may still in some measure meet and parry this inconvenience and difficulty. We may still deceive ourselves in such an estimate, but generally the probability of error will be lessened as the observations are more numerous. We have, moreover, the valuable advantage of being able to prove the law of development, by passing from one nation to another, and seeing how the maximum is influenced by locality.

In the review I have made of dramatic works, I have thought proper to take, not the period at which the works were written, which is generally impossible, but the time when they were represented, which, on an average, will generally be two or three years later.

Ages.	French Theatre.			English Theatre.		
	Principal Works.	Authors who have produced them.	Works which might have been produced.	Principal Works.	Authors who have produced them.	Works which might have been produced.
20 & under,	0	47	0	1	24	1
20 to 25, -	5	47	5	6	24	6
25 to 30, - -	15	47	15	8	24	8
30 to 35, -	26	47	26	9	23	9
35 to 40, - -	26	46	27	7	22	8
40 to 45, - -	25	45	26	7	22	8
45 to 50, - -	28	43	30	6	19	8
50 to 55, -	23	41	26	0	15	0
55 to 60, - -	5	33	7	1	12	2
60 to 65, - -	6	28	10	1	11	2
65 to 70, - -	4	23	8	0	7	0
70 & upwards,	2	18	5	1	7	3

The first column for each country indicates the number of principal dramatic works; the second the

F

number of authors who composed them, and who survived to the ages pointed out; and the third column informs us how many works might have been produced, all things being equal, if the number of authors had not been reduced by death. Thus, between their 65th and 70th years, 23 authors have produced four works; and I have supposed that if the 24 others had continued to live, they would have been able to produce other four, which would give a total of 8 dramatic works. Admitting, then, that each had the same opportunity to produce, at a given age, I have multiplied each number of the first column, which gives the principal dramatic works, by the ratio $\frac{47}{a}$, in which a stands for the number of surviving authors.

Now, if we proceed to examine the results which the table presents, we shall perceive that, both in England and France, dramatic talent scarcely begins to be developed before the 21st year; between 25 and 30, it manifests itself very decidedly; it continues to increase, and continues vigorous, until towards the 50th or 55th year; then it gradually declines, especially if we consider the value of the works produced.

Moreover, it would appear that authors were rather more precocious in England than in France: this may be owing to the manner in which the numbers have been collected, and to the difficulty which French authors experience before they procure the representation of their pieces.

It would be interesting to compare these results with those which have been obtained by considering the number and relative merit of the different works. This I have endeavoured to do in the following table, which I only bring forward as an essay, not pretending that the classification of French works is according to their real merit. I have thought proper only to make three degrees of comparison of the works given by Picard as forming the French stage; and I have quoted a small number of those which I conceive to belong to the first rank:—

Ages.	Order of the Works.			Relative Aggregate.	Name of the Works of the First Order.
	1st.	2d.	3d.		
20 and under,	0	0	0	0	
20 to 25, -	1	0	4	7	Œdipe.
25 to 30, - -	3	3	9	24	Le Cid, Andromaque, Britannicus.
30 to 35, -	4	8	14	42	Les Horaces, Cinna, Polyeucte, Iphigénie.
35 to 40, - -	4	8	14	42	Phèdre, Le Joueur, Zaïre, Le Méchant.
40 to 45, -	2	9	14	38	Le Distrait, Alzire.
45 to 50, - -	6	10	12	50	Le Misanthrope, Le Tartuffe, L'Avare, Mahomet, Mérope, La Métromanie.
50 to 55, -	3	8	12	37	Les Femmes Savantes, Athalie, Le Glorieux.
55 to 60, - -	0	3	2	8	
60 to 65, - -	0	2	4	8	
65 to 70, - -	0	1	3	5	
70 & upwards,	0	1	1	3	

In the approximative estimate I have made of the relative degrees of merit of works of the first, second, and third orders, I have taken the numbers 3, 2, and 1; and from them I have deduced the values of the last column, which entirely confirm those given by the former table. It is also easy to see, whatever numbers we may employ to express the relative degrees of merit of works, that the general results still remain the same.

Another very curious result which the tables I have formed show, although the details are here suppressed, is, that tragic talent is developed more rapidly than comic. The *chefs-d'œuvre* which enrich French comedy, were not begun until the 38th or 40th year; and we scarcely find any works belonging to elevated comedy before the 30th year; though I am only speaking of the French authors included in the Repertory of Picard. But I leave this discussion to more competent judges; here I confine myself to just pointing out the plan to be adopted. Others are more able to ascertain if the talent of the tragic author really arrives at maturity earlier than the comic author; and if this maximum is more precocious because it is naturally connected with the time of life when the passions are in the highest state of exaltation. The best mode of analysing this question will be, to ascertain the law of development of musical talent and the art of design, and things generally which excite the passions; and, on the other hand, to study our faculties, the development of which does not so much require the conjunction of the passions and an exalted imagination, as observation and reflection. I shall soon present a remarkable example of analysis of the development of the passions, which tends to show that their maximum of energy takes place about the 25th year; so that, if an art existed, the exercise of which would follow a ratio proportional to the development of the passions, and where previous studies were dispensed with, its maximum of development would also take place about the 25th year: this maximum will afterwards draw near to that which reason attains, according as the intervention of this faculty becomes more necessary. It will also be necessary to take into account the time required for the studies which are indispensable in the production of works.

Our intellectual faculties arise, increase, and decay: each one attains its energy towards a certain period of life. It would be of the highest interest to ascertain those which occupy the two extreme limits of the human scale; that is to say, those which are the first and those which are the last in arriving at maturity; because they have the property of being simple, and not resulting from combination: thus, for example, dramatic talent is a combination of several other faculties, such as imagination, reason, &c.; but, I again repeat, such an analysis requires infinite care, numerous researches, and great shrewdness of observation.

After having rapidly sketched the course to be pursued in studying the development of the intellectual faculties, I think it will be proper to speak of their diseases, which are dreadful affections, the intensity and number of which seem to keep pace with the development of the mind.

2. Of Mental Alienation.

" Sloth and misconduct give birth to poverty; immorality and intemperate passions lead to crime; insanity may attack the most honourable, and does not always spare the wisest men."* This opinion, put forth by a man whose name has great weight in science, will be sufficient to convey an idea of the importance I attach to any thing bearing on the statistics of the deranged. If it be true that diseases of the mind increase in proportion to the development of this faculty, we shall have a new measure or standard, which may regulate what I have previously attempted to establish. However, it is well to be aware that, by taking all insane persons indiscriminately, we may be led to very inaccurate results. Moreover, it is right to distinguish the two classes of insane persons carefully: for, according to M. Esquirol, it is insanity, properly so called, with which idiocy has been confounded, that is in a direct ratio with civilisation. Idiocy is a state depending on soil and material influences, whilst insanity is the product of society and of moral and intellectual influences. In idiocy, these causes have prevented the development of the organ, and, consequently, the manifestation of intelligence. In the production of insanity, the brain

* *Remarques sur la Statistique des Aliénés*, &c., par M. Esquirol (*Annales d'Hygiène*, Décembre 1830).

is over-excited, and goes beyond its physiological power.*

To form an idea of the influence of this fatal malady, we shall commence by a glance at some of the principal countries where its influence has been most decided.

Countries.	Population.	Deranged Persons.	Population to one Deranged Person.
Norway, - -	1,051,318	1,900	551
England, - -	12,700,000	16,222	783
Wales, - -	817,148	896	911
Scotland, 1825, -	2,093,454	3,652	573
New York, 1821,	1,616,458	2,240	721
France.† - -	30,000,000	30,000	1000

In Norway, idiots form one-third of the total number of deranged persons, and one-half in Scotland and Wales: it is the great number of idiots which makes the proportion of deranged persons in Scotland so much greater than it is in England. In general, we observe that in mountainous countries there are many more idiots than in level ones; and in plains where agriculture is solely pursued, we find more idiots than in towns. In France and New York, the number of idiots is very small.

From numerous researches into the ratio in which the sexes are affected, collected from several countries, having great differences in temperature, customs, and laws, M. Esquirol has enumerated 37,825 males to 38,701 females; from which it appears that difference of sex has not much influence on mental derangement. But this is not the case with the seasons; their influence is very marked; at least we may infer this from the following returns of insane persons admitted at Charenton:—

Months.	Admissions: 1828–1829.		Admissions before 1829.	Cures.	Deaths.
	Men.	Women.			
January, -	42	21	37	11	21
February,	40	33	49	10	24
March, -	49	25	53	10	16
April, - -	50	38	58	16	22
May, - -	58	36	44	15	18
June, - -	55	34	70	19	18
July, - -	52	36	61	23	18
August, -	45	24	64	22	13
September,	48	26	47	22	11
October, -	44	47	49	24	30
November,	47	22	35	22	22
December,	35	28	52	15	8
Total,‡ -	565	370	619	209	221

Thus, the summer months have produced the greatest number of cases: the cures have also been most numerous in summer and autumn. We may conceive that, from cases of acute insanity breaking out during the hot season, and being more readily cured, also, than chronic ones, the three months of autumn ought to furnish the greatest number of cures.

If we examine what influence age has on the development of mental alienation, we shall again find very curious results. It would appear that mental alienation may be divided, according to ages, into imbecility in infancy, mania in youth, melancholy in mature age, and madness in advanced age.§

The following table will show us the degree of frequency of this disease at different ages. It is constructed from the data given by M. Esquirol in the

* M. Esquirol. The data of this chapter are extracted principally from articles inserted by this philosopher in the *Annales d'Hygiène*.

† These numbers relating to France are from casual not statistical observation. See also the *Memorial Encyclopedique*, May 1833.

‡ The numbers for the five years from 1829 to 1833, given in this and the following table, have been kindly furnished me by M. Esquirol, from an unpublished work.

§ See the article *Folie* of the Dict. des Sciences Médicales.

Annales d'Hygiène for April 1829. To estimate the degree of frequency of mental alienation, I have thought it necessary to count the number of individuals between 15 and 20, 20 and 25, &c., years of age. In this table I have also included the number of cures, and their ratio to the number of patients.* Lastly, the numbers of both the last columns are those which M. Esquirol has kindly permitted me to take from his work about to be published.

Ages.	At Charenton before 1839.		Ratio.	Lunatics to the Population.	At Charenton 1829 to 1833.	
	Admissions.	Cures.			Men.	Women.
15 to 20 years,	22	11	2·0	24	24	11
20 to 25 „	67	30	2·2	79	65	23
25 to 30 „	86	40	2·2	109	76	31
30 to 35 „	98	36	2·7	134	79	47
35 to 40 „	81	25	3·3	125	65	64
40 to 45 „	79	21	3·8	129	64	59
45 to 50 „	72	14	5·1	131	52	44
50 to 55 „	52	12	4·3	108	54	37
55 to 60 „	21	6	3·5	51	32	20
60 to 65 „	21	9	2·3	63	33	18
65 to 70 „	6	1	6·0	24	14	9
70 & upwards,	14	4	3·5	45	6	7

We have already seen that, all things being equal, it is between the 30th and 50th years that the greatest number of standard dramatic works have been produced in France—that is, the period when imagination and reason are most productive; and, by a singular contrast, it is also about the same age that mental alienation is most frequent, and the cure of it most difficult. The intellectual life of man, and the diseases of his mind, especially develop themselves about the age of 25 years, when physical development has almost ceased: man, indeed, at this age, is almost entirely developed in stature, weight, and strength; and it is at this time that the greatest tendency to crime is manifested. Again, it is remarkable from another comparison, namely, that the period of reproduction falls between the 25th and 30th years. Thus, the average man, between 25 and 30 years of age, has completed his physical development, and this is also about the period when his intellectual life is most vigorous.†

M. Esquirol, in a work published in 1830, in the *Annales d'Hygiène*, has given the following numbers, which establish a difference between sexes and ages :—

Ages.	Paris.			Norway.		
	Men.	Women.	Total.	Men.	Women.	Total.
Before 20 years,	436	348	784	188	141	329
From 20 to 25,	624	563	1,187	101	83	184
„ 25 to 30,	635	727	1,362	97	88	185
„ 30 to 40,	1441	1607	3,048	214	173	387
„ 40 to 50,	1298	1479	2,777	150	155	305
„ 50 to 60,	847	954	1,801	128	115	243
„ 60 and upwards, „}	875	1035	1,910	117	140	257
Total, - -	6156	6713	12,869	995	895	1890

* According to a work by M. Klotz, *De Vesaniæ Prognosi*, the annual ratio of admissions to dismissions in the principal lunatic hospitals of Europe, would fall within the limits 0·330 and 0·590. In the generality of the establishments in Belgium, the entries are to the exits as 390 to 1000.—*Traite sur l'Alienation Mentale*, &c., par *J. Guislain*, 2 vols. 8vo. 1826.

† M. Pierquin, in his *Arithmetique Politique de la Folie*, finds, as the principal conclusion of his researches, that "crimes are always, from being proportionate to the population, also in a relative proportion to the degree of insanity," and seeks to refute the assertion of M. Esquirol, that insanity is a disease of civilisation. I certainly think, with him, that in general, the causes which tend to produce alienation, also influence the number of crimes, and especially crimes against persons, but without there being a direct and necessary ratio between the number of insane and that of criminals, because all crimes have not their source necessarily in mental alienation.

We may first observe, that at Paris insane men, up to the age of 25 years, are rather more numerous than women ; after this age, the contrary takes place. In Norway, the number of insane women only exceeds that of men towards the end of life. In the latter country, the number of insane under 20 years is 329, which is one-sixth of the total number existing in the kingdom ; whilst at Paris, the number of insane under 20 years of age, is only 784, or one-fourteenth. This difference arises, no doubt, from the great number of idiots entered in the returns of Norwegian statistics. If in Norway there are more imbecile persons from the time of infancy or early youth, the contrary takes place for the periods beyond 60 years of age. In Norway, scarcely one-eighth of the insane are more than 60 years old; whilst in Paris one-sixth exceed that age.

To form a better opinion of the influence of age, I have reduced the preceding numbers to 1000, and I have compared them with the corresponding numbers of the same ages, given in the tables of population in the *Annuaire du Bureau des Longitudes* of France, and those of Sweden for 1820 :—

Ages.	Paris.			Norway.		
	Population.	Insane.	Ratio.	Population.	Insane.	Ratio.
Before 20 years,	0·402	0·061	0·15	0·411	0·174	0·42
20 to 25 „	0·084	0·092	1·09	0·087	0·097	1·11
25 to 30 „	0·080	0·106	1·32	0·084	0·098	1·17
30 to 40 „	0·140	0·237	1·69	0·136	0·205	1·51
40 to 50 „	0·114	0·216	1·90	0·109	0·161	1·48
50 to 60 „	0·091	0·140	1·54	0·086	0·129	1·50
60 & upwards,	0·089	0·148	1·66	0·087	0·136	1·56
Total, -	1·000	1·000	1·00	1·000	1·000	1·00

The numbers for France also concur to show that mental alienation is most frequent between the 40th and 50th years. In Norway, its frequency becomes great between the 30th and 40th years, and preserves the same value almost to the end of life.

These results agree well with the observation of M. Esquirol, that insanity is a disease which attends and increases with civilisation. The fortress of the understanding is attacked, either by too much mental labour, or by passions and disappointments which are too acutely felt.

We cannot collect too many documents to verify, with still greater accuracy, the results of the tables which I have just given. It is with this object that I now bring forward some new documents taken from a *Rapport Statistique sur la Maison d'Aliénés de Bon-Sauveur à Caen*, during the years 1829 and 1830, by M. Vastel.* The author classes the insane in the following manner, according to age. In the last column, the total numbers are reduced to 100 :—

Ages.	Insane.	Men.	Women.	Insane.
From 15 to 20 years,	10	7	3	0·03
„ 20 to 30 „ -	54	39	16	0·17
„ 30 to 40 „ -	94	44	50	0·29
„ 40 to 50 „ -	82	32	50	0·25
„ 50 to 60 „ -	57	18	39	0·17
„ 60 to 70 „ -	25	6	19	0·08
„ 70 to 80 „ -	3	1	2	0·01
Total, -	325	146	179	1·00

Here, again, we find the same analogies, the same laws of development, proceeding, as it were, in a parallel manner.

M. Falret has written a work on insanity, suicide, and sudden death, of which at present we only know the general contents, from a report made by M. Serres to the Institute.† The principal conclusions of this

* Annales d'Hygiène, Oct. 1832.

† The work of M. Falret has gained the prize for Statistics, founded by M. de Monthyon.

work, on the influence of season, sex, and age, are the following :—" Of the total number of the insane, women form one-third more than men. Women are most subject to the attack of insanity in July; but for men this month is in the third rank; with a reference to civil statistics, we find that more than one-fourth of the men are bachelors : as to age, we find mental diseases develop themselves in men between the 30th and 39th years, and in women between the 40th and 49th years ; as to the nature of the affections, melancholy predominates in women, and the tendency to homicide in men.   The same contrast is found in the cures, deaths, and relapses."

~~~~~~~~

CHAPTER II.

DEVELOPMENT OF MORAL QUALITIES.

1. Of Foresight, Temperance, Activity, &c.

I HAVE already observed, that it is not so much a method which we want, when endeavouring to appreciate the development of moral qualities, as sufficient and trustworthy data. For example, if we are considering the virtues most essential to the social state, we have scarcely any data, and those which exist, having been collected with intentions very different from our own, are either unfit for purposes of comparison, or utterly incomplete. For example, let us suppose that we want to ascertain the degree of foresight at different periods of life, as well as the modifications of this virtue by the differences of sex, locality, profession, &c. We are obliged to recur to actions by which this foresight has been manifested; and if we cannot collect them all, it is at least necessary to unite as great a number as possible, and to take care that the classes of individuals who are the subject of comparison are in the same circumstances. It is in choosing, classing, and reflecting upon the materials, that discernment and unprejudiced reasoning are so essentially necessary, since the examples to be followed have not yet been laid down. Those who first enter upon this field of research, will no doubt often go astray; but their efforts will be valuable and useful, if they are conducted with candour and impartiality. Nothing is more injurious to the interests of science, than to undertake such researches with notions previously formed.

If we had authentic documents respecting savings' banks, assurance societies, and the different institutions which encourage foresight—if these documents gave the age, sex, profession, and every other requisite information concerning the individuals who take part in the operations of these establishments—it is evident that we should already have very satisfactory elements to enable us to obtain an approximation to the values we are seeking. We may conceive, moreover, how much discernment is necessary, in placing the individuals concerned in similar circumstances, and distinguishing those among whom it is impossible to establish any comparison; not to mention other data necessary to enable us, from the time at which they were taken, to render all chances equal on both sides. We should be able, with due precautions, to make other documents, furnished by establishments of another nature, available for the same purpose, and which would serve in this manner to verify the former conclusions. Thus, the number and value of the objects placed in pawnbrokers' hands, will better exemplify the want of foresight of a community than any misery in its condition. For, if it be true that accidents and reverses of fortune sometimes compel men, even the most prudent, to have recourse to such establishments, it much more frequently happens that the deposits are placed there from want of due care and economy. The passion for gambling, the number of failures, the frequenting of coffee-houses and low haunts, drunkenness, and many other circumstances, would furnish

useful elements for our purpose in appreciating the want of order and foresight. On most of the subjects of inquiry which I have just mentioned, there exist evidences which are more or less complete, but which are little understood in general, as I have already observed.

Drunkenness is a vice of which we ought to have exact records in countries where the police are active ; yet it is to be regretted that they are altogether unknown to those who have the greatest interest in making use of them. As drunkenness is a common source of many other vices, and also of crimes—tending to demoralise and to deteriorate the species—governments ought to favour the researches of learned men, who seek to ascertain the condition of the people, and who try to improve them. Drunkenness is influenced by a great number of causes which are easily estimated, because the necessary data require less investigation than those relating to other analogous estimates. I am persuaded that a work, well written, which would endeavour to make known the injuries this pestilence inflicts on society, would be of the greatest utility, and would furnish an explanation of a great number of isolated facts which depend upon it, and which we are in the habit of considering as purely accidental.

In England, about half a century ago, strong drinks and liquors were used in excess ; and authors were not long in finding out to what extent this vice led to thoughtlessness and injury in the nation, how much the health of man suffered, and how much the mortality increased with the demoralisation of the people. Their observations have not been lost ; and a progressive reformation took place, commencing with the better classes. This defect, formerly so common, and of which they were almost proud, is not to be seen now, except in the lower orders, from among whom it will gradually disappear, as much as the nature of a moist climate will allow, where cordials, taken moderately, are calculated to produce a useful effect. When climate creates a necessity, it is very difficult to prevent the public from abusing it. I am obliged to Mr Babbage for the communication of some curious documents, containing a list of all the drunken persons who have been arrested by the London police in the year 1832, and who were immediately released, because no charge was brought against them. Although the results of one year cannot be very useful, I have thought proper not to omit them. If we possessed an extensive series of similar documents, we should find in them the most precious memorials of the manners of the English people, and, in particular, all which relates to changes in the condition of the population.

Number of Drunken Persons taken up by the London Police in 1832.

Months.	Men.	Women.	Ratio.
January, - - -	1,190	825	1·44
February, - - -	1,175	740	1·59
March, - - -	1,190	710	1·67
April, - - -	1,150	690	1·67
May, - - - -	1,200	730	1·64
June, - - -	1,225	780	1·57
July, - - -	1,355	990	1·37
August, - - -	1,305	935	1·39
September, - - -	1,198	975	1·23
October, - - -	1,560	1,100	1·42
November, - - -	1,360	880	1·55
December, - - -	1,425	935	1·52
Total, - - -	15,333	10,290	1·49

The number of drunken people taken up by the police was then 25,623 ; to which we ought to add 3505 individuals brought before the magistrates, and compelled to pay a fine, as well as 3429 others, who have likewise been conducted before the magistrates, but without undergoing condemnation ; so that the total amounts to 32,557. We must remark, that we only know those cases of drunkenness which were so great as 'to disturb the public tranquillity. Also, in comparisons which we should like to establish between other towns, it would be necessary to be extremely circumspect, and consider the degree to which its suppression was carried; or, rather, in comparing one town with itself at different times, it would be necessary to take into account the effect of the police, and the changes they may have produced.

One would require to have long inhabited London, and to know perfectly the peculiarities which it presented in 1832, to draw all the conclusions inferable from the preceding numbers; still there are some results which it may be very interesting to point out. And, firstly, we have to notice the great number of women, compared with the number of men, which is at least as 2 to 3. This disproportion is great, and must make us think unfavourably of the moral restraint of women in the lower class, especially in a country where the sex is so well conducted in the ranks of society a little higher. This ratio varies according to the different months, and in a manner which would make us think that the variation is not purely accidental. Towards the end of winter, and at the commencement of spring, the men are comparatively the most numerous: the contrary takes place in summer.

If we take the numbers in their absolute value, we find, for men, that they sensibly increase from the commencement to the end of the year; for women, the smallest number is in spring, and the largest in summer and the commencement of autumn. Classing them according to the seasons, we find—

	Men.	Women.
For January, February, and March,	3555	2275
.. April, May, and June,	3575	2200
.. July, August, and September,	3831	2900
.. October, November, and December,	4345	2915

It must be remarked, that this is during the latter months of the year, when the feasts of Christmas and St Andrew take place, which are not always celebrated by the people with the greatest degree of temperance.

If we seek to form an idea of the activity of a people, of the state of its industry, and of its productive faculties, in the absence of direct data, we have, for the means of appreciating its revenue, the value of that which it is able to pay to government, the nature of its contribution, the quantity of imports or exports, the price of ground, of hand work, &c., but particularly the state of the population, because, as we have been able to see, the population is regulated by the number of things produced. I shall present an example of such a valuation, a very poor one, no doubt, but one which will explain my idea:*—

Countries.	Quantity of Pasturage.	One Horse to	One head of Cattle to	Number of Sheep.
British Isles,	¼ of territory.	12 inhab.	2 inhab.	2 to 1 inhab.
France,	½ ..	19 ..	5 ..	1 to 1 ..
Low Countries,	½ ..	13 ..	3 ..	1 to 3 ..
Prussian monarchy,	⅓ ..	10 ..	3 ..	1 to 6 ..
Austrian empire,	⅔ ..	27 ..	8 ..	1 to 3 ..
Spain,	1·65 ..	75 ..	11 ..	1 to 1 ..

Countries.	Population.	Inhabitants to one square mile.	Ratio of the Army to the Population.
British Isles,	23,400,000	257	229
France,	32,000,000	208	138
Low Countries,	6,118,000	339	142
Prussian monarchy,	12,464,000	155	80
Austrian empire,	32,000,000	165	118
Russian empire,	56,500,000	37	57
United States,	11,800,000	7·5	1977

* The first table is taken from the *Revue de Paris* of M. Moreau de Jonnes; the numbers of the second and third tables are from the works of M. Balbi—*La Monarchie Française Comparée aux Principaux Etats*, and *L'Abrégé de Geographie*.

Countries.	Inhabitants living in Town.	Part of the Population employed in Manufactures.	Part of the Population employed in Agriculture.	Revenue to each Inhabitant.	Debt to each Inhabitant.
				francs.	francs.
British Isles,	0·50	0·45	0·34	65·2	869
France,	0·33	0·36	0·44	30·9	145
Low Countries,	0·29	?	?	26·3	635
Prussian monarchy,	0·27	0·18	0·66	17·2	29·3
Austrian empire,	0·23	0·09	0·69	10·9	45·6
Russian empire,	0·12	0·06	0·79	6·6	21·4
United States,	?	?	?	12·1	34·8

If, in the beginning, we compare France to England, we shall find the first kingdom proportionally less peopled than the latter: there are fewer inhabitants in town, and also fewer employed in manufactures: the Englishman pays into the treasury twice as much as the Frenchman, and his exports are much more considerable: the proportion, as regards the two countries, according to M. Ad. Balbi, is nearly as 3 to 1. The Prussian monarchy bears almost the same proportion to France which France does to England. It is remarkable, according to our table, that the countries which have the largest population, are generally those which have the most town inhabitants, the greatest number of hands employed in manufacture, and proportionally the fewest in agriculture; they have fewer men in the army, pay most taxes to the state, and have the largest debt.* Land armies appear to be numerically in inverse ratio to maritime ones: the latter require fewer men, but more expense.

In Europe, with the exception of Russia, nearly the same number of hands are employed in agriculture, and the surplus population turn to manufactures (*industrie*). It then becomes necessary to change the nature of the products by exportation; and the country which has the most manufactures is generally that which has the most exports. Manufactures are always and every where of more importance than agriculture, and those who pursue them possess the greatest riches and pay the most to the state; but since the revenues from manufactures are more uncertain, their wealth is less secure: we also see that the public debt rises immensely in value, and every thing which tends to confine the scope of trade, and to diminish the exchange of produce, will cause a considerable mortality.

It is to be regretted that, at the present time, we do not possess, for different countries, exact accounts of the prices of manual labour, of ground, of lodgings, of the food necessary to the life of an individual, of the carriage of letters, and the means of communication for travellers and merchandise; these accounts would give data for comparing the activity of the inhabitants and the price of time—valuable elements, but of which some people do not yet appear to understand the importance.

I had proposed, at this place, to compare the donations made for the use of the poor, of hospitals, and benevolent institutions in general; but I must omit this investigation, from want of exact documents: I particularly regret that M. Guerry, when considering this subject in France, has only given ratios, and no absolute numbers, nor any of the sources whence he has extracted them.

It appears to be still more difficult to speak on the influence of religious ideas, and the condition of people in this respect.

A very useful addition to moral statistics, would be to point out the dates at which certain practices and customs existed, and also the time when they commenced, and when they ceased. For example, at what period prosecutions for witchcraft were most

* According to M. le Baron de Morogues, states in which the people are most given to agriculture, are those which are the least loaded with pauperism.—*Recherche des Causes de la Richesse et de la Misère des Peuples Civilisés*, p. 395.

numerous, when they began to take place, and when they were discontinued; in what countries men were tortured and put to death for religious opinions, without having disturbed the public peace, at the same time what were the extreme limits of the period, and the epochs of greatest severity; what kind of fanaticism, either political, religious, or otherwise, has prevailed at any period, in any country; what gave rise to it, and what caused its decline; what was its nature, intensity, and results, &c. I shall not stay longer to make such enumerations; these are researches which henceforth must necessarily be considered as pertaining to the history of nations, and will assist us in determining their laws of development. However, I do not think we ought to abandon this subject without giving an example of a particular kind of mania or fanaticism, so to term it, which appears to be making sensible advances every day.

2. Of Suicides and Duels.

The destruction of man by his own hands, although generally repugnant to the notions of modern society, has nevertheless found panegyrists, and those who have proclaimed its advantages. Suicide, among some nations, continues to be branded with infamy by the public. The ancients were not entirely of this opinion: it was often practised by the most illustrious men, and has been mentioned with admiration by their gravest historians. We are naturally excited by the death of Cato, who wished not to survive the liberty of his country; by the death of Lucretia, who wished not to survive her dishonour; or even by the death of the criminal, who seeks to spare his family the shame of seeing his head fall on the scaffold.

The destruction of one man by another, excites horror; yet this dreadful crime may also, in our manners and modern institutions, present the appearance of a virtue under certain circumstances. We can only comprehend these apparent contradictions, by admitting that the crime consists, not in the action, but in the intention of him who commits it; so that, if the intention was noble or generous, the action may also be considered of the same character. This is the only manner in which we can explain the diversity of opinions on duelling especially, which was unknown to the ancients, and which had its rise in the middle ages.

We possess few data on the number of suicides; and what information we have on the number of duels, is so incomplete or inaccurate, that we cannot make use of it. From the table of M. Balbi, entitled *La Monarchie Française Comparée aux Principaux Etats du Globe*, suicides appear to take place in the following proportions:—

France (1827),	1 suicide to 20,740 inhabitants.
Prussian monarchy,	.. 14,404 ..
Austrian empire,	.. 20,900 ..
Russian empire,	.. 49,182 ..
United States—New York,	.. 7,797 ..
.. Boston,	.. 12,500 ..
.. Baltimore,	.. 13,656 ..
.. Philadelphia,	.. 15,875 ..

According to Casper, who has paid much attention to this subject,[*] the number of suicides is particularly great in towns; indeed, we annually enumerate as follows:—

	To 100,000 Inhabitants	1 Suicide to
At Copenhagen,	100 suicides	1000 inhabitants.
.. Paris,	49 ..	2040 ..
.. Hamburg,	45 ..	2222 ..
.. Berlin,	34 ..	2941 ..
.. London,	20 ..	5000 ..
.. Elberfeld,	20 ..	5000 ..

The General Records of the criminal courts of France, present, from 1827, annual accounts, not only of suicides but also of accidental deaths and duels

* Beitrage, &c., 1 vol. 12mo. Berlin: 1825.

which have come to the knowledge of the public magistrate. According to these accounts, we find—

Years.	Accidental Deaths.	Suicides.	Duels.	
			followed by Death.	not followed by Death.
1827,	4,744	1542	19	51
1828,	4,855	1754	29	57
1829,	5,048	1904	13	40
1830,	4,478	1756	20	21
1831,	5,045	2084	25	36
Total,	24,170	9040	106	205

This table gives 4834 accidental deaths, and 1808 suicides, as the annual average; which, to a population of 32,000,000 souls, gives one accidental death to 7000, and 1 suicide to 18,000 inhabitants; as to the number of duels, it may be supposed that the values in the table are too low.

A very great number of suicides takes place in the department of the Seine. They have been committed in the following manner, during the years from 1817 to 1825 inclusive:—

Years.	Total.	Submersion.	Fire-arms.	Asphyxia.	Voluntary Falls.	Strangulation.	Cutting Instruments.	Poisoning.
1817,	352	160	46	35	39	36	23	13
1818,	330	131	48	35	40	27	28	21
1819,	376	148	59	46	39	44	20	20
1820,	325	129	46	39	37	32	28	14
1821,	348	127	60	42	33	38	25	23
1822,	317	120	48	49	33	21	31	15
1823,	390	114	56	61	43	48	47	21
1824,	371	115	42	61	47	38	40	28
1825,	396	134	56	59	49	40	38	20
Total,	3205	1178	461	427	360	324	280	175

The average number of suicides, therefore, in the department of the Seine, annually reaches 356; which, for a population of 860,000 souls, gives 1 suicide to 2400 inhabitants; Geneva gives the ratio of 1 to 3900, for the years between 1820 and 1826 inclusive.[*] The following are the modes of destruction, according to 95 observations:—36 individuals perished in water; 34 blew out their brains; 6 hanged themselves; 5 were poisoned; 2 died from wounds; 2 cast themselves from an eminence. Thus, with regard to the preference shown for particular modes, these numbers are almost the same as at Paris.

The means of destruction are not every where the same: thus, at Berlin, according to Casper, 535 suicides have taken place in the following manner:— 234 by strangulation, 163 by fire-arms, 60 by submersion, 27 by cutting the throat, 20 by cutting instruments, &c., 19 by voluntary falls, 10 by poisoning, and 2 by opening veins.[†]

In all the preceding numbers, one may perceive an alarming concordance between the results of the different years, as they succeed each other. This regularity, in an act which appears so intimately connected with volition, will soon appear before us again in a striking manner, as connected with crime. However, society in a country may undergo modifications, and

* Hertha, August 1828; and Bulletin de M. de Férussac, May 1829.

† Studying the circumstances connected with suicides, duels, and certain kinds of crimes, we may be disposed to think that man is frequently actuated by a propensity to imitation. M. Chevreul, in a letter addressed to M. Ampère (*Sur une Classe Particulière de Mouvemens Musculaires*), has brought forward some philosophical considerations of great interest, and which show how much human nature deserves to be studied more deeply, in some relations which have been perhaps too much neglected.

thus produce an alteration in what at first presented a remarkable constancy for a short time. According to Casper,[*] at Berlin, between 1788 and 1797, only 62 suicides took place; and 128 between 1797 and 1808, and 546 between 1813 and 1822. It has been remarked, that suicides have become more numerous; this conjecture would be very probable, if it be true that they are a result of civilisation, and if we consider that legislation endeavours to repress them in some countries. It is to be doubted, however, whether there are not some errors in the numbers, depending on the circumstance that statistical researches were made with much less care formerly than at present.

M. Casper, in his researches on the subject, has attentively discussed the influence of states of the atmosphere on suicide, and also the influence of seasons, which, despite the few observations we possess, is manifested in a remarkable manner, as may be seen in the following table, where the suicides occurring during each season are noted:—

Months.	Berlin: 1812-1822.	Hamburg: [†] 1816-1822.	Westminster :[‡] 1812-1821.	Paris :[§] Six Years.
Jan., Feb., & March,	109	39	67	42
April, May, & June,	155	31	55	53
July, Aug., & Sept.,	173	41	60	61
Oct., Nov., & Dec.,	145	38	46	31

Here, again, summer appears to exercise a greater influence on the number of suicides than the other seasons, as well as on the number of those affected with insanity, and, as we shall soon perceive, also on the number of crimes against person.

M. Casper also finds that, all things being equal, suicides in town and country have been numerically as 14 to 4. With respect to difference of sex, he has observed, for Berlin, that, of 727 suicides, 606 were committed by men, and 121 by women, which gives a ratio of 5 to 1. According to the *Recherches Statistiques sur Paris*, the ratio for this city would be 1 nearly. At Geneva, the ratio has been 4 to 1 for the seven years from 1820 to 1826.

We scarcely possess any researches on the ages at which suicide takes place. I only know of those published by Casper for Berlin,[||] and those published for Geneva.[¶] M. Guerry has given the number of suicides for Paris;[**] but only those of men, and which have taken place by suspension or fire-arms. The following table presents a summary of the documents for Berlin and Geneva:—

Ages.	Berlin: 1818-1824.	Geneva: 1820-1826.
Below 10 years,	1 }	
From 10 to 15 years,	17 }	5
.. 15 to 20 ..	32 }	
.. 20 to 25 ..	30 }	
.. 25 to 30 ..	25 }	
.. 30 to 35 ..	12 }	24
.. 35 to 40 ..	9 }	
.. 40 to 50 ..	34 }	
.. 50 to 60 ..	32 }	45
.. 60 to 70 ..	17 }	
.. 70 to 80 ..	9 }	21
.. 80 and upwards,	2 }	
Total,	220	95

To have a better idea of these numbers, it will be preferable to class them in periods, each of 10 years' duration, and to reduce the number to 1000. At the same time, we may compare them with those of Paris,

and with a population of 1000 individuals arranged according to their respective ages.

Ages.	Suicides at Berlin.	Suicides at Paris by Shooting.	Suicides at Paris by Suspension.	Suicides at Geneva.	Population Divided according to Age.
10 to 20 years,	224	61	68	53	312
20 to 30 ..	251	283	51 }		188
30 to 40 ..	96	182	94 }	252	100
40 to 50 ..	156	150	188 }		136
50 to 60 ..	146	161	256 }	474	100
60 to 70 ..	77	126	235 }		68
70 to 80 ..	41	35	108 }	221	30
80 and upwards,	9	2	0 }		6
Total, -	1000	1000	1000	1000	1000

The number of suicides between 10 and 30 years of age, is extremely high at Berlin; it would further appear, that between 30 and 40 years of age, the minimum number occurs, or at least that the number of suicides, which was very great between the 10th and 30th years, then diminishes, to regain fresh intensity towards the end of life. Will not the circumstance have some influence, that a father separates himself from his family with more difficulty when his children are young than when they can already provide for their own necessities? It would be very interesting to have more documents on the motives which lead to the commission of suicide.

It is sufficiently evident, that some particular cause exists at Berlin, which induces such a great number of young persons between 16 and 20 to destroy themselves. Removing the effects of this agency, the results agree sufficiently with those of Paris and Geneva, and tend to show that the number of suicides increases with age, though we must take care to bear in mind the number of individuals of each age who are found in a population.[*] This tendency, in its first development, almost progresses in the same ratio as the development of intelligence and mental alienation.

It would also appear that the hours of the day have some influence on suicide by suspension. M. Guerry has given the following numbers in the *Annales d'Hygiène* for January 1831:—

	Suicides.
From midnight to 2 in the morning,	77
.. 2 to 4 o'clock,	45
.. 4 to 6 ..	58
.. 6 to 8 ..	135
.. 8 to 10 ..	110
.. 10 to 12 ..	123
.. 12 to 2 ..	32
.. 2 to 4 ..	84
.. 4 to 6 ..	104
.. 6 to 8 ..	77
.. 8 to 10 ..	84
.. 10 to 12 ..	71
	1000

MM. Benzenberg and Casper have compared the number of suicides with the number of homicides and mortal blows, to infer thence the probability that an individual found dead has perished by one or the other.[†] The towns of Prussia give the following numbers:—

	Suicides.	Homicides.
1818,	339	27
1819,	452	24
1820,	475	40
1821,	456	40
1822,	442	45
	2164	176

* Beitrage zur Medicinischen Statistik, &c. 8vo. Berlin: 1825. See also the researches of Dr Heyfelder, entitled Der Selbsmord, &c. 8vo. Berlin: 1828.
† Grohmann in Hufel, Journal, l c.   ‡ Falret, l c.
§ Esquirol, l c. || Beitrage, p. 53.
¶ Beitrage, and Bulletin de M. de Férussac, Mai 1829.
** Annales d'Hygiène, Janvier 1831.

* In the *An. d'Hygiène*, Oct. 1829, there are two very remarkable Memoirs by M. Devergie, one on the mode of ascertaining how long a person has been drowned, the other containing some researches on those who have been hanged.
† Beitrage, &c., p. 94.

This ratio is about 1 homicide to 12 suicides. M. Hermann has found that, in Russia, the number of suicides is almost equal to that of homicides, and that this ratio does not vary much in the different parts of the empire, although the number of suicides and homicides are far from preserving the same comparative value to the population.* In France, the suicides are to the population as 1 to 20,000 nearly, and the homicides as 1 to 48,000 : this ratio of suicides to homicides is therefore nearly as 5 to 3.

In concluding this chapter, I shall lay before the reader the principal conclusions contained in the work of M. Falret on suicides, from the report of M. Serres to the Institute of France, which gives the only results hitherto published. "Suicides present, in both sexes, a very remarkable contrariety, according to the results furnished by tables. Thus, the month of April, attended with the greatest number of suicides among men, is only so in the fifth degree among women; with the latter, the month of August occupies the same rank as April does for men.

The social position of the parties presents a no less remarkable contrast. Of the men, it is bachelors who form the largest number; and of the women, we find the greatest number among those engaged in the bonds of matrimony. We cannot omit to observe here the difference between women and men, as respects the influence of concubinage on the production of voluntary death : this influence, for women, is almost treble.

We observe still more striking differences, if such can be, between the two sexes, as respects the influence of age. In men, it is from 35 to 45 that the greatest number of suicides take place; in women it is from 25 to 35. The next period for men is 45 to 55; whilst in women this only holds the fifth rank : but, by a singular compensation, we observe twice as many suicides among young girls as among boys who have not reached their fifteenth year.

If we inquire into the mode of self-destruction which is practised, we shall see that men give a decided preference to cutting instruments and fire-arms, while women destroy themselves by poison, falls from a great height, or asphyxiate themselves by means of burning charcoal."

CHAPTER III.

OF THE DEVELOPMENT OF THE PROPENSITY TO CRIME.

1. Of Crimes in General, and of the Repression of them.

SUPPOSING men to be placed in similar circumstances, I call the greater or less probability of committing crime, the *propensity to crime.* My object is more especially to investigate the influence of season, climate, sex, and age, on this propensity.

I have said that the circumstances in which men are placed ought to be similar, that is to say, equally favourable, both in the existence of objects likely to excite the propensity and in the facility of committing the crime. It is not enough that a man may merely have the intention to do evil, he must also have the opportunity and the means. Thus the propensity to crime may be the same in France as in England, without, on that account, the *morality* of the nations being the same. I think this distinction of importance.†

* Mémoires de l'Académie de Pétersbourg, 1830; and Bulletin de M. de Férussac, Nov. 1831.

† This has been very clearly established by M. Alphonse de Candolle, in an article entitled *Considérations sur la Statistique des Délits,* inserted in the *Bibliothèque Universelle de Genève,* Feb. 1830. The author regards the propensity of individuals to crime as depending on their morality, the temptation to which they are exposed, and the greater or less facility they may find to commit offences. Of these three causes, the first belongs more especially to the man; the other two are, properly speaking, external to him. As it is with man that I am occupied, I have endeavoured, in the course of my researches, that the causes external to him might be constantly nearly equal, so that they might be left out

There is still another important distinction to be made; namely, that two individuals may have the same propensity to crime, without being equally criminal, if one, for example, were inclined to theft, and the other to assassination.*

Lastly, this is also the place to examine a difficulty which has not escaped M. Alphonse de Candolle in the work above mentioned : it is this, that our observations can only refer to *a certain number of known and tried offences, out of the unknown sum total of crimes committed.* Since this sum total of crimes committed will probably ever continue unknown, all the reasoning of which it is the basis will be more or less defective. I do not hesitate to say, that all the knowledge which we possess on the statistics of crimes and offences will be of no utility whatever, unless we admit without question that *there is a ratio, nearly invariably the same, between known and tried offences and the unknown sum total of crimes committed.* This ratio is necessary, and if it did not really exist, every thing which, until the present time, has been said on the statistical documents of crime, would be false and absurd. We are aware, then, how important it is to legitimate such a ratio, and we may be astonished that this has not been done before now. The ratio of which we speak necessarily varies according to the nature and seriousness of the crimes : in a well-organised society, where the police is active and justice is rightly administered, this ratio, for murders and assassinations, will be nearly equal to unity; that is to say, no individual will disappear from the society by murder or assassination, without its being known : this will not be precisely the case with poisonings. When we look to thefts and offences of smaller importance, the ratio will become very small, and a great number of offences will remain unknown, either because those against whom they are committed do not perceive them, or do not wish to prosecute the perpetrators, or because justice itself has not sufficient evidence to act upon. Thus, the greatness of this ratio, which will generally be different for different crimes and offences, will chiefly depend on the activity of justice in reaching the guilty, on the care with which the latter conceal themselves, on the repugnance which the individuals injured may have to complain, or perhaps on their not knowing that any injury has been committed against them. Now, if all the causes which influence the magnitude of the ratio remain the same, we may also assert that the effects will remain invariable. This result is confirmed in a curious manner by induction, and observing the surprising constancy with which the numbers of the statistics of crime are reproduced annually—a constancy which, no doubt, will be also reproduced in the numbers at which we cannot arrive; thus, although we do not know the criminals who escape justice, we very well know that every year between 7000 and 7300 persons are brought before the criminal courts, and that 61 are regularly condemned out of every 100; that 170,000 nearly are brought before courts of correction, and that 85 out of 100 are condemned; and that, if we pass to details, we find a no less alarming regularity; thus we find that between 100 and 150 individuals are annually

of the computation. I have necessarily been obliged to take into account natural influencing causes, such as climate, seasons, sex, and age.

* In an article on *Hygiène Morale,* M. Villermé has fully shown how fatal the *regime* of prisons may become to the unfortunate person who is often confined for slight offences, and cast into the midst of a collection of wicked wretches, who corrupt him. " I have been told," says he, " by a person who accompanied Napoleon to the Isle of Elba, that, in the particular and at that time philosophical conversations of the ex-emperor, he has several times been heard to say, that under whatever relation we may view man, *he is as much the result of his physical and moral atmosphere as of his own organisation.* And the idea, now advanced by many others, which is contained in this phrase, is the most general as well as the most just that can be formed on the subject before us.—*Annales d'Hygiène Publique,* Oct. 1830.

condemned to death,* 280 condemned to perpetual hard labour, 1050 to hard labour for a time, 1220 to solitary confinement (*à la réclusion*), &c.; so that this budget of the scaffold and the prisons is discharged by the French nation, with much greater regularity, no doubt, than the financial budget; and we might say, that what annually escapes the minister of justice is a more regular sum than the deficiency of revenue to the treasury.

I shall commence by considering, in a general manner, the propensity to crime in France, availing myself of the excellent documents contained in the *Comptes Généraux de l'Administration de la Justice* of this country; I shall afterwards endeavour to establish some comparisons with other countries, but with all the care and reserve which such comparisons require.

During the four years preceding 1830, 28,686 accused persons were set down as appearing before the courts of assize, that is to say, 7171 individuals annually nearly; which gives 1 accused person to 4463 inhabitants, taking the population at 32,000,000 souls. Moreover, of 100 accused, 61 persons have been condemned to punishments of greater or less severity. From the remarks made above with respect to the crimes which remain unknown or unpunished, and from mistakes which justice may make, we conceive that these numbers, although they furnish us with curious data for the past, do not give us any thing exact on the propensity to crime. However, if we consider that the two ratios which we have calculated have not sensibly varied from year to year, we shall be led to believe that they will not vary in a sensible manner for the succeeding years; and the probability that this variation will not take place is so much the greater, according as, all things being equal, the mean results of each year do not differ much from the general average, and these results have been taken from a great number of years. After these remarks, it becomes very probable that, for a Frenchman, there is 1 against 4462 chances that he will be an accused person during the course of the year; moreover, there are 61 to 39 chances, very nearly, that he will be condemned at the time that he is accused. These results are justified by the numbers of the following table :—

| Years. | Accused Persons present.† | Condemned Persons. | Inhabitants to one accused Person. | Condemned in 100 accused Persons. | Accused of Crimes against | | Ratio between the two kinds of Crime. |
					Persons.	Property.	
1826,	6,988	4,348	4,557	62	1,907	5,081	2·7
1827,	6,929	4,236	4,593	61	1,911	5,018	2·6
1828,	7,396	4,551	4,307	61	1,844	5,552	3·0
1829,	7,373	4,475	4,321	61	1,791	5,582	3·1
Total,	28,686	17,610	4,463	61	7,453	21,233	2·8

Thus, although we do not yet know the statistical documents for 1830, it is very probable that we shall again have 1 accused person in 4463 very nearly, and 61 condemned in 100 accused persons; this probability is somewhat diminished for the year 1831, and still more for the succeeding years. We may, therefore, by the results of the past, estimate what will be realised in the future. This possibility of assigning beforehand the number of accused and condemned

* The number of persons condemned to death has, however, diminished from year to year; is this owing to the increasing repugnance which tribunals feel to apply this punishment, for the abolition of which we have so many petitioners at the present day?

† The number of accused persons absent was—

| In 1826, | 1827, | 1828, | 1829, |
| 603 | 845 | 776 | 746 |

I have taken the documents of 1826, 27, 28, and 29 only, because the volume for 1825 did not contain the distinction of age or sex, of which I make use further on. Moreover, in 1825 the number of accused was 1 to 4211 inhabitants, and 61 in 100 were condemned.

persons which any country will present, must give rise to serious reflections, since it concerns the fate of several thousand men, who are driven, as it were, in an irresistible manner, towards the tribunals, and the condemnations which await them.

These conclusions are deduced from the principle, already called in so frequently in this work, that effects are proportionate to their causes, and that the effects remain the same, if the causes which have produced them do not vary. If France, then, in the year 1830, had not undergone any apparent change, and if, contrary to my expectation, I found a sensible difference between the two ratios calculated beforehand for this year and the real ratios observed, I should conclude that some alteration had taken place in the causes, which had escaped my attention. On the other hand, if the state of France has changed, and if, consequently, the causes which influence the propensity to crime have also undergone some change, I ought to expect to find an alteration in the two ratios which until that time remained nearly the same.*

It is proper to observe, that the preceding numbers only show, strictly speaking, the probability of being accused and afterwards condemned, without rendering us able to determine any thing very precise on the degree of the propensity to crime; at least unless we admit, what is very likely, that justice preserves the same activity, and the number of guilty persons who escape it preserves the same proportion from year to year.†

In the latter columns of the preceding table, is first made the distinction between crimes against persons

* After the preceding paragraphs were written, two new volumes of the *Comptes Rendus* have appeared. As the results which they contain show how far my anticipations were just, I thought it unnecessary to change the text, and shall merely give in a note the numbers corresponding to those I availed myself of before.

| Years. | Accused Persons present. | Condemned Persons. | Inhabitants to one accused Person. | Condemned in 100 accused Persons. | Accused of Crimes against | | Ratio between the Numbers of the two Classes of Criminals. |
					Persons.	Property.	
1830,	6,962	4,130	4,576	59	1,666	5,296	3·2
1831,	7,607	4,098	4,281	54	2,046	5,560	2·7
Aver.	7,284	4,114	4,392	56	1,856	5,428	2·9

Thus, notwithstanding the changes of government, and the alterations in consequence of it, the number of accused persons has not sensibly varied: "the slight increase observed in 1831, may principally be attributed to the circumstance, that in consequence of renovations in the criminal court arrangements, the operation of the judiciary police was necessarily abated in the latter months of 1830; so that many cases belonging to this period were not tried until 1831, which has increased the figure for this year."—*Report to the king.* The number of acquittals is rather greater than in the preceding years; and the same remark will be made further on in the case of Belgium, the government of which country was also changed.

The number of accused persons absent in 1830 was 787, and in 1831, 672; thus, the results of this year again agree with those of the preceding years.

† If the letters A, A¹, A², &c., represent the numbers of individuals annually committed for crimes, and a, a^1, a^2, &c., the corresponding numbers of individuals annually condemned; if we suppose, also, that the ratios $\frac{A}{a}$, $\frac{A^1}{a^1}$, $\frac{A^2}{a^2}$, &c., are sensibly equal to each other, that is to say, if $\frac{A}{a} = \frac{A^1}{a^1}$, we shall also have $\frac{A}{A^1} = \frac{a}{a^1}$. So that, if the number of the condemned A and A¹ is annually nearly the same, it will be the same with the number of those who are guilty; that is to say, the propensity to crime will preserve the same value. It is thus that the almost unchangeableness of the annual ratio of the accused to the condemned, allows us to substitute for the ratio of the condemned of any two years the ratio of the accused for the same two years.

and crimes against property: it will be remarked, no doubt, that the number of the former has diminished, whilst the latter has increased; however, these variations are so small, that they do not sensibly affect the annual ratio; and we see that we ought to reckon that three persons are accused of crimes against property to one for crimes against person.

Beside the preceding numbers I shall place those which correspond to them in the Low Countries, whilst the French code was still in force.

Years.	Accused Persons present.	Condemned Persons.	Inhabitants to one accused Person.	Condemned in 100 accused Persons.	Accused of Crimes against		Ratio.
					Persons.	Property.	
1826,	1389	1166	4392	84	304	1085	3·5
1827,	1488	1264	4100	85	314	1174	3·7

Thus, the probability of being before a court of justice was almost the same for France and for the inhabitants of the Low Countries; at the same time the number of crimes against persons was fewer among the latter, but the repression of them was also greater, since 85 individuals were condemned out of 100 accused, which may be owing to the absence of a jury, their duties being fulfilled by the judges. This modification made in the French code should be taken into consideration. Indeed, it causes a very notable difference in the degree of repression; for when once accused, the Belgian had only 16 chances against 84, or 1 to 5, of being acquitted; whilst the Frenchman, in the same circumstances, had 39 chances to 61, or nearly 3 to 5, that is to say, thrice as many. This unfavourable position in which the accused person was placed with us, might be owing to the circumstance, that the judges before whom he appeared were indeed more severe than a jury, or perhaps that they were more circumspect in acquitting a person in the Low Countries. I shall not determine which of these was the case, but simply observe, that in courts of correction the French judges are even more severe than ours, and the same is the case in courts of police.

Thus, during the four years before 1830, in France, the reports gave 679,413 arraigned persons, or 1 to 188 inhabitants. Moreover, of this number, 103,032 individuals only were acquitted, or 15 in the 100 of those arraigned. There was then 1 chance against 187 that the Frenchman would be brought before a court of correction in the course of one year, and 85 chances to 15 that when there he would be condemned.

During the years 1826 and 1827, there were 61,670 persons arraigned, in the Low Countries, before courts of correction, of whom 13,499 were acquitted; and there was one arraigned person to 198 inhabitants. Therefore, the probability of a Frenchman being before a court is rather greater than for an inhabitant of the Low Countries, as also is the probability of his being subsequently condemned.

Setting aside the northern provinces of the ancient kingdom of the Low Countries from those which at the present time form the kingdom of Belgium, and which are more intimately connected with France, we find, for the latter provinces, during the years previous to 1831:—

Years.	Accused Persons present.	Condemned Persons.	Inhabitants to one accused Person.	Condemned in 100 accused Persons.	Accused of Crimes against		Ratio.
					Persons.	Property.	
1826,	725	611	5211	84	189	536	2·8
1827,	800	682	4776	85	220	580	2·6
1828,	814	677	4741	83	230	584	2·5
1829,	753	612	5187	81	203	550	2·7
1830,	741	541	5274	73	160	581	3·8
Aver.,	767	625	5031	82	200	566	2·8

Each year, then, in Belgium, we have had, as an average, 1 person accused to 5031 inhabitants; and in France, 1 to 4400 inhabitants nearly. It is remarkable, that although these numbers do not differ much, yet the particular values for each year have not once given as great a number of accused persons for Belgium as for France.

We may observe, that in Belgium, as in France, there was a slight diminution in the number of accused persons in 1830, which originated in the same cause, namely, the closing of the tribunals for a certain period, in consequence of the revolution.

We see also that the repression of crime has sensibly diminished. This, no doubt, is thus accounted for: after revolutions men are more circumspect in their condemnations, since they are not always screened from personal danger, even in the judgments which they pronounce.

The jury has been established in Belgium since 1831; we shall soon be enabled to judge what influence this has had on the repression of crime, and what are its most remarkable consequences.

2. Of the Influence of Knowledge, of Professions, and of Climate, on the Propensity to Crime.

It may be interesting to examine the influence of the intellectual state of the accused on the nature of crimes: the French documents on this subject are such, that I am enabled to form the following table for the years 1828 and 1829; [*] to this table I have annexed the results of the years 1830 and 1831, which were not known when the reflections which succeed were written down.

Intellectual state of the Persons Accused.	1828-1829: Accused of Crimes against		Ratio of Crimes against Property to Crimes against Persons.	1830-1831: Accused of Crimes against		Ratio of Crimes against Property to Crimes against Persons.
	Persons.	Property.		Persons.	Property.	
Could not read or write,	2072	6,617	3·2	2134	6,785	3·1
Could read and write but imperfectly,	1001	2,804	2·8	1033	2,840	2·8
Could read and write well,	400	1,109	2·8	408	1,047	2·6
Had received a superior education to this 1st degree,	80	206	2·6	135†	184	1·4
	3553	10,736	3·0 aver.	3710	10,856	2·9 aver.

Thus, all things being equal, the number of crimes against persons, *compared with the number of crimes against property*, during the years 1828 and 1829, was greater according as the intellectual state of the accused was more highly developed; and this difference bore especially on murders, rapes, assassinations, blows, wounds, and other severe crimes. Must we thence conclude that knowledge is injurious to society? I am far from thinking so. To establish such an assertion, it would be necessary to commence by ascertaining how many individuals of the French nation belong to each of the four divisions which we have made above,[‡] and to find out if, proportion being considered, the individuals of that one of the divisions commit as many crimes as those of the others. If this were really the case, I should not hesitate to say

[*] The intellectual state of 474 accused persons for the year 1828 has not been noted, as also 4 for the year 1829, and 2 for 1831.

[†] The number of the accused of this class is increased in consequence of political events, and crimes against the safety of the state.

[‡] See the *Tableaux Sommaires faisant connaître l'Etat et les Besoins de l'Instruction Primaire dans le Departement de la Seine*. Paris: L. Colas; a pamphlet in 8vo, 1828, anonymous, but probably by M. Jomard. See also the *Rapport General sur la Situation et les Progrès de l'Enseignement Primaire en France et à l'Etranger*, by the same person. 8vo. Paris: L. Colas. 1832.

that, since the most enlightened individuals commit as many crimes as those who have had less education, and since their crimes are more serious, they are necessarily more criminal; but from the little we know of the diffusion of knowledge in France, we cannot state any thing decisively on this point. Indeed, it may so happen, that individuals of the enlightened part of society, while committing fewer murders, assassinations, and other severe crimes, than individuals who have received no education, also commit much fewer crimes against property, and this would explain what we have remarked in the preceding numbers. This conjecture even becomes probable, when we consider that the enlightened classes are presupposed to possess more affluence, and consequently are less frequently under the necessity of having recourse to the different modes of theft, of which crimes against property almost entirely consist; whilst affluence and knowledge have not an equal power in subduing the fire of the passions and sentiments of hatred and vengeance. It must be remarked, on the other hand, that the results contained in the preceding table only belong to two years, and consequently present a smaller probability of expressing what really is the case, especially those results connected with the most enlightened class, and which are based on very small numbers. It seems to me, then, that at the most we can only say that the ratio of the number of crimes against persons to the number of crimes against property varies with the degree of knowledge; and generally, for 100 crimes against persons, we may reckon fewer crimes against property, according as the individuals belong to a class of greater or less enlightenment. In seeking the relative annual proportion, we find the following numbers for France, to which I annex those furnished by the prisons in Belgium in 1833, according to the report of the inspector-general of prisons :—

Intellectual state of the Accused.	Absolute Number.			Relative Number.		
	Accused in France:		Condemned in Belgium: 1833.	Accused in France :		Condemned in Belgium: 1833.
	1828-29.	1830-31.		1828-29.	1830-31.	
Could not read or write, -	8,689	8,919	1972	61	61	19
Could read and write imperfectly, -	3,805	3,873	472	27	27	15
Could read and write well,	1,500	1,455	776	10	10	24
Had received a superior education to the 1st degree,	286	319		2	2	
Total, -	14,289	14,566	3220	100	100	100

Thus, the results of the years 1828 and 1829 are again reproduced identically in 1830 and 1831, in France. Sixty-one out of one hundred persons accused could neither read nor write, which is exactly the same ratio as the Belgic prisons presented. The other numbers would also be probably the same, if the second class in Belgium took in, with the individuals *able to read only*, those who could write imperfectly.

The following details, which I extract from the *Rapport au Roi* for the year 1829, will serve to illustrate what I advance :—

" The new table, which points out the professions of the accused, divides them into nine principal classes, comprising,

The *first*, individuals who work on the land, in vineyards, forests, mines, &c., 2453.

The *second*, workmen engaged with wood, leather, iron, cotton, &c., 1932.

The *third*, bakers, butchers, brewers, millers, &c., 253.

The *fourth*, hatters, hairdressers, tailors, upholsterers, &c., 327.

The *fifth*, bankers, agents, wholesale and retail merchants, hawkers, &c., 467.

The *sixth*, contractors, porters, seamen, waggoners, &c., 289.

The *seventh*, innkeepers, lemonade-sellers, servants, &c., 830.

The *eighth*, artists, students, clerks, bailiffs, notaries, advocates, priests, physicians, soldiers, annuitants, &c., 449.

The *ninth*, beggars, smugglers, strumpets, &c., 373. Women who had no profession have been classed in those which their husbands pursued.

Comparing those who are included in each class with the total number of the accused, we see that the first furnishes 33 out of 100; the second, 26; the third, 4; the fourth, 5; the fifth, 6; the sixth, 4; the seventh, 11; the eighth, 6; the ninth, 5.

If, after that, we point out the accused in each class, according to the nature of their imputed crimes, and compare them with each other, we find the following proportions :—

In the first class, 32 of the 100 accused were tried for crimes against persons, and 68 for crimes against property. These numbers are 21 and 79 for the second class; 22 and 78 for the third; 15 and 85 for the fourth and fifth; 26 and 74 for the sixth; 16 and 84 for the seventh; 37 and 63 for the eighth; 13 and 87 for the ninth.

Thus, the accused of the eighth class, who all exercised liberal professions, or enjoyed a fortune which presupposes some education, are those who, relatively, have committed the greatest number of crimes against persons; whilst 87-hundredths of the accused of the ninth class, composed of people without character, have scarcely attacked any thing but property." *

These results, which confirm the remark made before, deserve to be taken into consideration. I shall observe that, when we divide individuals into two classes, the one of liberal professions, and the other composed of journeymen, workmen, and servants, the difference is rendered still more conspicuous.

The following table will assist us in arriving at the *influence of climate* on the propensity to crime ;† it is

* See the *Comptes Generaux*, p. 9, 1830. The *Comptes Generaux* for 1830 and 1831 present the following results for each of the classes given in the text; here again we find the same constancy of numbers :—

	For 1829.	For 1830.	For 1831.
1st, -	2453	2240	2517
2d, -	1932	1813	1985
3d, -	253	225	272
4th, -	327	309	300
5th, -	467	455	425
6th, -	289	310	327
7th, -	830	848	320
8th, -	447	374	391
9th, -	373	388	469
Total, -	7373	6962	7006

† It has seemed to me that these numbers might give us a satisfactory idea of the state of knowledge in each department, especially of the lower classes, among whom the greatest number of crimes take place. This method, by which we take for each department some hundred individuals whose intellectual state we can determine, appears to me to be more certain than that of M. Dupin, which is, to judge of the education of the province by the number of children sent to school. It may be that there is generally very little knowledge in those places where schools have been but recently established, and have not as yet been able to produce any appreciable effects. In order to render the results obtained by this method more comprehensible, I have constructed a small map of France (*Plate 5*), which, by the varying depths of shade, points out the intellectual state of the different parts of this kingdom. Allowing that this map differs a little from that which M. Dupin has given, we shall, however, easily see from both maps, that Northern France, especially near Belgium and the Rhine, is the most enlightened, whilst we find the greatest darkness along a line which traverses France diagonally from Cape Finisterre to the department of the Var. With this dark line is connected a second one, which leaves the centre of France, passing to the base of the Pyrenees. Thus, the results, obtained

formed from the documents of the *Comptes Généraux de l'Administration de la Justice* in France, for the five years previous to 1830. The second and the third columns give the numbers of those condemned for crimes against persons and property; the two following columns show the ratio of these numbers to the respective population of each department in 1827; a sixth column gives the ratio of crimes against property to crimes against persons; and the last column shows how many in 100 accused were unable to read or write; the numbers which are given there only relate to the years 1828 and 1829.

Departments.	Condemned for Crimes against		Inhabitants to one Person Condemned for Crime against		Crimes against Property to one Crime against Persons.	Accused Persons in the 100 who could neither Read nor Write.
	Persons.	Property.	Persons.	Property.		
Corse, -	287	107	3224	8649	0·36	50
Haut-Rhin, -	144	295	14,192	6928	2·05	33
Lot, -	98	110	14,312	12,751	1·12	80
Ariége, -	82	78	15,118	15,893	0·95	83
Ardèche, -	108	99	15,205	16,587	0·92	67
Aveyron, -	99	160	17,677	10,938	1·62	69
Pyrenees-Orient,	41	55	18,460	13,761	1·34	76
Seine-et-Oise,	112	377	20,034	5953	3·36	56
Vaucluse,	56	118	20,090	9875	2·03	65
Moselle, -	95	274	21,534	7466	2·88	49
Lozère, -	31	53	22,384	13,092	1·71	47
Var, -	67	117	23,216	13,295	1·75	71
Bas-Rhin, -	111	341	24,120	7851	3·07	31
Seine, -	197	2496	25,720	2030	12·67	34
Bouches-du-Rhin,	63	208	25,897	7844	3·25	56
Eure, -	80	296	26,354	7123	3·70	63
Doubs, -	48	146	26,491	8909	3·04	35
Marne, -	61	244	26,643	6661	4·00	54
Tarne, -	59	169	27,767	9694	2·86	75
Seine-Inférieure,	123	850	27,980	4049	6·91	59
Drôme, -	49	133	29,163	10,744	2·71	71
Calvados, -	84	394	29,819	6357	4·69	52
Hautes-Alpes,	21	47	29,840	13,333	2·24	42
Landes, -	44	153	30,149	8690	3·48	86
Basses-Alpes, -	25	62	30,613	12,344	2·48	66
Vosges, -	62	132	30,632	14,388	2·13	45
Gard, -	53	129	32,788	13,471	2·43	67
Loiret, -	46	215	33,068	7075	4·67	70
Vienne, -	40	170	33,459	7873	4·25	81
Ille-et-Vilaine,	82	318	33,747	8702	3·88	66
Hérault, -	50	92	33,956	18,454	1·84	62
Aude, -	39	75	34,102	17,733	2·42	72
Rhone, -	61	302	34,146	6895	4·95	51
FRANCE, -	4662	17,543	34,168	9080	3·76	60
Puy-de-Dome,	82	157	34,547	18,044	1·91	75
Loire-Inférieure,	66	160	34,628	14,284	2·42	76
Aube, -	34	206	35,553	5868	6·06	54
Isère, -	73	220	36,101	11,958	3·01	62
Dordogne, -	64	149	36,256	15,573	2·33	76
Jura, -	33	123	37,344	12,613	2·96	50
Haute-Marne,	32	94	38,254	13,023	2·93	46
Indre-et-Loire,	37	131	39,211	11,075	3·54	79
Charente, -	45	92	39,295	19,220	2·05	60
Haute-Loire,	36	35	39,677	40,810	0·97	75
Allier, -	35	124	40,757	11,504	3·54	91
Pas-de-Calais,	76	568	41,751	5660	7·38	65
Basses-Pyrenees,	47	142	43,880	14,524	3·02	73
Gers, -	35	91	43,943	16,901	2·60	70
Corrèze, -	32	56	44,513	25,430	1·75	77
Orne, -	48	183	45,248	11,868	3·81	66
Seine-et-Marne,	35	167	45,459	9527	4·77	58
Maine-et-Loire,	50	197	45,867	11,641	3·94	81
Haute-Vienne,	30	120	46,058	11,515	4·00	79
Hautes-Pyrenees.	24	64	46,263	17,349	2·67	71
Eure-et-Loire,	30	231	46,592	6013	7·70	63
Ain, -	36	84	47,448	20,335	2·33	60
Deux-Sèvres,	30	124	48,043	11,623	4·13	61

(*Table continued.*)

Departments.	Condemned for Crimes against		Inhabitants to one Person Condemned for Crime against		Crimes against Property to one Crime against Persons.	Accused Persons in the 100 who could neither Read nor Write.
	Persons.	Property.	Persons.	Property.		
Charente-Infé-rieure, }	44	257	48,199	8252	5·84	66
Meurthe, -	52	249	48,788	10,189	4·79	42
Sarthe, -	45	177	49,613	12,614	3·93	87
Haute-Garonne,	41	190	49,636	10,711	4·63	71
Haute-Saône,	33	134	49,643	12,225	4·06	43
Mayenne, -	35	146	50,591	12,128	4·17	82
Morbihan, -	41	183	52,129	11,679	4·46	78
Cantal, -	25	75	52,403	17,468	3·00	61
Loir-et-Cher,	22	142	52,424	8122	6·45	68
Nord, -	91	543	52,893	8783	6·02	71
Loire, -	34	104	55,252	18,063	3·06	54
Côte-d'Or,	35	160	55,992	11,592	4·57	48
Nièvre, -	24	109	56,620	12,467	4·54	65
Saone-et-Loire,	45	168	57,308	15,350	3·73	74
Vendée, -	28	106	57,648	15,228	3·62	77
Lot-et-Garonne,	29	111	58,084	15,181	3·83	68
Meuse, -	26	105	58,911	14,588	4·04	39
Yonne, -	29	140	58,986	12,219	4·83	45
Cher, -	21	98	59,188	12,683	4·67	86
Finistère, -	42	252	59,863	9977	6·00	79
Manche, -	51	247	59,922	12,373	4·84	62
Tarn-et-Garonne,	20	89	60,397	13,572	4·45	88
Côtes-du-Nord,	47	292	61,881	9960	6·21	90
Gironde, -	41	207	65,628	12,999	5·05	67
Aisne, -	36	259	67,995	9451	7·20	62
Oise, -	23	163	83,723	11,814	7·09	52
Somme, -	31	257	84,864	10,230	8·29	64
Ardennes, -	15	92	93,875	15,346	6·13	37
Indre, -	12	96	99,012	19,377	8·00	77
Creuse, -	6	40	210,777	31,617	6·67	80

To the preceding documents I shall join those concerning the ancient kingdom of the Low Countries* and the dutchy of the Lower Rhine, where the French code is still in force, and allows comparisons to be still established:—

Provinces.	Condemned for Crimes against		Inhabitants to one Person Condemned for Crimes against		Crimes against Property to one Crime against Persons.	Inhabitants to one Pupil at School.
	Persons.	Property.	Persons.	Property.		
Brabant, Southern,	61	168	16,336	5932	2·75	13
Flanders, Eastern,	82	154	17,100	9104	1·88	14
Limbourg, -	32	120	20,384	5436	3·75	15
Overyssel, - -	16	42	20,385	7765	2·62	7
Brabant, Northern,	30	66	22,031	10,014	2·20	9
Anvers, -	29	113	22,562	5800	3·90	12
Groningen and Drenthe, }	18	98	23,611	4296	5·44	7
Liege, - -	26	82	25,107	7961	3·15	15
Flanders, Western,	46	142	25,222	8171	3·09	15
Namur, - -	14	66	27,433	5819	4·71	9
Gueldres, -	21	114	27,633	5090	2·20	9
Holland, Southern,	28	216	32,000	4148	7·71	11
Holland, Northern, and Utrecht, }	28	242	37,560	4000	9·42	10
Luxembourg, -	14	47	42,208	12,572	3·34	8
Hainault, - -	21	76	52,712	14,565	3·62	10
Zealand, -	5	86	53,450	3106	17·20	10
Friesland, -	3	103	132,248	3852	34·33	8
Low Countries,	474	1956	25,747	6239	4·13	10
Low Countries (crimes),	424	1691	28,783	7217	4·00	10
Dutchy of the Lower Rhine, }	296	994	33,784	10,060	3·36	13
France, -	7160	20,308	21,648	7632	2·84	27

by two different modes, nevertheless agree with each other in a very satisfactory manner. We may say that we find the greatest enlightenment where there is the greatest freedom of communication, and in the course of large rivers, such as the Rhine, the Seine, the Meuse, &c. In Southern France, the trading sea-coasts, and the banks of the Rhone, are also less obscure, while the absence of enlightenment is perceived chiefly in those parts of France which are not traversed by great commercial roads. We naturally look for instruction in those places where the need of it is greatest.

* The numbers for the Low Countries embrace the years 1826–27, and for the dutchy of the Lower Rhine the years from 1822 to 1826, according to the *Revue Encyclopedique* for the month of August 1830. Since this summary gives us the number of crimes and not of the condemned, I have thought proper to give the number of crimes for France and the Low Countries, in order to render the results comparable.

As it would be very difficult to form an idea of the whole of the results contained in the preceding tables, and as at the same time it would be impossible to embrace the whole at one glance, I have endeavoured to render them perceptible by shades of greater or less depth, placed on a map of France and the Low Countries, according to the greater or less number of crimes against persons or property, in proportion to the population (*See plate 6*). The first figurative map belongs to crimes against persons; it shows us at first, by the darkness of the shades, that the greatest number of crimes are committed in Corsica, in the South of France, and particularly in Languedoc and Provence, as well as Alsace and the Valley of the Seine. The southern part of the Low Countries, with the exception of Hainault and Luxembourg, present also rather deep tints. However, it is proper to observe, that the shades are perhaps more obscure than they ought to be, if we consider that they represent the number of condemned people, and that in general, in the Low Countries, the repression has been much stronger than in France, since in the latter country only 61 individuals are condemned in every 100 accused, whilst in the Low Countries, 85 is the proportion. On the contrary, Central France, Brittany, Maine, Picardy, as well as Zealand and Friesland, present much more satisfactory shades. If we compare this map with that which indicates the state of instruction, we shall be disposed to believe, at first, that crimes are in a measure in inverse ratio to the degree of knowledge. The figurative map of crimes against persons and those of crimes against property presents more analogy. In like manner, the departments which show themselves advantageously or disadvantageously on either side, may be arranged in the following manner, making three principal classes :—

FIRST CLASS.—*Departments where the number of those condemned for crimes against persons and property exceeds the average of France.*

Corse, Landes, Rhône, Bouches-du-Rhône, Doubs, Haut-Rhin, Bas-Rhin, Moselle, Seine-Inférieure, Calvados, Eure, Seine-et-Oise, Seine, Marne, Loiret, Vienne, Ille-et-Vilaine—17 departments.

SECOND CLASS.—*Departments where the number of those condemned for crimes against property and persons has been less than the average of France.*

Creuse, Indre, Cher, Nièvre, Saône-et-Loire, Jura, Ain, Isère, Loire, Haut-Loire, Cantal, Puy-de-Dôme, Allier, Corrèze, Haut-Vienne, Basses-Pyrénées, Hautes-Pyrénées, Haute-Garonne, Gers, Tarn-et-Garonne, Lot-et-Garonne, Gironde, Dordogne, Charente, Deux-Sèvres, Vendée, Loire-Inférieure, Maine-et-Loire, Sarthe, Orne, Mayenne, Manche, Finistère, Morbihan, Côtes-du-Nord, Somme, Oise, Aisne, Ardennes, Meuse, Meurthe, Haute-Saône, Haute-Marne, Côte-d'Or, Yonne, Seine-et-Marne—47 departments.

THIRD CLASS.—*Departments where the number of those condemned for crimes against persons only, or against property only, has been less than the average of France.*

Var, Hautes-Alpes, Basses-Alpes, Drôme, Vaucluse, Gard, Ardèche, Lozère, Aveyron, Lot, Tarn, Hérault, Aude, Pyrénées-Orientales, Ariége, Charente-Inferi-cure, Loir-et-Cher, Eure-et-Loire, Nord, Pas-de-Calais, Aube,-Vosges—22 departments.

In making the same distinction with regard to the provinces of the Low Countries,* we find—
FIRST CLASS—Southern Brabant, Anvers, Limbourg, Groningen, and Drenthe—5 provinces.
SECOND CLASS—Hainault, Luxembourg—2 provinces.

* See, for the most ample accounts, La Statistique des Tribunaux de la Belgique, pendant les Années 1826, 1827, 1828, 1829, and 1830, published by MM. Quetelet and Smits. 4to. Brussels : 1832.

THIRD CLASS—Namur, Liege, Western Flanders, Eastern Flanders, Zealand, Northern Brabant, Southern Holland, Northern Holland, Utrecht, Guelderland, Overyssel, Friesland—12 provinces.

Before endeavouring to deduce conclusions from the preceding calculations, I shall remark that certain ratios cannot be rigorously compared, on account of the defective valuation (or census) of the population, or from an unequal degree of repression in the different courts of justice. It will be difficult enough to find out the errors arising from the first cause, as we have only, for the elements of verification, the relative numbers of births and deaths ; as to the unequal degree of repression, such is not exactly the case, for, besides that we are led to believe that the activity of justice in finding out the authors of crimes is not every where the same, we see that acquittals are not always in the same ratio. Thus, according to the documents from 1825 to 1829, 61 individuals out of every 100 accused have been condemned in France, yet the degree of repression has generally been stronger in the northern than in the southern part of the country. The Court of Justice of Rouen has condemned the greatest number, and it has condemned 71 individuals out of 100 accused at the least ; the courts of Dijon, Anjou, Douai, Nanci, Orleans, Caen, Paris, Rennes, have also exceeded the average ; the courts of Metz, Colmar, Amiens, Bordeaux, Bourges, Besançon, Grenoble, Lyons, and La Corse, have presented nearly the same average as France ; whilst the acquittals have been more numerous in the southern courts, such as Toulouse, Poitiers, Nismes, Aix, Riom, Pau, Argen, Limoges, and Montpellier—the two last courts having condemned, at an average, only 52 individuals of 100 accused. It yet remains for examination, whether these decisive inequalities in the number of acquittals in the north and south of France are owing to a greater facility in bringing forward accusations, or to indulgence to the accused. It appears to me probable, that it may be in part owing to crimes against persons being more common, all things being equal, in the south, and crimes against property in the north ; we know, also, that more acquittals take place in the first class of crimes than in the second. However the case may be, I think it will be proper not to lose sight of this double cause of error which I have just pointed out.

If we now cast our eyes over the departments of France which have exceeded the average of crimes against persons as well as of crimes against property, we shall first find Corsica and Landes to be, from their manners and customs, in peculiar circumstances, and which will scarcely permit of their being compared with the rest of France.

The Corsicans, indeed, impelled by cruel prejudices, and warmly embracing feelings of revenge, which are frequently transmitted from generation to generation, almost make a virtue of homicide, and commit the crime to excess. Offences against property are not frequent, and yet their number exceeds the average of France. We cannot attribute this state of things to want of instruction, since the number of accused who could neither read nor write was comparatively less than in France. This is not the case in Landes, where almost nine-tenths of the accused were in a state of complete ignorance. This department, where a poor and weak population live dispersed, as it were, in the midst of fogs, is one where civilisation has made the least progress. Although Landes is found in the most unfavourable class as regards crimes, it is nevertheless proper to say that it does not differ much from the average of France : we may make the same observations on the departments of Vienne and Ille-et-Vilaine. As to the other departments, we may observe that they are generally the most populous in France, in which we find four of the most important cities, Paris, Lyons, Marseilles, and Rouen ; and that they also are the most industrious—those which present the greatest changes and intercourse with strangers. We may be surprised not to find with them the departments of the Gironde and Loire-Ihferieure, which seem to be almost in the same circumstances as the departments of Bouches-du-Rhône and Seine-Inférieure, especially if we consider that, with respect to knowledge, they seem less favoured than these last,`and the repression of crime also has generally been effective. This remark is particularly applicable to the department of the Gironde, for the Loire-Inférieure does not differ so much from the average of France. I shall not hesitate to attribute these differences to a greater morality in one part than the other. And this conjecture becomes more probable, if we observe that the whole of the departments of the south of France, which are on the shores of the sea from the Basses-Pyrénées to La Manche, except Landes and Ille-et-Vilaine which have already been mentioned, fall below the average of France for crimes against persons; and that, on the contrary, all the departments, without exception, which are on the shores of the Mediterranean, as well as the ones adjacent to them, exceed this average. We may also remark, that the shores of the Atlantic, from Basses-Pyrénées to La Manche generally fall below the average for crime against property.

The third class presents us with fifteen departments, on the border of the Mediterranean, and which all exceed the average of France in crimes against persons and are below the average in crimes against property. The districts on the Mediterranean appear, then, to have a very strong propensity to the first kind of crimes. Of seven other departments of the same class, one only exceeds the average for crimes against person, and that is Vosges in Alsace; the others exceed the average of crimes against property.

The departments of the second class, where the fewest condemnations for crimes against persons and property take place, are generally situated in the centre of France, on the shores of the Atlantic, from the Basses-Pyrénées to La Manche, and in the valleys watered by the Somme, the Oise, and the Meuse.

The following is a summary of what has been said:—

1. The greatest number of crimes against persons and property take place in the departments which are crossed by or near to the Rhone, the Rhine, and the Seine, at least in their navigable portions.

2. The fewest crimes against persons and property are committed in the departments in the centre of France, in those which are situated in the west towards the Atlantic, from the Basses-Pyrénées to La Manche, and in those towards the north, which are traversed by the Somme, the Oise, and the Meuse.

3. The shores of the Mediterranean and the adjacent departments show, all things being equal, a stronger propensity to crimes against persons, and the northern parts of France to crimes against property.

After having established these facts, if we seek to go back to the causes which produce them, we are immediately stopped by numerous obstacles. And, indeed, the causes influencing crimes are so numerous and different, that it becomes almost impossible to assign to each its degree of importance. It also frequently happens, that causes which appear very influential, disappear before others of which we had scarcely thought at first, and this is what I have especially found in actual researches: and I confess that I have been probably too much occupied with the influence which we assign to education in abating the propensity to crime; it seems to me that this common error especially proceeds from our expecting to find fewer crimes in a country, because we find more children in it who attend school, and because there is in general a greater number of persons able to read and write. We ought rather to take notice of the degree of moral instruction; for very often the education received at school only facilitates the com-

mission of crime.* We also consider poverty as generally conducing to crime; yet the department of Creuse, one of the poorest in France, is that which in every respect presents the greatest morality. Likewise, in the Low Countries, the most moral province is Luxembourg, where there is the greatest degree of poverty. It is proper, however, that we come to a right understanding of the meaning of the word poverty, which is here employed in an acceptation which may be considered improper. A province, indeed, is not poor because it possesses fewer riches than another, if its inhabitants, as in Luxembourg, are sober and active; if, by their labour, they can certainly obtain the means of relieving their wants, and gratifying tastes which are proportionally moderate; according as the inequality of fortune is less felt, and does not so much excite temptation: we should say, with more reason, that this province enjoys a moderate affluence. Poverty is felt the most in provinces where great riches have been amassed, as in Flanders, Holland, the department of the Seine, &c., and above all, in the manufacturing countries, where, by the least political commotion, by the least obstruction to the outlets of merchandise, thousands of individuals pass suddenly from a state of comfort to one of misery. These rapid changes from one state to another give rise to crime, particularly if those who suffer are surrounded by materials of temptation, and are irritated by the continual aspect of luxury and of the inequality of fortune, which renders them desperate.

It seems to me that one of the first distinctions to be made in our present inquiry, regards the different races of mankind who inhabit the countries which we are considering; as we shall shortly see, this point is of the greatest importance, although not the first which presents itself to the mind. "The population of France belongs to three different races—the *Celtic race*, which forms nearly three-fifths of its inhabitants; the *German race*, which comprehends those of the late provinces of Flanders, Alsace, and part of Lorraine; and the *Pelasgian race*, scattered along the shores of the Mediterranean and in Corsica. The changes of manners," adds Malte-Brun, " to which this division is exposed, may alter the character of a people, but cannot change it entirely." † If we cast our eyes over the figurative map of crimes against persons, this distinction of people is perceived in a remarkable manner. We shall see that the Pelasgian race, *scattered over the shores of the Mediterranean and in Corsica*, is particularly addicted to crimes against persons; among the Germanic race, which extends over Alsace, the dutchy of the Lower Rhine, a part of Lorraine, and the Low Countries, where the greater proportion of persons and of property gives rise to more occasions of committing crime, and where the frequent use of strong drinks leads more often to excesses, we have generally a great many crimes against property and persons. The Batavians and Frieslanders, who also belong to the Germanic race, are more especially prone to crimes against property. Lastly, the Celtic race appears the most moral of the three which we have considered, especially as regards crimes against persons; they occupy the greatest part of France and the Wallone of Belgium (*et la partie Wallone de la Belgique*). It would appear, moreover, that frontier countries, where the races are most crossed with each other, and where there is generally the most disturbance, and where the customhouses are established, are the most exposed to demoralisation.

After having admitted this distinction, based upon

* M. Guerry has arrived at conclusions similar to mine, and almost at the same time, in his *Essai sur la Statistique Morale de la France*, p. 51, and has expressed them almost in the same terms; the same results have also been obtained in England, Germany, and the United States.

† Précis de la Géographie Universelle, livre 159.

the differences of races, it remains to be examined what are the local anomalies which influence the morality of the people and modify their character.

The most remarkable anomaly which the Celtic race seems to present, is observed in the department of the valley of the Seine, especially below Paris ; many causes contribute to this. We first observe that these departments, from their extent, contain the greatest proportion of persons and property, and consequently present more occasions for committing crimes ; it is there that there are the greatest changes in the people, and the greatest influx of people from all countries without character, in a manner which must even have altered the primitive race more than any where else ; lastly, it is there also where the greatest number of industrial establishments are found ; and, as we have already had occasion to observe, these establishments maintain a dense population, whose means of subsistence are more precarious than in any other profession. The same remark is applicable to the valley of the Rhone, and with the more reason, as the Pelagian race has been able, in ascending this river, to penetrate farther into the interior of the country than any where else.

The commercial and industrious provinces of the Low Countries are likewise those in which the greatest number of crimes are committed.

As to the greater number of crimes against property to be observed as we advance towards the north, I think we may attribute it, in a great measure, to the inequality between riches and wants. The great cities, and the capitals especially, present an unfavourable subject, because they possess more allurements to passions of every kind, and because they attract people of bad character, who hope to mingle with impunity in the crowd.

It is remarkable that several of the poorest departments of France, and at the same time the least educated, such as Creuse, Indre, Cher, Haute-Vienne, Allier, &c., are at the same time the most moral, whilst the contrary is the case in most of the departments which have the greatest wealth and instruction. These apparent singularities are, I think, explained by the observations which have been made above. Morality increases with the degree of education in the late kingdom of the Low Countries, which would lead us to believe that the course of education was better.

The influence of climate is not very sensible here, as we may see by comparing Guienne and Gascoigne with Provence and Languedoc, and the inhabitants of the Hautes and Basses Pyrénées to the inhabitants of the Hautes and Basses Alpes, which, notwithstanding, are under the same latitudes. We may also say that the influence of knowledge and of climate partly disappears before more energetic influences ; and that they are moreover far from effacing the moral character of the three races of men who inhabit the country which we are considering. Nevertheless, we cannot but allow, when bringing the ratios of the sixth column of our table together, that the number of crimes against property, in proportion to the number of crimes against persons, is increased considerably in advancing towards the north.

It is to be regretted that the documents of the courts of justice of other countries cannot be compared with those of France and the Low Countries. The difference in laws and the classifications of crime render direct comparisons impossible. Yet the countries of some extent, and which give the distinction of crimes against persons and crimes against property, allow at least of our drawing a comparison between their different provinces under this head. It perhaps will not be without some interest to our inquiry to compare the different parts of Prussia and Austria with one another. The data of criminal justice in Austria are extracted from the *Bulletin des Sciences* of M. de Férussac, for November 1829, and relate to the five years from 1819 to 1823 ; those of

Prussia are extracted from the *Revue Encyclopédique* for August 1830, and relate to the three years from 1824 to 1826 inclusive. I have followed the same form of table as the above : nevertheless, I regret that I could not give the number of children in the schools of the different parts of Austria. For Prussia, I have taken the number of children in 1000 of those who attend the schools, according to the statement of the *Revue Encyclopédique*.

Arrondissements.	Crimes against		Inhabitants to one Crime against		Crimes against Property to one Crime against Persons.	Inhabitants to one Scholar.
	Persons.	Property.	Persons.	Property.		
AUSTRIA.						
Dalmatia,	2986	2,540	535	625	0·85	?
Gallicia & Bukovina,	5234	14,105	3,955	1470	2·70	?
Tyrol, - -	658	2,516	5,707	1492	3·82	?
Moravia & Silesia,	753	3,545	12,662	2689	4·71	13
Gratz-Leibach & Trietz, or Internal Austria,	589	*2,479	13,311	3188	4·21	10
Lower Austria (or, Cotes de l'Ens),	573	7,099	17,130	1382	12·37	10
Bohemia, -	737	*7,221	18,437	1881	9·90	9
						Scholars in 1000 Children.
PRUSSIA.						
Prussia, - -	249	8,875	22,741	639	35·65	451
Saxony, - -	147	5,815	27,588	697	39·56	491
Posen, - -	97	3,481	31,440	875	35·88	490
Silesia, -	228	7,077	33,714	1086	31·04	584
Westphalia, -	92	3,383	38,436	1045	36·77	525
Brandenburg, -	112	5,431	39,496	688	57·42	468
Pomerania, -	27	1,622	92,131	1533	60·11	940

It would be very difficult to point out the various races of men who have peopled the countries mentioned in the preceding table, because they are so much mixed in certain parts, that their primitive character is almost lost. The German race predominates in the Prussian states, and is mixed with the northern Sclavonians, particularly along the shores of the Baltic and ancient Prussia, and with the western Sclavonians in the Grand-Dutchy of Posen and Silesia. In the Austrian states, and especially in the northern and eastern parts, the Sclavonian race is again mixed with the German ; Malte-Brun even thinks that in Moravia the Sclavonians are three times as numerous as the Germans :[†] they are divided into several tribes, of which the most remarkable is the Wallachians ; "they are brave in war, tolerant in religion, and scrupulously honest in their habits." The Tyrolese, formed of the ancient Rhœti, would be, according to Pliny (book iii. chap. 19), originally from Etruria ; the Dalmatians, of Sclavonic origin, are also mingled with Italians.

It will appear, then, also, from the table which has just been given, that crimes are more numerous in Dalmatia, where the blood of the south is mixed with the blood of the people of the north. Among the Tyrolese, we find also the traces of more energetic passions than among the other people under the Austrian dominion, excepting, however, the inhabitants of Gallicia, descendants of the Rosniacks, who proceeded, together with the Croatians and Dalmatians, from the Eastern Sclavonians.[‡] Classing the people according to the degree of crime, it would appear that they are in the following order :—Etruscans or Italians, Sclavonians, and Germans.[§] It would also appear

* The numbers for Bohemia and Internal Austria only relate to the four years 1819, 1820, 1822, and 1823.

† Précis de Géographie Universelle, livre 145.   ‡ Ibid. l. 116.

§ The western Sclavonians are composed, according to Malte-Brun, of Poles, Bohemians or *Tcheches*, of the *Slovaques* of Hungary, the Serbes in Lusatia.—*Livre* 116. " The distinctions that the eastern Sclavonians have a greater propensity to crime than the northern and western ones, who are more mixed with the Germans, and are in a more advanced state of civilisation. We see from the preceding table, that the state of instruction in Prussia is in a direct ratio to the number of crimes; it appears to be nearly the same in the countries under the Austrian dominion.

3. On the Influence of Seasons on the Propensity to Crime.

The seasons have a well-marked influence in augmenting and diminishing the number of crimes. We may form some idea from the following table, which contains the number of crimes committed in France against persons and property, during each month, for three years, as well as the ratio of these numbers. We can also compare the numbers of this table with those which I have given to show the influence of seasons on the development of mental alienation, and we shall find the most remarkable coincidences, especially for crimes against persons, which would appear to be most usually dependent on failures of the reasoning powers :*—

Months.	Crimes against Persons.	Crimes against Property.	Ratio: 1827-28.	Crimes against Persons.	Crimes against Property.	Ratio: 1830-31.
January, - -	282	1,095	3·89	189	666	3·52
February, - -	272	910	3·35	194	563	2·90
March, - -	335	968	2·89	205	602	2·94
April, - - -	314	841	2·68	197	548	2·78
May, - - -	381	844	2·22	213	569	2·67
June, - - -	414	850	2·05	208	602	2·90
July, - - -	379	828	2·18	188	501	2·66
August, - - -	382	934	2·44	247	596	2·41
September, -	355	896	2·52	176	584	3·32
October, - -	285	926	3·25	207	586	2·83
November, -	301	961	3·20	223	651	2·95
December, - -	347	1,152	3·33	181	691	3 82
Total, - - -	3847	11,205	2·77	2428	7159	2·94

First, the epoch of maximum (June) in respect to the number of crimes against persons, coincides pretty nearly with the epoch of minimum in respect to crimes against property, and this takes place in summer; whilst, on the contrary, the minimum of the number of crimes against persons, and the maximum of the number of crimes against property, takes place in winter. Comparing these two kinds of crimes, we find that in the month of January nearly four crimes take place against property to one against persons, and in the month of June only two to three. These differences are readily explained by considering that during winter misery and want are more especially felt, and cause an increase of the number of crimes against property, whilst the violence of the passions

between the Sclave (Sclavonian) and the German are, the care which the former takes of his property, and his constant desire to acquire more; he is not so industrious, not so capable of attachment and fidelity in his affections, and more disposed to seek for society and dissipation. He prides himself on greater prudence, and is generally distrustful, especially in his dealings with Germans, whom he always regards as a kind of enemy."—*Livre* 114. Malte-Brun also makes a distinction of Germans of the north and Germans of the south. "The Thuringerwald divides Germany into two regions—the north and the south. The German of the north, living on potatoes, butter, and cheese, deprived of beer and spirits, is the most robust, frugal, and intelligent: it is also with him that Protestantism has the most proselytes. Delicate in his mode of life, accustomed to wine, sometimes even given to drunkenness, the German of the south is more sprightly but also more superstitious."—*Livre* 148.

* The observations which we possess are neither so numerous nor so carefully compiled as to enable us to affirm that any direct ratio exists between the propensity to crimes against persons and the tendency to mental alienation; yet the existence of this ratio becomes more probable if we consider that we find again the same coincidence regarding the influence of age.

predominating in summer, excites to more frequent personal collisions.

The periods of maxima and minima also coincide with those of the maxima and minima of births and deaths, as we have already shown.

The *Comptes Généraux* of France also contain data on the hours at which crimes have been committed, but only for thefts in Paris and the neighbourhood. These data are hitherto too few to draw any satisfactory conclusions from them.

4. On the Influence of Sex on the Propensity to Crime.

We have already been considering the influence which climate, the degree of education, differences of the human race, seasons, &c., have on the propensity to crime; we shall now investigate the influence of sex.

At the commencement, we may observe that, out of 28,686 accused, who have appeared before the courts in France, during the four years before 1830, there were found 5416 women, and 23,270 men, that is to say, 23 women to 100 men. Thus, the propensity to crime in general gives the ratio of 23 to 100 for the sexes. This estimate supposes that justice exercises its duties as actively with regard to women as to men; and this is rendered probable by the fact, that the severity of repression is nearly the same in the case of both sexes; in other words, that women are treated with much the same severity as men.

We have just seen that, in general, the propensity to crime in men is about four times as great as in women, in France; but it will be important to examine further, if men are four times as criminal, which will be supposing that the crimes committed by the sexes are equally serious. We shall commence by making a distinction between crimes against property and crimes against persons. At the same time, we shall take the numbers obtained for each year, that we may see the limits in which they are comprised :—

Years.	Crimes against Persons.			Crimes against Property.		
	Men.	Women.	Ratio.	Men.	Women.	Ratio.
1826, -	1639	268	0·16	4073	1008	0·25
1827, - -	1637	274	0·17	4020	998	0·25
1828, - -	1576	270	0·17	4396	1156	0·26
1829, - -	1552	239	0·15	4379	1203	0·27
Averages,	1601	263	0·16	4217	1091	0 26
1830, - -	1412	254	0·18	4196	1100	0·26
1831, - -	1813	233	0·13	4567	993	0·22
Averages,	1612	243	0·15	4381	1046	0·24

Although the number of crimes against persons may have diminished slightly, whilst crimes against property have become rather more numerous, yet we see that the variations are not very great; they have but little modified the ratios between the numbers of the accused of the two sexes. We have 26 women to 100 men in the accusations for crimes against property, and for crimes against persons the ratio has been only 16 to 100.* In general, crimes against persons are of a more serious nature than those against property, so that our distinction is favourable to the women, and we may affirm that men, in France, are four times as criminal as women. It must be observed, that the ratio 16 to 26 is nearly the same as that of the strength of the two sexes. However, it is proper to examine things more narrowly, and especially to take notice of individual crimes, at least of those which are committed in so great a number, that the inferences drawn from them may possess some degree of probability. For this purpose, in the following table I have col-

* These conclusions only refer to the results of the four years before 1830. The numbers of the following years, which have been since added to the table, give almost the same ratios.

lected the numbers relating to the four years before 1830, and calculated the different ratios; the crimes are classed according to the degree of magnitude of this ratio. I have also grouped crimes nearly of the same nature together, such as issuing false money, counterfeits, falsehoods in statements or in commercial transactions, &c.

Nature of Crimes.	Men.	Women.	Women to 100 Men.
Infanticide, - - -	30	426	1320
Miscarriage, - -	15	39	260
Poisoning, - - -	77	73	91
House robbery (vol domestique),	2648	1602	60
Parricide, - - -	44	22	50
Incendiarism of buildings and other things, - - -	279	94	34
Robbery of churches,	176	47	27
Wounding of parents (blessures envers ascendans), - -	292	63	22
Theft, - - -	10,677	2249	21
False evidence and suborning, -	307	51	17
Fraudulent bankruptcy, -	353	57	16
Assassination, - - -	947	111	12
False coining (fausse monnaie), counterfeit making, false affirmations in deeds, &c. - -	1669	177	11
Rebellion, - - -	612	60	10
Highway robbery, - -	648	54	8
Wounds and blows, - -	1447	78	5
Murder, - - -	1112	44	4
Violation and seduction, - -	685	7	1
Violation on persons under 15 years of age, - - -	585	5	1

As we have already observed, to the commission of crime the three following conditions are essential—the will, which depends on the person's morality, the opportunity, and the facility of effecting it. Now, the reason why females have less propensity to crime than males, is accounted for by their being more under the influence of sentiments of shame and modesty, as far as morals are concerned; their dependent state, and retired habits, as far as occasion or opportunity is concerned; and their physical weakness, so far as the facility of acting is concerned. I think we may attribute the differences observed in the degree of criminality to these three principal causes. Sometimes the whole three concur at the same time: we ought, on such occasions, to expect to find their influence very marked, as in rapes and seductions; thus, we have only 1 woman to 100 men in crimes of this nature. In poisoning, on the contrary, the number of accusations for either sex is nearly equal. When force becomes necessary for the destruction of a person, the number of women who are accused becomes much fewer; and their numbers diminish in proportion, according to the necessity of the greater publicity before the crime can be perpetrated: the following crimes also take place in the order in which they are stated—infanticide, miscarriage, parricide, wounding of parents, assassinations, wounds and blows, murder. With respect to infanticide, woman has not only many more opportunities of committing it than man, but she is in some measure impelled to it, frequently by misery, and almost always from the desire of concealing a fault, and avoiding the shame or scorn of society, which, in such cases, thinks less unfavourably of man. Such is not the case with other crimes involving the destruction of an individual: it is not the degree of the crime which keeps a woman back, since, in the series which we have given, parricides and wounding of parents are more numerous than assassinations, which again are more frequent than murder, and wounds and blows generally; it is not simply weakness, for then the ratio for parricide and wounding of parents should be the same as for murder and wounding of strangers. These differences are more especially owing to the habits and sedentary life of females; they can only conceive and execute guilty projects on individuals with whom they are in the greatest intimacy: thus, compared with man, her assassinations are more often in her family than out of it; and in society she commits assassination rather than murder, which often takes place after excess of drink, and the quarrels to which women are less exposed.

If we now consider the different kinds of theft, we shall find that the ratios of the propensity to crime are arranged in a similar series: thus, we have successively house robbery, robbery in churches, robberies in general, and, lastly, highway robbery, for which strength and audacity are necessary. The less conspicuous propensity to cheating in general, and to fraudulent bankruptcy, again depend on the more secluded life of females, their separation from trade, and that, in some cases, they are less capable than men—for example, in coining false money and issuing counterfeits.

If we attempt to analyse facts, it seems to me that the difference of morality in man and woman is not so great as is generally supposed, excepting only as regards modesty; I do not speak of the timidity arising from this last sentiment, in like manner as it does from the physical weakness and seclusion of females. As to these habits themselves, I think we may form a tolerable estimate of their influence by the ratios which exist between the sexes in crimes of different kinds, where neither strength has to be taken into consideration, nor modesty—as in theft, false witnessing, fraudulent bankruptcy, &c.; these ratios are about 100 to 21 or 17, that is to say, about 5 or 6 to 1. As to other modes of cheating, the difference is a little greater, from the reasons already stated. If we try to give a numerical expression of the intensity of the causes by which women are influenced, as, for example, the influence of strength, we may estimate it as being in proportion to the degree of strength itself, or as 1 to 2 nearly; and this is the ratio of the number of parricides for each sex. For crimes where both physical weakness and the retired life of females must be taken into account, as in assassinations and highway robberies, following the same plan in our calculations, it will be necessary to multiply the ratio of power or strength ½ by the degree of dependence 1·5, which gives 1·10, a quantity which really falls between the values 12·100 and 8·100, the ratios given in the table. With respect to murder, and blows and wounds, these crimes depend not merely on strength and a more or less sedentary life, but still more on being in the habit of using strong drinks and quarrelling. The influence of this latter cause might almost be considered as 1 to 3 for the sexes. It may be thought that the estimates which I have here pointed out, cannot be of an exact nature, from the impossibility of assigning the share of influence which the greater modesty of woman, her physical weakness, her dependence, or rather her more retired life, and her feebler passions, which are also less frequently excited by liquors, may have respectively on any crime in particular. Yet, if such were the characters in which the sexes more particularly differ from each other, we might, by analyses like those now given, assign their respective influence with some probability of truth, especially if the observations were very numerous. I do not speak of modes of justice, of legislation in general, of the state of knowledge, of means of providing for physical wants, &c., which may powerfully contribute to increase or diminish the number of crimes, but whose influence is generally not very evident as regards the ratio of the accused of each sex.

Perhaps it may be said, that if it be true that the morality of woman is not greater than that of man, house robbery should be as frequent for the one as for the other. This observation would be just, if it were proved that the class of individuals by whom house robberies are committed, were equally composed of men and women; but there are no data on this subject. All that can be laid down is, that men and women who live in a domestic state, rather commit crimes against property than against persons, which very materially confirms the observations made above, on the influence of retired life and sedentary habits. The *Compte Général de l'Administration de la Justice* in 1829, for the first time, gives the professions of the accused; and in the article *Domestiques*, we find 318 men and 147 women employed as farm-servants; and 149 men and 175 women as personal domestics: the total number of men is greater than that of women. Now, of these numbers, there were 99 accused of crimes against persons, and 590 of crimes against property: the ratio of these numbers is 1 to 6 nearly, and it has preserved exactly the same value in the years 1830 and 1831. But we have had occasion to see that this ratio for the mass of society is 1 to 3, when particular circumstances are not taken into consideration; and it would be only as 263 to 1091, or 1 to 4 nearly, if society were composed of women alone: thus, in all the cases, I think it has been sufficiently shown that men and women, when in the state of servants, commit crimes against property in preference to others.

As to capital crimes, we may arrange them in the following manner:—

Apparent Motives: 1826-1829 inclusive.	Accused for				Total.
	Poisoning.	Murder.	Assassination.	Incendiarism.	
Cupidity, theft,	20	39	237	66	362
Adultery, -	48	9	76	..	133
Domestic dissensions, -	48	120	131	34	333
Debauchery, jealousy, - -	10	58	115	37	220
Hatred, revenge, & divers motives,	23	903	460	229	1615
Total, - -	149	1129	1019	366	2663

Adultery, domestic quarrels, and jealousy, cause almost an equal number of poisonings in both sexes; but the number of assassinations, and especially of murders, of women by their husbands, is greater than that of husbands by their wives. The circumstances bearing on this subject have been stated already.

Of 903 murders which have taken place from hatred, revenge, and other motives, 446 have been committed in consequence of quarrels and contentions at taverns; thus, more than one-third of the total number of murders have taken place under circumstances in which women are not usually involved.

The four last volumes of the *Comptes Généraux*, contain some interesting details on the intellectual state of the accused of both sexes: they may be stated as follows:—

Intellectual State.	Men.	Women.	Ratio: 1828-29.	Men.	Women.	Ratio: 1830-31.
Unable to read or write, - -	6,537	2152	3·0	6,877	2042	3·3
Able to read and write imperfectly, - -	3,306	497	6·6	3,422	451	7·6
Could read and write well, -	1,399	110	12·7	1,373	82	16·7
Had received an excellent education to the 1st degree, - -	283	5	56·6	314	5	62·8
Intellectual state not mentioned,	374	104	3·6	2	..	..
	11,901	2868	4·2	11,988	2580	4·6

These numbers give us no information on the population, since we do not know what is the degree of knowledge diffused in France; but we see, at least, that there is a great difference in the sexes. I think we might explain these results by saying, that in the lower orders, where there is scarcely any edu-

cation, the habits of the women approach those of the men; and the more we ascend in the classes of society, and consequently in the degrees of education, the life of woman becomes more and more private, and she has less opportunity of committing crime, all other things being equal. These ratios differ so much from each other, that we cannot but feel how much influence our habits and social position have on crime.

It is to be regretted that the documents of justice for the Low Countries do not contain any thing on the distinction of the sexes; we only see (according to the returns of the prisons and the houses of correction and detention, in the *Recueil Official*), that on the 1st of January 1827, the number of men was 5162, that of women 1193, which gives 100 women to 433 men. Making use of the documents which have been disclosed to me by M. le Baron de Keverberg, I found that in 1825 this ratio was 100 to 314.

According to the report of M. Ducpétiaux, on the state of prisons in Belgium, we enumerated 2231 men and 550 women, as prisoners on the 1st of January 1833, which gives a ratio of 405 to 100: among these prisoners were found 1364 men and 326 women who could not read or write; so that the intellectual state of the prisoners of both sexes was nearly the same; the ratio of the whole population to those who could neither read nor write, was as 100 to 61 among the men, and 100 to 60 among the women. To the number of prisoners just mentioned, may be added 419 individuals confined in the central military prison, of whom 282 could neither read nor write; this gives a ratio of 67 in 100.*

If we examine the accounts of the correctional (or minor) tribunals of France, we find the ratio between the accused of both sexes to be 529,848 to 149,565, or 28 females to 100 males. Thus, with respect to less serious offences, which are judged by the correctional tribunals, the women have there been rather more numerous compared with the men than in the case of weightier crimes.

5. Of the Influence of Age on the Propensity to Crime.

Of all the causes which influence the development of the propensity to crime, or which diminish that propensity, age is unquestionably the most energetic. Indeed, it is through age that the physical powers and passions of man are developed, and their energy afterwards decreases with age. Reason is developed with age, and continues to acquire power even when strength and passion have passed their greatest vigour. Considering only these three elements, strength, passion, and judgment† (or reason), we may almost say, *à priori*, what will be the degree of the propensity to crime at different ages. Indeed, the propensity must be almost nothing at the two extremes of life; since, on the one hand, strength and passion, two powerful instruments of crime, have scarcely begun to exist, and, on the other hand, their energy, nearly extinguished, is still further deadened by the influence of reason. On the contrary, the propensity to crime should be at its maximum at the age when strength and passion have attained their maximum, and when reason has not acquired sufficient power to govern their combined influence. Therefore, considering only physical causes, the propensity to crime at different ages will be a property and sequence of the three

* According to the statistical tables of France, of young persons inscribed for military service in 1827, we enumerate (Bulletin de M. Férussac, Nov. 1829, p. 271)—

	Absolute No.	Relative No.
Young persons able to read, -	13,794	5
" " read and write,	100,787	37
" " not able to read or write,	157,510	58
	272,091	100

This ratio of 58 in 100 is a little less unfavourable than that of prisons, which is 60 in 100.

† I am not speaking of the intellectual state, of religious sentiments, of fear, shame, punishment, &c., because these qualities depend more or less directly on reason.

quantities we have just named, and might be determined by them, if they were sufficiently known.* But since these elements are not yet determined, we must confine ourselves to seeking for the degrees of the propensity to crime in an experimental manner; we shall find the means of so doing in the *Comptes Généraux de la Justice*. The following table will show the number of crimes against persons and against property, which have been committed in France by each sex during the years 1826, 27, 28, and 29, as well as the ratio of these numbers; the fourth column points out how a population of 10,000 souls is divided in France, according to age; and the last column gives the ratio of the total number of crimes to the corresponding number of the preceding column; thus there is no longer an inequality of number of the individuals of different ages.

Individuals' Age.	Crimes against Persons.	Pro- perty.	Crimes against Property in 100.	Population according to Age.	Degrees of the Propensity to Crime.
Less than 16 years.	80	440	85	3304	161
16 to 21 years,	904	3723	80	887	5217
21 to 25	1278	3329	72	673	6846
25 to 30	1575	3702	70	791	6971
30 to 35	1153	2883	71	732	5514
35 to 40	650	2076	76	672	4057
40 to 45	575	1724	75	612	3757
45 to 50	445	1275	74	549	3133
50 to 55	288	811	74	482	2280
55 to 60	168	500	75	410	1629
60 to 65	157	395	71	330	1642
65 to 70	91	184	70	247	1113
70 to 80	64	137	68	255	788
80 and upwards,	5	14	74	55	345

This table gives us results conformable to those which I have given in my *Recherches Statistique* for the years 1826 and 1827. Since the value obtained for 80 years of age and upwards is based on very small numbers, it is not entitled to much confidence. Moreover, we see that man begins to exercise his propensity to crimes against property at a period antecedent to his pursuit of other crimes. Between his 25th and 30th year, when his powers are developed, he inclines more to crimes against persons. It is near the age of 25 years that the propensity to crime reaches its maximum; but before passing to other considerations, let us examine what difference there is between the sexes. The latter columns of the following table show the degrees of propensity to crime,† reference being had to popu-

* Here we are more especially considering crimes against persons; for crimes against property, it will be necessary to take notice of the wants and privations of man.

† To give a new proof of the almost identity of results of each year, I have thought proper to present here the numbers collected between 1830 and 1831; we may compare them with those of the preceding tables, which are nearly exactly double, because they refer to four years:—

Individuals' Age.	Crimes against Persons.	Pro- perty.	Crimes against Property in 100 Crimes.	Accused. Men.	Accused. Women.	Women to 100 Men.
Under 16 years,	27	214	88	211	30	14
16 to 21	394	1,888	83	1,911	371	19
21 to 25	643	1,706	72	1,913	438	23
25 to 30	738	1,872	70	2,185	445	20
30 to 35	662	1,741	72	2,004	399	20
35 to 40	376	1,083	74	1,167	297	26
40 to 45	279	725	72	800	204	25
45 to 50	200	643	76	692	151	21
50 to 55	161	426	73	487	100	21
55 to 60	91	245	73	270	66	24
60 to 65	55	147	73	162	40	25
65 to 70	31	100	77	113	18	16
70 to 80	29	58	66	67	20	30
80 and upwards,	6	1	14	6	1	16
All ages,	3712	10,856	74	11,988	2580	22

lation, and the greatest number of each column being taken as unity:—

Individuals' Age.	Accused. Men.	Accused. Wo- men.	Women to 1000 Men.	Degrees of the Propensity to Crime. In Gene- ral.	Men.	Wo- men.	Calcu- lated.
Under 16 years,	438	82	187	0·02	0·02	0·02	0·02
16 to 21	3,901	726	186	0·76	0·79	0·64	0·66
21 to 25	3,762	845	225	1·00	1·00	0·98	1·00
25 to 30	4,260	1017	239	0·97	0·96	1·00	0·92
30 to 35	3.254	782	240	0·81	0·80	0·83	0·81
35 to 40	2,105	621	295	0·59	0·56	0·75	0·71
40 to 45	1,831	452	256	0·55	0·54	0·60	0·60
45 to 50	1,357	363	267	0·46	0·44	0·51	0·51
50 to 55	896	203	227	0·33	0·33	0·33	0·42
55 to 60	555	113	204	0·24	0·24	0·22	0 34
60 to 65	445	97	218	0·24	0·24	0·23	0·27
65 to 70	230	45	196	0·16	0·17	0·14	0·21
70 to 80	163	38	233	0·12	0·12	0·12	0·12
80 & upwards,	18	1	56	0·05	0·06	0·01	0·04
All ages,	23,270	5416	233	0·41	..	..	..

Women, compared to men, are rather later in entering on the career of crime, and also sooner come to the close of it. The maximum for men takes place about the 25th year, and about the 30th for women; the numbers on which our conclusions are founded are still very few; yet we see that the two lines which represent the relative value for each sex are almost parallel. The latter column contains results calculated by the following very simple formula:—

$$y = (1 - \sin. x)\frac{1}{1+m}, \text{ supposing } m = \frac{1}{2x-18}.$$

In this manner the degree of the propensity to crime is expressed according to age (*en fonction de l'âge*) x. We must take, as we see, for the axis of the abscissæ, one-fourth of the corrected circumference (*circonférence rectifiée*), and divided into decimal parts. The results of this formula generally agree better with the results obtained for women. I have endeavoured to render them sensible by the construction of a curve, the greater or less divergences of which from the axis AB (see *plate* 4) indicates the degree of the propensity to crime. The equation becomes a sinusoide:—

$$y = 1 - \sin. x,$$

for ages above 30 years, because m evidently is equal to unity. It is not to be expected that we should find mathematical precision, for several reasons, of which the principal are—

1. The numbers obtained for four years are not so great that we may adopt their results with perfect confidence.

2. To calculate the propensity to crime, we must combine these numbers with those which the tables of population have furnished; and it is pretty generally agreed that the table of the *Annuaire* does not give the state of the population of France with sufficient accuracy.

3. The propensity to crime can only be calculated from the whole of the individuals who compose the population; and as those who occupy the prisons are generally persons of more than 25 years of age, and who, from their state of captivity, cannot enter into the ratio for persons above 25 years of age, there must necessarily be a void (*lacune*). If, instead of taking crimes collectively, we examine each in particular in proportion to age, we shall have a new proof that the maximum of crimes of different kinds takes place between the 20th and 30th years, and that it is really about that period that the most vicious disposition is manifested. Only the period of maximum will be hastened or retarded some years for some crimes, according to the quicker or slower development of certain qualities of man which are proportioned to those crimes. These results are too curious to be omitted here; I have presented them in the following table, according to the documents of France, from 1826 to 1829 inclusively, classing them according

to the periods of maxima, and taking into account the population of different ages. I have omitted the crimes which are committed in smallest number, because the results from that alone would have been very doubtful.

Nature of the Crimes.	Under 16 Years.	16 to 21.	21 to 25.	25 to 30.	30 to 35.	35 to 40.	40 to 45.	45 to 50.	50 to 55.	55 to 60.	60 to 65.	65 to 70.	70 to 80.	80 and upwards.
Violations on children under 15 years,	4	120	71	96	73	39	34	45	22	18	26	17	21	2
House robbery,	54	965	845	766	528	351	249	207	112	56	61	34	14	~
Other thefts,	332	2479	2050	2292	1716	1249	1016	707	433	263	190	98	65	10
Violation and seduction,	9	155	156	148	99	38	40	27	9	5	3	1	2	~
Parricide,	6	13	12	13	6	3	2	1	4	2	~	~	~	~
Wounds and blows,	6	180	300	359	219	129	101	95	55	35	23	10	7	1
Murder,	15	139	198	275	172	103	84	49	48	30	25	17	9	~
Infanticide,	1	40	99	134	76	44	30	8	7	1	8	4	2	~
Rebellion,	5	67	129	156	115	51	51	35	29	16	16	5	5	~
Highway robbery,	21	80	111	149	107	60	62	46	22	21	8	6	4	~
Assassination,	10	90	144	203	183	100	104	89	53	32	24	13	15	1
Wounding parents,	2	47	64	73	72	40	30	16	8	2	1	~	~	~
Poisoning,	5	6	17	30	27	15	20	12	6	2	5	4	1	~
False witnessing and suborning,	2	23	46	48	44	42	42	35	23	15	15	11	7	~
Various misdemeanours,	8	86	202	276	312	244	207	185	129	78	75	28	28	2

Thus the propensity to theft, one of the first to show itself, prevails in some measure throughout our whole existence; we might be led to believe it to be inherent to the weakness of man, who falls into it as if by instinct. It is first exercised by the indulgence of confidence which exists in the interior of families, then it manifests itself out of them, and finally on the public highway, where it terminates by having recourse to violence, when the man has then made the sad essay of the fullness of his strength by committing all the different kinds of homicide. This fatal propensity, however, is not so precocious as that which, near adolescence, arises with the fire of the passions and the disorders which accompany it, and which drives man to violation and seduction, seeking its first victims among beings whose weakness opposes the least resistance. To these first excesses of the passions, of cupidity, and of strength, is soon joined reflection, plotting crime; and man, become more self-possessed and hardened, chooses to destroy his victim by assassination or poisoning. Finally, his last stages in the career of crime are marked by address in deception, which in some measure supplies the place of strength. It is in his decline that the vicious man presents the most hideous spectacle; his cupidity, which nothing can extinguish, is rekindled with fresh ardour, and assumes the mask of swindling; if he still uses the little strength which nature has left to him, it is rather to strike his enemy in the shade; finally, if his depraved passions have not been deadened by age, he prefers to gratify them on feeble children. Thus, his first and his last stages in the career of crime have the same character in this last respect: but what a difference! That which was somewhat excusable in the young man, because of his inexperience, of the violence of his passions, and the similarity of ages, in the old man is the result of the deepest immorality and the most accumulated load of depravity.

From the data of the preceding tables, it is scarcely possible not to perceive the great influence which age exercises over the propensity to crime, since each of the individual results tend to prove it. I shall not hesitate to consider the scale of the different degrees of the propensity to crime, at different ages, deserving of as much confidence as those which I have given for the stature, weight, and strength of man, or, finally, those for mortality.

Account has also been taken of the ages of accused persons, who have appeared before the minor or correctional courts of France, but only preserving the three following heads, which refer but to the four years preceding 1830:—

Ages.	Criminal Courts.		Correctional Courts.	
	Men.	Women.	Men.	Women.
Under 16 years,	2	2	5	6
From 16 to 21,	17	13	14	16
More than 21,	81	85	81	78
	100	100	100	100

Thus, the correctional cases are, in early age, all things being equal, more frequent than criminal cases; they are the first steps of crime, and consequently those most easily ascended. In Belgium, only four heads of ages have been made, and the results of correctional and criminal courts have been united, which renders our comparisons more difficult, since, as we have just seen, the numbers in each are not the same; it is also to be regretted that care has not been taken to distinguish the sexes. Be this as it may, by taking the total number of the accused and suspected (*prévenus*) as unity, we obtain the following results:—

Ages.	Suspected (or Committed) and Accused.				
	1826.	1827.	1828.	1829.	Average Number.
Under 16 years,	4	5	5	5	5
From 16 to 21,	13	11	12	11	12
21 to 70,	81	82	81	82	81
Above 70 years,	2	2	2	2	2
	100	100	100	100	100

These results are very similar to those of the correctional courts of France, and the latter elements ought certainly to predominate, when we make no distinction between the accused and those merely committed, since the latter are always more numerous than the accused. Yet it would seem that with us there are fewer offences between the ages of 16 and 21 than in France.

We do not find that the number of children brought annually before the courts of Belgium has diminished, either in an absolute sense, or compared with the numbers of other accused and committed persons. The same is nearly the case with France, as we see by the following table, in which I have preferred giving the absolute numbers:—

Years.	Under 16 Years.	16 to 21.	More than 21.	Total.
Accused.				
1826,	124	1,101	5,763	6,988
1827,	136	1,022	5.771	6,939
1828,	143	1,278	5.975	7,396
1829,	117	1,226	6.030	7,373
1830,	114	1,161	5,687	6,962
1831,	127	1,121	6,358	7,606
Committed.				
1826,	5,042	12,799	86,196	104,037
1827,	5,233	13,291	73,588	92,112
1828,	5,228	14,902	71,622	91,752
1829,	5,306	14,431	79,438	99,175
1830,*	2,852	6,452	47,812	57,116
1831,	5,651	17,659	84,433	107,743

We must not, however, conclude from these results that education, which for some time has been diffused

* Those committed for different kinds of offences are not included in these numbers.

with such activity, has been of no effect in diminishing the number of crimes committed by young persons; several years more are necessary before its influence can become apparent, and before it can carry its effects into the bosom of families.

It is a matter of regret, that as yet we possess so few accounts of the ages of criminals, calculated to render appreciable the influence of places and the customs of different nations. In general, we remark, that the number of children in prisons in England is much greater than with us; this would appear to be owing, especially in the metropolis, to children being trained in a manner to theft, while the really guilty act through their intermediation. In the penitentiary of Millbank, in the year 1827, 1250 individuals were registered as under 21 years of age out of a total number of 3020, which gives a ratio of 41 to 100, being more than double that of France and the Low Countries.*

The condemned persons in the jail of Philadelphia in 1822, 1823, and 1824, were proportioned as follows:†—

Ages.	1822.	1823.	1824.	Totals.
Under 21 years, -	52	72	58	182
From 21 to 30 years, -	151	143	122	416
— 30 to 40 — -	72	67	79	218
Above 40 years, - -	55	49	28	132

The total for the three years was 948. Taking the ratio of this sum to 1000, we find the following values, opposite to which I have placed those of France:—

	Philadelphia.	France.
Under 21 years, - - -	19	19
From 21 to 30 -	44	35
— 30 to 40, - - -	23	23
Above 40 years, - - -	14	23
	100	100

Thus the prisons of Philadelphia present exactly the same number of criminals as those of France for individuals under 19 and for those between 30 and 40 years of age; they have fewer old men, but more men between 21 and 30, which may be owing to the nature of the population of the two countries.

France, Belgium, and Philadelphia, agree then pretty nearly as to the number of criminals in proportion to the ages; but England differs very sensibly from the average values presented by these countries, and that is owing, no doubt, as I observed before, not so much to the character of the English people as to the modes of eluding the rigour of the laws which the malefactors make use of, acting through the intermedium of children whom they have trained up as instruments of crime.

Conclusions.

In making a summary of the principal observations contained in this chapter, we are led to the following conclusions:—

1st, Age (or the term of life) is undoubtedly the cause which operates with most energy in developing or subduing the propensity to crime.

2d, This fatal propensity appears to be developed in proportion to the intensity of the physical power and passions of man: it attains its maximum about the age of 25 years, the period at which the physical development has almost ceased. The intellectual and moral development, which operates more slowly, subsequently weakens the propensity to crime, which, still later, diminishes from the feeble state of the physical powers and passions.

3d, Although it is near the age of 25 that the maximum in number of crimes of different kinds takes place, yet this maximum advances or recedes some years for certain crimes, according to the quicker

or slower development of certain qualities which have a bearing on those crimes. Thus, man, driven by the violence of his passions, at first commits violation and seduction; almost at the same time he enters on the career of theft, which he seems to follow as if by instinct till the end of life; the development of his strength subsequently leads him to commit every act of violence—homicide, rebellion, highway robbery still later, reflection converts murder into assassination and poisoning. Lastly, man, advancing in the career of crime, substitutes a greater degree of cunning for violence, and becomes more of a forger than at any other period of life.

4th, The *difference of sexes* has also a great influence on the propensity to crime: in general, there is only 1 woman before the courts to 4 men.

5th, The propensity to crime increases and decreases nearly in the same degrees in each sex; yet the period of maximum takes place rather later in women, and is near the 30th year.

6th, Woman, undoubtedly from her feeling of weakness, rather commits crimes against property than persons; and when she seeks to destroy her kind, she prefers poison. Moreover, when she commits homicide, she does not appear to be proportionally arrested by the enormity of crimes which, in point of frequency, take place in the following order:—infanticide, miscarriage, parricide, wounding of parents, assassination, wounds and blows, murder: so that we may affirm that the number of the guilty diminishes in proportion as they have to seek their victim more openly. These differences are no doubt owing to the habits and sedentary life of woman; she can only conceive and execute guilty projects on individuals with whom she is in constant relation.

7th, The *seasons*, in their course, exercise a very marked influence on crime: thus, during summer, the greatest number of crimes against persons are committed, and the fewest against property; the contrary takes place during winter.

8th, It must be observed that age and the seasons have almost the same influence in increasing or diminishing the number of mental disorders and crimes against persons.

9th, *Climate* appears to have some influence, especially on the propensity to crimes against persons: this observation is confirmed at least among the races of southern climates, such as the Pelasgian race, scattered over the shores of the Mediterranean and Corsica, on the one hand; and the Italians, mixed with Dalmatians and Tyrolese, on the other. We observe, also, that severe climates, which give rise to the greatest number of wants, also give rise to the greatest number of crimes against property.

10th, The countries where frequent mixture of the people takes place; those in which industry and trade collect many persons and things together, and possess the greatest activity; finally, those where the inequality of fortune is most felt, all things being equal, are those which give rise to the greatest number of crimes.

11th, Professions have great influence on the nature of crimes. Individuals of more independent professions are rather given to crimes against persons; and the labouring and domestic classes to crimes against property. Habits of dependence, sedentary life, and also physical weakness in women, produce the same results.

12th, *Education* is far from having so much influence on the propensity to crime as is generally supposed. Moreover, moral instruction is very often confounded with instruction in reading and writing alone, and which is most frequently an accessory instrument to crime.

13th, It is the same with *poverty*; several of the departments of France, considered to be the poorest, are at the same time the most moral. Man is not driven to crime because he is poor, but more generally

* Bulletin de M. de Férussac, Mai 1828.
† American Review, 1827, No. 12.

because he passes rapidly from a state of comfort to one of misery, and an inadequacy to supply the artificial wants which he has created.

14th, The higher we go in the ranks of society, and consequently in the degrees of education, we find a smaller and smaller proportion of guilty women to men; descending to the lowest orders, the habits of both sexes resemble each other more and more.

15th, Of 1129 murders committed in France, during the space of four years, 446 have been in consequence of quarrels and contentions in taverns; which would tend to show the fatal influence of the use of *strong drinks.*

16th, In France, as in the Low Countries, we enumerate annually 1 accused person to 4300 inhabitants nearly; but in the former country, 39 in 100 are acquitted, and in the second only 15; yet the same code was used in both countries, but in the Low Countries the judges performed the duty of the jury. Before correctional courts and simple police courts, where the committed were tried by judges only, the results were nearly the same for both countries.

17th, In France, crimes against persons were about one-third of the number of crimes against property, but in the Low Countries they were about one-fourth only. It must be remarked, that the first kind of crimes lead to fewer condemnations than the second, perhaps because there is a greater repugnance to apply punishment as the punishment increases in severity.

I cannot conclude this chapter without again expressing my astonishment at the constancy observed in the results which the documents connected with the administration of justice present each year. "Thus, as I have already had occasion to repeat several times, we pass from one year to another, with the sad perspective of seeing the same crimes reproduced in the same order, and bringing with them the same punishments in the same proportions." All observations tend likewise to confirm the truth of this proposition, which I long ago announced, that *every thing which pertains to the human species considered as a whole, belongs to the order of physical facts :* the greater the number of individuals, the more does the influence of individual will disappear, leaving predominance to a series of general facts, dependent on causes by which society exists and is preserved. These causes we now want to ascertain, and as soon as we are acquainted with them, we shall determine their influence on society, just in the same way as we determine effects by their causes in physical sciences.* It must be confessed, that, distressing as the truth at first appears, if we submit to a well followed out series of observations the physical world and the social system, it would be difficult to decide in respect to which of the two acting causes produce their effects with most regularity. I am, however, far from concluding that man can do nothing for man's amelioration. I think, as I said at the commencement of this work, that he possesses a moral power capable of modifying the laws which affect him; but this power only acts in the slowest manner, so that the causes influencing the social system cannot undergo any sudden alteration; as they have acted for a series of years, so will they continue to act in time to come, until they can be modified. Also, I

* M. Guerry comes to the same conclusions from his researches on crimes, *Essai sur la Statistique Morale,* p. 69 :—" One of the most general conclusions we can make is, that they all concur to prove that the greater number of facts of a moral nature, considered in the mass, and not individually, are determined by regular causes, the variations of which take place within narrow limits, and which may be submitted, like those of a material nature, to direct and numerical observation." As this idea has continually presented itself to me in all my researches on man, and as I have exactly expressed it in the same terms as those of the text, in my conclusions on the *Recherches sur le Penchant au Crime,* a work which appeared a year before that of M. Guerry, I have thought it necessary to mention the point here, to prevent misunderstanding.

cannot repeat too often, to all men who sincerely desire the well-being and honour of their kind, and who would blush to consider a few francs more or less paid to the treasury as equivalent to a few heads more or less submitted to the axe of the executioner, that there is a budget which we pay with a frightful regularity —it is that of prisons, chains, and the scaffold : it is that which, above all, we ought to endeavour to abate.

BOOK FOURTH.

OF THE PROPERTIES OF THE AVERAGE MAN, OF THE SOCIAL SYSTEM, AND OF THE FINAL ADVANCEMENT OF THIS STUDY.

CHAPTER I.

PROPERTIES OF THE AVERAGE MAN.

In the three preceding books I have presented the results of my inquiries on the development of the physical and moral system of the average man, and on the modifications which he undergoes from different influences. These results can only be considered as the first essay towards an immense work, which, to be completed, would require long and painful researches, and which would only be really useful by being extremely exact.

This determination of the average man is not merely a matter of speculative curiosity; it may be of the most important service to the science of man and the social system. It ought necessarily to precede every other inquiry into social physics, since it is, as it were, the basis. The average man, indeed, is in a nation what the centre of gravity is in a body; it is by having that central point in view that we arrive at the apprehension of all the phenomena of equilibrium and motion; moreover, when considered abstractly, it presents some remarkable properties, which I am now going to state succinctly.

1. Of the Average Man considered with reference to Literature and the Fine Arts.

The necessity of veracity in faithfully representing the physiognomy, the habits, and the manners of people at different epochs, has at all times led artists and literary men to seize, among the individuals whom they observed, the characteristic traits of the period in which they lived; or, in other words, to come as near the average as possible. I do not wish to be understood as implying that it is necessary to give the same traits, the same tastes, and the same passions, to every individual, whatever may be his age, rank, country, or the period at which he lives; but that the most characteristic marks must be studied, still keeping in view these differences. Thus we should investigate what are the predominating elements in any people or in any age; for example, whether fanaticism, piety, or irreligion—a spirit of servility, independence, or anarchy. No one will hesitate to allow to me that man is more courageous at 20 than at 60, and more prudent at 60 than at 20; or that persons of the south have more liveliness of thought and feature than the inhabitants of the north : these are common observations, which every one admits, and which we should be shocked to find unattended to in works of imagination. But can it be thought wrong to give more precision to these vague ideas ?—is it altogether conformable to the actual state of our knowledge, to receive relations which have only been slightly observed, when they may be determined with certain precision? If it had been demanded some years ago at what age a man has the greatest propensity to crime, we should no doubt have been much embarrassed to find the true answer; and perhaps the most erroneous opinions would have been put forth, especially on the influence of sexes and the intellectual state. Yet who would assert that these researches are useless to philosophers and men of letters, or even to the artist, who only truly deserves this name according as he has studied the human heart deeply? The time is passing away when men were contented with indistinct ideas, and relations determined at a glance; when numerical determinations become applicable, they are especially consulted by the observer and lover of truth.

I am far from pretending, however, that even a profound knowledge of the different faculties of man will be sufficient to obtain success in the fine arts and literature; but I think that, to produce a work truly capable of moving and agitating the passions, we must be acquainted with man, and especially man as it is desired to represent him. Thus, to take but one example, the artist who has only studied the type of the Grecian physiognomies, however admirable this type may appear to us, if he reproduces it in modern subjects, will produce but a chilling effect on the spectator, who, though he admires the art and composition, will never be deeply excited. Grecian figures, however varied they may be according to age, passion, and sex, have notwithstanding a general likeness, which carries us, in spite of ourselves, back to antiquity, and distracts our attention from the subject sought to be represented before us. If such figures are represented in action, the anachronism only becomes more sensible. Artists, at the revival of the fine arts, fully comprehended the necessity of painting what they had before their eyes, and on that account they produced such astonishing effects. The noble and severe figure of Christ has nothing in common with those of the Apollo or the Jupiter of ancient mythology; a Madonna of Raphael has an enchanting grace, which is not surpassed by the finest forms of the antique; and these beauties have a greater influence on the imagination, because they are more similar to the natures around us, and act more directly upon us. Even we ourselves, in more remote situations and circumstances, feel the necessity, when retracing our national facts, of not bringing forward Grecian or Italian figures: in the midst of a battle, where men are found, all nearly of the same age, and all alike dressed in the same kind of armour, our eye seeks to recognise, by the physiognomic traits and expressions, the Frenchman or the Englishman, the German or the Russian. In the French army itself, the soldier of the old guard had an expression which has become classical, and is identified in some measure with the remembrances of the empire.

If the arts have already admitted such imperceptible shades, and have the power of awakening the remembrance of an era by recalling the physiognomic traits which seem to belong to it, what value ought we not to affix to an accurate determination of these traits, if they are capable of being appreciated? Some men of genius have penetrated very far in these researches, and their ideas, which at first were rejected, have since been more favourably judged of, when experience came to their support. Lavater has not hesitated to analyse the human passions by the inspection of the features, and Gall has endeavoured to prove that we may arrive at similar results by inspecting the cranial protuberances. There is an intimate relation between the physical and the moral of man, and the passions leave sensible traces on the instruments they put in continual action; but what are these traces? It is agreed that they do exist; the artist studies and seeks to seize them; yet, by a singular prepossession, we reject the possibility of this being determined with any degree of accuracy, or the utility of the determination. But how comes it that such artist or such poet labours to no purpose, and presents constantly to us the Greek or Italian type, according as he had more especially studied the antique or the Italian school?—how is it that Rubens, despite his genius, when painting the divinities of ancient mythology, gives forms which

antiquity would have disavowed? It is because Rubens had also a type, and this type had been chosen from among the moderns.

It is undoubtedly owing to the want of care taken in studying the shades of the moral and physical qualities of man among different people and in different ages, that the greater number of works of imagination have been so monotonous and lifeless. The necessity of studying nature and truth has indeed been felt; but the fact has not been sufficiently attended to, I think, that nature is not invariable. The ancients have represented the physical and moral man with infinite art, such as he then was; and the greater number of the moderns, struck with the perfection of their works, have thought they had nothing to do but servilely to imitate them; they have not understood that the type has been changed; and that, when imitating them for the perfection of art, they had another nature to study. Hence the universal cry, "Who shall deliver us from the Greeks and Romans?" Hence the violent dispute between the classics and romanticists; hence, lastly, the necessity of having a literature which was truly the *expression of society*. This great revolution was accomplished, and furnishes the most irrefragable proof of the variability of the human type, or of the average man, in different men and in different ages.

As for ancient subjects, the artist or the poet who wished to reproduce them might constrain us to admire his art; but we should always feel that he placed a nature before our eyes, which, so to speak, was dead —a type which is extinct. We must undoubtedly make concessions to the fine arts, and give ourselves to their illusions; but we must not let the sacrifices demanded exceed certain limits. We cannot, for a moment, go back several centuries, forget our religion, social institutions, and habits, and feel sympathy for men not having our tastes, manners, or the same traits which we are accustomed to see around us. The ancients themselves never required such sacrifices on the part of the public; and such men as Euripides and Sophocles took good care not to introduce on the stage an Osiris, and the mysterious feasts of the Egyptians, who, nevertheless, had been their patterns.

A few ages are of little moment in the annals of the human race; and we cannot assure ourselves that man will not undergo any modifications—in form, for example—and that a type which once existed may not be completely lost some day. This supposition may appear extraordinary; yet we see that all the elements relating generally to man undergo changes; who, therefore, can assure himself that the type of the Grecian figure shall not be lost, either in the flight of time, or in some great catastrophe involving the destruction of the Caucasian race? Such overthrows are in the nature of possible things. The consequences of such an event might be, that another race—the Mongolian, for instance—which, after much difficulty, might people the earth, and find the remains of the fine arts, would only see in all these fine Grecian figures, which we are accustomed to admire, things entirely artificial and conventional, such as the Egyptian forms appear at present to us. They might admire these antiques as specimens of art; but I doubt if they would prefer the ancient form to their own, if they had to represent their divinity in a human shape. What has just been said, will no doubt be rejected by those who have pre-established ideas regarding a fixed standard of beauty. I shall not discuss that question here; I only publish my views with diffidence, not seeking to impose them on any one.

I think I have sufficiently shown, in what has preceded, that the determination of the average man is not useless, even to the fine arts and literature; and that he who shall arrive at this determination, will have no difficulty in obtaining the attention of artists and men of literature. It would inform them more precisely of things which they now know but vaguely;

it would discover others to them of which they are ignorant, or at least clear their minds of a mass of prejudices. They would receive these notions as a painter learns perspective, which, in geometrical outline, is not very *pittoresque* either. Moreover, artists have received the researches of Gall and Lavater probably with greater eagerness than savants: indeed, it is to their care that painters are indebted in a great measure for the knowledge of the proportions of different parts of the human body, in each sex, at different ages. This knowledge was so important to them, that it was an object of study of the greatest painters at the revival of the arts: we may see, especially, what care the celebrated Albert Durer took in regard to it in his works.

At the same time, I admit that the artist and the literary man can, and even ought, to search out the prominent traits, exaggerate rather than diminish them, and contrast the most different physiognomies and characters; but the truth must always lie between the extremes which they present to our view, and these extremes themselves lie within *limits* defined by nature. Going beyond, we only create fantastic beings and monstrosities; these reveries of a disordered imagination may astonish, and even amuse, but they can never produce those deep sensations and lively emotions which we only feel for beings of our own caste.

To conclude the exposition of my views of the average man, I remark, that it will first be necessary to study, in the most complete manner, the development of his different faculties, and every thing which may influence their development, every other consideration being laid aside. The artist, the man of literature, and the savant, will afterwards choose from among these materials those which are best suited to the subject of their studies, as the painter borrows from optics the few principles bearing on his art.

2. Of the Average Man considered in reference to the Natural and Medical Sciences.

It will not be necessary to insist forcibly, to natural philosophers, on the importance of the investigation of the different laws of the development of man; indeed, without the knowledge of these laws, the science of man cannot be complete or philosophic. I think the utility of the methods of determining them, which I propose, needs not to be explained to them again; several of these have been familiar to them for a long time, and others form a part of their usual modes of proceeding in fathoming the secrets of nature.

In the eyes of the naturalist, the average man is only the type of a people; numerous observations have shown that this type is not unique, and consequently that there are different races of men. But the characters on which these distinctions are established have not been sufficiently defined; indeed, how can we study the modifications which the elements relative to man, as well as their laws of development, undergo in the different races, when we have not settled the point of commencement?

Hence, also, proceeds the difficulty of surmounting the greater number of the most interesting and philosophical questions of natural history. It is frequently asked if the human species has deteriorated, or if it is capable of deteriorating at any time; but this problem, for want of the elements for its solution, remains without a satisfactory answer.

It is also asked if there is a type or standard of the beautiful for the human species, which is proportionate to the development of intelligence. Comparative anatomy has been thought to find an affirmative solution of this question, in the magnitude of the brain and the size of the facial angle, which, according to the delicate researches which have been made, diminishes in proportion to the lowering of intelligence in men and animals; and it has been inferred from this, that

the maximum of intelligence will be found in the species which have the facial angle most nearly approaching to a right angle; which would give the pre-eminence to the Caucasian. I do not know if any observations have been made on a somewhat larger scale, having in view the measurement of the degrees of size of the facial angle at different ages, in order to determine if these are at all proportionate to the degrees of the development of intelligence.

Naturalists are also occupied in determining carefully what are the *limits* of the extent of the different elements belonging to man; these *limit values* have always been objects of attention, and ought to be carefully registered in the natural history of man, so that we might know, not only what is, but also what is possible.

The anatomical researches of Gall on the brain tend to show that the development of its different parts is proportionate to the development of certain corresponding faculties, which appear to have their seat there. Without entering into an examination of the doctrine of this learned physiologist, one must regret that his principles have not yet been submitted to more direct observations, and that it has not been examined whether the law of development of our faculties at different ages corresponds to the law of development of the presumed corresponding parts of the brain;[*] indeed, so far from knowing the relative proportions on these different points, it appears that, up to the present time, we have but very few data on the law of development of the brain itself, or upon its size and weight at different ages, either as regards average value or extreme limits.[†]

[*] Since the above was written, M. Broussais, to whom science is indebted for so many useful works, has read a memoir to the Academy of Moral and Political Sciences, on the influence of the physical on the moral, and, in particular, on the actual state of our knowledge on phrenology. M. Edwards has presented some considerations in support of this work, agreeing with it, also, in requiring scientific experiments on this new science. The principal conclusions of this learned physiologist are contained in the following note, for which I am indebted to his friendship:—

" The proofs on which we found our convictions are referred to two principal classes; the first includes proofs which may be called *individual*, and the second those which we shall call *scientific.*

In the first case, we cannot be convinced of the truth of certain relations without verifying them ourselves. Thus it is necessary that every individual who wants to form an opinion, must himself make the proof which others have done. In the second case, on the contrary, when we are considering a *scientific* proof, if it has been properly obtained, it is enough to receive the knowledge to be convinced of the truth. Thus we dispense with the necessity of personally making the proof again.

In general, the kind of proofs on which phrenology rests belong to the first class, or those here called *individual;* because it is always necessary that each *individual* who wishes to know what to maintain should repeat the proof.

This is the condition in which phrenology stands. It is evident that, if the relations pointed out are generally true, any one who has sufficient knowledge may convince himself by a sufficient number of observations; but he could not transmit to another his conviction, unless one could know the extent and measure of his experience.

Now, if that could be expressed in a determinate manner, the proof would be no longer individual but scientific; and not only he who had acquired could communicate his conviction, but the latter would also be able to impress it on others; for it is the peculiarity of scientific proof that it forces general conviction on those who can understand it. Other persons are obliged to admit on hearsay, that is, on the authority of the first class. Now, phrenology, if true, is really capable of scientific proof.

It is by forming a sort of statistics, the plan of which might be readily designed, that the scientific proof of this doctrine is practicable. It is greatly to be desired that phrenologists would do this."

[†] M. Guerry wrote to me in 1831—" I am now occupied, along with M. le Docteur Esquirol and M. le Docteur Leuret, with the statistics of insanity. We measure the head, in every direction, of every person at Charenton, the Bicêtre, and the Salpétrière. We

We ought also to state with more care than has yet been done, the capacity of our organs, and the limits they can attain.

If the average man were completely determined, we might, as I have already observed, consider him as the type of perfection; and every thing differing from his proportions or condition, would constitute deformity and disease; every thing found dissimilar, not only as regarded proportion and form, but as exceeding the observed limits, would constitute a monstrosity.

The consideration of the average man is so important in medical science, that it is almost impossible to judge of the state of an individual without comparing it to that of another imagined person, regarded as being in a normal condition, and who is intrinsically no other than the individual we are considering. A physician is called to a sick person, and, having examined him, finds his pulse too quick, and his respiration inmoderately frequent, &c. It is very evident, that to form such a decision, we must be aware that the characters observed not only differ from those of an average man, or one in a normal state, but that they even exceed the limits of safety. Every physician, in forming such calculations, refers to the existing documents on the science, or to his own experience; which is only a similar estimate to that which we wish to make on a greater scale and with more accuracy.

Moreover, the data which the average man presents, can themselves only serve to furnish others more important, and which relate to the individual observed. To explain my idea, I shall suppose that every man has the knowledge and prudence necessary to examine himself carefully, and to determine all the elements which compose him, and the limits within which they may vary, in a state of health: he will form a table differing more or less from that of the average man, and which will assist him in recognising whatever is more or less anomalous in his own case, and whatever imperiously demands attention. It would be this table which the physician should consult in the case of illness, in order to estimate the extent of the divergences from the normal state, and what are the organs more especially affected. But as, in the greater number of cases, the sick person can make no satisfactory observations on his own person, nor any elements which are peculiar to him, the physician is obliged to have recourse to the common standard, and compare his patient with the average man; a course which, in fact, seems to present less difficulty and inconvenience, but may also cause serious mistakes in some circumstances. For here, again, we must observe that general laws referring to masses are essentially imperfect when applied to individuals; but we do not mean to say that they can never be consulted with advantage, or that the divergences are always considerable.

A prudent man, who studies and observes his con-

also measure the cerebrum and cerebellum of those who die. I have thus been led to undertake the *Histoire du Developpement de la Tête Humaine Moyenne*. I have been led to it entirely from having read your excellent Memoir on the Stature of Man. Fifteen days ago, we noted the state of the pulse of ninety maniacal persons, between five and seven o'clock in the morning, and whilst they were at breakfast. We already have found certain periodic returns in the number of the pulsations; these observations will be continued to the end of the month.

I hope to be able to measure the angles of the head very exactly, so as to obtain the proportions and form of an average maniacal head, of one hallucinated, of an idiotic, imbecile, and epileptic one, &c."—(Notes on my *Recherches sur le Penchant*, &c.) It is to be regretted that this announced work has not yet appeared.

At the end, however, of the work, *De la Frequence du Pouls chez les Alienés*, MM. Leuret and Mitivié give the result of their researches on the specific weight of the brain of the insane, which prove that there is no marked difference in this respect between insane and healthy persons. The specific weight has an average value, represented by 1·031, water at 15° of temperature being considered as unity.

stitution, may prevent many diseases, and scarcely needs to have recourse to professional men, except in severe and extraordinary cases. His habit of observing himself, and the knowledge which he has thus obtained, form, in some measure, a kind of table giving him the elements of his constitution. In general, we only call in the physician when indisposed: I think it would be useful were he also to see us when in a state of health, so that he might obtain a better knowledge of our normal state, and procure elements of comparison necessary for cases of anomaly and indisposition. It is very evident that a physician, called to a patient whom he sees for the first time, and of whose constitution he is absolutely ignorant, will, in certain circumstances, commit errors by submitting him to the common rule.

I shall not pursue these remarks, the truth of which, I venture to think, will be appreciated. The constitution of the average man serves as a type to our kind. Every race has its peculiar constitution, which differs from this more or less, and which is determined by the influence of climate, and the habits which characterise the average man of that peculiar country. Every individual, again, has his particular constitution, which depends also on his organisation and his mode of existence. It is consequently interesting to know each of the elements which concern us individually, and we have a general interest in knowing each of the elements which bear on the average man, who is the type to which we should incessantly have recourse.

3. Of the Average Man considered with respect to Philosophy and Morals (la Morale).

Human nature (*humanité*) is modified by necessities of time and place. The development of the different faculties of the average man ought to be closely proportionate to these necessities: this is a condition essential to his existence and continuance. If the average man, at different epochs, had been determined carefully, we might at this day perceive what laws of development have undergone the greatest change: we should possess the most valuable means of analysis; and we should also learn what have been the qualities which have successively predominated and exercised the greatest influence on our social system.

The laws of development of the average man, at such or such a period, must not be confounded with the laws of the development of human nature* (*humanité*). There is but little general conformity betwixt them: thus, I should be much disposed to believe that the laws of development of the average man continue almost the same through successive centuries, and that they only vary in the magnitude of maxima. Now, it is really these maxima, relating to the developed man, which give the measure of the development of human nature in each century. We do not possess any exact documents to guide us in such a research, but it would appear that, physically considered, collective man is scarcely progressing; yet it has been observed that a civilised man is generally stronger than a savage. As to intelligence, his progress cannot be questioned, and his existing state of develop-

* To render my idea sensible by a figure (see *plate* 4), I suppose that we construct the line indicating the development of the strength of man at any given period; and that on the same axis of the abscissae we also construct the corresponding similar lines for other periods, so that these lines succeed each other at the distance of a century, for example, proceeding from points whose distance from each other increase as the time; it will happen that the maxima of the ordinates will not correspond to the same ages or have the same magnitude. Now, connecting all the points of maxima by a line, which will evidently be the container (*l'enveloppe*) of all the curves representing the law of individual development in all the modifications which it has undergone in the course of time, we shall have the curve which represents the general law of the development of human nature (*humanité*). By similar processes, we may render equally apparent all the laws of development of the different faculties of the human species.

ment undoubtedly exceeds what it has been at any other time. Also following, with history in our hands, the average type of human nature through different centuries, we see man, at first, in possession of all his strength, blindly taking advantage of it, and attaching to the world of matter a power and a range altogether limitless : the king of nature, he has plants, animals, and even the stars, as tributaries. But, as his reason becomes developed, a new world is unrolled before his eyes, contracting the limits of the former one; the intellectual man gradually supplants the physical one; and it is this continually increasing triumph of the intellectual man, which the history of the arts and sciences presents to us at every page.

I have said that, although the laws of the development of human nature were not generally the same as those of the average man of any one period, yet these laws might, in certain circumstances, be identically the same; and that human nature, under certain relations, might be developed in a manner similar to a single individual. I should be much disposed to believe that this is the case with the collective human mind; indeed, following it in its uncertain and irregular course, we see it endeavour to strengthen itself from the very beginning, reach in due time the highest conceptions, and present almost the same phases as the intellect of the individual man from infancy to maturity. The human mind is at first astonished at the sight of any thing beyond the ordinary course of things, and attributes the most simple occurrences to the caprice of supernatural beings, instead of deducing them from immutable laws, which are alone worthy of a divine intervention. We see it afterwards pursuing a course which is more certain and conformable to reason, observing facts, isolated at first, then classing them, and inferring the consequences. Still later, the mind learns to interrogate nature by experiment, and to reproduce transitory phenomena at will, under the most favourable circumstances for observing them. And when its reasoning powers have reached full maturity, then it studies the nature of causes, seeks to value their reciprocal intensities, and thus raise itself to a knowledge of the attendant phenomena which they produce. Such is the development which we see the human mind undergoing when we study its progress in the history of the sciences; such, also, is the course which the intellect of man pursues from infancy to maturity.

I have said before, that the average man of any one period represents the type of development of human nature for that period; I have also said that the average man was always such as was conformable to and necessitated by time and place; that his qualities were developed in due proportion, in perfect harmony, alike removed from excess or defect of every kind, so that, in the circumstances in which he is found, he should be considered as the type of all which is beautiful—of all which is good.

If human nature were stationary and not susceptible of amelioration, it is evident that the average man would also continue invariable; and his different qualities, instead of presenting the type of the beautiful and excellent of the period at which he lives, would present the type of the absolutely beautiful and excellent in the most general sense. Thus, when we say that the type of the beautiful, as to the form of man, is absolute, we mean that the average man ought not to differ from this proportion, and that human nature cannot advance further. It is not so with reason: the vast conquests of science, by giving more accurate notions of an infinite multitude of things, and by destroying errors and prejudices, have necessarily furnished our reason with the means of rising to a still greater height, and arriving at a relative degree of perfection, the idea of which could not so much as be conceived some ages ago.

Such should also be our criterion as to morals. Human qualities become virtues, when they are equally removed from all the excesses into which they may be disposed to fall, and confined within due limits, beyond which every thing is vice.* If these limits do not vary in the course of time and among different people, we have strong probabilities for believing that this virtue has an absolute value. Now, this is what we remark generally concerning most moral qualities : they admit a type which we may with great probability consider as absolute, so that human nature, considered in reference to these qualities, will not be progressive. Yet there are qualities the importance of which has varied in the course of time, and which has increased or diminished with the development of reason, on which they depend, at the same time that the physical has yielded preponderance to the intellectual man. Thus courage, which, in the earliest ages, raised a man to the first rank, and, in some manner, assigned to him a place near to divinity, has diminished in importance beside other qualities more in harmony with our manners and present actual necessities. The qualities of a contingent value, if I may so express myself, are in a measure subordinate to the law of development of human nature, and to the different principles of conservation; they generally produce more renown than the others, because men have a more direct influence in encouraging them.

The natural consequence of the ideas which I have just stated, is, that an individual who should comprise in himself (in his own person), at a given period, all the qualities of the average man, would at the same time represent all which is grand, beautiful, and excellent. But such an identity can scarcely be realised, and it is rarely granted to individual men to resemble this type of perfection, except in a greater or less number of points. M. Cousin, setting out from very different considerations to those which are the object of this work, has nevertheless been in some measure led to conclusions similar to those I have just deduced from the theory of the average man. Speaking of the character peculiar to great men, he finds that this character consists in comprising people, periods, all human nature, nature, and universal order.† " Thus," says this learned academician, " all the individuals of which a people is composed, represent the whole mind of this people. But how do they represent it? One people is one in mind; but this is a multitude in its external composition, that is to say, a great multiplicity. Now, what is the law of all multiplicity ? It is, to have differences (d'être diverse), and, consequently, to be capable of more and less. Apart from absolute unity, every thing comes within the sphere of difference (and has degrees) of greater and of lesser. It is impossible but that, in a given multitude, such as a people, which, as has been shown, has a common type, there should be individuals who represent this type more or less. As there are those who represent it less clearly, more confusedly and imperfectly, so there are also those who represent it more clearly and perfectly, and less confusedly. Hence a line of demarcation between all the individuals of one and the same people. But those who are on the first plane, and represent the entire mind of their people more completely, are nevertheless a multitude, a great number, and are still subject to shades of difference: whence, again, a new selection of individuals who eminently represent the mind of their people. It is impossible for the case to be otherwise. From this we infer two things: first, the necessity of great men; second, their peculiar character (caractère propre). The great man is not an arbitrary creature, who may be or may not be. He is not simply one individual, but he has reference to a general idea, which communicates a superior power to him, at the same time that it gives him the determinate and real form of individuality. Too much and too little individuality equally destroy the great

* This is what the ancients thought generally, and in particular, Aristotle—Eth. ad Nic 2, ch. 2.

† Cours de Philosophie, leçon 10.

man. In the one case, the individuality in itself is an element of misery and littleness; for the particularity, the contingent, the finite, incessantly tend to division, to dissolution, to nothingness. On the other hand, every generality being connected to universality and to infinity, tends to unity, and absolute unity: it possesses greatness, but runs a chance of losing itself in chimerical abstraction. The great man is the harmonious union of particularity and generality: it is the possession of this character alone which makes him great—this added representation of the general mind of his people; and it is his relation to this generality which makes him great; and, at the same time, to represent this generality which confers his greatness on him, in person and in a real form, that is to say, in a finite, positive, visible, and determinate form; so that the generality does not encumber the particularity, and the particularity does not destroy generality; so that particularity and generality, infinite and finite, are united in this measure or standard, which is true human greatness.

This measure, which constitutes true greatness, also constitutes true beauty," &c.

The passage which has just been quoted, expresses my ideas better than I could have succeeded in doing myself. A man can have no real influence on masses —he cannot comprehend them and put them in action —except in proportion as he is infused with the spirit which animates them, and shares their passions, sentiments, and necessities, and finally sympathises completely with them. It is in this manner that he is a great man, a great poet, a great artist. It is because he is the best representative of his age, that he is proclaimed to be the greatest genius.

It is never sufficient for a man merely to resemble the average man in many things as much as possible, to enable him to produce great things himself; it is moreover necessary that he has occasion and possibilities for action. Newton, for example, deprived of all the resources of science, would always have had the same strength of intellect; he would always have been a type of several eminent qualities, and, in particular, of correctness of judgment and imagination; but if only a greater or smaller amount of science had been laid within his reach, he would have been Pythagoras, Archimedes, or Kepler; with all the resources which his period possessed, he has, and must have been a Newton. This appears to me incontestible: in the favourable position in which he found himself, it was a matter of necessity for him to put his eminent faculties in action, and to advance as far as circumstances permitted him. Now, the sciences had arrived at such a point, as to render it necessary that the theory of the motion of the celestial bodies should be reduced to correct principles; and Newton was then the only man who combined the necessary conditions to accomplish this work.

It appears to me that science only is truly progressive, and I use this word in its widest sense. All the faculties of man which are not based on science are essentially stationary, and their laws of development are constant. As to the other faculties, their laws of development, as has already been observed, probably remain the same also, or at least each only undergoes changes in the degree of its maximum, which depend on the development which science has attained. The development of science would therefore give the measure of the development of human nature.

Consequently, I participate in the following opinion of M. Cousin, that "entire history, not that of one people or one epoch only, but that of all epochs and all human nature, is represented by the great men. Thus, give me the series of all the known great men, and I will give you the known history of the human race."*

And, indeed, from what we have seen, the great

* Cours de Philosophie.—Introduction à l'Histoire de la Philosophie, leçon 10.

man, in his individuality, is the best representative of the degree of development to which human nature has attained in his times, and his works show the extent in which he himself has aided that development.

We are more convinced of the necessity of great men, and the error we commit in supposing that they spring up accidentally, when we consider the immense time required for a great truth, after it has been shadowed forth, to diffuse itself, and descend to the mass of people, and produce its effects; in general, it is not until centuries after, that we see the man come forward who developes or personifies it and secures its triumph. Thus, the germ of the great revolution, which has marked the close of the last century, was brought forward long ago, and was slowly developed, descending from high intellects to the lower ranks of society; but its course had not escaped the sagacious observer. Great events are, like great men, necessitated; and how can we be surprised at this, when we have seen that even the actions of ordinary individuals are necessitated, and when we have seen that a given social organisation induces a certain number of virtues and crimes as a necessary consequence, and that these crimes are of such or such a kind, and are performed by such and such means? This necessity is found both in good and evil—in the production of good things as well as of evil—in the production of chefs-d'œuvre and noble actions which are an honour to a country, as well as in the appearances of scourges which desolate it.

4. Of the Average Man considered with reference to Politics.

Whatever may be the difference of opinion observed in the same people, there must exist, even in the most opposite minds, some common ideas, which in moments of excitement of the passions are unobserved, but which would soon show themselves spontaneously if any one attempted to do violence to them. There are also common necessities; and even between opinions which seem utterly opposed to each other, we sometimes find more relations than at first sight we should suppose.

It is evident that, of all the political systems which any people would incline to adopt, there must be one which would suit best with the ideas and ordinary requirements, and which would most advantageously reconcile the interests of different parties; it is also evident that such a system could not be established by unanimous consent, since, even supposing that it is meditated upon most rationally and calmly, it must necessarily jar against certain passions, and meet opinions which are unfavourable to it. This system must not be confounded with that which would consist in taking a sort of average between two dominant ideas, and which must always be essentially defective in principle, since it is always impossible to conciliate minds, by placing between their opposed opinions another opinion which they equally repel. On the contrary, that which we have in view is based on elements common to all, and on ideas, which, though differed from by some, are still those of the majority.

It will perhaps be objected that, if the generality of men desired unjust or absurd things, it would be unreasonable to apply a political system to them equally unjust or absurd. I begin by declaring, that I do not think such a desire can exist in the generality of men; and, that, in the second place, if this wish could exist, it would even be necessary to gratify it, from the fear of being compelled to do so by some violent crisis.* This naturally leads me to considerations more or less connected with my subject, and which appertain to my mode of viewing the social system.

* See, on the same subject, the work of Sir T. C. Morgan, Sketches of the Philosophy of Morals, p. 244. 1 vol. 8vo. London: 1812. We find some very judicious observations in it, and which are deserving of more attention.

Revolutions, even those which have the most happy effects on the future, are never accomplished without certain actual sacrifices; as sudden changes, in a corporeal system, never take place without a certain loss of vital power. Independently of the real losses which bring no advantage to any body, changes of fortune, more or less manifest, take place; and it is in this case almost the same as in gaming, where the moral chances are not the same, that is to say, what is lost on the one side is not compensated by what is gained on the other. The great art of those who conduct revolutions should especially consist in making the transition with the least possible degree of violent change; and in this respect governments themselves are in the position best calculated to effect reforms. As for myself, I think that *the measure of the state of civilisation at which a nation has arrived is found in the mode in which its revolutions are effected.* This principle presupposes another, which is always true where states of equilibrium and motion are possible, in physical phenomena as well as in political facts; it is this—*the action is equal to the reaction.*

This wants some explanation: it will perhaps be asked, how I understand the application of this principle to morals and politics. An example taken from the material world will render this more manifest. When a force acts against a flexible body which yields and bends, each particle of this body successively leaves its primitive position and takes a new one; with respect to the compressing force, it is extinguished by successive and partial reactions, so that the action may be very energetic, without producing any apparent reaction; the only effect produced is a change in the flexible body, which is more or less sensible. If, on the contrary, the power acts against an elastic body, each particle of this body momentarily leaves its primitive state, but with a tendency to return to it immediately; the reaction is then general and instantaneous, it is also very evidently equal to the action. These examples are applicable to a social body. If each one is fully imbued with a knowledge of his rights and duties—if he invariably desires to do that which is just—if he energetically strives to re-enter the course he has traced out as soon as any one attempts to make him swerve from it—and if the reaction be allowed to manifest itself immediately after the action, both will be very *evidently* equal. But this state of irritability, so to say, presents itself with very different degrees of energy in different people, and we may say that the reaction, in its visible results, is generally less than the action.*

Revolutions are only *reactions* exercised by the people, or a part of the people, to correct abuses, real or supposed. They cannot be of a serious character if the apparent provocation has not been so also. Now, among an enlightened people, where the government is necessarily supposed to be wise and far-sighted, abuses cannot accumulate to such a degree as to take an alarming aspect; the more they are seen to increase, the more would the government be accused of want of foresight or evil, and the people who tolerate them of baseness and apathy; possessed of a feeling of their own dignity, they would have reacted against each of the abuses in proportion as they were manifested. When the degree of irritability is less, they yield to abuses, or only react when the number of them

* It is remarkable that the principle of the equality of action and reaction is also applicable to morals. Without being entirely destitute of sentiment, we cannot, in fact, withdraw ourselves from the consequences of this principle. The calmest and most moderate man, having made the firmest resolution not to depart from his habitual condition, will forget all his intentions on beholding a feeble person unjustly and brutally oppressed by a stronger one. In proportion to his degree of sensibility, so will he react with greater or less energy according as the offending person commits excesses. However, in similar circumstances he would have protected the aggressing party against the oppressed, if both had changed their relative positions.

has become too great to be endured any longer. The explosion is then the more terrible, because the power has been accumulating. Now, it is this extent or degree of accumulation which gives us, as I said previously, the measure of the state of civilisation of a people.

Frequently the reaction is manifested with symptoms apparently more serious than the action; but this is owing to the real reaction being conjoined with irrelevant causes. Thus in revolutions, amongst those who react under the influence of real abuses which are deeply felt, we almost always find turbulent men mixed with them, who delight themselves with the disorder, or are actuated by interested views. Such a state of things renders the position of a government very critical, and requires so much the more circumspection, in proportion as there is less good faith in the parties who oppose it. Enlightened and conscientious men, who have thoroughly acquainted themselves with causes,—and their number is always very small—will certainly support the government by their authority; but, in the midst of a general conflict, such auxiliaries are in general of little use, because they rarely act in person, and only on very serious occasions; they confine themselves to the development of the moral causes, which have always a very remote bearing on action, so that the effects which they produce do not manifest themselves until towards the end of revolutions, and only lead to an ultimate appreciation of morality, and to an insensible return to a state of equilibrium. This was manifested in the first French revolution, when abuses of every kind had accumulated to a deplorable extent, and the reaction was perhaps still more deplorable. The succeeding revolutions have been less serious, because more enlightened and provident governments took greater pains to prevent the causes of reaction, and make them disappear as soon as they assumed an alarming character. In this respect, England is placed in a very happy position; her reforms are accomplished successively and without sudden changes, and yet we cannot look without fear on reactions which may arise in consequence of the inequality of fortunes, and the state of the finances of this kingdom.

Despotism requires to be very powerful, and very able to depend upon its resources, to maintain itself where the people are irritable and prompt to react; it cannot long endure, whatever may be its power, in countries such as ours, where action, when at all serious, is spread with the greatest rapidity. In this respect, the liberty of the press has been of essential service—a service which perhaps has not been duly appreciated —namely, in having singularly contributed to facilitate reaction, and consequently to render great revolutions almost impossible; it possesses this immense advantage, that it does not allow force to accumulate to an alarming degree, causing reaction to manifest itself almost immediately after action, and sometimes even before action has had time to propagate itself. This has been observed during the late revolution in France, which was purely local, and the effects of which were confined within the walls of Paris. Among a people easily acted upon, and where action is readily transmitted, the greatest revolutions take place in parts, and reaction is extinguished by successive efforts, or at least overturns the cause which gave rise to it, without a violent shock.

Governments, like things, have also their states of equilibrium; and this equilibrium may be stable or unstable. This is an important distinction, and one easily understood. The stable equilibrium exists, when, in consequence of action and reaction of every kind, a government constantly regains its normal state; if, on the contrary, under the action of slight causes, a government tends to diverge more and more from its normal state, and if, each year, it change its form and institutions without adequate motives, its downfall is at hand, and it will infallibly sink, unless it finds assistance in the adjacent governments; but even then its fall cannot be long retarded. Examples are not wanting to support the distinction I have just made.

I have said above that civilisation tends to render the shocks which political revolutions cause in the social system both less violent and less frequent; I ought to add, that it also tends to make wars between nations less frequent. We no longer have the idea that these scourges are necessary things, from which we can never extricate ourselves, but 'regard them as an evil inevitable, in the absence of those laws which ought to regulate the rights of nations, and of sufficient power to secure the execution of them. In the beginning of communities, the strongest threw himself on the weakest, to wrest from him privileges and wreak vengeance; we find them renewing incessantly the most unjust and bloody contentions, until the time when equitable laws finally regulated the rights of every one, and put a period to such violences. Alas! this deplorable state of early times is still our own, if we look to nations instead of individuals. Indeed, without going far back, have we not seen nations cast themselves on nations, and tear each other for the most frivolous reasons?—the feeble or the least active fell in these cruel struggles, and the injury is still so recent, that we are yet scarcely aware of the extent of it. Far am I from wishing to cast odium on the warrior who exposes himself in defence of his country. His noble zeal deserves all our admiration, and has supplied the place of those protecting laws which ought to have defended him and his. But whilst groaning under a necessary evil, human nature should show the path of justice, in which it ought henceforth to go. Let us allow the same rights to nations which we grant to individuals—let there be laws for one as for the other—and let there be some power great enough and sufficiently enlightened to execute them. We have lately seen a judgment given by neutral nations in the case of a recent difference between two others which had arms in their hands. This judgment has been carried into execution; notification, citation, bodily restraint, none of the ordinary forms of justice, have been neglected. This event, which has not been sufficiently observed, and which has probably saved Europe from another struggle, indeed presents itself under appearances which are not very poetic to our imaginations, still warmed by the recitation of great deeds of arms, but it is not the less a real progress in the career of civilisation.

CHAPTER II.

ON THE ULTIMATE PROGRESS OF OUR KNOWLEDGE OF THE LAWS OF HUMAN DEVELOPMENT.

IN this work I have only been able to present an incomplete sketch of the vast labour which still remains to be done; but the difficulties were too numerous, and the materials which I had to work up too defective, for me to venture any farther into a territory almost entirely new. This study, however, has too many attractions—it is connected on too many sides with every branch of science, and all the most interesting questions in philosophy—to be long without zealous observers, who will endeavour to carry it farther and farther, and bring it more and more to the appearance of a science. At the same time, it will be very difficult to proceed on a safe course, before more information and more exact observations than we now possess, have been collected. The solidity of the edifice must depend on the soundness of the material.

In researches of this nature, it will be necessary always to produce original documents with caution, point out their sources, and give all the data which may lead us to appreciate their value. These docu-

ments ought to be of such a nature, that we can rigorously deduce the averages and limits between which the particular values lie. I have myself been more than once obliged to deviate from the course which I wish to see pursued by others, because, in order to render my ideas plain, I have been obliged to take the assistance of examples.

It will be equally desirable, whenever numbers are used, and results deduced from them, that we calculate the probable degree of error carefully. It is not enough to possess materials; it is also necessary to know the full value of them. One of the greatest defects of actual statistics is, that in the same line they present all the numbers indistinctly which can be collected, and make them concur to one result, without taking their importance or probable value into account. This confusion must necessarily produce great obstacles to the progress of science, and cause dangerous errors to prevail for a long time.

There is another research which deserves no less attention. It is not sufficient to perceive that an effect depends on several causes; it is extremely important that we be able to assign the proper degree of influence of each of these causes: in bringing this work to a conclusion, I shall now employ myself in demonstrating the possibility of finding a suitable measure for such an appreciation.

In the first place, it is necessary to admit, as a principle, that where variable causes do not exist, the effects produced will constantly be the same; and that the more variable the causes are, the effects will also generally vary within wide limits. Thus, supposing that human volition acts independently of all fixed laws, and in the most varied and irregular manner, we must necessarily find the effects produced presenting the greatest anomalies also, and differences varying within the widest limits. Now, it is these differences which it is desirable to examine and *measure*.

To define our ideas, let it be supposed that we want to examine if any general causes exist which modify the repression of crime; in other words, which modify the severity wit' which the guilty are punished. We must necessarily have recourse to observations which have been very carefully collected; and, if the annual results are not constantly the same, we shall be obliged to admit that the variations proceed either from errors of observation, from the influence of local causes, or from the influence of moral causes inherent in man. Going deeply into these researches, we really find that these elements vary according to time and place. Now, since the number of probable influential causes may be extremely great, it is proper to investigate them individually: it is in this manner that we are (at) first enabled to separate from our results the influential causes depending on locality, all our observations being taken in the same country; and that we may also eliminate the influential causes depending on periodicity of season, by carrying our researches over the whole year, whence we return to the appreciation of all the influential causes, taken separately.

Uniting the statistical documents of the courts of assize in France for the six years before 1831, we find:—

Years.	Accused.	Condemned.	Repression.
1825, - -	7,234	4594	0·635
1826, - - -	6,988	4348	0·622
1827, - - -	6,929	4236	0·610
1828, - - -	7,396	4551	0·615
1829, - - -	7,373	4475	0·607
1830, - - -	6,962	4130	0·593
Average, -	7,147	4389	0·6137

This table shows us that the repression of crimes

in general, has been annually decreasing, certainly not very much, but yet manifestly. Now, of the causes influencing repression, some act in a constant and others in a variable manner. By virtue of the former, the number 0·6137, which expresses the repression of crimes in general, should have a constant value from one year to another; by virtue of the action of the variable causes, the same number would undergo greater or less modifications. I shall first be occupied with the measurement of the influence of the constant causes.

To give a better conception of my idea, I suppose an individual labouring under an accusation; as we have just seen, the chance of being condemned will be as 614 to 1000; this probability should be understood in the most general sense, admitting that as yet we know nothing of the nature of the crime, the age, or the sex, of the accused, or of the state of education, or any of the constant causes modifying the repression of crime. But if we learn the fact, that the accusation is for a crime against persons, the probability of being condemned is altered; indeed, experience proves that the repression of crimes against persons is less than that of crimes against property. In France, the average values have been from 0·477 to 0·665, for the six years previous to 1831. Thus the chances are only 477 in 1000 that the individual will be condemned when accused of crime against persons; 655, when the crime is one against property. The principal cause of this inequality appears to be, as has been frequently remarked, that we are averse to apply punishment when it has a certain degree of severity, or appears severe in proportion to the crime; this is especially the case with crimes against persons.[*]

The sex of the accused has, moreover, a marked influence over the repression of crime: the severity is not so great towards females. All these shades will be more evident on inspecting the following table, which points out the different degrees of probability which exist of an accused person being condemned, according as the causes are favourable or the contrary:—

State of the Accused Person.	Probability of being Condemned.
Possessing a superior education,	0·400
Condemned who has pleaded guilty,	0·476
Accused of crime against person,	0·477
Being able to read and write well,	0·543
Being a female,	0·576
Being more than 30 years old,	0·586
Being able to read and write imperfectly,	0·600
Without any designation,	0·614
Being a male,	0·622
Not being able to read or write,	0·627
Being under 30 years of age,	0·630
Accused of crime against property,	0·655
Condemned in absence, or for non-appearance (*contumax*),	0·960

Experience, therefore, proves that the most influential cause diminishing the repression of crime consists in the appearance of the criminal before the judge with the advantage of a superior education, which supposes a certain degree of affluence, and the ready means of making a defence. The most advantageous position an accused person can possibly be in, is to be more than 30 years of age, a female, to have received a superior education, to appear under an accusation of a crime against person, and to come when cited, previously to being taken into custody; on the contrary, the most disadvantageous state is to be under 30 years of age, unable to read or write, to be a man, and accused of crime against property, and not to be

* [Here, as in other places, M. Quetelet gives his important sanction to the principle upon which the amenders of the criminal laws of England chiefly found their arguments for reform. The severity of the punishment leads to the escape of the criminal.]

able, as refusing to appear when cited, to produce the means of defence.

The causes which modify the probability of being condemned, according to the state of the accused person, appear to me so evident, as to render it superfluous to insist on them. Such is not the case with the degree of influence of these causes; this estimation is attended with difficulties. Reflecting upon it, it has appeared to me that, of all the numerical elements subject to variation, we might very easily *estimate the importance of the deviations from the average, or the importance of the causes which produce them, by comparing these deviations with the magnitude of the average*. It is almost in this manner that the first geometricians who studied the theory of probabilities as applied to facts bearing upon man (and Buffon, in particular), have estimated the importance of a whole, for one individual, by comparing it with what this individual possessed.

According to this estimation, it will be necessary to take the deviations from each of the ratios calculated above, and compare these with the number 0·614, the measure of the repression in France, when we do not pay attention to any modifying cause; the respective magnitude of the deviations will give this measure of their importance, and consequently that of the causes which produce them, effects being considered as proportional to their causes. Let us suppose, for example, that we seek to ascertain the value of the respective influences which are exercised on the repression of crime in France, by possessing the advantage of a superior education, and being a female; we find the values of the repression are 0·400 and 0·576, and the differences between these numbers and the general average, 0·614, are 0·214 and 0·038. From what has been said, the importance of these differences, or of the causes which produce them, will be $\frac{214}{614}$ and $\frac{38}{614}$, or otherwise, 0·348 and 0·062. From this we perceive that a superior education has five times the influence which being a woman has, in diminishing the repression of crime before the tribunals. The following table presents the degrees of influence of the different causes modifying the repression of crime, and has been calculated upon the same bases :—

State of the Accused.	Relative degree of the influence of the state of the Accused on the Repression of Crime.
Possessing a superior education,	0·348
Appeared to plead after having been declared absent or contumacious,	0·224
Accused of crime against persons,	0·223
Being able to read and write well,	0·115
Being a female,	0·062
Being more than 30 years of age,	0·045
Being able to read and write imperfectly,	0·023
Without any designation,	0·000
Being a man,	0·013
Being unable to read or write,	0·022
Being under 30 years of age,	0·026
Accused of crime against property,	0·067
Having withdrawn from justice, or for non-appearance when cited (*contumax*),	0·563

Thus, as I have already observed, there is not any cause which has more influence in varying the repression of crime, than the reluctance or non-appearance of the accused to answer charges. The preceding table does not merely possess the advantage of showing this clearly, but also shows the degree of influence of the cause producing it.

And here there is a question of another kind, viz., how far those causes may be regarded as constant which have now been pointed out. For, before one can say that they are absolutely constant, it must be shown that the results which they produce continue the same from year to year. Now, this is what does not take place: the deviations from the average, which we have taken as constant quantities, annually undergo slight modifications, which we have attributed to *variable* causes : these modifications are in general very small, when we only take a small number of years into account; but still it is necessary to notice them. The repression of crime in general, for example, has not been constantly of the value 0·614 during the six years which have furnished the elements of our calculations; small annual differences have been observed, and the repression, in its greatest deviations from the average, more and less, has been 0·635 and 0·593; the deviations are consequently 0·021 and 0·021; and consequently their ordinary value is $\frac{21}{64}$, or 0·034. Thus the variable causes which have produced alterations of the degree of repression, have had, in their maximum and minimum of energy, influences which have equalled or even surpassed the influences of some causes which we have been considering as constant. To have a juster idea of the variable causes, it will be proper to examine the effects which they have annually produced on each of the elements considered above. The following tables will supply us with data on this subject :—

Years.	Repression of Crimes		Repression.	
	against Persons.	against Property.	Men.	Women.
1825, - -	0·46	0·66	..	..
1826, - -	0·51	0·67	0·63	0·60
1827, - -	0·50	0·65	0·62	0·60
1828, - -	0·47	0·66	0·63	0·57
1829, - -	0·46	0·65	0·62	0·57
1830, - -	0·46	0·64	0·61	0·54
Average, -	0·477	0·655	0·722	0·576

Years.	Repression in Individuals		Repression.	
	under 30 Years.	above 30 Years.	Not Appearing.	Appeared to stand Trial.
1826, - -	0·64	0·60	0·93	0·49
1827, - -	0·64	0·58	0·97	0·45
1828, - -	0·64	0·58	0·97	0·46
1829, - -	0·62	0·59	0·97	0·50
1830, - -	0·61	0·53	0·96	0·48
Average, -	0·63	0·586	0·96	0·479

Years.	Repression in Individuals			
	unable to Read or Write.	able to Read and Write imperfectly.	able to Read and Write well.	who had a Superior Education.
1828, - -	0·63	0·62	0·56	0·35
1829, - -	0·63	0·60	0.55	0·48
1830, - -	0·62	0·58	0·52	0·37
Average, -	0·627	0·60	0·543	0·40

These different tables teach us that the greatest variations which any of the constant causes modifying the repression of crime have undergone, have scarcely exceeded the value of the intensity even of these causes: or, in other terms, that in the very circumstances most unfavourable to observation, the effects of constant causes have been but little effaced by the effects of variable and accidental causes. We shall be enabled to judge better on this point by the following table, which discriminates for us the importance of the greatest deviations which the causes modifying repression have presented in each of the cases above enumerated :—

Causes which Modify Repression.	Difference from the Average.	
	Less.	Greater.
The accused has a superior education, - -	0·200	0·125
ʺ ʺ appears to answer charge, -	0·050	0·056
ʺ ʺ is prosecuted for crime against person, - - - - }	0·069	0·035
ʺ ʺ is able to read and write well,	0·031	0·042
ʺ ʺ is a female, - - - -	0·042	0·062
ʺ ʺ is upwards of 30 years of age,	0·024	0·027
ʺ ʺ is able to read and write imperfectly, - - - - }	0·033	0·033
ʺ ʺ *is without any designation*, -	0·034	0·034
ʺ ʺ is a male, - - - -	0·013	0·019
ʺ ʺ is unable to read or write, -	0·005	0 011
ʺ ʺ is under 30 years of age, -	0·016	0·032
ʺ ʺ is prosecuted for crime against property, - - - - }	0·039	0·018
ʺ ʺ does not appear when cited, -	0·010	0·031

I have always reasoned on the hypothesis that our results were founded on so great a number of observations, that nothing fortuitous could affect the value of the averages: but this is not the case here. Some results are deduced from observations which are yet small in number, and we know that, all things being equal, *the precision of results increases as the square root of the number of observations.* This is especially applicable to any thing concerning the repression (punishment) of the accused persons who have received a superior education. The values obtained are deduced from a small number of observations, and the deviations from the average of them have consequently been greater: now, by employing the method of the smallest squares, I have found that the accuracy of the numbers 0·400 and 0·6137, previously obtained for repression in general, and for repression exercised in particular against the accused who have received a superior education, is in the ratio of 0·0870 to 0·0075, or as 11 to 1.

In separating, pursuant to the preceding observations, what is purely fortuitous in the deviations from the averages, so that we may only consider the causes which have had a greater or lesser regularity of influence on the repression of crime, I think that we may pretty nearly represent their influence by 0·034. These deviations are such that it is easy to perceive that the repression of crime has gradually diminished. Now, this progressive diminution must have its causes; and one of them, undoubtedly the most influential, is pointed out in the *Compte Général de l'Administration de la Justice Criminelle en France pendant l'Année* 1830 :—" Six years have passed away since the *Comptes Généraux* of the administration of criminal justice have been published. During the former half of this period (1825, 1826, and 1827), the lists of the jury were formed according to the rules laid down in the code of criminal instruction (*instruction criminelle*); during the second half (1828, 1829, and 1830), these lists have been made according to the law of the 2d of May 1827, which has changed the basis of juries, and called a greater number of citizens to fulfil its duties. By taking the totality of the results of the accusations during the entire period of six years, as well as during each part of it, and by comparing these different results, we find that the only difference betwixt juries formed according to the code of criminal advice, and those which the legislature has subsequently made, is this, that the latter class appear to have a slight tendency to look upon accusations less severely. The proof of this assertion is found in the following table :—

Years.	Totality of Accusations.		
	Acquitted.	Condemned to Punishments.	
		Ignominious.	Correctional.
1825, 1826, 1827, 1828, 1829, and 1830, }	0·39	0·38	0·23
1825, 1826, and 1827,	0·38	0·41	0·21
1828, 1829, and 1830,	0·39	0·36	0·26

In a few years we shall be enabled to compare these conclusions with those resulting from the declarations of the present juries, whose constituent elements have been further enlarged by the reduction of the electoral franchise, and who at present only pronounce condemnation with a majority of seven voices."

Thus the preceding table shows us that not only the number of acquittals has diminished, but even the punishments awarded have been less severe: there have been fewer ignominious and more correctional ones.

This observation on the tendency to value accusations more leniently, presents itself with a still greater degree of probability when we examine the nature of the crimes in detail: it is there, especially, that we can see if they have recoiled more readily from the application of punishments, on account of their severity. We find, in effect, that condemnations to death have diminished very manifestly. The same observations recur when we make the distinction between crimes against persons and property; a proof of which, also, is found in the following table:—

Years.	Accused of Crimes against Persons.			Accused of Crimes against Property.		
	Acquitted.	Condemned to Punishment.		Acquitted.	Condemned to Punishment.	
		Ignominious.	Correctional.		Ignominious.	Correctional.
1825, 26, 27, 28, 29, 30,	0·52	0·28	0·20	0·34	0·42	0·24
1825, 26, 27,	0·50	0·30	0·20	0·33	0·45	0·22
1828, 29, 30,	0·53	0·26	0·21	0·35	0·39	0·26

On both hands we see fewer condemnations, and the condemnations are less severe.* It appears, therefore, to be probable, that some causes exist, whatever may be their nature, which have had an influence in France in slightly diminishing the repression of crime: time will show us better if we are to seek for one of the causes of this in the introduction of that law which has changed the constitution of the jury, and also if this cause is single. However the case may be, it is very evident that the causes which from year to year have modified the repression of crime in general, have had a weaker influence than the constant causes which modify it according to the nature of the crimes: for, still preserving the two established periods, we find that the first-mentioned causes have had the effect of producing, on an average, only two or three additional acquittals out of 100 accusations, taken promiscuously; while the second causes have almost invariably produced eighteen acquittals more for accusations of crimes against persons than for those against property. This indeed has been already seen, when comparing the two tables given above.

I have hinted that the change introduced in the formation of juries was perhaps not the sole cause which had modified the repression of crime: and, indeed, I think that the events of 1830 have not been without some influence on this matter. The repression, for crime in general, is at that period much less than during the other years, and this conjecture gains still more weight when we enter into the consideration of details. Thus, out of the twelve modifying causes which have been pointed out, the repression for this year has presented nine minima, and the three other values approach their minima very nearly. Indeed, it is natural to suppose that, to those causes which might then predispose to indulgence, there would also be added apprehensions of individual safety, fears of reaction, and other causes which are developed in the heart of man in the midst of political agitation. Generally speaking, a revolution ought to produce a greater

* See the *Comptes Généraux*, for the repression of each crime in particular.

or less modification of each element of the social system, and especially in what relates to crime.

I shall here observe, that analogous effects have also been observed in Belgium, where a revolution took place at the same period. The results of the repression of crime for this country are sufficiently interesting to find a place here.

Years.	Crimes in General.		
	Accused.	Condemned.	Repression.
1826,	725	611	0·843
1827,	810	682	0·852
1828,	814	677	0·832
1829,	753	612	0·811
1830,	643	483	0·759
Average,	747	613	0·821

This table shows us that the degree of repression in 1830 was weaker than during the other years; the difference is here even more sensible, for the measure of its importance is 0·075, whilst in France it was 0·034; but our revolution was also less local than that of France, and the provisional government lasted longer.

Another observation which must strike us on examining this table is, that the repression has in general been much higher in Belgium than in France; the respective values have been on an average 0·821 and 0·614, nearly as 4 to 3. This great disproportion is owing to the circumstance, that, up to that time, the jury had not been instituted in Belgium, although the people were governed by similar criminal laws; and these numbers may, to a certain degree, give us the measure of the influence exercised on the fate of an accused person, in case of his appearing before judges or before a jury. Now that the institution of jury is established in Belgium, we shall be still better enabled to appreciate its influence, from the modifications which it may produce in the repression of crime.

I have presented the circumstances bearing on repression with some detail, that I may give a better idea of the light in which I view the possibility of measuring the influence of causes. I shall now offer the results of the calculations which I have obtained for other elements of the social system, and their approximation will lead us to very remarkable conclusions. I have been careful to point out the years in which the maxima and minima of the deviations have occurred, by the side of the degree of importance of these deviations.

BELGIUM.	Importance of the Difference.		Epochs.	
	More.	Less.	Of Max.	Of Min.
Stature of the Militia—Town,	0·003	0·005	1825	1827
,, ,, Country,	0·001	0·003	1826	1827
Repression of crime in general,	0·038	0·075	1827	1830
Condemnations in general,*	0·112	0·212	1827	1830
Births in town,	0·084	0·120	1825	1817
,, in country,	0·083	0·139	1826	1817
Deaths in town,	0·158	0·047	1826	1816
,, in country,	0·170	0·071	1826	1824
Marriages,†	0·135	0·212	1815	1817
Receipts of the treasury,	0·188	0·096	1826	1820
Expenditure of the treasury,	0·143	0·133	1826	1820
Price of wheat,	1·134	0·447	1816	1824
,, of rye,	1·374	0·500	1816	1824

* The importance of the deviations, and especially of the maximum deviation of the lesser, is sensibly greater for Belgium than for France: this arises from the circumstance that, during the year 1830, there were much fewer condemnations than in the preceding years, the operation of the tribunals having been suspended during a longer or shorter time. This year is a complete anomaly, and perhaps ought not to have been included in our calculations, except we took the time only during which the courts were open.

† These ratios have been taken from the numbers found in the whole of the ancient kingdom of the Low Countries.

(*Table continued.*)

FRANCE. *	Importance of the Difference.		Epochs.	
	More.	Less.	Of Max.	Of Min.
Repression of crime in general,	0·034	0·034	1825	1830
Condemnations in general, -	0·047	0·057	1825	1830
Condemnations for crimes against property, - - -	0·056	0·056	1828	1827
Condemnations for crimes against person, - - -	0·153	0·144	1825	1830
Births, - - - - -	0·021	0·054	1819	1818
Deaths, - - - -	0·071	0·049	1828	1823
Marriages, - - - -	0·117	0·125	1823	1817

The two preceding tables demonstrate clearly different facts, which I shall successively examine.

In the first place, by only regarding the facts themselves, and without having regard to the influence of causes taken individually, we see that, among the elements observed, the least variable are the stature of man and the repression of crime (or the severity which the tribunals display in punishments); we afterwards see, in the adjoining lines, the facility which man shows to commit crime, and the facility with which he reproduces his kind, or dies. Thus, whatever be the determining motives of his actions, in point of fact, they modify no more the number of deaths than the number of births, or even the number of crimes which annually scourge society.† Marriages also take place with regularity, but their number varies at the same time within wider limits than the preceding elements; the same has been the case with the receipts and expenses of the Belgic treasury; but no element has undergone greater variations than the price of rye and wheat.

In passing, we shall observe, that the prices of grain have a very close (*étroite*) relation to every thing bearing on the other elements. Thus, in the years 1816 and 1817, the prices of grain were very high, and marriages numerous; on the other hand, it was the same with births. It would appear as if the maximum of deaths should also have taken place in this year, in place of the minimum, which we observe in the towns, in 1816. Examining the numbers for 1817 attentively, we really find that they will form maxima for town and country, if we consider the increase of the population, another influential cause, which it is easy to calculate. The minimum would then be carried to 1824, which is the period when grains were at the lowest price, and which year was followed by a year of very great fruitfulness of women both in town and country.

Taking notice of the annual increase of the population, which has been considerable in Belgium, we find values which closely resemble those furnished by France; we find, moreover, that the year 1817 presents the minimum of marriages and births, both for town and country, and, at the same time, the maximum of deaths, both for town and country.

It is to be observed, that the maximum of the number of marriages has taken place in 1815, notwithstanding the increase of the population in subsequent years. This year, which brought the wars and disasters of the empire to a close, allowed a great number of young men to return home; and, being attended by peace, gave rise to many new establishments in life.

* See the *Comptes Généraux, &c.*, and the *Annuaire du Bureau des Longitudes de France*, 1832, for what relates to the movement of the population from 1817 to 1829.

† It may be objected, that the observations on crime only refer to five years, whilst those on births and deaths extend to twelve years; and that we ought, in the same manner, to expect to find smaller differences between the extreme values of the effects produced by variable causes. But I shall reply, on the other hand, that births and deaths being annually much more numerous than crimes, what is casual leaves fewer traces behind it, and must have a less sensible influence in modifying regular causes.

H

We may further see, from the preceding numbers, that a residence in town or country has not manifested a well-marked influence in varying the elements we have now been considering.

Until now, I have omitted the influence of season and time of the day; yet it may be interesting to know the respective influences of annual and diurnal periods, which I have eliminated to the extent of my present materials, carrying my observations to annual average results.

To ascertain the influence of an annual period, I shall compare the average results obtained for each month, and, as hitherto, I shall value the importance of the maximum deviation from the average, whether on the side of surplus or the reverse. This calculation gives the following results. Those for births and deaths relate to Belgium, the others are calculated for France:—

	Periods of		Importance of the Difference.	
	Min.	Max.	Min.	Max.
Births in town,* -	July,	Feb.	0·107	0·122
~ country, -	..	..	0·162	0·177
Deaths in town, - -	..	January,	0·126	0·153
~ country, -	..	..	0·191	0·212
Crimes against property, -	..	Dec.	0·113	0·233
~ ~ person,	January,	June,	0·121	0·289
Mental alienation, -	..	..	0·288	0·346

What must strike us at first is, that the influence of season only has more effect in causing the elements relating to man to vary (those at least which I have considered), than all the united influences of nature and of men have had in causing variations of the average annual results during the same period. These monthly variations take place, moreover, in the most regular manner, as I have elsewhere shown. To form an idea of the influence of the seasons, compared with the combined influences of all the causes operating to modify the annual results, I shall take the same elements and compare the extremes with which the greatest deviations to one side or another have been comprised, and I shall assume as unity the sum of the differences of each annual average. It will be understood that here the conclusions are deduced from the same observations, classed either according to years or months:—

	Sums of the Differences of Max. and Min.		Ratio.
	Annual.	Monthly.	
Births in town,	0·204	0·229	1·13
~ country, -	0·222	0·339	1·53
Deaths in town,	0·205	0·284	1·39
~ country,	0·241	0·403	1·67
Crimes against property, -	0·112	0·346	3·09
~ ~ person, -	0·297	0·410	1·38
Mental alienation, -	?	0·634	?

Thus, the results taking place in different years have varied less than those produced by seasons, and the respective influences of the causes which give rise to them, as concerns the movement of population, are more dissimilar in the country than in town. We may remark, in general, that the country is, physically speaking, more easily acted upon than towns, and that the deviations from the average there have greater values, undoubtedly because more hold is given to modifying causes of different kinds.

The epochs at which the maxima and minima take place have also very singular relations. Thus, deaths and crimes against property are more numerous in

* M. L'Avocat Guerry has given, in the *Annales d'Hygiène* for April 1829, some drawings (*dessins*) representing the influence of the seasons on physiological phenomena: it is to be greatly regretted that these designs are not accompanied by the numbers according to which they have been made.

winter, in consequence of the rigours of the season and the privations to which man is subjected. Crimes against person are more frequent at periods when the passions are most in force, and when mental alienation manifests itself with the greatest intensity.

As to the diurnal period, it is to be regretted that calculations are still wanting to enable us to appreciate its decided influence on the human species. From the numbers which I have obtained for Brussels, births appear to be more numerous during night than in the day time. The deviation from the average both on the side of surplus and the reverse, amounts to 0·114.* M. Buek has since arrived at the same results for the city of Hamburg, and found the ratio to be 0·136. M. Villermé himself, at the Hospice de la Maternité in Paris, has obtained similar results. The deviations are more important when we compare the different hours of the day separately. M. Guerry, in the *Annales d'Hygiène* for January 1831, has presented some researches on the influence of the different parts of the day on suicide by suspension; and he has found, during a period of 14 years, that the greatest number of cases have taken place between the hours of 6 and 8 o'clock in the morning, and the fewest number between 12 at noon and 2 in the afternoon. The deviations, more and less, have been in relative importance as the numbers 0·625 and 0·614: these deviations are considerable, compared with those hitherto observed.

It is sufficiently apparent, that the smallest period, that of the day, has still greater influence than the monthly period (which depends on the succession of seasons), and consequently more influence than the totality of the causes, which produce variations betwixt the average results of one year and another—always supposing it to be understood, that these average results are not deduced from too large a number of years, during which the men observed may have completely changed, so as in a manner to present a different social condition.

If we now sum up what has been said, we may deduce the following conclusions:—

1st, The regular and *periodic* causes, which depend either on the annual or diurnal period, produce effects on society which are more sensible, and which vary within wider limits, than the combined *non-periodic* effects annually produced by the concurrence of all the other causes operating on society; in other terms, the social system, in its present state, appears to be more dissimilar to itself in the course of one year, or even in the space of one day, than during two consecutive years, if we have reference to the increase of the population.

2d,.The *diurnal* period seems to exercise a somewhat stronger influence than the *annual* period, at least so far as births are concerned.

3d, The annual period produces more sensible effects in the country than in town; and this appears to be the case with those causes in general which tend to modify the facts relating to man.

4th, The price of grain has a very marked influence on the elements of the social system; and although we still want sufficient data to appreciate the comparative values of this influence, yet we may very safely range it among the causes operating most energetically.

5th, If we wished to class, according to our observations, the elements relating to man in an order which should indicate the degree of variation to which they are subject, we should find the succession as follows, commencing with the *least variable* :—The stature of man; the repression of crime, or the degree of severity with which it is punished; the births; the propensity to crime, or the facility with which it is committed; deaths; marriages; receipts and expenses of the treasury; and, finally, the prices of grain.

* See my *Recherches sur la Population, &c., dans le Royaume des Pays-Bas*, p. 21.

Thus man commits crime with at least as much regularity as is observed in births, deaths, or marriages, and with more regularity than the receipts and expenses of the treasury take place. But none of the elements which concern him, and which have been calculated in our table, vary within wider limits than the prices of grain.

From what has been said, we may draw the two following principal conclusions :—

Since the price of grain is one of the most influential causes operating on the mortality and reproduction of the human species, and since, at the present day, this price may vary within the widest limits, it is the province of the foresight of governments to diminish as much as possible all the causes which induce these great variations in prices, and consequently in the elements of the social system.

On the other hand, since the crimes which are annually committed seem to be a necessary result of our social organisation, and since the number of them cannot diminish without the causes which induce them undergoing previous modification, it is the province of legislators to ascertain these causes, and to remove them as far as possible : they have the power of determining the budget of crime, as well as the receipts and expenses of the treasury. Indeed, experience proves at first as clearly as possible the truth of this opinion, which at first may appear paradoxical, viz., that *society prepares crime, and the guilty are only the instruments by which it is executed.* Hence it happens that the unfortunate person who loses his head on the scaffold, or who ends his life in prison, is in some manner an expiatory victim for society. His crime is the result of the circumstances in which he is found placed : the severity of his chastisement is perhaps another result of it. However, when matters have come to this point, the punishment is no less a necessary evil, were it only as a preventive mean : it would only be desirable that the other means of prevention might afterwards become sufficiently efficacious for us not to be obliged to have recourse to the former severe means.

I shall conclude this chapter by a final observation, which is as it were a consequence of all the preceding, viz., *that one of the principal facts of civilisation is, that it more and more contracts the limits within which the different elements relating to man oscillate.* The more knowledge is diffused, so much the more do the deviations from the average disappear; and the more, consequently, do we tend to approach that which is beautiful, that which is good. The perfectibility of the human species results as a necessary consequence from all our researches. Defects and monstrosities disappear more and more from the physical world ; the frequency and the severity of diseases are combated with more advantage by the progress of medical science ; the moral qualities of man experience not less sensible improvements ; and the farther we advance, the less are great politic overthrows and wars (the scourges of humanity) to be feared, either in their immediate effects or in their ultimate consequences.

It would seem at first sight that the fine arts and literature must suffer from this state of things. For if it be true that individual peculiarities tend to disappear more and more, and that nations assume a greater resemblance to each other, whatever is most picturesque in society and in the aspect of different parts of the globe, ought insensibly to disappear. Even during the last half century, and within the limits of Europe alone, we see how great the tendency is for people to lose their national character and be amalgamated in one common type: yet nature will always be so prodigiously varied, that the talented man will never have to fear lest the source of the picturesque be exhausted ; on the contrary, he every day finds for himself new sources from which his imagination may take the noblest and most elevated inspiration, and bring out treasures unknown to his predecessors.

APPENDICES.

APPENDIX—CONTAINING THE ADDITIONS MADE BY THE AUTHOR (M. QUETELET TO THE GERMAN TRANSLATION OF HIS WORK, PUBLISHED AT STUTTGART IN 1838, BY DR V. A. RIECKE.

No. I.

ADDITION TO THE INTRODUCTION.

Extracts from the Bulletin de l'Académie Royale des Sciences et Belles Lettres de Bruxelles : 1835. No. 8.

M. QUETELET communicated the other day to the academy several statistical notices published by the French government, confirming more and more the ideas expressed by him regarding the constant return of the same phenomena in every thing having a reference to the physical and moral man, provided society undergoes no violent change :—First, It may be seen from documents which refer to the recruiting of the French army, that annually nearly the same number of young men liable to serve as conscripts must be exempted on account of a deficiency in, fingers and in teeth ; on account of deafness, goitres, lameness, diseases of the bones, weak constitution, insufficient size of body ; or on account of being the first-born, or of being orphans, or sons of widows, blind people, &c. Just as constant appear the numbers of young people who are able to read and write, and those who have received no instruction ; the number of those self-mutilated in order to avoid military service, &c. From the following table, it will be more evident in what degree conditions which appear to depend on entirely accidental causes have a constant recurrence. It is an accurate extract from a Report to the King, lately published in France, regarding the recruitment of the army :*—

Number of Young Men in France who have been excused Military Service on account of Bodily Infirmities.

Causes of Unfitness.	1831.	1832.	1833.
Wanting fingers, - - -	752	647	743
„ teeth, - -	1,304	1,243	1,392
Deafness and dumbness, - -	830	736	725
Loss of other limbs or organs, -	1,605	1,530	1,580
Goitres, - - -	1,125	1,231	1,298
Lameness, - - - -	949	912	1,049
Other deformities, -	8,007	7,630	8,494
Diseases of bones, - -	782	617	667
Short-sighted, - - -	948	891	920
Other affections of the eyes, -	1,726	1,714	1,839
Itch, (?) - - -	11	10	10
Scald head, - - -	749	800	794
Leprosy, - - - -	57	19	29
Other cutaneous diseases, -	937	983	895
Scrofulous affections, -	1,730	1,539	1,272
Affections of chest, - -	561	423	359
Hernia, - - - -	4,044	3,579	4,222
Epilepsy (falling sickness), -	463	367	342
Different other diseases, -	9,168	9,058	10,286
Weakness of constitution, -	11,783	9,979	11,259
Insufficient size of body, -	15,935	14,962	15,078
Amount of whole class of certain age,	295.978	277,477	285,805

M. Quetelet further mentions, that he knows, from sources to be depended on, that not only the number of letters delivered at the post-office of Paris remains nearly the same every year, but that also every year nearly the same number of letters are found, which have been forgotten to be sealed, or which could not be delivered in consequence of illegible handwriting, or insufficient addresses, &c. &c. For a long time he had endeavoured to prove, that society pays a fearful budget to crime, which perhaps shows a greater regularity than the financial budget : and in a work which he lately published—" An Attempt at the Natural Philosophy of Society"—he felt himself entitled to say, that if the statistical details published by the government were also to make mention of those crimes the perpetrators of which have remained unknown, their occurrence would not be less regular. This supposition has actually found a complete confirmation in our country, in the reports made to the minister of justice, and which will be published forthwith. There exists too strict a connexion between the phenomena presented by society, and between the causes of which they are the effects, to be neglected any longer by the philosopher and statesman ; and, without doubt, the science which has this study for its object, will occupy, in course of time, a high rank in the scale of human knowledge.

No. II.

ADDITION TO THE SECOND DIVISION OF THE FIRST BOOK.

Influence of the Seasons upon Births.

M. Ramon de la Sagra, in his History of the Island of Cuba,* has given a comparative view of the number of births of the white and coloured population in Havanna, according to the months of the year. From the ciphers we reprint here, it will be seen how much geographical latitude modifies the results which we have observed in our climates, although the place mentioned is situated in the northern hemisphere. The following ciphers include the observations of five years, from 1825 to 1829 :—

Months.	Births.		
	Among the White Population.	Coloured Population.	Total.
January, -	624	703	1,327
February, - -	573	596	1,169
March, - -	600	627	1,227
April, - -	636	638	1,274
May, - -	634	651	1,285
June, - -	659	620	1,279
July, - -	661	698	1,359
August, - -	694	741	1,435
September, -	736	760	1,496
October, - -	772	736	1,508
November, -	713	706	1,419
December, -	700	774	1,474
Total, -	8002	8250	16,252

---

* *Compte rendu au Roi,* p. 128 and 129. Similar examinations take place in the kingdom of Wirtemburg, and, as in the above case, the results form a source of valuable materials for medical statistics.

* Historia Economico-Politica y Estadistica de la Isla de Cuba, p. 35. Havanna : 1831. 4to.

According to this table, the greatest number of births in Havannah occurs in October, and the fewest between February and May. This is nearly the opposite of that distribution of births for the seasons observed in Europe.

No. III.

ADDITION TO THE THIRD SECTION OF THE FIRST BOOK.

Mortality of Lying-in Women.

M. Casper communicates, in his excellent work on the Relations of Mortality (*Die Wahrscheinliche Lebensdauer des Menschen, &c.*), " The probable Duration of Human Life," p. 51, the following results relative to the mortality of women at child-birth in the Prussian monarchy. There were—

	Born.	Died in Child-Bed.
In the years 1817 till 1826 (inclusive),	4,955,672	44,772
" 1826 ~ 1828 "	499,507	4,539
" 1828 ~ 1829 "	495,483	4,615
" 1829 ~ 1830 "	497,241	4,441
" 1830 ~ 1831 "	490,524	4,710
" 1831 ~ 1832 "	481,959	4,677
Total, - - - -	7,420,386	67,754

If from this number of births the regular recurring number of twins and triplets, amounting to about 94,000, are deducted, it follows that of 108 women in child-bed, one died. According to Lubbock, there died in the ten years, from 1818 to 1827, only one woman in child-bed of 117.

No. IV.

ADDITION TO THE FIFTH SECTION OF THE FIRST BOOK.

Extract from the Bulletin de l'Académie Royale des Sciences de Bruxelles: 1835. No. 1, p. 129.

M. Quetelet communicated, in consequence of a paper transmitted by M. Villermé on the population of Great Britain, the following accounts regarding the mortality in Belgium :—" Science has of late been enriched by several important works * on the statistics of Britain, especially on the relations of mortality in that country. The different documents they contain have confirmed most distinctly a fact which I have for some time believed to exist, and which ought to have been pointed out by MM. Villermé and François d'Ivernois—the fact, namely, that the population of Britain has not so great a claim as commonly supposed to a much smaller mortality than the other states of Europe.

I have already observed, in a paper which was read to the Royal Academy of Sciences at Paris,† that in Britain, for every two children there are only to be found three individuals above fifteen years of age, and in the United States even fewer; whilst in France, Sweden, and Belgium, at least four are to be found. Indeed, this disproportion principally arises from the rapid increase of population, as it subsisted of late in Britain and the United States. Most of the children who are the fruit of this great development of fertility not yet being far advanced in the career of life, the number of adult individuals resulting from them

* The principal works are :—

Abstracts of the Answers and Returns, &c. By Rickman. 3 vols. 4to. 1831.

Tables of the Revenue, Population, Commerce, &c. By Porter. 2 vols. folio. 1833.

A Digest of all the Accounts, &c. By Marshall. 1833.

On the Natural and Mathematical Laws concerning Population, &c. By Francis Corbaux. 1 vol. 8vo. 1833.

† 8th September 1834. See the journal *L'Institut*, No. 71, 20th September 1834 ; and *Le Temps*, 18th September 1834.

must be proportionally small. M. Villermé, our correspondent, as member of the French Institute, has considered the question under another point of view. This gentleman has, in a paper on the population of Great Britain,* compared Rickman's tables of mortality for England, those of Duvillard for France, and those I have published for Belgium (the one in my *Annuaire de l'Observatoire,* the other in a manuscript paper read at a meeting of the Academy for Moral and Political Science at Paris): it results from this comparison, that the ' probable duration of the life of children at their birth, is in Great Britain about two years longer than in Belgium.' With individuals of 1 to 30 years of age, the case is the reverse. We may wager 100 to 100 that a person may live in Belgium from 1 to 3 years longer than individuals of the same age born and brought up in Britain. Further, the probability of the duration of life with individuals from 30 to 40 years of age is in both countries precisely the same ; and only at the age of 45 the probable duration of life is somewhat more in favour of the English than of the Belgians ; but the difference amounts at most to only one year. In the face of these facts, from which it is evident that the mortality in Britain is not lower than in Belgium, it appears very probable that life, at the moment of birth, in the former is the safer possession than in the latter, where, with the child of one year old, the probable duration of life is at least for a year and a half longer than in England ; and that on the other side of the channel there dies every year 1 in 49, whilst in Belgium, according to the results of the years from 1825 to 1829, the proportion of deaths in relation to the population is about 1 to 43 years, because every where, one annual death for 40 or 41 inhabitants is a low mortality, at least when the country in question is of a pretty large size. Herein, also, are to be found new reasons to consider the list of mortality for England, more especially regarding those for young children as incomplete.

To facilitate forming an opinion on this subject, M. Villermé has compared the tables of population for England and Belgium,† concluding from his table that there is a marked advantage in favour of Belgium, which proportionally has fewer children, but keeps them better, and has proportionally more grown-up individuals. It will be, moreover, advisable, as I have already observed, to pay attention to the rapidly increasing population in England, which contributes to place that country in a less favourable position than ours. According to Duvillard, the ciphers of France are on the whole less favourable than those of Belgium and England.

MM. Hayer and Lombard have of late also compared the mortality of Geneva with that of Belgium and France :‡ it results from their investigations that in the two latter countries the number of deaths in the first year of life are far more numerous than in Geneva. The following are the principal results of the comparison which they have made regarding the probable duration of life between the three countries, proceeding on the base of their tables of mortality, and on those of Duvillard and my own for cities :—

Probable Duration of Life.			
	In France.	In Belgium.	In Geneva.
At Birth, -	20½ years.	25 years.	47½ years.
At 5 years of age,	45½ "	50 "	52¾ "
" 30 "	29⅖ "	34 "	34 "
" 50 "	16⅔ "	19⅜ "	18½ "

From this comparison, the advantage in the early period of life is on the side of Geneva ; but at the age of 30, the probable duration of life is not longer than

* Annales d'Hygiène, tome xii. par.ie 2.

† Annuaire de l'Observatoire de Bruxelles.

‡ Recherches Statistiques sur la Mortalité de la Ville de Genève, and Bibliothèque Universelle. August 1834.

in Belgium, and it even then diminishes. The scientific men of Geneva observed, that if 90 years were to be taken as the extreme old age, the proportion of individuals of this age to the number of births would be the standard for longevity. Thus, we shall find— in Geneva for males, 0·0113 for females ; average, 0·0089 : in Belgium, 0·0068 : in England, from the official tables from 1813 to 1830, only 0·0065. It follows, from the preceding comparisons, that Belgium, with regard to its mortality, does not labour under any disadvantage when compared with England and Geneva—two countries which have hitherto been considered the most favoured—excepting, perhaps, in regard to the mortality of children.

~~~~~~~~~~

No. V.

ON THE MORTALITY (NATURAL AND ACCIDENTAL DEATHS INCLUDED) OF THE EUROPEAN TROOPS OF THE ENGLISH ARMY IN THE EAST INDIES, IN A PERIOD OF FIVE YEARS, FROM 1826 TO 1830.

On the whole, we possess few notices on the mortality of Europeans who have lived within degrees of latitude differing much from their natural climate. The following documents, therefore, which I owe to the kindness of A. M'Culloch, Esq., of the War-Office, must be acceptable to the reader. This able statistician, to whom we owe very interesting investigations, observes, that hitherto it has been possible to arrive at results only somewhat correct regarding children and females :—

Place.	1826.	1827.	1828.	1829.	1830.	Mean.
PRESIDENCY OF BOMBAY.						
Number of troops, -	2793	3135	3175	3632	3876	3322
Cases of death, -	305	162	204	107	147	185
Usual number of patients,	481	347	368	358	383	387
PRESIDENCY OF BENGAL.						
Number of troops, -	7976	8761	8916	8630	9520	8770
Cases of death, -	774	522	549	575	362	556
Usual number of patients,	846	888	882	879	721	843
PRESIDENCY OF MADRAS.						
Number of troops, -	6626	6686	7986	8084	8774	7630
Cases of death, -	614	509	386	266	199	395
Usual number of patients not given under this head.						

From these ciphers, the following proportions result :—

	Per 1000 Men.		
	Bombay.	Bengal.	Madras.
Cases of deaths, - -	55	63	52
Sick, - - -	116	96	(?)

This gives an average of about 57 cases of deaths per 1000 men, or 1 death for 17·5.

In respect to the kinds of diseases producing these deaths, they may be arranged as follows :—

Names of Diseases.	Cases of Deaths.			Annual Number per 1000.		
	Bombay.	Bengal.	Madras.	Bombay.	Bengal.	Madras.
Fever, - - -	267	735	405	15·9	16·8	11·0
Affections of the lungs, -	43	100	82	2·5	2·2	2·2
" of the liver, -	80	180	170	4·2	4·1	4·5
" of the stomach and bowels, -	272	872	819	16·2	19·7	21·2
Cholera morbus, -	173	623	306	10·0	14·2	8·0
Affections of the brain, -	21	98	27	1·2	2·1	0·6
Dropsy, - -	12	25	28	0·7	0·5	0·7
Other cases of deaths, -	57	149	141	4·3	3·4	3·8
Total, - -	925	2782	1978	55·0	63·0	52·0

The mean mortality (expressed in per cents.), shows, amongst the European officers of the Indian army, the following results :—

Rank.	Bombay.	Bengal.	Madras.
Colonels, - -	5·74	5·94	5·40
Lieutenant-colonels, -	5·45	4·84	6·11
Majors, - -	3·77	4·10	5·42
Captains, - -	3·78	3·45	5·02
Lieutenants, - -	3·96	2·75	4·17
Ensigns, - -	3·15	2·34	3·80

The general mean of all ranks, including surgeons and assistant-surgeons, was 3·85.

During the last 20 years, there died of the army of Bengal 1184 officers, or 59·2 annually of the average number of 1897 individuals : this gives 3·12 per cent.

The mean duration of life of the deceased was, in

81 Colonels, - - - -	61 years.
97 Lieutenant-colonels, - - -	51 ~
78 Majors, - - - -	40 ~
277 Captains, - - - -	36 ~

We add to the comparative view another, pointing out the mortality of civilians in the India Company's service in Bengal, during the years from 1792 to 1836, according to their several ages and number of years of service :—

Number of Years of Service.	Age.	Number of Civilians.	Cases of Deaths.	Retired from the Service.
1	20	975	19	2
2	21	933½	22	3
3	22	906½	18	7
4	23	874½	19	5
5	24	835½	12	7
6	25	790½	10	
7	26	754	17	4
8	27	694½	17	3
9	28	638	20	4
10	29	577½	8	3
11	30	545	6	2
12	31	519½	14	1
13	32	489	8	2
14	33	468	5	6
15	34	448	8	2
16	35	424	6	6
17	36	403	9	2
18	37	376½	11	7
19	38	351	10	2
20	39	324½	8	7
21	40	293½	11	9
22	41	270	10	6
23	42	239	10	6
24	43	216	5	2
25	44	196	7	10
26	45	167½	7	9
27	46	148	7	8
28	47	129	3	8
29	48	114½	4	1
30	49	101½	3	5
30 to 45	50 to 64			

If we put together these ciphers in periods, we arrive at the following comparative view :—

Number of Years of Service.	Age.	Number of Civilians.	Cases of Deaths.	Cases of Deaths per 10,000.	Retired from the Service.
1 to 5	20 to 24	4525	90	199	26
6 to 10	25 to 29	3454½	72	208	21
11 to 15*	30 to 34	2469½	41	166	13
16 to 20	35 to 39	1879	44	204	24
21 to 25†	40 to 44	1214½	43	354	33
26 to 30	45 to 49	660½	24	364	31
30 to 45	50 to 64			486	

In the *United Service Journal*, we find several notices by Mr M'Culloch on the mortality of officers of the British army.

* After ten years of service in India, every officer may return for three years to England. Many avail themselves of this permission, which evidently contributes to the decrease of mortality.

† After twenty years' service, many officers return to Britain, which likewise contributes to the decrease of the mortality

No. VI.

EXTRACT FROM THE "BULLETIN DE L'ACADEMIE ROYALE DES SCIENCES DE BRUXELLES": 1835. No. 10. CONCERNING THE MORTALITY AT BRUSSELS.

M. Quetelet communicated to the academy the results of the late census, according to which the number of inhabitants of Brussels amounts to 102,702, the garrison not included, which consists of from 2000 to 3000 men. According to the tables of population, there took place in the year 1834—

4230 Births,	Consequently, 1 to 26 inhabitants.	
3862 Deaths,	„ 1 to 29 „	
1092 Marriages,	„ 1 to 100 „	
8 Divorces.		

Before the census, the number of inhabitants for Brussels was calculated at 94,000. M. Quetelet thinks that even the present cipher is still too low; and, in the preceding calculation, he believes he is entitled to estimate it at 110,000, the garrison included. He supports his supposition, by considering the number of births, deaths, and marriages, according to which, Brussels would present less favourable conditions than most of the great cities of Europe, as he has already shown in his *Essay on the Natural Philosophy of Society.* However, we must not lose sight of the circumstance, that the number of deaths in a great city is always augmented by the number of diseased strangers who swell up the tables of mortality in the hospitals, or by those who go there to receive efficient assistance in their sufferings.

No. VII.

REMARKS ON THE MORTALITY IN EPIDEMICS.

Epidemics modify the mortality in a very remarkable manner, and the importance of the phenomena of disease in individuals bears by no means a proper ratio to the general result of the tables of mortality. If the study of epidemics had been properly followed, we should have tables as interesting for science as useful to mankind. Several instances might be adduced to prove this. I shall here content myself with citing one: the cholera morbus and influenza are diseases which differ greatly from each other; the one is a dreadful scourge, which manifests itself in the most fearful manner; the other, in its ordinary external appearance, resembles a catarrh or common cold; and yet the tables of mortality prove that, although the latter disease is not so deadly, it nevertheless, in consequence of its universality, and in consequence of the sufferings it causes, produces results nearly as extensively fatal as cholera. Facts, serving to confirm this opinion, may be found in the excellent work published by Dr Gluge on the History of Influenza.[*] They show, moreover, that mortality in epidemics is principally confined to childhood and to old age—those periods which, in the common course of things, have the smaller probability of life.

No. VIII.

INFLUENCE OF SEASONS UPON MORTALITY.

In the work of M. Ramond de la Sagra, may be found several interesting notices regarding the mortality in Havannah. The following ciphers are the results of five years, namely, from 1825 to 1829:—

* Die Influenza oder Grippe u. s. w. Minden: 1837. 8vo.

Months.	Cases of Deaths.		
	White Population.	Coloured Population.	Total.
January,	545	938	1483
February,	536	831	1367
March,	597	900	1497
April,	487	760	1247
May,	535	731	1266
June,	501	668	1169
July,	589	793	1382
August,	550	736	1286
September,	492	689	1181
October,	548	752	1300
November,	416	709	1125
December,	508	756	1264
Total,	6304	9263	15,567

The mortality in the hospital, amongst strangers, does not exhibit quite the same proportion. The following table gives a view of the mortality in the Hospitals of San Ambrosio and San Juan de Dios, in the years 1825 to 1829, and the mortality of strangers during the years 1820 to 1824:—

Months.	San Ambrosio.	San Juan.	Strangers.
January,	76	162	44
February,	65	133	65
March,	92	184	91
April,	103	145	84
May,	146	149	169
June,	167	195	170
July,	158	203	169
August,	132	198	140
September,	128	247	113
October,	123	240	73
November,	93	196	50
December,	97	277	56
Total,	1830	2329	1229

As far as the first ciphers are concerned, it will be seen that the winter months, and the months of July, August, and October, exhibit the greatest mortality; but the unfortunate individuals received into the hospitals, and the strangers, are especially subject to the deleterious influence of the summer heat. If we compare, in respect to strangers, the mortality of the month of December with that of June and July, we find an increase in the latter nearly fourfold. However, we ought to know, in order to arrive at a correct opinion, what the average number of strangers may be in Havannah during the seasons thus contrasted.

We owe to the kindness of Mr M'Culloch, information regarding the mortality in the island of Malta, during 14 years, in a population oscillating between 96,000 and 103,000 inhabitants; thus giving an average of 100,000 souls. They are as follows:—

Months.	Cases of Deaths.
January,	2920
February,	2773
March,	2786
April,	2404
May,	2292
June,	2568
July,	3075
August,	2919
September,	2675
October,	3081
November,	3013
December,	2995
Months unknown,	802
Total,	34,303

We observe here again, as in the ciphers of Havannah, a tendency to a maximum of deaths during summer, as a consequence of heat.

Here follow a few notices regarding the mortality of tropical climates, to be found in the work of Mr A. S. Thomson, on the influence of climate on health.[*]

* *Observations on the Influence of Climate on Health and Mortality.* 8vo. Edinburgh: 1837. See also the work by Dr Annesley, *On the Climate of India.* London: 1825. Also the *Medical Almanac*, by Farre, for 1837.

The first numbers inform us of the relative monthly mortality of the English troops in the Windward and Leeward Islands. The others refer to 3149 individuals of the native troops in the Presidency of Madras, and 3017 of the English troops, who were received during 1815 into the hospitals.

Months.	Mortality in the Windward and Leeward Islands.	Presidency of Madras—Sick.	
		Native Troops.	English Troops.
January, - -	65	125	74
February, - -	48	63	64
March, - - .	42	60	70
April, - -	57	48	74
May, - -	59	54	84
June, - -	69	85	87
July, - -	87	104	109
August, - -	119	93	81
September, -	114	74	73
October, -	133	113	105
November, -	109	94	82
December, - -	97	87	97
Total, -	1000	1000	1000

Also here we observe, in the time of the great summer heat, and in consequence of it, a greater mortality and more numerous cases of sickness. We may therefore be well assured, that extremes of cold and heat are equally deleterious to our species.

~~~~~~~~~~~~

No. IX.

ADDITION TO THE SEVENTH SECTION OF THE FIRST BOOK.

On the Law of the Increase of Population.

Since the publication of my work, M. Verhulst, of the Military Academy of Brussels, has submitted to analysis my hypothesis on the law of the increase of population. This hypothesis rests on the supposition of an analogy between the movement of the population, under the difficulties which oppose the increase, and between a moveable body which falls through a resisting medium. The results of this comparison agree very well with the data furnished by statistics, and with those derived from calculation, if we suppose an infinitely increasing density in the different layers of the resisting medium. The formulas on which the calculations and the results regarding the population of Belgium, France, and Prussia, are based, may be found in the second part of the series of the *Correspondance Mathématique de l'Observatoire de Bruxelles.* (See p. 113, and following.) We may say that the statistical data have not yet been collected in so comprehensive a manner as accurately to permit us to reduce from our hypothesis, by calculation, all the consequences to be derived from it regarding the intensity of the difficulties met with by the population in its increase.

~~~~~~~~~~~~

No. X.

ADDITIONS TO THE THREE FIRST SECTIONS OF THE SECOND BOOK.

On the Results of Experiments made on the Weight, Height, and Strength of above 800 individuals. By JAMES D. FORBES, *Esq., F.R.S.S. L. & E., Professor of Natural Philosophy in the University of Edinburgh.**

The interesting and remarkable experiments published by M. Quetelet, of Brussels, on various points of physical development in man, under a variety of circumstances, as to climate, station, age, and sex, induced me to take the opportunity which my professional position presented of obtaining the measure of physical development as to the weight, height, and strength of natives of Scotland, between the ages of 14 and 25, students in our university.

In the prosecution of this plan, separate lists were kept of persons not born in Scotland, and of these the English and Irish lists have likewise been subjected to calculation. Though of these the numbers are comparatively small, the results present some pretty decisive characters. These experiments were continued during two winters (1834–5, 1835–6): every experiment was made by myself, and noted down by myself. The weights were ascertained by Marriot's spring-balance, which was verified from time to time, and found to have undergone no change in its elasticity. The weight of clothes is included.* The heights are in English inches, shoes included. For the measure of strength, Regnier's dynamometer was employed, and these experiments were somewhat less satisfactory than the others. The error of the instrument had been ascertained before the commencement of the experiments, and was found to be pretty constant throughout the scale. But after the experiments were finished, this was by no means the case, the error having become variable, owing to the interfering action of a small spring employed to bring the index to zero. As this, however, only affects the absolute results (or, at least, its relative influence is trifling), I have contented myself with applying an interpolated correction deduced from the mean of the errors before and after, which cannot differ much from the truth. But the instrumental errors are not the only ones to be contended with. To avoid errors in the *use* of the dynamometer, requires vigilant superintendence on the part of the observer; and as the first pull is generally (though not always) greater than the second or third, this also must be allowed for. I have invariably repeated the experiment three times, and often much more frequently. When extraordinary cases have occurred, I have taken the precaution of observing at distinct intervals of time.

In ascertaining the mean results, the following method has been adopted:—The natives of each country were separated, and each class divided, according to age, into twelve sets, from 14 to 25, the greatest number being of the age of 18 years. The mean weight, height, and strength for each year was computed, and the result projected upon ruled paper. Curves were drawn through the points thus projected, in such a way as to represent most satisfactorily the whole observations. These curves, with the determining points, are now exhibited to the society. It is proper to add, that the ages registered being the ages *at last birthday*, the weight, &c., registered, is not that due to the age noted, but at a mean to an age half a year later. Thus, all the persons who were 20 last birthday, are *between* the ages of 20 and 21, or 20½ at a mean. This has been attended to in making the projections.

Besides the English, Scotch, and Irish curves, I have exhibited those of the Belgian development, from M. Quetelet's experiments, reduced to English measures. The thickness of the shoes not being included in these experiments, half an inch (perhaps too little) has been added to make them comparable with the others. It is important to add, that M. Quetelet's experiments here quoted, as well as my own, were made upon persons in the higher ranks of life—in both cases, in fact, upon persons having the benefit of academical instruction.

The number of persons examined by me in the two winters before stated, was thus divided:—Scotchmen, 523; Englishmen, 178; Irishmen, 72; from the colonies, &c., 56; total, 829. I was careful to obtain a fair average of persons of all degrees of height and

---

* Read to the Royal Society of Edinburgh, and communicated by the author.

* According to Quetelet, this amounts to one-eighteenth of the weight.

strength, in which respect the Scotch average is more unexceptionable than the others. There is always a tendency in such cases to get too high a development, because diminutive persons are the least likely voluntarily to come forward. An example of this is found in the mean height obtained by M. Quetelet, from a register of 80 individuals at Cambridge, between the ages of 18 and 23, giving a mean of 69·6 inches, instead of 68·7, as my experiments indicate.

The numerical results derived from the graphical process before described, are given at the close of the paper, and seem to warrant the following conclusions :—

1. That in respect of weight, height, and strength, there is a general coincidence in the form of the curves with those of M. Quetelet.

2. The British curves seem to have more curvature for the earlier years (14 to 17), or the progress to maturity is then more rapid, and somewhat slower afterwards. If we may depend upon the English curves, this is more strikingly the case in natives of that country than of Scotland, at least in point of weight and strength.

3. The tables incontestibly prove the superior development of natives of this country over the Belgians. The difference is greatest in strength (one-fifth of the whole), and least in weight.

4. In comparing natives of England, Scotland, and Ireland, more doubt arises, owing to the difference in the number of experiments ; those for Ireland are confessedly most imperfect. Yet I conceive that the coincident results in the three tables, entitle us to conclude that the Irish are more developed than the Scotch at a given age, and the English less. Some qualification is, however, due, in consequence of the remark (2) ; for in the earlier years (14–17), it would even appear that the English so far get the start of the Scotch, as not only relatively, but also absolutely, to surpass them (in strength and weight) ; but between 17 and 19 they lose this advantage. I am disposed to think that this appearance of a result is not accidental.

5. The maximum height seems scarcely to be attained even at the age of 25. This agrees with M. Quetelet's observations. Both strength and weight are rapidly increasing at that age.

6. In the given period of life (14–26) all the developments continue to increase ; and all move slowly from the commencement to the end of that period. Hence the curves are convex upwards. [This is not the case below the age of 14, for weight and strength. —*Quetelet.*]

Weights in Pounds (including clothes).

Age.	English.	Scotch.	Irish.	Belgians.
15 years,	114·5	112	..	102
16 ~	127	125·5	129	117·5
17 ~	133·5	133·5	136	127
18 ~	138	139	141·5	134
19 ~	141	143	145·5	139·5
20 ~	144	146·5	148	143
21 ~	146	148·5	151	145·5
22 ~	147·5	150	153	147
23 ~	149	151	154	149·5
24 ~	150	152	155	149·5
25 ~	151	152·5	155	150

Heights in Inches. Full Dimensions (with shoes).

Age.	English.	Scotch.	Irish.	Belgians.
15 years,	64·4	64·7	..	61·8
16 ~	66·5	66·8	..	64·2
17 ~	67·5	67·9	..	66·1
18 ~	68·1	68·5	68·7	67·2
19 ~	68·5	68·9	69·4	67·7
20 ~	68·7	69·1	69·8	67·9
21 ~	68·8	69·2	70·0	68·0
22 ~	68·9	69·2	70·1	68·1
23 ~	68·9	69·3	70·2	68·2
24 ~	68·9	69·3	70·2	68·2
25 ~	68·9	69·3	70·2	68·3

Strength in Pounds.

Age.	English.	Scotch.	Irish.	Belgians.
15 years,	..	280	..	204
16 ~	336	314	..	236
17 ~	352	340	369	260
18 ~	364	360	389	280
19 ~	378	378	404	296
20 ~	385	392	416	310
21 ~	392	402	423	322
22 ~	397	410	427	330
23 ~	401	417	430	335
24 ~	402	421	431	337
25 ~	403	423	432	339

No. XI.

Extract from the Correspondance Mathématique et Physique, 1st Series, vol. ii. part 1.   January 1838.

M. Horner's Investigation into the Development of the Growth of Boys and Girls.

Several years ago we published tables to show the degree of growth in both sexes at different ages. These tables, which at first sight might seem merely curious, became afterwards of real utility, especially in England. Their importance, indeed, was so much felt, that it was deemed advisable to repeat our experiments in several places, in order to find a measure of the modifications likely to be produced in our results by circumstances to which we could pay no attention. Thus, Mr Forbes of Edinburgh has measured a great number of young Englishmen, Scotchmen, and Irishmen, and a comparison of his results with ours has shown a remarkable correspondence in respect to the gradual development ; at the same time, however, it has, notwithstanding, exhibited a real difference between the mean height of individuals belonging to different nations.[*]

In order to find out the influence produced on the development of the growth by working in manufactories, Mr J. W. Cowell has made different interesting observations at Manchester and Stockport. The result of these has been published in the first volume of the Factory Reports, and in an essay On the Philosophy of Society.

Hitherto we have only seen, from No. 339 of the Penny Magazine, July 1837, that the same experiments have also been repeated by Mr Horner, another English factory inspector. Mr Horner thought that he had observed that the people, in order to evade the law excluding young children from the heavy work in the factories, had hit on the plan of using false certificates of age, and Mr Horner, to discover the fraud, resorted to a direct test. He made use of a table similar to ours, and in order to arrive at a nearer approximation of the truth, he resolved to institute collateral observations. Mr Horner, therefore, procured from twenty-seven surgeons, the measure of 16,402 individuals, of whom 8469 were boys, and 7933 girls, of the age from 8 to 14 inclusive, and from the following places—Manchester, Bolton, Stockport, Preston, Leeds, Halifax, Rochdale, Huddersfield, and Skipton, and the neighbouring rural districts. The following table is an extract from one of greater dimensions, in which the distinction has been noted between towns of first and second rate magnitude and the country :—

* See the *Correspondance Mathématique,* volume ii. page 205 and following ; and Transactions of the Royal Society, Edinburgh.

Age.					Number of Children Measured.	Mean Height.		Average Height of Boys & Girls taken Together.	
						foot.	inch.	foot.	inch.
From	8 to 8$\frac{1}{2}$ years,				327 boys.	3	9$\frac{5}{8}$	3	9$\frac{1}{4}$
~	~	~			267 girls.	3	8$\frac{11}{16}$		
From	8$\frac{1}{2}$	& below	9	years,	339 boys.	3	11	3	10$\frac{3}{4}$
~	~	~	~	~	272 girls.	3	10$\frac{3}{8}$		
~	9	~	9$\frac{1}{2}$	~	527 boys.	3	11$\frac{3}{8}$	3	11$\frac{1}{2}$
~	~	~	~	~	438 girls.	3	11$\frac{3}{8}$		
~	9$\frac{1}{2}$	~	10	~	418 boys.	4	0$\frac{1}{8}$	4	0
~	~	~	~	~	375 girls.	4	0		
~	10	~	10$\frac{1}{2}$	~	574 boys.	4	1	4	1
~	~	~	~	~	506 girls.	4	1		
~	10$\frac{1}{2}$	~	11	~	550 boys.	4	1$\frac{7}{8}$	4	1$\frac{3}{4}$
~	~	~	~	~	421 girls.	4	1$\frac{5}{8}$		
~	11	~	11$\frac{1}{2}$	~	664 boys.	4	2$\frac{3}{8}$	4	2$\frac{1}{4}$
~	~	~	~	~	577 girls.	4	2$\frac{1}{8}$		
~	11$\frac{1}{2}$	~	12	~	559 boys.	4	3$\frac{1}{16}$	4	3$\frac{1}{4}$
~	~	~	~	~	478 girls.	4	3$\frac{1}{4}$		
~	12	~	12$\frac{1}{2}$	~	767 boys.	4	3$\frac{3}{4}$	4	0
~	~	~	~	~	712 girls.	4	3$\frac{7}{8}$		
~	12$\frac{1}{2}$	~	13	~	660 boys.	4	4$\frac{1}{4}$	4	4$\frac{3}{8}$
~	~	~	~	~	618 girls.	4	4$\frac{3}{4}$		
~	13	~	13$\frac{1}{2}$	~	1269 boys.	4	5$\frac{1}{6}$	4	5$\frac{1}{4}$
~	~	~	~	~	1260 girls.	4	5$\frac{1}{3}$		
~	13$\frac{1}{2}$	~	14	~	864 boys.	4	6$\frac{3}{8}$	4	6$\frac{1}{2}$
~	~	~	~	~	980 girls.	4	6$\frac{1}{2}$		
~	14	~	~	~	951 boys.	4	7$\frac{3}{4}$	4	7$\frac{7}{8}$
~	~	~	~	~	1029 girls.	4	8		

The average, or the mean height of the young people between 14 and 18 years, has been ascertained according to the particular accounts given by Mr Harrison, surgeon at Preston.

Age.	Number of Young Persons Measured.	Average Height.		Total of Mean Height in both Sexes.	
		foot.	inch.	foot.	inch.
From 14 to 15 years,	117 male sex.	4	8$\frac{1}{4}$	4	8$\frac{3}{4}$
~ ~ ~	140 fem. ~	4	9		
~ 15 to 16 ~	82 male ~	4	10$\frac{1}{2}$	4	10$\frac{2}{3}$
~ ~ ~	106 fem. ~	4	10$\frac{3}{4}$		
~ 16 to 17 ~	43 male ~	5	0$\frac{1}{2}$	5	0$\frac{1}{11}$
~ ~ ~	90 fem. ~	4	11$\frac{1}{2}$		
~ 17 to 18 ~	47 male ~	5	0	5	0
~ ~ ~	112 fem. ~	5	0		

In order to compare the height at similar ages in England and in Belgium, we have expressed, in the following table, the ciphers given in the Penny Magazine in metres; and in order to get, for instance, the height of a child of nine years of age, we have taken the mean of the child's height in the age between 8$\frac{1}{2}$ and 9 years, and the height of the age of 9 and 9$\frac{1}{2}$, &c. &c.

Age.	English.		Belgians.	
	Boys.	Girls.	Boys.	Girls.
	metres.	metres.	metres.	metres.
9 years, -	1·202	1·191	1·219	1·195
10 ~ -	1·234	1·232	1·275	1·248
11 ~ - -	1·273	1·267	1·330	1·299
12 ~ -	1·306	1·310	1·385	1·353
13 ~ - -	1·338	1·347	1·439	1·403
14 ~ -	1·400	1·403	1·493	1·453
15 ~ - -	1·457	1·420	1·546	1·499
16 ~ -	1·511	1·502	1·594	1·535
17 ~ - -	1·530	1·518	1·634	1·555

Of measurements which have been made in Cambridge, we have seen that, in general, Englishmen at the time of their complete bodily development are taller than the Belgians; yet we drew our conclusions also from the measurement of students. The results we communicate here are derived from young labourers.

From this it may be seen that the heavy work in manufactories forms an obstacle to the bodily development of men. We have already obtained analogous results from the numbers communicated by Mr Cowell, which refer to the youth employed in manufactories, and from others who were not so employed. In the following table we have placed together notices which, up to the present moment, we have procured on this matter; they may thus be compared with the preceding observations, and it is to be desired that in other countries similar observations should be made.

[*Note.*]—We have also inquired into the law of growth of plants, and in several animals; and although we have not as yet had time to pursue them with the requisite care and to the necessary extent, they have already afforded very interesting results, and some remarkable points of comparison.

Mean Height of Youth from 9 to 25 Years.

Age.	Boys.*		Girls.*		English.†	Scotch.†	Irish.†	Belgium.‡	
	Working in Manufactories.	Not so Employed.	Working in Manufactories.	Not so Employed.				Boys.	Girls.
	metres.	metres.	metres.	metres.	metres.	metres.	metres.	metres.	metres.
9 years, - -	1·222	1·233	1·218	1·230					
10 ~ - - -	1·270	1·286	1·260	1·254				1·227	1·200
11 ~ - -	1·302	1·296	1·299	1·323				1·282	1·248
12 ~ - - -	1·355	1·345	1·364	1·363				1·327	1·275
13 ~ - -	1·383	1·396	1·413	1·399				1·359	1·327
14 ~ - - -	1·437	1·440	1·467	1·479				1·403	1·386
15 ~ - -	1·515	1·474	1·486	1·502	1·635	1·643		1·487	1·447
16 ~ - - -	1·565	1·605	1·521	1·475	1·689	1·696		1·559	1·475
17 ~ - -	1·592	1·627	1·535	1·542	1·714	1·724		1·610	1·500
18 ~ - - -	1·608	1·775	1·593	1·645	1·729	1·739	1·744	1·670	1·544
19 ~ - -					1·740	1·750	1·762	1·700	1·562
20 ~ - -					1·744	1·754	1·772	1·706	
21 ~ - -					1·747	1·757	1·777	1·711	1·570
22 ~ - -					1·750	1·757	1·779		
23 ~ - -					1·750	1·760	1.784		
24 ~ - -					1·750	1·760	1·784		
25 ~ - -					1·750	1·760	1·784	1·722	1·577

* These results were ascertained in the neighbourhood of Manchester.

† These by Mr Forbes of Edinburgh.

‡ These by measurement of the wealthy class.

No. XII.

Remarks on the Quality of the Blood, according to the Age and Sex.

We are of opinion that all the relations which may vary in different individuals, either according to age or to sex, ought to be subjected to investigations such as the preceding. In this respect the quality of the blood merits our attention, for it undergoes very remarkable changes. The investigations of MM. Lecanu and Denis have furnished, in respect to these variations, the following results :*—

We observe, in the blood of the fœtus, which is necessarily the same as that of the placenta, comparatively little serum and much cruor; this quality of the blood also continues for some time after birth, and seems to remain the same so long as the new-born child preserves the peculiar rosy colouring, that is, for two or three weeks.

From this period to about the fifth month, the quantity of serum increases and that of the cruor decreases.

From the fifth month to the fortieth year, the quantity of cruor increases and that of the serum decreases. From the fortieth to the fiftieth year, again, the serum increases and the cruor decreases.

The following are the mean proportions obtained by a comparison of the blood of individuals of different ages :—

Proportions.

7 persons from	5 months to 10 years,		830 Serum,		11 Cruor.	
13 ..	.. 10 years	.. 20 ..	800	..	14	..
11 ..	.. 20 ..	.. 30 ..	760	..	17	..
12 ..	.. 30 ..	.. 40 ..	790	..	17	..
6 ..	.. 40 ..	.. 50 ..	760	..	16	..
8 ..	.. 50 ..	.. 60 ..	780	..	15	..
2 ..	.. 66 ..	.. 70 ..	790	..	14	..

These are the results at different periods of life.

As to the different quality of the blood in the male and female sex, M. Lecanu has found that in the male there exists comparatively less serum in the blood than in the female. He found, in the

	Blood of the Male.	Blood of the Female.
Maximum,	805·263 Serum.	853·135 Serum.
Minimum,	778·025 ..	790·394 ..
Mean,	791·944 ..	821·764 ..

The blood of the male has consequently 29·820 less serum than that of the female.

On the other hand, the proportion of cruor is greater in the male, as may be seen by the following table:—

	Blood of the Male.	Blood of the Female.
Maximum,	148·450 Cruor.	129·999 Cruor.
Minimum,	115·850 ..	68·349 ..
Mean,	132·150 ..	99·169 ..

Thus the blood of the male sex contains 32·981 more cruor than that of the female.

No. XIII.

Remarks concerning the Highest Development of the Passions.

The author of a kind notice of our work, published in a periodical, considers the opinion very bold that the passions of men attain their highest energy at the twenty-fifth year, and that, consequently, those talents which presuppose the development of the passions, and especially imagination, ought to produce at this

period of life the most distinguished works. With the view of opposing our opinion, the critic cites the instance of J. J. Rousseau, who began to write his best works when about forty. Even if this instance were completely applicable to the question, it proves nothing : as we see that even the most accomplished scientific men commit mistakes, it cannot be often enough repeated, that the result of calculations of probability can only apply to masses, and cannot be applied to individual cases. J. J. Rousseau did not die at that age which is usually reckoned the mean duration of the life of man; and yet no one would think of doubting on that account the correctness and the real value of the bills of mortality.

No. XIV.

Extract from the Bulletin de l'Académie Royale des Sciences de Bruxelles. 1836. No. 5.

Remarks on the Influence of Age on Insanity, and on the Disposition for Crime, by M. Quetelet.

In my work on Man, and on the development of his faculties, I have endeavoured to lay before the public the few documents which science possesses concerning the age most liable to mental disease. The accounts of Paris, Caen, and Norway, the only ones I could procure, all agreed in showing that most diseases of the mind occur between thirty and forty. In order to be able to compare the results, I took the total of the insane as unity, and thus I deduced for the different periods of life the following proportions :—

	Paris.	Caen.	Norway.
Below 20 years,	0·06	0·03	0·17
From 20 to 30 years,	0·20	0·17	0·19
.. 30 to 40 ..	0·24	0·29	0·21
.. 40 to 50 ..	0·22	0·25	0·16
.. 50 to 60 ..	0·14	0·17	0·13
Above 60 years,	0·14	0·09	0·14

Since the publication of the work containing these investigations, I have received, through the kindness of Sir Charles Morgan, some interesting communications regarding the statistics of the lunatic asylums in Ireland, collected by Mr Radcliffe. Amongst these notices, there is a tabular view of 5021 insane, whose age was extracted from the tables of the institutions. Besides this, I found in the work of Mr Porter—Tables of the Revenue, Population, &c., 1834—a view of the insane in bedlam, which likewise contains information regarding the age of the insane who were received into this institution and not considered incurable. According to this view, there were, in the years—

	Insane.	Mean Age of the Insane.
1830,	201	37 years.
1831,	212	35 ..
1832,	163	37 ..
1833,	184	26 ..
1834,	217	36 ..

They remained in the institution an average period of 204 days. The age of 977 of these insane will be found in the following table, in which also the notices concerning Ireland have been entered.

	Bethlem Hospital.		Irish Lunatic Asylums.	
Age.	Insane.	Proportion.	Insane.	Proportion.
Below 20 years,	61	0·06	560	0·10
From 20 to 30 years,	261	0·27	1551	0·31
.. 30 to 40 ..	292	0·30	1284	0·25
.. 40 to 50 ..	203	0·21	939	0·19
.. 50 to 60 ..	107	0·11	609	0·12
Above 60 years,	53	0·05	138	0·03
Total,	977	1·00	5021	1·00

It may be seen that the numbers of the Bethlem Hospital agree pretty well with those of France and

---

* S. Lecanu—*Etudes sur le Sang Humain.* Paris: 1837. 4to. And Denis—*Recherches Expérimentales sur le Sang Humain*, p. 287.

Norway, according to which most insane exist between the years of thirty and forty; as far as Ireland is concerned, the maximum in this country appears somewhat earlier. However, we must not conclude from the circumstance that "in general the greatest number of insane are to be found between thirty and forty years of age," that also at this age the greatest number of outbreaks of this disease occur. In order to ascertain the critical age, we must take into account the population and the number of individuals from the different classes given in our table. If we then take the average number of the ciphers for those countries of which we now speak, we find—

	Mean of the Insane in the above 5 Tables.	Distribution of the Population.	Proportion of the Population.
Below 20 years, -	0·08	0·40	0·20
From 20 to 30 years, -	0·23	0·17	1·25
.. 30 to 40 .. -	0·26	0·14	1·86
.. 40 to 50 .. -	0·21	0·11	1·91
.. 50 to 60 .. -	0·13	0·09	1·44
Above 60 years, -	0·09	0.09	1·00
	1·00	1·00	1·00

Thus it appears, that if we have regard to the population, and if we may be allowed to generalise the preceding results, *that the age between forty and fifty, or rather the fortieth year, is the period of life most subject to insanity.* In my essay on the Natural Philosophy of Society, I have shown that it is the same age in which most masterpieces of dramatic literature are produced in England and France, with this only difference, that England has in that respect a slight advantage over France. May we draw from this the conclusion, that the human mind is affected by diseases which are in proportion to its energy or exercise? This is still a problem, the solution of which is of great importance to society, and which unquestionably will be elucidated by the theory of probabilities which is founded on correct observation.

To the preceding question another may be added, which perhaps is even of more direct importance to society, the question, namely, What influence does age exercise over the disposition to crime? Several years ago I had shown, what the results of the following years have confirmed, that in France not only the number of crimes committed by individuals at certain periods of life almost always recur in the same proportions, but also that the proportions, notwithstanding their difference, are equally regular, if we draw a distinction between the different kinds of crimes on account of the sex of the criminals.

Heretofore, the documents which have been afforded by the administration of justice in Belgium have shown that the same regularity is also to be found with us; further, that in like manner the proportion of the sexes in criminals of different ages is in both countries nearly the same. From this correspondence of the results, we must therefore conclude that they are either reproduced year after year by a kind of miracle, or that they arise in a very great similarity of the social organisation in the two countries, in so far at least as regards those relations which influence crime. I have even observed that this phenomenon of moral life shows a greater regularity of occurrence than many phenomena of the material world.

A short time ago, documents have been published regarding the administration of criminal law in the grand-dutchy of Baden, which likewise furnish information respecting the age of the accused individuals; *

---

* *Uebersicht der Strafrechtespflege u. s. w.* Karlsruhe: 1834. 4to. (Account of the Administration of Criminal Justice, &c.) The celebrated jurist, Mittermaier, in communicating this remarkable work to me, had the kindness to express his opinion regarding the investigations in which I was engaged, in the following terms:—" I am convinced that the manner in which you view things, proceeding, as you do, by combining facts, is the only way in which we may hope to penetrate the mysteries of nature.

---

and here again we meet with a remarkable correspondence of numbers, as may be seen from the following table:—

Age of the Accused.	Grand-dutchy of Baden: 1833.		France 1826-1829.
	Number of the Accused.	Proportion.	
14 to 18 years, -	93	0·06 } 54	0·53*
18 to 30 .. .. -	784	0·48 }	..
30 to 40 .. -	381	0·24	0·23
40 to 50 .. -	211	0·13	0·14
50 to 60 .. -	106	0·07	0·06
60 to 70 .. -	33	0·02	0·03
70 years and above,	1	0·00	0·01
	1609	1·00	1·00

At what conclusion must we then arrive from so many documents which show so surprising a correspondence, although the ciphers are not very large? Must we entirely deny the free will of individuals, or must we suppose that it is without influence if we consider the phenomena of society on a large scale—as happens with the phenomena of the material world, where the internal action and reaction of a system do not disturb the equilibrium? This at least seems to be deducible from observation, if we do not perhaps prefer blindly to reject what it teaches us.

That which in my opinion modifies the results of different years, is not the influence of free will, as far as it can in fact be active, but rather the changes which society undergoes by degrees, through the gradual reform of its institutions—as through the oscillations of its habits and wants—changes which fortunately take an extremely slow course. If the social organisation could experience sudden changes, the influence of free will would continually defy our foresight, which is of course based on a knowledge of past ages. Of what use would it be then to introduce wise institutions, or to think of a reform in our legislation? Experience convinces us more and more that, with the same social organisation, we may be prepared year after year for the return of the same moral phenomena. Violent changes or revolutions may indeed take place, which, for the moment, disturb the common course of things, the influence of which may even produce lasting modifications; but there is the same relation to be here observed as in epidemics and famines with regard to mortality. Do we reject the tables of the mean duration of life, upon which insurance companies found their speculations, on account of the disturbances their operations may experience from the occurrence of an epidemic? We may even foresee a revolution, or any other important shock society receives, at least to a certain extent; whilst this is not the case as regards an epidemic, and most other calamities which devastate mankind. Every country has its table of mortality, as every country must have its table of disposition to crime; therefore, we cannot conclude that, if we had found regarding the influence of age upon crime in France, Belgium, and the grand-dutchy of Baden, the same results, we necessarily also should arrive at the same results in England. We may, perhaps, find others, but I do not hesitate affirming that the ciphers of 1835 will also recur in 1836, as the same ciphers have occurred year after year in France, always under the supposition that the state of society undergoes no remarkable change.

All my investigations regarding the nature of crime lead me to the same results as yours, and the inferences which the legislature might draw from them are of the highest importance. It is a sad truth which you profess in your work, that it is society which prepares the crime. This truth is especially confirmed by the statistics of *recidive cases* (relapses.)

* The French tables do not follow the same divisions according to the age.

Mr Porter, to whom we owe very interesting statistic contributions, has, sometime ago, published the first accurate tables respecting the age of the accused throughout the whole of England, for the year 1834 ;[*] and his results agree with those of France, Belgium, and the grand-dutchy of Baden, in so far as the maximum of the number of criminals belongs to the same age.

Age of the Accused.	England : 1834.		France : 1826-1829.
	Accused.	Proportion.	
Below 16 years, -	2,604	0·12	0·02
From 16 to 21 years,	6,473	0·29	0·16
·· 21 to 30 ··	7,069	0·32	0·35
·· 30 to 40 ··	3,146	0·15	0·23
·· 40 to 50 ··	1,525	0·07	0·14
·· 50 to 60 ··	685	0·03	0·06
Above 60 years,	303	0·02	0·04
	21,806	1·00	1·00

A remarkable difference between the tables of England and those of France is to be found in the circumstance, that in the former country there is comparatively a much greater number of juvenile accused than in the latter. This is partly owing to the circumstance, that the English assizes have also to decide on most of those crimes which in France are brought before the correctional police. Before the bar of the latter there appear, however, far more juvenile accused than before the assize or criminal courts. On the other hand, there is in England a class of criminals who train up children as implements for theft and all kinds of petty larceny.[†] But if we set aside these two causes, and other deviations which render difficult the comparison between two countries whose institutions and laws are so different, I think I require to yield nothing of the views with which I concluded several years ago a paper on the disposition to crime, which the academy directed to be inserted in the seventh volume of its Transactions, namely, that this afflicting condition seems to be developed in proportion to the intensity of the bodily strength and the passions of men, attaining their maximum about the twenty-fifth year. the period when the body has nearly reached its full development.

Afterwards the intellectual and moral development, which follows a slower course, contribute to the decrease of this disposition to crime, which in after life becomes still more striking in consequence of the decrease of the bodily strength and of the passions.

No. XV.

Extract from the Bulletin de l'Académie Royale des Sciences de Bruxelles : 1836. No. 6.

Influence of Age upon the Disposition to Crime.

Addition to the foregoing remark :—" Every country has its table of mortality, as every country must have its table of the disposition to crime," &c. &c.

When I communicated, about a month ago, the preceding remarks to the academy, I did not imagine that so soon thereafter facts would confirm, in the most decided manner, my opinions. I was then citing the proportional number of criminals of different ages, as the result from the statistical documents regarding England for 1834 ; and observing that they agreed with those of Belgium, France, and the grand-dutchy

* Tables showing the Number of Criminals Offenders in the Year 1834, &c.

† The cause which likewise must influence the results respecting the number of juvenile criminals, is, that the population of England has proportionally more children than that of France. From the tables of population for the two countries, it results, that in England, for 100 below 15 years, there are only 150 adults, whilst in France there are more than 200.

of Baden only in so far as the age of 25 years appears as that when most crimes are committed, I had no hesitation in saying, that the differences which are exhibited in other respects are by no means accidental, but must be the result of the social organisation of England ; so that, as their organisation has been the same in 1834 and 1835, the ciphers observed during the former year ought also to occur, without change, in the latter. The documents of the English tribunals for the year 1835, which Mr Porter kindly communicated to me a few days ago, have just now decided the question. The following is an extract from the two reports :—

Age of the Criminals.	Proportion for each Age.	
	1834.	1835.
12 years and less, ·· - - -	1·78	1·67
12 to 16 years, - - - -	9·82	9·70
16 to 21 - - - -	28·83	29·65
21 to 30 ·· - - - -	31·49	31·92
30 to 40 ·· - - - -	14·01	14·01
40 to 50 ·· - - - -	6·79	6·60
50 to 60 ·· - - - -	3·06	3·24
60 and above, - - - -	1·35	1·30
Age unknown, - - - -	2·87	1·91
Total, - - - -	100·00	100·00

These results, which differ considerably from those of France, agree, as we see, with each other in a remarkable manner ; especially if we take into account that we have not to refer to Poisson's *Law of great numbers.* These were, in fact, during the two years the documents of which we have compared, founded on 22,451 and 20,731 criminals : this makes, according to Mr Porter—

In 1834, - - 1 criminal to 619 inhabitants.
·· 1835, - - 1 ·· ·· 631 ··

The same regularity appears, also, in respect to the sex of criminals ; for of 100 criminals, there were

84 men and 16 women in 1834.
83 ·· ·· 17 ·· ·· 1835.

The same regularity is also observed in other relations which come under our view. Thus we find, for instance, if we distinguish between the different crimes,

	1834.	1835.
Crimes against person, - - -	10·94	9·72
·· ·· property, with violence, -	6·50	6·53
·· ·· ·· without violence, -	73·97	74·66
Injury to property, - - - -	0·72	0·75
Forgeries, &c., - - - - -	1·92	1·78
Crimes not included under the preceding categories, - - - -	5·95	6·56
Total, - - -	100·00	100·00

This regularity is certainly as great as that which has been observed in the annual number of births and deaths, and still greater than that which has been observed in the recurrence of certain phenomena considered as purely physical. England, then, forms no exception to the following thesis : " *There is a budget which is paid with frightful regularity—a budget, namely, of prisons and scaffolds.*" I repeat once more, because I attribute a great importance to this observation, that " Human society, considered on a large scale, exhibits laws similar to those which regulate the material world ;" that the greater the number of observed individuals may be, the more will disappear all bodily and intellectual peculiarities ; and the series of general phenomena, by means of which society erects and maintains itself, predominates with remarkable regularity in their recurrence. Thus the possibility may be explained of analysing the different faculties of men in an inductive manner ; and what in future will be wanting to us are, not methods of observation, but *observations* made in sufficient number and with sufficient care to claim full confidence for the deduced results.

TRANSLATOR'S APPENDIX.—PHYSIOLOGICAL AND PATHOLOGICAL STATISTICS.

It was originally my intention to have added extensively to the admirable work of M. Quetelet, now submitted for the first time to the criticism of the British public; but two considerations have induced me to lay aside this idea, at least for the present. The first is, that accurate and official details, upon either general or national statistics, are not yet procurable, to a proper extent, in Great Britain. Secondly, the additional matter, even admitting it to be perfectly accurate, which could scarcely have happened, must to a certain extent have led the attention of the reader from the main object—the leading idea, if I may so speak, of the work—that bright and original conception of a great mind, which those who have perused the preceding pages must now fully understand.

Hitherto the attempts to apply to human physiology and pathology the science of numbers and weight, have neither been very numerous nor very successful. I shall merely select a few instances as illustrative of the principles advocated by M. Quetelet.

I.—PULSATIONS OF THE HEART.

The left ventricle or cavity of the heart acts as a powerful piston, and by its contractions discharges into the great artery of the body a certain quantity of arterial blood at each contraction. These contractions constitute, in fact, the pulse of the heart; but as the blood so discharged passes rapidly along the arteries to every part of the body, it is usual for the physiologist, and more especially the medical man, to reckon the number of these contractions at some of the more remote arteries, and the radial artery at the wrist is for many reasons the vessel usually selected. The phenomenon called the *pulse*, is erroneously supposed by many to reside in the arteries; but it is, in man at least, dependent solely on the heart's action and on the pressure of the observer's finger. It will now be understood, then, that by the number of the "pulsations" is meant the number of contractions which the left ventricle of the human heart performs in a given time.

The statistics of these pulsations, also of the number of respirations, had not escaped the observation of medical men. The reader is by this time aware of the extent of the valuable researches of M. Quetelet on these points—correct so far as they go, but requiring modification in consequence of an important element or two having been overlooked in the inquiry.

About one hundred years ago, Dr Bryan Robinson* made many accurate observations respecting the human pulse. If Kepler was the first to endeavour to arrive at the "constants" of the human pulse, yet he probably failed to discover that remarkable law, so clearly stated by Dr Robinson, which rests on the influence of posture (and muscular action generally) over the number of the human pulsations. "I took," says he, "the pulses in a minute, and measured the lengths of a

great number of bodies. I took the pulses when the bodies were sitting, that they all might be situated alike with respect to the horizon; and in the morning before breakfast, that their hearts might be as free as possible from the influences of all disturbing causes; and when I had got a very large stock of observations, I took the means of the pulses." Unfortunately, he has not published the tables of observations on this point—a great neglect in an original observer, rendering it impossible for future experimenters to verify his observations. Instead of this, he says that he found those means "to be nearly as the biquadrate roots of the cubes of the lengths of the bodies inversely." Language of this kind has happily disappeared from most modern physiological works.

In the following table he lays down two other laws of the human pulse, tending to prove that the quickness of the pulse is, to a certain extent, inversely as

Ages in Years.	Length in Inches.	Pulse from Observation before Breakfast, and Sitting.	Pulse by Theory.
	72	65	65
	68	67	68
	60	72	74
14	55	77	79
12	51	82	84
9	46	90	91
6	42	97	97
3	35	113	111
2	32	120	119
1	28	126	132
½	25	137	144
0	18	150	184

the *age* and *height*. Having exemplified these laws of the pulse by a variety of observations and remarks, he next attempted to measure the effects of *diet and stimulants*, and of the *time of day*; but in this he failed, as was shown in 1812-14 by Dr Knox, whose inquiries and experiments led to the following conclusions:—

"1. That Dr Bryan Robinson was the discoverer of the 'differential pulse in man;' that he described it perfectly, and ascribed it to its real cause.

2. That he appreciated correctly enough the influence of food, and other disturbing causes of the heart's action, but that he knew nothing of the precise nature of the laws regulating these actions, not having submitted them to any statistical inquiry.

3. He first proved indisputably, that from birth to adult age, the rapidity of the pulse constantly declines, and he has given an accurate statistical table to prove this.

4. He endeavoured to show, by the same numerical method, that the rapidity of the pulse was inversely as the height of the person: or, to give an example, let A be five feet, and let B be six feet, then the pulse of A is to that of B as 72 to 65. But this table is not carefully drawn up, and the actual conclusions are not legitimate, though the law may be a correct one.

* A Treatise on the Animal Economy. Dublin: 1732.

5. He suspected a diurnal movement in the rapidity of the pulse; namely, that it decreased during sleep, and increased from morning until night. With several of his conclusions I do not agree.

Lastly, He attempted to ascertain, statistically, the effects of muscular motion on the pulse *in health*; the ratio of the pulsations to the inspirations; and the immediate result on the heart's action, of a temporary deprivation of air."

The true nature of the fourth law, regulating the human pulse, was discovered by Dr Knox in 1812–13: he calls it "*the diurnal revolution of the pulse*," and he proved that there was not only a *natural, numerical, diurnal revolution in the heart's action*, but that there existed a fifth law, namely, "a diurnal revolution in the *excitability* of the heart to stimulants of all kinds." These remarkable laws being opposed to the received medical notions and physiological theories of the day, were much disputed; but they have been completely proved by subsequent observers. The following remarks, quoted from his Memoirs, will readily explain these laws to the general reader:—

"The question of an average pulse for any particular age can only be put, at least in this form, by those ignorant to a great extent of the physiology of the pulse. Systematic writers on physiology, by stating such questions and replying to them, display a desire to satisfy the general reader at the expense of truth. The pulse varies every hour of the day and night, and after every meal; it is extensively influenced by merely rising from the sitting to the erect posture; and how, without a special attention to these circumstances, any one can arrive at an average pulse, it is somewhat difficult to imagine. Nothing can be more vague and more unsatisfactory than the following table:—

Average of the Human Pulse at Different Ages, according to BRYAN ROBINSON.

Age.				Length in Inches.	Pulse.
At birth,	-	-	-	18	150
~ ½ year,	-	-	-	25	137
~ 1 ~	-	-	-	28	126
~ 2 ~	-	-	-	32	120
~ 3 ~	-	-	-	35	113
~ 6 ~	-	-	-	42	97
~ 9 ~	-	-	-	46	90
~ 12 ~	-	-	-	51	82
~ 14 ~	-	-	-	55	77
				60	72
				68	67
				72	65

MAGENDIE.		ELLIOTSON. (last Edition.)		MAYO.	
		Before birth,	128		
At birth,	130 to 140			At birth,	- 140
~ 1 year,	120 to 130	At 1 year,	- 124	At 1 year,	- 120
~ 2 ~	100 to 110	~ 2 ~	- 110	~ 2 ~	100 to 110
~ 3 ~	90 to 100	When the first			
~ 7 ~	85 to 90	teeth drop out,	86		
~ 14 ~	80 to 85	At puberty,	80	At puberty,	- 80
Adult age,	75 to 80	At manhood,	75	Adult from 70 to 75	
First old age,	65 to 75	Old age, about	60	Old age,	- 60
Confirmed do.	60 to 65	Scarcely found it twice alike.			

Here the oldest writer is not only more minute, but approaches perhaps nearest to the truth.

Such tables as the above, are, for the most part, slightly varied copies of each other, and in respect to them I would make the following remarks:—

No mention is made how the averages of these three last tables were struck. We are left to guess, 1st, at what time of the day the pulse was noted, and if in all the individuals at the same time of day; 2dly, in male or female; 3dly, sitting, lying, or standing;

4thly, before or after meals; 5thly, morning, noon, or night; 6thly, whether sleeping or waking.

A little reflection clearly shows that there can be no such thing as an average pulse, unless counted under circumstances precisely similar in all the individuals experimented on; and even then we should only obtain the average for that particular hour and time of day. This would be an average pulse in a certain sense. In the absence, however, of such data, the practical utility even of which I question, there still are some, imperfect as they are, which merit attention.

In order to arrive at even an attempt at a fair average, we are forced to go back to Dr Robinson's Treatise, written nearly a hundred years ago, and find it to contain the only approach at an analysis of this subject. He gives, in Table II., the average pulse of two men at every hour of the day (whilst sitting), from 8 A.M. until 11 P.M., taken for several weeks: the mean of these waking hours was—for A, 76; for B, 78. But still there is a meagreness of detail, and a narrowness of observation, rendering it impossible to base, on such observations, any important conclusion.

The mid-day pulse of 25 young gentlemen, taken between the hours of 12 and 2, in July 1836, was as follows:—

No.	Age.	Height.	Pulse Sitting.	Pulse Standing.
1. H.	- 21	5 feet 5¾ inch.	66	64
2. H.	- - 22	5 ~ 7 ~	74	82
3. R.	- 27	6 ~ 1¼ ~	70	76
4. H.	- 18	5 ~ 6 ~	68	72
5. G.	- 19	6 ~ 0 ~	56	56
6. M'G.	- 18	5 ~ 5 ~	74	76
7. S.	- 20	5 ~ 7½ ~	68	74
8. W.	- 20	5 ~ 10 ~	82	82
9. T.	- 17	6 ~ 0 ~	96	96
10. E.	- - 17	5 ~ 5½ ~	61	70
11. H.	- 20	5 ~ 0 ~	68	68
12. W.	- 20	5 ~ 5 ~	60	72
13. W.	- 20	5 ~ 8 ~	86	84
14. S.	- 22	5 ~ 6 ~	68	76
15. D.	- 18	5 ~ 8 ~	76	82
16. F.	- - 22	5 ~ 3½ ~	66	68
17. W.	- 19	5 ~ 6 ~	64	64
18. C.	- - 18	5 ~ 9 ~	84	92
19. K.	- 39	5 ~ 11 ~	66	74
20. B.	- 24	5 ~ 11 ~	52	56
21. T.	- 20	5 ~ 11½ ~	69	81
22. D.	- 17	5 ~ 7 ~	84	86
23. S.	- 22	5 ~ 10 ~	82	82
24. M'D.	- 16	5 ~ 8 ~	80	80
25. O.	- 29	5 ~ 10½ ~	70	72
Mean,	- 21		72·4	75·4

This table, which was drawn up with the greatest attention to accuracy, discloses some curious facts in the history of the pulse. So far as could be determined, all these young gentlemen were in good health, with one exception; and yet we find two, in whom the pulse constantly decreased on rising from their seat, and became accelerated on sitting down; being the very reverse of a law which all physiologists had thought to be universal.

Besides these two, in whom the pulse showed so singular a character, there were six others who had no differential pulse, that is, in whom the muscular action required to maintain the body erect did not accelerate the pulse a single beat.

Is there, or is there not, a "diurnal revolution" of the pulse in respect merely to numbers, independent of stimulation by food or exercise? Now, I fancy that this has been completely proved in my first memoir, published more than twenty years ago. But some have asserted that this morning acceleration and evening retardation depends altogether on the use of food and other stimulants, and that, were it not for these, the pulse would not rise early in the morning and fall towards evening, but would sink constantly. This opinion is incorrect, as the following table, given as a specimen of the experiments by which the existence of a differential pulse was established, will tend to show :—

Table showing the differential pulse, observed in Mr S., aged 20, morning and evening ; proving a diurnal revolution, both as to numbers and as to excitability, altogether independent of food or exercise, and proving the morning pulse to be quicker than the evening one.

Date.	Hour.	Horizontal.	Sitting.	Standing.	Differential.
April 5,	10 P.M.	53	64	78	25
„ 6,	7 A.M.	60	75	90	30
„ 7,	7 A.M.	65	80	90	25
„ 8,	10 P.M.	57	66	78	21
„ 9,	7 A.M.	65	80	90	25
„ 10,	{10 A.M.	60	82	95	35
	{10 P.M.	58	70	76	18

Average Differential Pulse.

Morning, - 26·7   Evening, - 21·3

	Horizontal.	Sitting.	Standing.
Average morning pulse,	62	78·3	90
Average evening pulse,	56	67	77

The apartments occupied by Mr S. (a gentleman of the most regular habits and in excellent health) seemed to me cold, and exposed to the boisterous westerly winds of this climate. I have no doubt but that the temperature of the room had fallen greatly during the night, otherwise the difference between the morning and evening pulse would have been still more marked.

The morning pulse was of course noted before breakfast.

Without doubt, were we to continue long without food, the pulse would first sink, and then become exceedingly quick on the slightest excitement. No one doubts this; but that the morning pulse is quicker than the evening one, altogether independent of any stimulants, is proved, I think, beyond a doubt by this and other tables.

The next question, which is a more important one in many respects, is as to the existence of a diurnal revolution in the excitability of the heart; by this I mean a varying susceptibility, according to the time of day, for a healthy powerful action of the heart, when influenced by food, exercise, &c.

The numerous observations detailed throughout this paper, and in my former memoir, published in 1814-15, may, it is hoped, settle this question with unprejudiced persons. The excitability of the heart diminishes regularly from an early hour until late in the evening. Indeed, I have reason to think that, since the publication of my first memoir in 1815, few have doubted this fact; and I beg leave, therefore, to refer at once to that memoir."

The following observations will explain to the reader the nature of the "elements" omitted by M. Quetelet :—

" I can nowhere find in the valuable works of M. Quetelet, that he was aware of the effects of position on the pulse, or of its diurnal revolution, or of the diurnal change in its excitability ; and this lessens, I regret to say, the otherwise entire confidence I and all others would be disposed to place in the results arrived at by this profound and ingenious philosopher. In the tables, for example, constructed to determine the influence of sleep on the pulse and respiration, compared with the waking state, no mention is made of the time of day or night, nor of the position of the person whilst awake, whether horizontal, sitting, or standing upright. The pulsation of the person sleeping would, in all probability, be reckoned in the evening, at a time when the pulse sinks naturally, altogether independent of sleep.

Again, he found that in a male child from four to five years old, the pulsations and inspirations were—

Asleep.		Awake.	
Pulsations, -	77·3	Pulsations, -	93·4
Inspirations, -	24·5	Inspirations, -	29·3

In the construction of these tables, two great data have been neglected, namely, the position of the person and the time of the day.

If the pulsations and inspirations were reckoned during the night, as an index of the effects of sleep, then the effects of the time of day are mistaken for the effects of sleep ; for at midnight the pulse numerically is low in a healthy and stout person, whether asleep or not, and the excitability of the heart is nearly at its zero. Again, the pulse would be counted at one time whilst the person was in a horizontal position, and at another time whilst sitting, or even standing. This would also make a difference of 10 or 12 beats, which M. Quetelet has not taken into account. I question much if any effects arise from sleep, excepting of a very trivial nature; but restlessness and watchfulness, arising from any cause, when the body ought to sleep and requires it, would produce a highly excited pulse, the result of weakness and temporary ailment.

In this climate, the temperature of our rooms often sinks very much during winter, and especially towards the morning ;* with the temperature the pulse sinks, and this may be one cause why, as I have just remarked, some have doubted the fact of the pulse being quicker in the morning than towards evening.

The effects of a cold room in depressing the pulse, is such, that even the active exercise of writing fails to counteract it.

The following table shows that the pulse remained much depressed under circumstances in which it ought to have risen very much :—

1st December.

2 A.M.—In bed, - - - - -	60
5 A.M.—Sitting and writing for some hours,	60
(There was no fire in the room).	
6 A.M.—Still writing, - - - -	62
7 A.M.—Ditto, - - - - -	60

Here the pulse ought, but for the cold room, to have risen very much, for the action of writing raises the pulse considerably ; that of composition still more. Those whose minds are much occupied with business, are not fair subjects for experiments on the pulse.

The use or abuse of wine and spirituous liquors, renders all observations on the pulse inaccurate. These liquors, in my opinion, are purely medicinal. Their daily, or even frequent use in any climate, or in any quantity, I apprehend to be a great error in regimen, and can never be required. I think them directly opposed to the enjoyment of perfect health and strength."

I shall conclude these remarks by adding the general results :—

" 1. The velocity of the heart's action is in the direct ratio of the age of the individual, being quickest in young persons, slowest in the aged. There may be exceptions to this, but they do not affect the general law.

2. The question of an average pulse for all ages has hitherto been determined upon insufficient data.

3. There is a morning acceleration and an evening retardation in the number of the pulsations of the heart, independent of any stimulation by food, &c.

* The thermometer being seldom above 61 or 62 degrees of Fahrenheit, even with a strong fire in the room. It is unnecessary to remark to any medical person that, if he sits before a strong fire, his pulse will rise almost at any time, and that if he sits still in a cold room until his feet feel chilled, his pulse will sink proportionally; hence, if possible, all observations on the pulse ought to be made in summer. I attribute to an inattention to the fact of the coldness of apartments in this country generally during the night and towards morning, why some have thought that there is no diurnal revolution of the pulse as to its numbers, independent of stimulation by food and otherwise ; or, in other words, that the pulse will not accelerate towards morning spontaneously.

4. The excitability of the heart undergoes a daily revolution, that is, food and exercise most affect the heart's action in the morning and during the forenoon, least in the afternoon, and least of all in the evening. Hence we should infer that the pernicious use of spirituous liquors must be greatly aggravated in those who drink before dinner.

5. Sleep does not farther affect the heart's action than by a cessation of all voluntary motion, and by a recumbent position.

6. In weak persons, muscular action excites the action of the heart more powerfully than in strong and healthy individuals; but this does not apply to other stimulants—to wine, for example, or to spirituous liquors.

7. The effects of the position of the body in increasing or diminishing the number of pulsations, is solely attributable to the muscular exertion required to maintain the body in the sitting or erect position; the debility may be measured by altering the position of the person from a recumbent to the sitting or to the erect position.

9. The law of the differential pulse is not universal. There are exceptions to be found even in those in perfect health. It is also possible that there may be some in whom the diurnal revolutions of the pulse takes place only in consequence of the use of stimulants. But this has not been proved satisfactorily.

10. The most powerful stimulant to the heart's action is muscular exertion. The febrile pulse never equals this.

11. The law of relation between the inspiration and pulsation of the heart has been stated by M. Quetelet."

II.—CLIMATE.

Since the publication of M. Quetelet's work, the different effects of various climates on the sickness, mortality, and invaliding of British troops, have been carefully and admirably investigated by Major Tulloch.* These researches are not confined exclusively to British troops, as they include an inquiry into the effects of climate on the Negro or black troops in the British service, when removed from the tropical to colder but yet comparatively warm, or at least mild, regions of the earth. Previous to laying before the reader some of the more important results deduced by Major Tulloch, from the data placed in his hands by the unwearied exertions of Sir James Macgrigor (to whom the chief merit of these reports is due), I shall take the liberty of making the following observations.

The various climates of the globe may practically be arranged under two zones or belts—inter-tropical and extra-tropical, north and south of the equator. The extra-tropical regions may again be subdivided into two or three regions, which may be designated as warm, temperate, and cold or frozen. These respective regions differ much in climate, and, to a great extent, in their botanical and zoological sections, including man himself; for, whilst the tropical regions of the Old World have been inhabited from the earliest historic period by the Negro and other dark-coloured races, the warm climates have equally been held by the Pelasgic, Copt, Syrian, Arab, and Jewish (on the supposition that these are distinct races of men); the temperate by the Celtic and Saxon; and *probably* (for the fact is not certain) the cold or frozen by a race, the Fin and Laplander, differing from all the others. The following observations may conveniently form an introduction to the subject of emigration, which I shall discuss in the next section.

* See Statistical Reports ordered to be printed by the House of Commons.

The influence of climate over the health of Europeans of the Saxon and Celtic races, in tropical regions possessing no countervailing advantages, such, more especially, as *great elevation* (this being seemingly the only security), had been ascertained, at least practically, and on a great scale, long prior to Major Tulloch's researches. The first report of that gentleman referred to the West Indies. "The main object kept in view," says the major, "has been merely to determine the extent of sickness and mortality at each station, the diseases by which it has been induced, and such causes of these diseases as appear sufficiently obvious or tangible to admit of remedy." This report was followed by a second on the sickness, mortality, and invaliding among the troops in the United Kingdom, the Mediterranean, and British America; and this by a third on Western Africa, St Helena, the Cape of Good Hope, and the Mauritius.

It would appear, from these documents, that neither the Saxon, nor Celtic, nor mixed race, composing the troops of Great Britain, can withstand, even under the most favourable circumstances, the deleterious influence of a tropical climate. Disposed at one time to ascribe this sad result to the deplorable habits of intemperance, the besetting vice of all soldiers, I am now, though most reluctantly, compelled to admit that even temperance, however it may diminish the effects of the climate, and add to the chances in favour of the European, is by no means a permanent security. So far as regards the vast regions of the earth—the most fertile, the richest—the question as to their permanent occupancy by the Saxon and Celt—I mean as *Britain and France are now occupied*, or any other country, by its *native* inhabitants—will be regarded as settled by almost all who peruse these reports. The Anglo-Saxon is now pushing himself towards the tropical countries; Mexico has been invaded and partitioned; another battle of San Jacinto will shortly decide the fate of California; Central Mexico may follow, and Peru: but can the Saxon maintain himself in these countries—in Brazil, Columbia?—It is to be feared not. Experience seems to indicate that neither the Saxon nor Celtic races can *maintain themselves*, in the strict sense of the word, within tropical countries. To enable them to do so they require a *slave population of native* labourers, or of coloured men at least, and, in addition, a constant draught from the parent country. The instances of Cuba, Brazil, Mexico, Columbia, &c., where the Spanish and Portuguese seem to be able to maintain their ground, do not bear so directly on the question as many may suppose: for, in the first place, we know not precisely the extent to which these have mingled with the dark and native races; and, secondly, the emigrants from Spain and Portugal partook, in all probability, more of the Moor, Pelasgic, and even Arab blood, than of the Celt or Saxon.

But can these latter maintain their ground in the warm but extra-tropical regions of the earth? This question has not yet been fully answered. The Dutch have held possession of the Cape for nearly two hundred and fifty years, and have thriven well; have been free of disease, and multiplied exceedingly; *but*—and here comes the trying part of the question—*they have never laboured*. So with Algeria, which the Celt now attempts to colonise. Can he *stand labour in the field*? I doubt it exceedingly. Time alone can satisfactorily offer a solution of this question. Yet in many parts of Southern Australia, the Saxon and Celtic races can withstand labour in the field; but the experiment has been made on too limited a scale to warrant important deductions. But the cold and frozen regions they tolerate easily; it seems, indeed, to have been their congenial soil. Yet even here, fever, that scourge of the human race in all climates, commits sad ravages, and consumption of the lungs, by its numerous victims, causes many ever-recurring woes. But the reproductive principle is equal and even much superior to all the diseases incident to these climates when inhabited by their indigenous races; not so, however, when the natives of tropical countries attempt to settle in them. Major Tulloch has proved that to them such climates are at least as disastrous as the tropical regions have proved to Europeans.

Before concluding these general remarks, I take the liberty of adding a single one in respect to acclimatation. When our troops occupied Walcheren and Flushing, during the deplorable scheme of invading Europe, the mortality assumed a most alarming character : it more than decimated the British troops, as it seems always to have similarly affected the French, the Dutch or Saxon inhabitants suffering, as was said, in no shape from fever, wondering at the mortality amongst the British, and asserting the climate to be as good as any other. Now all this, if true, must arise from acclimatation, seeing that both races, English and Dutch, arise from one parent stock ; and it seems probable, therefore, that in progress of time the descendants of those very men who fell in the prime of life at Flushing, cut off by fever, might experience no ill effects from a climate to which they and their forefathers, for several generations, had become inured. This is merely thrown out as a hint for future inquirers. In the mean time, it has been proved that the mortality of our troops *increased* with length of residence in the West Indies and in all tropical countries, so that acclimatation is the reverse of salutary, at least in so far as regards the first emigrants. This law holds even in cold climates, such as Britain, at least in regard to large towns, a residence in which, by persons who have come to reside in them from the country, is constantly injurious to health ; the longer always the worse. So much for the theories of medical men in respect to acclimatation ; on careful inquiry they have proved (a not unusual occurrence) the reverse of truth.

Upon the whole, every reliance may be placed in the following deductions by Major Tulloch, the result of the first series of his inquiries.

" It has been supposed by many, that the diseases which prove so fatal to Europeans in these latitudes, especially fevers, are, if not a necessary, at least a very general, consequence of continued exposure to a high temperature. The sufficiency of this, however, as a uniform cause of sickness and mortality, is contradicted by the fact, that these vary considerably in different stations, the mean temperature of which is nearly alike. The range of the thermometer, for instance, in Antigua and Barbadoes, is rather higher than in Dominica, Tobago, Jamaica, or the Bahamas; yet we find that the troops in the latter stations suffer nearly three times as much as those in the former. There are also several instances in which epidemic fever made its appearance, and raged with the utmost virulence during the winter months—a circumstance not likely to have taken place if that disease had originated in increased temperature.

If elevated temperature was an essential cause of the mortality to which Europeans are liable in this climate, we might expect it in every year to produce similar effects ; whereas, on the contrary, it appears, from the tabular statements in the preceding report, that the mortality in one year is sometimes twenty times as high as in another, without any perceptible difference in the range of temperature. This fact has already attracted the notice of some medical authors, who, in treating of yellow fever, adduce instances of various epidemics both within and beyond the tropics, during which the temperature was not above the average, and was sometimes even a little below it, and inversely where the existence of a high temperature was not attended with the prevalence of fever.[*]

In accounting for the unhealthiness of these colonies, great influence has been ascribed to excess of moisture.

That neither heat nor moisture can be the primary causes which influence the health of troops in the West Indies, is at once established by referring to the comparative view of the ratio of mortality in each year at every station, in which there are numerous instances of two adjacent islands, or even of two contiguous stations in the same island, being subject in an equal degree to the operation of these agencies ; and yet, while the one has been desolated by the ravages of fever, the other has been enjoying a degree of salubrity equal to that of Great Britain.

Though heat and moisture are not the primary causes of fever, however, it is highly probable their operation tends in some measure to increase its intensity. The tables illustrating the influence of the seasons on the health of the troops in each station, show, that the greatest number of admissions into hospital, and deaths, has, on the average of a series of years (though not uniformly or equally in each year), taken place in those months when the greatest degree of heat was combined with the greatest moisture ; and it may be observed, as a striking exemplification of this fact, that as the sun proceeds northward in the ecliptic, carrying heat and moisture in his train, the period generally termed the unhealthy season is later in the northern colonies than in those to the south.

The unhealthy character of that period of the year in which the greatest degree of heat and moisture is combined, is not, however, confined to the West Indies, but extends also to the East, as well as over a large portion of the northern temperate zone. Hence (Major Tulloch continues) these causes cannot specially render the West Indies so unhealthy. He also shows, by a comparison of stations, that neither can the rank vegetation of marsh or savannah be held the primary cause of West Indian maladies, and concludes with the following suggestion, which chimes in with an idea gradually acquiring more and more importance in medical statistics :—

" We are too sensible of the difficulty of the subject to venture on any theory of our own, which might on subsequent examination prove as futile as those which preceded it ; but we merely wish to call the attention of such persons as may be disposed for further inquiry, to the circumstance that as yet no experiments have been made on the electrical condition of the atmosphere in the West Indies, during periods of epidemic ; and as it is possible either an excess or deficiency of that powerful though unseen agent, may exercise an important influence on the vital functions, the subject seems worthy of attention. Heat and moisture are well known to be intimately connected with the development of electrical phenomena, and its influence on vegetation has also recently been established by experiment ; consequently, if the prevalence of disease could be satisfactorily traced to that source, the reason why heat, moisture, and vegetation should have been mistaken as the causes, when acting only as auxiliaries, would be readily accounted for ; and even should the results leave the cause of disease as undetermined as before, science will at least be benefited by the inquiry." The main practical result accruing from the researches of Major Tulloch, has reference to the effect of an elevated site on the health of a resident population within the tropics.

This is a point deeply affecting all such colonisation schemes as that proposed for the Darien isthmus, and other tropical localities. The report demonstrates, beyond a doubt, as regards remittent fever, " that, at an elevation of from 2000 to 2500 feet, settlers or troops are likely to be either wholly exempt from that disease, or to encounter it in so very modified a form, that the mortality from all causes will not, on the average of a series of years, materially exceed that to which an equal number of European troops would be subject in the capital of their native country. The diseases of the tropics seem, like the vegetable productions of the same regions, to be restricted to certain altitudes and particular degrees of temperature. The researches of Humboldt on this subject have tended to establish that yellow fever is never known beyond the height of 2500 feet, so that the nearer this boundary can be approached the more likely is the health of the troops to be secured."

In the second report by the same able statistician, we find the following deductions. They refer chiefly to the comparative salubrity of the Mediterranean stations, and those occupied by our soldiery in North America. After showing that the Mediterranean troops, from many causes *independent of climate*, are less exposed to the influences producing pulmonary disease, Major Tulloch proceeds thus :—

"When we find, notwithstanding all these circumstances apparently so favourable to the greater development of these diseases in Canada and Nova Scotia, that the troops there do not suffer from them to a greater extent than in the Mediterranean, it would manifestly be incorrect to attribute their prevalence in North America to the reduced temperature, and sudden atmospherical vicissitudes, incident to that quarter of the globe, seeing that the sufferings of the troops from these diseases are equally great in other climates where no such causes are in operation to induce them.

The caution necessary to be exercised in attributing to certain peculiarities of climate the prevalence of any class of diseases, is so strikingly exhibited by the proportion of rheumatic affections ascertained to have occurred among the troops in different colonies, that the following abstract will best serve to illustrate our observations on this head :—

	Admissions from Rheumatic Affections annually per 1000 of mean Strength.
Jamaica,	29
Nova Scotia and New Brunswick,	30
Bermudas,	33
Malta,	34
Ionian Islands,	34½
Gibraltar,	38
Canada,	40
Mauritius,	46
Windward and Leeward Command,	49
United Kingdom,	50
Cape of Good Hope,	57

Thus we find that in the mild and equable climate of the Mediterranean, or the Mauritius, the proportion of rheumatic affections is even greater than in the inclement regions of Nova Scotia and Canada, and that, though some of the provinces of the Cape of Good Hope have occasionally been without rain for several years, these diseases are more frequent in the dry climate of that command than in the West Indies, where the condition of the atmosphere is as remarkably the reverse; yet have extreme cold and atmospheric vicissitudes, coupled with excess of moisture, been assigned as satisfactory causes for their prevalence.

Considering that medical officers have hitherto possessed no means of comparing the influence of such diseases in different climates, any erroneous impressions which may be entertained on that subject, need not excite surprise. The information now collected, in regard to those prevalent among troops in every colony, will best serve to counteract such impressions, and afford a surer basis for future theories on that subject.

The results of this report, in regard to the relative prevalence, at different stations in British America, of remittent and intermittent fevers, add still further

to the difficulty of establishing any uniform connexion between the presence of marshy ground and the existence of those febrile diseases to which the exhalations from it are supposed to give rise.

When, in subsequent reports, we come to investigate the operation of these diseases on the west coast of Africa and other colonies, we shall be able to adduce still more satisfactory evidence on this subject; in the mean time, we have felt it our duty to place the preceding facts in a prominent point of view, not for the purpose of establishing any particular theory, but to show how inadequate, in many instances, is the supposed influence of emanations from a marshy soil to account for the origin of these diseases. All the evidence obtained seems only to warrant the inference, that a morbific agency of some kind is occasionally present in the atmosphere, which, under certain circumstances, gives rise to fevers of the remittent and intermittent type; and that, though the vicinity of marshy and swampy ground appears to favour the development of that agency, it does not necessarily prevail in such localities, nor are they by any means essential either to its existence or operation.

Notwithstanding the doubt in which this branch of the investigation is still involved, we may venture, from the facts adduced in all the reports hitherto submitted, also to draw the conclusion, that when this morbific agency manifests itself in the epidemic form, its influence is frequently confined to so limited a space, as to afford a fair prospect of securing the troops from its ravages, by removal to a short distance from the locality where it originated. The history of the epidemic fevers at Gibraltar furnishes several remarkable instances of this kind; and we have also shown that, both in the West Indies and Ionian Islands, one station has frequently suffered to a great extent from yellow fever, while others, within the distance of a few miles, have been entirely exempt. In the epidemic cholera at Montreal and Halifax, which seems to have been in this respect somewhat analogous in its operation, we have also had occasion to remark the sudden cessation of the disease immediately on the removal of the troops, even to a short distance.

Instead of entering, therefore, into any discussion as to the causes which seem thus to limit the range of these epidemics to particular localities, we shall merely call the attention of medical officers to the fact, that on the outbreak of any serious disease of that nature, they may forthwith take into consideration the expediency of removing the troops from the locality where it originated—a measure which, whenever camp equipage can readily be procured, or the necessary accommodation obtained for them, is likely to be attended with but little temporary inconvenience, and may probably lead to the happiest results. We are aware that this suggestion is by no means a new one, having already been made and acted upon in various colonies, and we only advert to it now, for the purpose of bearing testimony to its apparent efficacy, and encouraging the adoption of it whenever circumstances will permit."

It may be interesting to many of our readers to have placed before them the following section on the "Influence of the Seasons in producing Sickness and Mortality among the Troops serving in North America":—

"The following table, illustrative of this subject, has been prepared from the returns of the Canada command. In Bermuda, Nova Scotia, &c., the dates of the admissions and deaths have not been recorded with sufficient regularity to admit of similar results being exhibited on as extensive a scale, and we have therefore confined our calculations to Canada, where, on account of its severity, we might expect to find the influence of winter on the health of the troops very strongly manifested :—

Table showing the Influence of the Seasons on the Sickness and Mortality of Troops in British America.

Months.	Admissions into Hospital in 20 Years of Troops in Canada.				Deaths in 20 Years of Troops in Canada.			
	By Acute Diseases.	By Chronic Diseases.	By Surgical Diseases.	Total by all Diseases.	By Acute Diseases.	By Chronic Diseases.	By Surgical Diseases.	Total by all Diseases.
January, - -	2,142	273	2,270	4,685	36	35	5	76
February, - -	1,918	227	2,026	4,171	31	23	3	57
March, - -	1,950	266	1,910	4,126	31	41	3	75
April, - - -	2,551	294	2,038	4,883	33	39	1	73
May, - -	2,820	303	2,216	5,339	28	34	2	64
June, - \ -	3,063	298	2,479	5,840	58	37	9	104
July, - -	4,183	352	2,570	7,105	53	29	8	90
August, - -	5,144	354	2,678	8,176	103	21	4	28
September, -	4,440	332	2,436	7,208	54	24	4	82
October, - -	3,055	241	2,280	5,576	38	27	6	71
November, - -	2,798	229	2,241	5,268	32	27	3	62
December, - -	2,252	197	2,072	4,521	35	23	3	61
Total,	36,316	3366	27,216	66,898	532	360	51	943

Thus, so far from the extreme severity of the winter in Canada operating very prejudicially to the health of the troops, we find, that in January, February, and March, when the minimum of the thermometer is many degrees below zero, the admissions from acute diseases, in which the influence of the seasons is most likely to be manifested, are not half so numerous as in July, August, and September, while those from chronic and surgical diseases are also lower, though not in the same proportion. In fact, so rare are the cases of sickness during winter, that not more than five and a half per cent. of the force come under treatment monthly; whereas, during July, August, and September, the monthly admissions average more than ten per cent. of the force. The ratio of deaths follows the same law, though the influence of the cholera during the summer and autumn of 1832 and 1834 increased the relative mortality at that period in a still greater proportion than the admissions.

The numbers reported sick on each muster-day, establish the same results in regard to the comparative salubrity of the winter season, not in Canada alone, but also in Nova Scotia, New Brunswick, and Bermuda.

	Mean Sick.		
	Canada.	Nova Scotia and New Brunswick.	Bermuda.
January, -	124	72	28
February, - -	125	73	27
March, - -	124	72	30
April, - -	127	69	31
May, - -	123	78	30
June, - - -	135	81	30
July, - -	144	82	32
August, - -	161	89	35
September, -	162	84	33
October, - -	136	80	34
November, - -	124	67	32
December, - -	116	67	30

The general prevalence of febrile affections in Upper Canada during summer, might be supposed to account for the preponderance of sickness there at that season ; but the same peculiarity extends also to the lower province, where febrile diseases are more rare. The same feature is observable among the civil inhabitants, as will be seen from the following abstract of the deaths in each month among the population of the several districts in the lower province, made up pursuant to an order of the House of Commons, dated 6th December 1832.

Deaths in each Month, from 1829 to 1831 inclusive, in the following Districts of Lower Canada :—

Months.	Quebec.	Montreal.	Three Rivers.	Gaspar.	St Francis.	Total in whole Province.
January,	974	1186	194	10	1	2365
February,	986	1241	244	16	2	2489
March, -	1005	1325	292	10	3	2735
April, -	1012	1293	318	6	—	2629
May, - -	978	1382	392	14	6	2772
June, - -	1129	1496	307	10	1	2943
July, - -	1464	2221	368	13	2	4068
August,	1395	2178	358	9	5	3945
September,	1147	1562	240	11	1	2961
October,	956	1392	215	15	—	2578
November,	950	1130	186	11	2	2279
December,	1070	1236	176	14	2	2498

Thus, even in the lower province, where intermittents are comparatively rare, June, July, August, and September, prove much more fatal to the civil inhabitants than the most severe of the winter months. The preponderance of mortality during that period may in a slight degree be accounted for by the influx of emigrants in summer, but is by far too great to be entirely attributable to that source ; especially as the preceding abstract shows that it commenced prior to the month of April, while the ports were closed, and again fell to its former level in November, though many of the emigrants must have been still in the province.

In the state of New York, the seasons are found to exercise a corresponding influence on mortality, even when no visitation of yellow fever is experienced. From 1816 to 1826, the dates of decease of 24,852 persons were carefully recorded, and of every thousand of these deaths the relative proportion in each month was found to have been as follows :—

January,	-	75	July,	- -	95½
February,	- -	75½	August,	-	108½
March,	- -	74	September,	-	109½
April,	- -	73	October,	-	97
May,	- -	72	November,	-	79½
June,	-	65	December,	-	75½
	Total,	-	-	1000	

From all these facts, then, we are forced to arrive at the conclusion, that the constitution of the soldier, serving in these commands, is not affected in any material degree either by the extreme severity of a North American winter, or the sudden transitions he undergoes at that season, in passing from a heated guard-room, with the thermometer at 80 degrees, to his sentinel duties in the open air, under a temperature of 25 or 30 degrees below zero. On the contrary, the degree of health enjoyed by the troops during winter is not exceeded in any quarter of the globe.

The extreme rarity of sickness and mortality among the crews of vessels employed in the arctic regions, when exposed to a lower temperature, and still more sudden vicissitudes than any we have had to record, affords a striking illustration how little the constitution of our countrymen is likely to be affected even by the severest climate to which they are exposed.

While febrile affections of the intermittent and remittent types prevail during spring and autumn, bowel complaints during summer, catarrhs and all the train of pulmonary affections during spring and the commencement of the winter, there are comparatively few diseases of any kind during the severest part of the season, except those of the eyes, induced by the reflection of the snow, frost-bites from exposure, and a few cases of acute rheumatism and pneumonia, which, however, may be said to prevail with equal severity at other periods of the year."

The following table is also curious and interesting, as contrasting the soldier and the civilian.

	Ages.	By Tables of Scotch Benefit Societies.	By Tables of English Benefit Societies.	Returns of East India Company's Labourers in London.	Returns of Portsmouth Dock Labourers.	Returns of Woolwich Dock Labourers.
Constantly Sick per 1000,	20 to 30	11·4	15·4	13·6	19·9	23·4
	30 to 40	13·2	18·3	13·8		
		Days.	Days.	Days.	Days.	Days.
Average number of Days Sick in each Year, -	20 to 30	4·1	5·6	4·02	7·3	8·5
	30 to 40	4·8	6·6	5·06		
Average Duration of each Attack of Sickness, -	20 to 30	··	··	18·7	13·2	··
	30 to 40	··	··	22·6		

In the third report by Major Tulloch, the two extremes are happily contrasted, viz., Western Africa and the Cape of Good Hope; the latter, perhaps—nay, almost certainly—the healthiest climate in the world, the former proverbial for being a grave to Europeans. His details fully bear out the general character of the stations. In conclusion, it may be remarked, that, independent of all other important results, these reports are peculiarly valuable from the ample refutation they afford, to all minds open to conviction, of the more generally received medical theories in respect to the causes of many fatal and harassing diseases. They may also prove of much practical benefit, in freeing the minds of emigrants from those terrors which the very thought of particular localities has long been apt to induce. Rheumatism and ague rise to the mind, whenever men think of a Canadian winter; but we find that, in reality, the soldiery in the Mauritius suffer more severely from that disease than they do in British America. In short, Major Tulloch's elaborate researches lead to the conclusion, that atmospheric causes, operating on all climes in common, and modified only to a comparatively slight degree by local circumstances, form the great source of the morbific influences affecting mankind. When this point is more fully investigated, and fitting remedial means discovered, emigration will be stripped of half its difficulties, and a new lease given to civilised man, as it were, of a large portion of the globe, of which at this moment he can scarcely be called the occupant.

END OF TREATISE ON MAN.

PLATE 1.

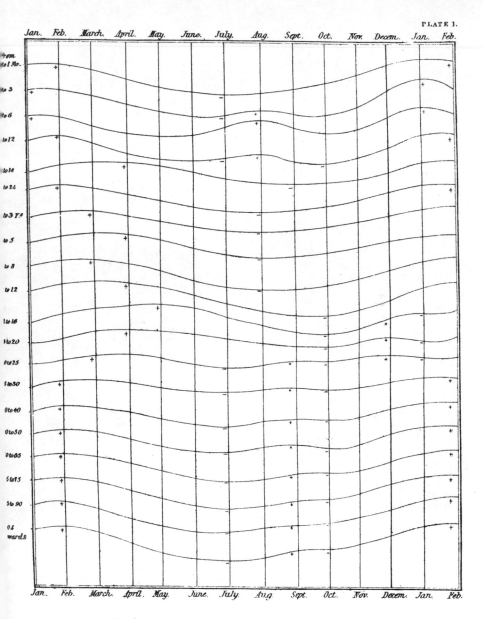

Lines indicating the Mortality of each Month for different ages. page 36.

J. Gellatly Edit.

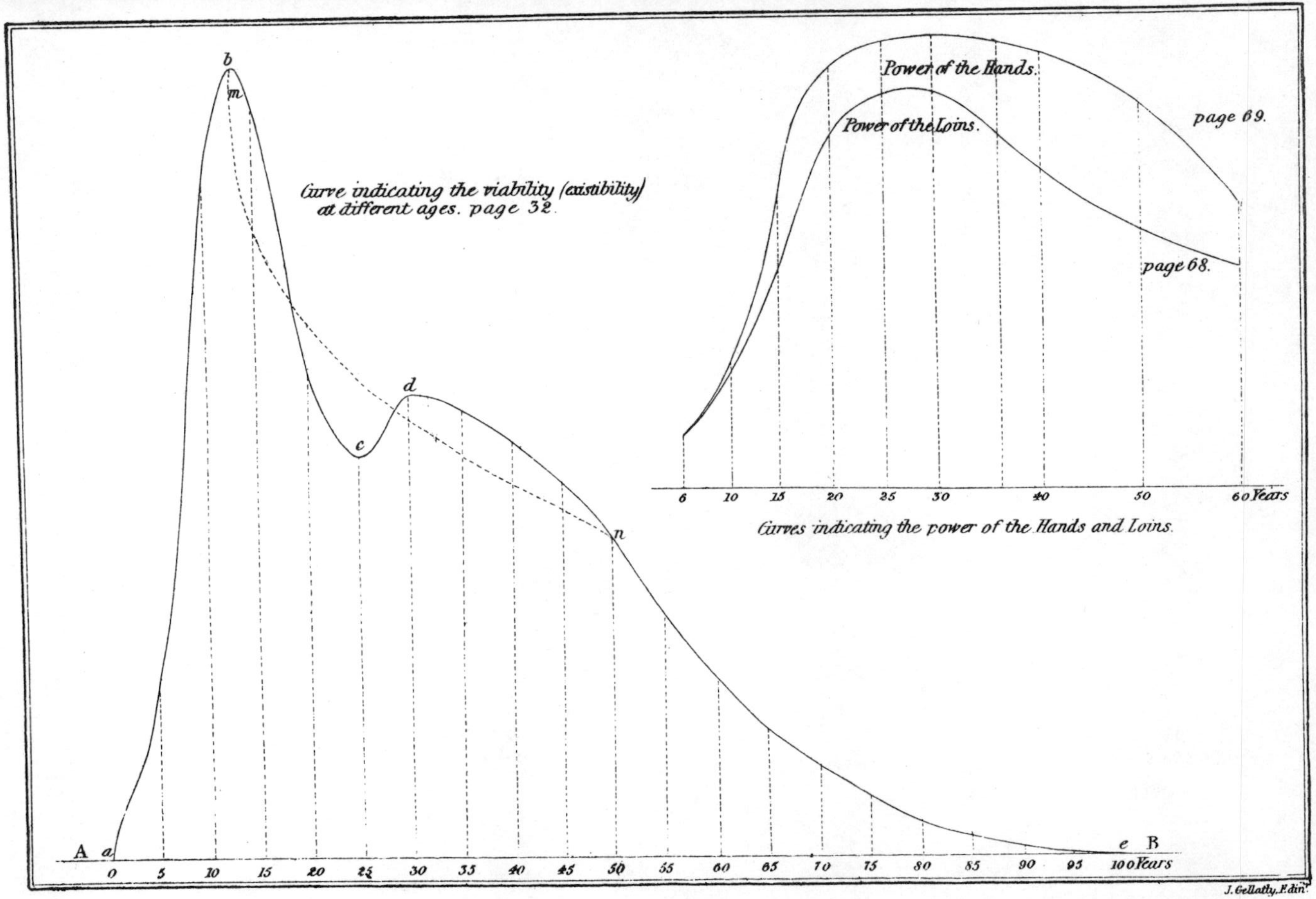

PLATE 2.

page 69.

page 68.

Power of the Hands.

Power of the Loins.

Curves indicating the power of the Hands and Loins.

Curve indicating the viability (axistibility)
at different ages. page 32.

60 Years

6   10   15   20   25   30   40   50   60 Years

0   5   10   15   20   25   30   35   40   45   50   55   60   65   70   75   80   85   90   95   100 Years

J.Gellatly, Edin.

PLATE 3.

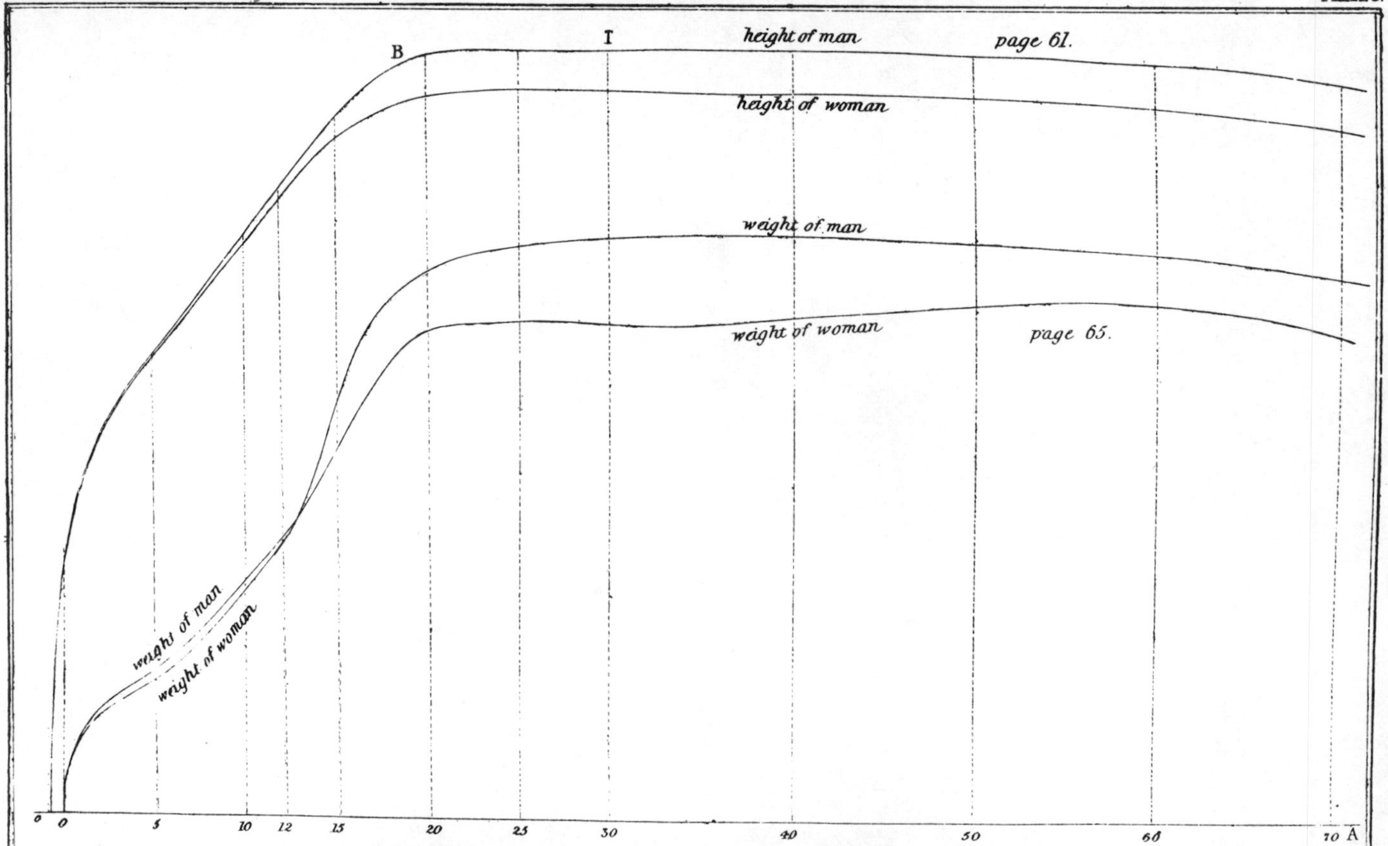

Curves indicating the development of the height & weight of man & woman at different ages.

height of man.

page 61.

height of woman.

weight of man.

weight of woman.

page 65.

weight of man

weight of woman

T

B

A

0   5   10 12 15   20   25   30   40   50   60   70

J. Galbraith Delin.

PLATE 4.

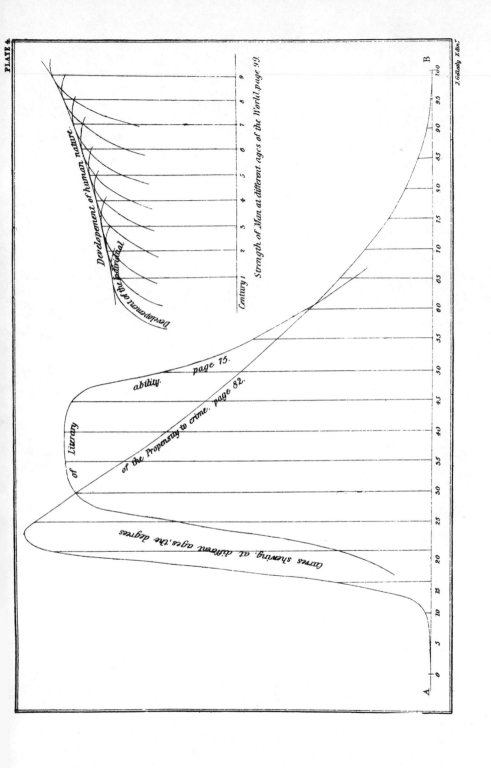

Development of human nature.

Development of the individual

Century I   2   3   4   5   6   7   8   9

Strength of Man at different ages of the World. page 49.

ability.   page 75.

of Literary

of the Propensity to crime. page 82.

Curves shewing at different ages, the degrees

A   0   5   10   15   20   25   30   35   40   45   50   55   60   65   70   75   80   85   90   95   100   B

J. Gellatly Edin.

PLATE 5.

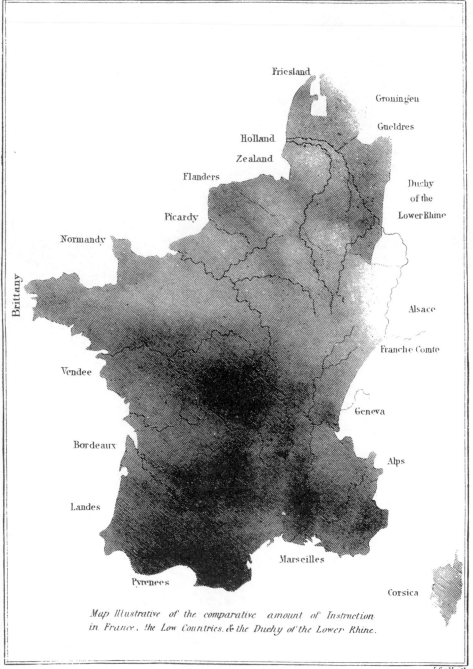

Map Illustrative of the comparative amount of Instruction in France, the Low Countries, & the Duchy of the Lower Rhine.

J. Gellatly

PLATE 6.

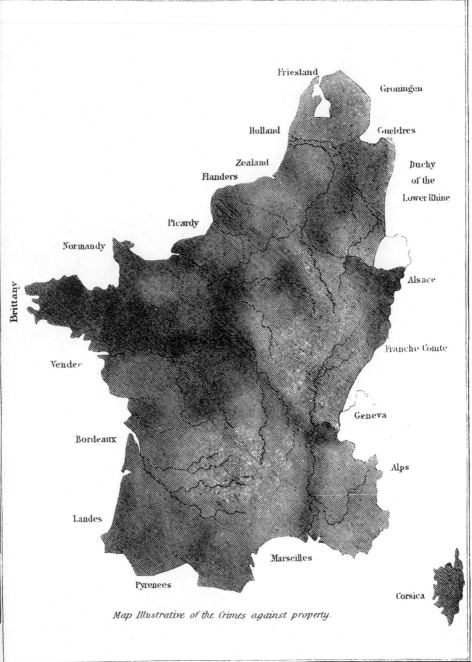

Friesland

Groningen

Holland

Gueldres

Zealand

Duchy
of the
Lower Rhine

Flanders

Picardy

Normandy

Alsace

Brittany

Franche Comte

Vendee

Geneva

Bordeaux

Alps

Landes

Marseilles

Pyrenees

Corsica

Map Illustrative of the Crimes against property.

J. Gellatly

PLATE 7.

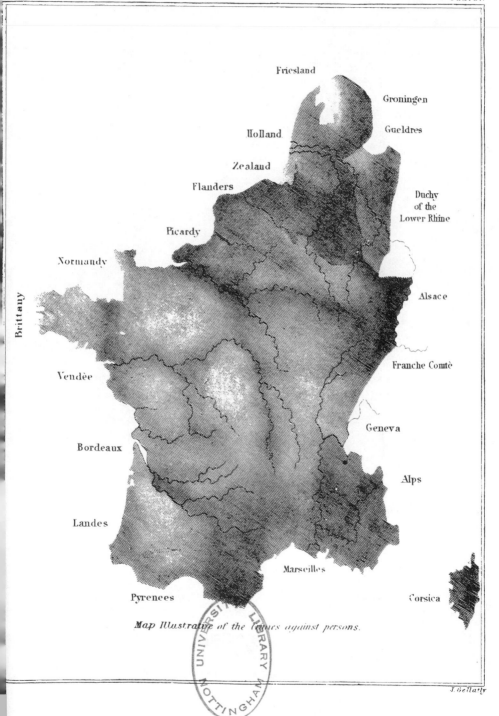

Friesland

Groningen

Gueldres

Holland

Zealand

Flanders

Duchy
of the
Lower Rhine

Picardy

Normandy

Alsace

Brittany

Franche Comtè

Vendèe

Geneva

Bordeaux

Alps

Landes

Marseilles

Corsica

Pyrenees

Map Illustrative of the Crimes against persons.

J. Gellatly